LONGMAN LINGUISTICS LIBRARY

HISTORY OF LINGUISTICS VOLUME

LONGMAN LINGUISTICS LIBRARY

General editors

R. H. ROBINS, *University of London*
GEOFFREY HORROCKS, *University of Cambridge*
DAVID DENISON, *University of Manchester*

For a complete list of books in the series, see pages v and vi.

History of Linguistics

edited by Giulio Lepschy

Volume IV: Nineteenth-Century Linguistics
Anna Morpurgo Davies

LONGMAN
London and New York

Addison Wesley Longman Limited
Edinburgh Gate
Harlow, Essex CM20 2JE
England

and Associated Companies throughout the world

*Published in the United States of America
by Addison Wesley Longman Inc., New York*

First published 1998

ISBN 0 582 29478-9   Paper
ISBN 0 582 29477-0   Cased

British Library Cataloguing-in-Publication Data

A catalogue record for this book is
available from the British Library

Library of Congress Cataloging-in-Publication Data

A catalog entry for this title is available from the
Library of Congress

Set by 35 in 10/11pt Times
Produced by Longman Singapore Publishers (Pte) Ltd.
Printed in Singapore

LONGMAN LINGUISTICS LIBRARY

General Editors:

R. H. Robins,
University of London

Geoffrey Horrocks,
University of Cambridge

David Denison,
University of Manchester

History of Linguistics Vol. IV
Edited by GIULIO LEPSCHY
Nineteenth-Century Linguistics
ANNA MORPURGO DAVIES

History of Linguistics Vol. III
Renaissance and Early Modern
Linguistics
Edited by GIULIO LEPSCHY

History of Linguistics Vol. II
Classical and Medieval Linguistics
Edited by GIULIO LEPSCHY

History of Linguistics Vol. I
The Eastern Traditions of Linguistics
Edited by GIULIO LEPSCHY

The New Comparative Syntax
Edited by LILIANE HAEGEMAN

Grammar and Grammarians in Early
Middle Ages
VIVIEN LAW

Greek: A History of the Language and
its Speakers
GEOFFREY HORROCKS

A Short History of Linguistics
Volume IV
R. H. ROBINS

Causatives and Causation
A Universal-typological perspective
JAE JUNG SONG

An Introduction to the Celtic Languages
PAUL RUSSELL

Frontiers of Phonology: Atoms,
Structures and Derivations
Edited by JACQUES DURAND and
FRANCIS KATAMBA

Modern Arabic
Structures, Functions and Varieties
CLIVE HOLES

Dialects in English
Studies in Grammatical Variation
Edited by PETER TRUDGILL

Modality and the English Modals
F. R. PALMER

Generative and Non-linear Phonology
JACQUES DURAND

A Linguistic History of Italian
MARTIN MAIDEN

Latin American Spanish
JOHN LIPSKI

The Meaning of Syntax
A Study of Adjectives of English
CONNOR FERRIS

English Historical Syntax
DAVID DENISON

Aspect of the English Verb
Process and Result in Language
YISHAI TOBIN

Historical Linguistics
Problems and Perspectives
Edited by CHARLES JONES

A History of American English
J. L. DILLARD

Verb and Noun Number in English
A Functional Explanation
WALLIS REID

English in Africa
JOSEF SCHMIED

Linguistic Theory
ROBERT DE BEAUGRANDE

An Introduction to Bilingualism
CHARLOTTE HOFFMANN

The English Verb
F. R. PALMER

Generative Grammar
GEOFFREY HORROCKS

Principles of Pragmatics
GEOFFREY LEECH

A History of English Phonology
CHARLES JONES

Contents

Introduction

This work originated in the discussions held by a group of advisors for linguistics of the Italian publishers il Mulino. Examining the areas in which new and useful initiatives could be encouraged, it was thought that a large-scale history of linguistics would meet a widely felt need, and I was asked to elaborate a plan for such a work. The preparation and the completion of the project took about ten years, and the work, written by scholars from different countries, began appearing in Italian in 1990. This English edition has been reorganized into five volumes. In this introduction I shall say something about the nature and contents of this work, and its place within the present panorama of linguistic historiography.

What I proposed was a history of linguistic thought, rather than an account of the development of linguistic science. In other words, for different societies and in different periods a presentation of the prevailing attitudes towards language was therefore required: its social, cultural, religious and liturgical functions, the prestige attached to different varieties, the cultivation of a standard, the place of language in education, the elaboration of lexical and grammatical descriptions, the knowledge of foreign idioms, the status of interpreters and translators, and so on.

This implies of course a 'view from within', that is, presenting the linguistic interests and assumptions of individual cultures in their own terms, without trying to transpose and reshape them into the context of our ideas of what the scientific study of language ought to be. The purpose is an understanding of what certain societies thought about language rather than an assessment of their ideas on a scale of scientific progress.

The content of the five volumes of the English edition is as follows: Volume I includes the ancient traditions, each of which develops in a manner which is, from a viewpoint both cultural and chronological, largely independent, apart from obvious connections, like those between

Arabic and Hebrew thought in the Middle Ages. (The Graeco-Roman tradition, which is the basis of those reflections on language which we present chronologically in Volumes II–V, appears at the beginning of the second volume). Chapter 1, by Göran Malmqvist, of Stockholm University, describes the development of Chinese linguistics, analysing the relevant lexicographical and grammatical works, and throwing light on the particular shape imposed on phonological analysis by the logographic nature of Chinese script. Chapter 2, by George Cardona, of the University of Pennsylvania, presents the Indian grammatical tradition, its cultural and religious implications, and particularly the contribution of Pāṇini, illustrating its systematic character and its attention to detail. Chapter 3, supervised by Erica Reiner, of the University of Chicago, presents and interprets the documents which bear witness to linguistic interests and knowledge in the civilizations of the ancient near East; the chapter is divided into three sections, devoted to Ancient Egyptian (by Janet Johnson), Sumerian (by Miguel Civil), and Akkadian (by Erica Reiner). Chapter 4, by Raphael Loewe, of the University of London, examines the place of language within the Hebrew tradition, from the Biblical period, through the Talmudists, the mystics, the enlightenment, down to the rebirth of Hebrew as an everyday language, paying particular attention to the philosophical and cultural implications of these trends. Chapter 5, by the late Henri Fleisch, of Saint Joseph University in Beirut, probably the last essay to flow from the pen of this eminent scholar, deals with the original system of grammatical analysis elaborated by the great Arabic civilization of the Middle Ages.

The successive volumes present the main stages of the European tradition, in their chronological order. In Volume II, the first chapter, by Peter Matthews, of Cambridge University, deals with classical linguistics and offers a reading of the main texts of the Graeco-Roman world which elaborate the grammatical categories on which we still base our analysis of language. The second chapter, by Edoardo Vineis, of Bologna University and (for the philosophy of language) by Alfonso Maierù, of Rome University, presents a detailed discussion of language study from the end of the sixth to the end of the fourteenth century, not limited to the late medieval period which has received most attention in recent years (with particular reference to Modistic philosophy), but extending to the less frequently studied early Middle Ages.

In Volume III, the first chapter, by Mirko Tavoni, of Pisa University, covers the fifteenth and sixteenth centuries, and is completed by two sections, one on Roman Slavdom, by M. D. Gandolfo, and one on Orthodox Slavdom, by S. Toscano; the bibliography of this chapter takes advantage of the great Renaissance Linguistic Archive set up by

M. Tavoni at the Istituto di Studi Rinascimentali in Ferrara. The second chapter, by Raffaele Simone, of Rome University, offers a detailed map of the varied terrain constitued by seventeenth- and eighteenth-century culture, in which many of the roots are found from which the great plant of later comparative linguistics derives its nourishment; R. Simone, who is a professional linguist, keeps in mind the philosophical perspective that is particularly relevant for this period.

In Volume IV Anna Morpurgo Davies, of Oxford University, examines the flowering of historical and comparative linguistics in the nineteenth century, stressing in particular some aspects which traditional presentations, focusing on the Neo-grammarians, sometimes leave in the shadow, such as the interest in typological classifications, and the importance for comparative philology of the newly constitued German university system in the first three decades of the century.

Volume V, by the editor of this history, offers a synthesis of the main developments in twentieth-century linguistics, extending from the progress of comparative studies to linguistic theory, philosophy of language, and the investigation of language use in different areas, from literature to social communication. (The Italian edition also includes a chapter on the history of Italian linguistics and dialectology, by Paola Benincà, of Padua University, which is omitted from the English edition.)

Let us briefly look at the present state of linguistic historiography. Over the last three decades, there has been a considerable revival of interest in this field. In 1974 Konrad Koerner, a German scholar teaching in Canada, founded the journal *Historiographia Linguistica*, which has become a forum for international discussion on the history of linguistics; in 1978 he was the organizer of the first international congress on the history of linguistics (the meetings are held at three-yearly intervals). There are also several other associations devoted to the history of linguistics, like the Société d'histoire et d'épistémologie des sciences du langage, created in 1978, presided over by S. Auroux, which publishes a Bulletin, and the journal *Histoire Epistémologie Langage* (1979–); the Henry Sweet Society for the History of Linguistic Ideas, founded in 1984 on the initiative of Vivian Salmon, which organizes regular meetings and publishes a *Newsletter*; the North American Association for the History of the Language Sciences, founded in 1987. *Beiträge zur Geschichte der Sprachwissenschaft*, edited by K. Dutz and P. Schmitter, started to appear in Germany in 1991. The interest in the history of linguistics over this period is also indicated by the publication of monographs and collections of studies, such as Hymes (1974), the two tomes devoted to the historiography of linguistics by Sebeok (1975), Parret (1976), Salmon (1979), Grotsch (1982), Schmitter (1982), Chevalier and Encrevé (1984), Bynon and Palmer (1986), Formigari and Lo Piparo (1988), Koerner (1989, 1995), Koerner and Asher (1995), Salmon (1996), Stein (1997).

A separate study would be necessary to examine the main available histories of linguistics, from the great works of the nineteenth century devoted to Classical linguistics by Steinthal (1863), to Oriental philology by Benfey (1869), and to Germanic philology by R. von Raumer (1870). Subsequent studies witness the triumph of Neogrammarian comparative philology, from Delbrück (1880) to Meillet (1903) to Pedersen (1924). Since the 1960s numerous historical presentations have been published, from the large and well-informed work by Tagliavini (1963), lacking however in historical perspective and theoretical insight, to the two-volume contribution by Mounin (1967–72), the neat and well-balanced book by Robins (1967), the acute and comprehensive synthesis by Law (1990), the disappointing attempts by Malmberg (1991) and Itkonen (1991). Large-scale works have also started appearing in the last few years under the direction of Schmitter (1987; 1991; [Ebbesen] 1995; 1996) and of Auroux (1989; 1992); one is being edited by Koerner for De Gruyter's *Handbücher*. Stammerjohann (1996) is an important biographical dictionary. There is no space to mention in this context the great many studies devoted, since the 1960s, to individual periods and problems in the history of linguistics, although they often provide the detailed groundwork that makes possible over-all synthetic assessments (some titles will be quoted in the list of references).

What is the place of our history of linguistics against this background? To me it seems to be in an advantageous position, in the middle ground between the concise, one-author profiles on the one hand, and the extended, multi-authored, multi-volume series on the other. Compared to the former, it has more richness of detail, which is made possible by the greater space available, and the higher degree of reliability that derives from the authority of contributors who are specialists in the individual areas. Compared to the latter, it is more compact and coherent in perspective and basic assumptions, and it can not only be consulted for single questions, or studied in individual sections, but also be read in its entirety.

If I were asked to present a schematic précis of the main features which I see as inspiring this work and characterizing its realization, I would list the following points:

1. A perspective directed towards understanding the past, rather than dealing with present-day concerns. The aim is to reconstruct and illustrate different epochs and traditions within their own context and on the basis of their own values, rather than of their appeal to present-day preoccupations: to highlight their linguistic interests, rather than our own.

2. This is a history of linguistic thought, of interests and attitudes toward language. These may or may not find a place within the elaboration of a 'scientific' study of language (however we may want to define it), but in any case I feel that an account of the preoccupations with linguistic matters in different societies proves to be an interesting and worthwhile object of historical investigation.

3. I have considered it essential, in my choice of authors for individual chapters, that they should be specialists, able to analyse the relevant texts in the original languages, and to present them to a lay readership. I aimed at obtaining not an account of what is known, derived from current literature, but a series of original contributions based on first-hand study of the primary sources.

4. From what precedes it is clear that this work is prevalently concerned with a historical and philological study of ideas, with texts from the past, rather than with methodological and theoretical problems posed by historiography. It is an 'extroverted', rather than an 'introverted' history, dealing with the facts it analyses, rather than with the theoretical and ideological assumptions which lie behind the work of the historian. This obviously does not imply that methodological questions are not a legitimate object of study; but I believe that it is possible to offer useful contributions on the history of linguistics, without dealing in the first instance with the theory of historiography.

5. One of the main linguists of our times, Yakov Malkiel, observed some years ago (Malkiel and Langdon 1969) that to produce good work on the history of linguistcs it is not enough to be a linguist: one has also to be a historian, and to fulfill the expectations normally raised by a historical essay. Here of course, one can only observe that the ability to set some episodes of the history of linguistics within their social and cultural context, is the exception rather than the rule (examples that come to mind are those of Dionisotti (1967a, b, 1972) or Timpanaro (1963, 1965, 1972, 1973)). What I had in mind for this history of linguistics was the more modest aim of providing information about ideas on language, in different periods and societies, which are not easily (and in some cases not at all) accessible elsewhere.

I know from direct experience that linguists feel the need for a work of this kind, and I hope it may also appeal to readers who are interested to know how people, at different times and within different cultural traditions, have looked at one of the most essential and challenging features of our common humanity – that is, language.

Giulio Lepschy

References

AARSLEFF, H. (1982) *From Locke to Saussure. Essays on the Study of Language and Intellectual History*, University of Minnesota Press, Minneapolis.

AMIROVA, T. A., OL'KHOVIKOV, B. A. and ROŽDESTVENSKIJ, JU. V. (1975) *Očerki po istorii lingvistiki*, Nauka, Moskva (German tr. *Abriss der Geschichte der Sprachwissenschaft*, Veb Bibliographisches Institut, Leipzig, 1980).

AUROUX, S. (ed.) (1989) *Histoire des idées linguistiques. Tome I: La naissance des métalangages. En Orient et en Occident*, Mardaga, Liège-Bruxelles.

AUROUX, S. (ed.) (1992) *Histoires des idées linguistiques. Tome 2: Le développement de la grammaire occidentale*, Mardaga, Liège.

BENFEY, T. (1869) *Geschichte der Sprachwissenschaft und orientalischen Philogie in Deutschland, seit dem Anfange des 19. Jahrunderts mit einem Rückblick auf die früheren Zeiten*, Cotta, München.

BORST, A. (1957–63) *Der Turmbau von Babel. Geschichte der Meinungen über Ursprung und Vielfalt der Sprachen und Völker*, Hiersemann, Stuttgart.

BRINCAT, G. (1986) *La linguistica prestrutturale*, Zanichelli, Bologna.

BYNON, T. and PALMER, F. R. (eds) (1986) *Studies in the History of Western Linguistics. In Honour of R.H. Robins*, Cambridge University Press, Cambridge.

CHEVALIER, J.-C. and ENCREVÉ, P. (eds) (1984) *Vers une histoire sociale de la linguistique* (Langue Française, 63), Larousse, Paris.

CHOMSKY, N. (1966) *Cartesian Linguistics. A Chapter in the History of Rationalist Thought*, Harper and Row, New York.

DELBRÜCK, B. (1880) *Einleitung in das Sprachstudium. Ein Beitrag zur Geschichte und Methodik der vergleichenden Sprachforschung*, Breitkopf und Härtel, Leipzig.

DIONISOTTI, C. (1967a) La lingua italiana da Venezia all'Europa. Il Fortunio e la filologia umanistica. Niccolò Liburnio e la letteratura cortigiana, in *Rinascimento europeo e Rinascimento veneziano*, edited by V. Branca, Sansoni, Firenze, 1–46.

DIONISOTTI, C. (1967b) *Geografia e storia della letteratura italiana*, Einaudi, Torino.

DIONISOTTI, C. (1972) *A Year's Work in the Seventies. The Presidential Address of the Modern Humanities Research Association delivered at University College, London, on 7 January 1972*, reprinted from *The Modern Language Review*, Vol. 67, No. 4.

EBBESEN, S. (ed.) (1995) Sprachtheorien in Spätantike und Mittelalter (Geschichte der Sprachtheorie, edited by P. Schmitter, 3), Narr, Tübingen.

FORMIGARI, L. and LO PIPARO, F. (eds) (1988) *Prospettive di storia della linguistica*, Editori Riuniti, Roma.

GRAFFI, G. (1991) *La sintassi tra Ottocento e Novecento*, il Mulino, Bologna.

GROTSCH, K. (1982) *Sprachwissenschaftsgeschichtsschreibung. Ein Beitrag zur Kritik und zur historischen un methodologischen Selbstvergewisserung der Disziplin*, Kümmerle Verlag, Göppingen.

HYMES, D. (ed.) (1974) *Studies in the History of Linguistics*, Indiana University Press, Bloomington.

ITKONEN, E. (1991) *Universal History of Linguistics*, Benjamins, Amsterdam.

KOERNER, K. (1978) *Towards a Historiography of Linguistics. Selected Essays*, Benjamins, Amsterdam.

KOERNER, K. (1989) *Practicing Linguistic Historiography. Selected Essays*, Benjamins, Amsterdam.

KOERNER, K. (1995) *Professing Linguistic Historiography*, Benjamins, Amsterdam.

KOERNER, K. and ASHER, R. E. (eds) (1995) *Concise History of the Language Sciences. From the Sumerians to the Cognitivists*, Pergamon, Elsevier Science, Oxford.

LAW, V. (1990) Language and its Students: the History of Linguistics, in *An Encyclopedia of Language*, edited by N.E. Collinge, Routledge, London/New York, 784–842.

LEPSCHY, G. (ed.) (1990–94) *Storia della linguistica*, 3 vols, il Mulino, Bologna.

MALKIEL, Y. and LANGDON, M. (1969) History and Histories of Linguistics, *Romance Philology*, 22, 530–74.

MALMBERG, B. (1991) *Histoire de la linguistique de Sumer à Saussure*, Presses Universitaires de France, Paris.

MEILLET, A. (1903) *Introduction à l'étude comparative des langues indoeuropéennes*, Hachette, Paris (eighth edition, 1937).

MOUNIN, G. (1967–72) *Histoire de la linguistique*, 2 vols, Presses Universitaires de France, Paris.

OL'KHOVIKOV, B. A. (1985) *Teorija jazyka i vid grammatičeskogo opisanija v istorii jazykoznanija. Stanovlenie i evolucija kanona grammatičeskogo opisanija v Evrope*, Nauka, Moskva.

PARRET, H. (ed.) (1976) *History of Linguistic Thought and Contemporary Linguistics*, De Gruyter, Berlin.

PEDERSEN, H. (1924) *Sprogvidenskaben i det Nittende Aarhundrede. Metoder og Resultater*, Gyldendalske Boghandel, København (English tr. *Linguistic Science in the Nineteenth Century*, Harvard University Press, Cambridge, Massachusetts, 1931; and with the new title *The Discovery of Language. Linguistic Science in the Nineteenth Century*, Indiana University Press, Bloomington, 1962).

RAUMER, R. VON (1870) *Geschichte der germanischen Philologie vorzugsweise in Deutschland*, Oldenbourg, München.

ROBINS, R. H. (1967) *A Short History of Linguistics*, Longman, London (fourth edition, 1997).

SALMON, V. (1979) *The Study of Language in Seventeenth-Century England*, Benjamins, Amsterdam (second edition, 1988).

SALMON, V. (1996) *Language and Society in Early Modern England. Selected Essays 1981–1994*, Benjamins, Amsterdam.

SCHMITTER, P. (1982) *Untersuchungen zur Historiographie der Linguistik. Struktur – Methodik – Theoretische Fundierung*, Narr, Tübingen.

SCHMITTER, P. (ed.) (1987) *Zur Theorie und Methode der Geschichtsschreibung der Linguistik. Analysen und Reflexionen* (Geschichte der Sprachtheorie, 1), Narr, Tübingen.

SCHMITTER, P. (ed.) (1991) *Sprachtheorien der abendländischen Antike* (Geschichte der Sprachtheorie, 2), Narr, Tübingen.

SCHMITTER, P. (ed.) (1996) *Sprachtheorien der Neuzeit II. Von der Grammaire de Port-Royal (1660) zur Konstitution moderner linguistischer Disziplinen* (Geschichte der Sprachtheorie, 5), Narr, Tübingen.

SEBEOK, T. (ed.) (1975) *Historiography of Linguistics* (Current Trends in Linguistics, 13), Mouton, The Hague.

STAMMERJOHANN, H. (ed.) (1996) *Lexicon grammaticorum. Who's Who in the History of Linguistics*, Niemeyer, Tübingen.

STEIN, G. (1997) *John Palsgrave as a Renaissance Linguist. A Pioneer in Vernacular Language Description*, Clarendon Press, Oxford.

STEINTHAL, H. (1863) *Geschichte der Sprachwissenschaft bei den Griechen und Römern mit besonderer Rücksicht auf die Logik*, Dümmler, Berlin (second edition, 1890–91).

TAGLIAVINI, C. (1963) *Panorama di storia della linguistica*, Pàtron, Bologna.

TIMPANARO, S. (1963) *La genesi del metodo del Lachmann*, Le Monnier, Firenze (new edition, Liviana, Padova, 1985).

TIMPANARO, S. (1965) *Classicismo e illuminismo nell'Ottocento italiano*, Nistri Lischi, Pisa (second, enlarged edition, 1969).

TIMPANARO, S. (1972) Friedrich Schlegel e gli inizi della linguistica indoeuropea in Germania, *Critica Storica*, 9, 72–105 (Eglish tr. Friedrich Schlegel and the Beginnings of Indo-European Linguistics in Germany, in F. Schlegel, *Ueber die Sprache und Weisheit der Indier*, edited by E.F.K. Koerner, Benjamins, Amsterdam, xi–lvii).

TIMPANARO, S. (1973) Il contrasto tra i fratelli Schlegel e Franz Bopp sulla struttura e la genesi delle lingue indoeuropee, *Critica Storica*, 10, 53–90.

Acknowledgements

In the preparation of the Italian edition I availed myself of the advice of many friends and colleagues. For Volume I, I should like to thank in particular Zyg Barański, Verina Jones, Anna Morpurgo Davies, Joanna Weinberg (Introduction); Michael Halliday and Michael Loewe (Chapter 1); Anna Morpurgo Davies (Chapter 2); Arnaldo Momigliano (Chapter 3); Ada Rapoport and Joanna Weinberg (Chapter 4); Bernard Lewis (Chapter 5); for Volume II, Tullio De Mauro (Chapter 2); for Volume III: Giuseppe Dell'Agata (Chapter 1), Tullio De Mauro (Chapter 2). I am grateful to Emma Sansone, who sensitively performed the difficult job of translating into English chapters originally in other languages (Volume I, Chapter 5; Volume II, Chapter 2; Volume III, Chapters 1 and 2; Volume V). I should also like to thank the series' editors for their comments during the preparation of the English edition. This introduces some updatings and improvements on the previous Italian edition. In particular Volume I, Chapter 4 includes a more detailed discussion of Hebrew grammatical ideas, and Chapter 5 profited from the suggestions of Edward Ullendorff and of the late A. F. L. Beeston. I am grateful to Chiara Cirillo, Rolando Ferri and Helena Sanson for their help with the proofs and the index of Volume III.

GCL

Preface

This volume was originally intended as a chapter for the *History of Linguistics* edited by Giulio Lepschy. During its composition the chapter acquired a life of its own and expanded well beyond its original limits until it became necessary to modify the original plans in order to accommodate its new size. I am grateful to Giulio Lepschy, to the series editors and to the publishers who have shown far more patience and flexibility than I deserved or could have hoped for.

The text was originally written in English but an Italian translation (by Dr. Francesca Nassi) has already appeared in two different versions: in 1994 as a section of the third volume of the *Storia della linguistica* edited by Lepschy for Il Mulino; in 1996 as a revised and somewhat extended independent volume (*La linguistica dell'Ottocento*, Il Mulino, Bologna). In this English edition I have introduced some further corrections and additions.

In the Introduction (pp. xiii–xvii) Lepschy lists some of the general features of his *History of Linguistics*. The aim, he states, is relatively modest: to concentrate on a historical-philological account of facts, ideas and works of the past. Space constraints do not allow any protracted discussion of method or an attempt at linking the history of the subject with the social and cultural history of the period. On the other hand history of linguistics, in Lepschy's view, is best interpreted broadly as history of linguistic thought; to concentrate merely on linguistic theory or on the science of language excluding the attitudes to language and other linguistic concerns would have been too limited and limiting.

The first point I find reassuring when I consider my own limitations: most of my work has been in historical and comparative linguistics and I lack philosophical or historical training. The second point has general validity, but in the nineteenth century a different option becomes available. I have preferred to concentrate on the interests, theories and achievements of the professional linguists of the time, even at the cost of neglecting some of the more popular discussions about language.

Admittedly in our period language and linguistic problems played an
increasingly important part for the general public. The increase in literacy
linked to the spreading of school education called for the compilation
of a greater and greater number of grammars and dictionaries. At the
same time the formation of the new national languages prompted extensive discussions about the merits of the one or the other form of speech
and about the contrast between spoken and written language; the change
in religious attitudes which introduced stricter requirements in the translations, editions etc. of the sacred texts, led to protracted debates about
hermeneutics and the nature of translations; the new conception of race,
tied as it was to linguistic differences, brought out the social and political role of language. Yet the great novelty of the nineteenth century
is the creation of a linguistic profession and a linguistic discipline which
found their initial support in the research ethos of the German universities. Among the achievements of this professional linguistics there is
a series of 'positive' results (to use the terminology of the time), which
were seen as testable and verifiable and had remarkable repercussions
on the general ideology of the period and on the way in which the
layman came to perceive linguistic facts. These are unique events and
must be given priority in any account of nineteenth-century linguistic
thought, even if obviously they do not exhaust it. A correct analysis is
all the more necessary at a time when the technical and crucial part of
nineteenth-century work, which is largely historical and comparative,
has become impenetrable not only to the historian of ideas but also to
the linguist who has not had a traditional training. In the last forty or
fifty years the concerns of linguistics have changed. We now risk not
understanding any longer the motivation and the methodological assumptions of a number of results which are still valid, but are known only
to a few historical linguists; at the same time, however, we also fail to
understand the intellectual background of those linguistic theories which
prevailed at the beginning of the twentieth century and in spite of the
later changes in attitude were – and are – still influential at a much later
period.

Even within my self-imposed limits this book suffers from noticeable
gaps. Some choices are inevitable since nobody can be equally competent in all subjects; my account of Indo-European studies is more complete than my account of Romance, and within Indo-European I lay
more emphasis on the classical languages than on e.g. Slavic or Celtic.
I have occasionally referred to work on non Indo-European languages
but here I have had to take a great deal on trust. The concentration on
Europe and the United States of America is due to institutional facts;
these are the areas in which professional linguistics developed. The
influence of German learning and German universities on the subject
has been immense and German-speaking linguists have a privileged

position in this story; for the rest I have tried to keep track of the developments in England, France and Italy and occasionally the United States, not because they were necessarily more important than those in e.g. the Netherlands or Denmark or Russia, but because in my view they are representative of the different ways in which linguistics was understood and developed. The bibliographical notes should compensate for the gaps in the information provided.

Intellectual movements do not normally start at the beginning of a century and end at its end nor do the individual scholars operate in an intellectual vacuum. The earlier view that 'scientific' linguistics sprang fully armed from the heads of Schlegel or Bopp or even Sir William Jones is of course too simplistic. I have tried to highlight the diversity and vitality of linguistic thought which marked the beginning of the century and to indicate how closely linked the various tendencies were to those of the earlier period. Yet by the late 1830s scholars came to believe that they were moving within a new paradigm and at that stage a break in continuity did in fact take place: the older books were no longer read. The historiography of the late nineteenth century magnified the break and that of the early twentieth century followed suit. Historiography now becomes an essential component of our history. A second component is institutional. Lists of newly-founded university chairs and their holders are tedious; yet it is just the creations of these chairs, initially in Germany, and then in the rest of Europe and North America, that gave to linguistics its new status and was instrumental on the one hand in creating a break between the eighteenth and the nineteenth century, on the other in guaranteeing the continuity between the linguistics of the nineteenth century and that of the following century.

At the other end of the century the position is different. In my view the continuity with the twentieth century is not only institutional but also intellectual. The shift from historical and comparative to descriptive and structural work, from technical to theoretical approach, which characterizes the twentieth century happened gradually and was to a large extent prepared by the earlier discussions. For my purposes a stopping point was necessary, but no obvious date offered itself; my choice of a round figure, the years 1899–1900, is meant to underline the arbitrary and conventional nature of such a division.

Lepschy gives a brief account of the present historiography; I see no need to repeat it or to dissent from it. The multi-author and multi-volume histories edited by Auroux, Koerner and Schmitter respectively which he mentions (p. xvi) are now reaching the nineteenth century and will bring yet another perspective to the subject. They will no doubt fill some of the gaps which I pointed out above even if it is likely that a comparison between the various works will reveal how personal each choice necessarily is. They may also help the reader to make an

enlightened selection in the recent bibliography. One of the problems
– and the advantages – of the recent developments has been the multiplication of monographs and detailed analyses of special points in the
history of linguistics. It is now almost impossible to keep up-to-date
with the secondary literature and we have all read two or more authors
who discuss exactly the same subject without knowing of each other.
No doubt my book will offer other instances of the same phenomenon.
I have had to ignore some very recent works; in particular I regret not
having been able to use the second volume of the *Spractheorien der
Neuzeit*, edited by Peter Schmitter (Narr, Tübingen, 1996) and the recent
Histoire de la pensée linguistique (PUF, Paris, 1997) by Pierre Swiggers,
both of which appeared after I had submitted my manuscript to the
editor. A recent survey of the history of French linguistics by P. Desmet,
L. Melis and P. Swiggers in *Travaux de linguistique*, 33 (1996), 133–
78 can fill some of my bibliographical gaps.

*   *   *

In writing this book I have incurred a series of debts – all of which are
impossible or almost impossible to repay.

The first is with Giulio Lepschy. It is a truism to say that if he had
not asked me to contribute to his history of linguistics this book would
not have been written, but if I have not given up the attempt on more
than one occasion this is entirely due to him. With his typical unassum-
ing authority he has offered and produced help at all stages, while
cheerfully and patiently accepting my perennial delays and showing
with his example how much more useful the carrot is than the stick. It
is not surprising that my respect and admiration have increased over the
years; it is more surprising that our long-standing friendship has survived through a period in which I felt, and was, permanently guilty.

My interest in the history of linguistics dates from some thirty years
ago when Arnaldo Momigliano asked me to read a paper about
Brugmann to his seminar at the Warburg Institute. To my protestations
that I knew nothing about the subject and cared less he replied with a
firm 'nonsense' and refused to take no for an answer. My first reading
of the neogrammarians opened a new world: on the one hand historical
linguistics in the making with all the opportunities to rethink what I had
learned as acquired facts often without understanding their rationale, on
the other hand a chance to see how distorted the normal second-hand
accounts of the figures of the past can be. I owe to Momigliano the
discovery, new for me, that historiography and the history of historiography are necessary parts of history.

In those same years I was lucky enough to have almost daily meetings with Eduard Fraenkel; in his Oxford seminars I not only learned
to read Greek and Latin authors and to respect our predecessors but

also had a glimpse of what it means to be part of a living tradition. It is impossible to write about the academic world of nineteenth-century Germany without realizing how important the link was between the teacher and the student and how great the tension between what one learned and what one thought, school loyalty and individual research. Thanks to Eduard Fraenkel, who had studied with Wilhelm Schulze and Jacob Wackernagel and, through Johannes Schmidt, his teacher's teacher, traced his intellectual ancestry to the middle of the nineteenth century, I had first-hand contact with a world which otherwise I would have known only through the printed text.

Yet my greatest debt of gratitude is to Henry Hoenigswald. I owe him what seems to me the central idea of this book. Starting with the nineteenth century there is or may be a chasm between what linguists do and what they say they do. The method and the achievements of the historical and comparative linguists of the nineteenth century must be extracted from their technical work rather than from their prefaces or their rhetoric. They may not have been aware of their modus operandi but at some point in my narrative this is what joins together people from very different schools and allows rivals and enemies, such as those who took opposite sides in the neogrammarians' controversy, to do the same type of work and reach the same conclusions. Our first task is then that of extracting the method from the actual work. The task does not end there; the general works are important and often very important; at present they are enjoying a renaissance after the initial neglect. Yet they cannot be used as tools to interpret the technical work, while the converse may occasionally be true.

The recent explosion of interest in the history of linguistics has changed the picture of the subject. I hope that the pages that follow will show how much I owe to those who have contributed to it. Other debts are too numerous to be listed, but I want to thank my two Oxford colleagues, John Penney and David Langslow, for the help they have given me over the years and for their willingness to allow our joint Indo-European seminars to include constant references to the earlier history of the problems discussed. I am also grateful to the librarians of the Ashmolean library, the Bodleian library, the Taylor Institution, and of my Oxford college, Somerville, for the patience with which they have helped me to trace my sources in the most recondite parts of their libraries. Finally, Pamela Catling, with equal patience, has compiled the index of names included in general index.

My mother, Maria Morpurgo Castelnuovo, died while I was writing this book. Others tried to teach me how to think of linguistics or philology, but she tried to teach me how to think. The book is dedicated to her memory.

Anna Morpurgo Davies

1

Historiography and institutions

1.1 The first 'scientific' linguistics?

In a number of standard textbooks written between the 1860s and the 1960s the early nineteenth century is taken as the point of departure for the history of 'scientific' linguistics. The implicit or explicit claim is that only at that date linguistics entered 'la voie rationelle' (Leroy 1971, 17). Yet it is clear that serious concern with language at a descriptive or philosophical level existed at a much earlier stage. If so, why this arbitrary starting point? This is a question in the history of historiography, but is equally relevant to the history of linguistics. An answer may help to define the specific characters of nineteenth-century linguistic thought and to provide an account of the links between that thought and modern linguistic work.

1.1.1 A unitary purpose?

The first impression of someone reading in, or about, the literature of the period is that the scholarly linguistic work of the nineteenth century in, e.g. France, England, Italy, Germany and to a certain extent in the United States is characterized by a unity of intent and purpose, which, if allowance is made for the predictable academic squabbles and the necessary divergencies of opinion about individual points, allows the observer to produce a coherent characterization of the work of the time. In brief, as has often been stated, the main concern of the century is with linguistic history and linguistic comparison. The main achievements are, on the one hand, the establishment of a set of discovery procedures which are used to classify languages from a genetic point of view in language families, to determine their subgrouping, to establish the main points of their historical developments, and to a certain extent to reconstruct unattested protolanguages; on the other hand, the collection and classification in the terms indicated of an immense amount of linguistic data and philological material. The most spectacular results concern the Indo-European linguistic family and the reconstruction reached by the end of the century of the main features of Indo-European, the unattested parent language. Thus in the history of nineteenth-century linguistics it seems possible to trace a straightforward line of development conceived in terms of linear progress based on increased factual information and on the solution of a series of technical problems; the very coherence of the century's work would then explain our attitude towards it.

1.1.2 A monolithic subject?

This analysis is partly correct but is heavily oversimplified. Above all our impression of a monolithic subject is to a certain extent the result of a selection consciously or subconsciously operated on what was actually written and published. Among other things it ignores national differences, which especially in the first part of the century were considerable, and tends to concentrate on the German development as paradigmatic. The slow arrival in England, for instance, of the 'new philology', i.e. of what is normally taken to be the typical approach of nineteenth-century linguistics, breaks the general pattern (Aarsleff 1983). Similarly in France the new discipline was slow to become established (Hültenschmidt 1987) and even at the end of the century, thanks to Bréal, preserved closer links with the earlier centuries than it had done in Germany. But 'German' linguistics too is less monolithic than it seems. There is a multitude of German and Austrian nineteenth-century publications on linguistic matters which the main-stream practitioners hardly ever mention. An obscure dissertation published in 1829 (Loewe 1829) lists some 25 books about 'philosophical grammar' published in German between 1800 and 1828; most of these authors were hardly ever quoted by their more famous successors or contemporaries and are now unknown (see below, p. 25). Much later the reviews written by established scholars are often more instructive about what was being published and discussed than the references which we find in their substantive work. As late as 1877, the young Karl Brugmann reviewed under the same heading no less than three books by reputable authors (Marty, Steinthal, Noiré) about the origin of language (Brugman 1877). These books could not have had much general impact in a period in which the newly founded Société de Linguistique de Paris had undertaken not to discuss the question of the origin of language. In fact our historiography has blotted away not only 'minor' authors, but also unpalatable work by 'major' authors; the forms of glottogonic thought which so frequently accompany the achievements of the century in historical linguistics are normally ignored (Vallini 1987). Similarly, nobody remembers the time and effort spent by the best brains of the period in Germany and elsewhere in the attempt to define criteria for a typological classification of languages, an attempt which later fell into discredit and consequently into obscurity (Morpurgo Davies 1975).

1.1.3 Institutional facts and historiographical assumptions

How do we explain the selectivity of our account? Internal data are not sufficient. Two 'external' factors are also important: institutions and historiography.

Aarsleff (1982, 4) has argued that a coherent history of 'the craft of linguistics' as such cannot be pushed back behind the creation of comparative and historical philology as academic disciplines in the early decades of the nineteenth century. This is probably correct; the institutionalization of linguistics in the Universities (starting with the German Universities) is a nineteenth-century phenomenon. It marked off the 'new' linguistics from that of the earlier period, it helped to give the subject a new identity, and finally established a link between our linguistics and that of the previous century. The selection of University teachers largely from within the University system guaranteed an element of continuity which previously had been lacking and opened new possibilities for a coherent development. When we speak of main-stream linguists we in fact refer to those who were accepted by the academic establishment.

The period was also characterized by public self-analysis and/or hagiography to a level previously unheard of. Institutionalization predictably led to the multiplication of that published matter which rates half-way between history and ephemera: obituaries, elogia, institutional accounts are the necessary by-products of academies, periodicals, Universities, etc. But linguists were also tireless in trying to write the history of their subject and of their own achievements. For no earlier period do we have an equal wealth of secondary literature which classifies and defines the work done, reconstructs its development and traces its intellectual ancestry. This contemporary historiography is bound to have had an influence on our own views and our approach to our predecessors.

If so, we cannot any longer postpone a brief exploration of institutional facts and historiographical assumptions.

1.2 Linguistics and academe

In the nineteenth century, linguistic scholarship came to find in the Universities its natural habitat. This was not so in the previous two centuries. A history of linguistics (admittedly incomplete) such as Arens (1969) lists among the influential authors of the seventeenth and eighteenth centuries: Bacon, Wallis, Holder, Locke, Arnauld, Nicole, Comenius, Leibniz, Junius, L. Ten Kate, J. Ludolf, Condillac, Maupertuis, Rousseau,

Ch. de Brosses, Beauzée, Herder, Lichtenberg, Monboddo, Horne Tooke. Of these authors only a few have been labelled linguists rather than e.g. philosophers (such as Bacon, Locke, Leibniz, Condillac, etc.); even fewer would count as professional academics. Wallis, who is among the latter, was in fact a professor of geometry (not of anything to do with language) at Oxford. By contrast, the names mentioned by Arens for the middle or the second half of the nineteenth century (Pott, Böhtlingk, von Raumer, Steinthal, Brücke, Schleicher, Georg Curtius, Whitney, Scherer, Johannes Schmidt, Leskien, Sievers, Verner, Brugmann, Henry Sweet, Baudouin de Courtenay, Wenker, Ascoli, Saussure, Schuchardt, Gaston Paris, Paul Meyer, Rousselot, etc.) belong to scholars who can mostly be called linguists and held relevant University or research positions mainly in Germany but also, to judge from this list, in Austria, Denmark, England, France, Italy, Poland, Russia, Switzerland and the United States. If we look at the end of the century and the more modern period, Arens' selection, which is certainly not afflicted by anti-German prejudice, reveals a disappearance of the German predominance; even so all scholars included were professional academics holding chairs in linguistics or allied disciplines.

1.2.1 University expansion

This superficial test then confirms our first impression about the institutionalization of linguistics and its link with the newly formed or remodelled Universities. Three phenomena of different nature contributed. The first is a tremendous increase in the number and/or size of higher education institutions in Europe and North America. The German data are particularly impressive, partly because of the special nature of University development in the German states (especially in North Germany), partly because they are fuller than those available for other countries and have been the object of more intense scrutiny. A few figures, even if not absolutely exact, make the point: in Germany during the Napoleonic wars the number of University students fell to c. 5,500 but by 1889–90 the number had reached 28,820, by 1914 60,748 (Jarausch 1982, 27ff.). In Germany as elsewhere the increase in student numbers was accompanied by an increase in the number of teachers. In 1840 the German states had a total of 1,212 University teachers (including Ordinarii, Extraordinarii and Privatdozenten), in 1892–3 the total was 2,275 (Conrad 1893, I, 144). In other European countries the development was much slower but, in general, Universities show strong numerical expansion towards the end of the century. The examples that follow are arbitrarily chosen but significant.

In England and Wales (as contrasted with Scotland) the century starts with higher education limited to two Universities only, Oxford and Cambridge, but ends with a number of additional new institutions and the impulse for the creation of further Universities. We can speak of 17,839 students in higher education in 1901 as contrasted with 3,385 in 1861 (Lowe 1983) and less than 1,500 in 1800 (Sanderson 1975). At Oxford – to offer an example which was statistically significant at the time – the teaching staff increased from 50 to 191 between 1814 and 1900 while the undergraduates increased from 945 to 3,091 (Engel 1983, 288).

France is a special case. The French revolution had abolished all Universities, and the *facultés*, which were formed later, were not devoted to research but were mainly concerned with administering the *baccalauréat*; the Universities come seriously to the fore only in the 1880s. The data available are far less circumstantial than for Germany but between 1861 and 1865 we assume that there was an annual average of 91 *licences* (degrees which qualified graduates to teach in schools) in letters and 95 in sciences for the whole country (Prost 1968, 243); between 1881 and 1885 the numbers had risen to 256 and 309, and between 1906 and 1910 to 537 and 532.[1]

If we exclude the preparatory schools for the faculties of medicine and pharmacy, in 1876 there were *c*. 9,400 students. These rose to *c*. 15,200 in 1890 and *c*. 40,300 in 1914 (Weisz 1983, 236). In the faculties of letters according to Weisz (*loc. cit.*) the figures were of 238 students in 1876, 1,834 in 1890 and 6,586 in 1914. In 1865 there were 79 professors in the faculties of letters, as contrasted with 116 in 1888 and 178 in 1919 (Weisz 1983, 318). Seminars and research institutes begin to appear on the German model only at the end of last century and the beginning of our century (Charle 1994, 47ff.).

For Italy good statistical data are available from 1861, the creation of the Italian kingdom. In that year 20 Universities had a total of 6,504 students; by contrast in 1900 26 universities had 26,033 students, and the number increased to 29,624 in 1914. In 1861 we are told that there were only 163 students in all faculties of letters as contrasted with 2,049 in 1900 and 2,734 in 1914 (*Sommario* 1958, 78–9).

At the same time the North America Universities began to make their impact known. Here higher education did not necessarily imply a form of instruction similar to that of German Universities but the number of students involved in 1800 has been reckoned to be 1,237 as contrasted with 12,964 in 1840, 62,000 in 1870 and 256,000 in 1900 (Burke 1983, 111).

1.2.2 The academic class
Statistics about student numbers are perhaps not as important as the other facts to which we referred earlier: the creation in Europe and North America of an academic professional class underpinned by new possibilities of a regular academic career and the beginning of a new attitude

towards research and scholarship. The increase in student numbers was accompanied by an increase in the number of professors; the scholarly life was open even to those of middle-class origin who depended on a salary for their livelihood. At the same time, specialized research and its publication came to be seen as part of the duties of University teachers. Here too the German Universities had a leading function: 'By 1835 much professorial learning had narrowed into disciplinary channels oriented toward research, discovery and specialization' (Turner 1975, 530). The other European and American Universities lagged behind. In 1893, in a statement not entirely deprived of chauvinistic pride, F. Paulsen (in Lexis 1893, 3ff.) noted that the pursuit and advancement of *Wissenschaft* ('science') were typical of all German Universities. In England, he argued, well-known names such as those of Macaulay, Gibbon, Darwin, H. Spencer, Grote, Bentham, Ricardo, James Mill and John Stuart Mill were not connected with Universities (cf. for the same point Perkin 1983, 209), but in Germany the position was different. There the reaction to the name of any important *Gelehrte* ('scholar') was bound to be: 'At what University is he?' and to the name of any professor: 'What has he written?'. Paulsen also noted that there were signs that in England and in France the situation was changing and that the United States was following suit. Yet in 1928 a great Italian classicist partly trained in Germany could still maintain that in England the greatest scholars had no connection with the Universities and that these were half finishing schools and half institutions of learning (Pasquali [1928] 1968, 392f.). This is exaggerated but it is certainly true that the creation of a professorial class which owed its allegiance both to a University institution and to the advancement of a discipline (Turner 1975) occurred in England and France only towards the end of the century. During the bad period of French Universities, research and scholarship had been associated with some *écoles spéciales*, with the Collège de France and with the academies but the other *facultés* had had little to contribute. As has been said, until the 1860s in higher education one could speak of 'Paris and the desert' (Charle and Verger 1994, 71). The foundation of the École Pratique des Hautes Études in 1868 is to a certain extent the result of the frustration of a minister, Duruy, who had not succeeded in his projects of University reform. A serious role of the Universities in the advancement of learning can only be seen in the last two decades of the century and after the impact of the process of University reform which was then initiated.

In the United States the Association of American Universities, founded in 1900 to promote research as the essential function of the Universities, was initially able to admit only 13 institutions (Light 1983, 352ff.). Here too specialization and advanced research in University teaching came to the fore at a late stage in the course of lively discussions.

Almost everywhere this movement towards a research ethos in the European and American Universities is consciously associated with a German model. As Renan put it in 1867, 'ce qui a vaincu à Sadowa c'est la science germanique' ('at Sadowa the victor was German science'; Prost 1968, 228). In England in 1868 Thomas Huxley quoted the Royal Commissioners, who had reported on the University of Oxford in 1850, and one of the Oxford reformers, Mark Pattison, in order to say that 'in Germany the Universities are exactly what the Rector of Lincoln [*sc.* Mark Pattison] and the Commissioners tell us the English Universities are not; that is to say, corporations of "learned men devoting their lives to the cultivation of science, and the direction of academical education"'. He had previously said that the German Universities had in the course of a century become 'the most intensely cultivated and the most productive intellectual corporations the world has ever seen' (Huxley [1868] 1971, 95f.). In 1885, in the preface to a translation of Conrad's book about German Universities, an Oxford professor stated that 'the prosecution of inquiry and research . . . in Scotland is not provided for at all and in England is being somewhat awkwardly attempted' (cf. Conrad 1885, xxv). The German model, he argued, had to be studied very seriously. Conrad himself had written (I quote from the English translation) that in Germany 'the entire body of university teachers . . . may be regarded as a standard of the purely scientific activity of the nation' (1885, 213).

1.2.3 Linguistics as a University discipline

Against this background, linguistics came to be established as a University discipline, first in Germany and then, through developments which in part were inspired by the German model, in the other European countries and in North America.[2]

In Germany the first University position with a title which specifically referred to the study of linguistics was established in 1821 for Franz Bopp; its name (*Orientalische Literatur und allgemeine Sprachkunde*) perhaps represented a compromise between the old and the new order (Wackernagel 1904). Yet it is significant that the chair belonged to the newly founded University of Berlin, Humboldt's creation and the most advanced and forward-looking product of Prussian education. Some eighty years later, in 1902, all German Universities, ancient and new, had at least one official position in linguistics and often more than one – though at the time linguistics often meant comparative linguistics or *Indogermanistik* (Wackernagel 1904, 206). By the second part of the century, in Germany at least, a brilliant scholar could have reasonable expectations of an academic career in a linguistic subject; this was certainly not the case at the beginning of the century.[3] But again in Germany the creation of the new chairs of linguistics was not an isolated fact. In the expansion of German Universities the *Philosophische Fakultät* (which included all arts and sciences, but not medicine, law and theology) had had the lion's share. In 1881–6 it was the largest of the four faculties and in the last part of the century more than half of all University teachers belonged to it (Conrad 1893, 145ff.). Yet within the *Philosophische Fakultät* the greatest increase in chairs was due to comparative linguistics and to the non-classical languages (oriental and modern languages) (Conrad 1884, 169; cf. also Christmann 1985). Conrad, himself a professor of 'Government', observed that in the field of non-classical languages a series of new scientific subjects had recently arisen or reached greater independence; they were new and differentiated disciplines which required a professor each and consequently had led to the creation of a series of new chairs. He quoted by way of example German, Egyptian, Indian, Romance and English philology, and added that richer Universities could afford even Slavic and Celtic philology (Conrad 1884, 170). In other words, in Germany at least, even the outsider was struck by the success of the linguistic disciplines in the Universities and by the creation of new chairs in linguistics or related subjects. Conrad gives us some figures: in 1835 in Leipzig there was only one Ordinarius in the fields of Sanskrit, oriental and modern languages, but in 1882–3 there were 9 Ordinarii for these subjects; Berlin had 3 Ordinarii in 1835, but 8 in 1882–3. The academic position of Sanskrit is relevant here; at present we do not necessarily expect a professor of Sanskrit to be interested in linguistic matters but a German Sanskritist in nineteenth-century Germany was likely to have much in common with a professor of *Vergleichende Sprachwissenschaft*. By 1850 there were at least 10 chairs of Sanskrit in German Universities; the first of these had been founded as early as 1818 for A. W. Schlegel.[4]

Other European countries followed suit but at a much slower pace, as one might have predicted in view of the different speed of development of their University systems. The newly formed University of London (then to become University College) appointed as Professor of Oriental Languages in 1828 a German pupil of Franz Bopp and a friend of Eugène Burnouf (Barthélemy-St Hilaire 1891, 108f.), the 23-year-old F. A. Rosen, who held the chair for a short period but inspired his classical colleagues with interest in German-type philology (Chambers 1939, 345f.). In 1842 University College appointed one of these, T. Hewitt Key, to the chair of Comparative Grammar (Szemerényi 1987, I, 21). Ten years earlier (1832) Oxford had established its chair of Sanskrit, but the aim was the diffusion of the Holy Scriptures in India. It was only in 1848 that it succeeded in appointing Frederick Trithen (a Swiss-born Russian trained in Germany, who published on Sanskrit, Greek and on the Slavonic languages) to a new chair of Modern European Languages (Simmons 1980, 10f.). After his premature death in 1854 he was succeeded by Friedrich Max Müller, a German Sanskritist and comparativist and the same scholar for whom in 1868 the chair of Comparative Philology was created; this was the first chair which the University established at its own expense and not as the result of a donation. In this period a few other chairs of linguistic subjects were established (Posner to appear).

In France there was a tradition of advanced studies in oriental languages, both at the Collège de France and at the École des Langues Orientales Vivantes (founded in 1795), but here too Sanskrit was the forerunner of the 'new' linguistics. Antoine-Léonard de Chézy was appointed to teach Sanskrit at the Collège de France in 1814 (the first Sanskrit chair in a European 'University') and was replaced in 1832 by the great Avestan, Sanskrit and Pali scholar Eugène Burnouf (1801–52), who was in close contact with Bopp. Yet, in spite of the greatness of these two scholars, in the first part of the century linguistics and Sanskrit were not interchangeable in the way in which they mostly were in Germany.[5] In 1852 a chair of *Grammaire comparée* was founded at the Faculté des Lettres de Paris by the minister Fortoul to replace a chair of Philosophy which was politically tiresome (Zeldin 1967); the professor appointed was Carl Benedikt Hase (1780–1864), who was already 72 (Auroux 1983, 248) and had no impact on French intellectual life. More important was the creation of the École d'Anthropologie (1867) with a chair of Linguistic Anthropology which was held by Abel Hovelacque until 1896 and by André Lefèvre after that (Auroux 1984, 299f.). However, it is only with the appointment of Michel Bréal as *Chargé de cours* at the Collège de France (1864), the creation for him of a chair of *Grammaire comparée* (1866), the foundation of the Société de Linguistique de Paris (1866) and the creation of the École Pratique des Hautes Études (1868), with a section of *Sciences historiques et philologiques*, where a number of the members of the Société de Linguistique found their home (Auroux 1983, 253; 1984, 304ff.), that a linguistic institutional establishment starts, ready to exploit the new University developments of the end of the century. Round the same period, the Romanists led by Gaston Paris, who was trained in Germany, also concentrate round the École des Hautes Études (Bergounioux 1984). Yet, even as late as 1905 complaints were registered that in this field Germany was much better off than France; it was pointed out that there was no chair of Provençal in France and that all the major linguistic chairs were in Paris only (Zeldin 1967, [1973] 1993, 2, 324).

In Italy the position was very different. The first chairs of Sanskrit precede the chairs of linguistics (Flechia at Turin from 1852, Bardelli at Florence from 1859) but with the formation of the new kingdom in 1861 the official ministerial policy encouraged the establishment of new chairs of Sanskrit and of Comparative Linguistics, even if the latter had varying titles: *Filologia indogermanica*; *Lingue e letterature comparate*;

Lingue indogermaniche; *Grammatica comparata e lingue orientali* (the title of the chair which Ascoli held in Milan from 1861 before he changed it to *Storia comparata delle lingue classiche e neolatine* in 1868). By the 1870s Turin, Florence, Bologna, Pisa, Naples, Rome and Milan all had relevant chairs (Timpanaro 1979, 418f.; Dovetto 1994b). In this form of institutionalization Italy lagged behind Germany but was ahead of both France and England.[6]

1.2.4 The first University chairs

The introduction of linguistics in the Universities appears then as a development which goes hand in hand with the introduction of a research ethos in higher education and is to a large extent led by Germany. At its clearest it leads to the creation of chairs variously called *Vergleichende Sprachwissenschaft, Allgemeine Sprachwissenschaft, Grammaire comparée*, Comparative Philology, *Filologia indogermanica*, etc., but these are not the only examples of linguistic chairs. Not altogether incongruously, the newly founded chairs of Sanskrit, Anglo-Saxon, Ancient Germanic Languages, etc., on the one hand, and of Modern Languages (English, French, German, Russian), etc., on the other, all contributed to the feeling that linguistic disciplines had made their impact on the Universities. Hebrew, some other oriental languages and the two classical languages were established in European Universities before our period. At some stage they too came, to a certain extent, within the orbit of linguistic disciplines; for some countries at least the reconciliation of classics and linguistics had a particularly profound impact. At different periods and in different ways two newly established disciplines, anthropology and psychology, also made their contribution to the institutional establishment of linguistics. The position in *Anthropologie linguistique* at the École d'Anthropologie in Paris has already been mentioned. In Germany, just to give an example, the impact which the University of Leipzig had on linguistics and on a number of foreign students during the last decades of the nineteenth century was based as much on the leading Indo-Europeanists who taught there (Leskien, Brugmann, Sievers, etc.) as on the prestige of Wilhelm Wundt, a professor of philosophy (from 1875), trained as a physiologist, who counts as one of the founders of experimental psychology but also opened his monumental *Völkerpsychologie* with two volumes on language (*Die Sprache*, 1900). Again in the second part of the century the development of phonetics brought together physiologists and linguists and eventually led to the creation of some University posts in Phonetics. Once more it may not be chance that the same University, Leipzig, employed at different times a medical scholar, Karl Ludwig Merkel (1812–76), who was the author of one of the most significant books on the physiology of speech (*Physiologie der menschlichen Sprache*, 1866), and an Indo-Europeanist and Germanist, E. Sievers, who

in 1876 published the extremely important *Grundzüge der Lautphysiologie*, then re-edited under the title of *Grundzüge der Phonetik* (1881)
(Kohler 1981, 162f.).

1.2.5 The linguistic periodicals

By the end of the century, linguistics had a firm institutional basis in the
Universities of a good part of Europe (and perhaps of the United States).
In Germany it even seemed necessary to one of its leading practitioners,
B. Delbrück (1875), to write a booklet about the study of linguistics
in German Universities which provided advice about the best way of
arranging courses during a student's first years at University.

A different form of institutionalization, which also reflected the new
research ethos of the century, led to the creation of specialist periodicals,
some of which still survive. In most Western countries the periodicals
dedicated to Asiatic or oriental studies are the oldest; they are not exclusively linguistic but contain linguistic articles. We may remember, without making a full list, the *Indische Bibliothek*, directed by A. W. Schlegel
and C. Lassen (1820–30), or the still-existing *Journal Asiatique* (Paris
1822–), *Journal of the Royal Asiatic Society* (London 1823–), *Journal of
the American Oriental Society* (from 1843–9), *Zeitschrift der Deutschen
Morgenländischen Gesellschaft* (1847–). At a later stage, periodicals
for Romance philology, Germanic philology, Slavic philology, etc., were
created but the nineteenth century also saw the foundation of new linguistic societies and new reviews dedicated to linguistics as such. In
Germany there was the *Zeitschrift für die Wissenschaft der Sprache*
(1845–53), the *Zeitschrift für vergleichende Sprachforschung auf dem
Gebiete des Deutschen, Griechischen und Lateinischen* (later . . . *auf
dem Gebiete der indogermanischen Sprachen*), edited by [F.F.] A. Kuhn
from 1852; the *Beiträge zur vergleichenden Sprachforschung auf dem
Gebiete der arischen, celtischen und slawischen Sprachen* (edited by
Kuhn together with Schleicher and started in 1858), *Orient und Occident*, edited by Benfey, 1860–6. In 1859/60 two relatively isolated scholars, Lazarus and Steinthal, founded the *Zeitschrift für Völkerpsychologie
und Sprachwissenschaft*, which died, in that form at least, in 1890 (cf.
p. 205). In the 1870s we observe a number of new reviews, some of
which survived into the twentieth century. A. Bezzenberger founded in
1877 the *Beiträge zur Kunde der indogermanischen Sprachen*. The
Morphologische Untersuchungen edited by Brugmann and Osthoff
published only 5 volumes between 1878 and 1890 and a sixth in 1910,
but the *Indogermanische Forschungen* founded by Brugmann in 1891
are still being published in the 1990s. In 1884 Friedrich Techmer started
the *Internationale Zeitschrift für allgemeine Sprachwissenschaft*, which
ended with its editor in 1890 (cf. p. 269).[7] Outside Germany, the Philological Society, which had mainly linguistic interests, was reconstituted

in London in 1842 on the basis of an older society; its *Transactions* have appeared continuously since then.

In France the foundation of the Société de Linguistique de Paris in 1866 (but in fact in 1863) and the publication of its *Mémoires* from 1868 and of its *Bulletin* from 1869 are well-known facts, but there had been earlier linguistic societies and earlier periodicals: an Institut des Langues, then renamed Société de Linguistique, was founded in Paris in 1837 (Auroux 1983) in connection with the third series (1837–40) of the *Journal de la langue française et des langues en général*. The existence of a *Revue de linguistique et de philologie comparée* from 1867 to 1916 is often forgotten, partly because its contributors, who included Hovelacque, Chavée, etc., did not belong to what later came to be regarded as mainstream linguistics (Auroux 1984, 303ff.; Desmet 1994). From 1868 the *Revue critique d'histoire et de littérature*, among whose editors were the Romanists Gaston Paris and Paul Meyer, published numerous linguistic articles (Nicolas 1988, 58f.). The *Revue des langues romanes* and the *Revue celtique* begin in 1870, and the end of the century sees the first periodicals dedicated to dialectology: the *Revue des patois gallo-romans* (1887–93), edited by J. Gilliéron and the abbé Rousselot (then *Bulletin de la Société des parlers de France*, until 1898), and the *Revue des patois* (1887–89), edited by L. Clédat (then *Revue de philologie française*).

In Italy, the *Archivio Glottologico Italiano* was founded by Ascoli in 1873 and continues in modern times. The *Rivista di filologia e istruzione classica* founded less than a year earlier also contained a number of linguistic articles (Timpanaro 1972c, 411–18). Some of Ascoli's first articles appeared in an old and glorious periodical, *Il Politecnico*, which Carlo Cattaneo had resurrected in Milan in 1859 and directed until 1864. Much later, in 1899, Giacomo de Gregorio founded in Palermo the *Studi glottologici italiani*, which survived until 1931 (Benincà 1994, 588ff.; 1996, 109ff.).

In the United States the *International Journal of American Linguistics* was founded by F. Boas as late as 1917 and *American Speech* started in 1925 (Andresen 1990, 3), the same year that saw the birth of the Linguistic Society of America and of *Language* (cf. Pedersen 1962, 310; Bloomfield 1925). Before that articles of general linguistic interest were frequently printed in the *Journal of the American Oriental Society* (from 1843–9), in *Transactions of the American Philological Association* [TAPA] (from 1870) and in the *American Journal of Philology* [AJPh] (from 1880). W. D. Whitney, the professor of Sanskrit at Yale, was the first president of the American Philological Association and published both in TAPA and in AJPh (Gildersleeve's journal) articles about general linguistics, Indo-European Studies, and Sanskrit.[8] From a much earlier period, discussions of linguistic interest had taken place in less specialized outlets, the *North American Review* (from 1815) and the

Transactions of the American Philosophical Society (started 1771, new series 1818; cf. Andresen 1990, 40).

1.2.6 Historical and comparative linguistics

Both chairs and periodicals, two clear signs of academic respectability, document through the whole century the prevailing of historical and comparative linguistics. Though in a very few instances general linguistics was practised and taught as a separate subject, in general the teaching of linguistic theory and of the general principles of language description and development was entrusted to the holders of chairs with an explicit comparative or historical bias. At Geneva, Ferdinand de Saussure taught first Sanskrit and Indo-European languages (as Ordinarius from 1896) and then (from 1906–7) *Linguistique générale et histoire et comparaison des langues indo-européennes.* In Leipzig, one of the largest and linguistically perhaps the most successful German University, courses in *Allgemeine Sprachwissenschaft* were held in the 1880s by Hans Georg Conon von der Gabelentz, though his official position was that of 'Extraordinarius der orientalischen Sprachen'. J. D. Whitney, who offered regularly to undergraduates in Yale College a course in general linguistic science, was in fact a Professor of Sanskrit and Comparative Philology (Silverstein 1971, x–xiii).

Similarly, the more successful linguistics periodicals, those which survived or are remembered, were dedicated to comparative linguistics or to Indo-European linguistics or, even more specifically, to a specific sub-branch of Indo-European. Even those whose title does not reveal a historical bias have a preponderantly historical content. This is certainly the case for the *Mémoires de la Société de linguistique de Paris* or the *Transactions of the Philological Society* or the *Archivio glottologico.*

1.3 Historiography

Historiography joins institutionalization as one of the two factors which contribute to the break in continuity between eighteenth- and nineteenth-century linguistics. The link with the newly formed University institutions is obvious: all accounts are due to academics who in the development of linguistics act both as protagonists and as chroniclers. The first full history of linguistics appeared in 1869, predictably in Germany, as part of a projected 22-volume *Geschichte der Wissenschaften in Deutschland* ('History of Sciences in Germany') commissioned by the Bayerische Akademie der Wissenschaften. The title chosen by the author, Theodor Benfey, a Sanskritist, classicist and comparativist, who because of his Jewish origin had not had the speedy career that he deserved, is in itself significant: *Geschichte der Sprachwissenschaft und orientalischen Philologie in Deutschland seit dem Anfange des 19. Jahrhunderts mit einem*

Rückblick auf die früheren Zeiten ('History of Linguistics and Oriental Philology in Germany from the Beginning of the Nineteeenth Century with a Look at the Earlier Period'). It indicates that, as the series required, the emphasis is on the German achievements of the nineteenth century. Some 240 pages are dedicated to the great events (the discovery of Sanskrit) and the great men of the beginning of the century (F. Schlegel, Bopp, Grimm, Humboldt), another 100 to a survey of recent work on Indo-European languages, while a further 100 pages cover the work on all other linguistic families of the world. Finally, some 7 pages describe the German studies in general linguistics (*Allgemeine Sprachwissenschaft*). All this is preceded by some 300 pages which give a summary of the development of linguistic thought before the nineteenth century. One year later (1870) the same series published a *Geschichte der germanischen Philologie* by Rudolf von Raumer; here too some 290 pages were dedicated to the first period and some 440 pages to the work done during and after German Romanticism. In this last part the names of Fr. Schlegel, Bopp and Grimm also recurred, with the two brothers Grimm having the lion's share. After ten years, and within the different framework of the *Bibliothek indogermanischer Grammatiken*, a series of neogrammarian inspiration, we have a brief *Einleitung in das Sprachstudium* ('Introduction to the Study of Language') with the subtitle *Ein Beitrag zur Geschichte und Methodik der vergleichenden Sprachforschung* ('A Contribution to the History and Methodology of Comparative Linguistics') (1880) by Berthold Delbrück. Here the story started with Bopp, briefly discussed Humboldt, A. W. Schlegel and Jacob Grimm, and then, through Pott and Benfey, reached Schleicher and eventually the neogrammarians.[9] By this time the conventional hagiography, which is to a certain extent of neogrammarian inspiration, is fully established (Hoenigswald 1986, Koerner 1989, 3–12). There are three generations of linguists: the founders (with perhaps the precursors), the consolidators, who also introduce methodological innovations, the developers, who join to a new methodological perception an emphasis on concrete work well done, sometimes on the basis of collective work, and who, we are told, have brought the subject to its highest level. In the terms of Indo-European comparative linguistics for which the hagiography was first established, the names which fill the various slots are those of Sir William Jones and Friedrich Schlegel (precursors), Franz Bopp, Jacob Grimm, Wilhelm von Humboldt (founders), Georg Curtius, August Schleicher and August Fick (consolidators), and finally Leskien, Verner, Brugmann, Delbrück, etc. (developers). August Pott counts both as a founder and as a consolidator, and the Italian Graziadio Isaia Ascoli as a consolidator and a developer, while the role of the Dane Rasmus Rask as either a precursor or a founder varies according to the accounts. Later authors follow the same basic pattern (with variations); cf. e.g.

Oertel (1901), Thomsen (1927; first published in 1902), Pedersen (1983; written in 1916), and ([1931] 1962; written in 1924), Jespersen (1922), Leroy (1971), Jankowsky (1972), etc. At an earlier stage, the extraordinarily popular *Lectures on the Science of Language* by F. Max Müller ([1861] 1862) included an account of the development of linguistic thought which started with Greece and Rome, but deliberately led to a climax marked first by Friedrich Schlegel (1808) and then by Rask, Bopp, Grimm, etc.

1.3.1 The creation of the *fable convenue*

It has been observed (Aarsleff 1982, 313) that this basic agreement in the way in which the story of the subject is told is typical of a discipline which has become institutionally successful and creates its own history in order to meet the ideological needs of its practitioners. This is so, but the first part at least of the *fable convenue* (Hoenigswald 1986, 177) is earlier than the institutional successes. It appears, with some modifications, in two 1850 articles by Steinthal (1970, 114–27 and 128–38), where the beginning of the new *deutsche Sprachwissenschaft* is found in works by Bopp, Jacob Grimm and W. von Humboldt. Before that we already see it in print in Pott's introduction to his *Etymologische Forschungen* published in 1833 (Pott 1833–6, I, xx). Here, after a reference to the importance of the discovery of Sanskrit and of Friedrich Schlegel's 1808 book, Bopp's 1816 book is hailed as marking the beginning of a new period in linguistics. Just as the later epigones will do, to Bopp's name Pott joins the constellation of A. W. Schlegel, Humboldt and Grimm and lists F. Schlegel as a precursor. In other words, the view which then became canonical about a new linguistics started by Bopp, the founder and herald of a new era, already existed, in Germany at least, in 1833: at that stage A. W. Schlegel's Sanskrit chair (1818) and Bopp's chair in Berlin (1821) had been founded but little else had happened. This no doubt explains why in Pott (1833) we find a far less confident attestation of the German nature of linguistics than in later authors and more understanding of the continuity between earlier and later work. G. Hermann, the Greek scholar, A. F. Bernhardi, the author of a very successful *Sprachlehre*, and J. Chr. Adelung, the editor of *Mithridates*, are all highly praised. Of Adelung, Pott says that, thanks to him, Germany, the heart of Europe and of European science ('das Herz Europas und Europäischer Wissenschaft'), can now challenge even in linguistics the other countries which produced great collections of materials. But Pott also states that linguistics is still deficient in a systematic understanding of its object (1833–6, I, xxiii). Here he differs from the arrogance of some at least of his successors, but at the same time gives them the lead in implying that the theoretical results of the previous centuries could be disregarded.

Between 1833 and Benfey (1869) the official version of the story was consolidated and found acceptance outside Germany. In 1861 Max Müller (1862, 3) wrote in England and in English that the 'science of language' could not trace its lineage much beyond the beginning of the nineteenth century, and later on stressed (*ibid.* 22) that Germany was the birthplace of this science. Earlier than Max Müller and in France, Renan had spoken in 1848 of the immense progress made in the 'science des langues' and had linked this progress with Friedrich Schlegel (1808), who had indicated the main features of the comparative method, with Bopp (1816), where the new method found its first application, and finally with a series of rivals and disciples such as Humboldt, Jacob Grimm and Burnouf, who definitively founded 'la science experimentelle du langage' (Renan [1848] 1883, 85f.). Still in France, but almost twenty years later, the young Bréal contrasted in the preface to his translation of Bopp's comparative grammar the disjointed, haphazard nature of the linguistic work done in France with the numerous works of comparative grammar which appeared in Germany checking and emending each other's conclusions as happens in the real sciences (1866–72, I, ii–iv); he also expressed the hope that his translation would introduce the new linguistics into France too. At the same time he mentioned that the *philologie comparative*, created only half a century earlier, was now taught in the whole of Europe and had its chairs, its books, its periodicals, its specialized societies (*ibid.*, lv). He too then referred to Bopp as a founding father: 'L'auteur de ce grand mouvement scientifique est un homme modeste' ('the author of this great scientific movement is a modest man').

Later on a more muted view came from America. Whitney ([1875] 1882, 317ff.) treated Schlegel as a forerunner and attributed primacy to German scholars: Bopp and Grimm had raised the historical study of language to the rank of a science. Yet for Whitney, who unconsciously echoes Pott's earlier sentiments, Germany, the home of comparative philology, had not yet been able to produce a real science of language, i.e. that discipline which 'makes the laws and general principles of speech its main subject, and uses particular facts rather as illustrations' (*ibid.*, 315). Consequently, 'accustomed as the world is to look to Germany for guidance in all matters pertaining to this subject, until they shall come to something like agreement it will hardly be possible to claim that there exists a world's science of language' (*ibid.*, 319).

1.3.2 Continuity or break with the past?

To sum up: through most of last century among the members of the newly created linguistics establishment there was widespread, even if not general, agreement in a set of historiographical assumptions: a new 'linguistic' discipline had arisen at the beginning of the century, the founders were German scholars (with a few exceptions) and the great success of the discipline was due to German scholarship. However, there was no unanimity in the assessment of (a) the importance of pre-nineteenth-century background, (b) the status and limits of the new discipline. An extreme position (which is almost a parody of the far more thoughtful views held e.g. by Benfey 1869) might have held that no serious linguistic work had been done before Bopp or Schlegel or Sir William Jones and that serious linguistics was only concerned with comparative and historical work. A more moderate position (represented e.g. by Whitney), while agreeing that some form of breakthrough had happened at the beginning of the century, would have been more doubtful about assuming that all problems had since been solved or were approaching a solution and, as we have seen, supported a much broader concept of linguistics. Even in Germany, someone such as Gabelentz (1891, 16–30) offered a version, however simplified, of linguistic historiography which was closer to that of Whitney's than to the more extreme views. He recognized the importance of Bopp and Grimm, but on the one hand distinguished between various types of research (historical and descriptive analysis of single languages, comparative and historical work, general linguistics), and on the other hand saw in nineteenth-century comparative linguistics a much greater element of continuity with the seventeenth and eighteenth centuries than the other authors quoted above.

1.3.3 Specific features

If in the nineteenth century, main-stream linguistics is indeed character-ized by some common features which separate it from earlier linguistic thought, how were these features seen at the time? On this point it is neither possible nor profitable to distinguish between explicit histori-ographical comment and the various declarations of faith by the prac-titioners of the subject; in what follows we shall refer to both sorts of evidence.

There is a variety of elements. At the beginning of the century those who will later be labelled as 'founders' constantly use terms such as 'empirical' and 'scientific', together, of course, with 'historical' and 'comparative'. Yet some of these adjectives are also used by authors who are later treated as chronologically or intellectually 'different'. Hervás, Adelung, Denina and, to a certain extent, Vater saw their work as funda-mentally empirical and based on observation. In this they did not differ from Jacob Grimm, who in 1822 (vi) declared that observation is the soul of linguistic inquiry, or from Pott, who in 1833 (1833–6, I, xxiv) reported that at long last *der Weg Bako's*, which is based on observa-tion, had entered linguistics. But, as we shall see, Hervás and Adelung, in contrast with Grimm and Pott, do not belong to the official canon; at best they are labelled as precursors. Also, some terms, though con-stantly repeated, were not sufficiently specific to provide the touchstone which distinguished the old from the new: 'empirical' is again a case in question. At its vaguest, a defence of empiricism turned into a generic anti-philosophical or anti-metaphysical statement, without any explanation of what philosophical view was under attack.[10] At its most definite, it turned into a plea for favouring the study of languages or of a particular language, over that of language as such. Similarly 'scientific' is as ambiguous as the German *wissenschaftlich* which it translates. For some (the most extreme), linguistics was a natural science; for others (a more moderate group), linguistics was comparable with the natural sciences because of the method that it used and the solidity of the results that it achieved; for a third group, scientific was synonymous with scholarly. In other words, the 'scientificity' of linguistics, though frequently referred to, underwent a continuous process of redefinition all through the century. The comparison between comparative anatomy and comparative linguistics so fashionable at the beginning of the century, the organicistic terminology of that period, Renan's 1848 reference to linguistics as a 'science experimentelle', Max Müller's preferred term 'the science of language', could all be seen as supporting the extreme view or the more moderate position. A redefinition was prompted by the polemics of the 1870s; at that stage Delbrück, in discussing the level of certainty reached by linguistic enquiry, argued that this was as high as is possible for a **historical** discipline.

'Comparative' and 'historical' were of course omnipresent, but here too the meanings changed. There is, first of all, a basic lexical problem which mainly concerns Germany: *historisch*, at the beginning of the century, could mean 'empirical', and sometimes *geschichtlich* had the same value (Telegdi 1966); the diachronic meaning was established later. 'Comparative', or its equivalents in the major European languages, originally referred to any study based on the analysis of more than one language; after F. Schlegel (1808) it slowly acquired a genealogical and evolutionary value. Yet what effectively prevents us from arguing that comparison provides the defining character of contemporary linguistics is the fact that attempts at, and interest in, genealogical comparison considerably precede the beginning of the century.

In fact though all the features mentioned were important, none of them can count as the unifying element which characterizes the intellectual climate of the period. And yet the new institutionalization had an intellectual counterpart. The Bopps, the Grimms, the Bréals, the Schleichers, the Ascolis, the Sweets, the Brugmanns, all shared a firm belief in the accumulation of knowledge. The work of the 'new linguistics' could be shared and organized because, as in the sciences, individual achievements built on earlier achievements and consolidated them. In some of its manifestations this was again an antiphilosophical motif, but the primary focus was not polemical. Most of the new linguists and their historiographers were quietly confident that their work was not done in isolation; it was shared with their colleagues and was above all a contribution to the grand edifice whose foundations were laid at the beginning of the century. They also thought that, though the grand scheme would perhaps need revision, some or most of the individual concrete results would never be faulted; they were an acquisition for ever. This set of assumptions is largely responsible for the feeling of continuity and coherence that dominated the century's work while it also accounts for the main features of nineteenth-century historiography. The characteristic distinction between precursors, founders, consolidators, etc. was based on an elementary concept of progress; in its turn progress was seen as defined by the accumulation of concrete results and by the diminishing number of unsolved problems.[11] The starting point was fixed at the beginning of the century because, on the one hand, the 'discovery' and exploitation of Sanskrit (see below) gave the impression that much of the earlier work was outdated, and, on the other hand, previous achievements had begun to be conveniently summarized in new books so that earlier authors could be easily forgotten.

Within this context the various meanings of 'scientific' and 'empirical' can also be shown to have something in common – they all presupposed a belief in the validity of the concrete results achieved and in the accumulation of knowledge that they allowed. The example of Bréal and Schleicher shows that this view was shared even by scholars whose theories deeply diverged. The former constantly reacted against all suggestions that language was an object separate from the speakers, while for the latter, language was a *Naturorganismus* subject to unchangeable natural laws (Schleicher 1869b, 120). And yet Bréal spoke of the edifice of comparative grammar as of something which was slowly being built; in Germany works of comparative grammar followed, checked and complemented each other, just as happened in France for physiology or botany; detailed observations accumulated, leading to laws which opened the way to new discoveries (Bréal 1866–72, I, iv; cf. Ascoli 1873a, xxxiv). In his turn, Schleicher ([1861–2] 1871, I, iii) emphasized that, after all doubtful conclusions had been rejected, there was still in his field a rich store of knowledge which would remain for all times; these were the results which warranted collection in a compendium.

1.4 Conclusions

We have now come full circle and can draw some conclusions. The introduction of linguistics into the Universities, which was made possible by the impressive expansion of all academic institutions and by their newly acquired research ethos, had a determining effect in creating a set-up in which the subject could develop in a unified manner; it also allowed the prevailing of one type of linguistics over the others and encouraged a series of scholars to build on each other's work. In its turn this rapid institutional development helped to create the conditions for the multiplication of a historiographical or quasi-historiographical literature which was bound to be influential. Institutions and historiography agree in supporting the picture which we have drawn at the beginning (see above, Section 1.1); indeed it is doubtful that without such powerful allies any picture could have emerged with that degree of unnuanced clarity. Yet this is not to say that the picture was wrong; it was incomplete and to a certain extent biased. But it accurately reflected the new development of the period which consisted in the creation of a 'craft of linguistics', to use Aarsleff terminology, as distinguished from a series of views about language which can arise even among people who are not primarily linguists. The unquestioned acceptance of the nineteenth-century view of itself by our own century (until very recently) is again due to a concomitance of causes. Our own institutions and our own historiography continue the institutions and historiography of the nineteenth century.[12] But in addition two factors contributed. First, some of the conclusions of the comparative and historical work of the nineteenth century became part of common everyday knowledge. No one now rejects the suggestion that German and Sanskrit are related and continue an earlier Indo-European language. Secondly, and perhaps more importantly, historical and comparative work is still done in this century by scholars who see themselves as the direct followers of nineteenth-century scholars; neither the methodology nor the results achieved have been forgotten, nor do the practitioners see any reason to assume that this will ever happen (Watkins 1983). In other words, continuity does not only belong to institutions; we must allow for a factor of intellectual continuity which is bound to be influential on any historiographical assessment.

Notes

1. These figures are based on Prost (1968, 263). They differ from those found in Bréal (1872, 371) who, given his involvement with public education, must have known his facts. Yet both sets of figures serve to demonstrate how few students were involved in the work of the *facultés*. According to Bréal, 179 examinations for the *licence* in sciences, and 272 for that in letters took place in 1865; of these only 94 and 187 were not in Paris. Since students could be examined twice or even three times in the same year Bréal reckons that the correct figures for the number of students examined in the provinces were 70 and 140 respectively. The figures given by Weisz (1983) are again different.

2. Amsterdamska (1987, 63–89 and 129–37; see especially p. 288, note 13) produces a number of facts and figures to illustrate the institutionalization

of linguistics in German Universities (she also briefly contrasts the French position). Her tables at pp. 130–1 document on the basis of Conrad (1893) and Ferber (1956) the dramatic increase in student numbers and chair numbers in Germany from the first to the second part of the century.

3. Gabelentz (1891, 31) offers a rare example of a nineteenth century linguist aware of the importance of institutional facts. He points out that before his time people came to linguistics from a number of different disciplines: F. and A. W. Schlegel, Adelung, Vater, Bopp, Klaproth from philology and oriental studies; Castrén and Wilhelm Schott from theology; Wilhelm von Humboldt, Jacob Grimm, Silvestre de Sacy, Eugène Burnouf and H. C. von Gabelentz from law, just as the more modern Lucien Adam; Abel-Rémusat and the Sanskritist Wilson from medicine.

4. Max Müller's statement (1862, 166) that 'in almost every continental university there is a professor of Sanskrit who lectures likewise on Comparative Grammar and the science of language' is exaggerated but not too remote from the truth, if we take it as referring to German Universities only.

5. E. Burnouf lectured about general linguistics and comparative grammar between 1829 and 1833 only (Barthélemy-St Hilaire 1891, 15). Émile Egger (1813–85), a classicist who in 1852 became Professor of Greek at the Sorbonne, taught some notions of comparative grammar at the École Normale Supérieure from 1839 to 1861 (Bréal 1866–72, 1, lvii). The other forerunners were the Romanists led by François Raynouard (1761–1836). For the history of linguistics and philology in the French *facultés des lettres*, see Bergounioux (1990 and 1994), with the essential bibliography about French Universities.

6. The countries mentioned above have been selected exempli gratia. For Spain, cf. some very interesting general reflections about the late appearance of an institutionalized comparative and historical linguistics in Gutierrez-Cuadrado (1987); see also Mourelle-Lema (1968), Quilis and Niederehe (1986); for the Netherlands see Van Driel (1992) and the other articles collected in Noordegraaf, Versteegh, Koerner (1992), as well as Noordegraaf (1993, 1994). In the United States Sanskrit was again the first born from an institutional point of view; W. D. Whitney (1827–94) started teaching Sanskrit and, later, comparative grammar at Yale in 1854 but he followed E. E. Salisbury (1814–91), who was professor of Arabic and Sanskrit Language and Literature. Admittedly John Pickering (1777–1846), who had worked on American Indian languages, had been offered chairs at Harvard which he had refused, but they were chairs of Hebrew and Greek (Andresen 1990, 105, 120ff.). The American Oriental Society, founded in 1842, was more geared to Asiatic languages and more influenced by the German model (Andresen, *ibid.*). On the other hand, Samuel Haldeman (1812–80), a great admirer of Sir William Jones, who taught at the University of Pennsylvania first as Professor of Zoology and Natural History and then (from 1869) as Professor of Comparative Philology, worked on Amerindian languages (Firth 1957, 114ff.) and had good knowledge of phonetics and the right ideas about registering phonetic observations (Firth, *ibid.*, 166), though he was also responsible for a great number of absurd etymologies.

7. Some data and statistics about linguistic and philological periodicals in Germany are provided by Amsterdamska (1987, 86f. and 133f.). We should of course remember that periodicals existed long before the nineteenth century and the list given above could be extended backwards. One aborted attempt to create a linguistic periodical at the beginning of the nineteenth century was made by J.-S. Vater and F. J. Bertuch with the *Allgemeines Archiv für Ethnographie und Linguistik*, whose only volume appeared in Weimar in 1808.

8. Bloomfield (1925, 4, note 1) deplores the English use of philology as synonymous with linguistics and much prefers the American usage, which contrasts linguistics with philology, 'the study of culture'. In fact British use was and still is ambiguous; this probably fooled Pedersen ([1931] 1962, 310), who assumes that England has no linguistic periodicals until the twentieth century (ignoring the *Transactions of the Philological Society*). On the other hand, in the nineteenth century Bloomfield's distinction was not always clear even in America; from this point of view it is interesting to read the address read by the Rev. Dr W. H. Ward to the 1894 session of the First American Congress of Philologists dedicated to W. D. Whitney. Whitney is constantly referred to as a philologist and is treated as the Father of American Philological Science (Ward 1897). Perhaps only in Germany there is a clear terminological distinction: cf. Curtius ([1862] 1886, 1, 133), who observes that in France and in England 'philology' meant *Sprachstudium*. In general see Belardi ([1984] 1990, 8ff.); and for the links, both substantive and terminological, between philology and linguistics (and hermeneutics), cf. also Koerner ([1982] 1989, 233–44) and Jäger (1987).

9. Later editions of the book differed considerably (Koerner 1989, 6–8); the fourth edition (1904) was enlarged with, *inter alia*, brief accounts of classical and pre-nineteenth-century linguistics and an extensive discussion of Humboldt's thought; the sixth edition (1919) gave more space to syntax. From the fourth edition the title is *Einführung in das Studium der indogermanischen Sprachen* ('Introduction to the Study of the Indo-European Languages').

10. A latent anti-philosophical, anti-theoretical note is present from the beginning to the end of the century in the work of comparativists and historical linguists. Grimm's attitude will be discussed below, but cf., at one end, Pott's declaration that 'Grimm's historical exposition of the sound mutations in the Germanic languages has by itself more value than many a philosophical theory all full of onesided or meaningless abstractions' (Pott 1833–6, I, xii), and at the other (well into the twentieth century), Pedersen's statement ([1916] 1983, 44) that 'philosophy has never produced anything but trouble when it has raised its head in the area of linguistics'.

11. According to Delbrück (1875, 11), in the last part of the century nobody could any longer maintain that linguistics was in its infancy; this was all the more misguided if it was meant to imply that 'the sum of our linguistic views must be compared to a philosophical system, which one good day will get buried under the waves of the next system'. On the contrary, Delbrück continued, there was now a significant series of scientific results which are as certain as is possible to be for the results of historical research.

12. Recent attacks against the limitations of our historiographic tradition (such as that by Andresen 1990, 11ff.) are welcome because they highlight new data which allow us better to understand our period, but in my view are counterproductive when they try to demolish the results of last century's Indo-European linguistics on the basis of supposed methodological revolutions in Indo-European studies. The new reconstructions of the consonantal system of Indo-European proposed by Gamkrelidze and Ivanov (1973, 1984) are not generally accepted, but in any case these two authors would be the first to recognize that they have not 'tumbled' Grimm's law; on the contrary they have accepted in full the correspondences quoted by Grimm and his results, but have diverged from Brugmann, more than from Grimm, in their attempt to identify the phonetic reality which corresponds to the symbols of our reconstructions.

2

The old and the new: data collection and data comparison

2.1 Multiplicity of approaches

The later historiography has created the impression that the first two decades of the nineteenth century were marked by a thought and research vacuum which was slowly being filled by the new comparative-historical linguistics. This is not so; linguistic thought was neither vacuous nor idle – but it was not monochord either; as shown by the contemporary sources, the discussion was extraordinarily wide-ranging.

2.2 A German survey: M. L. Loewe

The contemporary publications trace a picture which is partially unexpected. In 1829 M. L. Loewe, who described himself as a professor of philosophy in the *Academia medico-chirurgica* of Dresden, published a short dissertation entitled *Historiae criticae grammatices universalis seu philosophicae lineamenta,* which concentrated on German achievements. The booklet has no originality and is hardly more than a bibliographical list. It offers a brief survey (with the occasional critical remark) of the work done on philosophical grammar (broadly understood) from the second part of the eighteenth century to the author's times.[1]

The starting point is a basic classification of the possible lines of enquiry about language. **Universal** or **philosophical grammar**, we are told, is a universal system through which the faculties of the soul (*functiones animi*; cf. e.g. Monboddo's 'operations of the mind') are represented in articulated sounds. Because of its systematic nature it differs from that type of **philosophy** which asks general questions about language and has no definite limits; because it rests on the nature of the soul, it contrasts with **harmonic** or **comparative grammar**, which is empirically based and cannot formulate rules endowed of natural necessity. On the other hand, its universality distinguishes it from **special**

grammar, which may also be philosophical (and needs to be so according to Herder) but is always geared to a specific language. Finally, universal grammar should not be confused with the *disciplina repraesentandi generalis* because this has a much wider scope while universal grammar is concerned only with representations which use articulated sounds as their medium.

Some categories require explanation. Philosophical grammar clearly refers to the French tradition exemplified e.g. by Du Marsais, but Loewe also lists two British scholars, Harris and Monboddo. In Germany he gives due prominence to Herder's 1772 work on the origin of language, but also stresses that in a number of points Herder agrees almost verbatim with his French predecessors. In his view, the German tradition reaches its acme with A. F. Bernhardi's *Sprachlehre* (1801–3) and *Anfangsgründe der Sprachwissenschaft* (1805), two books that look at language not only from the point of view of rational thought but also from that of other human faculties and operations.[2] Afterwards, he argues, the work continued but was less impressive; some texts discussed the role of psychology in language, others that of Kant's transcendental forms. Some important work was concerned with German: the reference is to Becker (1827) and Schmitthenner (1826). With a few exceptions, most of the authors quoted do not appear in the later histories of linguistics; yet the extensive list produced by Loewe is sufficient to demonstrate that in Germany at the beginning of the century there still was a prolific line of research in universal grammar and that the contemporary authors saw it as connected with the work of the previous century.[3]

Loewe does not discuss harmonic or comparative grammar but it is clear that the term did not have the exclusively genealogical or evolutionary meaning which it assumed later. It referred rather to the eighteenth- and early-nineteenth-century attempts to extract general rules from the evidence of many languages (Naumann 1986, 50, 57) and to collections of data from the various languages of the world. In mentioning a book by J. S. Vater (1808), Loewe (1829, 46f.) observes that in spite of its title (*Lehrbuch der allgemeinen Grammatik*) it really belongs within comparative grammar since it makes constant use of evidence from a multiplicity of languages.[4]

The distinction between general and special grammar is not new; it is found in the *Grammaire de Port Royal* (1660) and is discussed for instance in the article *Grammaire* of the *Encyclopédie* and in Destutt de Tracy ([1803] 1826, 9f.). But what does Loewe refer to? He speaks of the importance of universal grammar for the so-called special or empirical grammars and in a footnote (p. 3**) quotes a few such works while pointing out the immense disparity of subject matter and method. The list includes Greek, Latin and German grammars; between Gottsched, the author of the very successful *Grundlegung einer deutschen Sprachkunst*

(1748) with clearly prescriptive aims, and Schmitthenner, who in the first third of the nineteenth century moved uneasily between a general and a comparative approach (Naumann 1986, 76ff.), we find the name of Grimm, the historical linguist.

For anyone nurtured within the later historiography it is remarkable that some of the obvious names are omitted from this survey: Franz Bopp, Friedrich and August Wilhelm Schlegel, Wilhelm von Humboldt. Did Loewe think that none of these authors had anything to offer to universal grammar? Or was he not acquainted with their work?[5]

Whatever the answer, the conclusion is that in Germany in the first decades of the century, in addition to purely philosophical work, which necessarily impinged on language, we find (1) general discussions which continued the work of the previous century, or reacted to it, and were heavily influenced by French and English publications, but also by German philosophy (Kant's influence is all-pervasive); (2) empirical philological work which collected data from various languages sometimes for historical-ethnographic aims, but occasionally for its own sake; (3) work geared to individual languages; this could be descriptive or historical or merely philological; it could have scholarly or simply pedagogical aims. The study of the local language(s) of course prevailed: Naumann (1986, 354ff.) lists more than 110 grammars of German between the time of Adelung and 1850.

2.3 Volney and the philosophical study of language

In France, ten years earlier than Loewe, and with much greater wit, vivacity and elegance, the count of Volney (1757–1820), historian, politician, *idéologue*, had also discussed past and present linguistic work in a lecture delivered at a private session of the Academy and later published (Volney [1819] 1820). He spoke of philosophical study of language rather than of philosophical grammar and the definition he gave of his subject matter is noticeably different from that of Loewe. For Volney such a study dealt with 'the impartial enquiries aimed at learning all matters of general concern to language, at explaining how languages were born and formed, how they grow and become established, change and die, at showing their affinities and their differences, their filiation, at accounting for the very origin of the admirable faculty of speech which we share', a faculty which allows us 'to express the ideas of the mind through the sounds of the mouth, sounds which in their turn become, as basic elements, object of study' (*ibid.*, 7). There follows a brief history of linguistics from this point of view: Volney argues that nothing useful was done before the Renaissance because of the Greek and Roman absence of interest in languages, which was followed by the restrictive practices of the Church. He sees some signs of awakening in the sixteenth century and recognizes the beginning of a new era in the eighteenth century when Leibniz pleads for a study of language comparable with that of the exact sciences and then new collections of data (Pallas, Hervás, Adelung) start to appear. The French work on linguistics had been kept back by the heavily classical nature of French education but the Academy should now encourage the diffusion of the famous foreign works. Those who arrogantly assume that it is enough to know Greek and Latin in order to work on universal grammar should be reminded that these two languages are simply dialects of a 'Scythian' nation which originated north of the Indus and spread its language as far as the Ganges and Britain.

Remarkably, Volney does not enthuse about the glories of eighteenth-century French linguistics; he approves of de Brosses but prefers Monboddo's type of exposition. Court de Gebelin he dismisses as someone who is closer to fiction than to science ('appartient plutôt aux romans qu'à la science'); the great tradition of the *grammaire générale* is not discussed (cf. Auroux, Désirat and Hordé 1992).

2.4 Linguistics in France

We expect comparative grammar in Germany and *grammaire générale* in France but in Loewe (1829) and Volney (1820) the emphasis is reversed. In both countries the intellectual horizons were less narrow – and less coherent – than they are made out to be. Yet the traditional view is not altogether wrong. In France the great tradition of general or philosophical grammar does not die with the eighteenth century, though under this name we subsume very different and indeed opposite tendencies (see below). The *idéologues* belong to the nineteenth century as well, and Destutt de Tracy's *Grammaire*, the second part of his *Elémens d'idéologie*, appeared in 1803 and was reprinted again until 1826. If we turn from Volney to his friend and contemporary J. D. Lanjuinais, we find in his brief account of the history of linguistics ([1815] 1832, iv, 549–86) a reminder that three different editions of the 1799 *Principes de grammaire générale* by A. I. Silvestre de Sacy were published in 1803, 1810 and 1815 (the seventh edition appeared in 1840). Thiébault's *Grammaire philosophique* dates from 1802; the *Grammaire des grammaires* by Ch. P. Girault-Duvivier appeared in 1812 (9th edn, 1840). The *Journal grammatical et didactique de la langue française* founded in 1827 was renamed *Journal philosophique, grammatical et littéraire de la langue française* in 1831 (Bruneau 1948, 469–71). On the other hand, Volney took an excessively dismal view of the lack of French achievements in empirical linguistics. Admittedly there was in his time no French equivalent of Adelung's *Mithridates* or of Hervás' *Catalogo*; the French had to wait until Balbi (1826a, b) for something similar, though in 1804 *La clef des langues* by Carlo Denina described the languages of Europe and was written in French. Yet there was serious work on languages which oscillated between philology and linguistics. In the Romance field, F. J. Raynouard (1761–1836) and somewhat later Claude Fauriel (1772–1844) produced fundamental work on Provençal in a philological mode. In the field of oriental languages, A. I. Silvestre de Sacy (1758–1838) gained fame as an Arabic and Persian scholar; one of his pupils, J. F. Champollion (1790–1832), started the decipherment of Egyptian Hieroglyphics; J. P. Abel-Rémusat (1788–1832), professor at the Collège de France from 1814, did notable work on Chinese and Asiatic languages, while A.-L. de Chézy (1773–1832), for whom the Collège de France in 1814 founded the first University chair of Sanskrit in Europe, started Sanskrit studies in France and taught the language to Eugène Burnouf, his successor and one of the greatest orientalists of his time. The École des Langues Orientales Vivantes was founded in 1795 and became a major centre for the study of oriental languages. In 1826 Balbi (1826a, cxxii) correctly assumed that serious linguistic and ethnological work was best done in Paris, both because of the native scholars, and because of the cosmopolitan character of the capital's intelligentsia (cf. Delesalle and Chevalier 1986, 147ff.).

2.5 Linguistics in Britain

Britain may illustrate the differences between the various types of linguistic work done in the first third of the century: the excellent account by Aarsleff ([1967] 1983) and the additional information collected by Beyer (1981) offer an adequate picture. Before the 1830s most British work is either in the framework of universal grammar (Harris, Monboddo, Beattie) or is influenced by Horne Tooke's *Diversions of Purley,* which was published between 1786 and 1805 and was regularly reissued until 1860. This professed to follow in the footsteps of Locke but went much further in its assumption that neither is language an imitation of thought, nor does thought depend on signs and language; for Tooke language **is** thought. Its constituent elements are nouns and verbs, which are simply the names of ideas; every other part of speech, including the relational elements, is derived from these through 'abbreviation'. In this context etymology acquires paramount importance as the only technique which can show, indeed demonstrate, the 'concrete' origin of all words and all parts of speech. The general conclusions fitted in with the radical philosophy of the time and were hailed by e.g. James Mill and Jeremy Bentham as of supreme importance; the philosophers had neither inclination nor competence to challenge the nitty gritty of Tooke's etymological work. On the other hand, Tooke's work, where the decomposition of words reminded the reader of the techniques of the most popular of sciences, chemistry, gave the impression that Tooke had made the study of language scientific by providing a method which could support the conclusions of the philosophers. What, of course, he had not done was to provide a solid foundation for etymology; indeed if one compares his practice and the methodology outlined by Turgot in the article *Étymologie* (1756) of the *Encyclopédie*, the impression is that Tooke is far more of a dilettante. However, etymology was used to confirm a general theory, as Turgot had advocated, and the bulk and coherence of the evidence adduced seemed too impressive to be dismissed. Tooke found imitators who produced a series of etymological works now forgotten (Aarsleff 1983, 76ff.), which include, for instance, an *Etymologicum universale* published in 1822–5 in three volumes by Walter Whiter, a fellow of Clare College, Cambridge. The other side of the coin is that linguistics came to be seen by Tooke and his admirers as a science with a methodology of its own (based on etymology) which was based on empirical data and led to conclusions of general importance (cf. Droixhe 1978, 258f.). Dugald Stewart objected on philosophical grounds, but Tooke's influence did not come to an end until much later, when a more rigorous form of philology became available and the inconsistence of his etymologies was revealed (Aarsleff 1983, 111f.).

Though Tooke had all the prestige, other linguistic work was being published in Britain in the first three decades of the century. After the publication of Halhed's *Grammar of the Bengal Language* in 1778, British authors published in 25 years no less than five Sanskrit grammars and two dictionaries as well as a number of editions and translations of texts and some important linguistic articles. Most of this work is philological (in the German sense), rather than linguistic, but its influence on general linguistic studies, especially abroad, was considerable (cf. p. 62ff.). At the same time, and in very different circles, a certain amount of dialect work was being done, mainly in the form of glossaries, accompanied in some instances by etymological discussions. In 1836 the Rev. Richard Garnett (1789–1850) published in the *Quarterly Review* an account of ten such glossaries which had appeared between 1808 and 1832 (Garnett 1859, 41–77). He was in general favourable to the simple collections of data but highly critical of etymological attempts, though showing considerable respect for John Jamieson's *Etymological Dictionary of the Scottish Language* (1808). Finally there was the comparative work described at some length by Beyer (1981, 22–46), a very mixed bag of books which tried to produce a demonstration of monogenesis or continued the old discussions about the kinship of English and Persian, the kinship of Germanic and Greek languages, etc., and which in part ignored, in part were aware of, the contributions which the newly discovered Sanskrit could bring to their subject. A good example, which contains the familiar mixture of hard argument and unsupported suggestions, is *Hermes Scythicus* by John Jamieson (1814). The thesis is that the similarities between Greek and Latin on the one hand and Gothic or the Germanic languages on the other cannot be explained on the assumption that Germanic borrowed from Greek; it is more likely that Greek and Latin originated from the ancient Scythian, which is taken as the prototype of Germanic languages. Jamieson proposes to demonstrate his suggestion through a close comparison of prepositions, conjunctions, particles in general, derivational suffixes, pronouns, names of numbers, verbal inflections and forms of adjectival comparison. The philological analysis is competent and at times impressive, the method used certainly shows that the languages considered are related, but the apparent isolation of the work is striking; no references to other authors or to the recent work on Sanskrit, no serious attempt to distinguish between old and more recent Greek forms or between various forms of possible kinship. In contrast, James Cowles Prichard's book on *The Eastern Origin of the Celtic Nations*, published in 1831 but apparently written earlier, has some at least of the now familiar apparatus of scholarship, even if the author was not 'officially' a linguist but a doctor of medicine and an ethnologist.

2.6 Philosophical grammar vs. data-oriented linguistics

The interest in languages and linguistics in this period is beyond doubt, but the various strands are not easy to separate. Two tendencies emerge: on the one hand the data-oriented linguistics which Volney was asking for, and on the other the tradition of universal or philosophical grammar in which Loewe was interested. In France J. P. Abel-Rémusat with his work on Chinese and his *Recherches sur les langues tartares* (1820) belongs in the first group; Destutt de Tracy with his *Grammaire* ([1803] 1826) belongs in the second. But is Horne Tooke an exponent of the eighteenth-century tradition of universal or philosophical grammar or does his interest in etymology make him a precursor of the later historical linguistics? This question could be repeated *mutatis mutandis* for a number of other scholars. In some instances specific works can be classified but individual scholars cannot. A. I. Silvestre de Sacy was both a notable orientalist, a decipherer of unknown scripts etc., and the author of an extremely successful *Principes de grammaire générale mis à la portée des enfans et propres à servir d'introduction à l'étude de toutes les langues*.[6] Similarly J. S. Vater is both the author of a series of data collections and of a *Versuch einer allgemeinen Sprachlehre* (1801). Obviously the distinction was not always clear and not always relevant, but it was accepted by the contemporary authors: Vater ([1801] 1970, viii) contrasted a *philosophische* and a *historische* (i.e. empirical/

inductive) point of view, though he had difficulties in finding a way to reconcile the two (Schmitter ap. Nerlich 1988, 43f.). What trend should we now pursue?

The theory-oriented work of the early nineteenth century is closely linked with the eighteenth-century tradition. It would be difficult, if not impossible, to consider the French *grammaire générale* or the German *allgemeine Grammatik* (and this includes the work on the origin of language) without making constant reference either to Locke's and Condillac's influence or to Herder's work (which may well be related) or to the tradition of e.g. Port Royal and James Harris' *Hermes*. All authors in question were aware that they belonged in a certain tradition. If so, this work must be considered in the right context, which is that of earlier linguistic thought. By contrast, the data-oriented work came to be felt – rightly or wrongly – as marking the beginning of a new tradition. This is not entirely correct, but offers an obvious starting point for our enquiry. We shall now concentrate on the 'new linguistics' and on its more concrete aspects though we shall have to return to the theory – but from a new angle.

2.7 The 'new linguistics'

Somewhat earlier than Volney, another learned Frenchman, the count of Lanjuinais, had deplored ([1815] 1832, iv, 557) the fact that 'the general science of languages, which covers their filiations, their histories, their boundaries, their alphabets, their lexica, the methods of teaching them and their grammatical literatures' ('la science générale des langues, celle qui embrasse leurs filiations, leurs histoires, leur débornemens, leurs alphabets, leurs lexiques, les méthodes de les enseigner et leurs littératures grammaticales') was barely known in France. A few years afterwards, in his review of *Asia polyglotta* by J. Klaproth, Lanjuinais added a revealing note ([1823] 1832, iv, 541f.): 'scholars still said in the eighteenth century that in the world there are four mother languages and seventy-two idioms. *Linguistics* [*linguistique*], or the general science of languages, was established relatively recently and Adelung's *Mithridates* . . . has taught us that there are among men more than two thousand idioms'.[7] The Italian geographer, ethnologist and polymath A. Balbi (1782–1848) explains further (1826a, ix): the 'science nouvelle' which the Germans call linguistics, is divided into two parts 'étude pratique des langues' and 'étude comparative'.[8] Among the names of those who have contributed most to the new science he lists, in addition to the French orientalists mentioned above, the Germans Bopp, Schlegel, Humboldt and Klaproth, as well as some Englishmen (Colebrooke, Jones, Wilkins) and a Dane, Rasmus Rask. Obviously Volney, Lanjuinais and Balbi refer to data-oriented linguistics based on detailed analyses

of actual languages; genealogical classification and history are specifically mentioned but are not the only objects of study. Years earlier a
Königsberg professor, C. J. Kraus (1753–1807), had also spoken of a
'philosophical comparison of languages' ('philosophische Sprachvergleichung') and of a 'philosophische Universallinguistik' in an extremely
impressive review of the first part of Pallas' *Vocabularia comparativa*
published in 1787, where he in effect produced a plan for a descriptive
and comparative study of the known languages (both written and unwritten), which would give due weight to a phonetic, semantic and grammatical description while also defining the ethnological characteristics
of each language. The aim was on the one hand philosophical (to provide information about the connection of language and thought, human
faculties, etc.), on the other historical – it did not differ considerably
from that of Volney.[9]

As we have seen, we need to turn to Pott (1833–6, 1, xxiii) to find
the view that, though Adelung with his collection of languages had
given immense lustre to Germany, it was Bopp (1816) that marked the
beginning of a new epoch in linguistics. Afterwards the new linguistics
will be identified with the comparative linguistics of Bopp and the
historical and comparative linguistics of Grimm. We then notice a shift
in terminology: *comparatif, comparé, vergleichende*, which referred
to the older harmonic grammar, i.e. as Meiner had put it in 1781 (cf.
Naumann 1986, 50), to the grammar which is built on the comparison (*Vergleichung*) of several languages, acquire the evolutionary and
genealogical sense which they kept for the whole of the nineteenth century and the first part of this century (cf. p. 80 note 18). Round 1830
there is still a great variety of attitudes (cf. Swiggers 1993), but the
change in atmosphere (even if not necessarily in terminology) is more
than complete when in 1858 Louis Benloew (1858, 3), a German scholar
settled in France as professor at the *Faculté des lettres* of Dijon, writes
that the type of grammar which uses examples and rules from many
languages is called *grammaire comparée* but for the comparison to be
at all profitable the languages must be related.[10]

Yet it is only with hindsight that we see a contrast between a data-
oriented linguistics which aims at collecting facts about languages – all
languages – for typological or ethnological or historical or philosophical
reasons and the equally data-oriented work which is mainly concerned
with establishing a method to study the development of languages and
their genealogical classification. For us the 'new' science of language
is in a sense double. It is doubtful that this was so for its practitioners
– for the first decades at least. What they had in common was a concern
for the collection of linguistic data, either in the field or through the
philological study of texts, an increasing interest in the detailed analysis
of several languages, and, in some instances though by no means all,

a fundamental distrust in the 'esprit de système' which they saw as characteristic of the old concern for language and which they wanted to counteract with 'l'examen des faits positifs' (Balbi 1826 a, xlix). For the rest, aims and methodology differed; how and why did not become clear till later.

2.8 'L'appel de l'histoire'

From this broader angle we see the starting point of the new linguistics not only, as is usually done, in the climate of Romanticism, but in a much earlier period. Authors such as Volney, in their eagerness to highlight the brave new world which lay ahead of them, underrated the importance of the earlier work, though they knew that there was a connection between their interests and the post-Renaissance enquiries. Later on, the nineteenth-century authors whose work was mostly historical saw themselves as belonging to a new paradigm and dismissed all earlier research, thus introducing a gap of considerable magnitude between themselves and their predecessors. It is only very recently that attempts have been made to bridge the gap; an impressive example is that of Daniel Droixhe (1978, 1984) who has aimed at reconstructing the various phases which marked 'l'appel de l'histoire' between 1600 and 1800. The details belong in the earlier parts of this history of linguistics, but some basic strands must at least be mentioned. First, starting with the Renaissance, the knowledge of – and interest in – languages increases. Numerous collections of linguistic data (glossaries, translations of the Bible and of the Lord's Prayer, etc.) are published and necessarily the new material leads to a more sophisticated approach to the problems of classification. In the eighteenth century we witness a real explosion of linguistic knowledge, due both to the changed historical circumstances which made it possible and to 'that extraordinary accumulation of learning and knowledge' (Venturi [1960] 1972, 14) which characterized the Enlightenment not only in France but in the whole of Europe. Secondly, during the whole of the period considered by Droixhe there are attempts at classifying the known languages into language families; if there was an earlier belief that all languages were derived from Hebrew, this gradually disappears; the standard monogenetic assumptions begin to lose their predominance and the criteria for defining linguistic similarity begin to be formulated. Thirdly, there is a considerable interest in the earlier linguistic phases, which is accompanied by an increasing sophistication in philological techniques. Pioneering work on Anglo-Saxon and Gothic is done in the seventeenth century; the first decipherments of unknown scripts belong to the eighteenth century; the end of the eighteenth century sees in Germany, partly as a result of Winckelmann's neo-Hellenism, a new interest in reconstructing the history of classical texts (Wolf) and consequently a new concern for textual criticism and a closer attention to linguistic data.

2.9 From theory to history

If the empirical work necessarily preludes to the 'new linguistics', the theoretical discussions of the eighteenth century are not necessarily hostile. The tradition linked with the *Grammaire de Port Royal* (1660) is important and survives well into the nineteenth century but not all the eighteenth-century thought on language belongs within that framework. There is also a strong tradition of philosophical empiricism (De Mauro [1965] 1970a; Rosiello 1967) which comes to the fore in the Enlightenment and, as we shall see, is indirectly responsible for some of the later concerns. For Locke words corresponded to ideas and not to things, and language was a social institution, conventional and man-made; this view was adopted in the French Enlightenment by Condillac and his followers (including Destutt de Tracy and some of the other *idéologues*), but for them language acquired an even more important role: it became the precondition of thought. The study of the origin and development of language now becomes a history of the human mind; this view prevails in France but also in England with Monboddo and in a somewhat different manner with Horne Tooke (Aarsleff 1982, 27ff.). In Germany, though in a different framework, the 'genealogical priority' of language was asserted by Hamann and by Herder (Formigari 1977b, 35ff.). The numerous essays about the origin of language, which were criticized so harshly in the following century, did in fact aim at understanding from a philosophical point of view how ideas were formed and how knowledge was acquired; they were not meant as pieces of historical research. Yet in the context of these discussions we find constant reference to two types of evidence which, within a different framework, will play a considerable role in the next century: etymology and exotic or primitive languages. In his 1746 *Essai sur l'origine des connoissances humaines*, Condillac (1947–51, I, 87 = *Essai* II, 1, x, § 103) refers to Locke's statement that, 'if we could trace them to their sources, we should find in all languages the names which stand for things that fall not under our senses to have had their first rise from sensible ideas'. Etymology could play a role in this search for the first sources. Its importance for the general theory of language and for a reconstruction of the philosophical history of man is clearly stressed in the article *Étymologie* (1756) which Turgot wrote for the *Encyclopédie*.[11] But the same thoughts about the value of etymology are found everywhere, not only in France but also in Britain with Monboddo and then of course with Tooke, in Germany with Michaelis, Herder and so on.

Equally significant are the references to exotic languages. We find
e.g. in Maupertuis' 1748 *Réflexions philosophiques sur l'origine des
langues et la signification des mots* a reference to the interest of those
remote languages 'which seem to have been formed on systems of ideas
so different from ours that it is almost impossible to translate into our
languages what has been expressed in those languages' ('qui semblent
avoir été formées sur des plans d'idées si différentes de nôtres, qu'on
ne peut presque pas traduire dans nos langues ce qui a été une fois
exprimé dans celles-là'). And Maupertuis continues, 'It is from the comparison of those languages with the others that a philosophical mind
would gain great benefit' ('Ce serait de la comparaison de ces langues
avec les autres qu'un esprit philosophique pourrait tirer beaucoup
d'utilité') (Grimsley 1971, 31f.). Turgot, who round 1750 replied to
Maupertuis, objected to these sentiments but concluded: 'it is true, however, that the study of primitive languages [*langues sauvages*] would be
very useful' (*ibid.*, 62).[12] In different works, such as Herder's *Ursprung
der Sprache*, we also find frequent, even if superficial, references to
remote languages.

The omnipresent references to etymology and exotic languages cannot be separated from the recurrent discussions about the genius of
language and its link with the genius of the nation. Here too different
people may speak of different things; the background changes from
Condillac's *Essai* (Part 2, Chapter 15) to Herder to Monboddo or even
to James Harris, and, in Italy, to Melchiorre Cesarotti (Rosiello 1967,
79ff.; Simone 1990, 367ff.), not to mention Vico. Condillac (1947–51,
I, 103 = *Essai* II, 1, xv, § 162) argued that the way in which ideas are
linked in combinations which are then consecrated by usage is peculiar
to each language and that 'if the customs had influence on the language,
this, once its rules were fixed by famous writers, had influence on the
customs'. But Condillac's views are tied to his particular brand of
empiricism; Herder interprets 'genius of the language' differently. Yet
the essential point is that during the whole of the eighteenth century we
find in constant use everywhere and under different ideological umbrellas
a phrase which emphasizes the non-triviality of linguistic differences.

Why are these views relevant to the new linguistics? Partly because
if etymology, exotic languages and language diversity are perceived as
philosophically interesting, this may also lead to a more intensive study
of these subjects and to data-oriented study; partly because it is easy to
reinterpret the concern with origins in a historical rather than philosophical key. Etymology in particular offers a clear lead to a philological and historical study of languages. Similarly the concern with exotic
languages and language diversity may lead away from philosophy
towards a typology based on fieldwork or philological study. A passage
by a notable *idéologue* illustrates both the contrast between theory- and

data-oriented approaches and the starting point of the reinterpretation. In his *Grammaire* ([1803] 1826, 86f.), Destutt de Tracy argued that just as the adjectives are originally nouns altered to indicate a specific function, the prepositions are originally adjectives or nouns fossilized in certain functions. He was then obliged to admit that in modern languages this is not always obvious. Yet, he continued, Horne Tooke, 'grammairien vraiment philosophe', has succeeded in demonstrating that almost all English prepositions derive from nouns and adjectives; similar research, if extended to all languages, would be useful in many respects and would demonstrate through facts ('par les faits') what has been established through theory and according to the generation of ideas ('par la théorie et suivant la génération des idées').[13] There follows a disclaimer about the author's ability or willingness to undertake this task. Destutt de Tracy's words are enlightening in view of the later developments. Aarsleff ([1974] 1982, 161) has observed that the eighteenth century's search for origin 'concerned the present state of man, not the establishment of some "historical" fact or "explanation" of how things actually were at some point in the past'. On the other hand, the nineteenth century 'was so saturated with a factual historical view that it could not see the attempt to deal with origins in any other light, thus failing utterly to comprehend what the previous century had been up to'. In our passage (and in similar ones) we may see the origin of the misapprehension.[14] We also have here a blueprint for two possible but opposite developments. The eighteenth century research done in a theoretical mode (to use again Aarsleff's terminology) could continue in that vein but if so it was bound to fall foul of the new factual and historical mood of the following century, and be rejected (which did indeed happen) or be relegated to pure philosophy (which also happened). The alternative was to aim at a rapprochement with the other line of enquiry. If so, however, the question arose whether the theory was simply looking for factual confirmation of its results (thus admitting, as was implicitly done by Destutt de Tracy, that its models were capable of factual confirmation and opening the way to the misunderstanding mentioned above) or was ready to accept radical changes, i.e. to abandon part at least of its methodology and aims and to turn into an inductive discipline.

We may now reconsider Volney's text quoted above. Volney's wish, as we have seen, is for data-oriented work which starts inductively from the comparison of different languages. Yet he also wants to know what is the origin of our *faculté de parler*. For him the transition from theory- to data-orientation and from philosophical to historical approach either has happened or is beginning to happen. However, differently from his successors, he has not broken the bridge with the earlier tradition – he is still very much an *idéologue* and a philosophical empiricist. Similarly, J.-M. Degérando ([1800] 1969, 61) mantained in general terms

that 'the pursuit of learning has settled at last on the way of observation' and then – to put it anachronistically – sketched a procedure for
linguistic fieldwork, while arguing at the same time that 'the art of properly studying these languages [viz. the languages of savage tribes], if
it could be reduced to rules, would be one of the master-works of philosophy; it can be the result only of long meditations on the origin of
ideas' (*ibid.*, 70).[15]

2.10 The collections of language data

The philosophical climate of the beginning of the century clearly was
not opposed to a data-oriented approach to language and languages,
but what knowledge was actually available? Volney himself referred
to Pallas (1787–89), Hervás (1800–5) and Adelung (1806–17).[16] Later
on, Balbi, with his *Atlas ethnographique du globe ou classification des
peuples anciens et modernes d'après leur langues*, published in 1826,
gave to France a less full but more up-to-date work. There are profound
differences between these collections both because of their methodology and aims and because of the material they contain. Yet to ignore
any of them means to yield too easily to the later historiography which
found all these works faulty because of their lack of sophistication in
historical and comparative techniques and dismissed them without further ado.

2.10.1 Pallas's universal dictionary

The project by Catherine II of Russia for a universal dictionary led to
the collection through a series of questionnaires, which were given very
wide diffusion, of the basic vocabulary (12 numerals and 273 other
words including nouns, adjectives, verbs, pronouns and adverbs) of 200
languages from Europe and Asia. This was edited by the famous natur-
alist P. S. Pallas (1741–1811), with a Russian title rendered in Latin as
Linguarum totius orbis vocabularia comparativa and published in two
volumes at St Petersburg in 1787–9 after a first Latin edition in 1786
(F. Adelung 1815; Gipper-Schmitter 1979, 20ff.). A later four-volume
Russian version edited by the Hungarian F. I. Jankovič de Mirievo in
1790–1 removed 7 Asiatic languages and added some 79 new languages,
including 30 African and 23 American; yet it had very little diffusion
and was still limited to vocabulary words transcribed in Cyrillic.[17]

Volney was one of those who pointed out that the work was full of
mistakes, but also stressed that it remained 'un des plus beaux présens
faits à la philosophie par un gouvernement'. In fact the actual linguistic
discussion or classification was tenuous or non-existing and the importance of the material collected was partly diminished by inaccuracies.[18]
Yet it served to highlight the magnitude of linguistic diversity and it

obliged readers and reviewers to consider the problems of language diversity from a more general point of view (Simone 1997, 189).

2.10.2 Lorenzo Hervás y Panduro

The Spanish Jesuit Lorenzo Hervás y Panduro (1735–1809) reached the study of language in the course of his search for encyclopedic knowledge. He is an eighteenth-century polymath rather than a nineteenth-century professional linguist. His *magnum opus*, written after he had had to leave Spain for Italy in 1767 because of the expulsion of the Jesuits from all Spanish territories, appeared under the general title of *Idea dell' Universo* and consisted of 21 volumes published between 1778 and 1787 at Cesena; of these the last five (XVII–XXI) were concerned with language and languages and contain a catalogue and classification of the known languages (XVII), a discussion of the origin of language (XVIII), an analysis of numerals and their origin (XIX), a *Vocabolario poliglotto* (XX) with 63 words translated in 154 languages, and finally a *Saggio prattico delle lingue* (XXI) with the Lord's Prayer in more than 300 languages and a few grammatical comments on the texts.[19] Between 1800 and 1805 Hervás also published in Madrid a *Catálogo de las lenguas de las naciones conocidas* in five volumes and six tomes which included more data than the previous work, but remained unfinished: the analysis of the European languages is incomplete and the African languages, which appeared in the Italian version, are missing.

Hervás is convinced that languages provide the best evidence for the history and above all the prehistory of nations (Bustamante 1986, 83f.; Val-Alvaro 1987). Yet he is dissatisfied with simple word-lists, such as those collected at the same time by Catherine the Great. Ideally he would like to have a complete series of grammatical descriptions; failing that, reasonable stretches of text with translations may provide adequate data. Hervás partly finds his own material in the Roman libraries, but he also explains that he has been in touch with numerous Jesuits returned from foreign parts and has collected from them written and oral information, though unfortunately this human reservoir of knowledge was disappearing fast. The data are arranged in a rough geographic order by continent or subcontinent but in addition Hervás distinguishes between *lingue matrici* and dialects accepting the terminology and basic concepts adopted by J. J. Scaliger at the end of the sixteenth century; the *lingue matrici* are not related to each other but each one of them is seen as the origin of a number of dialects. For Europe, Hervás (1784) lists: Illyrian (from which the various Slavic languages are derived), Scythian (with Hungarian, Finnish, Lappish, etc., but also Gothic), Turkish (which Hervás treats as a dialect of 'Tartar Mongolian'), Greek, Teutonic (from which he derives the Germanic languages except Gothic), Celtic (with Irish, Welsh, Breton, etc. but definitely not with Basque or other languages), Latin (with the Romance languages including Romanian), Basque or Cantabrian (which in Hervás' view was also the main Italic substratum).

Hervás' work is important because of the vastness of the linguistic material collected: his list and analysis of American indigenous languages was far richer than anything done earlier. Yet this is not all. There is a wealth of observations and thoughts which anticipate later developments, and his general statements, even if misguided, are often far sharper and clearer than those of his successors.[20] First there is his confident belief in the importance of languages as historical sources. This is not new, but in Hervás' case it leads to careful accounts of the historical context against which the known languages must be considered; it also explains his attempts to offer for some languages (such as Latin) evidence for both early and later phases. Indeed in the case of Latin and Romance we find already in the 1784 *Catalogo* what amounts to brief external histories of these languages. Hervás' views also have something to contribute to the general theory of typology and to that of language development. For him a language is defined by its vocabulary, its phonological characteristics and above all its *artificio grammaticale*, i.e. that part of language which is incapable of fundamental changes. Without in any way attempting a typological classification in grammatical terms, Hervás is in effect defining the basic principles on which this can be founded and saying that a language can in no sense alter its structure while remaining meaningfully the same language. This view (which is fundamentally an eighteenth-century view) underlies a large part (even if not all) of nineteenth-century work but is hardly ever expressed so clearly. It follows from this assumption that in no way can we say that all attested languages are related, nor is there any question of a common descent from Hebrew. The differences between dialects can indeed be shown to be secondary but those between *lingue matrici* cannot be explained away. It is not stated, however, how the structure or *artificio grammaticale* of a language is defined and what counts as structural difference. In the article *Langue* (1765) of the *Encyclopédie*, Beauzée (if he was the author) had argued that a common vocabulary did not prove common origin, i.e. etymology was of no use for this purpose. What characterized related languages was that they shared 'the same syntax, the same construction, in a word, the same genius'. Beauzée then followed l'abbé Girard in denying that French, Spanish and Italian derived from Latin and proceeded to argue that these three languages and English seemed to descend from Celtic and to have taken from it 'la marche analytique'.[21] By contrast, Hervás (e.g. 1784, 179ff.) has no hesitation in deriving French, Spanish and Italian from Latin, i.e., if he is coherent with his general statements, in attributing to both Latin and the Romance languages the same *artificio grammaticale*. Could it be that the experience of structurally very different languages such as the Amerindian languages or Basque had given him a new conception of what structural difference meant? And if so, is this an example of how a set of purely empirical data can insensibly alter the whole general approach?

2.10.3 Adelung's *Mithridates*

Even though Volney did not read German, he seems to have felt (with most of his contemporaries) that Hervás' work was to a certain extent superseded by the *Mithridates oder allgemeine Sprachenkunde mit dem Vater Unser als Sprachprobe in bey nahe fünfhundert Sprachen und Mundarten* written by J. C. Adelung (1732–1806) and after his death by J. S. Vater in four parts from 1806 to 1817 (Volney [1819] 1820, 35ff.). He also noticed that its approach was less historical and more philosophical and grammatical than that of Hervás – a statement which is at least questionable. In his turn, Benfey (1869, 272), who observed that the last volume of this gigantic compilation appeared one year later than Bopp's first work, pointed out that *Mithridates* should count as the conclusion, by no means an unworthy one, of the old linguistics. On the whole Benfey's judgement has been accepted but we should at least qualify it (Wyss 1979, 96–100). *Mithridates* cannot be said to have brought a new methodology or essential new material to comparative linguistics, i.e. it does not belong with Bopp's discipline, but from the point of view of language classification and typology the book is far more important than Benfey seems to imply. When the first edition of *Les langues du monde* by A. Meillet and M. Cohen appeared in 1924 it showed that, with the exception of Friedrich Müller's *magnum opus*, published between 1876 and 1888, no other work had even attempted to cover the same ground as *Mithridates* with the same richness of details. The work consists, as also did Hervás' *Catalogo*, of an account of the history, spread, etc. of the known languages and of the evidence available; basic grammatical and/or lexical information is also provided. The languages are classified geographically (by continent or subcontinent), typologically (according to whether the words are monosyllabic or plurisyllabic) and genealogically, though Adelung's fundamental belief in monogenesis and his assumption that all polysyllabic languages started as monosyllabic blurs the distinction between typology and genealogy.[22] The justification given for the enterprise is double: first, the natural desire to collect information about various types of human endeavour; secondly, and most important, the desire to contribute through the study of languages to historical knowledge and the assessment of the relationship and origin of different peoples (Adelung 1806–17, i, *Vorrede*, iii–iv). Adelung is convinced, like Hervás, whose work he quotes and uses, that mere word-lists are not sufficient to define a language, and he aims at giving samples of actual discourse. For the rest he protests (somewhat too loudly) that he has no

'Lieblingsmeinung', no thesis that he will defend at all costs irrespective of the evidence,[23] and that he does not want to derive all languages from a specific language. Kinship, he continues, cannot be established through the mere comparison of vocabulary words; nor does grammatical structure help because similar grammatical features can appear in numerous languages without particular significance. It is necessary to compare roots, but this is only possible if in the vocabulary of each language the meaningful roots have been previously segmented – something which requires considerable knowledge of the structure of the language and has not been done, or not been done correctly, except perhaps for German. Adelung is rehearsing here, admittedly without great originality, a sequence of old and in some instances relatively new motifs. His general views are less impressive than those of Hervás, though he does not hesitate to label Hervás (1784) as 'ganz unkritisch und unphilosophisch' (Adelung 1806–17, i, 671), but differently from Hervás he was a man who had had notable influence in things linguistic and who was treated with respect by his contemporaries (his work on German is now undergoing a revaluation).[24] Some points are important in his general statements and in his accounts of the various languages. First, his preferring for the historical rather than the philosophical aim, his denial of any preconceived theory (both if put into practice or not), fitted better with the mood of his successors than is normally assumed. Bopp's school abandoned Hervás' and Adelung's ethnographic interests in order to concentrate on language *per se* (Schmitter in Nerlich 1988, 34), but even so a historical-ethnographic approach was far more congenial to the future developments than the more theoretical philosophical problems of others. Also, we find in *Mithridates* (in spite of all its inaccuracies and mistakes) the general appearance and perhaps substance of a scholarly and philological approach to language.[25] In his Basque chapter (even though it is not one of his best efforts) Adelung starts with a brief historical account, then turns to the language and mentions the words that it has in common with other languages, stresses its uniqueness, illustrates it with reference to its phonological or grammatical characteristics, lists the bibliography and sources available, makes brief mention of the relevant dialects, and eventually offers some passages (partly taken from Hervás) with an interlinear translation and in one instance a grammatical commentary based on Hervás. The arrangement of the data has an air of modernity and the bibliographical information strikes a note which was absent from Hervás. At Vater's invitation, Wilhelm von Humboldt (1817) rewrote this particular section for the fourth part of *Mithridates*, revealing the inconsistencies and inaccuracies of the original text. This too has modern overtones: the period of the independent polymath is coming to an end and the way is open to specialization and teamwork, i.e. to what Bréal most admired in German scholarship (cf. p. 19).

2.10.4 Adriano Balbi

Balbi's work has often been ignored (e.g. by Benfey 1869) and yet Du
Ponceau admired it (Swiggers 1992, 11) and Pott ([1884] 1974, 270)
noted that it deserved recognition. We deal again with a polymath but
this time with a 'professor of geography, physics and mathematics', an
Italian who migrated to Berlin and Paris, and came to languages from
ethnography and geography. His purpose is once more to use 'l'étude
comparée des langues' in order to follow through the centuries the migrations of peoples, to clarify ancient and modern geography and to shed
light on the prehistory of mankind and on the development of its intellectual faculties (1826a, xii). Language is the most durable and indeed the
defining character of the individual nations but the linguistic evidence
must be used well (rejecting the wild hypothesis and nonsensical etymologies of previous centuries); if this is done, *la philologie ethnographique*
can play a considerable role in historical and geographical research (*ibid.*,
ix and cxvi). Balbi recognizes the inadequacy of Adelung's classification based on the monosyllabic/polysyllabic distinction and the incom-
pleteness of his evidence (neglect of Oceania, out-of-date information
about Africa and America, wrong classification of the languages of Europe, etc.) and aims at something different. The *Atlas* consists of a series
of tables arranged roughly by continent (including Oceania), which give
an extremely schematic account of the various families of languages
attested and of their main characteristics. Further tables give for each language a basic vocabulary of 26 words. Since Balbi clearly made great
use of the help of a number of illustrious specialists (who are constantly
referred to), it is indeed true that his data are more accurate than those
of Adelung, but that is not all: his general assumptions stated in the first
introductory volume are also remarkable. He discusses at length concepts such as those of language family, etymology, structural classification, use of comparison, etc., and does not hesitate to request written
opinions from some of his heroes or to excerpt from their writings: the
Danish geographer Malte-Brun, Alexander von Humboldt, Abel-Rémusat,
Klaproth, etc. are constantly quoted. In fact the general volume provides
a lively account of the problems discussed by his contemporaries in the
field of data-oriented linguistics. Like Malte-Brun, Balbi hesitates to
assume that there was an Indo-Germanic (as he calls it) family because
the evidence is too dispersed and some of its elements too badly known,
but while waiting for further information he prefers to speak of a 'kingdom' (*regne*) of such languages (1826a, 29): a kingdom in his terminology, which again he owes to Malte Brun (Malte-Brun ap. Balbi 1826a,
2–13), includes groups of languages or language families which at some
stage must have had a closer connection, while a family includes languages which clearly had a common origin such as the Slavic or Germanic languages (*ibid.*). It is unfortunate, Balbi argues, that the type of

evidence which allows us to distinguish between kingdoms and families is only available for Indo-Germanic (*ibid.*, 30). For no other group of languages do we have sufficient evidence. What we need in all instances is the type of analysis that Jacob Grimm produced for Germanic distinguishing old from new features and carefully contrasting the dialects (*ibid.*, 57).

We have here, in the context of an invitation to caution, the implicit definition of a working programme: Grimm's type of analysis must be extended to other languages and, if possible, to all other languages. In the case of the 'Indo-Germanic' languages, this may lead to the conclusion that they form a family rather than a kingdom; in the case of the other languages of the world, it may lead to the identification of other kingdoms and other families. With hindsight we notice that Balbi's programme was in fact the programme that future generations put into effect.

2.11 Language kinship

Our authors all share an interest in language as a source of historical knowledge. The aim is not new: Leibniz had repeatedly said as much (Aarsleff 1982, 84–100). Yet what is striking in Hervás, Adelung and Balbi is the fact that they agree in giving precedence to historical results over the more theoretical philosophical investigations based on language.

If languages are to provide information about the origins and earlier migrations of nations, it is necessary first of all to establish what languages exist, what is a language and what is a dialect, what evidence we have about the history of each language and of its speakers, what languages are related and therefore descend from the same language, etc. The general question of monogenesis or polygenesis may sometimes (though not always) be seen as less important because, if considered historically, it applies to periods so remote that we cannot hope to obtain information about them. On the other hand, the question of language kinship becomes crucial. How is this to be tackled?

The problem is old. Ever since the Renaissance (and indeed since the Middle Ages) attempts had been made to group languages into families (Bonfante 1953, Borst 1957–63, Metcalf 1974, Droixhe 1978, etc.). In fact most of the biological terminology which we still apply to languages (expressions such as 'linguistic family', 'mother language', 'cognate languages', 'daughter languages', 'language kinship') is not a product of the nineteenth century but of the earlier period (Metcalf 1974, 236; Percival 1987). A great deal of effort and erudition was deployed in those early attempts; a posteriori we distinguish between two lines of attack but it is doubtful that the contemporaries would have always found it useful to do so. On the one hand the linguistic data were looked at with the aim of identifying similarities and differences. On the other hand there were historical/ethnographic enquiries which linked languages and peoples and reached conclusions on the basis of historical/literary/religious sources or, more sweepingly, on the basis of similarities or dissimilarities between the names of the peoples or tribes in question. As late as 1814, John Jamieson in arguing, as his title page indicates, for 'The Radical Affinities of the Greek and Latin Languages to the Gothic', declared that 'although himself satisfied that the proof, arising from a comparison of the languages, is sufficient to demonstrate the national affinity of the Greek and Romans to the Scythians', nevertheless 'to remove, as far as possible, every ground of hesitations with others, he *had* prefixed a Dissertation on the historical evidence which bears on the same point' (Jamieson 1814, iv). The evidence used relied entirely on classical or immediately post-classical sources which discussed the languages spoken by specific tribes, the ethnographic/political/geographic distinctions between tribes, and the names of the tribes in question.[26] Jamieson fitted within a long-standing tradition: if two languages were declared to be related this was hardly ever done for exclusively linguistic reasons (Metcalf 1974, 240f.). The historical data were obtained in more or less scholarly fashion; the main point is that hardly ever was a distinction drawn between information which bore on the language and information which bore on ethnic characteristics. Nevertheless, structural considerations were also important (and were bound to become more so when languages 'without a history' were considered). Gradually a few methodological principles had emerged, even if in practice they were not followed by everyone. We shall now look briefly at some of the positive conclusions and then at a few points of principle and practice which the beginning of the nineteenth century inherited from the preceding generations.

2.11.1 Genealogical classification

It is often said that before the nineteenth century all languages were taken as derived from Hebrew so that no attempt was made at establishing other genealogical groupings. This is wrong for at least two reasons. First, a generic belief in a common descent from Hebrew did not necessarily prevent attempts at further subgrouping. Secondly, what Droixhe (1978, 45) calls 'faillite de la monogenèse hébraïque' was already apparent in the seventeenth century (Simone 1997, 163ff.). Sporadic attempts at deriving all languages from Hebrew obviously continued after that period as did some authors' belief in monogenesis, though this was not necessarily connected with the Adamic theory. Nevertheless we also find early attempts at genealogical classification in which Hebrew and/or monogenesis played no role. The famous classicist Joseph-Justus Scaliger (1540–1609) wrote in 1599 a pamphlet (published in 1605 and 1610) in which he attributed all European languages to four major and seven minor mother-tongues (*matrices*) which were not related among them-selves: the grouping revealed awareness of the special links of e.g. the Romance or the Germanic or the Slavic languages and had considerable influence in the seventeenth and eighteenth centuries (Droixhe 1993). But not everyone was as cautious: the increasing importance of the national languages and a considerable dose of incipient nationalism led to a number of mutually contradictory works which derived the known languages from e.g. Flemish or Swedish or German. At the same time some results came into the public domain: by the end of the seven-teenth century it had been recognized that languages such as Hebrew, Aramaic, Phoenician, Arabic, Ethiopic, etc., belonged to one family, which later (1781) was called Semitic by the Göttingen scholar A. L. Schlözer. Yet Hervás in 1784 still wondered whether all these languages descended from Hebrew or whether Hebrew itself was one of the daughter languages.[27]

Also important was the work done about Finno-Ugric languages (Gulya 1974). Adelung (1806–17, ii, 739ff.) linked Finnish with Lappish but treated Hungarian separately as a mixed language. However, Hervás (1784, 162ff.) had joined Hungarian, Finnish, Lappish, Lettish, etc. in a single family. This connection had been suggested at a much earlier stage, e.g. by the German Martin Fogel (1634–1675), who relied on lex-ical agreements and on structural similarities (Stehr 1957, 7–23; Lakó 1970), and later by the Swede P. J. T. von Strahlenberg (1676–1743), who anticipated the discovery of the Uralo-Altaic unity (Stehr 1957, 32–49). But in the last third of the eighteenth century two Hungarian scholars, the Jesuit János Sajnovics (1733–85) and the medical doctor Sámuel Gyarmathi (1751–1830), wrote monographs which conclusively demon-strated the kinship of Hungarian and Lappish-Finnish first and then that of these languages with Estonian and other Finno-Ugric languages.[28] The interest of the *Demonstratio idioma Ungarorum et Lapponum idem esse* published by Sajnovics in 1770 and of the *Affinitas linguae hun-garicae cum linguis fennicae originis grammatice demonstrata* published by Gyarmathi in 1799 does not only consist in the validity of the con-clusions reached but above all in the consistence of the method employed. Sajnovics fought the popular view that related languages must be mutu-ally comprehensible, emphasized the magnitude of linguistic change by contrasting early and late texts in the same language, considered the prob-lems caused by spelling vs. pronunciation and then proceeded to com-pare lexical and grammatical forms in a systematic manner. Gyarmathi followed the same method and went as far as to state that lexical cor-respondences are the least important criterion for kinship (1799, xiii). In both works the discussion is purely linguistic (no historical account is attempted) and the emphasis is on the comparison of grammatical **forms** (endings, suffixes, pronouns, etc.), though structural similarity is also mentioned; yet no clear account is given of what counts as similar and what does not.[29] Both authors were violently attacked in their country of origin largely because the Hungarians were not ready to be linked to countries which they considered culturally inferior (Zsirai 1951). Possibly because of this, but also because the languages which they considered were not widely known, their methodological impact on the development of comparative linguistics was limited (cf. Gulya 1974, 266ff.).

2.11.2 The 'Scythian' and 'Celtic' theories

Two other comparative trends, which were influential before the nineteenth century but were then forgotten, brought back most European and some oriental languages to a 'Scythian' or a 'Celtic' source.[30] We have seen the references to Scythian by Volney and John Jamieson (pp. 27, 30). Volney knew about Sanskrit, and his Scythian is in effect what others would have called Indo-European or Indo-Germanic, but the assumption that some of the Germanic languages were related with Persian and perhaps with Greek and Latin is much older. In various guises it appears from the sixteenth century onwards (Droixhe 1978, 55ff., 81ff.) and eventually takes the form of a consistent belief in a great Scythian nation extended from East to West, from Europe to Asia, which gave birth to Greek, Latin, Persian and the Germanic languages. This view was enthusiastically formulated in the mid seventeenth century, e.g. by Frenchman Claude Saumaise (1588–1653) and by the Leyden professor Marc Boxhorn (1602–53); it survived in the eighteenth century when some of the earlier work was reprinted (Metcalf 1974, 234f.) and when it influenced e.g. Monboddo (Muller 1984b); finally, as we have seen, it reached our period (Metcalf 1974, Droixhe 1978, 86–99). Arguments used in support were, on the one hand, the evidence of historical or literary sources, and, on the other hand, linguistic similarities in lexicon but also in inflectional patterns and in structure. Yet that same Monboddo who accepted some of Saumaise's conclusions did not hesitate to add Hebrew to the list of related languages and to share in the prevailing Celtomania; other authors were even more eclectic. This absence of sharpness in both methodology and conclusions explains how the Scythian theory could partly compete, partly interact with a theory which in its most extreme eighteenth-century form treated most of the world languages as derived from Celtic (Droixhe 1978, 147). The theory had been influential on e.g. Leibniz, who was ready to believe that most European languages belonged to a 'Celtic' family. Even more daringly, Monboddo (1773–92, i, 587ff.) argued that Eskimo and Basque were so close to each other that they were mutually intelligible and that, since undoubtedly Basque was Celtic, Eskimo too had to be Celtic.[31] As Hervás pointed out (1784, 170), 'if the Celtic language had been spoken by all nations that the Ancient called Celtic, we ought to say that the Celtic idiom was the language of almost all ancient nations of Europe'. At the beginning of the new century Celtomania diminished while the Scythian trend had a somewhat longer life until it was absorbed by the new Indo-European classification, with which to a certain extent it overlapped.[32]

2.12 Lexical comparison

The concrete proposals inevitably went hand in hand with some sort of methodology. Before the nineteenth century the simplest form of comparison was based on the lexicon: if two or more languages had words with similar meanings and similar forms they could be deemed to be related. At a relatively early stage, however, it came to be acknowledged that lexical similarities could also be due to chance, to onomatopoeia and to late borrowings, and it was emphasized that comparison ought to bear on the most stable part of the lexicon. In the seventeenth century Hugo de Groot (Grotius) had produced a small list of words in support of his view that the Amerindian languages derived from Scandinavian. The Belgian Jan de Laet (1582–1649) objected that lexical comparisons were not always sufficient to demonstrate kinship. Moreover, he argued, even when it was necessary to concentrate on the lexicon, not all word equivalences were equally significant; it was better to look at the 'ordinary' vocabulary, in particular at the words for the parts of the body, for the numbers from 1 to 10, at some kinship and geographic terms (Metcalf 1974, 246ff.; Droixhe 1978, 72f.). We are moving already towards a definition of 'basic vocabulary' which will play a role in much later investigations. As Droixhe has pointed out, Sir William Jones in 1789 also wrote in similar terms and specifically aimed at excluding from comparison terms which were likely to be introduced through secondary contacts of political, commercial or cultural nature. Similar views repeatedly occur between the sixteenth and the nineteenth centuries (Muller 1984a, 1986, 17ff.), though it is difficult, if not impossible, to establish for each author whether he reached them independently or took them from his predecessors. Long after Jan de Laet, Leibniz pleaded for word collections: his preferred list started with the numerals, kinship terms and words for parts of the body (Gulya 1974). Much later Balbi (1826b), who added to his *Atlas* word lists for some 700 languages, selected 26 terms which again included the words for some natural elements, some kinship terms, the parts of the body and the numerals and argued that these were sufficient to locate each language into the family to which it belonged. In all this, i.e. in the selection of the lexical material to be used for comparison, there was considerable agreement.[33] Yet there were divergences in the way in which words were equated across languages:

what degree of formal and semantic similarity was required to conclude that two words were cognate?

2.12.1 Phonetic equations

'Everyone who deals with them knows that the individual languages have sound alternations adapted to their genius [*suo genio accommodatas litterarum permutationes*] so that those who ignore them often treat as unrelated what is in fact closely linked' (Ihre 1769, 1, ii). In the second part of the eighteenth century this sentence and the analyses that follow it summarize the results of the somewhat desultory reflection about the nature of phonetic divergence which had taken place earlier. Both for the purposes of etymology and for those of comparison it was necessary to establish what degree of phonetic divergence was allowed in related words. Already the Latin grammarians had listed 'letters' which alternated because they were articulated in similar manner and consequently counted as *cognatae* (Diderichsen 1974, 28of.). In the Renaissance the problem came to the fore. There was general agreement that etymologically related words in the same language or in different languages could differ in their phonetic make-up. This could lead of course to a free-for-all. However, among the most cautious etymologists the view prevailed that the only alternations allowed were those among 'cognate letters'. In the seventeenth century further thought was given to the question of what 'letters' should count as 'cognate'. Similarity of articulation (intuitively established) was a natural starting point but other criteria were sometimes mentioned: morphophonemic alternations within the same language and occurrence of the alternation in different phases of the same language or in related words of other dialects or languages. Hence [t] and [d] could be labelled 'cognate' for at least three different reasons, each of which – most people would have agreed – was sufficient by itself: (a) they were similarly articulated, (b) [t] alternated with [d] within the same language (e.g. in Latin *at-tendo* was a compound of *ad* and *tendo*), (c) [t] of one language could correspond to [d] of other languages (cf. e.g. English *eat* and Latin *edere*).[34] Once this form of 'letter kinship' was established it was treated as a sort of linguistic universal and was used to provide support for any word-correspondence where either of the two 'letters' occurred. If the alternation (*permutatio*) X occurred in language Y in stage T there was no reason why it should not also occur in different stages of the same language or in an altogether different language (Metcalf 1974). The Président de Brosses (1765) did not hesitate to link the Romance FORT and the Germanic VALD on the ground that F and V were both labials, R and L were liquids and T and D were dentals. Later authors made fun of this attitude but we should not forget that the various attempts at establishing rules of *literarum permutatio* on the one hand were responsible for the increased attention to the 'decomposition' of the word into its elements and consequently for the growing phonetic knowledge, and on the other hand led to the discovery of impressive regularities in the phonetic correspondences between related languages and to an awareness of how many mutations were language-specific. In the eighteenth century this last point was mentioned by J. C. Wachter in his *Glossarium Germanicum* (1737) and firmly stated by Turgot in his *Étymologie* article for the *Encyclopédie* (Diderichsen 1974). The Swedish Germanist Johan Ihre (1707–80), the author of the *Glossarium suiogothicum* (1769) from which we quoted at the beginning of this section, published, as some of his predecessors had done, a long list of word correspondences (mostly Swedish, Greek and Latin) aimed at showing the validity of the *permutationes* which he had set up; *de facto*, if not *de jure*, he operated in terms of language-specific developments.[35] Since he was almost certainly influential on Rask, together with Wachter and Turgot he provides us with a clear link between the old and the new. At the end of these forms of 'paleo-comparativism', to adopt the term used by Marazzini (1992), we find the Italian Carlo Denina (see note 16), who in *La clef des langues* (1804) calls for a rejection of nonsense etymologies in favour of a serious study of the ways in which Romance words are derived from Latin. According to Denina (1804, 3, ix–x), it is possible to define specific rules like that according to which the derivation of French *tête* from Latin *testa* indicates the loss of the sibilant and 'its replacement with a circumflex accent'. This 'key' can then explain the contrast between a series of French words and equivalent words in Italian and Spanish.

A final point concerns the meaning of *litera* or 'letter'. We should not think that no distinction was made between graphic and phonetic phenomena; the often repeated observation that two *literae* were *cognatae* when they were pronounced with the same organ, proves the contrary.[36] However, the phonetic knowledge of those involved in linguistic comparison varied considerably. Often the *literarum permutationes* were established on the basis of correspondences of letters with little or no attempt to go back to their pronunciation. There were of course exceptions: a notable one was Sajnovics, who in 1770 (37) said that it was impossible to compare Hungarian and 'Lappish' words without previously reducing them to a mutually consistent spelling on the basis of their pronunciation and then proceeded to give a rudimentary indication of the value of each letter or sound.

2.13 Grammatical comparison

Lexical comparison was not the only linguistic method adopted to establish language kinship. Hervás had given weight to the *artificio*

grammaticale and the later historiography has highlighted the importance that grammar acquired at the very end of the eighteenth century
and the beginning of the nineteenth century. Indeed it is often assumed
that the emphasis on grammatical comparison is a discovery of this
period and is largely responsible for the breakthrough associated with
the new comparative linguistics (cf. e.g. Pedersen [1916] 1983, 34f.;
[1931] 1962, 240ff.). Yet here too we must look at an earlier period. The
same Jan de Laet, whom we quoted before, had argued in the seventeenth
century that to show that two languages were related it was necessary
to consider 'linguae aut dialecti genium, pronunciandi rationem, con-
structionis modum' in addition to the basic vocabulary (Metcalf 1974,
246f.; Droixhe 1978, 72f.). In the same period the supporters of the
Scythian thesis also referred to morphology and grammar as important:
Claude Saumaise in his *Commentarius de lingua hellenistica* (1643),
which was used as a source by Monboddo, spoke of a common 'Scythian'
origin for Greek, Latin, Persian and German on the basis, *inter alia*, of
similarities in verbal inflection, noun composition, etc. (Droixhe 1978,
90); in 1647 M. Z. Boxhorn, professor at Leyden and one of the main
upholders of the Scythian thesis, argued in favour of the same views,
comparing in addition to lexical items inflection, pronouns, diminu-
tives, infinitives, etc., i.e. grammatical forms in general (Droixhe 1978,
91ff.).[37] Were these principles forgotten and then rediscovered? The
truth seems to be more complicated. Obviously the first encounters of
the eighteenth century with 'exotic' languages favoured lexical collections rather than grammatical descriptions (Gulya 1974). On the other
hand, grammar, in the broad sense of the word (which included syntax),
was far from neglected at the time. In 1715 a Dr William Wootton, a
Cambridge graduate and a divine, a friend of Newton and Bentley, published an essay *De confusione linguarum Babilonica* where he argued
that the essential differences between one language and another were to
be found in their grammars (i.e. structural make-up) rather than in their
vocabulary (Salmon 1974, 351ff.; Pope 1989, 31ff.). As we have seen
in the article *Langue* of the *Encyclopédie*, syntax was considered the
defining characteristic of each language and provided e.g. a reason for
linking French with another *analogue* language such as Celtic rather
than with the very different Latin.[38] In fact the Enlightenment's concern
with syntax, which was in tune with the philosophical mood of the period,
and its interest in typology, which was undoubtedly connected with the
new linguistic discoveries, had the effect that grammar, structure, 'analogy' were the object of far greater attention than previously. Hence it
is not surprising that at the end of the eighteenth and the beginning of
the nineteenth centuries a number of authors insisted on the importance
of a study of grammar as a proof of linguistic kinship. Yet different
things were meant on different occasions. Hervás' *artificio grammaticale*

is mainly concerned with syntax. Kraus (1787) on the other hand thought that syntax was likely to be similar even in unrelated languages and looked for 'individual similarities', in grammatical formation, position, etc., while pointing out that the grammar was far more resistent to change than the lexicon. Adelung (1806–17, I, *Vorrede* xii f.) argued that for the purposes of genealogical classification it was useless to compare grammatical features across languages because these could be shared by many different languages. Even so, grammatical analysis was crucial because it was the only method through which it was possible to segment the roots of words, and language relationship could only be established through the comparison of roots (not of whole words). Balbi (1826a, xlii f., note), while pleading on the authority of Alexander von Humboldt for a structural description of languages, also stated that grammatical comparison cannot be used to establish kinship and quoted as example the fact that English and Omagua, a language of Brazil, were clearly not related, though their grammars contrasted in similar ways with the grammars of other languages in their families (*ibid.*, 28). The title of Gyarmathi (1799) contains a reference to grammar, but Gyarmathi actually compared the **forms** of declensions, conjugations, comparatives of adjectives, etc., and argued that the evidence they provided was more powerful than that of the lexical similarities. J. Sajnovics in 1770 had stressed that he intended to compare words of both languages (Hungarian and Lappish, i.e. Finnish) and 'quod praecipuum est, nomina, ac verba construendi modum, affixis et suffixis utendi rationem'; he had then compared the inflectional elements of the two languages. In conclusion, grammar was not neglected in comparative work. The problem is rather that the frequent, but generic, appeals to grammar were ambiguous. Under that heading it was possible to argue that two languages were related because they had similar grammatical **structures**, i.e. they were both inflected for case, or had a similar phonological system, or similar word-order patterns. Yet it was also possible to compare grammatical **forms**: the case endings, the verbal endings, the suffixes used to mark comparable functions, the pronouns, etc. Neither type of comparison is a novelty of our period. Nevertheless they now come to the fore not least because the increased linguistic knowledge had, on the one hand, drawn attention to the importance of structural, i.e. grammatical, differences between languages, and, on the other, called for some criteria on which a classification of languages could be based. Typologically it was natural to distinguish e.g. those languages which had complicated verbal paradigms from languages with simpler grammar; the lexicon could not provide the same classificatory criterion. For a genealogical classification both similarity in structure and similarity in grammatical forms seemed to provide useful criteria. At a later stage – and this will be the novelty – it became possible to make an **explicit** distinction between the two types of 'grammatical' comparison, but this was not easily achieved, even if the **practical** work just mentioned, from Saumaise to Sajnovics and Gyarmathi, pointed in that direction.[39]

Notes

1. Pott (1833–6, I, xvii) refers to Loewe in tones which are not very complimentary, but see also Haase (1874–80, I, 41f.), who is less scathing. Loewe was in fact marginal but had made an honest effort to read the literature available in Germany in his field. I have not seen his *Grundriß der deutschen Sprachlehre in steter Beziehung auf allgemeine Sprachlehre, als Leitfaden für seine Zuhörer und Zöglinge, doch auch für jede Art des Unterrichts und mit Andeutung eines dreifachen Lehrganges* (Dresden 1828), listed in the bibliography of Naumann (1986, 358).

2. For August Ferdinand Bernhardi (1770–1820) and his background, see Schlieben-Lange and Weydt (1988), Gessinger (1990); the former stress the importance of a scholar who can count as a precursor of Humboldt, who reformulated the ideas of the Enlightenment in the light of Idealism and Romanticism (*ibid.*, 94). Part of the novelty of Bernhardi's work consists in his attempt to discuss the role of language in science and poetry under the heading of *Angewandte Sprachlehre* (applied linguistics).

3. Pott (1863) discusses the German tradition of *allgemeine Grammatik*, but is mostly hostile, as one would expect. Cf. also Haase (1874–80, I, 42f.), who sees the beginning of *Sprachphilosophie* in England (with James Harris) and pays little attention to the French Enlightenment. More recently, see Naumann (1986, 46ff.), who lists some 25 books on general grammar written in Germany between 1800 and 1830; in Loewe we find at least 10 additional titles. There is now a revival of interest in this German tradition; see in general Schlieben-Lange and Weydt (1988) (with earlier bibliography), Gessinger (1990).

4. J. S. Vater (1771–1826), who completed Adelung's *Mithridates*, also published a *Literatur der Grammatiken, Lexica und Wörtersammlungen aller Sprachen der Erde* (1815), which listed all the publications that gave information about the known languages. About him see Breckle in Vater (1970, 11*–16*); Schmitter in Nerlich (1988, 41–4).

5. Loewe does not mention the new developments in philology connected with the names of C. G. Heyne at Göttingen and his pupil F. A. Wolf at Halle and then Berlin, though these were relevant for special grammar at least (cf. Leventhal 1987). Later on, Pott (1833–6, I, xviii) stated that at the turn of the century Bernhardi, Adelung and the classicist Gottfried Hermann had notable influence on the development of linguistics, but the last of these names does not appear in Loewe (1829).

6. Pott (1863, 109) clearly found it odd that a famous Arabist such as Sacy had written such a book and in quoting its title added an exclamation mark after *toutes*.

7. This figure is excessive and does not correspond to that of the *Mithridates*; yet F. Adelung (1820) boasted of having listed the name of 3,064 lan-

guages and dialects. Cf. Pott ([1884] 1974, 251–2), who has some interesting observations about the supposed total of 72 languages previously
known.

8. For the term 'linguistics' and its first use in Germany and then in France,
cf. Koerner ([1982] 1989, 233ff.; 1995, 173), Auroux (1987) with the earlier bibliography, and Swiggers (1996).

9. See Arens (1969, 136–46) and the English translation and commentary in
Kaltz (1985). Cf. also Gipper and Schmitter (1979, 22f.), who draw atten-
tion to Kraus' views about linguistic relativity. For the contrast between
Volney and Kraus, cf. De Clerq, Desmet and Swiggers (1992).

10. Note, however, that Benloew still has in mind the old meaning. The distinction between the two values of comparative is at its clearest in the
contrast between two French authors. In 1778 A. Court de Gebelin, polymath and linguist of some superficiality, wrote in the fifth volume of his
Monde primitif (1777–82, v, 558): 'Special grammars are simply the principles of the Universal and Primitive Grammar, modified by the genius of
each language; they can all be brought back to a general standard. In this
way we shall establish the COMPARATIVE GRAMMAR which indicates
the relationship of all special grammars and points out in which way the
principles which they all share are modified in each and the necessary
reasons for such modifications'. In 1866 Bréal (1866–72, 1, iv) observed
that 'among all linguistics books that by Bopp is the one where the comparative method can be most easily learned' and added later (*ibid.*, lvii)
that 'in our country the first regular courses of comparative grammar are
due to M. Egger, who introduced the comparative method in the lectures
which he held at the École Normale Supérieure from 1839 to 1861'. For
the typological use of 'comparative' made by Du Ponceau under the influence of the *idéologues* and of Humboldt, see Swiggers (1994, 225).

11. For Turgot the final aim was that of understanding 'la théorie générale de
la parole, et la marche de l'esprit humain dans la formation et le progrès
du langage', but he also stressed that the theory constantly needed to be
compared with the facts. Well before Turgot, Leibniz had aimed at using
etymology, not only for historical purposes, but also to gain insights into
the operations of the mind (Aarsleff [1969] 1982, 84–100).

12. It may be relevant that in 1815 Maine de Biran, whose concerns were
entirely philosophical, regretted that Maupertuis had not substantiated his
point with some real examples and argued that, in the absence of definitive
evidence, it was legitimate to assume that translation was always possible
(Grimsley 1971, 87f.).

13. Destutt de Tracy ([1803] 1826, 86, note 1) exploits the occasion to make
a dig against James Harris, 'who has been so celebrated here, though he
does not deserve it'.

14. Even elsewhere there was ambiguity as to whether the perspective adopted
was historical or philosophical. As a good empiricist, Condillac rejected
the theory that a natural word order is that which reflects the logical ordering, as in *Alexander vicit Darium* 'Alexander conquered Darius', with the
subject which precedes the verb and the object; he preferred to call natural
that order which is based on the 'liaison des idées'. From this point of view

the original order, according to him, called for the object before the verb. Ricken (1978, 96) points out that Condillac finds support for his hypotheses in the comparison of French with Latin: 'What is new in contrast with the comparisons of the French and Latin constructions made in the seventeenth century, and still pursued by Du Marsais on the basis of the theory of natural order, is that Condillac inserts the two languages into a historical development'.

15. In his 1800 pamphlet Degérando advised the explorers who wanted to study the articulate language of the Savages to follow an order as close as possible to the generation of the ideas, i.e. to start eliciting first the names of concrete objects such as the parts of the body and to graduate only later to more abstract concepts.

16. Volney (1820, 32, note 1) does not take seriously Court de Gebelin's *Monde primitif*, though this listed a number of languages, including non-European ones; in this he was later followed by Balbi (1826a, xlii) and much later by Max Müller (1862, 136). Volney also ignores *La clef des langues* (1804), published in three volumes at Berlin by the Italian Carlo Denina (1731–1813), which provides analyses and etymologies for European languages (Denina 1985; Marazzini 1989, 118ff.; 1992); this may be due to political reasons, as suggested by Marazzini (1984), but also perhaps to the fact that Volney was more interested in exotic non-Indo-European languages than in the material discussed by Denina. For information about the earlier collections of words and versions of the Lord's Prayer, cf. Adelung (1806–17, 1, 645–76).

17. We must remember that e.g. Neapolitan and Italian counted as two separate languages.

18. Even so the book was still felt to be useful a number of years after its publication. In 1821 Vater (1820–1, ii, 126) thought that he was doing a service to the readers of one of his books by alerting them to the availability of some copies of Pallas's book in a Berlin bookshop. For Pallas in general, cf. Wendland (1992), and for parts of the *Vocabularia*, Fodor (1975), Haarmann (1979).

19. The Italian work was difficult to find (cf. Tovar 1986, 14) and, for instance, was inaccessible to Benfey (1869, 269).

20. For Hervás in general, see Tovar (1986), Tonfoni (1988), Sarmiento (1990), Calvo Pérez (1991); for his notion of substratum, Coseriu (1978); for his ideas on linguistic relativity, Val-Alvaro (1987).

21. Cf. Droixhe (1978, 146f.). Turgot, in the article *Étymologie* of the *Encyclopédie*, reaches similar conclusions. See also below, p. 50.

22. See Metcalf (1984). Adelung's classification of the European languages contrasts with that of Hervás. He recognizes the following groups: (I) Cantabrian or Basque, (II) Celtic (Irish and Gaelic), (III) Celtic-Germanic (Welsh, Cornish and Breton), (IV) Germanic (Low and High German, Scandinavian, English), (V) Thracian-Pelasgian-Greek-Latin (with the Romance languages except for Romanian), (VI) Slavic, (VII) Germanic-Slavic (Prussian, Lithuanian, Lettish), (VIII) Roman-Slavic (Romanian), (IX) 'Tschudisch' (Finnish and Lappish), (X) Mixed languages (A. Hungarian, B. Albanian). In the fourth part of *Mithridates*, which contains

corrections to the second part by F. von Adelung, Adelung's nephew, and by J. S. Vater, the latter points out (in Adelung 1806–17, iv, 383–5) that it might be better to abandon the reference to Thracian and Pelasgian in group V; he also argues (*ibid*. 407–11) that Romanian is one of the daughter languages of Latin and supports this with arguments both from the vocabulary and from the grammar. On the other hand, he accepts the separation of Hungarian from Finnish and Lappish; the problem had been discussed at length in Part 2 (771ff.) with an extremely interesting analysis of Gyarmathi (1799). The conclusion is that the important grammatical correspondences between Hungarian, Finnish and Lappish are not sufficient to exclude the possibility (minuscule) that Hungarian is a 'Turkisch-Tatar' language which underwent the influence of Finnish.

23. But see Metcalf (1984), who also draws attention to Adelung's pet theory, that he had discovered the original site of Paradise.

24. We must ignore this work, but cf. e.g. Strohbach (1984), Bahner (1984), Schmidt (1986), Naumann (1986), etc. For the *Mithridates*, see Lüdtke (1978) with Malkiel (1979).

25. In considering the impact of *Mithridates* it is superfluous to distinguish between Adelung and Vater even if the latter, as we know from his preface to Part 2, did not always agree with his predecessor. In general, Part 1 (Asiatic languages and odd notes about the languages of the Pacific) is due entirely to Adelung and so is most of Part 2 (languages of Europe). For the rest, i.e. for the various sections of Part 3, dedicated to African and Amerindian languages, Vater is largely responsible and certainly follows higher standards of completeness and accuracy. Benfey (1869, 279) somewhat unfairly remarks that in 1817 Vater, while quoting Bopp (1816), which had just appeared, did not realize how important that book was going to be for the future of linguistics.

26. An example may show how these arguments worked. Jamieson (1814) was convinced, on the authority of Herodotus and other historians, that the Greeks descended from the Pelasgians. But he also knew that according to ancient sources the earliest inhabitants of Greece were barbarians (39ff.) and that the Phrygians were among the barbarians. Herodotus and others guaranteed that the Phrygians came from Thrace. For Strabo, the Getae were a Thracian nation (12ff.) and we know from Thucydides that they bordered with the Scythians (10). Hence the Thracians were Scythian, the Phrygians were Scythian and the barbaric first inhabitants of Greece (i.e. the Pelasgians or their predecessors) were Scythian. It followed that the Greeks were descended from the Scythians and the Greek language was a Scythian language. Moreover, Jordanes used *Gothi* and *Getae* promiscuously so that it was possible to conclude that the Goths were also Scythian and so were the Greeks.

27. For the secondary literature on the possible influence of Semitic comparative studies on the later Indo-European studies, cf. Muller (1986, 19f.).

28. Cf. Muller (1986, 22f.), and for the development of Finno-Ugric linguistics and the scholars involved, see Stipa (1990).

29. For an outsider it is difficult to determine the difference between the two works even if Gyarmathi's *Affinitas* is the best known of the two. Gyarmathi

covers a much wider range than Sajnovics and deserves the title of founder of Finno-Ugric comparative grammar, but the method he follows does not seem to differ fundamentally from that of his predecessor. His attempt at dismissing the possibility of a Hungarian-Turkish kinship clearly shows that, though he aimed at comparing grammatical forms rather than structures, he did not altogether spurn structural considerations: the presence of more moods and tenses in Turkish than in Hungarian is used as an argument against a possible connection of the two languages (Gyarmathi 1799, 240ff.).

30. Basic bibliography in Droixhe (1978) and Muller (1986, 9–14). For Boxhorn, cf. Droixhe (1989).

31. Adelung (1806–17, ii, 14) reports Monboddo's statement that, according to a Jesuit whom he knew, Eskimos and Basques spoke mutually comprehensible languages, but concludes: 'The good father can only have seen this in a dream'.

32. The terminology is confusing. For Volney, Scythian refers to what we would now call Indo-European, for Hervás, to the Finno-Ugric languages (with Gothic), while Adelung (1806–17, ii, 739) calls these languages 'tschudisch' (Russian *čud'*) after having reproached O. Rudbeck (1630–1702), who wanted to derive this word from 'Scythian'. Even those exponents of the Scythian theory who leave Finno-Ugric aside may use the term either by itself or linked with Celtic (Scytho-Celtic), sometimes to refer to the parent language of Celtic, sometimes as coterminous with Celtic, sometimes as synonymous with Germanic or Teutonic (cf. Metcalf 1974, 235). The demonstration that the Celtic languages were Indo-European had to wait until the 1830s–1850s and the various works by Prichard, Pictet, Zeuss and Bopp (Poppe 1992).

33. The reasons were not always the same. Sometimes authors relied on purely empirical observations: our own experience of languages tells us that some terms are more likely to be borrowed than others. Sometimes the motivation was more 'philosophical': some parts of the vocabulary were deemed to be more 'essential' and 'original' than others. Monboddo (1773–92, i, 600ff.; cf. Muller 1984b) argued that the comparison of the names of the elements and of the words for numbers and for close relatives was particularly significant because these words were among the first to exist in every language and indeed were coeval with language. With keener historical sense, Sajnovics (1770, 14) insisted that for the purposes of comparative Finno-Ugric linguistics it was useless to compare religious terms (*de Deo Summo, de vita aeterna*, etc.) when the Finns knew nothing about these subjects before the arrival of missionaries. Practical considerations were also important: the basic vocabulary was preferred because it included words easier to obtain in a 'fieldwork' situation (cf. Degérando [1800] 1969, 73). On the other hand, Balbi (1826a, cxxxii f.) stated that he had deliberately chosen terms which had already been collected for most languages; any other choice would have obliged the researcher to start the work from the beginning.

34. My use of square brackets ([t], [d], etc.) to mark phonetic symbols corresponds to the modern convention, but is of course entirely anachronistic for the nineteenth century. Cf. Lepschy (1990–4, iii, 492).

35. Vowels and consonants were treated differently and it was often assumed that no special *literarum permutationes* could be set up for the vowels; cf. e.g. the full title of Whiter (1822–5) quoted in the list of references. This view was rejected by Turgot in the article *Étymologie* (1756) of the *Encyclopédie* in the context of an attack against the attempt to find general principles of phonetic evolution rather than to identify the historical changes on the basis of the actual data. Yet Ihre (1769, I, xli), who shared some of the same views, refused to discuss correspondences between vowels because 'in almost all languages they alternate in an haphazard manner' ('illae in omnibus fere linguis locum promiscue permutent'). The difference may be due to the data considered. Ihre worked on Germanic, where the history of the vowels is notoriously difficult, while the Greek and Romance examples quoted by Turgot have given far less trouble.

36. Protestations against the confusion of letters and sounds are frequent and explicit in the eighteenth century and earlier (Droixhe 1978, 249ff., 262ff.). Authors as different as Ch. de Brosses and A. Court de Gébelin concentrate on a physiological description of speech and the latter does so in the context of what is meant to be (even if unsuccessful) a 'comparative' grammar (cf. also Savoia 1981).

37. Boxhorn here implicitly disagrees with another popular assumption according to which inflectional endings could not be used for comparison because they were too variable (Metcalf 1974, 246). On the other hand, J. J. Scaliger had earlier implied that *analogia*, i.e. the grammatical system, was an important criterion of language affinity.

38. L'abbé Girard (1747, I, 27ff.) makes this clear. Syntax or 'construction', we are told, 'changes in the various peoples just like the words, marks the most important difference between languages and speaks against the opinion of those who would have us believe that French, Spanish and Italian are daughters of Latin' ('varie chez les Peuples ainsi que les mots, fait la différence la plus essencielle entre les Langues, & s'oppose à l'opinion de ceux qui assûrent que la Françoise l'Espagnole & l'Italienne sont filles de la Latine'). This last belief, he argues, is based on etymology, but words can be borrowed; nowadays one can see these living languages characterized by an article which they cannot have taken from Latin, which does not have it, and totally remote from the 'transpositive' constructions and the case inflections typical of Latin.

39. Sometimes one wonders whether the distinction between similarity in grammatical **forms** and similarity in grammatical **structures** is clear to all modern historiography. It is always said (e.g. Benfey 1869, 236; Arens, 1969, 105; Diderichsen 1974, 283; Droixhe 1978, 39, etc.) that, according to the famous Semitist Job Ludolf (1624–1704), in order to argue that two languages were related it was necessary to demonstrate not only that they shared a part of the lexicon but also that they had the same *grammaticae ratio,* as was the case in the Semitic languages (for Ludolf's law, cf. now Collinge 1995, 30f.). However, no one explains what Ludolf meant in the brief passage of the *Dissertatio de harmonia linguae aethiopicae cum ceteris orientalibus* (1702) which all these authors quote, but which I have not been able to identify. It is likely, however, that Ludolf had in mind both

grammatical forms and grammatical structures, if we can rely on the observations made in the first page of the *Dissertatio de origine, natura et usu linguae aethiopicae*, which is printed at the beginning of the second edition of the *Grammatica aethiopica* (1702). In general see Swiggers (1993) for a useful discussion of the concept of grammatical form in the early nineteenth century.

3

Friedrich Schlegel and the discovery of Sanskrit

3.1 An historiographical break

Polymaths such as Adelung, Vater (in his more empirical work) and Balbi were in different ways aware of the new data-oriented direction that linguistics was taking but also felt the need to rehearse and classify the previous knowledge. This led both to collections of the *Mithridates* type and to bibliographical repertories such as Marsden (1796, 1827), Vater (1815), F. Adelung (1820).[1] By contrast in the 1830s and 1840s we begin to find a different attitude. At that stage, it is conceivable, and almost natural, to say, as A. W. Schlegel put it ([1833] 1846, iii, 57), that 'the comparative study of languages . . . , if systematically treated, is a science newly created' ('l'étude comparée des langues . . . , traitée méthodiquement, est une science toute de nouvelle création'). Pott, as we have seen, refers in 1833 to the new epoch when linguistics (*Sprachwissenschaft*), thanks to Bopp but also to other authors such as A. W. Schlegel, Humboldt and Grimm, became an independent discipline. Even outside Germany we find statements of the same tenor: in 1835 and in England the Rev. Richard Garnett ([1835] 1859, 9), a basically self-taught man who became an Assistant Keeper of Printed Books at the British Museum, complained that his compatriots knew no German and referred to 'the writings of Grimm, Bopp, and their coadjutors – men who seem likely to effect the same sort of revolution in European philology that Cuvier wrought in the sciences of comparative anatomy and geology'.[2] These statements are as crucial for an understanding of the new linguistics as they are for that of its historiography. Benfey (1869, 332) explains why. In his view, after Bopp the change in outlook was so drastic that the whole of the previous work had become of merely historical importance; even what was correct could not be retained since it rested on different foundations. The implication is that it is no longer necessary to read the scholarly work written before the beginning of the century. At this point a real break is not only on the cards, but has actually occurred. In German Universities the generations of Bopp and perhaps Pott deliberately rejected most of the previous work; the generation that followed hardly knew that it existed (Benfey being a shining exception). They inherited a number of earlier assumptions and conclusions, but they were not aware of their origins.

3.1.1 Linguistics as an autonomous discipline

According to Benfey, at the beginning of the century linguistics had become an independent *Wissenschaft*. This in his view was prompted by a multitude of causes. First, there was the realization that state, law, religion, language, customs, art and science evolved according to laws of development which are inbuilt in the nature of mankind (1869, 320–1) and consequently could be the object of study in their own right. But such study had to be based in the empirical work of each discipline; after Schelling and Hegel it was no longer possible to keep apart practical concrete work and philosophical discourse.[3] Secondly, a new *Philologie* had arisen; it was more scholarly and more broadly based than the earlier attempts; it was also prepared to explore the whole culture instead of a few textual or antiquarian questions;[4] it was, above all, capable of rescuing the old *Sprachenkunde* from its servile status. While previously this could only help ethnology to determine the kinship or otherwise of peoples, it had now revealed that language was one of the most significant elements for the understanding of the development of a nation. And yet, for Benfey, a mere change in attitude would not have been sufficient to 'produce' the new linguistics; a triggering factor was needed and this had been provided by the discovery of Sanskrit in the West. In other words, Benfey here identifies the new linguistics with comparative-historical work, which he sees as the product of a combination of new data (the discovery of Sanskrit), a new philology and a new philosophy. Every one of these points is of course challengeable and we have already argued that the break was due as much to the cumulation of a series of institutional and historiographical factors as to a sudden intellectual revolution. Nevertheless the traditional account has its force and we must now turn to Sanskrit and the East.

3.2 The 'discovery' of Sanskrit in the West

In the eighteenth century the travels of discovery, the new colonial powers, the missions, all yielded various types of information – anecdotal data, rudimentary grammars, vocabulary lists, etc. Of such material were formed the great collections (Pallas, Hervás, Adelung) that we have described. Yet the 'discovery' of Sanskrit in the West stands out for a number of reasons: the high level of the learned amateurs who collected the data, the increasing sophistication of the information available, the excitment it produced among the intelligentsia in Europe, the intellectual and even political consequences which it had, and finally the way in which the arrival of the new information coincided with a change of direction in the study of linguistics (Simone 1997, 212).

3.2.1 The sacred languages of India

Early news about a sacred language of India written in a syllabic script reached Europe through letters which remained unpublished for a long time. As early as 1583 the English Jesuit Thomas Stephens (1549–1619) and the Italian merchant Filippo Sassetti (1540–88) had noticed similarities between Sanskrit, the most ancient language of India, and the European languages (Muller 1986, 14ff.). Further work by Jesuits and other missionaries and travellers to India occasionally referred to Sanskrit as well as to other Indian languages. The manuscript of a Sanskrit grammar written in Latin round 1660 by Heinrich Roth, SJ (1620–68), a German Jesuit who worked as a missionary in India and studied the language at Agra for six years, has recently been published in facsimile (Roth 1988). Unfortunately it remained unknown in its time.[5] Sanskrit and Vedic manuscripts reached the 'bibliothèque du roi' in Paris before the middle of the eighteenth century and in that period references to the languages of India and to Sanskrit in particular became far more frequent. We also have from the same period more detailed statements about the main characteristics of the Sanskrit language: the enthusiastic reports about the 'harmony, abundance, and energy' of the language and the greatness of its literature by Father Jean François Pons, S. J. (1698–1752) written in 1740 and published in 1743, the vocabulary lists which the père Cœurdoux sent from India to the abbé Barthélemy and which were read by Anquetil-Duperron in 1768 to the Académie des Inscriptions et Belles-Lettres (but not published until 1808; cf. Mayrhofer 1983, 154ff.); the Latin version of a native grammar also sent by Father Pons to Paris and later used by F. Schlegel, etc. The first Sanskrit grammar ever published (in Latin but based on Indian work) was written by an Austrian Carmelitan, J. Ph. Wessdin, known as Fr Paulinus a Sancto Bartholomaeo, and appeared in Rome in 1790; the same author also produced a second grammar in 1804, thus describing, as A. W. Schlegel put it (1832, 27), a 'language which he taught without knowing it'.[6] Before that (1798) he wrote about the similarities of Sanskrit with Zend (Avestan) and Germanic. But in a sense it is not the early knowledge of the language which was influential as much as the accounts, more or less garbled, of Sanskrit literature which reached the West and which, for instance, found an echo in Voltaire; an important factor, which should not be forgotten, is the fascination with all things oriental which characterized the end of the eighteenth century and the next decades (Schwab 1950, Gérard 1963, Willson 1964).

3.2.2 India and Great Britain

The missionaries and travellers who brought back news of Sanskrit and Indian civilization to the West came from various parts of Europe even if a great deal of information eventually converged in Paris, but, as Windisch (1917–20, i, 22) stated, it was the work of Englishmen that inaugurated the new science. In the second part of the eighteenth century the East India Company brought to India in various capacities a number of young men of considerable ability and culture who were trying to make their fortune as 'writers' (such as Colebrooke, Halhed and Wilkins) or as soldiers (such as Alexander Hamilton). Natural curiosity might have induced them in any case to acquire as much as possible of the local culture but political events also played a role; at least from 1772 Warren Hastings, soon to be appointed Governor General, encouraged the respect and use of both Hindu and Muslim law in criminal courts.[7] The Judicature Act of 1781 also confirmed that matters of inheritance and contract had to be dealt with according to local law and usage. Hence the practical necessity to explore the local rules and to understand the local languages, so that the British judges could have at their disposal a body of comprehensible information. A *Code of Gentoo Laws*, which Nathaniel Brassey Halhed (1751–1830) published in 1776, is a translation (from Persian) of a Sanskrit compilation commissioned by Hastings and then translated into Persian, the first answer to this need. In the preface to the *Code* and in that to his later *Grammar of the Bengal Language* (1778) Halhed commented on the 'copious and nervous' nature of Sanskrit, on its venerable antiquity and above all on the similarity of its basic vocabulary with that of Greek and Latin; in a private letter written in 1779 he advocated a Sanskrit origin of Greek and Latin (Rocher 1980b, 1983). He also provided some samples of Sanskrit, while explaining that the local scholars were singularly unwilling to allow foreigners to learn the language. Another employee of the East India Company, Charles Wilkins (?1750–1836), round 1778 found a Pandit 'of a liberal mind' willing to help him and he succeeded in learning enough of the language to make use of the Indian grammars and to become, as has often been stated, the first Westerner who really knew Sanskrit. His translation of the *Bhagavad-gītā*, a poem which was bound to impress for its beauty and for the depth of its philosophical conception, appeared in London in 1785; there followed in 1787 a translation of the *Hitopadeśa*, a famous collection of fables, and in 1808 his even more famous Sanskrit grammar. Wilkins also succeeded in creating fonts for printing the local scripts. In 1784 an event of considerable importance for the subject occurred, the foundation at Calcutta of the Asiatic Society, 'a Society for inquiring into the History, Civil and Natural, the Antiquities, Arts, Sciences and Literature, of Asia';[8] its transactions soon began to appear under the title of *Asiatick Researches* (the first number for 1786 was published in 1788). The Society enjoyed the support of Warren Hastings (Brockington 1989) but the president and founder was Sir William Jones (1746–1794) FRS, a well-known man of letters, a trained orientalist who had translated from Persian and published a Persian grammar, a translator of the classics and a distinguished lawyer, who had arrived in Calcutta in 1783 to be one of the judges of the Supreme Court appointed by the Crown. *Asiatick Researches* published articles on practically anything to do with Asia or India from the method for catching wild elephants (Vol. iii), to the 'spikenard of the antients' (Vol. ii), to a fundamental article by Colebrooke on the Sanskrit and Prakrit languages (Vol. vii) and to the president's 11 anniversary discourses, some of which discuss the classification of languages and nations.[9] Sir William Jones himself produced in 1789 a translation of *Śakuntalā*, a classical Sanskrit drama, which had an enthusiastic reception; another important translation (1796) was that of the Laws of Manu. He was also instrumental in establishing transliteration rules for *devanāgarī* which won general acceptance, in editing for the first time in the West a Sanskrit text in Sanskrit characters, and in collecting a number of manuscripts which eventually reached England.

This list of learned and productive Englishmen cannot finish without a mention of the most scholarly of them all, the judge Henry Thomas Colebrooke (1765–1837), a professor of Sanskrit at Fort William College, who had a fine understanding of language differences, promoted the first publication of Pāṇini's grammar in Calcutta (1809), was an enthusiastic collector of manuscripts, an editor and translator of all types of texts, including mathematical and astronomical works, and the author of a detailed grammar (on Indian models) which began to appear in Calcutta in 1805 but was never finished.

In general we may reconstruct, among the select few, an atmosphere of irrepressible excitement for the new culture and the language in which it was expressed and of relentless work done by people who had to steal time from other professional concerns. There was also a minimum of nationalistic pride; Sir William Jones stated in 1788 that if European culture owed to the Dutch the knowledge of Arabic and to the French that of Chinese, it was suitable that it should owe to the English that of Sanskrit (Windisch 1917–20, I, 24).[10] Yet, though this work is infinitely impressive, we should not think of it in purely 'linguistic' terms. All British Sanskritists of this period were impressed by the language and interested in learning it as well as possible, but language does not seem to have been their primary concern. Even Sir William Jones, who in the popular hagiography appears as the founder of comparative linguistics, declared in his First Anniversary Discourse of 1784 (published in early 1789) that languages for him had always been a means to an end. His contemporaries concentrated on translations, on understanding cultural facts through the texts and eventually on editions. We owe to them the first usable grammars of the language, even if these were all built on Sanskrit models. But they were definitely ancillary work; they served as preparatory work for research but also as textbooks for the one or two colleges mantained at any one time by the East India Company for the training of its civil servants.[11] Between 1804 and 1810 three grammars were published in Calcutta and one in London (Wilkins 1808), but Colebrooke (1805) and Forster (1810) were never completed. Carey ([1804] 1806) was, according to A. W. Schlegel (1832, 30), simply based on notes taken under dictation from a Pandit. Wilkins (1808) is at a different (and very high) level but it is still a textbook. The preface makes clear where Wilkins' own interests lie: he quotes Halhed for the comparison of Sanskrit with Greek and Latin, Jones (the philologer's passage quoted at p. 65) and Colebrooke for the beauties and interest of Sanskrit, but he then feels confident enough to talk about the literature and culture without appealing to any authority.

3.2.3 The rest of Europe

So far we have been dealing with internal British and Indian developments; but what determined the 'success of Sanskrit' outside India and Britain? A rough answer must appeal to a curious mixture of linguistic and non-linguistic facts. First, in our period the spread of cultural information in Europe, in spite of the tense political situation, was often rapid and effective. In the course of two years from its publication, Wilkins' translation of the *Bhagavad-gītā* (1785) was translated into Russian and French; later on a German edition appeared. Sir William Jones' *Sacontalá* (i.e. *Śakuntalā*) was translated into German, admired and reviewed by Herder, and greeted by Goethe with two enthusiastic distichs; there were also French and Italian versions. At an earlier stage, Halhed's *A Code of Gentoo Laws or Ordinations of the Pundits* (1776) had appeared in French and in German. Even the *Asiatick Researches* were translated; four volumes of selected articles in German were published at Riga in 1795–7; Langlès, the keeper of oriental manuscripts in the National Library of Paris, in 1805 helped to edit, and comment on, a French adaptation of the first seven years. The beauty and interest of the Sanskrit texts (in translation) conquered the European intelligentsia; the language remained unknown. And yet this meant that all knowledge depended on the results obtained at Calcutta through something which very much resembled an act of faith. Bréal (1866–72, I, xiii) describes the group of Paris people interested in things oriental: 'all that concerned religious doctrine, literary works, Indian legislation strongly attracted the interest of those writers and thinkers, but purely grammatical works were kept in low estime' ('tout ce qui touchait aux doctrines religieuses, aux œuvres littéraires, à la législation de l'Inde, sollicitait vivement l'attention de ces écrivains et de ces penseurs; mais les travaux purement grammaticaux jouissaient auprès d'eux d'une estime médiocre'). And he quotes an 1810 article by Chézy to illustrate the total dependence on the Asiatic Society at Calcutta: 'we were like travellers in foreign land obliged to depend on the good faith of interpreters' ('on ressemblait à des voyageurs en pays étranger, contraints de s'en reposer sur la bonne foi des truchemans').

3.2.4 Sanskrit and the classical languages: Sir William Jones

Statements about the similarity of Sanskrit with Greek and Latin did of course appear at an early stage; even if the reports by père Cœurdoux were not printed till later, and if the Rome publications by Paulinus were both later and less diffused, the observations by Halhed appeared in print in 1776 and 1778. However, the observations which most caught the imagination were those by Sir William Jones in the third of his anniversary discourses 'On the Hindus' pronounced at the Asiatic Society at Calcutta on 2 February 1786 and published in 1788. The general context was that of an attempt at establishing the origins, similarities and differences of the main nations of Asia on the basis of their languages and letters, philosophy and religion, sculpture and architecture, and finally sciences and arts. Linguistic comparison had definitely a part to play for the early period and it is with this in mind that Jones wrote the paragraph which, removed from its context, has now become one of the most quoted passages in the history of linguistics:

> The *Sanscrit* language, whatever be its antiquity, is of a wonderful structure; more perfect than the *Greek*, more copious than the *Latin*, and more exquisitely refined than either, yet bearing to both of them a stronger affinity, both in the roots of verbs and in the forms of grammar, than could possibly have been produced by accident; so strong indeed, that no philologer could examine them all three, without believing them to have sprung from some common source which, perhaps, no longer exists: there is a similar reason, though not quite so forcible, for supposing that both the *Gothick* and the *Celtick*, though blended with a very different idiom, had the same origin with the *Sanscrit*; and the old *Persian* might be added to the same family, if this were the place for discussing any question concerning the antiquities of *Persia*. (Jones [1788] 1807, iii, 34)

Jones refers to the roots of verbs and forms of grammar as proof of kinship but does not provide a detailed **linguistic** demonstration of his assertions.[12] Indeed from the rest of the anniversary discourse it emerges that, according to him, the Hindus had 'an immemorial affinity with the old Persians, Ethiopians and Egyptians, the Phoenicians, Greeks, and Tuscans, the Scythians or Goths, and Celts, the Chinese, Japanese, and

Peruvians' and that they all 'proceeded from some central country'. In the ninth discourse, pronounced on 23 February 1792, the conclusion is that Persians and Indians, Romans and Greeks, Goths and the old Egyptians or Ethiops 'originally spoke the same language and professed the same popular faith' (Jones 1807, iii, 185f.), while the judgement about China and Japan is less sanguine. Even so – and if we forget the Egyptians or Ethiops – Jones' statement, as Rocher (1980b) put it, turned out to be right and, we might add, influential.[13] The argument is based on the familiar mixture of linguistic and non-linguistic data – anything else at this period would be unexpected. Yet that Sanskrit was extraordinarily similar to Latin and Greek was so immediately obvious that no one moderately knowledgeable in the three languages could fail to notice it. How this could be explained was a different problem and Cœurdoux had suggested various solutions (including common origin) but had eventually opted for language mixture. Halhed had spoken for a genetic connection and what Jones did was to provide an authoritative voice for a different version of the genetic hypothesis (Sanskrit as a sister rather than as a parent language of Greek and Latin) in the expectation that future Sanskritists would validate it, as they in fact did. It is difficult to argue that he created a methodology but his influence on that European intelligentsia which depended on Calcutta for its information on things Indian was nevertheless considerable. First, he was by far the best known of all British Sanskritists thanks to his previous work on Persian and in general to his political and intellectual standing.[14] Secondly, his approach had immediate appeal for those who, like Hervás, Adelung and Balbi, aimed at an increase in historical learning through the study of language, while at the same time it was particularly authoritative because it used the new linguistic evidence from India, which was otherwise unavailable and which must have seemed to offer the solution to a number of problems.[15]

3.3 Friedrich Schlegel

Twenty years after the publication of the third anniversary discourse the 'philologer's passage' was quoted in the preface to Wilkins' Sanskrit grammar (1808) and less obviously referred to in a work which was to become extremely influential: Friedrich Schlegel, *Über die Sprache und Weisheit der Indier*. In the meantime, however, thanks to the East India Company and the Napoleonic wars, direct knowledge of Sanskrit had reached Paris. Alexander Hamilton (1762–1824) was a Scottish cadet in the Bengal army who, after his arrival in India in 1783, spent a great deal of time learning languages and joined the Asiatic Society at Calcutta soon after its foundation. He kept his interest in Sanskrit after his return to Edinburgh in 1797 and went to Paris sometime after the peace of Amiens (1802) to consult manuscripts in the National Library; the worsening political situation obliged him to remain there until 1806, though, thanks to the intervention of Volney, he was not treated as a war prisoner. He spent most of this time compiling a catalogue of Indian manuscripts in the library, which in 1807 was published by Langlès in a French translation with some additional notes. Most importantly he was admitted into the circle of the French orientalists, instructed some of them in Sanskrit and ended up living in the house of Friedrich Schlegel (who was in Paris from 1802 to 1805) and giving him regular Sanskrit lessons. On his return to England in 1806 he was appointed 'Professor of Sanscrit and other Hindoo languages' at Hertford College, thus becoming the first professor of Sanskrit in Europe and also the first man to publish in Europe an edition of a Sanskrit text (the *Hitopadeśa* in 1810). Yet, given that he wrote little and always anonymously, he is best known for the way in which he introduced some knowledge of Sanskrit in France and indirectly in Germany, for the influence he had on the content of Friedrich Schlegel's 1808 book and for the help which he gave in London to the two German Sanskritists Othmar Frank and Franz Bopp between 1814 and 1819 (cf. Rocher 1968, 73ff.). But Hamilton is also interesting from a more strictly linguistic point of view: though he declares that 'to the science of philology he has never devoted a moment' and that he is 'unambitious of the reputation of a linguist' [i.e. of 'someone who knows languages'], in the first decade of the century he stresses on more than one occasion that the connection between the ancient languages of India and of Greece is undoubtedly true and important, speaks of the study of languages as 'the most imperishable guide to the history of the nations', constantly refers to Jones' conclusions, but in spite of his veneration for Sir William, is able to reject his view that ancient Egyptian was connected to Sanskrit and Greek.[16] Rocher (1968, 124) is certainly right in saying that his work shows that before 1816 the ground for comparative Indo-European studies was well established.

3.3.1 *Über die Sprache und Weisheit der Indier*

The early history of Sanskrit studies in Europe provides a background – and a contrast – to the work of Friedrich Schlegel (1772–1829), a man who was neither a Sanskritist nor perhaps a pioneer of linguistics in the strict sense of the word, but was immensely influential in calling attention to the Sanskrit language and in exploiting the new information within the context of a grandiose, if nebulous, linguistic and literary panorama. With Schlegel and his older brother August Wilhelm (1767–1845) we enter the world of German Romanticism and we are confronted with the perennial question whether the progress of the new discipline is of necessity tied to Romantic views.[17]

When Friedrich Schlegel reached Paris in 1802 he was already well known as a man of letters who at Göttingen had been trained in philological techniques, had written extensively about Greek literature and literary subjects in general and was prominent in German intellectual circles. He and Wilhelm were the main exponents of that Jena group which was propounding the new tenets of Romanticism. In Paris at the beginning he formulated a project to collect a number of Provençal poems, 'die Quellen der romantischen Poesie' (Richert 1914, 11ff.). Later this was abandoned because everything had to yield to his enthusiasm for Persian and, above all, Sanskrit studies. The result was the 1808 book *Über die Sprache und Weisheit der Indier*, which started from Sir William Jones' conclusions and firmly asserted at the beginning the close linguistic affinity of Sanskrit with Greek and Latin, Persian and German, and its more remote links with Armenian, Slavic and Celtic. Schlegel went further than Jones and argued that all these languages derived from Sanskrit or its ancestor. On the other hand, he denied any connection with Coptic or Hebrew, with Basque, with most north and south Asiatic languages and with the languages of the Americas. He then proceeded to demonstrate the connection through comparison of full words, but above all of grammatical forms and grammatical structure: 'the decisive point, which here will clarify everything, is the internal structure of languages, or comparative grammar, which will lead us to completely new conclusions about the genealogy of languages in the same way in which comparative anatomy has spread light over the natural history of the higher organisms [*höhere Naturgeschichte*]' (1808, 28).[18]

The exemplification that followed was based both on general structural observations and on the comparison of endings, suffixes, etc. For Greek, Latin and Sanskrit the crucial principle was that all relations and definitions of meaning were not indicated by particles or auxiliary verbs but through inflection, i.e. through an internal modification of the root (*ibid.*, 35).[19] Yet here too examples of close similarity in grammatical **forms** were included. The conclusion argued for the superiority of Sanskrit over other languages, not least because of its higher structural regularity; on this basis it could then be argued that Sanskrit was more 'original' than either Greek or Latin, which already showed signs of decay. Further discussion identified a basic dichotomy in the languages of the world: a first group operated, in true 'organic' fashion, on the basis of an internal inflection of the root as described above, a second group indicated grammatical relationships merely through the ordering of words or the use of additional words or particles. The latter could eventually progress to an apparent inflection through the agglutination of particles to roots but the principle remained fundamentally different from that at work in the inflected languages, even if these, the truly organic languages, in their process of decay tended to move towards an increased use of particles, auxiliaries, etc. This conclusion – Schlegel argued – revolutionized all assumptions about the origin of language. Other languages could conceivably arise from grunts or onomatopoeia, but the inflected group – which was formed exclusively of the languages related to Sanskrit – could not, since the earlier phases were more perfect and sophisticated than the later ones. The same deep feeling and intellectual clarity which manifested itself in Indian thought and religion were responsible *ab initio* for a language which 'even in its first and simplest parts succeeded in expressing not in symbols but with immediate clarity the highest concepts of the world of thought as well as the whole foundation of perception' (1808, 63).

3.3.2 The structure of the book
The book starts with the section about language which we have summarized but continues with an analysis of Indian philosophical and religious ideas and, in its third part, with a consideration of how migrations may have brought a number of people west from an original Asiatic place. It concludes with a dithyramb in favour of the study of oriental language and literature; this also includes an attack against the Enlightenment's preference for the present as against the past, a statement about the intrinsic cohesion of language, law, philosophy, literature and religion, and a plea for a historical and comparative approach to these subjects:

> as in the history of nations the Asians and the Europeans form one large family and Asia and Europe form an indivisible whole, so we ought to aim more and more at envisaging the literature of all civilized peoples as one large whole, an on-going development, a single internally structured edifice and product. Many one-sighted and limited views will then disappear of their own accord and much will become comprehensible for the first time when seen in its proper connection; but above all everything will appear as new when seen in this light. (1808, 217f.)

The last section, dedicated to an anthology of new translations from Sanskrit, is preceded by a grand finale:

> And if the excessively one-sided and simplistic concern with the Greeks which prevailed in the last centuries has taken us away from the old earnestness and the source of all higher truth, then the more deeply we shall penetrate into this totally new knowledge and perception of oriental antiquity the more we shall be led back to an understanding of the divine and to that power of thought which first gives light and life to all art and all science.

3.3.3 A new approach to the origin of language
We should not allow these quasi-mystical flights of fancy, which foreshadow Schlegel's conversion to Catholicism, to conceal the interest of

the work. The technical part at the beginning includes the most detailed analysis published until then of the similarities between Sanskrit and some of the old European languages; with hindsight we recognize mistakes and imperfections but these are to be expected in a non-professional writer.[20] Equally important are the implications of the book's structure. Schlegel starts *in medias res* with a purely linguistic demonstration of the genealogical links between Sanskrit and the other languages; all historical discussion is relegated to a final, somewhat perfunctory, section. This supreme confidence in linguistic data, if not new, is at least noticeable; Gyarmathi had similarly argued for the kinship of Finno-Ugric languages on the basis of the language only, but he had had no general impact. And yet, though the book adopts a clearly empirical stance, it moves in a different atmosphere from that of e.g. the great linguistic collections. Language, and Sanskrit in particular, provide Schlegel with the evidence he needs to attack some of the tenets of his predecessors. The most ancient language of them all turns out to be the most regular, the most effective, the most poetic, the most untainted by confusion. What better proof of the Romantic view that the present does not necessarily represent a progress on the past? Further, if it can be empirically shown that grammatical structure can only change within certain limits and that languages with totally different structures cannot be related, it follows that we can no longer think in terms of monogenesis. But is this not a first step in revolutionizing on empirical bases the problem of the origin of language? Schlegel here seems to break completely away from the attitude of the Enlightenment and, we may add, of the *idéologues*; the philosophical problem *par excellence*, that of the origin of language, is looked at in (apparently) empirical terms: 'The hypotheses about the origin of language would all disintegrate or at least take a completely different form, if, instead of being left to poetic fancy, they were based on historical research' (F. Schlegel 1808, 60). This view, which Schlegel himself later modified or rejected (Nüsse 1962, 56f.), marks the beginning of that reinterpretation of the problem of the origin in a historical key which Aarsleff deplores (cf. above, p. 36) and which eventually led to the formal rejection of such discussions by the Société de Linguistique de Paris in 1866.

In fact the whole book – for all its woolliness, incoherence, exaggerated claims, etc. – must have read as an attempt at providing a concrete exemplification of the main Romantic assumptions. The somewhat naive insistence on the parallelism between the beauties of Sanskrit and the depth of Indian philosophy and religion rests on the view that law, religion, philosophy, language and culture are all linked as organic expressions of the *Volksgeist*, the character of a people or nation. This is not a new concept; versions of it were present in Vico, in the French Enlightenment and also e.g. in James Harris, but, after Herder, it had acquired in Germany the increasingly emotional and nationalistic overtones which found their expression, for instance, in Fichte's *Reden an die deutsche Nation* (also published in 1808). The enthusiasm for the past and for 'primitive' poetry or folklore was typical of Romanticism and of various German movements which preceded it (and it also had political overtones); Schlegel himself had intended to publish a collection of Old Provençal texts. Orientalism was a general passion but here it acquired a new twist which linked it with the interest in the Middle Ages prompted by the German search for a national identity. The assumption that the derivation of the Western languages from Sanskrit had been empirically demonstrated meant that the new task was that of tracing the roots of Western civilization in the East and of reconstructing the development from that original culture and language to modern days.[21]

All these motifs have a long history but their combination in this form strikes a new chord, all the more so because they seem to be supported by factual data which were relatively unknown until then. In time they will all become part of the standard stock in trade of nineteenth-century linguists, from the general claims made in favour of an empirical and an historical approach to the distinction between organic and mechanical and the typological distinction between two main classes of languages, to the more specific points about the existence of language decay, the need for a *vergleichende Grammatik*, etc. Even if *Über die Sprache und Weisheit der Indier* was received with indifference by some of the German *literati* (Struc-Oppenberg 1975), in the end its influence was considerable. In its youthful enthusiasm it seemed to open new vistas and to show that the data-oriented empirical approach to language, which had already begun to attract attention, had much greater potential than it was normally assumed: it did not lead only to ethnographic and historical conclusions but also to a new view of the development of man and culture.[22]

3.3.4 Language classification and the two Schlegels

Traditional historiography treats Friedrich Schlegel as a pioneer both in the field of linguistic typology (or classification – the distinction is not always clear) and in that of Sanskrit studies. Given the developments that followed, we must explore further these two points, starting with typology.

The general context is all important. Friedrich Schlegel was not the first author to come across the multiplicity of languages. All the earlier linguistic collections had had to classify their data. The most common model was a compromise between a geographic and a more or less reliable genealogical arrangement. As we have seen, Hervás too adopted this model, spurred perhaps by his belief in polygenesis; for him the different mother tongues could not be derived one from the other, since their syntactic structures were too different to allow a common origin. Adelung, on the other hand, had started from a 'structural' distinction between monosyllabic and polysyllabic languages, but beyond this he moved both in geographic and genealogical terms; his faith in monogenesis induced him to believe that the polysyllabic languages arose from monosyllabic ancestors.

Linguistic diversity had also been discussed in other contexts. First there were numerous attempts at evaluating languages from an aesthetic viewpoint. When in 1794 the Berlin Academy offered a prize for the best essay on 'the idea of a perfect language and on the comparison between the best known languages of Europe' (Jespersen 1922, 29) it continued in the tradition of similar comparisons. The subject of the 1783 competition concerned the merits which had made French the universal language of Europe; the winners mentioned in their essays the natural order of words which was typical of French and imitated the rational order (Ricken 1978, 136).

Secondly, the idea of *génie* or *esprit de la langue*, omnipresent in the eighteenth century, was constantly used to highlight the link between the different structures of languages and the characters of the nations to which each language belonged (Simone 1997, 197ff.). Sometimes the discussion went further: it was stated that language could influence thought (see above, p. 35) and in its turn this view introduced new evaluative criteria.

Thirdly, there were also attempts at defining in general terms the structural characters of languages so that they could be exploited for classification or typology.[23] As we have mentioned (p. 57, note 38), the abbé Girard distinguished in 1747 (i, 22–5) between 'langues analogues', 'langues transpositives' and 'langues mixtes' or 'amphilogiques'. In the languages of the first type, word order corresponded in general terms to the 'natural' order of ideas (i.e. the subject preceded the verb as in French), while in the 'langues transpositives' the word order was determined by imagination and at first sight seemed to be arbitrary (as in Latin and in the Slavic languages).[24] The distinction was not based exclusively on word order; the 'langues transpositives' were also inflected, and Girard admitted that in the 'langues analogues' the fixed word order was necessary because of the lack of inflection. The 'langues mixtes' included Greek and German, which were both inflected (like the 'langues transpositives') but also had an article (which normally belonged only to the 'langues analogues'). Beauzée, if he was the author, employed the same terminology in 1765 in the article '*Langue*' of the *Encyclopédie*, even if he eliminated the third category. In 1761 Adam Smith, who knew Girard's proposals (Noordegraaf 1977), distinguished 'compounded' languages (i.e. mixed languages) and more primitive or non-compounded languages. The contrast this time was between inflected, simple and primitive languages, with free word order, and uninflected languages in which inflection is replaced by various types of constructions (such as auxiliary + participle, or preposition + noun), while the word order is normally fixed. More interesting than the typology is the development process: according to Smith, inflection is abandoned in favour of simpler structures as the result of contacts with other languages. For Smith, language is comparable to mechanical engines, which, when invented, are extremely complex but gradually are perfected so that they require fewer wheels and fewer principles of movement; the difference, however, is that machines become more perfect, while languages become aesthetically less perfect.[25]

Even in Herder ([1767] 1877–1913, i, 233) we find, in passing, a distinction between three different ways of indicating the links between concepts, which may count as a more or less valid programme for a classification or a typology: (i) through a simple alteration of the expression of each idea, (ii) through the use of particles, (iii) through the simple collocation of the ideas. According to Herder, the first type is still preserved in modern languages of an archaic type; it is poetically useful but antiphilosophical. The second type, which is exemplified by German, is suitable for current linguistic usage, while the third type is philosophically the most perfect.

In other words, Friedrich Schlegel was less original than is normally thought when in 1808 he identified 'two main classes of languages according to their internal structure' and distinguished, as we have seen, between languages with roots which develop 'organically' to produce the different inflections and other languages which indicate the grammatical categories through separate words or affixes or prefixes, all endowed with an autonomous meaning. The novelty in Schlegel is rather in his use in this context of organicistic ideas and terminology. Whoever took seriously the organic metaphor was obliged to conclude that the two types could not derive one from the other; it was not possible that an organic language could lose its 'organicity' nor that a non-organic language could become organic. But how could one take seriously the idea of organic roots which sprouted infixes and suffixes? Did Schlegel produce some further definition? The answer to the second question is negative; that to the first question is more difficult and most probably must be sought in an analysis of the very concept of 'organic'. First of all in Schelling's (and Herder's) Germany, organicism enjoyed a great prestige and had a semi-mystical value (see below, p. 86ff.). There was in addition some empirical confirmation. It was indeed true that, as the classical languages demonstrated and the newly learned Sanskrit confirmed, among Indo-European languages at least, the most ancient languages had a degree of inflection much more developed; it seemed to follow that inflection was more 'original'. If so,

how could the inflection of the Indo-European languages with its complex system of endings and affixation be explained? Presumably not
through the composition of separate elements, given that the historical
process moved in the opposite direction and that in any case this would
not have been sufficient to justify the vocalic alternation of the roots.
If no 'mechanicistic' explanation of this type was available, within the
context of the contemporary Romantic dualism, the only alternative was
an organicistic account. The least mystic, the more positivistic among
Schlegel's followers could get away with an interpretation of 'organic'
as 'original', a meaning which the adjective acquired in the later linguistic literature (Morpurgo Davies 1987, 86, note 15). Even August
Wilhelm was inclined to treat the organic conception of the roots as a
metaphor (Timpanaro 1973, 560). There remained, however, the fact
that the basic dichotomy between organic and non-organic languages
was capable of a divisive and to a certain extent racist interpretation.
Within Schlegel's schema it was not possible to doubt the superiority
of the organic languages, and this meant giving a higher position to the
Indo-European languages in contrast with the others;[26] it also meant –
somewhat inconsistently – giving up any conception of language in its
entirety as an organic phenomenon.

The dichotomy caused also other problems. First of all, if understood as a form of classification (which was not necessarily the case in
its first formulation), it was ineffective: too many languages (with wildly
different structures) were included in the category of non-organic. Secondly, the so-called organic languages differed from each other just
because of that parameter, inflection, which was deemed to be their
defining characteristic. It was normally assumed that English or the
Romance languages had lost many of those inflectional features which
characterized ancient languages such as Sanskrit or Latin; if so, how
could they be called inflected? Nor was it helpful to refer to the auxiliaries and prepositions as forms which led to a sort of abbreviated
language, as hinted by Friedrich Schlegel himself (1808, 216). An answer
to both problems was suggested by the *Observations sur la langue et
la littérature provençales* by August Wilhelm Schlegel ([1818] 1846, ii,
158ff.), where Friedrich's dichotomy was replaced by a tripartition into
monosyllabic languages, affixed languages and inflected languages. The
last category, which for Wilhelm too included the only truly organic
languages, was prone to a shift from synthetic to analytic (Wilhelm's
terminology), without, however, losing its fundamental 'organicity'.[27]
This naturally opened again the question of the nature of inflection, all
the more urgently in a period when the concept of root, introduced by
the Indian grammarians, had become much clearer (Rousseau 1984).
Wilhelm concluded that the 'true' inflectional elements were characterized by absence of meaning (which must be understood as absence of

'lexical', 'concrete' meaning).[28] At a later stage the terminology changed (see below, p. 111f.) and linguists spoke of isolative, agglutinative and inflected languages accepting at the same time the distinction between analytic and synthetic. This so-called 'morphological' classification prevailed through most of the last century, even if its organicistic connotations disappeared or were reinterpreted (see below, p. 111f. and p. 212ff.). However, in contrast with what is normally argued, the later studies about classification or typology were not directly based on Friedrich Schlegel or his brother (nor for that matter on Adam Smith or Herder or the abbé Girard); Wilhelm von Humboldt, who knew far more languages and had thought at length about the problems of typology and classification, had a much deeper influence, even if this was partly based on a misunderstanding (see below, p. 113).

3.3.5 The influence of the two Schlegels
In Sanskrit studies, as contrasted with linguistics, Friedrich Schlegel's influence was great, but of another nature. His knowledge of the language was far from perfect, but he was the first Western scholar who learned Sanskrit and wrote about it without going to India. His example was influential on the first two men (except for Hamilton) who obtained chairs of Sanskrit in European Universities, Antoine-Léonard de Chézy, who taught himself Sanskrit in Paris and became professor at the Collège de France in 1814, and August Wilhelm Schlegel, for whom a chair of Sanskrit was created at the new University of Bonn in 1818. However, Wilhelm Schlegel, who became a much better Sanskritist than Friedrich and founded an important school of Sanskrit studies (Windisch 1917–20, i, 209ff.), did not pursue beyond certain limits his brother's comparative interests; he concentrated instead on applying rigorously to the texts 'les principes de la critique philologique', which he had learned from his classical studies (A. W. Schlegel 1832, 140).[29] His pupils and the pupils of his pupils oscillated between the two directions, with perhaps a preference for the latter. The scholar who under the influence of Friedrich's book dedicated himself to Sanskrit but aimed at comparison was Franz Bopp, whom we shall discuss later (p. 129ff.). With the creation of a number of chairs in German Universities and the establishment of Sanskrit at the Collège de France, where Eugène Burnouf succeeded Chézy in 1832, Sanskrit became one of the recognized disciplines in the European University system.[30] Its role in the development of comparative and historical linguistics was double: on the one hand it provided the basic data on which the techniques of comparison could be developed and tested; on the other hand, through its institutional successes, it helped to build up a system of support for the budding comparative linguistics; even the most philologically or literarily inclined members of the Bonn school did not wholly escape the comparative contagion.

Yet Friedrich Schlegel's great contribution consisted in highlighting to a wider public the role of Sanskrit in linguistic comparison. The contrast between his 1808 book and the earlier works emanating from Calcutta makes this understandable. H. T. Colebrooke, perhaps the most scholarly and most productive of the early Sanskritists, knew and stated that Sanskrit, Pahlavi and Greek derived from the same language, but for the rest concentrated in making available to the West Sanskrit texts and above all the Sanskrit grammarians. As Staal (1972, 34) put it, 'He was a practical scholar and saw to it that first things were done first'; *mutatis mutandis* this was true of all the early British scholars, with the partial exception of Sir William Jones, who had grander ambitions and a broader range of interests. Like him Schlegel caught the imagination of his successors but changed the focus of the enquiry; his speculations were more philosophical and theoretical than historical and ethnological. In the chapter of *De l'Allemagne* ([1810] 1833 [Part II, Ch. xxxi]) dedicated to the Schlegels, Mme de Staël had pointed out that in Germany, 'les connoissances et la sagacité philosophique . . . sont . . . presque inséparables'. Through his mixture of technical erudition, intuition and half real / half rhetorical depth, Friedrich Schlegel succeeded in giving the impression, to some at least, that Sanskrit had created an opening through which a new discipline **and** a new philosophy were emerging. He did not create a new subject. The results of comparative grammar could have been achieved without him and perhaps without Sanskrit; the method was defined by others. Nevertheless we may wonder whether without him the new discipline would have had the same level of intellectual and institutional success.

Notes

1. Cf. Auroux (1988a, 74).
2. For similar statements in the context of an onslaught against the 'extravagant and chimerical' results of the past etymology, cf. J. C. Prichard's book on Celtic (1831, 3f.).
3. Benfey (1869, 321) contrasts this attitude with that of Kant's pamphlet on *Der Streit der Fakultäten* (1798), according to which, of the four faculties in which traditionally the German University was divided, only the so-called *philosophische Fakultät* had scientific ('wissenschaftliche') concerns while the others (theology, law and medicine) simply expounded a set of arbitrary norms. This interpretation of Kant's views is probably forced (there was a question of guaranteeing freedom of thought in the philosophical faculty) but rightly or wrongly Benfey (1869, 321) wanted to argue that in the eighteenth century, in contrast with his own period, philosophy was seen as an abstract discipline entirely separated from the empirical results of the sciences and of the various fields of human endeavour.

4. Benfey emphasizes the importance of the foundation of Göttingen University (1837), which started what we would now call a new research ethos. Partly thanks to C. G. Heyne's classical teaching in Göttingen from 1763 and to his pupils – above all F. A. Wolf (1759–1824), professor in Halle and then in Berlin – there started a new school of classical philology characterized by an extraordinarily high level of linguistic and cultural research which was often devoted to a global concept of *Altertumswissenschaft* (classical antiquity) and was distinguished by world-famous classicists such as Gottfried Hermann (1772–1848), August Boeckh (1785–1867), etc. (for linguistics at Göttingen, cf. also Cherubim 1992).

5. Roth was in touch with the famous Father Athanasius Kircher, who inserted some *Elementa linguae Hanskret* in his book on China (1667); thus the first *devanāgarī* characters to be printed in the West were based on the drawings by Roth. The grammar was also known to Hervás, who recommended its publication but to no effect (Camps ap. Roth 1988, 10). For the early Sanskrit grammars written (and never published) by the missionaries, cf. Muller (1993).

6. Schlegel does not seem to know Paulinus' first grammar published in 1790. On the other hand his judgement is no more severe than that of other contemporaries. In 1801 Alexander Hamilton reviewed harshly one of Paulinus' books: 'It might be considered illiberal were we to insinuate that Fra Paolino did not understand a language of which he has published a grammar' (cf. Rocher 1968, 19). Anquetil-Duperron also doubted that all words and meanings of Sanskrit words quoted by Paulinus should be taken seriously (cf. F. Adelung in Adelung 1806–17, v, 56, but see also L. Rocher in Paulinus 1977, xiiff.).

7. There is of course no reason to believe that the decisions of the British rulers were determined by pure desire of scholarship and unselfish liberalism; political motives had a part to play. Majeed (1992, 22) has stressed the 'larger concern of British rule to legitimize itself in an Indian idiom'. There is nevertheless a considerable difference between the attitude of the British civil servants and that of the missionaries. Particularly in the nineteenth century, these latter were mainly concerned with the diffusion of Christianity and not with pursuing scholarly enquiries. Yet the first of the Sanskrit grammars due to British authors was written by a missionary. William Carey (1761–1834) published in 1804 *A Grammar of the Sungskrit Language, Composed from the Work of the Most Esteemed Grammarians* (new edn, Serampore 1806), and also edited part of the *Rāmāyana* with one of his fellow-founders of the Baptist mission at Serampore. For his grammar and the others that followed, cf. Law (1993).

8. For a good account of the background history and activity of the Society and its members (including Sir William Jones, the founder), cf. Kejariwal (1988); see also Mukherjee (1968).

9. Sir William Jones' justification for his article on the spikenard (a plant yielding an aromatic substance) captures well the flavour of the period and of the Society's work while accounting for the disparate subjects considered: 'Ignorance is to the mind what extreme darkness is to the nerves:

both cause an uneasy sensation; and we naturally love knowledge as we love light, even when we have no design of applying either to a purpose essentially useful' (Jones 1790, 405).

10. The British enthusiasm for all things Indian was not to last. The missionaries wanted to impose Christianity, and more evangelical and less tolerant trends began to prevail at the beginning of the century. But even a utilitarian thinker such as James Mill, who did not believe in the riches of India or in their usefulness to Britain (Majeed 1992, 151ff.), attacked all facets of Hindu culture as early as 1817. In the account of the creation found in the Laws of Manu 'it is all vagueness and darkness, incoherence, inconsistency, and confusion. . . . The fearless propensity of a rude mind to guess where it does not know, never exhibited itself in more fantastic and senseless forms' (Mill [1817] 1820, i, 286); the grammatical works 'afford a remarkable specimen of the spirit of a rude and ignorant age; which is as much delighted with the juggleries of the mind, as it it [sic] with those of the body, and is distinguished by the absurdity of its passion for both' (ibid., ii, 78f.); the celebrated copiousness of the language is in fact 'a defect and a deformity' (ibid., ii, 80). In 1835 Macaulay, as legal adviser to the Supreme Council of India and president of the Committee of Public Instruction, espoused the case of Western culture as against Indology and stated in a famous minute that no one could deny that 'a single shelf of a good European library was worth the whole native literature of India and Arabia' (Moon 1989, 465f.). Some fifty years earlier Warren Hastings had written that works such as Wilkins' *Bhagavad-gītā* 'will survive when the British dominion in India shall have long since ceased to exist, and when the sources which it once yielded of wealth and power are lost to remembrance' (cf. Brockington 1989, 97); the contrast could not have been greater. It was eventually decided that all funds available for the purpose of education (part of which had until then been employed to help the study of Arabic and Sanskrit) had to be used to promote English education alone. The losing party was headed by H. H. Wilson (1784–1860), also an employee of the East India Company, the author of the first Sanskrit dictionary (Calcutta 1819, 2nd edn, 1832), and the man who was to become the first professor of Sanskrit at Oxford (cf. Windisch 1917–20, i, 36–47). His failure to persuade public opinion had important political consequences but by this stage the progress of Sanskrit studies was no longer dependent on British support; Sanskrit had become a scholarly subject with a European momentum of its own.

11. The history of the College of Fort William (Calcutta), which was founded by the Governor General Lord Wellesley in 1800 to teach Indian languages, law and history to the Company's civil servants, was troubled, mainly for political reasons; by 1806 it had become a small institution mainly concerned with the teaching of Bengal civilians (until 1830), but previously Colebrooke and William Carey, a Baptist missionary, taught there. The Company also established a college in England (first at Hertford and then at Haileybury) in 1806 with the task of instructing the 'writers' destined to India; some at least of the students were supposed to learn Sanskrit and the college survived until 1857 (Philips 1940, 125–9; 295–7).

12. Rocher (1980b and 1983) makes a good case for a strong influence by Halhed on Jones and emphasizes the close similarity between the 'philologer's passage' and a letter written in 1779 by Halhed to the biblical scholar George Costard, which Jones probably saw before his departure for India (1783). Halhed's argumentation, as Rocher argues, shows a considerable degree of linguistic sophistication, but he prefers to assume that Sanskrit is the parent language of Greek and Latin. Jones reaches different conclusions but is probably moved both by non-linguistic considerations and by his acquaintance with the older Scythian theory which predisposed him towards an *Ursprache* no longer attested (Kispert 1978; Muller 1986, 25–31).

13. For Jones in general, cf. Cannon (1970, 1979 and 1990), Mukherjee (1968), Pachori (1993). His role in the history of linguistics (or more exactly of the comparative method) has been repeatedly disputed: should he be seen as a founder or as a precursor; as a summarizer or as a prophet? In addition to Aarsleff (1983, 124), a discussion of the problem, with earlier references, can be found in Morpurgo Davies (1975, 620–2), Kispert (1978), Szemerényi (1980), Mayrhofer (1983), Rocher (1980a, b and 1983), Muller (1986, 25–31), Robins (1987b). In some sense anything said about Sanskrit in 1786 by a famous orientalist (even if at that stage Sir William had studied Sanskrit for a few months only) was new and was bound to be influential. Whether 'On the Hindus' indicates a completely new departure it is legitimate to doubt; what it shows clearly, however, is that in some respects the gap between eighteenth-century and nineteenth-century outlook has been exaggerated. As Robins stresses, Sir William was above all an eighteenth-century man; but this did not prevent him from adopting a purely empirical attitude to language and from implicitly rejecting any question of universal grammar. When he spoke of strong affinity in the forms of the grammar it is indeed possible and perhaps likely that he had in mind the similarity in grammatical structure which joined Sanskrit to the two classical languages (Robins 1987b) but we cannot exclude that he **also** thought of more formal similarities. If it is indeed the case that the 'philologer's passage' was influenced by Halhed's letter to Costard (see note above), then Jones may have thought, like Halhed, of 'all the modes of declination and inflexion of . . . words' and taken this to refer to the formal similarity of the Sanskrit, Greek and Latin inflectional endings. As early as 1778 Halhed had noted that both Sanskrit and Greek had *mi*-verbs.

14. Sir William Jones' influence was felt, far less positively, when he attacked with an 'anonymous' French pamphlet Anquetil-Duperron's *Zend Avesta, ouvrage de Zoroastre* (Paris 1771), wrongly denying the authenticity of the manuscripts on which it was based: 'a charge which obscured the pioneering research for almost fifty years' (Cannon 1970, i, 107).

15. There has been some discussion of the reasons for the importance of Sanskrit in the development of comparative grammar. Was it due to the typical transparency of Sanskrit, which made its analysis particularly attractive in comparison with that of e.g. the classical languages, or was it rather due to the importance of the contacts with a different grammatical tradition, that of the Indian grammarians, which led to a deeper understanding of grammatical forms? For some literature, cf. Morpurgo Davies (1975, 619),

but see also Maggi (1986), with his discussion of John Cleland's morphological theories, and Romaschko (1991).

16. The life of A. Hamilton, or what can be known of it, has been studied in detail by Rocher (1968); the quotations given above are mostly taken from anonymous reviews written between 1809 and 1811 (cf. Rocher 1968, 95–101); for the contacts between Hamilton and Schlegel, cf. also Plank (1987b).

17. For F. Schlegel's linguistic thought in general, cf. Nüsse (1962) but also Fiesel (1927), Formigari (1977a, b); for his Sanskrit work, Oppenberg (1965) and Struc-Oppenberg (1975); for a general introduction and further bibliography, see Gipper-Schmitter (1979, 43–9) and Koerner (1989, 268–90); cf. also Plank (1987a and b). Particularly important are Timpanaro (1972a) (English translation in Timpanaro 1977) and Timpanaro (1973).

18. For the translation of *höhere Naturgeschichte* I follow Bolelli (1965b, 39); cf. Timpanaro (1973, 9). This passage is often quoted as the first example of the phrase *vergleichende Grammatik*. That this is wrong is shown by Timpanaro (1972a, 96 = 1977, xxx; cf. Koerner 1989, 274 and Plank 1993, 103), who argues that Schlegel's novelty consisted in giving a historical/genealogical dimension to the phrase. For the earlier use and the later developments see above, p. 32. Aarsleff ([1967] 1983, 157, note 115) has also noted that the phrase had been used five years earlier in 1803 by A. W. Schlegel in a review of Bernhardi's *Reine Sprachlehre* (see also below, p. 96, note 10).

19. It is not exactly clear what Schlegel refers to; no doubt he thinks of vocalic alternation in roots as e.g. in Latin *foedus/fides*, or English *drove/driven*. But he also seems to refer to the formation of endings as in the contrast between e.g. Sanskrit nom. sg. *pitā* 'father', acc. sg. *pitaram*, dat. pl. *pitṛṣu*.

20. Nine years earlier Father Paulinus had published a *De antiquitate et affinitate linguae zendicae, samscrdamicae et germanicae dissertatio* (Patavii 1798 but 1799). The contrast with Schlegel (1808) is remarkable; Paulinus refers back to William Jones' assertion that Sanskrit was related to Zend (the name then used for Avestan) but reports doubts on the subject, 'cum [Jones] nulla suae assertionis produxisset documenta' (1798, xvii, note 15); he then produces long lists of vocabulary words for Sanskrit and for Avestan (taken from Anquetil-Duperron) and adds much shorter lists of Germanic words taken from various Germanic languages. No grammatical analysis is attempted and no serious discussion of method, though Paulinus has learned from Jones that certain parts of the lexicon are less prone to borrowing than others and also points out in two separate notes (1798, xxii, note 18 and xxx, note 26) that Zend is similar to Sanskrit not only in nouns but also in verbs, particles, adverbs, some cases and numbers and that, as in all dialects, the most conspicuous changes concern the vowels while the consonants are steadier '& ex iis praecipue integritas dictionum, & affinitas linguarum innotescit'. In general the impression is that of a much less sophisticated approach (not least because Paulinus' transliteration of *devanāgarī* now looks singularly peculiar), but, differently from Schlegel, Paulinus extensively refers both to historical evidence offered by classical authors and to the earlier discussions on the Scythian theory (Boxhorn, etc.).

21. It is hardly ever noted that most of these points, including the rejection of the belief in eternal progress, the dichotomy between 'primitive', rough-

and-ready languages, such as that of the Hottentots, and perfected languages, such as Sanskrit, the appeal to the results of Sir William Jones, etc. are all present in an 1805 essay by A. W. Schlegel ([1805] 1846, i, 276–316: *Considérations sur la civilisation en général et sur l'origine et la décadence des religions*). The detailed argumentation, the point about the importance of *vergleichende Grammatik* and the distinction between organic and non-organic languages are missing, but the historical emphasis is there already.

22. The 1808 book was soon translated into French (1809) and had a definite impact on some at least of the future comparativists, including Franz Bopp. Friedrich Schlegel himself abandoned all specific work on Sanskrit or linguistic subjects until his much later lectures about language, which show a clear involution and perhaps a return to monogenetic views under the influence of religion (Timpanaro 1972a = 1977).

23. In this context it was sometimes possible to invoke the concept of *génie des langues*. Girard (1747, i, 21f.) explains: 'the most obvious difference between languages is that which first hits our ears. It arises from the difference of words; but the most essential difference is only apparent as the result of reflection; it arises from the difference in taste of each people for what concerns the turn of the sentence and the "idée modificative" of word usage . . . When this distinctive taste is considered in its universal character we are then confronted with what in the case of languages we call *GÉNIE*, and it is important for the grammarian to understand properly its nature'. There follows the passage about the three types of languages.

24. The distinction must be understood in the context of the French discussion about word order and its link with the logical order of ideas, a discussion which had an immense importance in the eighteenth century; cf. Ricken (1978); and about Girard, see Rosiello (1987).

25. After Pott (1880, i, xliii), Coseriu (1968) has highlighted the importance of Adam Smith as source of A. W. Schlegel; Rousseau (1984, 405f.) points out some important differences. Recently Plank (1987b) has recalled in this connection the ideas of Alexander Hamilton, Friedrich Schlegel's Sanskrit teacher. We owe to Plank (1987a) the reference to Herder and to Pott (1880, i, clv ff.), who quotes him; Plank observes that this type of classification was far more diffused than is normally assumed, so that it is very difficult to identify with certainty the sources of each view. On the typology of the eighteenth century, see Rosiello (1987), who stresses that Girard's typology is mainly descriptive and not evaluative in contrast with that of Adam Smith. Cf. also Nowak (1994).

26. This statement is deliberately anachronistic in its terminology. Friedrich Schlegel believed that Sanskrit was the ancestor of all those languages which we now call Indo-European. It is true, on the other hand, that Wilhelm thought of a common origin of Sanskrit, Greek, etc., but certainly did not call it Indo-European; the term that he used was *indo-germanique* (Timpanaro 1973, 357). For the various names used for the parent language see below, p. 147, note 8. From a different angle we ought to notice that Schlegel's decision to exclude the Semitic languages from the group of inflected languages cannot be explained in purely linguistic terms. Later on Bopp will treat Indo-European as mainly agglutinative and Semitic as truly inflected.

27. The distinction was clearly prompted by the wish to keep all the Indo-
European languages in the same 'organic' class. For the possible preced-
ents, cf. above, note 25. Wilhelm moves within the traditional classification
schemata (see below, p. 91ff.): synthetic and analytic are 'genders' which
count as divisions of a class. All the discussion obviously develops within
the framework of the French eighteenth-century discourse with which Adam
Smith too was familiar. Beauzée for instance had spoken of 'ordre analytique' or 'construction analytique' and Silvestre de Sacy (1808, 255f.), in
connection with a description of Coptic, had referred to a 'système de
synthèse'. Elke Nowak (1994, 12ff.) has called attention to the Schlegels'
uncle, Johann Heinrich Schlegel, who in a Danish treatise of 1763, translated into German in 1764, had discussed merits and defects of Danish and
had argued that all languages use one of two different procedures to indicate grammatical categories, inflection, i.e. change of word forms, or use of
additional elements (voces auxiliares). One of the differences between
Wilhelm and his brother is that the former adopted a more agnostic position about the possibility or otherwise of evolution from one to the other
class of his schema (A. W. Schlegel [1818] 1846, ii, 214, note 7); about
his more general views, cf. Timpanaro (1973) and Rousseau (1984).

28. The assumption obviously is that the presence of a 'concrete' meaning in
the forms which mark grammatical relations prevents the speakers or the
hearers from following closely the development of thought.

29. A. W. Schlegel also had an important role, as Diez's predecessor, in the
origins of Romance philology; his Observations sur la langue et la littérature
provençales of 1818, which in a sense are an analysis and review of
Raynouard's theories, contain a number of important observations about
the development of Romance languages and linguistic change in general.

30. The support for Sanskrit in German Universities (and especially in the new
Universities) was clearly a support for scholarship and documents the new
research ethos (cf. also Amsterdamska 1987, 64ff.). In Britain things were
different. As we have seen, Bopp's pupil, Friedrich Rosen (1805–37), was
appointed professor of Oriental Languages at the newly founded University of London in 1828 but his job was menial and it was only in 1836 that
he was given a chair of Sanskrit. The Oxford chair of Sanskrit was founded
in 1832 because of a benefaction by Joseph Boden, who wanted to encourage his countrymen 'to proceed in the Conversion of the Natives of India
to the Christian Religion'. Only a small number of votes guaranteed the
election of a real Sanskrit scholar, Horace Wilson, in preference to a clergyman with no such credentials (Gombrich 1978, 7ff.). However, Wilson and
most of his successors, faithful to the British tradition, did not contribute
to comparative studies except indirectly. Apart from what Rosen did in the
little time he had at his disposal and from the occasional reference to
Sanskrit data by people such as the Rev. Richard Garnett (1789–1850),
who were not Sanskritists, an effective link between comparative studies
and Sanskrit was only established by Max Müller in the middle of the
century (though Max Müller himself failed to obtain the Oxford chair of
Sanskrit when it fell vacant).

4

Historicism, organicism and the scientific model

4.1 Two new trends

We cannot plunge into a discussion of the more specific work that followed Friedrich Schlegel's 1808 book without looking first at two crucial trends which left their mark on the linguistic work of this period,
in Germany above all, but elsewhere as well: historicism and organicism.
The two movements pervade the whole of contemporary intellectual life;
here we shall focus on language only and shall use Schlegel's 1808 work
as one of our starting points. We shall then turn to a brief discussion
of the links between the 'new linguistics' and contemporary science.

4.2 Historicism

Historicism or *Historismus* is often taken as characteristic of the *Deutsche
Bewegung* (Oesterreicher 1986): in 1814 the jurist Savigny, who was
also Jacob Grimm's friend and patron, wrote that at last 'Historical
sense has woken up everywhere' ('Geschichtlicher Sinn ist überall
erwacht'; Savigny 1814, 5) and one year later he explained that 'history
is no longer a mere collection of examples but is the only way to a true
knowledge of our own condition' (1815, 4). The ultimate origin of this
approach, the relative importance of e.g. Vico or Leibniz, are not relevant for our purposes. Similarly the question of Herder's sources,
however interesting, is not immediately relevant, but some of the views
expounded by Herder (1744–1803), with greater or lesser consistency,
may serve as an introduction to the trend, even if not all are equally
important.[1] First, the belief (not a new one) that the character of a
language, like that of art, literature, etc. is indissolubly linked with that
of a people and, jointly to this, the constant highlighting of linguistic
and cultural variety. Hence the request in the *Ideen zur Philosophie der
Geschichte der Menschheit* (1784–5) for a 'philosophical comparison
[*Vergleichung*] of languages' since the 'genius of a people is nowhere

better manifested than in its speech'; hence also the regret that the wish
expressed by Bacon, Leibniz, Sulzer, etc. for a 'general physiognomics
of peoples on the basis of their languages' ('allgemeinen Physiognomik
der Völker aus ihren Sprachen') had never been realized; hence, above
all, the project of a history of the languages of individual nations which
would consider at the same time the revolutions which took place in the
relevant nations (Herder 1877–1913, xiii, 363ff.). Secondly, the search
for a genetic explanation: the nature of a thing, Herder repeats, is shown
by its origin. Thirdly, the constant reference to change: individuals, arts,
sciences and languages all are in perennial process of change. Finally,
the tendency to see the organism as the prototype of all dynamic wholes
and consequently to attribute a cyclical development to individuals and
institutions alike (Nisbet 1970, 70); language too, we are told in an early
work (1767), germinates, bears buds, flowers and eventually withers
away (Herder 1877–1913, i, 151–2).

Herder's views were infectious even for those who, like Friedrich
Schlegel, though prone to *herdisieren*, were ready to criticize his form
of historical relativism (Haym 1920, 246; Nisbet 1970, 68). If applied
to the study of language, they identified specific aims which were neither those of philosophical grammar nor those of the great linguistic
collections. Hervás, Adelung, Balbi all wanted to exploit language to
find out about historical **facts**: what tribe lived where, what migrations
had occurred when – even where Paradise was located. This was characteristic of an empirical data-oriented approach opposed to any metaphysical considerations, but the main concern was for history (of peoples
or events) and for linguistic facts which helped to establish historical
facts, not for the history **of languages**. On the other hand, Schlegel, if
we take him as our model, is actually interested in language development, and the capacity of language for infinite development ('einer
unendlichen Entwickelung'; Schlegel, 1808, 65) fascinates him. Passage after passage of the 1808 book (see above, p. 69ff.) hammers the
point home. Language is for Schlegel a living texture which is always
advancing and developing while being moved only by an internal force
(1808, 64f.). The differences in meaning between related words in
Persian, Sanskrit, Latin and Greek may lead to conclusions and observations about the way and the laws ('Gesetze') according to which the
meaning of words changes (1808, 26). We must study the grammar of
Persian to see how it was changed and whether in the earlier phases it
was closer to Sanskrit (1808, 31). A correct understanding of Greek
grammar can only be reached by abandoning all etymological juggling
and looking at language 'scientifically, i.e. historically through and
through' ('wissenschaftlich, d.h. durchaus historisch'; 1808, 41), etc.
That languages change is not a new discovery; Plato knew it and he
was not the first to do so. But the constant awareness of change, the

shift of interest from the static description of language to a dynamic view, the very importance attributed to change was felt to be new and of course was influential in leading to, and establishing, an actual method of research geared to the study of language development.[2] Schlegel is not prepared to write a history or an historical grammar of a language – this will be left to others – but is as aware as his followers that such a study is on the cards; to judge from the first part of his book he is closer to such a venture than Herder ever was. At the same time the principle of genetic explanation becomes all powerful. It would be foolish to state that linguistic data are no longer explained in terms of universal assumptions about language. In practice they are because the linguistics of the time takes an enormous number of assumptions for granted. In theory, however, the 'approved' type of explanation is that which accounts for linguistic facts in terms of their previous history.

Two concrete examples may support this view – all the more important because they come from fields which may be seen as marginal to the progress of the new linguistics. The first comes from Denmark, where a mineralogist felt impelled to write in 1821 a pamphlet about the causes of language change (Bredsdorff 1970). The author, Jacob Hornemann Bredsdorff (1790–1841), had no impact on the subject and remained largely unknown though his attempt to classify the various types of linguistic change is remarkably modern in outlook and, as indicated by Jespersen (1922, 70f.), would have been in order in the 1860s. The simple pamphlet, which shares none of the high-flung rhetorics of the Romantic authors, must at least serve to indicate how the historical approach was gaining ground in different quarters. The same lesson can be learned from the work of a German classicist, Franz Passow (1786– 1833), a pupil of Gottfried Hermann and Wolf, who first justified in a separate work (1812) his views about Greek lexicography and then brought out in 1819–23 his own re-edition of the standard Greek lexicon by Schneider: 'his leading principle was to draw out, wherever it was possible, a kind of biographical history of each word, to give its different meanings in an almost chronological order, to cite always the earliest author in which a word is found, – thus ascertaining, as nearly as may be, its original signification – and then to trace it downwards according as it might vary in sense and construction, through subsequent writers' ([Fishlake] 1834, 150). In other words, Passow, who also believed in an organic conception of language according to which each element was significant and worthy of study, introduced into Greek lexicography that historical approach which in England was to be imitated by H. G. Liddell and R. Scott in their *Greek–English Lexicon* (1843) and to be adopted by the authors of the *Oxford English Dictionary* (Aarsleff 1983, 253; Beyer 1981, 160ff.). At the beginning of the century classicists in general were not necessarily favourable to the activities of the historical and comparative linguists (see below, p. 153f.); it is all the more remarkable to see that this did not prevent one of them from adopting the historical approach which was so typical of the period.

4.3 Organicism

Organicism too has a role to play in this context and the omnipresence of organic metaphors in the German works of our period cannot be ignored. The comparison with organisms, the reference to biological processes in the discussion of all human events – from aesthetic creation to the various facets of human society and its institutions – are everywhere. The contrast is between 'organisms', which carry their own motivation and their own impulse for development (which may or may not be conceived in teleological terms), and 'mechanisms', which are formed from parts artificially added up. As August Wilhelm Schlegel explained in his 1808 Vienna lectures ([1808] 1817, I, iii), organic form is innate; mechanical form is imposed from outside as an accidental addition. At this point 'organic' becomes an adjective of praise; 'mechanical' implies rejection often tainted with contempt.[3]

Cassirer (1923, 96 = 1953, 1, 153) credits Schlegel (1808) with the full introduction of the new concept of 'organic form' into the discussion of language (cf. Nüsse 1962, 44ff.). In fact the definition of language as an organic whole or an organism, preceded as it was by Herder's organicism and by Schelling's vitalism, was in the air and is not specific to Schlegel.[4] The 1808 book does not explicitly compare languages with organisms (R. Wells 1987, 55) but this may be due to chance: the organic terminology is there, though it is idiosyncratically applied. In fact with Schlegel organicism has a special twist because 'organic' is not predicated of language in general but only of some languages characterized by their inflectional forms which do not arise through juxtaposition but through spontaneous 'organic' development of the roots. But in general what do 'organic' and 'organism' mean with reference to languages; how seriously must we take the metaphors?

The interpretation necessarily differs in different authors and even in different passages of the same author but in Germany at least the metaphor is regularly used in at least one of three senses and sometimes in all.

First, language like law, art, religion, etc. can be seen as an 'organic' expression of the people or the nation; here what matters is the natural, non-mechanical, non-superficial aspect of the connection. No contradiction is seen between this 'organic' connection and the fact that language may be treated as an organism in its own right. Indeed, as Humboldt put it in 1820, language is the unmediated emanation of an organic being and shares in the nature of all that is organic; in it every part exists only because of the existence of all other parts (Humboldt 1903–36, iv, 4).

Secondly, attention may also focus, as Humboldt indicates, on the organism as such, on its basic unity and on the mutual dependence or common purpose of all its parts; more emotionally than meaningfully the whole is sometimes said to be greater than the sum of its parts. This may be interpreted to mean that it is impossible to study isolated linguistic elements without looking at the whole structure. But there are further consequences: emphasis on structure comes to mean emphasis on grammar rather than on lexicon; in 1833 Bopp more than once glosses *Organismus* with *Grammatik* and a similar equation is partly implicit in F. Schlegel (1808).

Thirdly, when language is equated with organism the emphasis may be on development and possibly on autonomous development; organisms are living entities which develop according to a specific pattern or life history. The common metaphors about the birth, growth, decay and death of language are all much older than our period; as we have seen they were adopted by Herder in his particular brand of dynamic organicism and reinterpreted in this sense. A link can then be established between organicism and language history, and the way in which the latter is looked at may be influenced by the former. Pott (1833–6, I, xxvii) makes this clear: language 'as all organic objects has its periods of genetic development and training, times of progress and arrest, of growth, of flowering, of fading and of gradual death, in one word it has its own **history**'.[5] The development of organisms may be seen as determined by internal laws; if so, the same may be said of languages. Humboldt explained it with his normal caution ([1836] 1903–36, vii, 98 = 1988, 90): 'Since language, in direct conjunction with mental power, is a fully fashioned *organism*, we can distinguish within it not only *parts*, but also *laws* of procedure, or rather (since I would sooner pick terms here throughout, which do not even seem to prejudge historical research), *directions* and *endeavours*.' The stress is on laws of change and development but at the same time the organic conception provides an explanation of the why of change: it is a commonplace that all organisms are in continual process of development.

The analogy may be pushed further. It results both from the structural and the evolutionary view of the linguistic organism that language must be treated as an autonomous unit which requires separate study. In other words, the organic metaphor offers a justification for a study of language *per se*. Bopp explained in 1833 (1833–52, i, xiii–xiv) that his aim was to treat languages as objects and not as means of enquiry and to provide a study of their 'Physik und Physiologie'. Linguistics is now poised to become an autonomous discipline just as the natural sciences.

4.3.1 The use of the organic metaphor

One thing is certain: we are dealing with more than stereotype metaphors which entered linguistics due to the fashion of the period and were successful because of their overlap with a pre-existing biological terminology. For some, such as Jacob Grimm, the first and the third interpretations mattered most. For others the second, 'structural' interpretation was more important or the only one available. Karl Ferdinand Becker, the author of some works on the German language (syntax and word formation) which were very influential, saw nature as entirely dominated by an organic principle based on the dualism of opposing forces and proceeded to apply the same principle to syntactical analysis (Haselbach 1966).[6] Even in an austere and fundamentally anti-Romantic 'technician' like Bopp the organicistic conception had some influence (Morpurgo Davies 1987), but he concentrated on structure and development and paid only lip service to the organic connection between language and nation. In Humboldt we find all possible uses of the organic metaphor but also the awareness that the metaphor is just that, a metaphor, and cannot be pushed too far: speaking can never be called an organic act in the strict sense of the word. It is organic in so far as it is dominated by laws and is conditioned by the organism of physical organs ('das Reden kann niemals im eigentlichen Verstande eine organische Verrichtung gennant werden. Es ist zwar organisch, insofern es gesetzmässig und durch den Organismus körperlicher Werkzeuge bedingt ist') ([1824–6] 1903–36, v, 451).[7]

However, even with this disclaimer, problems remain. Friedrich Schlegel's distinction between organic and non-organic languages (cf. pp. 68, 73) was more influential than one might have expected but was never explained. Yet the real difficulties start in the second half of the century when the organic metaphor is taken literally and brought to its extreme consequences; language now becomes a real organism with a life of its own independent from that of the speaker, and linguistics becomes a science with no historical content. This is the conclusion reached by Schleicher and partly accepted and popularized (though with reservations) by e.g. Max Müller. Paradoxically the same organicism which had promoted an historical approach to language is now used to deny its validity. At the same time the extreme character of this view calls for a reaction which leads through various hesitations to the disappearance of most organic metaphors in scholarly work. For the layman, language remained, and to a certain extent still remains, an organism.

4.4 The influence of the sciences on linguistics

In Germany, but also elsewhere, organic metaphors are often accompanied by references to the natural sciences and/or to the scientific character of the new linguistics. How important is the connection? How much did Friedrich Schlegel and his followers know about sciences? How influential were these in the development of the new linguistics? A full enquiry is still a desideratum; in its absence we should enter a series of caveats. The scientific activities and/or concerns of German (and not only German) *Gelehrte* in the second part of the eighteenth century and in the following decades are well known and cut across school divisions; Goethe worked on comparative anatomy and botany as well as on *Farbenlehre*; Kant, as Herder put it (1877–1913, xviii, 324–5), investigated the natural laws of Newton, Kepler and the physicists and was familiar with the latest scientific discoveries; Lessing and Schiller had specialized in medicine; Schelling had a doctorate in philosophy and theology but had also studied natural science, especially physics and chemistry. In other words, there was in intellectual circles both some knowledge of contemporary scientific achievements and the expectation of such knowledge – all the more so at a time when sciences were making the sort of progress which impressed a wider public. Yet, even if the conditions for cross-fertilization were there, it is not clear what form this cross-fertilization could have taken, beyond the standard mentioning by the practitioners of one discipline of the successes of the other and the adherence to a general climate of opinion in which scientific knowledge, with its cumulative values, could easily be taken as the model of knowledge in general. First, the Schlegels, the Bopps, the Grimms, in other words the pioneers of comparative linguistics in Germany, were less involved in scientific pursuits than the authors we have quoted. From this point of view they also differed from some of the polymaths involved in the collection and/or classification of languages: Pallas, Alexander von Humboldt, Balbi. Secondly the arts/science divide should not be envisaged in modern terms: in France at the turn of the century it was still possible to discuss whether natural history was only pure science or also a part of philosophy and eloquence (Corsi 1983, 59ff.). Then and later the scientists themselves were often prepared, as Coleman put it (1977, 12), to borrow their science from their metaphysics; in Germany they felt strongly the influence of Schelling's philosophy of nature, though we now do not think of it as particularly scientific (Nordenskiøld 1929, 273ff.). Conversely, it was all too easy for e.g. a linguist to borrow from the scientists not their exact methodology or results, which were often difficult if not impossible to apply to the subject in hand, but their general assumptions and the speculative part of their work. K. F. Becker, who was a practising doctor and wrote some scientific pamphlets, was clearly influenced both in these and in his linguistic work by the Scottish doctor John Brown (1735–88), the founder of the 'Brunonian' system of medicine, and by J. F. Blumenbach (1752–1840), the professor of *Vergleichende*

Anatomie at Göttingen, but he acquired from them in the one case the
principle that a stimulus from outside causes a reaction in the organism
and a consequent dualism, and in the other case the belief in a formative power characteristic of the organism (Haselbach 1966, 15ff., but
cf. Koerner 1975, 735ff.)

In general we are left with the impression that the frequent references to organisms, organic development, the life of the plants or of the
animals do not **necessarily** reflect a specific knowledge of biology even
if this was often available. In most instances it is not possible to say
whether they originate in scientific works or e.g. in Kant's third *Kritik*,
in Herder's general discussions, or in Schelling's vitalism.

Other scientific analogies present us with the same problems. Friedrich
Schlegel's comparison between comparative anatomy and comparative
grammar (see above), which is quoted by Bopp (1820, 15) and used by
Grimm (1819, xii), makes us think of Cuvier and the recent French
developments in comparative anatomy (Timpanaro 1972a, 95ff. = 1977,
xxxiv ff.; Koerner 1989, 275f.; 1995, 57ff.), but Schlegel does not
really explain what he has in mind, though in his time there were serious disagreements about the nature, methods and aims of anatomy. He
may have wanted to refer to Cuvier's work, but he may have also
thought of an earlier tradition or more simply of comparative anatomy
in general without any further distinctions.[8] Certainly his brother alluded
to Cuvier when he pushed the comparison further and postulated the
future reconstruction of the lost parent language (A. W. Schlegel [1833]
1846, iii, 62ff.; cf. Timpanaro 1973, 561f.). Elsewhere we find references
to chemistry, another successful science of the period. Julius Klaproth,
the learned fieldworker and author of *Asia polyglotta*, defended his
thesis that genealogical comparison had to be based on words and
not on grammar, saying that 'Linguistic comparison works chemically
and analytically, without considering the form [i.e. the grammar]' ('Die
Sprachvergleichung geht chemisch und analytisch zu Werke, ohne auf
die Form zu sehen'; Klaproth 1823, x). It has also been argued that
Bopp too was influenced by chemistry (Zwirner and Zwirner 1966,
83f.).[9] But it is just this plurality of parallels which makes one inclined
not to give them too specific a meaning; their value may be generic or
they may mean different things. Thus when Friedrich Schlegel (1808,
41) spoke of the new linguistic study as really scientific (*wissenschaftlich*)[10] his formulation had different connotations from those of Max
Müller's phrase 'science of language'.[11] Much later, but still before
Max Müller, Jacob Grimm ([1851] 1864–90, i, 258ff.) saw at the age of
66 a similarity not only between the comparative methods of natural
history and those of linguistics but also between their modes of development. Botanists and anatomists, in his view, originally aimed at heal-
ing only; the advent of comparative studies led to a more scientific

approach characterized by the pursuit of knowledge for its own sake and by the removal of all restrictions in the scope of the enquiry. Similarly, classical philologists originally studied the ancient languages with the only aim of emending their texts; the advent of comparative linguistics, catalysed by the increase in linguistic knowledge and by the 'discovery' of Sanskrit, introduced a new scientific dimension. This is the type of sober account which would have probably been accepted by most of the early comparativists; it clarifies what is meant by science and at the same time postulates parallel developments between the natural sciences and linguistics rather than a definite influence of one on the other.[12] At the same time the organicism shared by both sciences and arts underlines and guarantees the unity of knowledge (Schmidt 1992).

4.4.1 Biology and linguistics: principles of classification

Some scepticism towards the repeated claims about a **concrete** influence of the sciences on linguistic thought or methodology is justified, but there is one field in which the connections between linguistic and scientific (mainly biological) work are real. The explosion of new linguistic material inevitably called the attention of those interested in language to the problems of classification and here they found themselves confronted with the much wider range of discussions about taxonomic principles which had dominated the study of plants and animals for more than a century. The Linnean classification, which gained incredible fame starting with the first part of the eighteenth century, was based on a series of hierarchical categories: each 'kingdom' dominated a hierarchy of four levels: class, order, genus and species (later a 'family' level was introduced between order and genus). Animals and plants were classified 'downward' by logical division on the basis of a character or set of characters previously identified. For the plants Linnaeus fixed on the reproduction system of the flowers, and the number, shape, proportion and situation of stamens and pistils allowed him to distinguish 24 different classes. The classification was, to use the contemporary technical term, 'artificial', in that the characters chosen were arbitrary and no overt attempt was made to justify the choice in terms of e.g. functionality or to base the classification on a combination of different characters or on differently weighted characters. The second part of the eighteenth century (after the publication in 1758 of the tenth edition of Linnaeus' *Systema Naturae*) saw a series of attempts to move towards a 'natural' classification: some characters had greater information powers than others and could be given prominence, different characters or character clusters could be used for different families. Changes in the general understanding of how organisms worked had a part to play. Whoever accepted the principles of correlation of parts and subordination of characters discovered by Georges Cuvier (1769–1832) would have found it difficult to use isolated features for classification. But also the followers of Étienne Geoffroy Saint-Hilaire (1772–1844), who was more interested in structural correlations and believed that structure determines function (rather than vice versa), did not operate in terms of isolated characters; on the contrary, homologies (analogies, in the language of the time) between very different organisms were established taking into account the position, the relation and the dependencies of the parts. Earlier on similar points had been made by the German supporters of idealistic morphology, headed by Goethe, who aimed at identifying for all major organisms an *Urbild* (archetype) which had the basic characteristics of the actual individuals. Gradually the downward classification based on logical principles was replaced by an upward classification based on inspection and on a multitude of empirical criteria which were used to classify plants and animals into hierarchical groups. At the same time the concept of 'natural' kept changing: for Linnaeus, who thought that a natural classification might eventually be possible, it referred to the true nature of things or species, i.e. to their essence (which was divinely determined); for others it meant rational and in agreement with the laws which determine natural events; for others it simply meant 'empirical'. The concept of *scala naturae* was also relevant. Scientists such as Blumenbach or Lamarck were ready to accept that organisms could be arranged according to their affinity on a scale of increasing perfection: a correct 'natural' classification ought to reveal the arrangement of the *scala naturae*. On the other hand, there were those such as Cuvier who believed that all animals were to be classified into four phyla, with no connection between them, thus denying the existence of a continuous scale. The question of evolution can be left aside at this stage since it will have to be considered later, but it is clear that every classification of organisms may end by asking whether there is an evolutionary link between them and whether a 'natural' classification must in fact be based on historical development.[13]

The linguists had similar problems, e.g. if classification was based on similar characters, what characters mattered? Was it useful to distinguish between artificial and natural classification for languages? The parallelism between their task and that of the zoologists, comparative anatomists and botanists was obvious – all the more so in a period in which languages were automatically equated with organisms. The young Rask proposed a categorization of languages into race, class, stock, branch, language and dialect which deliberately matched that of Linnaeus (Diderichsen 1960, 139; 1974, 298); his fellow countryman J. H. Bredsdorff wrote both about linguistic change and about the rules to follow in classifying natural objects ([1821] 1970, 1817). In 1812 Humboldt (1903–36, iii, 326) aimed at identifying 'natural classes of languages such as those established by natural scientists' ('des classes naturelles des langues telles que les établissent les naturalistes');[14] Balbi, as we have seen (p. 42), spoke of a 'kingdom' of languages; and finally the references to comparative anatomy which we quoted above may also be seen in the light of classification problems. However, on one point the linguists had the edge and did not take second place: differently from the scientists, they were ready to think in terms of genetic classification at a time when most biologists did not yet believe in the possibility of a classification of natural organisms based on descent. Yet this did not solve all problems. First, not all languages could be neatly slotted into language families: did that mean that they could not be classified? Secondly, it was not clear how far up the hierarchy the genealogical classification could go: Balbi's discussion is revealing (p. 42f.). In 1813 Thomas Young (1773–1829), the English physicist and Egyptologist to whom we probably owe the word Indo-European (see below, p. 147, note 8), in reviewing Adelung's *Mithridates* stressed the importance of the classification adopted. He continued: 'A perfect natural order of arrangement in treating of the peculiarities of different languages, ought to be regulated by their descent from each other and their historical relations; a perfect artificial order ought to bring together into the same classes all those genera which have any essential resemblances, that is, such as are not fortuitous, nor adoptive, nor imitative or derived from onomatopoeia' ([Young] 1813–14, 252). Here the natural vs. artificial distinction is seen as coterminous with genealogical vs. typological and Young takes for granted that the natural classification is that by descent. Yet Humboldt, who was perhaps of all comparativists the one who had the clearest ideas about the distinction between the two types of classifications, required a 'natural' classification 'indépendamment des affinités historiques'. When Pott (1833–6, I, xxvi) speaks of a physiological (i.e. typological) classification, the choice of the adjective is not unimportant: he must have in mind a classification which takes into account the whole organism of language (cf. Humboldt's similar usage, e.g. in GS iv, 7ff.; *Einl.* cxxi; GS vii, 98). Years later, Pott (1856, 191) wished for a linguistic Linnaeus who would classify the languages of the world into families, genera, species and other subdivisions, not on the basis of an artificial arrangement, but rather on that of a 'natural' classification in the sense of Jussieu; here the assumption is that languages can be 'naturally' classified in a non-genealogical manner. Pott also clarified aims and results of the two types of classification: the classification of natural history, if applied to languages, could not provide evidence about an original unity of languages as the genealogical classification. On the other hand, physiological classification could order all languages on a scale from the lowest to the highest and the noblest, as was done for the animal kingdom. Elsewhere (e.g. 1852, 514) Pott had also raised the other fundamental problem: change impinges on the whole organism of language, does it mean that if we established a non-genealogical classification like that of natural history we would then find that linguistic change can lead to a change of linguistic type? The question about the immutability or otherwise of the species had of course haunted scientific discussion; it now raised its head in linguistics. And indeed Friedrich Schlegel's distinction between two great classes of organic or inflectional and non-organic or non-inflectional languages (cf. above, pp. 68, 73) was based on the assumption that languages could not change type.

We shall return to linguistic typology in connection with Humboldt but at this stage we need to retain two points. First, in the case of classification there is a direct connection between linguistic and scientific theories; at the beginning of the century linguistics is still at the receiving end but things will change. Secondly, it is in the context of classification that the organic model comes into its own. Both for genealogical and for typological classification the emphasis is on the comparison of the whole organism: on the one hand the grammar rather than the lexicon, on the other not an individual character *à la* Linnaeus but a whole constellation of them (which again may mean grammar rather than lexicon). Here too the linguists are in tune with the scientists: the history of classification in the late eighteenth and early nineteenth centuries consists in an attempt to move away from 'une théorie de la marque' towards 'une théorie de l'organisme' (Foucault 1966, 158).

Notes

1. This is not the place to discuss Herder's importance and his influence on the German thought of the nineteenth century; cf. e.g. Gipper-Schmitter (1979, 60ff.) and for some more recent bibliography the essays collected in Koepke (1990).
2. Of course there is constant ambiguity – and not only in the terminology. *Historisch* may mean empirical; *Entwicklung* may refer to the development of a linguistic organism through (historical) time or to its unfolding while it progresses to its full form in a sort of metaphysical time. Some of Schlegel's passages quoted above (not all) could be 'ahistorical'; nevertheless the interest in the historical development of language is there.
3. The role of the organic concept in linguistics is widely discussed: see e.g. Cassirer (1945), Lepschy (1962), Haselbach (1966, passim), Rensch (1967), Brown (1967, 40ff.), Schlanger (1971), Picardi (1973 and 1977), Timpanaro (1972a = 1977 and 1973), Koerner (1975, 1989, 275ff., 1995, 50ff.), Löther (1984), Schmidt (1986, 1992), Percival (1987), R. Wells (1987), Morpurgo Davies (1987), Haßler (1991a, 114ff.), Schmitter (1992a and b).
4. Language as an organic whole (*organisches Ganze*) and the 'Organismus der Sprache' appear e.g. in a letter by Humboldt to Schiller written in 1795 (Seidel 1962, I, 150) and in a review of Bernhardi's *Sprachlehre* written

by A. W. Schlegel in 1803 (A. W. Schlegel 1846–7, xii, 152f.; cf. Percival 1987, 23, 35f. and Schmidt 1986, 61ff.).

5. The passage continues: '. . . history, which can be divided into internal and external'. This brings back considerably, at least from a terminological point of view, the distinction between internal and external history of a language; for its use in the last two decades of the century, cf. Varvaro ([1972–3] 1984, 25ff.), who regrets the lack of an early history of the dichotomy. Such a history should certainly refer to Renan's ([1855] 1858, x) very clear account of the contrast between 'extérieure' and 'intérieure' found in the 1855 preface to his *Histoire des langues sémitiques*.

6. Becker (1775–1849) is a complex figure. His work (see above all Becker 1827) belongs within the tradition of philosophical grammar and his aim is to produce a general grammar valid for all languages and based on the assumption that there is a universal semantic structure (Itkonen 1991, 281f.); from this point of view he is at opposite poles from Jacob Grimm. Yet his organicistic views are clearly derived from those of Schelling and of Romanticism. In his case, however, organicism is not connected with historicism nor with the link between language and nation; he uses it to justify his theory of grammar and above all his syntactical analysis, which is based on binary divisions (*Sein* and *Tätigkeit*, Subject and Predicate, etc.). The organic apparatus is singularly obscure and was attacked by Steinthal (1855), who, given his connection with Heyse (Becker's rival in the market of German textbooks), was not unbiased, as absurd and the 'emptiest nothing'. On the other hand, the syntactical analysis is extremely important. It dominated the tradition of German school grammars for more than half a century, was even accepted in the rival grammars by Karl Heyse (Chorley 1984), and exercised its influence also on Jacob Grimm (Lühr 1989) and later on anyone who wrote about syntax. It is Becker who reanalysed the sentence identifying in all phrases or constituents three fundamental relationships (*Satzverhältnisse*): predicative, attributive and objective, with the additional observation that e.g. predicative phrases can turn into attributive phrases ('the king is famous' into 'the famous king'). Thanks to an English translation, *A Grammar of the German Language* (1830), Becker's thought was also influential in English school grammars of the second part of the century (Beyer 1981, 136f.; Michael 1987, 370) and his influence reached Switzerland, Russia and the Netherlands (Haselbach 1966, 66; Van Driel 1992, 234ff.). See in general Weigand (1966), Haselbach (1966), Ott (1975), as well as the various monographs on the development of German grammar (Glinz 1947, Forsgren 1973 and 1990, Naumann 1986, etc.) and Graffi (1991, 34ff., 237ff., 272ff.). Knobloch (1989a and b) offers an analysis of pre- and post-Becker German grammars (cf. also Knobloch 1988, *passim*).

7. Steinthal (1855, 129) makes this clear: 'Organism, organ are in Humboldt, when applied to language, merely a clarifying image, without wisecracks, as those found in Becker and frequently elsewhere, and without mysticism, as in Friedrich Schlegel.' Picardi (1977), while also referring to this passage, stresses that the concept of organism adopted by Humboldt is in fact closer to that of the Kant of the third *Kritik* than to that of Romanticism. An 1827 letter by Humboldt to Becker, who had dedicated to him his

Organismus der Sprache (Haselbach 1966, 269–71), highlights the differences in their organicistic views. Humboldt is not ready to accept Becker's logicism, or to derive language wholesale from the idea of organism and the contrasts inbuilt in it; language is for him the necessary vehicle of thought in men and of communication in life; hence it must be derived 'from an examination of the whole nature of the individual man and of the whole position of mankind according to space and time'. Similarly, grammar arises for him 'from an enquiry into the conditions necessary for the formation of comprehensible discourse'.

8. To refer to comparative anatomy was fashionable; Herder does so frequently and once ([1784] 1877–1913, xiii, 69) he mentions in this connection the name of L.-J.-M. Daubenton, Buffon's assistant, together with that of an older pioneer, C. Perrault (1613–88) and that of Pallas. Humboldt ([1795] 1903–36, i, 377) in discussing in 1795 his plans for a comparative anthropology writes that comparative anatomy explains the constitution of the human body through the analysis of the body of animals. He may have thought of the Dutch professor P. Camper (1722–89), whom he quotes elsewhere and who had written on this subject, or of J. F. B. Blumenbach, who had obtained a chair at Göttingen thanks to his dissertation on human races and who had introduced comparative anatomy in Germany before Cuvier (Marino 1976, 16ff.). In any case, Humboldt had discussed comparative anatomy with Goethe and had followed courses in the subject (Quillien 1991, 369f.). Shortly before Schlegel and in a different context, James Ingram, the Rawlinson professor of Anglo-Saxon at Oxford, had spoken in his inaugural lecture (1807) of 'the comparative anatomy of the human language' (Aarsleff 1983, 172). In the same year the Göttingen orientalist, J. G. Eichhorn (1752–1827) aimed at 'grammatical anatomy of all languages' (Schmidt 1986, 72f.). As for Schlegel, probably he wanted to stress with his comparison the importance of an analysis of the internal structure, i.e. the grammar, of a language; animals, it had been argued even before Cuvier, should be classified according to the nature of their organs rather than to superficial characters (Corsi 1983, 46).

9. Aarsleff (1983, 89ff.) shows how relevant the contemporary successes of chemistry are to the persistent success of Horne Tooke in England: Tooke 'treated words as chemists do substances', as was said at the time. It is quite likely, as is hinted above, that the scientific parallels found in our authors had a similar effect in their time and in their country. What is more difficult to envisage is how a discipline which was moving towards very technical levels of work could borrow its exact methodology from another science, but for the later parallelism between chemistry and the argumentation first of Schopenhauer and then of Frege, cf. Picardi (1992).

10. Five years earlier August Wilhelm Schlegel ([1803] 1846–7, xii, 152f.), in tracing a programme for the combination of 'special grammar' and philosophy and for the comparison of what we now call the Indo-European languages, had concluded that as a result *Philologie* would increasingly become a real *Kunst*. We should probably remember the eighteenth-century distinction between *science, art,* and *pratique.* In the article *Grammaire* of the *Encyclopédie* the *grammaire générale* is treated as a science ('la science

raisonnée des principes immuables & généraux de la parole . . .') while the *grammaire particulière* is an art ('l'art d'appliquer aux principes immuables & généraux de la parole . . . les institutions arbitraires & usuelles d'une langue particulière'); cf. Auroux (1973, 67).

11. It is more difficult to know what Balbi (1826b, xliii) meant when he spoke of a *linguistique élevée au rang des sciences*. Balbi himself was trained as a scientist and was explicitly concerned with linguistic classification, i.e. with a field in which a certain amount of interdisciplinary contacts did indeed take place (see below).

12. Grimm's account was not new. In 1833 A. W. Schlegel (1846, iii, 62ff.) had also seen the development of comparative linguistics as matching that of comparative anatomy (cf. Timpanaro 1973, 561f.). Similar views were also expressed in England by the Rev. Richard Garnett (1859, 2; cf. above, p. 59). In 1835, while rejecting the etymologies *à la* Tooke, he attacked those who sneered at all interlinguistic comparison of words and reminded them that fifty or sixty years earlier it would have been equally easy to wonder why one should collect unsightly fragments of bones, while now 'after the brilliant discoveries of Cuvier and Buckland' no one would dare to ask such a question.

13. Most of what precedes is a grossly inadequate summary of the relevant parts of Mayr (1982, especially 147ff.).

14. Note, however, that Humboldt continues with a disclaimer: 'though in the case of an object of very different nature one must be careful not to want to follow the same path as they [viz. the natural scientists] do' ('quoiqu'il faille bien se garder de vouloir avec un objet d'une toute autre nature suivre la même route qu'eux'). Cf. Trabant (1986, 182).

5

Wilhelm von Humboldt, general linguistics and linguistic typology

5.1 An embarrassing thinker

Whoever is concerned with the development of the craft of linguistics in the nineteenth century must see Wilhelm von Humboldt as an object of both wonder and embarrassment. Historiographically everything about him is controversial. Does he intellectually belong in the eighteenth or in the nineteenth century? In linguistics does he count as an amateur or a professional? And where does his strength lie, in historical-comparative linguistics or in universal grammar? What do his most famous pronouncements about *innere Sprachform*, language as *energeia*, etc. really mean? In general do we understand his main tenets or is his obscurity overpowering? What led him to linguistics: German philosophy or the French Enlightenment? If the former, whose thought was most influential on him: Kant's or Herder's or Fichte's? And what about his fortune in linguistics: did he determine the future developments or did his successors see him as a negligible entity? Was he more influential in the nineteenth or in the twentieth century? Finally, what does Humboldt mean to us nowadays? Is he still a living force or someone long since forgotten? Each one of these questions has been answered, and reputably answered, in diametrically opposite fashions. Hence Humboldt has a place of honour in Chomsky's *Cartesian Linguistics* (1966), but also in Jespersen's (1922) and Leroy's (1971) accounts of nineteenth-century linguistics; is admired by a behaviourist such as Bloomfield and imitated by an idealist such as Vossler. For Cassirer and his later followers Humboldt's linguistic thought must be seen within a German tradition inspired by Kant and Herder, while for Aarsleff linguistics acquired a central position in Humboldt's thought as the result of his stay in Paris (1798–1801) and his main ideas were reached on the basis of his reading of Condillac done under the influence of the *idéologues*.[1] Finally, even in the historiography of the comparativists, Humboldt's fortune is varied: Benfey deeply respected him, even if with some reservations (Schmitter 1991b, 7), but Pedersen ([1931] 1962) hardly mentions him and he plays no real role in the first edition of Delbrück's *Einleitung* (1880), while the fourth edition (1904) gives a detailed account of his work (Koerner 1989, 6f.).[2]

5.2 Life and works

Chronologically Wilhelm von Humboldt's life is placed exactly between the two centuries: he was born in 1767 and died in 1835, leaving behind a series of essays of a literary, political/historical, anthropological and above all linguistic nature. His *Nachlass* included a large number of unfinished works on all subjects. An unfinished book was published posthumously with a preface by Wilhelm's brother, the famous explorer, geographer, ethnographer, polymath Alexander von Humboldt, and became perhaps the best known of his works: the *Einleitung über die Verschiedenheit des menschlichen Sprachbaues und ihren Einfluss auf die geistigen Entwickelung des Menschengeschlechts* (1836) is a lengthy theoretical introduction (a book in its own right) to the unfinished three volumes *Über die Kawi Sprache auf der Insel Java* (1836–39).[3] The two Humboldts belonged to the Prussian upper classes; this background allowed Wilhelm to alternate long periods of public service (often abroad) with equally long periods of study and reflection (mostly in Germany). Both his origin and his early training (at the Universities of Brandenburg in Frankfurt a.O. and of Göttingen) favoured his contacts with the most lively part of German culture: he became a friend of F. A. Wolf, of Schiller and of Goethe, but at Göttingen he also followed the courses of the great classicist C. G. Heyne and of the historian A. L. Schlözer, who, according to Humboldt's own statement (GS, vi, 136), was the first after Leibniz to have understood the real concept of linguistics and had drawn the guidelines for a reliable *Sprachkritik*, while also knowing 'an astonishing number of languages', including American Indian languages.[4] As minister in the Prussian legation at Rome, director of culture and education at Berlin responsible for a reform of secondary education and the foundation of the University of Berlin; Prussian ambassador at Vienna representing Prussia at the Vienna Congress; Ambassador in London; again Minister in Berlin, etc. Humboldt had considerable influence. Opinions about the value of his education reforms differ but, whatever their intrinsic validity, they had profound importance for the future of the new comparative linguistics. On the one hand in the Prussian Gymnasia the emphasis was firmly laid on the *humanistisches* side of training and particularly on Greek and Latin, two subjects which formed one of the indispensable foundations of the new discipline; on the other hand, the importance given to research and academic freedom in the University could only favour the new subject. Above all the appointment of Franz Bopp to a chair in the new University of Berlin provided that institutional breakthrough which determined the future of the subject. Finally, to have a patron such as Humboldt who was actively interested in languages as different as the classical languages, Basque, the indigenous languages of the two Americas, the Indonesian and Polynesian languages, who was so entirely au fait with the progress of the discipline, and who had actually taken the trouble to learn Sanskrit, could only give the new subject a very much needed accolade. Were it only for this Humboldt would deserve a place of honour in the history of the craft of linguistics. There is of course much more.

We can look at Humboldt the linguist in at least four different ways: first, as a theoretical linguist who tried to tackle within a new framework the problems about language which he had inherited from a long tradition which went back to the Greeks, but was also eager to base his work on an empirical basis. It is not difficult to see why Bloomfield (1933, 18) spoke of the posthumous introduction to the *Kawi Sprache* as of 'the first great book on general linguistics'; it was indeed the first book of general linguistics to be written by someone who had absorbed, and contributed to, the methods and results of the empirical approach of the nineteenth century. The 1836 book was not isolated: the numerous earlier monographs and essays do indeed count as works of general linguistics. Secondly, there is the descriptive linguist: starting with his work on Basque (from 1800), Humboldt was an indefatigable collector of linguistic data (mostly from written material; sometimes, as in the case of Basque, through fieldwork as well): from American Indian languages to Chinese, to the Polynesian languages, to Sanskrit. His linguistic library was second to none (Mueller-Vollmer 1993, 14ff.) and he himself prepared a series of grammars of different languages which remain largely unpublished (but see Humboldt 1994). Thirdly, Humboldt counts as one of the most important figures in the history of linguistic typology. The fact that already in the nineteenth century the highly successful typological classification of all languages of the world into isolating, agglutinative and inflectional (with a possible fourth category of incorporating languages) was wrongly attributed to Humboldt shows how influential he was believed to be. Round the middle of the century, when scholarship and above all German scholarship concentrated on the most technical questions of comparative reconstruction, Humboldt's followers, such as Pott and Steinthal, kept a lively interest in language typology and came to see its study as the contemporary replacement for the old *grammaire générale*. Fourthly, there is Humboldt the historical and comparative linguist. Delbrück (1880, 27) pointed out that it was

difficult to see any specific conclusion which Humboldt had contributed to Indo-European linguistics, though great Indo-Europeanists had
acknowledged his influence. One should remember, however, that
Humboldt's 'Essay on the Best Means of Ascertaining the Affinitiès of
Oriental Languages', read at the Royal Asiatic Society of London in 1828
and published in 1830 (GS, vi, 78–84), offers the most lucid explanation (and exemplification) of the basic principles of the comparative
method and at the same time makes the all important distinction between
structural similarity (which defines typological links) and similarity of
'grammatical forms, considered with respect to their system and their
sounds taken conjointly', which defines genetic affinity.[5] Moreover, and
this should not be forgotten, we owe to Humboldt the beginning of the
historical and comparative grammar of the Malayo-Polynesian languages
and it is exactly in the work about these languages that he showed his
mastery of the basic methodology of historical and comparative linguistics,constantly breaking new ground in an extraordinarily difficult
field (Percival 1974b; cf. also Buchholz 1986).[6]

5.3 The path towards linguistics

We must explore some of these motifs in more detail but first something must be said about Humboldt's progress towards linguistics. We
depend for this both on the work published during Humboldt's lifetime,
including some substantial essays presented from 1920 onwards to the
Prussian Academy at Berlin and published in its Proceedings, and on
a number of (mostly incomplete) manuscripts published after his death,
in addition to his voluminous correspondence and his diaries. In his
autobiographical fragment he remarks about his incapacity to complete
the numerous projects that he started.[7] There is little doubt that even the
very early work about literature or anthropology or indeed translation
(Humboldt was fascinated by the concrete problem of translating Greek
literature)[8] contains points which reveal considerable interest in language:
we quoted above (p. 94 note 4) Humboldt's 1795 reference to language
as an organism, which occurs in the context of a discussion about the
correct way to translate Homer. Humboldt was a notable classicist; from
his studies in classical philology and his contacts with Heyne's and
Wolf's scholarship he acquired a deep respect for that type of critical
analysis of both language and culture which was based on a detailed
knowledge of facts historically attested. On the other hand, an early unpublished fragment *Über Denken und Sprechen* (GS, vii, 581–3), which
belongs sometime in the 1790s, is far more abstract and represents
Humboldt's first explicit statement about thought and the articulation of
speech; he still thinks in terms of linguistic signs, a conception which
he will later reject. This is also the period of anthropological work and

of the projects for a comparative anthropology (Leroux 1958; Marino 1976; Quillien 1991, 333ff.).[9] Between the end of the eighteenth and the beginning of the nineteenth century, during or perhaps after a period spent at Paris, language becomes a primary interest. In 1802 a letter to Schiller confirms that *Sprachstudium* has kept him seriously engaged for a long time, that he has a plan for a general encyclopedia of all linguistic study and all languages, and that all linguistics must be combined in his view with philosophy and *Völkerstudium* (Seidel 1962, II, 221). And in 1805, writing to Wolf, he reiterates that all that he is doing is *Sprachstudium*. Meanwhile he had done a considerable amount of work about Basque to which he also brought his general anthropological interests; the results are the contribution to *Mithridates* (see above, p. 41) and a later (1821) book about the first populations of Spain, where he tried to link the Basques to the ancient Iberians.[10] Basque was just the beginning: during his Roman period (1802–8) Humboldt was able to exploit the Jesuits' archives and some of the data provided by Hervás in order to start a serious study of American Indian languages, which was later helped by the data provided by his brother on his return from his American travels (1799–1804) and even later by the important correspondence with North American scholars.[11] This he continued later on at Vienna (1810–15), when he also learned Hungarian and the Slavic languages, and the interest persisted after he relinquished his political offices in 1819 and dedicated himself to scholarship. At that stage he also found at long last the time to start seriously working at Sanskrit, a subject he had discussed in London with Wilkins and Bopp, and which came to occupy a considerable part of his intellectual life, not least because of frequent meetings with Bopp after his call to Berlin and of an increasingly important exchange of letters with A. W. Schlegel, now professor at Bonn. An article about the Sanskrit gerunds, papers about the *Bhagavad-gītā* and its translations prove that he reached a good level of competence. The bulk of his theoretical production belongs to the 1820s: two general essays, *Über das vergleichende Sprachstudium in Beziehung auf die verschiedenen Epochen der Sprachentwicklung* of 1820–1 (GS, iv, 1–34) and *Über das Entstehen der grammatischen Formen und deren Einfluss auf die Ideenentwicklung* of 1822–3 (GS, iv, 285–313), already contain *in nuce* most of Humboldt's general ideas about the intellectual development of language, the link between language and cognitive processes, the type of work to be done in comparative linguistics,[12] etc., as well as copious references to Amerindian languages.

Also between 1823 and 1824 some works (published and unpublished) reflect Humboldt's interest in writing, partly prompted by his interest in Champollion's findings, partly by his belief that it was possible to produce a typology of writing as important as that of language (De Meo 1990; Stetter 1990; Gessinger 1994, 704ff.). From this period dates his concern with Chinese and with the differences between its structure and that of the Western languages, which led to the publication of the famous *Lettre à M. Abel Rémusat sur la nature des formes grammaticales en général et sur le génie de la langue chinoise en particulier* ([1827] GS, v, 254–308) and of a further paper on the grammatical structure of Chinese presented to the Prussian Academy (*ibid.*, v, 309–24). Again in 1827 appeared the first detailed typological discussion of a grammatical phenomenon: *Über den Dualis* (GS, v, 4–143) discusses use and function of the dual in the languages of the world, starting with a brief account of the types of dual that are attested and of the language groups in which they appear (cf. Plank 1989); part of the material reveals Humboldt's newly found interest in the Indonesian languages. The promise of a further detailed analysis was never kept but at least another paper (about the relationship of local adverbs and pronouns in a number of languages) fits in the same typological mould (GS, vi, 304–30). The most productive years before the end of his life are dedicated to the study of language diversity from a theoretical point of view: the *Grundzüge des allgemeinen Sprachtypus* ([1824–6] GS, v, 364–473) preceded two major works, neither of which appeared in his lifetime: *Über die Verschiedenheiten des menschlichen Sprachbaues* (GS, vi, 111–203) and the Introduction to the Kawi work mentioned above (*Einl.*; GS, vii, 1–344). The latter was in fact the general introduction to two volumes of strictly descriptive and comparative analysis – on the one hand of the literary form of old Javanese (Kawi = the language of the poets), a language which we would now label as Western Malayo-Polynesian and which was very heavily influenced by Sanskrit, on the other hand of a number of other Indonesian languages. The work was prepared for publication and in parts integrated by Humboldt's assistant, J. C. Eduard Buschmann, who later acquired fame as one of the first scholars to attempt a genetic classification of the Indian languages of North America.[13]

5.4 Linguistic diversity and Humboldt's working programme

In the 1820s the count of Volney had conceived of a philosophical study of language which, while being data-oriented, would also be aware of more general problems such as that of the origin of the faculty of speech. Humboldt's work reminds us of this programme. From this point of view it naturally finds its place within a set of aspirations which were not alien to either the German tradition, as represented e.g. by Herder, or the French tradition, and which, in the last resort, went back to Leibniz. There is little doubt that one of Humboldt's aims was that of using language to solve more general problems, the link between language and thought, the progress of the intellectual development of mankind. At the same time, however, he knew that the empirical work was bound to call into question our understanding of what language is. Even more than his contemporaries he was obsessed by the existence of language variation both in time and in space. How could any general conclusion about e.g. cognitive processes be based on the study of language if the extent of the differences between languages had not been previously explored and its consequences assessed? One might say that in linguistics Humboldt dedicated his life work to an attempt at reconciling language variation with the universality of language.[14] Hence his efforts to acquire a firsthand acquaintance with the major language groups; hence, for instance, his turning to the Malayo-Polynesian languages when he began to feel that they perhaps provided an intermediate type between Chinese and, e.g. the languages of India. On the other hand, nothing of what he learned convinced him that there was no such thing as 'language' as a unitary faculty. The beginning of *Über die Verschiedenheiten des menschlichen Sprachbaues* is just a reiteration of his belief that the aim of linguistics, a subject which Humboldt deliberately called *allgemeine Sprachkunde* rather than *Sprachenkunde*, is that of identifying the unity of language while accounting for the variation (GS, vi, 111f.). The statement is even clearer in the conclusion of the same work (301f.). We are first told that it stands to reason that even languages of different families and different classes must have features in common, since this follows from the identity of human nature and human phonetic apparatus; this is also concretely demonstrated by the fact that speakers of different languages can learn to understand each other: 'the laws of thought are the same in all nations and the grammatical forms which depend on these laws can differ only within certain limits. . . . Just as one can affirm that every language, every dialect is different, from another point of view one can also bring forward the proposition that for mankind there is only one language and there has only been one from the beginning'.[15]

Yet general conclusions cannot be reached without first studying the individual languages. Humboldt defines for comparative study a programme of work which he tries to implement himself. What is needed is (a) individual monographs about all existing languages, (b) studies of individual linguistic features (e.g. the verb) through all languages.[16] Only when this is done will it be possible on the one hand to think in terms of a classification of languages, on the other to reach historical conclusions based on language kinship (GS, iv, 10f.).

For the first task the constant references to language as organism acquire a methodological value. As we have seen (p. 86ff.), the various meanings attached to this typical nineteenth-century metaphor are all present in Humboldt, together with a clear awareness that the metaphor is just that, a metaphor. In most instances, however, the organic meta-phor, and even more its concrete applications, acquire in him a struc-turalist flavour. General observations such as 'There is nothing isolated in language; each element appears only as part of a whole', (GS, iv, 14–15) are also translated into a firm working programme: 'The first rule is therefore to study each known language in its internal connec-tions, to follow all the possible analogies (in each language) and to order them systematically . . .', in other words, to prepare 'monographs for the whole language' (*ibid.*, 11) before the actual comparison starts. In the context of this programme it is necessary to define the correct criteria for description: 'since normally we come to the study of an unknown language from the point of view of a known language, be it our mother tongue or Latin, we try to see the grammatical relationships of this language expressed in the new one . . . ; to avoid this mistake we must study each language in its peculiarities, so that we may recog-nize through correct segmentation of its elements what special forms it employs, in terms of its own constitution, to indicate the grammatical relationships' (*ibid.*, iv, 288–9; cf. also v, 260–1; 1836–9, ii, 117).[17] The essay about the origin of grammatical forms lists a number of examples in Amerindian languages where the desire to find the well-known parts of speech in an exotic language led the observer to the wrong conclu-sions (GS, iv, 35ff.). In this general context attention is also drawn not only to the systematic, self-contained nature of each language as contrasted with other languages, but also to the difference between a descriptive approach which corresponds to the speaker's knowledge of his or her own language and a historical approach which calls for a work of reconstruction and analysis. The clearest application of these concepts emerges in the discussion of the Javanese verb. Humboldt (1836–9, ii, 86ff.) succeeds in showing, in contrast with earlier accounts, that in Javanese stems are nominal in character and verbs may be derived from them with a prefix which, because of a number of phon-etic changes, disappeared leaving behind a series of morphophonemic alternations between the first consonant of some verbs and that of the related nouns. He is at pains to explain that in this case speakers are not aware of prefixation and that for them the correct rule probably derives the nouns from the verbs, as was previously maintained. Hence, he argues, the earlier account was not wrong; we must realize that one thing is to set out rules which permit us to understand and speak a lan-guage (the aim of the first description), another is to enquire after the real and inner meaning of the grammatical forms and their original con-nection, or the way in which they originated (Humboldt's aim). The desire to return to the origins because of their explanatory value is not new, nor is the genetic approach; they belong both to the eighteenth and the nineteenth centuries. Yet the way in which the demonstration is conducted, the empirical, data-oriented analysis of linguistic data are new. Humboldt's argument is based both on internal evidence, since the morphophonemic rules are more comprehensible if the starting point is found in the nominal forms, and on historical-comparative evidence: the cognate forms of related languages and the Javanese nouns borrowed from Sanskrit show that while the consonantism of the verb changes, the nouns keep their original form. In his constant awareness of how a historical and comparative analysis can be conducted, in the primacy given to the data over the theory, Humboldt is a 'nineteenth-century' man, even if his range of interests and his philosophical awareness are so much wider than those of the nineteenth-century 'technicians'. His search for the origins does not lead him into the pitfalls of confusing synchrony with diachrony, meaning with etymology; not only does he point out the distinction, but he does not forget it when confronted with an actual problem of analysis.[18] Nor does he forget the lesson of empirical linguistics. As Stankiewicz (1974) has shown, Lord Monboddo, Herder, and the Dutch school had all argued for the priority (genetic and otherwise) of the verb on the noun in contrast with e.g. Condillac's view which pressed for a progress from the concrete (the noun) to the abstract (the verb). Humboldt himself elsewhere emphasizes the primary role of the verb, but in the context of an actual historical reconstruction the general 'philosophical' point is correctly ignored in favour of a strict adherence to the techniques of reconstruction.

5.5 Aims and justification

If the programme is that indicated, namely a twofold study of language diversity, what is the aim and what the justification? Here we find another form of tension in most of Humboldt's writings. On the one hand he pleaded for an autonomous linguistics; on the other he saw linguistics as one of the human sciences which obeys more general aims. Of comparative linguistics we are told in 1820 that it can only reach certain and meaningful results about language, the evolution of peoples and the *Bildung* of mankind, if it turns itself into a proper study which has its own use and purpose (GS, iv, 1).[19] Yet a few years later, after a statement that *Sprachstudium* must be pursued for its own sake, we are reminded that its ultimate aim is subordinate to the highest and most general aim of human spirit: mankind must clarify to itself what it really is and what its relations are to the visible and invisible things around it (GS, vi, 6; cf. Schmitter 1991b, 18ff.). The tension is only apparent. For Humboldt 'man is only man through language' and 'language, as *Sprachform*, is in fact the real condition of all intellectual activity and precedes, as their ideal essence, the actual linguistic manifestations' (Formigari 1988, 63). It should follow that to understand language (in its most general characteristics) also means to understand mankind. In fact this is the key to Humboldt's whole concept of language. He explains that it is all too natural for people to think of the different languages as different ways of indicating a mass of objects and concepts which have an independent existence of their own; the differences between languages are then taken as mere differences of sound. Yet this attitude is pernicious for linguistics. He continues: 'the real importance of linguistic study is in the participation of language in the formation of ideas [*Vorstellungen*]. Everything is included in this because the sum of these ideas is what makes man [*den Menschen*]' (GS, vi, 119). Language belongs to human beings, it has no other source than his existence; but, if language is identified with human beings, this is not merely with human beings conceived in general and metaphysical terms, but with a really existing, living man, conditioned by all the multifarious geographical and historical links typical of the physical world – not only with the individual, with the nations, with the generations of that specific time, but also with all peoples and all races which, however remote in time and space, have come in language contact with them (GS, vi, 120f.). In other words, it is languages rather than language that have the fundamental role. It then becomes possible to study on the one hand the various language organisms, on the other hand the languages in the course of their evolution and their intellectual maturation. The first study leads to an analysis of the physiology of language and of the speech faculty, the second considers the language in the phase of intellectual development as a means of formation of nations, of bondage between the elevated parts of mankind, but also of individuality and in the last resort of freedom (GS, iv, 8ff.). In this context the Humboldtian concept of language as inextricably tied to a worldview (*Weltansicht*) makes sense, as also makes sense Humboldt's desire to pursue the enquiry into the characters of languages and study languages, and this means literary languages, at the stage of their maximum perfection. Linguistics here falls together with art and science (GS, iv, 13ff.). Trabant (1990a, 138; cf. also 1986, 200ff.) explains Humboldt's statements about the autonomy of linguistics as being based on the Kantian discussion of the work of art which carries its purpose in itself, but one could extend to the language faculty Kant's statement in the third Critique that all higher faculties of the soul have an autonomy of their own. Moreover, if the supreme aim of linguistics is the understanding of mankind, linguistics contains its own purpose because in Humboldt's terms to understand mankind is to understand language.

The 'technicians' of the early and mid nineteenth century also called for an autonomous linguistics, or rather for a linguistics pursued for its own sake, but they sought no philosophical justification for their assertions, though implicitly or explicitly they accepted the view that language was an organism and that as all organized products of nature it contained its purpose (Morpurgo Davies 1987, 92ff.). Yet they were mostly reacting, as Humboldt also did, to the assumption that language studies were ancillary to those of history or literature. Some of the 'technicians', however, also took this fight for autonomy as a generic antiphilosophical fight, or, since 'philosophy' was an ill-defined concept, a fight against the old *grammaire générale* or against the use of logical concepts in language description or even against any attempt at generalization. Here Humboldt, while yielding to no one in his appreciation for a data-oriented approach which was actually based on the study of the existing languages, would have been reluctant to follow. His linguistics was *historische*, i.e. empirical, but also *allgemeine*, i.e. universal (GS, vi, 121), and he was keen to distinguish between those characteristics of each language which reflected 'the character of the nations' and those which were indeed universal. The passage of *Über die Verschiedenheiten des menschlichen Sprachbaues* quoted above continues with the statement that we owe to the Greeks all the fundamental ideas 'of the general philosophical grammar, from which all study of language must start' ('der allgemeinen philosophischen Grammatik, von welcher alle Sprachkunde zuerst ausgehen muss'; GS, vi, 112). [20]

5.6 The main problems

Any account of Humboldt's views must refer to those features of his thought which caught the imagination of future generations, even though they have been differently understood and their interpretation has been relentlessly discussed. They concern the old question of the origin of language, the concept of language as *energeia* rather than *ergon*, and the concept of *innere Sprachform*. We shall eventually turn briefly to his views of linguistic typology and to his concept of linguistic relativity. It goes without saying that anything said on subjects such as these and in this limited space is bound to be both incomplete and superficial.

'Man could not become man except by language; but in order to possess language he needed already to be man' (Humboldt GS, iv, 16). [21] If in Humboldt, who moves in a post-Kantian atmosphere, 'the notion of transcendental is moved from thought to language' (Formigari 1988, 63), it follows that there is no question of reconstructing an original language; mankind cannot get out of history to reconstruct a phase before history existed. Hence Humboldt's refusal to accept or reject the previous hypotheses about the origin of language – a step which led to a separation from the authors of the French Enlightenment but also from Leibniz, Herder and Fichte. [22] In this attitude Steinthal saw a complete alteration of the starting point of the discussion. Attention is necessarily translated from the problems of the origins to the problem of the nature of language and Humboldt reasserts his belief that this must exist as a whole (again the organic metaphor comes to the fore) in order to function at all; we cannot conceive of any form of communication which is half-way towards language and consequently any discussion of how man came to language is out of place.[23]

This clear rejection of a view of the origin of language grounded in time and space allows Humboldt to concentrate on what language is and how it is produced. Hence his insistence on language as product of a natural instinct like that of animals, with the difference, however, that this is an 'intellectual instinct of reason', it is less constricting and leaves room for the influence of individuals.[24] The product of human instinct can develop in different ways while the product of animal instinct keeps its homogeneity (GS, iv, 15f.). Here, as elsewhere, Humboldt is eager to explain the production of language in such a way that it can account for its universality and for its diversity. But language is not a mere product, a sort of object (*ergon*) which can be looked at and dissected; it is rather an activity, *energeia*, which is only capable of a genetic definition, 'the ever repeated mental labour of making the articulated sound capable of expressing thought' (*Einl.* lvii; GS, vii, 46; 1988, 49). This is true both of the individual act of speech and of the language; the customary sectioning into words and rules is merely a dead result of scientific analysis. Language is constantly created or re-created both by the individual and by the nation to which the individual belongs. The speaker (the individual) acts in unison with the hearer; both are involved in a creative activity (just like the child who learns to speak), both act as a limit and a stimulus for the activity and creativity of each other. One is unthinkable without the other, since 'understanding and speaking are but different effects of this power of speech [*Sprachkraft*]' (*Einl.* lxx; GS, vii, 56; 1988, 57). In this way Humboldt tackles the perennial problem of the nature of language which is dependent on the individual but is also dependent on the community, on the nation (cf. Steinthal [1851] 1858, 72ff.); while speech could in theory be an individual activity, listening or understanding could not. Yet all languages belong in a historical set-up and no nation or language of those known to us is original; it then follows that the mental activity which leads to the expression of thought operates on elements which are given and consequently is not a creative but a reshaping activity (*Einl.* lviii; GS, vii, 47; 1988, 49f.). In this way it becomes possible to account for historical development (the result of reshaping activity) and once again for linguistic diversity; in the act of production of speech the individuals exercise their own freedom. Different languages can then be tied to the differences in 'mental individuality' of each people; 'language is, as it were, the outer appearance of the spirit of a people; the language is their spirit and the spirit their language' (*Einl.* liii; GS, vii, 42; 1988, 46).[25]

In this context the omnipresent concept of 'form' in Humboldt can be explained. As shown by Coseriu (1970), the word is used in at least three different ways: with reference to language in general as form of comprehension of reality, with reference to an individual language and its own particular relationship with the extralinguistic world, and, finally, with reference to the forming principle of each language. In its more general meaning, form is any forming principle of language which has some character of generality and is dynamic rather than static: *forma formans* rather than *forma formata* (Beneš 1958, 3ff.; Gipper-Schmitter 1979, 82). *Innere Sprachform*, a term used but rarely in the *Einleitung* (Manchester 1985, 83), and which has given rise to endless discussion, may be taken as indicating the principle which determines the organization of grammar and lexicon in an individual language and which is invariably tied to the national character (Coseriu 1970). For Steinthal (1855, 374), who thought of himself as Humboldt's follower, languages differ because of their different phonological structures (*Lautform*) and their different *innere Sprachform*, but also because of the different way in which these two are linked: in different languages the same idea has different phonological expression.

Whatever the exact interpretation of Humboldt's theories, with hindsight there is no denying that they speak for a view of language as essentially a creative process in constant interaction with the result of this creation. It is of course this emphasis on creativity which has allowed Chomsky (1964, 1965, 1966), at the cost of some considerable anachronism, to see Humboldt as one of the precursors of generative grammar and to identify his *Gesetze der Erzeugung* with generative rules and his *innere Sprachform* with deep structure.[26] However, the same theories also underline the distinction between the work of the linguist, who in his analysis treats language as an object ready for the dissecting table, and the actual reality of language production, while stressing the various factors that conspire to make of language not only a tool for communication but also an expression of individuality and in some instances of aesthetic achievement: it is not surprising that later scholars such as Pott and Steinthal found in Humboldt support for their antinaturalistic views and that a much later exponent of linguistic idealism such as Vossler looked back at him as a source of inspiration. Finally, Humboldt's insistence on *innere Sprachform* as a principle of organization of the semantic and grammatical content of a language is taken as a starting point by the so-called neo-Humboldtians (Weisgerber, etc.) for their studies of the way in which the lexicon is differently structured in each language, thus revealing the particular *Weltansicht* of that language.[27]

5.7 Humboldt and linguistic typology

Humboldt, as we have seen, starts his essay *Über die Verschiedenheiten des menschlichen Sprachbaues* (GS, vi, 111) with a sentence which he will repeat at the beginning of the third volume of his Kawi book (1836–9, iii, 425): it is the important task of general *Sprachkunde* to investigate the variation in language structure. In *Über das vergleichende Sprachstudium* (*ibid.*, iv, 8f.) he had traced the programme of work which we have described above and which involves, on the one hand, the study of as many languages as possible, each considered as an organic whole, on the other hand, the examination of specific linguistic features which must be examined cross-linguistically while still bearing in mind the internal connection of each element with the other elements of the same language. It is important, of course, that Humboldt's own studies (description of American or Malayo-Polynesian languages on the one hand, analysis of e.g. the dual on the other) do to a certain extent follow this programme. The passage continues: 'Only in this way can we answer adequately the important question whether and how it is possible to subdivide languages, according to their internal structure [*Bau*], into classes, as one does for the families of plants' (GS, iv, 12).[28] In *Über die Verschiedenheiten* Humboldt defines for himself and his contemporaries the various ways in which languages may be seen to relate to each other:

1 Only languages in which we see identity or similarity of concrete grammatical forms belong to the same stock [*Stamm*];
2 Languages which do not have such a similarity of concrete grammatical forms but share a part of their vocabulary belong to the same area [*Gebiet*];
3 Languages which do not have common grammatical forms or common vocabulary but show similarity or identity of grammatical viewpoint [*Ansicht*] (in the linguistic form understood from a conceptual point of view) belong to the same class [*Classe*];
4 Languages which are not similar in either words, or grammatical forms or grammatical viewpoint, are unrelated [*fremd*] to each other and share only what is common to all human languages as such. (GS, vi, 294)

The clarity (particularly if compared with contemporary vagueness) is staggering.[29] There follows a discussion as to whether it is possible for genealogically related languages not to share concrete grammatical forms. Humboldt concludes that, even if that was possible, it would be likely that the languages in question belonged to the same class in the sense defined above. At this level then Humboldt operates with a concept of language class. Yet, in the very same work from which we have been quoting, Humboldt had explicitly renounced the possibility of a classification. He accepts the validity of a genealogical classification but doubts that it is feasible for all languages. He then considers the possibility of a structural classification of non-related languages based on some common structural characteristic, but rejects it because it would involve treating the languages as species, when in fact they must be treated as individuals, and also because it would be necessarily based on some specific character while languages must be considered as a whole. The passage ends with a denunciation of the parallelism with natural sciences, which never deal with the individual or the spiritual and consequently cannot provide a model for the classification of language (GS, vi, 150f.; cf. Trabant 1994, 22f.). In the Kawi *Einleitung*, however, it is stated that classificatory work may done for specific purposes, though it is doomed to failure if it aims at the essence of the languages and at their link with the spiritual individuality of nations (*Einl.* cccxlvii; GS, vii, 278). In other words, there is no necessary contradiction between Humboldt's references to language classes and his denial of a possibility of language classification. Nor is there contradiction between these statements and the observation that 'apart from Chinese, which dispenses with all grammatical forms' there are in languages 'three possible forms for the attainment of sentence making, the inflectional, the agglutinating and the incorporative' (*Einl.* cccxvii; GS, vii, 254; 1988, 216). Here Humboldt is simply defining three (or four) abstract **types** (or forms) of language and hastens to add that 'all languages carry one or more of these forms within them'.[30] There is no real attempt at introducing what later was taken to be the standard 'morphological' classification of languages into isolating (like Chinese), agglutinative (like Turkish), incorporating (like some Amerindian languages) and inflectional (like Indo-European). In a letter to Du Ponceau of 21 September 1827 Humboldt writes: 'I can say with certainty that it is not possible to divide languages into agglutinative and inflected languages. There is just a question of more or less which defines the character of languages, all of which are similar, since man is at the origin of all of them' (Swiggers 1994, 250; the last phrase is corrected from the text as suggested by Swiggers). On the other hand, there is here a first definition of the concept of language type in one of the two senses defined by Coseriu (1972, 1976), that of an ideal type against which actual languages can be measured. The other sense in which Humboldt uses linguistic type is even further from classification: for him the type or form of a language is the unifying and individuating principle of the structure of each language; it is what native speakers use as their guiding principle in the speech act and language learners must intuitively (and inductively) try to grasp before they can acquire the necessary competence in performance; it is the web of analogies which allows an external element to become acceptable because it is somehow annexed (cf. Di Cesare 1990b). Cassirer (1945) long since recognized in word and concept a sign of Goethe's influence on Humboldt.

Humboldt can then count as the real founder of nineteenth- and twentieth-century linguistic typology. He may have had predecessors, since it is a moot point whether e.g. l'abbé Girard and Adam Smith aimed at classification or at typology, but in his case the extent of the concern and the detailed level of discussion goes well beyond that of these earlier authors. With him the concept of type is also integrated into the general theory of language. On the other hand, he cannot count as the founder of language classification, as some of the nineteenth-century scholars wanted, nor should he be seen as the man who took over from August Wilhelm Schlegel and developed his thoughts.[31] This, as Steinthal knew, was due to a misunderstanding by Schleicher, which is comprehensible in the circumstances, but unfortunately had a much higher diffusion than it should have done.[32] Humboldt's merit in the history of the subject is to have shown the difficulties inherent in any attempt at linguistic classification and to have introduced a distinction between typology and classification which was far from clear in earlier (and later) authors (Coseriu 1972, 1976).

The passage about the various types of languages which we have just quoted continues: 'The distinction of **abstract** possible forms of language from the **concrete** ones that are actually present, will already contribute, I fancy, to a lessening of the uncongenial impression that I am singling out certain languages as the only legitimate ones, which automatically stamps the remainder as more imperfect' (*Einl.* cccxvii f.; GS, vii, 254; 1988, 216f.). This opens the way to a discussion of the different degrees of perfection in language types which reflects a number of similar statements elsewhere. While the organic/non-organic distinction of Schlegel is completely given up in Humboldt, and while he readily admits the typologically mixed character of individual languages, he nevertheless thinks that there is an ideal form of language and that in a sense all language types can be hierarchically arranged in a scale aiming at that ideal form, namely, inflection. It is easy to consider this attitude as determined by Eurocentrism, joined to incipient racism, but the latter is explicitly denied and we ought at least to try to find out what prompts Humboldt's attitude.[33] Since the categories considered are those that we mentioned earlier (isolating, agglutinative, inflected, etc.), and since these categories have been used for the so-called morphological classification, we must avoid assuming that they are morphological categories, in the modern sense of the word. Humboldt is concerned on the one hand with word formation, in so far as it defines syntactic categories, and on the other with syntax. The basic question concerns the way in which languages express concepts and their categorization in speech; the latter may have no formal identification or may be indicated by external additions to the word (which may or may not have a conceptual meaning of their own) or by an internal modification of the word (the *drive/drove* type). Inflected languages which make use of internal modification (as in the Semitic languages) or of accretions fused to the word (the endings of Greek or Sanskrit) reflect in the linguistic expression the mental phenomenon for which the concepts and their categorization form a unity. Those languages which use for the same purpose meaningful (i.e. conceptual) elements in sequence or in composition do not fulfil the purpose equally well because of the distracting value of the meaningful elements (*Einl.* cxxxv ff.; GS, vii, 108ff.). Isolating languages do not indicate categorization at all and in a sense do not fulfil the language's task. The categorized concept, however, must also enter into the sentence and indicate its relation to it. Here the inflected languages use inflection for this purpose just as they did for the categorization purpose; the isolating languages may use word order or *ad hoc* elements while the incorporating languages reduce the whole sentence to a word, though they often miss some basic indications or have to devise other schemata. The two extremes, isolating and inflected, have an internal coherence which is missing from the other type (*Einl.* clxxviii f., cc ff.; GS, vii, 143ff., 160ff.), but the inflected type again underlines the unit of the sentence while preserving the clarity of its component elements. Manchester (1985, 141) is probably right in assuming that for Humboldt inflection 'is "superior" because it is a method of symbolic designation which conforms more accurately to that which is symbolized (thought) than other methods do'. Hence also Humboldt's view that the inflected languages favour the process of thought in a way in which the less perfect languages do not – though Humboldt is eager to stress that everything can be expressed in every language, provided, of course, that the need arises. (GS, iv, 287).[34] Obviously Eurocentrism has a role to play in the theory, and no doubt was one of the reasons for its success, but it is difficult to deny that Humboldt went well beyond Schlegel in trying to justify it.

5.8 Linguistic relativism

We cannot abandon Humboldt without at least mentioning his view of language relativity or his concept of world vision (*Weltansicht*), subjects on which we have touched already.[35] Most introductions to linguistics written in the 1950s or 1960s make reference to the so-called Sapir-Whorf hypothesis according to which 'we dissect nature along lines laid down by our native languages', i.e. our language determines our cognitive processes. The same introductions then pay at least lip service to Humboldt, who would have been the first to support similar views. Other, more specific, works refer to the views of the German neo-Humboldtians centred round L. Weisgerber, for whom each language encapsulates an approach to the world and each language community is kept together by a vision of the world (*Weltbild*) provided by the mother tongue. Here too we are referred back to Humboldt but no attempt is made to go back further in time. We are again the victims of nineteenth-century historiography, which has deleted from scholarly awareness the assumptions and achievements of the previous century. Aarsleff ([1977] 1982, 345; 1988, xxxv ff.) rightly points out, as others had also done (e.g. Christmann 1967), that the idea that all languages to a certain extent determine the national character and the views of the speakers is commonplace in the eighteenth century and may be taken further back. Just to quote a few examples, similar views are found in France with Condillac, Diderot, etc.; in Italy, to a certain extent, with Vico, as well as Cesare Beccaria and Melchiorre Cesarotti (who depends on Condillac); in Germany they are reflected, for instance, in the title of the competition set in 1757 by the Berlin Academy, probably at the suggestion of Maupertuis (Aarsleff 1982, 189), about 'What is the reciprocal influence of the opinions of a people on language and of the language on opinions?'. The winner was the Göttingen Semitist J. D. Michaelis, who wrote an essay with this title which was then published in German and French and was influential on Herder. It is indeed the tradition of the discussion about the *génie des langues* which, through Herder and Humboldt and their influence on Steinthal and Pott, eventually reached our century. So much is not in doubt, though, in the context of the current polemics about Humboldt's background, it is of course disputed whether he was influenced directly by the French followers of Condillac or simply followed Herder's lead. In any case he must have been aware of the former: at a superficial level one can quote the statement by Dominique Joseph Garat (1749–1833), a Basque speaker who was a pupil of Condillac, and who in 1783 wrote in the *Mercure de France* apropos of his countrymen that 'je suis persuadé que tout ce qu'il y a de raison & d'étendue dans les idées de ce peuple, d'énergique, de fin & de délicat dans ces sentimens, il le doit beaucoup à la langue qu'il parle. Les belles langues sont comme des instrumens très faciles & très harmonieux, qui perfectionnent le talent qui s'en sert, qui inspirent réellement les idées qu'ils expriment'. Humboldt translated this text into German in his 1803 notebooks (Mueller-Vollmer 1991, 117). The ideas were in the air: at a deeper level we are struck by the quasi-verbal coincidences between some of Humboldt's statements and those of his contemporary, F. Schleiermacher (1768–1834), the famous religious reformer, theologian, philosopher and classicist, who was a friend of Friedrich Schlegel and one of the founders of the University of Berlin as well as its first theology professor (Gipper and Schmitter 1979, 92f.).[36] However, the real question is not so much one of influences as much as one of content: what did Humboldt have in mind? Should we attribute to him a sort of Whorfian determinism (mankind is bound by language and cannot break its barriers) or should we think simply that he was more aware than most of the links between language and culture in a way which harmonized with the romantic and historicistic views of the time? And in either case, are we talking of language as such or of the individual languages as Whorf was doing? The answer is implicit in most of what has already been said (cf. p. 111ff.). As early as 1806, Humboldt (GS, iii, 168) pointed out that only a shallow view of language would see the words as signs of objects or concepts which existed independently of them. Those who accepted that view also believed that all languages can be mechanically translated from one into the other and that in an ideal world language diversity had no *raison d'être* and one language would be adequate. According to Humboldt, the opposite is true. Words are signs in that they are used in lieu of things or concepts but otherwise they have an autonomy and individuality of their own. Language is an intermediate world between the outside world and that which acts within ourselves; it shows the analogy between mankind and the world. Formigari (1993, 178) stresses that this mediation of language is a transcendental mediation 'since it expresses the free agreement obtaining between subject and reality, man and the world, on which the possibility of knowledge is entirely dependent'. Humboldt accepts here a form of Kantian idealism, but the role that he attributes to language is new. At the same time, however, and already at this early stage, he emphasizes that the multiplicity of languages is what allows us to come closer to the 'spirit that reveals itself in the world' since each language represents a different point of view on which we can build our attempts at understanding. Later on (1810–11) in his project for a general study of language we are told that the real reason for the multiplicity of languages is the intimate need of the human spirit to produce a multitude of intellectual forms, which is parallel to the multitude of forms in nature (GS, vii, 622). A study of all languages can then establish the maximum growth that a language can reach.

The general question of how language influences thought or vice versa is in a sense a non-question for Humboldt since he envisages such close ties between language and thought that the two cannot be separated (Gipper 1987, 79); yet, given his rejection of the superficiality of language differences, in his system all reflection on language inevitably leads to reflection on languages. From there to the question of the ties between language and nation it is a small step: what is the link between a specific language with its own specific organization of lexicon and grammar and the character of the nation that speaks it? Here too we find a gamut of statements which at times may appear contradictory. Least controversial, at least for us, is Humboldt's belief (which he shares with the exponents of Romanticism and with e.g. Schleiermacher) that different languages do not divide semantic space in the same manner and consequently word-by-word translation is not be possible. If we consider the language of common discourse, we do not find exact synonyms across languages: the Latin *equus* does not exactly translate the Greek ἵππος any more than it does the German *Pferd* or, we might add, *horse* (GS, iii, 170; cf. *ibid.*, 311 and iv, 29, etc.).[37] But there is more to language diversity: 'the diversity of languages is not a diversity of sounds and signs but of world visions [*Weltansichten*]' (GS, iv, 28). Man can only approach the outside world through language but even so language is in some way external to him. Since it is the product of the nation and of the past, language, which is a fundamentally subjective entity, acquires an objectivity of its own and consequently it has the power to influence man in a way which is on the one hand constricting, on the other enriching (GS, iv, 28). The different languages, with their different *Weltansichten*, build a net round man: 'Man lives primarily with objects, indeed, since feeling and acting in him depend on his presentations [*Vorstellungen*], he actually does so exclusively, as the language presents them to him. By the same act whereby he spins language out of himself, he spins himself into it, and every language draws about the people that possesses it a circle whence it is possible to exit only by stepping over at once into the circle of another one' (*Einl.* lxxiv f.; GS, vii, 60; 1988, 60). Does it then follow that language is like a spider's web or a cage which imposes on man a view of the world from which he cannot escape; is this Humboldt's determinism? But immediately after the passage just quoted we are told that to learn a foreign language must lead to the acquisition of a new viewpoint in the vision of the world from which one starts and which is linked with (or determined by) one's first language, though one still brings into this new world the traces of the old one. In other words, an escape, however partial, is possible. Elsewhere, as we have seen (p. 114), Humboldt had explained that everything can be stated in any language if the speaker is led to new conceptions from different linguistic experiences (GS, iv, 287; cf. iv, 3). The conclusion must be, as Humboldt put it in 1820, that: 'the experience of translating even from very different languages and of using the rougher and least cultivated languages for teaching the most mysterious doctrine of a revealed religion shows that, even if with different results, every series of ideas can be expressed in every language. Yet this is simply the consequence of the universal relationship of all languages and of the flexibility of all concepts and their signs. However, for the languages themselves and their influence on the nations, what matters is simply what arises naturally from them; not that to which they can be compelled, but that to which they invite and inspire [*begeistern*]' (GS, iv, 17). As Trabant has noted (1985b, 194), Humboldt is neither an exponent of straight relativism nor of straight 'indifferentism' for which the different languages are merely different notations of the same entitities and the distinctions are purely superficial. His *Weltansicht* is not Weisgerber's *Weltbild* and his relativism is not Whorf's relativism.[38] As always, both facts and thoughts are more complicated and it is not chance that the same chapter of the Kawi *Einleitung* in which men are described as caught in the net of their language concludes underlining both the subjective and the objective aspects of language, the importance of history and the importance of renewed creativity, the depth of the difference between the various languages and their close link to the uniqueness of human nature: 'Language belongs to me, because I bring it forth as I do; and since the ground of this lies at once in the speaking and having spoken of every generation of men, so far as speech-communication may have prevailed unbroken among them, it is language itself which restrains me when I speak. But that in it which limits and determines me has arrived there from a human nature intimately allied to my own, and its alien element is therefore alien only for my transitory individual nature, not for my original and true one' (*Einl.* lxxix; GS, vii, 64f.; 1988, 63).

Notes

1. Cf. Aarsleff (1975; 1982, 335–55; 1988, xxxiii ff.). For the references to earlier literature and to some recent negative reactions, cf. Gipper-Schmitter (1979, 99–113), Gipper (1981), Oesterreicher (1981), Trabant (1986, 129ff.), Mueller-Vollmer (1990a); for an assessment of the debate 'from the outside', cf. Koerner ([1987] 1989, 32–5) and Sweet (1988). One of the main points that his opponents reproach to Aarsleff is that he has underrated the influence of Kant on Humboldt. On the other hand, there is also some agreement that the supposed break between the French Enlightenment (in a broad sense) and the German tradition has been exaggerated and that a number of Humboldt's (and Herder's) assumptions have an earlier and long history (cf. also Haßler 1991a, 114ff.).

2. The originality and complexity of Humboldt's thought may explain why the bibliography about him has now reached unmanageable proportions; here we can only refer to possible bibliographical sources. Gipper and Schmitter (1979, 77–91) discuss Humboldt's thought in general and also offer extensive bibliographic references; more recently Borsche (1990) offers a new account of all Humboldt's activities together with an admirable list of secondary literature (including the numerous collective volumes produced on occasion of the 150th anniversary of Humboldt's death). For the philosophical thought, see Liebrucks (1965), Formigari (1977b, 82–114; 1993, 169ff.), Borsche (1981), Manchester (1985), Carrano in Humboldt (1989, 11–53), Quillien (1991); cf. also Borsche *et al.* (1993) (I have not seen Müller-Sievers 1993). A short but impressively coherent interpretation of Humboldt's thought is found in the last chapter of Trabant (1986), and the introduction by Donatella di Cesare (1991) to her Italian translation of *Über die Verschiedenheit* is indispensable both for its content and its bibliography.

Heilmann (1976) collects a number of important articles. For Humboldt's concrete work, cf. Buchholz (1986) and Zimmermann, Trabant and Mueller-Vollmer (1994). For his biography one must still consult Haym (1856) but see above all P. R. Sweet (1978–80) with rich bibliography (in addition to Freese 1986). When possible, references are to the Berlin Academy edition of Humboldt's *Gesammelte Schriften* edited by Albert Leitzmann (GS = Humboldt 1903–36), even if this ignores the empirical work and, e.g. in the case of the Kawi Introduction, muddles the actual tradition; cf. the following note. Mueller-Vollmer (1993) presents an admirable account of Humboldt's linguistic *Nachlass,* which, *inter alia,* redresses the balance between the theoretical work (on which attention has largely concentrated) and the empirical work, which is largely unknown and unpublished. A major edition in 18–20 volumes of Humboldt's linguistic writing (published and unpublished) is being prepared under the general editorship of K. Mueller-Vollmer for Schöningh (Paderborn).

3. The textual tradition of this work is extremely complex. After Wilhelm's death his brother Alexander entrusted Eduard Buschmann with the task of seeing it through the press. In 1836 there appeared for the *Abhandlungen* of the Berlin Academy (officially of the year 1832) the first volume of the whole work; this was also printed in a more generally accessible form by the Berlin publisher Dümmler; most of the work was seen in its definitive form by Wilhelm von Humboldt himself. At the same time a somewhat different version which was meant as a self-contained book rather than as an introduction appeared also for Dümmler. Finally the Academy edition, prepared by Leitzmann (GS = 1903–36, vii, 1–344), is now revealed by the rediscovery of the *Nachlass* to be a not very successful contamination of the two previous versions (cf. Mueller-Vollmer 1990b; 1993, 73ff.). In this chapter I refer to the original Academy edition of the introduction (Humboldt 1836–39, I, i–ccccxxx) with the abbreviation *Einl.,* but I also provide references from the Leitzmann edition and take my English quotations from the 1988 translation by Peter Heath of the 1836 Dümmler edition (a better translation than that in Humboldt 1971).

4. August Ludwig Schözel (1735–1809) was a polymath who *inter alia* played a considerable role in Finno-Ugric linguistics. His original aim was that of introducing Linnean principles into the history of peoples, classifying them into classes, genera and species according to languages (Farkas 1952). He influenced Herder and the Göttingen historian J. C. Gatterer, the author of a famous *Weltgeschichte.* In general he is a good representative of the University of Göttingen, which at the time was far more forward looking than other Universities (cf. above, p. 77 note 4). For Humboldt at Göttingen, cf. Sauter (1989, 124ff.).

5. Cf. Morpurgo Davies (1975, 627f.). This is a recurrent motif in Humboldt's thought; it is already present *in nuce* in his contribution about Basque to Adelung's *Mithridates* (see above) and in an 1822 letter to A. W. Schlegel (cf. Hoenigswald 1984, 97f. and 1986, 175f.); see also Humboldt (GS, vi, 294) and Buchholz (1986, 155ff.).

6. Humboldt will remain a master in all these fields but it is likely that a serious study of his unpublished work, now made possible by Mueller-Vollmer's

(1993) catalogue, will alter our view of their respective importance in his intellectual life and indeed of his path to linguistics. For some of the American work cf. also the papers collected in Zimmermann, Trabant, Mueller-Vollmer (1994).

7. The constant accusations of obscurity (both in thought and style) directed against Humboldt have been partly answered by Gipper and Schmitter (1979, 79f.) who refer to Steinthal (1848, 30f.); they may nevertheless account for the controversial nature of Humboldtian historiography. Humboldt is not easy to understand nor is it easy to attribute to him a clear and systematic view of language and linguistics. Steinthal (1855, xx f.), who was a Humboldt admirer, wrote a propos of *innere Sprachform* that in no fundamental question of linguistic philosophy Humboldt ever reached a decisive opinion or a clear concept. Elsewhere ([1850] 1970, 135) he reiterated that Humboldt was not understood first because of the obscurity of his exposition and secondly because he was not clear about his own views. Humboldt himself wrote in an autobiographical fragment (GS, xv, 459) that he had all too rarely any certainty about truth and that he oscillated all too easily between two series of ideas, so that when he was about to accept the one he began to prefer the other. Yet in spite of Humboldt's own disclaimers about his intellectual power, the impression of the persistent reader is that he is a writer of supreme intelligence who anticipated a number of views some of which became comprehensible after his time, while some still remain to be understood. In this reader at least Humboldt's writings create a mixture of exasperation and exhilaration (both words are deliberately chosen), but the latter wins hands down.

8. And in general of all forms of translation; cf. Gipper (1986) who *inter alia* discusses the problems of translation from Sanskrit.

9. For Humboldt's anthropology, see Quillien 1991. Unfortunately I have not seen Quillien (1987).

10. For Humboldt's Basque work, see Gárate (1933), Michelena (1976), Buchholz (1986, 262–8), Mueller-Vollmer (1991).

11. We think especially of John Pickering (1777–1846) and P. S. Du Ponceau (1760–1844); see Mueller-Vollmer (1976), Aarsleff (1988), Swiggers (1992, 1993, 1994). The *Essai sur les langues du nouveau continent* (GS, iii, 9ff.) was written in 1812. Cf. the papers collected in Zimmermann, Trabant and Mueller-Vollmer (eds.) (1994).

12. The word is not used in the historical-comparative sense which it will acquire later (see above, pp. 25, 80 note 18) but simply refers to any enquiry based on the comparison of numerous languages belonging to different genetic and typological groups.

13. It is remarkable that, though the *Einleitung* was reprinted many times, translated into a number of languages, and in general frequently discussed, the other parts of Humboldt's *magnum opus*, though important both for the results achieved and the method adopted (see Buchholz 1986), are still available only in the original edition (1836–9).

14. That is different from saying that Humboldt was looking for substantive universals or that he was moving in the tradition of universal grammar, even if on a number of occasions he seems to adopt some of its formulations.

For Humboldt's (and Gabelentz's) view of implicational universals (to use anachronistic terminology), see Plank (1994).

15. Cf. in general and for the earlier literature, Buchholz (1986, 280).

16. Humboldt wrote numerous accounts of 'exotic' languages, most of which are still unpublished (cf. p. 100). On the other hand, his essay on the dual (see above) is an attempt to produce a monograph of the type described under (b) (cf. Plank 1989, 1994). Later on, the work on the passive by Hans Conon von der Gabelentz (1861a) tried to implement part of Humboldt's programme (Plank 1996).

17. Buchholz (1986, 146ff.) stresses how different this attitude is from that of the standard work on German grammar by Humboldt's predecessors and contemporaries.

18. Percival (1974b) discusses at length Humboldt's analysis of the Javanese verb; cf. also Buchholz (1986, 182ff.) for some of the general points.

19. Trabant (1990a, 137ff.) interestingly contrasts the attitude of Humboldt with that of the Leibniz of the *Brevis designatio meditationum de Originibus Gentium, ductis potissimum ex indicio linguarum* (1710), where, as indicated by the title, languages were used as documents for the reconstruction of the historical origins of peoples, something which, after Leibniz at least, was a normal aim for those interested in language variety. However, Trabant (*ibid.*) also refers to the Leibniz of the *Nouveaux essais* who asks for grammars and dictionaries of all languages of the world which will be useful both for knowing things and for 'the knowledge of our minds and of the wonderful variety of its operations' ('la connaissance de notre esprit et la merveilleuse variété de ses opérations').

20. The same passage is repeated in the Kawi book (Humboldt 1836–9, iii, 125) with some slight but interesting difference in wording: 'alle wesentlichen und bildenden Ideen der allgemeinen philosophischen Grammatik' is replaced by 'die wesentlichsten Ideen der allgemeinen Grammatik'. For the general distinction in Humboldt between philosophical and empirical linguistics, cf. Buchholz (1986, 147ff.).

21. 'Der Mensch ist nur Mensch durch Sprache; um aber die Sprache zu erfinden, müsste er schon Mensch seyn'. The translation given above is that quoted by Whitney (1875, 306), who, in his polemics against Max Müller, refers to it as one of those 'Orphic sayings' which is ridiculous to use as the 'foundation or test of scientific views' (Nerlich 1990a, 49). In fact, when Whitney compares Humboldt's saying with 'a pig is not pig without being fattened; but in order to be fattened he must first be a pig', he seems to have deliberately misunderstood the point.

22. Hence also Humboldt's statement that in principle both monogenesis and polygenesis are possible but there is no way to decide between the two (GS, iv, 5).

23. Cf. in general Trabant (1985a) and Di Cesare (1990a) with the previous literature, but see also Steinthal ([1851] 1858, 64ff.).

24. Cf. Trabant (1985a, 586) for a discussion of the Kantian origin of this concept.

25. The definition of language as *energeia* occurs only once in Humboldt (*Einl.* lvii, GS, vii, 45; 1988, 49). For the history of the interpretation, cf.

Jost (1960); the terminology goes back to Aristotle, and D. di Cesare (1988) has made a good case for interpreting the Humboldt usage in the Aristotelian sense of 'actuality', i.e. as a process of actualisation in contrast with potentiality (*dynamis*) but also with *entelekheia*, which refers to the complete fulfilment of the potentiality.

26. Chomsky's interpretation has been often – and rightly – attacked: cf. e.g. Baumann (1971), Coseriu (1970), Scharf (1983) (I have not seen Scharf 1994). However, e.g. Ramat (1976, 51) and Manchester (1985, 86) are right in recognizing some occasional similarity between Chomsky's own tenets and those of Humboldt.

27. For a summary of Humboldt's fortune in contemporary work, see Conte (1976).

28. Elsewhere, particularly in the early works, there are a few references to the desirability of a 'natural' classification like that of the scientists (e.g. in GS, iii, 326).

29. Even Buschmann, Humboldt's faithful assistant, did not make as clear a distinction between grammatical 'viewpoint' and grammatical forms. In his (more than justified) polemics against Bopp's derivation of Malayo-Polynesian from Sanskrit he argued – again correctly – that for mixed languages comparison of words is a very treacherous means to determine origin and kinship, but concluded that the only proof could come from 'der grammatische Typus und die grammatisch bedeutsamen Laute' (Mueller-Vollmer 1993, 35), i.e. from what Humboldt would have called grammatical viewpoint and grammatical concrete forms.

30. Coseriu (1972, 1976) suggests that the words *Isolierung* and *Agglutination* are due to Humboldt.

31. Humboldt rejected Friedrich Schlegel's distinction into organic and non-organic languages (e.g. in *Einl.* clxiv; GS, vii, 132 note; 1988, 118) and accepted from Bopp the view that agglutination could be responsible for some inflection. His attitude to August Wilhelm Schlegel's distinction between analytic and synthetic languages is not altogether clear but in general negative, as shown by Coseriu (1972, 1976): see e.g. GS, vi, 260. As for the idea that inflected languages could include agglutinative features, it is worth looking at Humboldt's defence of Bopp in his correspondence with August Wilhelm Schlegel. On 16 June 1829 he wrote that in his view Bopp was right to assume that personal endings of the (Indo-European) verb derived from pronouns, but in the attested languages this was irrelevant since the personal endings acquired their value not because they contained one or the other pronoun but because they occupied a definite slot in the schema of the verb's persons: 'in this way Sanskrit particularly is a language entirely inflected and all pervaded by form (and together with the related languages is alone among all other languages)' ('dadurch ist hauptsächlich das Sanskrit (mit den verwandten, wie ich glaube, einzig unter allen Sprachen) eine durchaus flectirte, ganz von Form durchdrungene'; Leitzmann 1908, 237).

32. Coseriu (1972, 1976) discusses at length Humboldt's typological views highlighting the misunderstanding; cf. also Gipper (1965), Pätsch (1967). Morpurgo Davies (1975, 659ff.), written before the appearance of Coseriu's article, also provides general bibliography about typology and language

classification. For Steinthal's and Pott's reactions, see Coseriu and Morpurgo Davies. In addition to Coseriu (who is fundamental), modern discussions of Humboldt's typology also include Telegdi (1970), Sgall (1971), Ramat (1976, 1985; cf. 1992), Di Cesare (1990b). Perhaps the clearest analysis of Humboldt's procedure in his concrete typological work is that by Plank (1989), who discusses the essay on the dual.

33. For Humboldt's views on the independence of language and race, see below, pp. 158, 182 note 16. Aarsleff (1988, lxi ff.) discusses the controversies between Humboldt and his American correspondents on the superiority of the inflected languages.

34. This is even more clearly expressed in the 1837 letter in French to Du Ponceau to which we referred earlier: 'I am much more concerned with studying languages and analysing their varieties than with defining their respective rank, but I think that it is my duty always to examine what influence one or the other character of a language can exercise on man's mind, except for the possibility that other characters counterbalance and prevent that influence' (Swiggers 1994, 250).

35. All analyses of Humboldt's thought discuss his linguistic relativism (cf. note 2); in addition, see Aarsleff ([1977] 1982, 335ff.; 1988), Brown (1967), Christmann (1967, 1981), Junker (1986), Haßler (1986a, b), Hoberg (1987b), Miller (1968), Penn (1972), Schmitter (1977). Cf. also Di Cesare (1991, 48ff.) with further references; for the later developments, Koerner (1995, 203–40) offers a good bibliography.

36. Gipper and Schmitter (*loc. cit.*) rightly deplore the absence of any reference to Schleiermacher in the history of linguistics. His 'hermeneutics' was not limited to philological analysis, but sought to formulate a general theory of interpretation and understanding which, as observed in Jäger (1987), opens the way to the autonomy both of hermeneutics and of philology or linguistics. It is certainly true that Schleiermacher's observations on the relativity of knowledge and the fact that its limits are determined by the various languages or on the difficulties of translating show non-superficial similarities with Humboldt's views. For the suggestion, unorthodox but interesting, that the real founder of hermeneutics was Humboldt and not Schleiermacher, cf. Quillien (1990); for hermeneutics in general, Ferraris (1989) and the essays collected in Laks and Neschke (1990).

37. The position is different for the terms of technical and scientific language which are indeed signs of well-defined entities. In 1820 Humboldt distinguishes between scientific and rhetorical use of language; in the former, words are legitimately used as signs of well-defined entities, in the latter, which is the use that we make of language in normal life intercourse as well as in poetry, history and philosophy, we have a mixture of the use of language as sign and of the free use determined by the will of the speaker (GS, iv, 29f.).

38. Cf. in general, Gipper (1972), but also Hoberg (1987b), and for the comparison with the neo-Humboldtians, Junker (1986). For the meaning of *Weltansicht,* which indicates man's original visual approach to reality, in contrast with *Weltanschauung,* 'conception of the world', and *Weltbild,* 'image of the world', see Di Cesare (1991, 1.f.).

Comparative and historical grammar: Rask, Bopp and Grimm

6.1 The 'new discipline' and the new technicism

In the second decade of the century the concentration of detailed monographs and learned articles documents the creation of the new 'craft'
and the new awareness of the cumulative nature of knowledge. In the
preface to the first volume of his *Deutsche Grammatik*, Jacob Grimm
(1819) expressed admiration for Rasmus Rask's work on the origin of
the Old Norse or Icelandic language, regretted that it had appeared too
late to be used in his own book and rejoiced about the points of agreement which nevertheless he found between that book and his own:
'historical [i.e. empirical?] studies lead necessarily to similar results'
('historische Studien führen notwendig zu ähnlichen Resultaten'; Grimm
1819, 11). He then pointed out that, while Rask had impressively highlighted the similarities of Germanic with Lithuanian, Slavic, Greek and
Latin, he had not pushed the comparison as far as Sanskrit, which was
the keystone of the whole enterprise. This work nevertheless had been
pursued by Franz Bopp (witness his 1816 book) and could not have
been entrusted to better hands.

Traditionally, Rask, Bopp and Grimm are seen as the initiators of
comparative and historical linguistics, Bopp *qua* founder of comparativism, Grimm *qua* founder of historical linguistics, Rask as the precursor
of both. The reverence bestowed on this trio is correct but the bi- or
tripartition must be justified more in terms of what followed than of
contemporary reactions. It is indeed the case that later comparativists,
the authors of the standard works on Indo-European, constantly referred
back to Bopp, while Grimm's work marked the beginning of a series
of contributions about the history of the Germanic languages and provided the model for Diez's comparative work on Romance, which in its
turn opened the way to historical work on Romance languages. Yet at
the time, and for a long while afterwards, the comparative element was

seen as subsuming the other. As late as 1863, Gaston Paris could write referring to this period: 'We were no longer limited to studying a language in isolation . . . All good grammars had to be comparative grammars, or at least the result of comparative studies' ('On ne dut plus se borner à étudier isolément une langue . . . Toute bonne grammaire dut être une grammaire comparée, ou au moins le fruit d'études comparatives'; Paris 1863, v).[1] Within this framework it is not extraordinary that Grimm felt that his work on Germanic belonged within the same sphere as that by Rask and Bopp.

6.2 Rasmus Rask

Rasmus Rask (1787–1832) remained relatively isolated both in the later historiography and among his contemporaries. He came from a poor Danish family, studied at the University of Copenhagen but never completed his studies, spent two years in Iceland and a further long period travelling as far as India and Ceylon with long stop-overs in Stockholm and St Petersburg, suffered from physical and mental illnesses, and even after his return to Copenhagen (after 1823) his career did not proceed as well as it should have done. For a long time he had financial difficulties as Professor of History of Literature and Assistant Librarian and did not obtain a chair of Oriental Languages until shortly before his premature death.[2] Most of his published contributions to linguistics consist of admirably concise grammars of various modern and classical languages (1811 Old Norse, 1817 Anglo-Saxon, 1824 Spanish, 1825 Frisian, 1827 Italian, 1830 Danish, 1832 Lappish and English); in addition there are editions of the two Eddas, a controversial essay on Danish orthography, books on Hebrew and Egyptian chronology, a grammatical description of an African language, a discussion of Avestan, and the famous prize essay about the origins of Old Icelandic (the essay praised by Grimm), which was written in 1814 and published in 1818 (*Undersøgelse om det gamle Nordiske eller Islandske Sprogs Oprindelse*).[3]

All Rask's grammars are basically descriptive and include, after a discussion of spelling and phonology, chapters about morphology, word formation and syntax. In the introduction to the Icelandic grammar of 1811 he explained that a grammar should not be merely prescriptive but should also describe usage and account for its causes and origins; to study Danish and Swedish properly it is necessary to have a knowledge of the language from which they derive because only in this way can the main phenomena of the two languages be explained. On the other hand, comparison, broadly understood, is only effective if the comparanda are similarly described; in an unpublished letter of 1825 Rask stated that he was particularly proud of the system of grammatical description which he had developed for the Germanic languages and which he thought was also applicable to Sanskrit and Avestan. At the same time, however, in an 1810 essay published in 1820 about the endings and forms of Danish, Rask (1932–7, ii, 50ff.) used Icelandic to explain the morphology of Danish and claimed priority for his concern not only with the origin of words but also with the origin of endings and inflections, i.e. with what we would now call historical morphology (Jespersen [1928] 1970, 29; cf. Diderichsen 1974, 296).

The prize essay starts with a discussion of etymology which deplores the excesses of the past but also includes a warm appreciation of Turgot's article in the *Encyclopédie*. Satisfactory etymology (the word has a broader meaning for Rask than for us) cannot be done on the basis of one language only; it must be based on comparison, which in its turn is concerned with both grammar and vocabulary. Grammatical agreement is the most certain indication of kinship because inflections are hardly ever borrowed. Nevertheless, languages are related when they share a basic vocabulary and when agreements in words are so frequent that it is possible to establish constant permutations of 'letters' (as for instance in Greek *p* vs. Germanic *f*, etc.). There follows an attempt to define the place of Icelandic and the other 'Gothic' (i.e. Germanic) languages; it is argued that they are not related to Celtic (Rask changed his mind on this later), Basque, Finno-Ugric, Eskimo, etc. but are much closer to Slavic and Baltic. The section about the 'Thracian' languages (Greek and Latin) establishes 'rules for the shift of letters from one language to the other' and in this context formulates without undue fuss the consonantal shift which we now call Grimm's Law and which accounts for the regular correspondences between e.g. Latin *p*, *t*, *k* and Gothic *f*, *þ*, *h* (see below). Here and elsewhere all discussion of morphology is preceded by phonological or orthographical observations. The grammatical elements of the classical languages are then analysed in detail and compared with those of 'Gothic': noun declensions, the comparative, pronouns, numerals, verbal forms, etc. In an earlier paper (written in 1810, published in 1820) about Danish 'grammatical etymology and etymological grammar' Rask had highlighted the novelty of his attempt to give a historical explanation of the endings and forms of Danish (mainly through comparison with Icelandic); the same system is followed here. Finally some 352 word correspondences are quoted. The conclusion is that the Germanic languages derive from a 'Thracian' stem whose oldest branches are Greek and Latin. The whole book is, as was stated, a first attempt at an Indo-European comparative grammar, with the disadvantage that the Eastern languages are not considered. However, it does show clearly that advance in this direction was possible even without Sanskrit. Since it appeared, as it did, after Bopp (1816) and was written in Danish, its influence was not as great as it could have been, but the impression it made on Jacob Grimm (and on other Germanists) was immense.

In a provocative article, Hjelmslev (1950–1), the theoretical linguist who was also the editor of Rask's works, argued that, far from being one of the founders of historical linguistics, Rask was in fact a 'rationaliste et systématisateur, . . . ni romantique, ni historien'. We have been the victims of a misguided historiography: Rask's wish was for a general and comparative grammar, a *grammaire générale empirique*; his classification of languages in families was fundamentally a typological not a genealogical classification. He did not believe in language change; languages do not change, but disappear. Though for him language was an organism and the study of language was similar to natural history, what he aimed at was a static classification *à la* Linnaeus. In other words, Rask is not the founder of historical linguistics but he rather foreshadows structuralism and modern general linguistics.[4]

In comparison with most of his contemporaries, Rask was singularly reticent and his general statements are few. The draft of a lecture on the philosophy of language, which he wrote in the last part of his life and never published, passionately argues for an empirical, data-oriented approach to language and rejects the type of philosophical grammar which starts from the ideas to move down to language: 'in any case it is not thought and its forms, but words, sounds and their forms and relationship or combination that one should concern oneself with in linguistics' (Christie 1985, 82). This phrase could serve as epitaph to most of nineteenth-century concrete work, but it is still too general to settle Hjelmslev's query. Rask's aim and method must emerge from his concrete work. It is certainly true that he aimed at defining some universal criteria of description and to link them to cognitive phenomena; so much emerges e.g. from Plank's analysis (1991b) of his attempt to establish a regular ordering for all inflectional paradigms. It is also true that Rask did not always distinguish between structural and genealogical arguments. Thus in his discussion of Thracian he compared all sounds of Greek with those of Icelandic and was satisfied when he found that they were 'the same' and obeyed similar morphophonemic rules. Here the general assumption was, once again, that related languages have similar structures. But Hjelmslev himself is the victim of the nineteenth-century historiography which saw a total break between the old 'bad' period and the new enlightened approach, between typology and genealogy. In Rask's time, structural arguments were constantly used to demonstrate kinship; it does not follow that those who used them were only interested in typological similarity. Similarly, even if Rask aimed at identifying the basic system of each language and did not share the Romantic view of language as an immediate emanation of the *Volksgeist*, it does not follow that he was not interested in linguistic history. If we look at the concrete conclusions and argumentation, we find that he developed not only techniques of genealogical comparison but also techniques for the study of historical development. He knew very well, for instance, that 'modern' etymology can avoid the excesses of the past because it is based on the knowledge of the older attested phases of languages. He also had enough feeling for language change to realize, to give a specific example, that irregular grammatical forms which have not been ironed out (as the Greek comparatives in *-iōn* vs. those in *-teros*, the ablauting forms of the Germanic languages, the pronouns which still preserve case distinctions in English, etc.) were likely to be old since that was the only way in which they could be explained (Rask 1818). As early as 1811, in his account of the Icelandic umlaut, he had seen that vocalic changes in the stem could be due to endings which had been pronounced at an earlier stage and were no longer there. Scattered through the 1818 essay we find instances of reconstructed proto-forms such as Greek ὀ-δοντ-ς (the antecedent of ὀδούς) or Latin *dent-s* for the attested *dens*, together with an account of the changes which led to the attested forms.[5] To reconstruct forms such as **dent-s* on the basis of e.g. the genitive *dent-is* was not a novelty; the ancient grammarians had done as much in order to show the basic regularity of some paradigms, and the Dutch schools of classical grammarians had followed the same procedure to the level of absurdity. Here, however, the reconstructed form is attributed historical reality and projected back in time; most importantly, this is guaranteed by comparison. Even in the absence of morphophonemic alternations, Greek ἀλλοδ is hypothesized as a proto-form for the attested ἄλλο; the final *-d* is reconstructed purely on the basis of comparison (cf. Latin *aliud*) and the reconstruction is supported by a phonological observation (final stops are not found in Greek). This interest in the distinction between innovations and preservations and in the identification of different types of changes gives Rask pre-eminence in both historical and comparative linguistics.

Rask's name will be for ever linked to his statements about the regularity of 'letter permutations' between related languages and his early formulation of 'Grimm's Law'. Yet he did not give particular methodological weight to these results (nor were they wholly new).[6] As most of his predecessors, he was probably more interested in trying to define general laws, physiologically determined, which would explain the permutation of letters in all languages (Diderichsen 1974, 299) than in explaining why the specific permutations were so important. Only later was the technique thoroughly exploited and only much later was it realized what technical and theoretical capital could be made of Rask's observations. It is characteristic of nineteenth-century linguistics that at various stages techniques, problem-solving and concrete results take the lead, exactly as in the natural sciences, while the theory is left behind.

Rask, as indeed Bopp, is just an example of this phenomenon; we may see him as an eighteenth-century man who produced nineteenth-century results, or, more plausibly, as a linguist of the early nineteenth century who had inherited or developed a series of assumptions and concerns which did not necessarily match his own concrete discoveries and indeed each other.

6.3 Franz Bopp

Rask's work was often neglected outside the Germanists' circles and he died too early to see it come to fruition. By contrast, Franz Bopp (1791–1867) was hailed when still alive as the founder of the new comparative linguistics and enjoyed both the intellectual and institutional honours which this involved.[7] He was educated in Aschaffenburg, first at the local *Gymnasium* and then briefly at the short-lived Karls-Universität, where he developed an interest in oriental languages largely through the influence of his teacher and patron, K. J. Windischmann, a doctor-philosopher of mystical inclinations who was well acquainted with some of the exponents of Romanticism and was fascinated by the religions and literatures of the East. From 1812 he studied Hebrew, Arabic, Persian and (largely on his own) Sanskrit in Paris, partially helped by a Bavarian grant. There he gradually began to concentrate on Sanskrit and on the study of language in preference to that of literature or religion, though at times he showed a Romantic desire to explore problems of comparative mythology. By 1815 he was able to help A. W. Schlegel, who was also trying to learn Sanskrit in Paris. As early as 1814 he had formulated the plan which determined his life work, that of writing a comparative grammar of Sanskrit and its daughters (Lefmann 1891–7, II, Anhang, 12*). In 1815 he had declared his intention to change the study of language into a 'philosophical and historical' (i.e. empirical) study, different from the practical endeavour of those who simply wanted to understand texts written in a different language from their own (*ibid.*, 33*). The first work, *Über das Conjugationssystem der Sanskritsprache in Vergleichung mit jenem der griechischen, lateinischen, persischen und germanischen Sprache,* was prepared for publication by Windischmann in 1816. How much it was influenced by F. Schlegel's *Über die Sprache und Weisheit der Indier* (1808) is shown *inter alia* by the format: after the main essay it included German translations from various Sanskrit texts. This is the book that has been celebrated again and again as the first comparative work about the Indo-European languages.[8] A second grant brought Bopp for a while to London, where he published an edition of a part of the *Mahābhārata* with a Latin translation (*Nalus carmen sanscritum e Mahâbhârato*, London 1819) and a substantially revised English version of the 1816 essay (Bopp 1820). After an unsuccessful attempt at obtaining a chair in Würzburg, and a brief period in Göttingen, eventually his financial worries came to an end when in 1821 he was offered a post of Extraordinarius in *orientalische Literatur und allgemeine Sprachkunde* at the new and forward-looking University of Berlin.[9] W. von Humboldt, who had met Bopp in London and was helped by him to learn Sanskrit, was obviously influential. Membership of the Academy, the Ordinariatus and further honours accompanied a stream of technical publications partly written in preparation for the two editions of his *magnum opus Vergleichende Grammatik des Sanskrit, Zend, Griechischen, Lateinischen, Litthauischen, Gothischen und Deutschen* (1833–52, 2nd edn 1857–61), partly meant to provide the indispensable tools for the knowledge of Sanskrit. Three different Sanskrit grammars appeared between 1827 and 1834 (the last reached four editions), and a *Glossarium Sanscritum* (with a wealth of comparative material) was published in 1828–30 and in two later editions. This looks to us like a typical academic career but at the time it was not so; with Bopp, more than with A. W. Schlegel, the institutionalization (and the specialization) of linguistics begins.

6.3.1 Bopp's technical work

Bopp's work exemplifies the new 'technical', aliterary and aphilosophical trend. The *Conjugationssystem* of 1816 (which we consider jointly with the 1820 version) started from the assumption that the kinship of the languages quoted in the title needed no demonstration and continued with a detailed comparative analysis of their verbal morphology. A verb is 'that part of speech by which a subject is connected with its attribute'. This definition is deemed to be logically correct; an analysis of the actual forms can show that it is also historically correct. In Latin *potest* 'he can' Bopp finds *pot-* 'capable', *-es-* 'is' and *-t* 'he', but this example remains isolated in the attested languages. The book sets out to demonstrate that in the earliest stages of language, verbal forms arose from the joining (we would say agglutination) of roots which carried the basic lexical meaning with other autonomous segments (forms of the verb 'to be', i.e. of the copula, or pronouns) which indicated grammatical relations. Systematic comparison between equivalent forms of different languages allows the linguist to distinguish the old forms from the new and to reconstruct a stage in which formal opacity had not yet set in. It then becomes clear that e.g. the Greek future in *-so-* can be connected with *eso-* 'I shall be' and the Sanskrit future in *-sya-* is also formed from the Sanskrit optative *syā-m* of the verb 'to be'. Similarly, the *-m* and *-t* endings which mark the first and third person singular in Sanskrit, Greek, Latin and Germanic can be compared with the *m-* and *t-* forms of the pronouns for 'I' and 'he, this'.

In the *Vergleichende Grammatik* the range is wider; we are told that the book aims at a general description of the 'organism' of the languages listed, but also intends to proceed to an enquiry into their 'physical and mechanical' laws and into the origin of the forms which indicate grammatical relationships. On the other hand, no attempt will be made to understand the mystery of the roots, why *i-* means 'to go' and not 'to stay', *sta-* 'to stay' and not 'to go'. There follows, after a few notes about the phonology of the various languages, a strictly morphological analysis arranged in the traditional manner: nominal cases, comparatives and superlatives, pronouns, verbs, word formation. Each morpheme is discussed language by language, with the aim of identifying and if possible explaining the original form. The vastness of the enterprise is unique; no similar cross-linguistic analysis at that level of detail had been attempted before.

6.3.2 Method and results

We can look at Bopp's achievements or at his method but the work's background and general assumptions must also be considered. First, the technical achievement: the edifice which is the comparative grammar of Indo-European. All through Bopp's work we find suggestions which are then checked and often replaced. In 1816 he was still hesitant (perhaps out of respect for Friedrich Schlegel) about the relative position of Sanskrit and the other languages. In 1820 he was clear that Sanskrit was just one of many related languages. He argued for this by showing that Sanskrit presented innovations which did not occur in e.g. Greek; in other words, he developed a method which allowed him to go beyond a mere statement of kinship and to define further the connection between two languages. The number of Indo-European languages recognized increased: Slavic appears in the second *Abtheilung* of the *Vergleichende Grammatik* and Armenian is present in the title page of the second edition, but meanwhile Bopp had also produced in 1838 a model demonstration (after Prichard, Pictet and Zeuss) of the Indo-European nature of Celtic and had argued in 1854 for a correct positioning of Albanian among the other Indo-European languages. The conclusions were constantly modified as the philological analysis of the older phases of the languages in question became known and could be exploited.

Methodological discussions are rare in Bopp's work; a few general points are reserved for the introductions and conclusions but otherwise the exposition is austere. The method emerges from the work without need for an explanation. Previous writers had underlined the importance of grammatical comparison, but no one had brought the analysis of morphology and its history to Bopp's level. The first step is morphemic segmentation (*Zergliederung*); the roots must be separated from the inflections: affixes, endings, etc. This is first done on synchronic principles and within a given language. Thus in a Greek paradigm such as that of the nom. *dus-menēs* 'hostile', gen. *dus-meneos*, dat. *dus-menei*, *-s* is treated as the nominative ending in parallel with the gen. *-os*, dat. *-i* (as in nom. *phulak-s* 'warden', gen. *phulak-os*, dat. *phulak-i*). Comparative evidence is then brought in to support or otherwise this first attempt. In Sanskrit the nom. is *dur-manas*, the gen. *dur-manas-as*, the dat. *dur-manās-e*. If so, *-s-* must belong to the stem and not to the ending. We must now check again the Greek data and we notice, first, that in Greek we have evidence for a loss of *-s-* between vowels so that *dusmene-os* could come from *dusmenes-os*; secondly, that an *-s* also appears in Greek *menos* 'anger', which is clearly related. Yet this is a neuter and Greek never has *-s* in neuter endings. We then conclude that the final *-s* in Greek *dusmenēs* is not a nominative marker but part of the stem and that the 'correct' segmentation is *dus-menēs*, not *dus-menē-s* (Bopp 1833–52, 171). When through this type of procedure all segments are identified and have been attributed the correct form and function, we again return to comparison in order to distinguish what is inherited from what is new. At this stage a second step becomes possible: we may ask why the original forms are what they are. To answer this question a new type of comparison is undertaken, this time between the forms which have been attributed to the parent language. The verbal endings of first and third person singular (*-mi/-m* and *-ti/-t*), which the early Indo-European languages inherited, show a striking similarity with Sanskrit *me*, Greek *moi* 'to/of me', etc., and Sanskrit *ta-*, Greek *to-* 'he, this'. It then seems possible to assume that the verbal form which means e.g. "I do X" includes *me* 'me' and that which means e.g. 'he does X' includes *ta-* 'he'. Further example: the inherited morph of the nominative singular is *-s*. This is compared by Bopp with the pronoun continued by Sanskrit *sa-* 'he', because *-s* is only masculine and feminine, not neuter, while the *sa-* root is also used only for masculines and feminines, not neuters. Clearly the reasoning is of a formal rather than semantic nature.

It is in the regular adherence to this procedure that Bopp's strength lies. Future generations rejected part at least of his speculations about the origin of individual morphemes (from pronouns, the copula, etc.) but this did not prevent them from accepting in most instances Bopp's segmentation and Bopp's distinction between inherited and newly created forms. One last example, however, shows some of the limitations of the method. Bopp points out that the augment (a prefix which is used to mark past tense in Sanskrit and Greek verbs) is formally identical to the prefix which forms negative compounds (cf. Sanskrit *a-bharam* 'I carried' vs. *bhar-* 'carry', *a-jnāta-* 'un-known' vs. *jnā-* 'know'). He concludes that the past may have been envisaged as a non-present. Yet, even in response to polemical attacks, he does not provide sufficient evidence for the type of semantic change from e.g. 'not-carry' to 'carried' that he wants to postulate. Moreover, though he considers it, he dismisses without convincing arguments the formal objection that the two *a*-s must be treated as separate morphemes, because (a) Sanskrit *a*- 'not' corresponds to Greek *a*-, while Sanskrit *a*- 'past' corresponds to Greek *e*-, (b) Sanskrit and Greek *a*- 'not' alternate with *an*- before a vowel, while Sanskrit *a*-, Greek *e*- 'past' never alternate with an *-n* form. The desire to account for all forms, whatever the cost, is left free rein and this is made possible on the one hand by a serious absence of detailed phonological and semantic discussion, on the other hand by the pre-eminence given to Sanskrit in the reconstruction. In general in Bopp's work, semantics and syntax barely exist and phonology takes second place. Morphology reigns supreme and Sanskrit is mostly (though not always) the touchstone which opens all doors.

But is the method entirely comparative or is it also historical? Here too, as for Rask, the answer is not simple. Bopp was not trying to write what we now call the history of a language, be it Indo-European or Sanskrit. A history would have required a different outlook and those cultural or ethnological interests which Bopp did not have. Morphology, the structured part of language, fascinated him, but little else. Moreover he was also reluctant to undertake the patient philological work which arranges texts or sources in chronological order with the aim of finding tangible evidence for language change; that smacked too much of the classicist or the literary scholar, while the same and often better results could be obtained through comparison. When somewhat polemically August Wilhelm Schlegel pointed out to him that the Vedas, the earliest Indian texts, provided concrete evidence for some of his reconstructed forms, he took this as a triumphal revendication of the validity of his method, not as a reproach for his neglect of existing data (Sternemann 1984a, 26). And yet it would be again mistaken to see Bopp as a pure comparativist who had no interest in language development. When he identifies *Wohllautgesetze*, i.e. laws of phonological change, or observes the re-creation of new grammatical forms according to the old patterns, or comments about the fact that apparently identical forms may be due to parallel innovations, he is in fact opening the way to an understanding of the how, if not the why, of language change. In a defence of his ill-fated demonstration that the Malayo-Polynesian languages were related to Sanskrit, he argued that an important task was to try to bring back the differences between related languages to the laws which determined them (1833–52, 4te Abth., xii).

6.3.3 Assumptions and cultural background
What is the background to Bopp's type of work? Through Windischmann, Bopp was in contact with the Romantic circles and there is little doubt

that he shared, to a limited extent, some of their assumptions. We also know that he was profoundly influenced by Friedrich Schlegel's 1808 book. With Schlegel, Bopp had in common, in addition to an enthusiasm for Sanskrit, an interest in early linguistic phases, some form of organicism, a view of language as subject to a form of decay which destroyed the original regularities, and a faith in comparison as a means of reconstructing lost phases of languages. Yet we do not find in him any real interest in that link between language and nation, which was so fundamental for Romantic theorizing, nor does he subscribe to the quasimystical or reactionary aspects of vitalism and historicism. On the contrary, the starting point of the *Conjugationssystem* is well grounded in the rationalistic tradition. The *Grammaire de Port Royal* (1660) stated that the basic sentence consists of a subject, an attribute and a copula (*la terre est ronde*) and that this is true even for sentences such as *Jean vit* ('John lives') because *vit* is equivalent to *est vivant* ('is living'), i.e. 'includes' an attribute and a copula (*est vivant*). These views were constantly repeated, not least in the *Grammaire générale* by Silvestre de Sacy, whose lectures Bopp attended in Paris.[10] No doubt when the young Bopp set out to demonstrate that the verbal forms arose from the agglutination of a root with forms of the verb 'to be', he was prompted by the desire to find in language the logical forms of universal grammar; the 'discovery' that the personal endings could be linked to pronominal forms fitted in the same mould. On the other hand, theories which supported the original autonomy of the bound morphemes and especially the identification of personal endings with the pronouns were not new; they went back at least as far as the seventeenth century but had also found favour in the two following centuries, in Holland, France and Germany, with linguists as different as Fulda, Adelung, Jacob Grimm and Abel-Rémusat (Timpanaro 1973, 22ff.). Bopp's originality consisted in his attempt to verify the theory through the new empirical method of comparative morphological analysis which he had developed for this purpose. But here too, as in Rask, the method was apt to take over; an analysis, which, even before it turned to its original aim, that of explaining the origin of the earliest grammatical forms, could account in genetic terms both for the irregularities and the regularities of the grammar of the individual languages, had a compelling interest of its own, all the more so because new data constantly called for its refinement and because the results of the method sometimes led to far more general conclusions. Technicalities and generalities here get inextricably confused.

Friedrich Schlegel, we have seen, had assumed that in the Indo-European languages roots were living germs ready to unfold into inflected forms; the organic unity of the word was for him the hallmark of a superior language-class. This quasi-mystical view could not appeal to Bopp, though at first he accepted it. On the one hand it was unnecessarily vague, on the other it seemed to contradict the clear segmentations prompted by comparative morphology. Bopp's successive works represent a constant effort to replace organic unfolding with agglutination. In 1816 he still assumes that part of the inflections arise organically by spontaneous alteration or growth of the root, while part arise through composition of the roots with other roots (verbal or pronominal); by 1820 'organic' in this context is restricted merely to reduplication and vocalic alternation, while the origin of all other inflections is due to agglutination (mostly with pronouns). Finally, the theory is advanced that even vocalic alternations are 'mechanically' determined by the form of the word and originally have no grammatical significance: Bopp thinks that he has discovered a correlation (operative in verbs) for which 'heavy' roots are accompanied by 'light' endings and vice versa: Sanskrit *as-mi* 'I am' has a light ending (*-mi*) and a 'heavy' root (*as-*) while in *s-mas* 'we are' *-mas* is a 'heavy' ending and *s-* a 'light' root.[11] In this way the last trace of organicism in inflection is removed. On the other hand, as Bopp knew and made explicit (1833–52, 108ff.), the demolition of Schlegel's concept of 'organic' root necessarily led to the rejection of his dichotomy of organic and 'mechanical' languages.[12] Timpanaro (1973) has shown how beneficial it was that at least one authoritative voice spoke against a theory which, partly because it pandered to Eurocentric beliefs, partly because it appealed to Romantic imagination, had an immense success but was also open to racialist exploitation. In the development of the craft of linguistics, controversies of this type demonstrated that even the most minute and pedantic arguments (such as those about the vocalism of Indo-European roots), were relevant to the higher discussions – and vice versa.

6.3.4 Style and influence

In his translation of Bopp's *Vergleichende Grammatik*, Bréal (1866–72, I, iv f.) stated that 'Bopp's work is that where the comparative method can be learned most easily' ('l'ouvrage de M. Bopp est celui où la méthode comparative peut être apprise avec le plus de facilité'). This was because: 'he says through which conjecture he succeeded in noticing certain identities, through which comparison he noticed certain laws; if the continuation of his research did not confirm one of his hypotheses, he has no hesitation in saying it and correcting his statements'. This is correct, but, just as Bopp himself was ready to check and correct or confirm his conclusions, so were his successors, for whom he provided an undoubted starting point. Bopp did indeed create a working style which survived when some of his assumptions and his conclusions had gone out of fashion or had been forgotten. A plain and factual way of writing where the very few rhetorical passages are left for the introductions and conclusions and questions of method are hardly ever discussed, a calm but unshakeable conviction that language can and must be studied *an und für sich* and there is no need to justify one's work in terms of philosophy or literature or history, an ability to define no-go areas where scholarly enquiry is likely to be unprofitable (be this the origin of the root or the genealogical definition of languages for which the right sort of evidence is not available) as well as a clear reluctance to formulate linguistic universals, a predilection for formal argumentation accompanied by a fascination for recurring patterns in language – all these features are typical of Bopp's style and that of the majority of his successors. Equally typical is a tendency to treat languages as self-contained well-defined objects which can be neatly displayed and dissected on the operating table and to accept the traditional linguistic categories without ever calling them into question. In more than one sense Bopp marks a beginning.

6.4 Jacob Grimm

'He felt, as no one had felt before, the natural poetry hidden in language' (Scherer [1883] 1886, ii, 253). This is a striking description for someone like Jacob Grimm, whom we want to list as the third of our technicians. Contrast Raumer's statement: 'Among all discoveries of comparative grammar hardly any had such lasting results as the law of *Lautverschiebung* found by Jacob Grimm' (Raumer [1837] 1863, 8). Jacob Grimm (1785–1863) is better known to Germanists, on whom he had a profound influence, than to linguists in general.[13] And yet his linguistic work deeply impressed his contemporaries; Heine wrote in 1837 that Grimm had done by himself more for *Sprachwissenschaft* than the whole French Academy from the time of Richelieu (Denecke 1971, 92). He and his younger brother Wilhelm, with whom he spent a large part of his life and did most of his work, were born in Hessen as the sons of a lawyer who died early, leaving his numerous children in precarious financial conditions. The two brothers studied law at Marburg, where it was their good fortune to meet Karl Friedrich von Savigny (1779–1861), one of the people connected with the 'historische Schule', and at the time a young teacher of law, who moved in Romantic circles (he married Brentano's sister) and had started work on a history of Roman law in the Middle Ages. It was in Savigny's library that Jacob saw the first medieval German texts and probably acquired that taste for books and for the Middle Ages which dominated the rest of his life. As Savigny's research assistant, Jacob spent some time in Paris in 1805, where he could browse in the local library collections. After successive positions as civil servant or librarian in Kassel, his home-town, he again visited Paris in various diplomatic capacities and attended the Vienna Congress in 1815. Eventually he returned to Kassel as second librarian in the Kassel library, a position which he kept until 1829 and which gave him time to dedicate to his studies. He then moved as Librarian and a professor of *Rechtsalterthümer* (later of German Grammar and Literature) to Göttingen, where Wilhelm followed him with a similar position. The peace and productivity of this period ended in 1837 when Jacob and Wilhelm were two of the seven professors (the *Göttinger Sieben*) who protested against the revocation of the constitution by the King of Hannover. They had to abandon their positions and returned to Kassel until in 1840 they received an invitation to go to Berlin as members of the Academy with the right to lecture in the University. Jacob still kept his political interests and round the troubled period of 1848 took part in political life; he died surrounded by honours in 1863, less than four years after Wilhelm. A stream of publications accompanies this curriculum: until 1818 they are mainly editions of German medieval texts, collections of fables (*Deutsche Sagen*), works on the Hildebrandlied and the Edda, a collection of Spanish *romances*, and the famous *Kinder- und Hausmärchen*, the collection of folk-tales edited together with Wilhelm (from 1812). There are also fantastic etymologies very much on the model of J. A. Kanne (1773–1824), a polymath who at some stage taught history at the Royal Institute in Nürnberg and had attracted Jacob's attention with his wildly speculative books about comparative religion and mythology. Yet as early as 1813 Jacob makes fun of these type of etymologies (he will later speak of the need to tame wild etymology) and after 1815, and a somewhat scathing review by A. W. Schlegel, he clearly manifests greater interest in the detailed study of language. In 1816 he describes to G. F. Benecke, a pupil of the classicist Heyne and an expert editor of early German texts, the new historical evidence which had convinced him, against his previous beliefs, of the correct interpretation of the German *Umlaut*; his analysis of Old High German texts had shown that older forms had a final *i*-vowel, while in later texts this was either lost or changed to -*e* while the vowel of the root was altered (hence Old High German *wari* 'fuisti' was replaced by Middle High German *wäre*). These observations convince Grimm of the importance of the genetic method in the explanation of linguistic facts and at the same time lead him towards a belief in the autonomy of phonetic facts (Ginschel 1967, 361f.). In 1819 there appears the first volume of the *Deutsche Grammatik*, soon to be followed in 1822 by a second edition, which, partly because of Rask's influence, includes a wholly new account of the phonology of the various Germanic languages. Three further volumes (1826, 1831, 1837) completed the grammar and a third edition of part of the first volume appeared in 1840 but was not continued. The work as a whole is in fact a comparative account of the Germanic languages starting from the oldest stages; in its final form it consists of separate accounts of the phonology and inflectional morphology of each language (ancient and modern), with a brief general explanation of common phenomena, followed by an account of word derivation and composition where each formation is considered in each stage of the Germanic languages. Finally, the syntactical categories and the syntax of the simple sentence are analysed. But the linguistic work does not stop here. In 1824 Jacob publishes a translation of Vuk's Serbian grammar with a long introduction which in fact discusses comparative Slavic grammar; 1848 is the year of the *Geschichte der deutschen Sprache* (2nd edn 1853), a series of independent essays about Germanic which mostly aim at cultural history done through a study of words. In 1851 the essay *Über den Ursprung der Sprache* appears, and finally Jacob and Wilhelm begin to publish the first parts of the *Deutsches Wörterbuch* (1854, 1860, 1864), for which work had begun as early as 1838 and which will be continued after their death and not finished until 1960. Non-linguistic work continues: various essays, more editions, *Deutsche Rechtsalterthümer* (1828), *Deutsche Mythologie* (1835), work on the Finnish epic poetry (1845), etc. The range is extremely wide but the main focus is on Germanic languages, literatures, law and religion. The first *Germanistentag* in Frankfurt in 1846 elected as its chairman the man who, rightly or wrongly, has been called the founder of *Germanistik* [14] (Ganz 1973, 10).

6.4.1 Empiricism and historicism

There are some recurrent motifs in Grimm's mature work on language. A starting point is his empiricism; for him, observation is 'the soul of linguistic enquiry' ('die seele der sprachforschung'; Grimm 1822, vi). No wonder then that in 1822 (*ibid.*) he declares himself hostile to the use of logical concepts in grammar and that previously, in the preface to the 1819 grammar, he had criticized both the 'philosophical' and the 'critical' (i.e. descriptive and prescriptive) analysis of language. But empiricism is joined to historicism. For Grimm the 'true' grammatical analysis is historical; his Germanic grammar will demonstrate that the forms of the modern language are incomprehensible unless they are brought back to earlier ones and that present-day grammatical structure can be set up only in historical terms (1819, 16).[15]

Grimm was no philosopher and we do not find in his work extended theoretical discussions, but through the whole of his life he never abandoned the view that language, literature, law, customs, beliefs and folklore are the true expression of the national culture and reflect its development: 'unsere sprache ist auch unsere geschichte' ([1851] 1984, 93). This led him to a commitment on the one hand to the study of all these forms of behaviour and on the other to that of the semantic and cultural aspects of language which others ignored; in his *Rede auf*

Lachmann of 1851 (Grimm 1984, 255) he divided *alle philologen* into those who work on words for the sake of things and those who work on things for the sake of words, and listed himself among the former. We find in him a naïve belief in a direct link not only between the history of words and the cultural and historical development of a nation but also between the development of the more structured parts of language and that of culture in the broadest possible sense. In 1822 (I, 590) he concludes his description of the Germanic consonant shift (Grimm's Law) with the observation that these are 'great events in the history of our language and neither is without inner necessity'; in 1848 (I, 416) he sees the same consonantal developments as 'connected with the violent progress and craving for freedom found in Germany at the beginning of the Middle Ages'. This deep conviction that even the study of e.g. phonology and morphology has a direct input into our understanding of the national culture allows him to get over what he himself saw at times as the disagreeable and dull character of his grammatical work (Tonnelat 1912, 381). The same conviction, joined to Grimm's erudition, so much impressed his contemporaries that, like Jean Paul, they spoke of the *Deutsche Grammatik* as of a *deutsches Sprachheroum*, a holy reliquary of linguistic prehistory (Scherer [1865] 1885, 172). At the same time we recognize in him the Romantic belief in the superiority of early linguistic phases: at least in the early work the loss of inflection is seen as a clear sign of deterioration and all through there is a clear assumption that the 'true' organization or structure of language is best identified in the earliest period.

6.4.2 Linguistics, philology and the attacks against prescriptivism

More than e.g. Bopp or even Rask, Grimm was aware of both the interdependence of, and the tension between, philology (understood as study of texts) and linguistics. His references to the achievements (and limitations) of classical philology are constant and in a sense he can be said to have done for his mother tongue what classicists had done for Greek and Latin. In 1840 (xii), when the 'antiphilosophical' battle was no longer so pressing, he drew a distinction between a study of language aimed at a better comprehension of the texts and a study of language *per se*, aimed at finding fundamental laws and regularities under the superficial anomalies. This, he argued, is the type of linguistics which most appropriately ought to be called *zergliedernde* because it dissects the real organism of language; it is comparative like comparative anatomy and finds its evidence not only in poetry but even in the humblest of dialects. As a literary man and a philologist, Grimm knew that at times 'wurzeln telben ... ist trocken, und in den quellen lesen süss' ('to dig out roots is dry, and to read in the sources is sweet';

Grimm 1840, xv), but he felt that in the end the more austere comparative approach had to be given priority because it yielded results that could not be dispensed with. On the other hand, his relentless perusal of texts and his willingness to explore all sources of information gave his work that sort of solidity which comes from the philological accumulation of data reunited for the first time. While in the Sanskrit field A. W. Schlegel was able to reproach Franz Bopp for his lack of concern for proper philological analysis, and a contrast was established between the more linguistic and comparative approach of the Berlin school headed by Bopp and the more textual and literary approach of the Bonn school headed by Schlegel, in the field of Germanic studies Jacob Grimm could use the same designation – *Philologe* – for himself and for editors of texts such as Karl Lachmann (1793–1851) or G. F. Benecke (1762–1844). The link was also apparent in the techniques used; the linguist Grimm and the philologist Lachmann produced similar analyses of medieval rhymes in order to establish the correct pronunciation of the vowels of the earlier language. The whole plan of the *Deutsche Grammatik* reflects this approach; it is explicitly a comparative work but the analysis is limited to Germanic and each language is treated in its own right. For the phonology, evidence from outside Germanic and general statements which, as we would now put it, bear on Proto-Germanic and Indo-European are restricted to a section on *Allgemeine Vergleichung* (Grimm 1822, 487–507) which takes little more than the 20 final pages in a volume of considerable size.

The combination of an empirical and historical approach with the devotion for German and its history also led Grimm to conclusions and works that had repercussions beyond the strictly scholarly field. In Germany more than in other countries where a standardized language had been in use for longer, the question of the correct form of the national language created strong passions. Grimm took from the start a strong anti-normative line. Every common peasant knows perfections and refinements of the language far superior to what a teacher can even dream of; the whole idea of teaching grammar in schools is fundamentally misguided (Grimm 1819, 2). Language must be allowed to develop on its own and no rules must be imposed from outside. Literary authors and school teachers were equally involved in the problem. In a famous skirmish with Jean Paul, who wanted to eliminate the linking -*s*- from German compounds (*Staatsmann*, etc.), Grimm spoke strongly for the retention of -*s*- on the basis of historical evidence (cf. Christmann 1977, 7–18). The times were moving with him; the *Berlinische Gesellschaft*, to which both Jean Paul and the two Grimms belonged and which had as its aim 'scholarly research in the German language', changed its emphasis from a normative to a historical approach (Faust 1983).[16] In 1838 the classicist Moritz Haupt in writing to Wilhelm Grimm with a first proposal for the compilation of the *Deutsches Wörterbuch* suggested that this should apply the results of historical *Sprachforschung* to the living language (Kirkness 1980, 54). In his turn in 1839 Wilhelm in describing the plans of the dictionary to Savigny stated that from it the reader would learn how people had spoken in the past or were speaking in the present but in no way would it be indicated how they ought to speak; thanks to this wholly historical attitude, the *Wörterbuch* would be distinguished from the 'gesetzgeberischen Weise' of most dictionaries (Dückert 1987, 13). We may wonder whether historicism here leads to a new form of prescriptivism based on history, but in fact Grimm's view is that use (past or present) and integration into the language structure are the only criteria for acceptability.[17]

6.4.3 The origin of language as an empirical problem

Finally, it is useful to summarize Grimm's short essay about the origin of language (1851), not because it opened new vistas or revealed unsuspected depths, but rather because, written as it was in the middle of the century by someone as authoritative as the sixty-six-year-old Grimm, it illustrates the change in attitude which had taken place between the eighteenth and the nineteenth century and at the same time clarifies Grimm's own *modus operandi*. For Grimm the main task is that of exploiting the new achievements of linguistics to look at the old problem. If we go back in time as far as we can, we find in the old phases of language highly inflected systems which presuppose an even higher degree of inflection at an earlier stage; yet historically we observe the disintegration of inflection followed sometimes by a re-creation of inflection through composition. If so, we may hypothesize a first period in which simple roots were created prior to their joining to create inflected forms; at this point consonants and vowels have some of their original value: *l* indicates what is soft, *r* what is rough, etc. Inflections then develop and reach a stage of perfection until abstract thought takes over and the process of continuous evolution, tied both to historical change and to human freedom, continues. English is the perfect example of a language which has become universal, shedding its inflection and mixing the sensuous basis of Germanic and the intellectual power of Latin.

There is here a mixture of old motifs which to Grimm were important (the vowels are feminine and the consonants masculine, etc.) joined to a relentless generalizing from what Grimm, largely following in the steps of Bopp, sees as the normal development of the Indo-European languages. What was a philosophical problem is treated inadequately as an empirical problem.[18] And yet if we want to understand how the climate of opinions had changed it may be worthwhile to compare Grimm and Friedrich Schlegel. For the latter, inflected languages can only decay; for Grimm there is a documented and quasi-cyclical process of loss and re-creation of inflections. Both authors speak for a rejection of the philosophical approach but otherwise they differ. For Schlegel, perfection is to be found in Sanskrit, the oldest language; for Grimm, and he is the man who was always ready to enthuse about the beauty of early linguistic phases, English is the language which has a claim to universality and will eventually dominate not because of its purity, but because of its mixed character. For Schlegel, the gap between inflected and non-inflected languages is total; Grimm is happy to assume that all languages show similar paths of development. Most significantly, while Schlegel speculates on the basis of his knowledge of some Indo-European languages and is confident about his conclusions, Grimm, who does exactly the same, ends by asking himself and his audience whether in fact this is a legitimate procedure.[19]

6.4.4 The technical discoveries and 'Grimm's Law'

Grimm's success as a linguist rests on the appeal that his more general assumptions had for his contemporaries but also on the cumulative impact of his technical achievements;[20] nor should we ignore the political circumstances which caused him to be seen as the prophet of the German language.[21] Yet the more specific results are remarkable in their own right. In essence they are based on a mixture of philological data, acutely analysed, and on a new understanding of some basic principles of historical and comparative analysis, not all of which had been clearly defined before him. Given Bopp's concentration on morphology, it is natural in Grimm's work to look mostly at the novelties in phonological and morphophonemic analysis. Ginschel (1967, 362) has highlighted the importance that the distinction between *Umlaut* and *Ablaut* acquired both in Grimm's own intellectual progress and in that of the subject. Vocalic alternations which indicated grammatical distinctions and were not immediately distinguishable either from a formal or a functional point of view (in English e.g. *foot/feet* and *drive/drove*), could be traced back to processes which were originally very different: one (*Umlaut*) was a Germanic innovation which depended purely on phonological factors (the vowel of *foot* was altered in the plural because it was originally followed by an ending which began with a front vowel), the other (*Ablaut*) was older and inherited. Historical considerations 'made sense' of what otherwise was a highly confusing and unpredictable set of alternations.

But even more than by *Umlaut* and *Ablaut* the contemporaries were impressed by Grimm's analysis of the Germanic consonantal shifts, which even during his lifetime came to be called Grimm's Law.[22] For Wyss (1979, 143) this is untypical of his interests and methodology but here one may differ. Admittedly, as has often been pointed out, Rask (and others before him) had already recognized that the Greek and

Latin stops had regular correspondences with the equivalent series of homorganic stops and fricatives in Icelandic and in the Germanic languages in general.[23] Grimm recognized similar correspondences between Gothic and Old High German: 'in the labial, lingual and guttural sounds the Gothic (Saxon, Frisian, Northern) *tenues* correspond to the High German aspirates, the Gothic *mediae* to the High German *tenues*, and the Gothic aspirates to the High German *mediae*. . . . Just as the Old High German has sunk one step down from the Gothic in all three grades, Gothic itself had already deviated one step from the Latin (Greek, Sanskrit)' (1822, 581–4). To use Grimm's symbols: because of a first shift (*Lautverschiebung*) common to all Germanic languages, Greek or Latin words with T, D, TH (Latin *tu* 'thou', Greek *damān* 'to tame', Greek *thugatēr* 'daughter') correspond to Gothic words with TH, T, D, (*þu, tamjan, daúhtar*), while, because of a second, parallel shift, limited to one language, the Gothic words correspond to High German forms with D, Z, T (*dû, zemen, tohtar*). In the *Deutsche Grammatik* these rules are supported by a rich exemplification but above all by a spelling-out of the principles on which they are based. Grimm makes a clear distinction between 'letter' similarity, which does not count for much in linguistic comparison, and historically observable correspondences which presuppose non-reversible change: a word with Greek T must match a Gothic form with TH; but a Gothic T does not match Greek TH but Greek D. Sound-correspondences of this sort on the one hand 'provide adequate proof of the original relationship of the languages involved', on the other offer a firm basis for etymology. Similar words of the relevant languages which do not observe these correspondences either are not related or are due to borrowing.

The clarity of these statements is impressive even though we are struck by two points: first, the low level of phonetic information (the two *Lautverschiebungen* can be treated as identical only because aspirates and fricatives are confused); secondly, the failure to distinguish, though this is perhaps a matter of formulation rather than of substance, between derivation from a reconstructed proto-language (Indo-European or Proto-Germanic) and derivation from a sister language. It is all too easy to get the impression that Gothic is derived from Greek, and Old High German from Gothic. On the other hand, the confidence with which Grimm is ready to exploit recurring phonological correspondences as proof of (a) the kinship of two or more languages, (b) the etymological connection of words, shows a remarkable change from the *wilde Etymologie* of some ten years earlier when he did not hesitate to compare the names *Tell, Bell, Bell-erophon, Egill* among themselves and with Latin *telum* 'javelin' and Greek *belos* 'arrow' (Ginschel 1967, 328f.). Methodologically there is little here which could not be found explicitly or implicitly in Rask but, even on the unwarranted assumption that Rask's work was as easily approachable as Grimm's, the impact of a discovery which identified a major sound change which, on the one hand, had its starting point not in Greek or Thracian, as Rask assumed, but in the parent language of Greek, Sanskrit and Latin, and, on the other hand, cyclically recurred in the historical period of Germanic was bound to be greater. Grimm's description brought out not only the parallelism between all voiceless stops, all voiced stops, etc., but also the internal coherence of the development which e.g. allowed all labials to change their mode of articulation without nevertheless abolishing their distinctions. We should not underrate the importance of these conclusions – they impressed both contemporary scholars and later generations; after 1822 no Germanist or Indo-Europeanist could ignore Grimm's Law. Indeed a detailed history of the various formulations and reanalyses of the law is exemplary for an understanding of the way in which the methodology of nineteenth-century linguistics developed.[24] From Grimm's point of view what perhaps mattered most was that the *Lautverschiebung* demonstrated that language development shows identifiable forms of regularity at all levels which can be revealed to the enquirer; the hope, as he pointed out, was that further discoveries might reach similar conclusions for the vowels. At a later stage the two *Lautverschiebungen* became the touchstone which served to define one language as against another; the 1854 *Vorrede* to the *Deutsches Wörterbuch* makes it clear that if the dictionary can ignore Low German this is also because Low and High German are separated by the impact on the latter of the second *Lautverschiebung* (Grimm 1864–90, i, xiv–xv). We see here the beginning of that diachronic definition of individual languages that will be extensively used (and misused) by later historical linguists.

6.4.5 *Ablaut* and *Umlaut*

It would be mistaken to see in Grimm a neogrammarian *ante litteram* who only lacks a knowledge of basic phonetics and of the family-tree model. The aim of his work is different. While for us e.g. Grimm's discovery and definition of *Umlaut* has the ring of modernity, his early conception of *Ablaut* brings us into another atmosphere. Wyss (1979, 144ff.) has acutely outlined the various threads which appear in Grimm's theory: in 1826 for him *Ablaut* is not a mechanical alternation, as it will be for the mature Bopp, nor is it determined by accent (as we now believe), but it is a dynamic process which goes back to the beginning of prehistory (Schlerath 1986, 7ff.). The basic form is that of the present (which carries the full meaning of the root, as in *niman*), while a second grade is used in the preterite (*nam*) and in nouns built on it and points to a change or a 'diminution' of meaning. In the clearest instances this is simply a negation of the meaning of the present: thus German *schwach* 'weak, feeble' is connected with OHG *swecchan* 'to smell badly, to stink' as something which has smelt but no longer smells (Grimm 1822–37, II, 79f.). Finally the grade of the preterite plural (*nêmum*) represents a further 'diminution' of meaning. The implicit assumption is that *Ablaut* has a direct link to meaning and perhaps that the choice of vowels and consequently their alternation is prompted by the symbolic value of the vowels themselves. Grimm here is close to the area that Bopp had declared taboo, namely the question of the origin of roots and of why some sounds are linked to specific meanings (Wyss 1979, 154): the general attitude could not find favour with future generations. At the same time, however, all the discussion of *Ablaut* is permeated by the belief that for the linguist formal considerations must take priority over other approaches: two roots, we are told, are different when they have different forms. If one form appears to have different meanings, this must be due to later semantic developments or to our incapacity to reconstruct correctly the earliest meaning. In this way an identification of the roots, on formal criteria, leads to powerful conclusions about meaning and the 'soul of words' (Grimm 1822–37, II, 77). Historicism here takes yet another twist; it is not only the grammatical structure that is explained by its prehistory; the very link between form and meaning is only comprehensible in the earliest stages of language. The paradoxical conclusion is that the priority of the form, which in a sense underlies the thinking of the whole century and which is the hallmark of Grimm's mature thinking, leads him on the one hand to some extreme conclusions about meaning, on the other to some wild etymologies which, though based on a very different approach, recall the 'wilde Etymologie' of his first works: OHG *lahs*, OE *leax* 'salmon' are seen as related to OHG *luchs*, OE *lox* 'lynx', because the vocalic alternation seems to match that of one of the acknowledged *Ablaut* types (Wyss 1979, 149). But the story does not end here; in 1840 (578) Grimm hesitates in assessing Bopp's view about the 'mechanical' origin of *Ablaut* and does not reject it outright because he is impressed by the connection found by Bopp between the length of the ending and the grade of the root in the Sanskrit verb. His position now is that Bopp's point cannot apply to Germanic where the law of vocalic alternation is a dynamic one, whatever its origin (cf. Benware 1974, 33ff.). For Germanic, Grimm does not hesitate to speak of the law's nobility and of the access it gives us to the deepest secrets of language, but he also quotes – almost in his own defence – the laws of *Umlaut*, which started as a mere phonetic development and became in German a real inflectional principle. In other words, the pattern observed by Bopp obliges Grimm to question his earlier view of a phenomenon to which he attributed immense importance; the results are, first, an implicit definition of diachronic grammaticalization (*Ablaut* may have started as a phonetic alternation but acquired different value and importance in Germanic and in German became the dominating principle),

and, secondly, an implicit rejection of the view that the oldest is the best
(cf. also Grimm [1847] 1984, 51). Here too empirical data lead to some
form of rethinking; in a similar manner the young Jacob Grimm had
been obliged by his own analysis of Old High German data to accept
Rask's explanation of *Umlaut*, which he had previously rejected. And
yet in the *Geschichte der deutschen Sprache* (1848, ii, 842–62) Grimm
ignores all these problems and concentrates only on the powerful effect
of *Ablaut* on Germanic and on the quasi-mystical value of the phenomenon. Even from a technical point of view, the history of nineteenth-
century linguistics is not one of linear and unimpeded progress.

Notes

1. We should not confuse the importance attributed in this period to the
   comparison of related languages with that attributed to the comparative
   method e.g. in Bloomfield (1933), where the chapter on comparison precedes that on linguistic change. As we shall see below, at the end of the
   century the neogrammarians, who never abandoned their uniformitarianism,
   maintained that the study of linguistic change has priority over that of comparison and linguistic reconstruction. On the other hand, when attention
   shifted from diachronic to synchronic linguistics, language history was seen
   as based on the comparison of successive synchronic stages; consequently
   one and the same method (the comparative method) could be used to compare both different stages of the same language and different languages
   (Hoenigswald 1987, 79).
2. For Rask's works and letters, see Rask (1932–37, 1941–68), Bjerrum (1959).
   First introductions in Raumer (1870, 470–86), Pedersen ([1931] 1962, 248ff.),
   Jespersen (1922, 36–40), Jankowsky (1972, 61–76), Petersen (1992, 103ff.),
   etc. More recent bibliography in Gipper and Schmitter (1979, 28–32). Background, development, etc. are impressively discussed in Diderichsen (1960
   and [1959] 1976, 254–72); cf. also Hjelmslev (1950–1), Diderichsen (1974),
   Percival (1974a), Petersen (1992, 9–29).
3. Most of this work was in Danish and therefore less accessible to non-
   Germanists. Part of the prize essay was translated into German for an obscure
   publication by J. S. Vater (1822); the Anglo-Saxon grammar was translated
   into English by Benjamin Thorpe in 1830 and was extremely influential
   in Old English studies (Aarsleff 1983, 182ff.). A German translation of
   the Frisian grammar appeared in 1834. In general, Rask's contributions to
   Germanic philology, the editions of early texts and the accurate philology
   of the grammars, are particularly important (Raumer 1870, 470–86). Also
   important was his work on Avestan (he succeeded in demonstrating that it
   was not a Sanskrit dialect) and his incidental, but crucial, contribution to
   the decipherment of cuneiform thanks to the identification of the Old Persian
   genitive plural ending and the consequent attribution of phonetic values to
   two signs.
4. Schmitter (1982, 137–42) discusses the methodology and presuppositions
   of Hjelmslev's essay on Rask.

5. Rask (1818, 167f.). The hyphenation of these forms, both reconstructed and not, is interesting; it indicates of course a form of segmentation similar to that independently operated by Bopp. It would be useful to know at what stage this begins to appear regularly in comparative work; it is absent, for instance, in Gyarmathi (1799) and F. Schlegel (1808).

6. Diderichsen (1960, 65ff.; 1974) shows that Rask's views about *cognatio literarum* are linked to those expressed by J. G. Wachter in the preface to his *Glossarium Germanicum* (1737). In any case, the principle as such is not new (cf. above); the application is.

7. For a tentative bibliography of Bopp's works, cf. Koerner (1989, 299–301), who also lists the English and French translations of the *Vergleichende Grammatik* (1845–50 and 1866–72). The basic biography is still Lefmann (1891–7). For the secondary literature, cf. Gipper-Schmitter (1979, 49–54), Morpurgo Davies (1987), Koerner (1989, 301–2), Schmitter in Nerlich (1988, 53–7) and, above all, Bologna (1992). Particularly important are the articles by Verburg (1950), Pätsch (1960), Neumann (1967, 5–20), Timpanaro (1973), Sternemann (1984a, b). Bopp's dualism has been discussed by Bologna (1992), who recalls Terracini (1949, 61–9).

8. At this stage Bopp certainly did not speak about Indo-European; the name *Indoeuropäisch* was adopted in the second edition of his *Vergleichende Grammatik*. In general for the origin of the various terms used, see Koerner (1989, 149–77). *Indogermanisch* prevailed in Germany, probably on the model of the orientalist and polymath Klaproth, who in his turn may have taken it from the French *indo-germanique* used by geographer C. Malte-Brun (cf. Bolognesi 1994). In English-speaking areas, *Indo-European* prevailed after the term (unhyphenated) was used by the physicist and Egyptologist T. Young in a review of Adelung's *Mithridates* (Young 1813–14). *Aryan* or *Arisch* had a period of favour and was used by F. Schlegel (1808).

9. Sternemann (1984b, 41–52) lists the courses offered by Bopp between 1822 and 1865; in the first period they are mainly in Hebrew, Arabic, Persian and Sanskrit, with a regular course in *Allgemeine Sprachengeschichte*. In 1830 regular courses in *Vergleichende Grammatik* (normally of Sanskrit, Greek, Latin and Germanic) start. Sanskrit remains but the other oriental languages tend to disappear, while the comparative grammar of German or Germanic is introduced.

10. Verburg (1950) sees the sources of Bopp's rationalism in Leibniz and excludes any influence of Sacy. This is possible but not strictly necessary; the views mentioned above were too general to be easily attributed to one source rather than another. Cf. also Savoia (1981, 1986).

11. These are the 'mechanical laws' to which Bopp refers in the introduction to the *Vergleichende Grammatik*, as Bréal explains (1866–72, I, 1). His theories about *Ablaut* brought Bopp to strong (but amicable) disagreements with Jacob Grimm (cf. Bopp [1827] 1836 and Schlerath 1986). The correlation between 'heavy' and 'light' syllables within a word is still accepted nowadays, but the prevailing explanation now operates in terms of an original pattern of accentuation which determined loss or shortening of vowels in non-accented syllables, a theory which was first hinted at in

a letter by Humboldt to Bopp (Lefmann 1891–7, Nachtrag 52*) and became more generally accepted in the 1860s.

12. Bopp himself, firm in his formal approach, distinguished between monosyllabic languages with no composition, such as Chinese, languages with monosyllabic roots and capacity for composition (as most languages, including the Indo-European ones) and languages with disyllabic roots and grammatical distinctions indicated by an internal modification of the root (as Semitic), a classification which, perhaps because of the absence of the extralinguistic overtones which characterized Schlegel's views, did not have great resonance.

13. Grimm's shorter writings are reprinted in his *Kleinere Schriften* (Grimm 1864–90); for a selection see the recent collection of lectures held in the Berlin Academy (Grimm 1984). His other major works are quoted below. The bibliography about the two Grimm brothers is immense. Cf. for a first introduction Denecke (1971), who also lists the main editions of the correspondence, Marini (1972), and Koerner (1989, 303–23). His linguistic thought is discussed extensively by Benfey (1869, 427–70) and Raumer (1870, 378–452, 495–539). Scherer's book (1885) is still interesting (but see Wyss 1979, 1–32). For Grimm's earlier work, cf. Tonnelat (1912) and above all Ginschel (1967); for an interesting attempt at an unconventional interpretation and a discussion of Grimm's fortune, see Wyss (1979). For the work on the *Wörterbuch*, see Kirkness (1980), Henne (1985, 1990), Dückert (1987, especially 7–48), Reichmann (1990) and Wiegand (1990), all with further bibliography. Denecke and Teitge (1989) attempt a reconstruction of the two brothers' library.

14. Wyss (1979, *passim* and 58ff.) has reasonably asked whether this interpretation of Grimm's role has any historical value.

15. It is often assumed that Grimm owes his historicism to Savigny and that e.g. his non-normative approach to grammar must be compared with the way in which Savigny opposed the introduction of a new code of laws into the German states on the ground that law, like language, must arise organically within a nation and cannot be imposed arbitrarily by the lawgiver. However, Grimm's progress towards linguistic studies seems to be independent of Savigny and some of the historicistic attitudes were in the air; Wyss (1979, 54–93) has made a strong case against the standard view.

16. School grammars necessarily preserved a normative element – and indeed this practice was defended with good arguments by R. von Raumer ([1855] 1863, 205ff.), one of Grimm's admirers – but here too attempts were made to introduce an historical perspective in textbooks or at least in their prefaces (Naumann 1986, 93ff.; Chorley 1984, 75, 134).

17. Wyss (1979, 175–82) asks a similar question about the *Deutsches Wörterbuch*, which, according to Grimm, was meant to be read and learned in the German family and included both current and old words and meanings. But, as Wyss points out, the contradiction is only apparent because Grimm starts from the assumption that the tangible, concrete meaning of a word is found in its first attestations and that to understand a word in full it is necessary to understand its concrete meaning. Admittedly, in the dictionary most foreign words are ignored but this is because a word to be

accepted must be (or have been) both 'popular' and 'deutsch', i.e. fully integrated into the structure of the language (Kirkness 1980, 17ff., Dückert 1987, 18–21).

18. Trabant (1985a, 577f.) points out how striking is the contrast between Grimm's approach to the problem (published as a *Berlin Akademie-Abhandlung*) and that of Humboldt (see above, p. 108); see also Di Cesare (1990a, 115). Ricken (1990c) sees the contrast somewhat differently and highlights some common elements in Humboldt and Grimm. For Grimm and Schelling, see Moretti (1991).

19. According to Pedersen ([1931] 1962, 40), Grimm believed that the comparative grammar of Indo-European 'leads us back to the very beginning of language'. This is an exaggeration, partly because of Grimm's final disclaimer, partly because all that he extracts from his studies is the identification of a pattern of development, not the reconstruction of a primitive language. On the other hand, Pedersen ignores the latent uniformitarianism of the essay, which in his eyes ought to have been a positive point.

20. The technical success is reflected in the success of the technical terminology that Grimm adopted or created. We owe to him technical terms which we still use such as 'strong' or 'weak' verbs, *Auslaut, Inlaut, Anlaut, Ablaut, Umlaut*, etc., even if the last two terms had been used by others before Grimm (cf. Ising 1956, 22; Skála 1961, 225; Lühr 1989, 33). The decision to adopt latinized rather than Germanic terminology in grammatical analysis goes back to the first edition of the *Deutsche Grammatik* (1819), where in the *Vorrede* Grimm speaks strongly for e.g. *Genitiv* and *Dativ* instead of *Zeugefall* and *Gebfall*.

21. How much Grimm had to offer is perhaps shown by his later reception. For two linguists as different as Benfey (1869, 451) and Henry Sweet (1910), the *Geschichte der deutschen Sprache* is either his most significant or one of his two most significant works; yet for Jespersen (1922, 47) the most impressive and lasting work is that dedicated to syntax in the fourth volume of the *Deutsche Grammatik*, i.e. exactly the type of work for which, according to Paul, Grimm was not particularly gifted (Lühr 1989, 130; see in general Rössing-Hager 1986 and Lühr, *op. cit.*).

22. 'Das Grimmsche Gesetz' appears in Raumer ([1837] 1863, 5, 9, etc.); in 1833 Pott (1833–6, I, xii) had referred to the laws (*Gesetze*) found by Grimm for Germanic. 'Grimm's Law' is apparently first found in English in an 1838 work by the Rev. W. B. Winning (cf. Aarsleff 1983, 209; Beyer 1981, 169–71). In 1864 (198) Max Muller entitled 'Grimm's Law' a chapter of his *Lectures on the Science of Language (Second Series)* and referred to 'one phonetic law, commonly called Grimm's Law', but the term already appears in his 1856 Comparative Mythology essay (Max Müller 1868–75, ii, 93).

23. The question of priority between Rask and Grimm has been debated at great length, particularly with reference to the 'discovery' of *Umlaut* (cf. Antonsen 1962; Ginschel 1967, 362) and of the first *Lautverschiebung* (cf. Collitz 1926; Jespersen 1922, 43–7; Jankowsky 1972, 69–76). Though Ginschel has shown that Grimm reached his concept of *Umlaut* on the basis of historical evidence which Rask did not have, it is still not clear how far he was influenced by Rask's previous observations. As for 'Grimm's

Law', no one would deny Rask's priority (though Rask too had been partly preceded by a number of earlier authors); the question is whether Grimm's global formulation did in fact change the nature of the results – it certainly had greater impact on his contemporaries. On the other hand, in 1872 A. J. Ellis (1873–4, 31) still wrote about the law 'of Rask or Grimm'.

24. After Grimm, important steps in the understanding of the *Lautverschiebung* are found in Raumer ([1837] 1863, 1–104), Lottner (1862), Grassmann (1863), Braune (1874), Paul (1874), Verner (1875). The neogrammarians tended to reject any connection between the first and the second *Lautverschiebung* and to treat even the changes summarized by the first *Lautverschiebung* as a series of unconnected events (cf. Streitberg 1896, 103ff.). A strong reaction against this attitude and a plea for a return to Grimm's unitary vision can be found in Fourquet (1948). For more modern developments, see the bibliography in Collinge (1985, 63–76) and even more recently van Coetsem (1990). Fifteen years after the appearance of Grimm (1822), the two points made above about phonetics and about the need for a clearer model of language relationship were highlighted by R. von Raumer (*loc. cit.*) in a monograph which is one of the first books by a linguist which stresses the need for an accurate articulatory analysis of all sounds discussed.

7

Comparative studies and the diffusion of linguistics

7.1 From individuals to schools

For the first part of the century it proved impossible to provide an account which ignored the individuals in order to concentrate on the results. Bopp, Grimm and Humboldt knew each other well and read each other's publications as they read those of Rask and of the two Schlegels, but they differed considerably both in their aims and in their theoretical underpinnings. Round the middle of the century the position changed: the *dramatis personae* increased drastically, operated on a wider geographical area, and tended to share, if not a common background, a common set of technical results on which to build. To provide here an account of the biography and motivation of all linguists of this period is impossible; it is preferable to try to identify the major trends and to refer to the individuals involved only in so far as they impinge on them.[1] A warning is necessary: the periodization adopted here follows the development of the technical work of comparison, which will be deeply influenced by the neogrammarian movement in the middle and the end of the 1870s. The more general discussion is less suitable for this type of classification; here it would perhaps be easier to opt for a simple distinction between the first and the second half of the century. However, it is not possible (nor perhaps reasonable) to distinguish the two forms of activity; nor should we forget that in the period in question the technical work has a guiding function (from an intellectual or institutional point of view). The compromise adopted here will oblige us to break occasionally the chronological limits indicated.

We must put the mid century in some perspective: Humboldt was dead, but Bopp and Grimm lived until 1867 and 1863 respectively. In Germany the last part of Bopp's *Vergleichende Grammatik* appeared in 1852 and the second edition started to appear in 1857; the publication of the English translation was concluded in 1853. Grimm's *Deutsche*

Grammatik was completed in 1837 but the *Geschichte der deutschen Sprache* appeared in 1848 and the *Deutsches Wörterbuch* started to appear in 1854. Humboldt's *Kawi Sprache* had appeared in 1836–9 and its editor, Eduard Buschmann, Humboldt's assistant and collaborator, started to publish a series of comparative works on American Indian languages in the 1850s.[2]

Between 1833 and 1836 August Friedrich Pott (1802–87), a student of Bopp at Berlin, and then an Ordinarius of *Vergleichende Sprachkunde* in Halle, had published the two volumes of his monumental *Etymologische Forschungen auf dem Gebiete der Indo-Germanischen Sprachen*, which produced the comparative evidence for a reconstruction of the bulk of the Indo-European lexicon, while also clarifying (even in its heaviness and obscurity) a number of methodological points of considerable importance. The first volume (pp. 180–284) listed (in their Sanskrit form) 375 roots which could be attributed to Indo-European and for which Pott mentioned the known correspondences in the various Indo-European languages;[3] in 1867–73 this was replaced by a *Wurzelwörterbuch der indogermanischen Sprachen* (part of Pott 1859–76) which listed 2,226 roots. It is easy to forget the importance of Pott's work, which spans a large part of the century, but his comparative results were essential to the progress of the subject, and the sharpness and thoughtfulness of his reflections about problems as different as those of sound laws, the language of gipsies, semantics, typology, race, etc. are infinitely impressive.[4]

7.1.1 The expansion of the discipline

Round the middle of the century an increase in the number and size of technical works accompanies the rapid diffusion and institutionalization of historical and comparative linguistics. The existence of an Indo-European family is now generally accepted;[5] the enquiry then turns to the history of the individual branches or to various fumbling attempts to compare Indo-European with other linguistic families (Semitic, Finno-Ugric) or even to exploitation of the comparative method for different families: Bantu with the studies of W. H. I. Bleek in 1862–9; Altaic with W. Schott and M. A. Castrén round 1850; Dravidian with R. Caldwell in 1856; Chinese and Tibetan with R. Lepsius in 1861; the languages of Melanesia with Hans Conon von der Gabelentz in 1861–73, etc. (cf. Tagliavini 1963, i, 81ff.).

In Germany Grimm's work is followed by similar studies on the comparative grammar of the Romance languages (Diez 1836–44), of the Slavic languages (Miklosich 1852–74), of the Celtic languages (Zeuss 1853), etc. Individual languages also acquire their major grammars written within the historical-comparative framework: an example is Eduard Adolf Maetzner's three-volume *Englische Grammatik* (1860–5), which covers some 1300 years of history and of variation in a sort of '"tele-ological" description which presents the now from the point of view of the past' (Leitner 1991b), while giving due importance to syntax. After Pott's list of roots, most Indo-European languages or language groups acquire an etymological dictionary or the equivalent, from Greek in 1839–42 (Benfey) and 1858–62 (Curtius) to Romance in 1853 (Diez), to Slavic in 1886 (Miklosich), to quote but a few examples. In 1868 August Fick produced a *Wörterbuch der indogermanischen Grunds-prache*.[6] Yet what gives the second part of the century its specific flavour is the move from a purely comparative approach to an approach which is at the same time comparative **and** historical **and** philological.[7] Here Grimm's model prevails; Diez (1794–1876), who held at Bonn from 1830 the first chair of Romance Philology, started as a literary scholar and editor of texts and, even when in his forties he turned to linguistic work, retained his devotion to 'exegetic philology' (Malkiel 1976a, 6f.). Franz Miklosich (1813–91), who was professor of Slavic Studies at Vienna from 1850, not only counts as the scholar who introduced the historical and comparative method into the study of the Slavic lan-guages, but was also an indefatigable editor of texts of ethnographic and historical importance. In Sanskrit studies a 'hero of scholarship', to use Delbrück's phrase, such as the Russian-born Otto Böhtlingk (1815–1904), who worked for some time at Bonn, produced an admirable edition of Pāṇini's grammar (1840) and was largely responsible for the monumental Sanskrit dictionary which he published with Randolph Roth at St Petersburg (1855–75). Yet he also did work on Vedic accentuation which was fundamental for further developments in Indo-European studies and produced in 1851 a description of Yakut, a Turkic language of North East Asia, which is impressive for its method as well as for the general reflections about language classification and comparison.

At least for those who were concerned with the Middle Ages or the earlier stages of languages, the techniques of historical linguistics become an integral part of philological training. Even the much older tradition of classical studies begins to yield. Some of the great classicists of the beginning of the century had remained aloof when confronted with the new comparativism: too many extravagant claims were made on behalf of the new discipline, often by scholars whose proficiency in the clas-sical languages was inadequate. The aims of classicists and comparat-ivists were also different: the former studied the language for the sake of the literary texts; the latter declared that language had to be studied for its own sake and that the primitive languages and non-literary texts were as interesting as the most perfect Greek poem (Rocher 1957–8). Gottfried Hermann (1772–1848), the main exponent of the grammatical and critical approach of the period, was often hostile. And yet 1839 saw the appearance of the first thorough account of the Greek dialects based both on the literary texts and on the inscriptions; this was due to H. L. Ahrens (1809–81), who, while dedicating the first volume of his work to August Boeckh, the *Altertumwissenschaftler par excellence*, did not hesitate to declare his indebtedness to Jacob Grimm and to use Sanskrit and Latin correspondences to explain the Greek forms.[8] In the same year, Ahrens' exact contemporary, Theodor Benfey (1809–81), the Sanskritist and historian of linguistics, began to publish what was in effect the first etymological dictionary of Greek (Benfey 1839–42). More importantly, from the late 1840s onwards, Georg Curtius (1820–85) dedicated most of his scholarly activity, which culminated when he held for all of twenty-four years a chair of *Klassische Philologie und indogermanische Sprachwissenschaft* at Leipzig, to the historical analysis of Greek, with results which enjoyed remarkable popularity among classicists as well (see below p. 186, note 40).[9] The Danish scholar J. N. Madvig (1804–86) not only counts as one of the great classicists of the century and had a considerable role to play in linguistic thought, but also was well acquainted with the principles of comparative linguistics and lectured on the subject.

Outside Germany we observe a slow diffusion and acceptance of the German approach (often muted in a less comparative and more historical and philological direction), first in the form of learned publications, translations, survey articles, etc. then at the institutional level. In Britain, Benjamin Thorpe (1782–1870) and John Kemble (1807–57), who had studied with Rask and Grimm respectively, started a vigorous programme of philological work in Old English inspired by the continental tradition and firmly attacked both the earlier amateurish philology and Horne Tooke's unscholarly etymologies (see e.g. Wiley 1971, 1990). In 1843 the new Greek–English Lexicon by H. G. Liddell and R. Scott deliberately followed the historical arrangement propounded by the German scholar F. Passow. In 1842 the foundation of the Philological Society at London brought together a number of people concerned with language at a time when German scholarship was having considerable impact (Aarsleff 1983, 221, but see also Beyer 1981, 177ff.) and opened the way to the start in the 1860s of the Society's great work, the *New English Dictionary on Historical Principles*. Soon after the middle of the century (1854), F. Max Müller (1823–1900), who had studied at Berlin and at Paris (with Burnouf) and was preparing a monumental edition of the RigVeda which he hoped to see published in Oxford, was appointed to the first of his Oxford chairs (see above, p. 9).[10] The new interest in linguistics even outside academic circles is best illustrated with the reference to an 1854 letter by Sir Charles Trevelyan, then Assistant-Secretary to the Treasury, who suggested that the war effort (the Franco-British Crimean War against Russia) required a small book which listed for the use of officers the languages spoken in the northern part of the

Turkish empire and in the adjoining Russian provinces, while also explaining the family to which they belonged and their general character and structure. Max Müller's ([1854] 1855) booklet, written in answer to this request, included a clear account of the principles of comparative philology and reached two editions in less than a year. At the time Max Müller's gift for popularization acquired significant importance: his extremely well attended 1861 Lectures on the Science of Language at the Royal Institution in London were later published in fourteen successive editions, translated into French, German, Italian, Russian, Swedish and Dutch, and chosen by Cardinal Newman as a prize-book for boys. Contemporary reviewers commenting on the size of the audience noticed with amazement that this was not attracted by the brilliant experiments or the revelations of a Faraday or an Owen, but simply by a 'philosophical exposition of the inner mysteries of language' (G. Müller 1902, i, 148).

In Italy from the 1840s and somewhat earlier we find Bernardino Biondelli's first articles, which aim at introducing comparative linguistics to an Italian public (De Mauro 1980, Santamaria 1981) and we begin to see the influence of German scholarship on Carlo Cattaneo's linguistic thought (Timpanaro 1969, 253ff.). Even less well known figures such as the Piedmontese Giovenale Vegezzi-Ruscalla in the 1850s deplored the ignorance of the linguistic work produced in Germany and asked for the creation in Piedmont of three linguistic chairs dedicated to the Romance, the Germanic and the Slavic languages respectively (Santamaria 1981, 25ff., 38). The study of Sanskrit in Universities was established from the 1850s. In the 1860s a remarkable programme of translations made accessible in Italian books such as Max Müller ([1861] 1862), Heyse (1856), some of the works by Georg Curtius, and Schleicher's *Compendium* (Timpanaro 1979, 406ff.). The enthusiasm for the new discipline reached unheard-of levels. Giacomo Lignana, Professor of *Lingue e letterature comparate* in the University of Naples and trained in Sanskrit at Bonn, saw linguistics as absorbing and replacing philology and in an anti-Hegel polemical outburst described Bopp's comparative grammar as the real discovery of the philosophy of history of our race ('la scoperta della filosofia della storia della nostra schiatta') (Timpanaro 1979, 440).[11] However, in spite of a remarkable tradition of efforts in Italian dialectology, most Italian work remained largely unknown abroad until Graziadio Isaia Ascoli (1829–1907) succeeded in obtaining international fame and Adolf Mussafia (1835–1905) obtained a chair in Vienna and wrote in German.[12] Ascoli, however, offers an interesting contrast with contemporary German scholars both because of his background and because of his achievements: while in Germany the new generation had been taught by accredited University professors, Ascoli was strictly an autodidact and was proud to be so. Also, while the contemporary German generation provided scholars who were either Indo-Europeanists or Romance scholars or general linguists or at best spanned two of these fields, in Ascoli we have someone who gained recognition in all of them. Curtius, who in the third edition of his *Grundzüge der griechischen Etymologie* (1869, xi) had spoken of a new enthusiasm for the studies started by Bopp in countries such as France and Italy, which previously had had little to contribute, in the fifth edition of the same work (1879, 83) referred to Ascoli's pioneering research, to his astonishing learning and his wonderful sharpness.

In France, as we have seen, there was a tradition of oriental learning, which Max Müller ([1854] 1855, x) envied, but the teaching was more geared to individual languages than to linguistics, and for good reasons the new discipline was slow to become established (Baggioni 1989a). Even so the principles of comparative grammar made their appearance in official courses at the École Normale by Eugène Burnouf (1801–52) and Émile Egger in the first half of the century (see above, p. 21 note 5) and of course in the achievements of Burnouf's research work. In the late 1860s we find two different groups of historical and comparative linguists who were responsible for the creation of two new periodicals (see above, p. 12). On the one hand, H. Chavée (1815–77), a Belgian settled in Paris, Abel Hovelacque (1843–96) and Lucien Adam (1833–1918) had a meeting point in the École d'Anthropologie and were influenced both by Comte's positivism and by Schleicher's biologism; on the other hand, a group headed by Michel Bréal (1832–1915) and Gaston Paris (1839–1903), who had studied in Germany with Bopp and Diez respectively, centred round the newly founded École Pratique des Hautes Études and the Société de Linguistique de Paris (from 1866), while rejecting the extreme forms of organicism in linguistics. We owe to Bréal (1866–72) the French translation, with an extensive set of notes, of the second edition of the comparative grammar by Bopp, deliberately chosen in a period in which the most up-to-date text was Schleicher's *Compendium* (see below, p. 12). In his turn, Gaston Paris helped to translate the third edition of the grammar of Romance languages by Diez (1863, 1874–6; see Desmet and Swiggers 1996). Yet the greatest propagandizer was perhaps Ernest Renan (1823–92), the man who in 1849 professed to owe to Burnouf his *vocation à la science* and who became one of the first members of the Société de Linguistique. A first version of his history of the Semitic languages had obtained the Prix Volney in 1847 (cf. Meillet 1938, 167ff.) and in the preface to the first edition of the book in 1855 he stated that his aim was to do for the Semitic languages what Bopp had done for Indo-European languages, 'i.e. an account of the grammatical system which showed how the Semites succeeded in giving through speech a complete expression to thought' ('c'est-à-dire un tableau du système grammatical qui montrât de quelle manière les Sémites sont arrivés à donner par la parole une expression complète à la pensée'). In fact nothing could be more remote from the style of Bopp's *Vergleichende Grammatik* than that of Renan's *Histoire*, which is fundamentally an external history of the Semitic languages. Yet the very fact that the wish was expressed is significant, as is the claim made in the same preface that three or four years had been enough to reveal, through the analysis of Indo-European languages, the most profound laws of language, while Semitic philology had remained isolated and almost alien to the general development of science ([1855] 1858, xii).[13] Round the middle of the century Renan contributed to the conditions which eventually introduced and institutionalized linguistics in France but, in spite of his total admiration for the German results and scholarship, both his *modus operandi* and some of his general views were *sui generis*. He remained to the end a dilettante of genius.

7.1.2 The new role of linguistics

We could discuss the successes and developments of linguistic subjects elsewhere; Denmark, which we have already mentioned, the Netherlands, Russia, Spain and the United States would be obvious ports of call and monographs or recent collections of essays contribute to such areas of study (Noordegraaf, Versteegh and Koerner 1992, Quilis and Niederehe 1986, Sarmiento 1987, Andresen 1990, etc.). Yet it may be better to use the available space to give a quick look at a wide penumbra of academic or non-academic activities, thoughts and beliefs which had always been 'language-related' but at this stage come considerably closer to the new 'craft of linguistics' or are inspired by it. We are dealing with a wildly disparate range of concerns and can only mention a few.

A first field which needs to be mentioned, even if it cannot be properly explored here, is that of writing and decipherments. Starting with the end of the eighteenth century but continuing all through the first half of the nineteenth century and later, there is a spate of impressive successes in this field. Previously incomprehensible scripts such as Egyptian Hieroglyphic, Persian cuneiform and Akkadian cuneiform yielded to their respective decipherers in the midst of considerable publicity; the Frenchman J.-F. Champollion (1790–1832), the German G. F. Grotefend (1775–1853) and the Englishman H. Rawlinson (1810–95) were the main protagonists of this work, but Rasmus Rask was influential in the decipherment of cuneiform. The work has more to do with philology than with linguistics, but came to be seen as part and parcel of the tangible successes of linguistics, as did the demonstration that languages as different as Welsh and Sanskrit were related. This led, on the one hand, to a great deal of interest in writing and in the connection between language and writing, between the evolution of language and that of writing, etc., and, on the other hand, to a greater faith in the power of linguistics to resolve all enigmas.[14]

As a result of this and other developments, we witness a remarkable change in the status of comparative linguistics; the newcomer, which had used for its justification the parallel with comparative anatomy, now acquires a leading role: at various times ethnology, anthropology, palaeontology, law, etc. came to look at it as a possible model (Stocking 1987, 56ff., 122). The comparative method understood in the historical genealogical sense spreads from linguistics to the social sciences (Leopold 1980, 58).

A consequence of the changed status is that linguistics now acquires a new semi-political role. Linguists were naturally prone to a form of Eurocentrism which brought them to conclude that the Indo-European languages were superior to the others. We have already seen Friedrich Schlegel's affirmations about the superiority of organic languages and Humboldt's faith in the importance of inflection. We may add, by way of example, Richard Lepsius's belief that languages with grammatical gender are better than those without[15] – among them only the Indo-European languages, he argued, have three genders and to them 'belong the future hopes of the world' (Lepsius [1863] 1981, 90). These views, accepted as much in Great Britain, France and Italy as in Germany (Römer 1985), could be easily reinterpreted in racist terms. The link between language and race is not a novelty of the middle of the century, nor is the theory of the inequality of races, but the belief that comparative philology had succeeded in providing a scientific demonstration of the genealogical links between some languages lent itself to political exploitation. Once a Germanic group of languages had been defined it became possible to exalt the Germanic or Saxon 'race' at the expense of other, less prominent, European nations. At a more general level, the Aryan race, which was mostly defined on linguistic bases as the race of Indo-European speakers, was contrasted with other supposedly inferior races, even if some linguists objected. A. F. Pott (1856; cf. 1852, 508), for example, violently reacted against the *Essai sur l'inégalité des races humaines* (1853–5) by Arthur, comte de Gobineau (1816–82) and against the use and abuse which he made of linguistic data (Leopold 1984, Ricken 1990b). Before him, Humboldt had expressly denied any correlation between language and race;[16] Whitney had views similar to those of Pott. Other linguists, however, accepted some form of racism: Renan believed in the inequality of races (Olender 1989, 75–114).[17]

Outside the linguists' circles, the linguistic-racial argument was all pervasive but could lead in different directions. The British attitude to India may serve as an example. If the Indians were Aryans, as Max Müller constantly repeated, it followed that they were, in Charles

Kingsley's words, 'our kinsfolk and equals'. This was likely to have consequences for the way in which colonial policy was envisaged – by the colonies at least (Leopold 1974). On the other hand, colonialism in India could be justified as prompted by the need to rescue the long-lost brothers, allowing them to benefit from the achievements of the most progressive Aryan nations. In general, the whole problem of language and race acquires considerable importance at this point in time and forms part of the background against which the history of linguistic thought ought to be considered.[18] In 1861 Max Müller remarked: 'In modern times the science of language has been called in to settle some of the most perplexing political and social questions. . . . in America comparative philologists have been encouraged to prove the impossibility of a common origin of languages and races in order to justify, by scientific arguments, the unhallowed theory of slavery' ([1861] 1862, 12).[19]

Other less contentious activities also gravitated towards the newly established academic discipline. From the beginning of the century onwards, work was going on which was prompted by the particular needs of each country and which was often entrusted to learned amateurs not necessarily linked with institutions. We can think of dictionary-making, of grammar-writing, of the spelling reform, of the 'language question', i.e. of the discussions about language standardization and the literary language in the emerging nations, and even of the description of 'exotic' languages in countries such as Russia or the United States where the need existed. Political and social events obviously influenced these needs; the increase in literacy called for more textbooks such as grammars or dictionaries, and the nationalistic movements which led to the creation of different states in the nineteenth century drew attention to language. Michael (1987, 7f.) records 377 different grammar books for English in 1821–70 as contrasted with 49 in 1721–70; further work (Michael 1991) has identified 456 grammars for the later period and a grand total of 856 grammars for the whole of the nineteenth century, which, it is suggested, could be a thousand, if all facts were available. At the same time we witness the explosion of textbooks meant to instruct in foreign languages; foreign-language teaching (in addition to, or sometimes to the exclusion of, the classical languages) becomes a feature of the schoolroom in Europe and practical needs cause some of the books meant for the traveller or self-taught person to acquire best-seller status (Howatt 1984, 129ff.). Languages such as Bulgarian, Serbian, Croatian, Slovenian, Ukrainian, Czech and Slovak acquired a more stable literary form in the nineteenth century in the midst of emotional debates (cf. e.g. Schenker and Stankiewicz 1980); the Italian *questione della lingua* is just as important, and so are the contemporary German discussions. The novelty is that to a certain extent all these multifarious activities and interests begin to be influenced (in general terms at least) by academic linguistics. Nowhere is this clearer than in the case of dictionaries. While writing in a self-congratulatory mode that 'in the Oxford [English] Dictionary, permeated as it is through and through with the scientific method of the century, Lexicography has ... reached its supreme development', James Murray ([1900] 1970, 49) listed in a footnote the great national dictionaries of the mid century: Grimm's German dictionary has already been mentioned (the first fascicle appeared in 1852); the work for the *Woordenboek der Nederlandsche Taal* also began in 1852 (the first volume appeared in 1882); the first volume of a new edition of the Italian *Vocabolario della Crusca* was published in 1863. Murray claimed superiority for his dictionary while implicitly acknowledging that the others too had to a greater or lesser degree adopted the historical method. Earlier on, while paying tribute to Noah Webster, the American lexicographer (1758–1843), Murray had pointed out that in the later editions of the *American Dictionary of the English Language* Webster's so-called etymologies had been cleared out *en masse* and the work placed in the hands of 'men abreast of the science of the time'. The reference was obviously to the purge of the Tooke-like 'derivations' of the first editions of Webster conducted in the 1860s by a German-trained linguist (Andresen 1990, 65f.). In other words, from the middle of the century the prevailing form of linguistics, historical linguistics, had spread not only into the Universities but also into works which were more widely diffused.

On the other hand, academic linguistics was not impervious to external influences. Phonetics, a subject which first became established at the end of the nineteenth century, offers an instructive example of the convergence of different needs and motifs which eventually come under the umbrella of linguistics. A brief digression may be in order even if it obliges us to move beyond the chronological limits of this chapter.

7.1.3 Converging trends: phonetics

It is normal to point out that the phonetic analysis of the Indian grammarians was far more advanced than that of their Western counterparts (see Cardona in Lepschy 1994–   , i, 27ff.). At the beginning of the nineteenth century, barring a few exceptions such as Rask, most of the scholars that we have mentioned so far had only inadequate notions of articulatory phonetics and, for the most part, no notions of auditory phonetics; instrumental phonetics did not really exist. Grimm (1840, xv) found unattractive the thought of substituting 'pure physiological functions' for his *Laute* or, as he more often called them, his 'letters' (*Buchstaben*).[20] In the last third of the century the position is very different. It seems likely that, if at that stage linguists become aware that at least some knowledge of phonetics is necessary, this is due to the convergence of many different paths which developed in the earlier period.

First, a universal phonetic alphabet was a desideratum for both practical and academic purposes. If it had been available, it would have been possible to express in writing the pronunciation of all known languages; the alphabet would also have been invaluable for such disparate purposes as helping with the learning of foreign languages, teaching to read, defining the pronunciation of new lexical elements in one's own language, teaching the deaf, writing down for the first time exotic languages so that missionaries could introduce writing (and the Bible) to remote tribes, documenting new languages or dialects for scholarly purposes, and, last but not least, even reforming the spelling system of the existing Western languages. Concerns of this type go back a very long way (Abercrombie 1981, Kemp 1981, Gessinger 1994) but become crucial in a wide range of circles at the beginning of the century, following in the steps of the first discussions by Sir William Jones. In the wake of the new explosion of linguistic knowledge, Volney was eager to promote a 'pasigraphy', i.e. a universal phonetic alphabet. The same interests were shared in America by Du Ponceau and John Pickering (Rousseau 1981; Andresen 1990, 98ff.; Swiggers 1994, 253ff.), though the phonetic bases of the latter's attempt were insufficient and were castigated in the more successful *Das allgemeine linguistische Alphabet* by K. R. Lepsius (1855, [1863] 1981). In the 1850s and the 1860s we find a number of different proposals for a universal alphabet: Pitman's Phonotypy, Max Müller's 'Missionary Alphabet', Lepsius's 'Standard Alphabet', Haldeman's 'Analytic Orthography', Brücke's phonetic transcription, Merkel's iconic system, Thausing's musical notation, Ellis's Palaeotype (as well as his other proposals), Fourner's *alphabet universel*, and above all Bell's 'Visible Speech', which aimed at constructing 'a Scheme of Symbols, which should embody the whole classification of sounds, and make each element of speech shew in its symbol the position of its sound in the organic scale' (Bell 1867, 18). In all instances these efforts (and the list is far from complete) called for an improved phonetic knowledge (Firth [1946] 1957, 92ff.); in some instances they led to interesting new analyses, as in that offered for the vocalic system by A. Melville Bell (1867), who lectured on speech and elocution at the University of Edinburgh and then at London, and who is often credited with the introduction of the concept of cardinal vowels. Henry Sweet had immense respect for his work, saw him as one of his teachers, and 'Visible Speech' influenced his Broad Romic Transcription, which in its turn was influential on the International Phonetic Alphabet. This work fed into the practical needs of language teaching; the so-called Reform Movement of the late nineteenth century brought phonetics to the classroom and was started and supported by leading phoneticians:

Henry Sweet, but also Paul Passy in France, who founded the Phonetic Teachers' Association (later renamed International Phonetic Association) and W. Viëtor in Germany (see below, p. 295ff.).

A second path to phonetics originates in the natural sciences. At the end of the eighteenth century, one of the first attempts at mechanical speech synthesis had come from the Austrian Wolfgang von Kempelen (1734–1804), a polymath, a jurist, and a mechanical genius who also wrote a *Mechanismus der menschlichen Sprache* (1791), which offers a remarkable physiological account of speech organs (Jespersen [1933] 1970, 47ff.; Malmberg 1991, 385ff.; Gessinger 1994, 398–400, 580ff. and *passim*). In 1865 A. J. Ellis, whom we quoted earlier in the context of universal alphabets or phonetic transcription, wrote an open letter in defence of Bell's 'Visible Speech' and found it useful to give an account of the bibliography on phonetics which he had been able to use (Ellis ap. Bell 1867, 23ff.). In addition to von Kempelen and to his own *Essentials of Phonetics* (1848), he referred to manuals of physiology and to the *Grundzüge der Physiologie und Systematik der Sprachlaute* by the Viennese doctor and physiologist E. W. Brücke (1856), which aimed at providing a classificatory system (based on articulation) of all human sounds. Ellis did not quote the second great work of the mid century, the monumental *Anatomie und Physiologie des menschlichen Stimm- und Sprach-Organs (Anthropophonik)* by C. L. Merkel (1857) Professor of Medicine at Leipzig, which concentrated on anatomical facts (a description of the organs of speech) and on an acoustic description of speech sounds including suprasegmental data. A later more approachable work by Merkel, *Physiologie der menschlichen Sprache (physiologische Laletik)*, appeared in 1866 and was conceived in the same spirit. It is in fact characteristic of the most important German and Austrian work in phonetics of the first three-quarters of the century that the main aim is the physiological analysis of the sounds used or usable in language rather than the description of actual linguistic systems and that the authors involved start with an original training in the sciences (Kohler 1981, 167). Equally impressive work, which led to the beginning of acoustic phonetics, the investigation of vocalic quality and the synthesizing of vowels, was conducted by scientists such as H. L. F. von Helmholtz (1821–94), who was both a physiologist and a physicist and whose fundamental monograph *Die Lehre von den Tonenempfindungen als physiologische Grundlage für die Theorie der Musik* (1863) was published in numerous editions and translated into English by A. J. Ellis. In this context we can also quote the works on aphasia by the French surgeon Paul Broca (1824–80), which opened the way to the studies on the localization of the linguistic faculty in the brain and to a *rapprochement* of the studies of neurology and linguistics (Bergounioux 1994, 209ff. with bibliography).

The third path is that of historical and comparative linguistics. We have already noticed how little interest in phonetics is shown e.g. by Bopp and Grimm; a few inadequate, often confused statements in terms of articulatory phonetics is all that we are offered. If we want to understand why this is so, we must turn to Pott's discussion. In his *Etymologische Forschungen* (1833–6, I, 69, 73) he pointed out that in the comparison of related languages what matters most is to link sounds 'etymologically' rather than phonetically. Obviously an etymological correspondence must depend on a 'physiological' relationship of the sounds in question, and to understand how a sound changes into another it is necessary to know about its articulation and its auditory impact as well as about the (phonetic?) relationship of the two sounds. Even so, Pott argued, this sort of knowledge is often incomplete and for the comparative linguist less essential than that of the 'etymologische Lautlehre'. Sanskrit *bh*, Greek φ, Latin *f* correspond etymologically; it is not indispensable, even if highly desirable, to know whether these letters indicate phonetically identical or similar or totally different units. Does this imply that Bopp, Grimm and even Pott compared letters rather than sounds? Admittedly, *Buchstabe*, 'letter', is often used interchangeably with *Laut*, 'sound', but that is not significant in itself;[21] Bopp and his contemporaries were perfectly capable of distinguishing writing and pronunciation (*Schrift- und Laut-System*), even if confusions occasionally occurred, but, as Pott indicated, they were mainly interested in comparing linguistic units without regard to their phonetic nature. The units in question were, in practice, whatever the theory, the functional units of phonology defined in terms of their number and distribution rather than of their articulatory and auditory features. In other words, as long as the emphasis was on the comparison of ancient written languages and as long as reconstruction concentrated on morphology, it was possible to proceed without any deeper knowledge of phonetics: the ancient alphabets were basically phonological. It fell to Rudolf von Raumer (1815–76), a Germanist who taught at Erlangen and was interested both in Indo-European and in the German spelling reform, to make a plea for the introduction of phonetics in historical discussion, while arguing that, in contrast with the attempts at establishing correspondences between languages, the attempts at reconstructing a process of sound change required a phonetic understanding of the point of departure and the point of arrival.[22] Karl Moriz Rapp (1803–83), who taught Indo-European at Tübingen, also wrote a *Versuch einer Physiologie der Sprache nebst historischer Entwickelung der abendländischen Idiome nach physiologischen Grundsätzen* (1836–41) and tried to exploit its results in his Indo-European studies (see below), but was largely ignored (Jespersen 1922, 68ff.). Yet, in spite of this exception, until the 1860s and the 1870s phonetics occupied a marginal position in the study of comparative and historical linguistics. The work on Germanic by Theodor Jacobi (1843), which also made use of articulatory phonetics, remained isolated (Benware 1974, 44ff.). In Germany the embargo was broken because of the impact of Brücke's and Merkel's work, the shift of emphasis from comparative to historical work and from ancient to modern languages, and because, once Pott's 'etymological' correspondences had been properly established, it became natural to turn to their phonetic explanation. In 1868 the Germanist Wilhelm Scherer (1868, 20), writing about *Ablaut*, exploded in indignation: 'is it too much to ask that a philologist who seeks a physiological explanation of phonetic processes, should read through some 60 pages of this classical book [*sc.* Brücke 1856]?' There is a direct link on the one hand between Scherer and the neo-grammarians and on the other between Scherer and Eduard Sievers, the Germanist and Indo-Europeanist, who in 1876 inaugurated the newly founded *Bibliothek indogermanischer Grammatiken* with a volume entitled *Grundzüge der Lautphysiologie zur Einführung in das Studium der Lautlehre der indogermanischen Sprachen* which was propaedeutic to a knowledge of phonetics in general and of the phonetics of the ancient Indo-European languages in particular. In England a straight line leads from Bell and Ellis to Henry Sweet (1845–1912), who wrote a *Handbook of Phonetics* in 1877 and was equally acquainted with articulatory and instrumental phonetics, spelling reform problems, etc., and with historical linguistics, the history of English and Indo-European studies. Bell was no historical linguist but Ellis was; Sweet spoke of the 'revolutionary investigations' contained in his *Early English Pronunciation* (1869–99) and confessed himself more than indebted to him. The English and German developments are to a certain extent independent, but it is remarkable that in the same period we begin to find both in England and in Germany historical linguists such as Sievers and Sweet who are also competent phoneticians. Obviously after the 1860s a great deal of phonetic work was done in complete ignorance of the historical approach, but the important point is that, for a short period at least, the two interests converged either intellectually or institutionally. Michel Bréal, Professor of *Grammaire comparée* at the Collège de France from 1864 to 1905, was responsible for the creation of a phonetic laboratory attached to his chair and for the appointment to it of the abbé Rousselot (1846–1924), who counts as the founder of instrumental phonetics. The novelty of the last quarter of the century is then provided, on the one hand, by the insertion of phonetics into the linguistic disciplines and the willingness of the linguists (or at least of some of them) to acknowledge that phonetics is the 'indispensable foundation of all study of language' (Sweet 1877, v), and, on the other hand, by the *rapprochement* of academic linguistics and the collateral disciplines which had led to the flourishing of phonetics.[23]

7.1.4 Historical linguistics and methodological awareness

So much for a sketch of the mid-century ambiance. Some leitmotifs recur. The urge to look diachronically at the facts of language does not disappear, on the contrary it is more explicitly formulated. Gaston Paris, the Romance scholar and French medievalist, in the preface to his translation of the introduction to Diez's grammar of Romance languages (Paris 1863, vi) pointed out that the hallmark of modern work was the persuasion that 'there is not in any language a single fact that can be explained without turning to the history of that language' ('il n'y a pas dans une langue un fait qu'on puisse expliquer sans avoir recours à l'histoire de cette langue') and that 'the present state of a language is only the consequence of its earlier stage, which is the only thing that can explain it' ('l'état présent d'un idiome n'est que la conséquence de son état antérieur, qui seul peut le faire comprendre'). We find here very clearly stated the view that history provides the only form of explanation of linguistic facts, a view which will form the basis of the prevailing linguistic theory of the 1880s. But Gaston Paris instantly moves to a question of method. He explains that in this context, etymology (that is to say the new critical form of etymology) had acquired a basic importance and quotes Diez's own preface to his *Etymologisches Wörterbuch der Romanischen Sprachen* (1853), where the new critical method was seen as based on *Lautlehre*. Paris concludes (*ibid.* vii): 'In effect it is thanks to comparison, history and phonology that not only etymological science but the whole of linguistics makes the progress that it does every day. Of these three guides, phonology . . . is one of the most reliable' ('C'est en effet grâce à la comparaison, à l'histoire et à la phonologie, que non seulement la science étymologique, mais la linguistique toute entière, doit le progrès qu'elle accomplit chaque jour. De ces trois guides, l'un des plus sûrs . . . est la phonologie').

This last statement is significant: theory is accompanied by a greater methodological awareness. It is not surprising to discover that this is provoked not so much by a change in theoretical perspectives as by the experience of actual work. The level of phonological (not phonetic) analysis found in the first edition of Diez's grammar (1836) is much lower (gaps, mistakes, a number of approximations) than that of the second edition (1856), no doubt because between the two there had been the experience of the *Etymologisches Wörterbuch* (Malkiel 1988, 11ff.).[24] The *Lautlehre* is, of course, still the phonological (rather than phonetic) analysis which we mentioned above, but it is important that Diez's preface to the *Wörterbuch* (1853) includes a brief account of the main causes of change which disturb the regularity of language:[25] assimilation, dissimilation, haplology, euphonic change of vowels, analogy (*Anbildung*), contamination, functional distinction of possible homonyms, popular etymology. Though this is not normally stated, the model (or at least one of the models) for Diez's four pages is clearly the long analysis of *grammatischer Lautwechsel* introduced by Pott in the second volume of his *Etymologische Forschungen* (Pott 1833–6, ii, 1–350), where he discussed assimilation, dissimilation, metathesis and additive or subtractive changes such as prothesis, epenthesis, syncope, apocope, etc., while offering examples of these phenomena from a number of often unrelated languages. The generalizations simplify the descriptions of the facts considered but also prompt a further conclusion: 'all languages depend in higher or lesser degree on the same physiological and psychological conditionings' (*ibid.*, 112). Another leitmotif of the mid-century decades is that in some authors at least the concern is less for the great theoretical problems (the origin of language, the link between language and thought, etc.) and more for the individual results, the plans for further historical and comparative work and the definition and justification of the method's successes. This does not mean, however, that the period was deprived of general views. On the contrary, as will emerge from what follows, two headings at least are necessary when we consider the actual work done at the time: that of comparative historical linguistics and that of the more general discussions about language. The distinction is useful for the sake of clarity, though the two areas of research are obviously connected and any account will have to depend on constant cross-referencing. It is significant that we may start our account with the more technical and concrete achievements, paradoxically leaving a discussion of the theory for a later stage. Why this is possible will become clear at the end of this chapter.

7.2 The model of Indo-European studies

In the semi-hagiographic account of the history of nineteenth-century linguistics which prevailed until recently, we were regularly presented with unimpeded progress from Bopp to the neogrammarians. The reconstruction of Indo-European provided the model: the 1833–52 grammar by Bopp was replaced by a second edition which started to appear in 1857, but was soon deemed to be outdated because of the appearance in 1861–2 of August Schleicher's *Compendium der vergleichenden Grammatik der indogermanischen Sprachen*;[26] in its turn this was believed to be superseded by the publication in 1886 of the first volume of the *Grundriß der vergleichenden Grammatik der indogermanischen Sprachen* (1886–93) by Karl Brugmann. This view, however simplistic, is justified by an analysis of the quotations and references of the time. After the 1870s it is difficult to find a reference to Bopp in the contemporary (German) literature (except of course for the recurrent hagiographic statements), just as in the 1890s the references to Schleicher disappear. The explanation is again to be found in the technical and cumulative aspects of the subject. On the one hand all later work is based on increased material: more Indo-European languages are used and all Indo-European languages are better analysed; on the other, it is possible to insert the old data and conclusions in the new manuals so that they do indeed make the earlier ones superfluous.[27] Large parts of Bopp's results are incorporated in Schleicher's book and we must now turn to this scholar and contemporary work.

7.3 August Schleicher

August Schleicher (1821–68), who during his short life held linguistic chairs at Prague and then at Jena, is indeed representative of the development of Indo-European studies (and perhaps of linguistic studies in general) round the middle of the century;[28] on the one hand, his *Compendium*, which had four editions (two posthumous) in the ridiculously short time of fifteen years and was translated into Italian and English, was seen as the basic textbook in the subject and created the model for such textbooks in future; on the other hand, he is normally credited with the introduction into comparative and historical work of some basic methodological innovations: the phonological reconstruction of Indo-European, the family-tree model of language descent, and an insistence on the importance of establishing regular sound laws. Needless to say these are also the features which according to the current historiography define the comparative work of the 1850–70s. There is no reason to challenge this view, but some qualifications are necessary under each of the headings mentioned.

7.4 The reconstruction of Indo-European

Reconstruction as such is not a novelty of the 1860s. The whole of Bopp's work was dedicated to an attempt at defining what forms Indo-European had and what forms were due to innovations of the individual languages, in other words to a reconstruction of Indo-European morphology.[29] Pott had in practice reconstructed the Indo-European lexicon.[30] Admittedly Bopp never attempted a systematic reconstruction of the phonology of Indo-European but it would be misleading to assume that no form of phonological reconstruction is found before Schleicher. The typical starred items of Schleicher, i.e. the proto-forms which, like *aus-ōs-ā*, were reconstructed to account for the attested Latin *aurōra* 'dawn', were less in evidence before him but not entirely absent.[31] We mentioned earlier Rask's reconstructions (p. 128) and Bopp's suggestion that Greek *dusmeneos* 'hostile' (gen. sing.) derived from *dusmenes-os*, a reconstructed form which we would now mark with an asterisk.

Bopp had also distinguished between the reconstructed forms of the parent language and the more recent forms due to the sound changes of the individual languages: he pointed out e.g. that the Sanskrit nominative *vāk* must go back to a form with final -*s* which was lost in Sanskrit itself since this change is not shared by Avestan or the European languages.[32] Rask's and Grimm's definitions of the Germanic *Lautverschiebung* were based on lists of phonological correspondences between languages, but it is in Pott (e.g. 1833–6, i, 82) that we first find a full set of standard correspondences (such as Sanskrit *bh*, Latin *f/b*, Greek φ/(β), Lithuanian *b*, Gothic *b*, OHG *p*, Persian *b*, etc.) which are based on lists of etymologically related words in a number of Indo-European languages, and, in their turn, form the base for phonological reconstruction. Pott had also discussed the criteria on which we establish whether one or the other sound in these lists of correspondences is the oldest. He had explained for instance (*ibid.*, 73–5) that Latin -*r*- derived from -*s*-, when in the equivalent Sanskrit words -*s*- or -*sh*- and not -*r*- were found. If so, when confronted with Greek *mues* 'mice' and Latin *mures* 'mice' there were reasons, in contrast with the *communis opinio* that derived Latin from Greek, to assume that the oldest form had an internal [*s*] which was lost in Greek and had changed into *r* in Latin (cf. Sanskrit *mūsaḥ* 'mice'). No more than four years later Rudolf von Raumer ([1837] 1863, 1–104) reiterated that sound correspondences (of the type set up by Pott) do not in themselves provide evidence about the direction of change, but the comparative material can nevertheless be used for this purpose: the fact that e.g. there are two languages like Sanskrit and Greek which share in equivalent words a *p*, while Gothic is alone (according to von Raumer) in having *f*, speaks for reconstructing *p*.

The novelty in Schleicher's *Compendium* is not in the use of reconstructed forms or even in the methodology of the reconstruction; it is rather in the commitment to an explicit and full reconstruction of **all** the forms which can be attributed to the parent language. Schleicher's (1868) attempt, which was much ridiculed later on, to write an Indo-European short story was prompted, as he implied in the introductory words, by a desire to extend the same commitment to the reconstruction of syntax.[33] But this commitment had its consequences: if the reconstructed forms were to be indicated in full, phonological reconstruction had to have priority. If so, it is not surprising that in the plan of the *Compendium*, in contrast with that of Bopp's grammar, the part dedicated to phonology is very extensive. Full reconstruction also allowed a different arrangement of the material. Bopp's account was basically inductive: we are first told what the evidence of the actual languages is and then how we can distinguish innovations and archaisms, i.e. we are first given the attested data and then some (morphological) reconstructions. Schleicher, on the other hand, starts with a description of the reconstructed sounds and forms of Indo-European and then discusses their developments in the individual languages. The plan may be misleading if it gives the impression that the reconstructions and the attested data have the same degree of validity, but has obvious advantages of clarity and simplicity. More important, it commits the linguist, perhaps *malgré lui*, to an explicit account of the parent language as a linguistic system and of the processes through which the attested forms have been derived from, or have replaced, the forms of the parent language; we lose Bopp's account of the discovery procedures and his various cautionary remarks, but we gain a sense of structure and, paradoxically, a sense of development.

No doubt each Indo-Europeanist had different views about the status of the reconstructed forms. Schleicher himself was fully aware, and said so in the introduction to the *Compendium*, that some reconstructions were more doubtful than others; he even went as far as to state that setting them out did not imply that they had really existed.[34] Yet the basic claim which Schleicher made for the importance of reconstructions – a claim the importance of which we now tend to underrate – was that they clarified once and for all the difference between Indo-European and Sanskrit by showing how different was the reconstructed proto-language from the attested Sanskrit language. The same point in favour of reconstructed roots had been made by Benfey at an earlier stage (see p. 179 note 3). Without too much fuss, Schleicher, his contemporaries or immediate predecessors, had found an algorithm which solved one of the basic problems of genealogical comparison: given that we can demonstrate that e.g. three languages L_1, L_2 and L_3 are related, how do we know whether two of them are derived from the third or all of them are derived from a fourth unattested language? Reconstruction provides the answer; if the first hypothesis is correct, the reconstructed L_x ought to overlap to a significant degree with one of L_1, L_2, L_3; if that is not the case, we must treat it as an independent language.[35] Max Müller made the point with extreme clarity in his *Lectures on the Science of Language* ([1861] 1862, 168ff.) and illustrated it with a retrospective attack on the old suggestion by Raynouard that French, Italian, etc. were all descended from Provençal, which would have been Latin's only daughter. Provençal *sem* 'we are', he argued, cannot be both the direct descendent of Latin *sumus* and the ancestor of French *sommes*, since the French form is closer to the Latin *sumus* than its supposed antecedent; similarly, Sanskrit *asi*, which must derive from the reconstructed Indo-European *as-si* 'thou art', cannot be the ancestor of Greek *essi* and Lithuanian *es-si*.[36]

7.5 The linguistic family tree

In effect it is reconstruction that allows the linguist to set up a genealogical tree of languages; if so, it is not surprising that the family-
tree model or *Stammbaumtheorie* is also associated with Schleicher and
with the specific instance of family tree of the Indo-European languages which appeared in all editions of the *Compendium*. The assumption is that a proto-language, an *Ursprache*, splits into a number of
Grundsprachen, which in their turn split into language families and
eventually into actual languages and dialects through a process which
can be repeated again and again. The tree model, where each attested
language corresponds to a branch of the tree and the language from
which they are descended corresponds to the trunk, fulfils two purposes
at the same time: it defines genetic relationship as implying descent from
a common ancestor, i.e. from the same proto-language (*Ursprache*), but
it also indicates the degree of relationship between the various members of the family. At the same time it serves a heuristic purpose in that
it indicates how, and through what intermediate stages, reconstruction
proceeds. Finally, the tree model was also seen as a representation of
the process of development of the various related languages; the length
of the branches could be used to provide a rough image of the chronology of the differentiation processes.[37]

The model, as used by e.g. Schleicher, also brought into the fore-
front the question of subgrouping. Given that three or more languages
belong to the same family, in what relation do they stand with each
other? What subgroups do we need to reconstruct? Once again Max
Müller addressed the problem ([1861] 1862, 168) and explained that,
while a comparison of numerals and certain grammatical forms could
at first sight establish that languages were related, 'a more accurate
standard was required for measuring the more minute degrees of relationship. Such a standard was supplied by Comparative Grammar; that
is to say, by the intercomparison of the grammatical forms of languages
supposed to be related to each other; such intercomparison being carried out according to certain laws which regulate the phonetic changes
of letters.'

Historiography may see the tree model (and the reconstructed forms
which go with it) either as a new form of technical notation for well-
known concepts or as the graphic representation of a new theoretical
stance. Whatever the conclusion, there is little doubt that the formalism,
however interpreted, calls for a much higher degree of precision than
that previously available to those involved in determining the genetic
relationship of languages. At the same time the notation, as could be
expected, also acquired a life of its own. In the tree of Indo-European
languages which appears in the introduction to the *Compendium* all

branching is binary: the Indo-European *Ursprache* splits into a Slavo-Germanic branch and an Aryo-Graeco-Italo-Celtic branch, which in its turn splits into 'Aryan' and Graeco-Italo-Celtic, which splits into Italoceltic and Greek, etc. Considering that at the time language divisions were mostly explained in terms of migration and division of tribes, there was no real reason why a tripartite division should not be considered; it seems likely that the formalism determined in a relatively stable manner the binary view of events.[38] When in 1870 August Fick (1833–1916) produced the second edition of his comparative dictionary of Indo-European roots, even though he adopted a different classification from that of Schleicher, he too operated in terms of successive binary divisions. Indo-European splits into 'Aryan' and 'European'; European splits into Graeco-Italic and Slavo-Germanic; Slavo-Germanic splits into Lithuanian-Slavic and Germanic, etc. Fick carried reconstruction well beyond what Schleicher had done. He produced a list of reconstructed roots not only for Indo-European but also for each major subdivision: 'Aryan', European, Graeco-Italic, Slavo-Germanic, etc.

7.6 Sound laws

Both Schleicher's and Fick's examples testify to the interdependence of reconstruction and the family-tree model. On the other hand, as Max Müller had explained, they both depend on an understanding of sound change. From the 1850s, 'sound laws' (the term *Lautgesetz* already occurs in Bopp) of the type 'Indo-European *p* became Germanic *f*' or 'Latin *s* became *r* between vowels' are in current use and the object of much discussion; it emerges clearly from the way in which these formulae are used that (a) they refer to the replacement of one sound with another in progress of time and in pairs of etymologically related words (a proto-form *ausōsa* becomes Latin *aurōra*), (b) the formula does not normally apply to one word pair only but to a larg(ish) number of word pairs, (c) the formula has some predictive value: if *s* becomes *r* we do not expect to find words which preserve *s*. While shared morphology had the dominant role in the earlier demonstrations of genetic relationship, as early as Pott the 'etymological parallelism of letters', to use Pott's terminology (e.g. 1833–6, I, 73; cf. already Grimm 1822, 592), had become the most important criterion, far more important than superficial phonetic similarity. For Pott (*ibid.*, I, xii), Grimm's Law had shown that 'letters' were 'a more secure guide through the obscure labyrinth of etymology than meaning', that linguistics (above all comparative linguistics) 'without an exact historical knowledge of letters lacks a solid foundation', and above all that 'even in the bare letters there is not arbitrary lawlessness, but rational freedom', i.e. a freedom restrained by laws (*Gesetze*) based on the nature of the sounds. Pott had also distinguished between conditioned (*bedingter*) or 'grammatical' sound change and what he called 'etymological' or 'dialectal' or 'lexical' sound change.[39] The former was determined by the phonological environment; the latter, of which Grimm's Law was the primary example, was empirically definable, but the primary cause remained mysterious (cf. e.g. Pott 1833–6, II, 2f.). In other words, by the 1850s no one doubted the importance of identifying the various *Lautgesetze* which accounted for divergences between two languages descended from the same proto-language (*Ursprache*) or between two phases of the same language. If so, where does Schleicher's novelty lie?

In the second edition of the *Compendium*, Schleicher ([1866] 1871, 15–16) refers to two contemporary schools of Indo-Europeanists: the first (to which Curtius, Corssen and Schleicher himself belonged) made sound laws the foundation of its work; the second (represented by Benfey and Leo Meyer) was far less strict about them (cf. Koerner 1989, 359). Benfey did in effect protest against those who denied the validity of an intuitively acceptable etymology because it was not supported by parallel sound changes, i.e. by a regular sound law (cf. e.g. [1865] 1890–2, I, ii, 155): sound laws for him were not eternal, had a beginning and an end, could be more or less widespread and could either be enforced in all forms which came within their range or be limited to one single instance. Curtius (1858–62, I, 70ff.), on the other hand, spoke of sound laws as natural laws (*Naturgesetze*) and recognized both major sound changes (*Lautveränderung*) which determine the whole phonological character of a language or a linguistic group (Grimm's Law is the standard example), and 'individual laws' which concern clusters of sounds often in connection with a specific position in the word (initial, internal, final), as when intervocalic -*s*- is lost in Greek. Yet he also admitted sporadic sound changes, as when Greek *p* sporadically replaces an inherited *k*, and interestingly enough argued that there was no way of drawing a clear line between sporadic changes and individual sound laws.[40] Similarly, Schleicher ([1861–2] 1871, 541 and 648), in his actual work of comparison, did not hesitate for instance to derive the Latin genitive singular in -*ī* from -*eis* or the Greek perfect λέλοιπα 'I was left' from *leloipma, assuming that the normal developments, which would have called for the retention of -*s* in Latin and -*m*- in Greek, did not operate in this case.[41] In general it seems that in the actual practice of reconstruction and historical explanation both e.g. Benfey and Curtius tried to work in terms of regular sound changes while being ready to admit exceptions when intuitively needed; yet Curtius, like Schleicher, was probably stricter than Benfey.

An example may clarify the whole argument. Our intuition tells us that words such as Latin *deus* 'god' and Greek θεός 'god' are etymologically related. Yet we expect an initial Latin *d* to correspond to Greek δ, as e.g. in Latin *domus* 'house', Greek δόμος 'house', and not to *th* (θ). In 1833 Pott (1833–6, I, 101f.) included in the list of etymological equivalents of Sanskrit *deva-* 'god' both Latin *deus* and Greek θεός (the traditional comparison), but mentioned the difficulty and offered a solution: the correspondence Sanskrit *d-*, Latin *d-*, Gr. *th-* (θ) was attested in other circumstances too. In a review of Pott's book, Benfey ([1837] 1890–2, I, ii, 5) took up the problem. He denied with good reason the validity of the parallels adduced by Pott and concluded without further ado that θεός was a dialect form which had replaced the expected Greek word with initial *d*. The discussion continued but in 1862 Curtius (1858–62, ii, 94ff.) picked up the question again. He rejected on philological bases the supposed evidence for a dialect origin of θεός; pointed out that the vocalism did not match that of the Sanskrit word (which pointed to an original diphthong) and that for Greek we had to postulate an internal *-s-*, as shown by compounds such as θέσ-φατος (literally 'said by the god(s)'), etc., and not a *-w-*, as predicted by the Sanskrit comparison; and ended (as Schleicher had done before him) rejecting the connection of the Greek word with the Sanskrit and Latin forms. Later authors followed this lead.[42] It is clear that from the time of Pott (at the latest) scholars had been aware of the phonological problem; various attempts at a solution had been proposed with greater or lesser success but it was only in the time of Curtius and Schleicher that an intuitively satisfactory comparison was rejected on the basis of a stricter adherence to sound laws and a stricter line of argumentation.

Some concrete results were partly responsible for this firmer line: the history of Grimm's Law after Grimm, parts of which we have hinted at already (see p. 150 note 24), may serve as illustration. Grimm himself had listed some exceptions; in his view these were sometimes due to the vagaries of languages which show phonological alternations among the dialects, sometimes to the complications always caused by the aspirates, sometimes to the fact that 'the sound shift takes place in mass, but never neatly in the individual items' (as shown, according to Grimm, by the comparison of Latin *dies* and Gothic *dags* 'day', which contradicts the sound law, and which, according to the current views, are not related). By the time of the second edition of Bopp's *Vergleichende Grammatik* (1857–61, i, 128), the main exceptions came to be codified in phonological terms: internally we find an unexpected voicing (*b* and not *f*) as in Gothic *sibun* vs. Latin *septem*; initially we find an unexpected voiced stop (*b* and not *p*) where Sanskrit has a voiced stop as in Gothic *band* 'I tied' vs. Sanskrit *bandh-*; after some consonants, such as *s*, the voiceless stops do not show any change, as in Gothic *fisks* 'fish' (with *k* and not *h*) vs. Latin *piscis*. Not much later, C. Lottner (1862) dedicated a lengthy article to the discussion of the exceptions to Grimm's Law, distinguishing false exceptions determined by wrong etymologies, onomatopoeia and borrowings from the real irregularities. Soon afterwards Hermann Grassmann (1863) demonstrated that one of the sets of exceptions listed by Bopp was only apparent; Sanskrit forms such as *bandh-* were due to the dissimilation of the first of two aspirates in adjacent syllables and called for an earlier **bhandh-*; consequently Gothic *band* was the expected treatment of the original form.[43] It was acknowledged that e.g. after *-s* the *Lautverschiebung* did not take place, so that after Grassmann's discovery the exceptions were now confined to the internal voiced stops (as in *sibun*) and the *Lautverschiebung* was seen as a far more regular process than before. Similarly, the example of sporadic sound change mentioned by Curtius (Greek *p* occasionally replaced an Indo-European *k*, though this was normally continued by *k* in Greek too) was clarified by the work initiated by Ascoli (1870) which led to the discovery of at least two different sets of consonants in Indo-European: velars (> Greek *k*, etc.) and labiovelars conventionally indicated with **k^w* (> Greek *p*, etc.). It is not surprising that in view of this type of observations the general attitude to sound laws changed.

In general, as far as the sound laws are concerned, the late 1850s are not characterized by sudden revolutionary change but rather by a steady progress towards the implementation and the closer definition of a paradigm which had previously been accepted in its fundamental lines. It was Schleicher's and Curtius's great merit that they succeeded in identifying a number of motifs that belonged to the first generation after Bopp and developed them in a coherent fashion. The ever-increasing quantity of data and the greater methodological awareness determined some remarkable changes in the state of the art. Present-day Indo-Europeanists are unlikely to look back beyond the late 1870s or 1880s; if they do, however, they will find Schleicher's *Compendium* (1861–2) and Curtius's *Grundzüge der griechischen Etymologie* (1858–62) or *Das Verbum der griechischen Sprache* (1873–6) far more accessible than any of the works that preceded them. From this point of view, Schleicher and Curtius undoubtedly mark a breakthrough in the work of the century.[44]

7.7 Indo-European origins: cultural reconstruction

We cannot abandon our account of historical-comparative work without considering two problems of increasing generality which are intimately connected to the development of the comparative method: the reconstruction of *realia* and/or *spiritualia* and the origin of the grammatical forms.

The desire to use linguistic facts to reconstruct prehistoric events is old (see Chapter 2); with the advent of reconstruction the urge to move from words to *realia* or to *spiritualia*, i.e. to cultural facts in general, was strong and was soon yielded to. In a sense Jacob Grimm's *Geschichte der deutschen Sprache* (1848) belongs to this trend. It was possible to identify words which were attributed to the parent language and conclude from them that specific objects or institutions or *formae mentis* also belonged to the primitive Indo-European tribes; if linguists could reconstruct words for 'plough' or 'dog' or 'wife' or 'god' then it followed that the Indo-Europeans had ploughs (and agriculture), dogs (and domestic animals), wives (and the institution of marriage), gods (and religion). As Max Müller put it ([1861] 1862, 235) the reconstructed lexicon 'will serve as evidence as to the state of civilisation attained by the Aryans [i.e. the Indo-European speakers] before they left their common home'. After Eichhoff (1836), works such as *Les origines indoeuropéennes ou les Aryas primitifs. Essai de paléontologie linguistique* (1859–63) by the Swiss Adolphe Pictet, even if exceedingly speculative and soon discredited, collected data and provided a name 'linguistic paleontology' for this type of enquiry.[45] We soon begin to find references to the problem of the *Urheimat*, the original locus of the Indo-Europeans and the point from which their diffusion started, a problem which is still with us nowadays: Pictet and Max Müller did not hesitate to put it in Asia. Adalbert Kuhn (1812–81) had from the 1840s onwards published articles which aimed at identifying those divine names which could be attributed to Indo-European, thus providing information about the Indo-European pantheon and Indo-European religion. This was still in the 'lexical' tradition, but Kuhn went further and recognized in the attested languages poetic and magic formulae inherited from Indo-European. For Max Müller's comparative mythology, which reached considerable fame in the second part of the century, the linguistic element was essential even if the comparison of myths could be separately pursued. In general both a lexical and a comparative approach were possible. The former extrapolated information about material and intellectual culture from the reconstructed lexicon and claimed scientific validity because of the 'scientific' nature of the new etymology; by contrast, the latter started from cultural (not necessarily linguistic) data and used comparison to reconstruct backwards; linguistic comparison provided the model and perhaps the testing ground but not the starting point. In both cases the results could be treated as a source for further, and even more general, conclusions. Pictet implied that since Indo-European languages agreed in their terms for 'god' but not in the names of the individual gods, it was possible to think of an original monotheism – with all the consequences that this may entail (Bologna 1988, 35). Max Müller, on the other hand, saw in his reconstructions a chance to demonstrate that mythology was inextricably connected with the metaphoric power of language. The Greek story of the beautiful Endymion loved by Selene but deeply asleep for most of his time can be explained, according to Max Müller ([1856] 1868–75, ii, 81ff.), if we realize that the word Endymion was originally an epitheton of the setting sun (from δύω 'to set') and was treated as a name when no longer understood. In more difficult cases we must refer to linguistic comparison to reconstruct the original meanings and the cause of the misunderstanding or reinterpretation; mythology, as Max Müller put it, is a 'disease' of the language ([1861] 1862, 12).[46]

7.8 Indo-European origins: grammatical forms

A wish to explain the origin of grammatical forms had prompted the type of morphological reconstruction which Bopp practised and had, indirectly at least, been responsible for the view that history and comparison offered the only way to the explanation of linguistic data. Did the increased sophistication of reconstruction now lead to further advances along this road? Or did it act as a deterrent?

At this point technicalities and broad-sweeping generalizations necessarily interact. Bopp, as we have seen (p. 135), had first assumed that grammatical distinctions based on *Ablaut* (English: *drive* vs. *drove*) were 'organic', as contrasted with normal inflection, which arose from agglutination; he had then tried to provide a mechanical explanation of *Ablaut* based on the assumption that of two adjacent syllables one had to be 'light' (hence Sanskrit *ás-mi* 'I am' vs. *s-más* 'we are'). In the following years the discussion about *Ablaut* continued; Bopp's rules of 'weight' were found to be contradicted by the evidence (Holtzmann 1841); meanwhile new studies about Sanskrit accentuation led to the observation that *Ablaut* was somehow linked with accentuation (Holtzmann 1841, Benfey [1846] 1890–2, I, ii, 58ff.). In the 1850s and 1860s opinions diverged, not least because in the absence of a satisfactory understanding of Indo-European vocalism a real analysis was not possible. Schleicher and Curtius agreed in attributing vowel gradation to the parent language and tended to assume that it had arisen in the pre-ethnic period in order to mark grammatical or semantic distinctions (Benware 1974, 47); yet the mysticism of Schlegel's organic analysis seems to have disappeared. By 1868 Lazarus Geiger, an isolated scholar, produced in a theoretical book entitled *Ursprung und Entwickelung der menschlichen Sprache und Vernunft* (1868–72, i, 164f.) the suggestion (still accepted nowadays) that the basic roots were accented and had a vowel which disappeared when the accent was removed in the inflection: hence a basic *ás-* 'to be' would appear as *s-* in e.g. *s-más* 'we are'; if so, *Ablaut* was no longer the mark of an organic or even a developed language.[47]

What about the origin of inflection? Bopp's theory that it was due to an earlier form of agglutination was now more widely accepted,[48] but a first difficulty arose from the increased attention given to phonology:

it was easier for Bopp than for his successors to say that the -*s* of the nominative derived from the pronoun (Sanskrit) *sa* or that the -*m(i)* of the first person singular ending was in origin the pronoun (Sanskrit) *ma*. By the 1850s and 1860s, someone was bound to ask what happened to the final vowel. But there was a further difficulty: the family-tree model made wonderfully clear that reconstruction based on the comparative method could only lead back to the period which immediately preceded the splitting of the basic proto-language; by itself it did not account for the origin of the forms of the proto-language. Writing at the end of our period, in 1867, Georg Curtius (1867, 200) had no doubts about these points and recognized the hypothetical character of all statements about the period which preceded the splitting of the reconstructed proto-language. Nevertheless, he was adamant: 'hypotheses of this type are absolutely indispensable for our science'. After fifty years of scholarly analysis of the various forms it was indispensable, he argued, to use the results in order to understand the *Urzeit*. Moreover, the experience of historical work had more and more drawn attention to the importance of establishing the correct chronological layering of linguistic events. But it had also become clear how necessary this chronological ordering was in any discussion of the formation of the linguistic organism; those who accepted that both the third person singular in -*t(i)* (Sanskrit *dadā-ti* 'he gives') and the *ta*-participle (Sanskrit *dā-ta-* 'given') were due to composition with the *ta*-demonstrative pronoun also had to accept that the two formations had both come into existence before the disintegration of the Indo-European unity. Yet they were also obliged to assume that this development had taken place at different times. Only in this way could one understand why in one instance the pronoun + 'give' is interpreted as {give} {he} → {he gives}, while in the other it is interpreted as {give} {there} → {the give}, {the given}. Curtius, in other words, realizes that the comparative method can only lead back to the period immediately preceding the division, but nevertheless takes for granted the connections established by Bopp between inflectional endings and pronouns and accepts Bopp's view that grammatical forms arose through agglutination. The linguist's task then becomes that of making plausible suggestions about the nature of the process and the various stages in which it happened. Curtius is far more aware than Bopp was of the need to justify the various hypotheses made; on the other hand, he is also willing to dismiss the phonological difficulties, projecting them back into a period earlier than that for which the normal development is expected.

7.9 The parent language: development and decay

So much for the practice; we may now turn to some presuppositions. Curtius is of course not alone in distinguishing in the prehistory of

Indo-European between a period of language formation in which the parent language is unitary while the main grammatical distinctions are created and a period of evolution (*Ausbildung*) associated with a plurality of daughter languages and a number of changes. As early as 1850, Schleicher (1850, 10ff.) had also recognized two main stages. Avoiding the question of the origin of language, i.e. of how the roots came to have the meaning that they have in each language family, he spoke in terms of a contrast between a phase of language development leading to the formation of a grammatical structure and one of language decay, characterized by considerable phonological change – the type of change governed by laws and rules which linguists were learning to recognize. In the phase of development, monosyllabic languages could change into agglutinative, and these in their turn could become inflected; there was no necessary progression but retrospectively it was clear to the linguist that all inflection arose from agglutination (as Bopp had argued for Indo-European) and that agglutination arose from composition in isolating languages. Once again, whatever the theory, the methodology is clear: the standard comparative method is used to reconstruct the starting point and the later developments of the second phase; the most audacious hypotheses concern the first phase. Very similar (and probably derivative) points were made by Max Müller, for whom 'the history of all the Aryan langages is nothing but a gradual process of decay' ([1861] 1862, 234).[49] There was a high level of agreement that in the formative period no real sound changes nor analogical changes occurred, since these were limited to the second period (decay) and were the main cause of linguistic differentiation. In other words, the theory was clearly anti-uniformitarian and as such was decisively attacked by those linguists who, either *motu proprio* or under the influence of Lyell's geology, believed that the same forces or causes had always operated in the language (see below, p. 160f.). However, Curtius himself was obliged by his method of reconstruction to attribute to the period before the start of linguistic differentiation those change processes which ought not to have been there. Thus for the first persons singular and plural Curtius reconstructed *da-dā-mi* 'I give' and *da-dā-masi* 'we give', but according to him the endings had to be compared with the pronominal forms *ma* 'I' and *ma+tva* 'I and thou'. It followed that the phonetic change from *ma* to *-mi* and from *matva* to *-masi* belonged to the period of unity. Uniformitarianism comes back and the comparativists may be obliged to accept that linguistic growth can be accompanied by phonetic change, i.e. by decay. However, it was advisable to limit one's losses and, in this context, one understands why Schleicher and Curtius found it difficult to accept the accent-based theory of *Ablaut* proposed by Geiger: *Ablaut* (vowel gradation) belonged to the parent language; to assume that it was due to a loss of vowels due to accentual shifts implied that there was sound change before the end of the common period, that is to say Geiger's proposal went against the basic tenets of the theory. In this case at least the contemporary views about growth and decay prevailed over the actual results of observation.

This is an isolated instance and in general the emphasis is on empirical data. The comparative method was seen as producing empirical evidence in favour of far-reaching theories: the nature of a primitive society, the priority of monotheism over polytheism, the origin of myths, the nature and origin of grammatical forms, the evolution of language, etc. It should now be clear why we have chosen to discuss the actual work of historical comparison before discussing the theoretical views of the period: the latter were all too often seen, rightly or wrongly, as directly dependent on, or inspired by, the concrete results. It is up to modern historiography to establish whether this is really so and what link there is, to modify Hoenigswald's words, between what the linguists were doing and what they thought they were doing or ought to have been doing.

Notes

1. More detailed information is available in Pedersen ([1931] 1962), who is mainly concerned with the technical aspects, and in Tagliavini (1968).
2. Cf. Mueller-Vollmer (1993, 20ff.) and Riese (1994).
3. Pott lists roots in the Sanskrit forms and according to the Sanskrit order, but in practice clearly examines elements which he would like to attribute to the parent language, even if he is not concerned with their phonetic aspect. Very interesting observations about the usefulness or otherwise of this procedure can be found in Benfey ([1837] 1890–2, I, ii, 5ff.), who argues for a different method, i.e. for phonological reconstruction, and in his discussion anticipates some of the discoveries of the end of the century on the reconstruction of Indo-European vocalism, on vocalic r, etc. For Pott's ideas, cf. Bologna (1990).
4. Pott's work would deserve far more study than it has received so far (though the position is changing), but the obscurity of his style acts as an effective deterrent. For some basic data, see the introductory material to Pott (1974) and above all Leopold (1983, 1984, 1989b, etc.). Cf. also Bense (1976), Ricken (1990b), Haßler (1991b) and Bologna (1988, 61ff., 1990, 1995). For Pott as the first exponent of *Allgemeine Sprachwissenschaft* in the German Universities, see above all Plank (1993).
5. The family name has not yet been settled, but in French the prevailing term is already *indoeuropéen*, in English *Indo-European*, and in German *indogermanisch*. In Italy we find *indoeuropeo*, *indogermanico*, *ariano* and *arioeuropeo* (the term introduced by Ascoli).
6. In addition to Pott (1833–6, 1859–76, etc.), others had collected Indo-European roots and lexical elements. F. G. Eichhoff (1836) listed 550 verbal roots in their Sanskrit form, together with the supposed equivalents

in other languages; the book also offered a list of nouns deemed to be inherited and organized in semantic fields: the world and its elements, animals and plants, the body, etc. The second part of the *Lexicologie indo-européenne* by H. J. Chavée (1849) also attempted a classification of verbal stems into rough semantic fields. In both works (and especially in Chavée) the proposed etymologies or correspondences were too unreliable to be generally accepted. About Pictet, who in 1859–63 aimed at reconstructing the material and moral culture of the Indo-Europeans and collected a set of lexical forms divided into semantic fields, see below, p. 188 note 45.

7. This is almost paradoxical in view of Schleicher's distinction between *Philologie* as a historical discipline and linguistics as a natural science (see below). On the other hand, Georg Curtius ([1862] 1886, i, 132–50), Schleicher's friend and sometime colleague, wished for a close connection between *Philologie* and *Sprachwissenschaft*.

8. The second volume (1843) was dedicated to Lachmann. According to the traditional view of classical studies, the Boeckh school represented *philologia perennis* and was dedicated to a view of *Altertumswissenschaft* as encompassing a unified knowledge of the ancient world as a whole, while Hermann's school had a narrower concept of classics as concerned with linguistic and textual studies. If so, it may seem remarkable that the link between the new linguistic approach and classics is made on the Boeckh side. Yet the phenomenon is not entirely surprising for three reasons at least: first, Grimm's approach, which Ahrens to a certain extent followed, was inspired by Romantic tenets which harmonized better with Boeckh's school than with the more traditional and rationalistic Hermann; secondly, as Pfeiffer (1968–76, ii, 188) points out, Ahrens' work would not have been possible without K. O. Müller's historical teaching at Göttingen, but Müller was Boeckh's favourite pupil and shared his concept of *Altertumswissenschaft*; thirdly, it is understandable that scholars steeped in the critical tradition such as Hermann reacted violently to the new arrivals who pretended to find easy comparative solutions for problems which had been debated for centuries. On the other hand, Hermann's own views were not always acceptable to the linguists. Bréal ([1864] 1877, 228) explains with an example where the divergences arose. Hermann maintained that the Latin ablative (a case unknown to Greek) was a recent innovation, and demonstrated 'with arguments based on the nature of the human mind' that no language could have more than six cases. Bréal ironically points out that at that stage it would have been possible to learn from the first Sanskrit grammars that Sanskrit had eight cases, which contradicts all the reasons deduced from Kant's philosophy (for us it is not uninteresting that Bréal does not refer to the cases of Russian or Finnish which, one may assume, were better known than those of Sanskrit).

9. Timpanaro (1981, 82f.) points out that the founders of the new textual criticism of the nineteenth century (Lachmann, Ritschl, Madvig) all showed considerable sympathy towards comparative linguistics well before the impact of Curtius's activities could be felt.

10. Max Müller's life is representative of the intellectual climate of contemporary Europe and Victorian England; see the hagiographic biography written

by his wife (G. Max Müller 1902) as well as Chauduri (1974); cf. also Jankowsky (1972, 117ff.), Leopold (1974), Dowling (1982, 1986, 46ff. and *passim*), Schrempp (1983), Stocking (1987, 56ff. and *passim*), Bologna (1988, 40–60), Harris and Taylor (1989, 165–75), Olender (1989, 113–26), Nerlich (1990a, 36–49), Salmon (1996).

11. A great wealth of data about Italian linguistics before Ascoli is collected in Santamaria (1981, 1983, 1986a, 1986b, 1993); for the earlier period, cf. Marazzini (1988, 1989, 1991, 1993) and Gensini (1984, 1993, 1994). Important work by Timpanaro (1969, 1972b, 1972c, 1978, 1979, 1980a, 1980b) is more informative than anything else about the atmosphere of the time and the problems discussed in Italy both in the first and the second part of the nineteenth century (cf. also Raicich 1970–4, 1981). See also Dovetto (1994a, b) and the essays collected in the recent volume about Giovanni Flechia (1811–92) (Cardinale, Porzio Gernia, Santamaria 1994). For Italian linguistics in general, cf. the essays collected in Ramat, Niederehe and Koerner (1986). See also the following note.

12. Ascoli has been extensively discussed, mainly in Italian sources; for a survey with previous references, see Bolelli (1962); for the terminology of his school, cf. De Felice (1954). One of the periodicals he founded, the *Archivio Glottologico Italiano* (1873ff.), is still one of the major Italian periodicals. Some work by Timpanaro is quoted in the previous note. Ascoli's diaries, letters, etc. which are being gradually published, are very interesting: cf. e.g. Timpanaro (1959), Gazdaru (1967), Prosdocimi (1969), Peca Conti (1978), etc. Ascoli (1986) collects a series of different contributions by various authors. Among Ascoli's contributions, those on Indo-European comparative philology (reconstruction of the velars and of the aspirates, work on Celtic and the language of the gypsies) attracted considerable attention, as did those on Italian and Romance dialectology (where he is undoubtedly a pioneer; cf. Benincà 1996, 98ff.). His name is also linked to a sober position in the Italian *questione della lingua* (cf. Dardano 1974, Grassi 1975, Vitale 1984, 461ff.) and to a more general theory about the importance of substratum in language development (Timpanaro 1969; Silvestri 1977–82, i, 73ff.; 1982, 1986). Finally, he is one of those few scholars who tried to go beyond the reconstruction of Indo-European and argued (on concrete linguistic evidence) for a common origin of Indo-European and Semitic and even further (and on more general motivation) for the possibility of monogenesis (Timpanaro 1969, 343ff.). Conceivably his Jewish origin may have contributed to his interest in 'gli studi ariosemitici', but after the discovery of Indo-European, it was a natural step to see how much further one could go; the same step was taken e.g. by the German Rudolf von Raumer (1815–76), who had a very different training and background. About Adolfo Mussafia, the great Romance philologist, see the introductory data in Mussafia (1983).

13. In his book on the origin of language, Renan ([1st edn 1848], 1858, 1883) argued that 'each family of idioms . . . has arisen from the genius of each race, without effort and without hesitations' (1883, 94); given that for him languages are imprisoned once and for all in their grammar, it is impossible to think of a common origin. Terracini (1949, 85) acutely observes that

this hypothesis can be tied to Humboldt's concept of internal form, but also depends on the results of comparative linguistics, which at that stage seemed to move against the hypothesis of a genealogical relationship between the great linguistic families.

14. For a general survey of the contemporary decipherments, see Pope (1975). During the nineteenth century we observe the development of an evolutionary (transformationist) view of the history of writing, which strongly resembled that postulated for language; in a first phase, pictograms would have been standardized into ideograms, the second phase would have developed on phonetic bases, beginning with a mixture of ideograms and syllabograms and ending with a purely syllabic system, which in the end was replaced by the alphabet (cf. Cardona 1981, 33ff.).

15. In his 1827 essay about the dual, Humboldt (GS, vi, 28) had expressed similar views and was rebuked by Madvig ([1836] 1971, 61); cf. Hauger (1994, 155ff.).

16. A passage from *Ueber die Veschiedenheiten des menschlichen Sprachbaues* (1827–9) is worth quoting in full (Humboldt GS, vi, 197f.): 'However different men may be in size, colour, body shape and features, nevertheless their mental structures are the same. The opposite view is contradicted by multiple experiences and has never been held seriously or from disinterested conviction, but only out of ridiculous pride in one's own colour or despicable greed, prompted by the opportunities of the traffic in negro slaves. Language, however, derives entirely from the spiritual nature of man. Even a difference in speech organs, which in general, as far as I know, has never been claimed for different races, could only lead to peculiarities of no importance, because the features on which articulation is based are also of a purely intellectual nature. The specific national character of an Hottentott certainly manifests itself in his language too and, since in men everything hangs together, the common negro nature takes its share, though it cannot be isolated in detail. If race, however, provided a necessary classification criterion for languages, then we would expect that the languages of peoples who belong to the same race would be differentiated from those of other races by identical structures, and this is definitely not the case.'

17. Often motives and reactions were complex and the holy indignation of modern authors may be misplaced. In 1938 (the date is significant) the Italian Semitist Giorgio Levi della Vida (1938, 2), who shortly afterwards had to leave Italy to escape from the consequences of his own anti-fascism and of the anti-Jewish laws, wrote, with more understanding than some of the modern historiographers: 'Renan, who had abandoned the religious dogma, remained under the dominance of the racial dogma. On the other hand it was the fashion of the times'. And he continued in a footnote: 'The antipathy which Renan felt for the "esprit sémitique" and his enthusiasm for Greece are the consequence of his rationalistic attitude; we may remember the *Prière sur l'Acropole' (ibid.*, 109).

18. If linguistics influenced the general opinions on race, the reverse is also true. To accept linguistic monogenesis, i.e. to believe that all languages had a common ancestor, normally meant to take an anti-racist attitude; this may account perhaps for the monogenetic views held by Ascoli, Max

Müller and by Baron C. J. K. Bunsen, Prussian minister in London and Max Müller's patron. On the other hand, to believe in polygenesis made it easier to believe in the theory that the differences between languages (and races) were fundamental and irreconcilable. Yet in our period the linguists were coming to the view that not only could monogenesis not be demonstrated, but also that the diversity of languages made a multiple origin more likely; this was the position of Schleicher, for instance, but also, within limits, that of Pott, which demonstrates that polygenesis did not necessarily go hand in hand with racism. Timpanaro (1979, 474ff.) highlights the difficulties created by the development of Darwinism. In theory the supporters of monogenesis ought to have been in favour of evolution, but in practice they were mostly prompted by religious considerations which were not compatible with it.

19. In the introduction to his book on *Die Mande-Neger Sprachen*, Steinthal (1867, xiv) expressed the worry that his evaluation of these languages as very *unvollkommen* in their organization could be exploited by the supporters of slavery. He concluded, however, that, were this to happen, he would have had to deplore it but would not have felt responsible, since he had already demonstrated how unjustified such a conclusion was from the scientific point of view.

20. *Buchstabenlehre* was the title of Grimm's phonology volume even if the term *Lautlehre* was introduced by Grimm himself in later editions (Kohrt 1985, 10).

21. The word 'letter', or its equivalents in Latin and the modern European languages, did of course fulfil a double function, that of indicating a written letter and a spoken sound. It would be foolish to assume that all those authors who speak of 'letters' while referring to sounds were not aware of the difference; cf. Abercrombie (1949) and for a deeper analysis see Kohrt (1985, 25ff. and *passim*).

22. Cf. Raumer (1863, 1ff. [1837], 368ff. [1858], 405ff. [1861]).

23. For the history of phonetics in general, see Panconcelli-Calzia (1940, 1941). More recently, cf. Kohrt (1984), Malmberg (1991, 377–404), Koerner (1994, x–xxxviii; 1995, 171–202). For the earlier history of attitudes to sounds etc., see Gessinger (1994).

24. Malkiel (*loc. cit.*) reaches this conclusion from an analysis of the texts; his view is supported by Gaston Paris' preface quoted above.

25. Diez (1853, xxii) observes that language may diverge from its own laws (*gesetzen*) and be directed 'von dem gefühle des wohllautes oder der zweckmässigkeit'. In this context I doubt that 'laws' refers to the regularity of sound change, as perhaps implied by Malkiel (1976a, 13); it is more likely that Diez had in mind the grammatical regularity of the language or its transparency, which are destroyed when, for instance, a reduplication is lost through haplology.

26. Schleicher's *Compendium* was followed in 1869 by an *Indogermanische Chrestomathie* which contained brief passages in the main ancient Indo-European languages accompanied by a short introduction and a glossary. The work was written together with other scholars, and Schleicher (1869a, iv) commented in the preface that in time it would become more and more

necessary to entrust such work to more than one author. In common with other histories of linguistics, we shall ignore the *Vergleichende Grammatik* (1852–9) by Moriz Rapp; the first volume is entitled *Grundriß der Grammatik des indisch-europäischen Sprachstammes* (1852) and the other five are devoted to nominal and verbal morphology. Rapp had studied with Rask and, in comparison with his contemporaries, showed greater interest in phonetics (cf. p. 163); one may notice the use which he made in the description of Indo-European of a (very simplified) phonetic transcription of his own creation. For the rest, as Pott observed ([1887] 1974, 2f.), the scientific level was not very high. However, two characteristics must at least be mentioned; first, the honest confession which Rapp makes in his introduction that he had experienced great difficulties in his attempt to learn the main Indo-European languages; secondly, his classification of *Sprachforschung* into, on the one hand, practical and historical philology (the latter was represented e.g. by Jacob Grimm) and, on the other, theoretical *Sprachwissenschaft*. Bopp is quoted under this second heading and is described as a scholar who, starting from Rask's achievements, aimed at universality in grammar but got lost in the details, because of the microscopic precision of his enquiry, and had not always succeeded in reaching a systematic overview (Rapp 1852–9, i, 3ff.).

27. As has often been noted, this German attitude makes all the more remarkable Bréal's decision to translate into French (between 1866 and 1872) not Schleicher's *Compendium*, but the second edition of Bopp's *magnum opus*. The reasons are both practical and theoretical: on the one hand, Bopp's plan is much easier to understand for the beginner and, on the other hand, Bréal was completely out of sympathy with Schleicher's 'scientific' and 'ahistorical' view of language (see below).

28. Schleicher studied classical philology and theology at Leipzig, Tübingen and, above all, Bonn, where he belonged to the seminar of the great Latinist and Plautine scholar F. Ritschl. He took his doctorate in 1846 with a dissertation about Varro and in the same year obtained his *venia legendi* in 'Indic language and literature and comparative grammar'. It is remarkable that, in spite of his classical training, he published very little about the classical languages; most of his work was dedicated to theory (mostly typology), to the Slavic and Baltic languages (he did fieldwork in Lithuania), to the Germanic languages, and, obviously, to Indo-European. Botany was his hobby. The progress of his career is again indicative of a midcentury generation. In 1850 he was appointed Extraordinarius in 'Classical Philology and Literature' at Prague (where Georg Curtius had a similar appointment), but in 1851 he obtained a similar position in 'Comparative Linguistics and Sanskrit' and in 1853 he became Ordinarius in 'Germanic and Comparative Linguistics and Sanskrit'. When in order to return to Germany he moved in 1857 to a less-rewarding position at Jena, he was made Honorary Professor of Comparative Linguistics and Germanic Philology. For his biography and works, see in general Lefmann (1870), Schmidt (1869, 1890), Delbrück (1880, 40–54), Dietze (1966), Bynon (1986), Koerner (1989, 322–75), all with further bibliography.

29. A similar interpretation can be found as early as Ascoli (1877, 9); cf. Morpurgo Davies (1994).

30. Cf. note 3. For other attempts at lexical reconstruction, cf. note 6. The aims varied: Pott had aims which were mainly linguistic; Eichhoff and Pictet aimed at cultural reconstruction, and so did Adalbert Kuhn (see p. 175); Chavée, however, wanted to reconstruct the oldest lexicon of all linguistic families, in order to identify the basic ideas which corresponded to the first roots (Leroy 1985; Bologna 1988, 78; Nerlich 1992, 126ff.). See in general Bologna (1988, 1990).

31. For Benfey, cf. note 3. The old view is that Schleicher is responsible for the convention for which an asterisk (*) marks the reconstructed forms (the so-called starred forms), but it has been pointed out that the same symbol occurs in the *Glossarium der Gothischen Sprache* published in 1843 by H. C. von der Gabelentz and J. Loebe (cf. Benware 1974, 37 note 8; Koerner 1989, 179ff.). It is worth remembering, moreover, that in 1833 Pott (1833–6, I, 180) used the same symbol (*ein Sternchen*) to indicate roots that were not attested as such but were reconstructed from their derivatives.

32. More or less valid reconstructions appear well before Bopp. It is enough to quote the 'Scythian' reconstructions produced by Claude Saumaise in the seventeenth century (cf. e.g. Droixhe 1978, 81ff.; Muller 1984a, 392f.).

33. Schleicher's short fable (58 words) about a sheep who saw some heavily loaded horses was rewritten by H. Hirt in 1939 and forty years later by Lehmann and Zgusta in 1979. The difference between the three versions offers a good running commentary on the development of Indo-European reconstruction through more than a century (cf. also Campanile 1986).

34. Kretschmer (1896, 8), mentioning the passage quoted above, observes that Brugmann was the first to attribute historical reality to the reconstructed forms, while Schleicher certainly did not do so. In fact this is at least doubtful. Probably Schleicher thought that there were some historical forms which corresponded to his reconstructions, even if the latter were not absolutely accurate from a phonological point of view.

35. Much before Schleicher, Bopp had tackled the same problem, when he had decided that Sanskrit was not the parent language of Greek, Latin, etc.; he had reached his conclusions without an **explicit** use of reconstruction, though the method used was not very different (see above p. 131).

36. The general point is impeccable but the Indo-European examples would now be considered flawed (Attic Greek *ei* must go back to *esi* and it is likely that *essi*, a dialect form, is in fact due to analogical remodelling). As for the French/Provençal example, an interesting feature is that Max Müller in this case either thinks in terms of an older version of French, though he does not feel necessary to specify it, or bases his observation that French *sommes* is closer to Latin *sumus* than to Provençal *sem* on spelling rather than pronunciation.

37. The origin of the linguistic family tree has been much discussed. As early as the 1640s, Claude Saumaise (1643, 438f.) spoke of the Greek dialects as of branches derived from a single trunk (Consani 1991, 86, 162; cf. Metcalf 1974). The tree diagrams appear in the early nineteenth century, both for biological families (Percival 1987, 26) and for the languages: Auroux (1990, 228ff.; cf. 1988b, 33) has republished the linguistic tree drawn by a certain Félix Gallet round 1800 which derives all languages from a 'langue primitive'. The tree has multiple ramifications and the branches can intersect and

join each other in contrast with the later trees. On the other hand, the information is old fashioned for the period: Greek and Latin, for instance, are derived from Hebrew. A table of languages in the form of a tree is found e.g. in Klaproth (1823, next to p. 217); otherwise see in general Koerner ([1987] 1989, 185ff.) and for a description of the various types of tree in biology and linguistics, R. Wells (1987, 52ff.). Is there a connection between the family trees used by linguists and the *stemmata codicum* used by classical scholars to give a graphic image of the relationship between the manuscripts of a given text? And is the idea of the reconstruction of the parent language based on that of the reconstruction of the archetype from which a family of manuscripts is descended? As Hoenigswald (1963 and 1975) pointed out, Schleicher was a pupil of the great classicist Ritschl, who round the middle of the century was introducing into textual criticism the *stemmata codicum* (but not the reconstruction of archetypes) which became *de rigueur* at a later stage. The contemporaries were aware of the similarities of the two techniques and in the late 1850s Curtius (1858–62, I, 22) drew the comparison between the two disciplines partly in order to attract classicists to linguistics (Timpanaro 1981, 85); later, Bréal ([1864] 1877, 225) did the same. However, though reciprocal influences are not to be excluded and Schleicher must have made the connection, it is possible that both disciplines developed their techniques independently from each other, favoured, as suggested by Timpanaro (1981, 84), by that 'comparative atmosphere' which prevailed in Europe at the time.

38. By contrast, Pictet (1859–63, i, 23) in order to represent the relationship of the Indo-European languages, drew a sort of ellipsis, with a central part which symbolized the parent language while various radia distinguished the different subgroups: Germanic, Latin, Indic, Iranian, etc. The arrangement was also meant to give some idea of the geographic distribution of the languages and of the place of origin of the parent language (the *Urheimat*).

39. The term 'unconditioned' (*unbedingter*) was first used by Benfey ([1837] 1890–2, I, ii, 5).

40. Nowadays Georg Curtius (cf. p. 154) is all too often forgotten while the limelight falls on Schleicher. Yet in a world in which every Indo-Europeanist, and indeed every linguist, was likely to have started as a classicist, his influence was considerable. He was trained at Bonn, where he heard Ritschl and A. W. Schlegel, and at Berlin, where he studied with Lachmann, Boeckh and Bopp; as Professor of Classical Philology at Prague from 1849 he partly overlapped with Schleicher before moving to Kiel and then, most importantly, to Leipzig (in 1861). His great institutional achievement consists in having fostered, as we have seen (p. 154), a *rapprochement* between classics and linguistics and in having been largely responsible for the initial successes of linguistic studies at Leipzig, which was to become the centre for such work: in the 1870s his courses about Greek Grammar or Comparative Linguistics attracted some 200 or 300 people each and the *Grammatische Gesellschaft* which he founded for classical students had 600 members in less than seventeen years (Windisch [1886] 1966, 344f.). The successes of his Greek school grammar, which reached eighteen

editions between 1852 and 1888, and was translated into most European languages, including English and (more than once) Italian, made his name known in an even wider area. But his major academic achievements are contained in the *Grundzüge der griechischen Etymologie* (1858–62, 5th edn 1879) and in *Das Verbum der griechischen Sprache* (1873–6, 2nd edn 1877–80), which gave a completely new standing to the study of Greek historical linguistics while providing perhaps the most detailed analysis of historical phonology of an Indo-European language available at the time. In both books the novelty was the combination of philological expertise (and sensitivity) and linguistic know-how. Good semi-contemporary accounts of his contributions are Windisch ([1886] 1966) and Pezzi (1889). Gippert (1994) offers an interesting analysis of his introductory lectures to comparative philology based on the notes taken in 1874 by Christian Bartholomae, the future comparativist and Iranian scholar.

41. Max Müller ([1856] 1868–75, ii, 133ff.) offers yet again an example of distinction between theory and practice or indeed between different kinds of practice. He explains that, in spite of all appearances, it is not possible to compare Sanskrit *Ushas* with Greek Ἔρως; there are numerous examples in e.g. Latin and Sanskrit of *s* turning into *r*, but 'whatever analogies other dialects may exhibit, no Sanskrit *sh* between two vowels has ever as yet been proved to be represented by a Greek *r*. Therefore *Eros* cannot be *Ushas*'. The most entrenched supporter of sound laws would have approved of these sentiments, but would have then reacted on very similar grounds against the comparison of Ἔρως and *arvat* 'horse' or of θάλασσα and ταράσσω favoured by Max Müller.

42. Or some of them did. Ascoli ([1867] 1877, i, 386ff.; cf. *ibid.*, 382ff.) accepted the validity of Curtius's points, but counteracted them with a series of alternative explanations which, though today do not convince, showed a similarity in method. Much later Max Müller (1868–75, IV, 238ff.) returned to the question, but still produced an *ad hoc* explanation to justify the irregular *d/th* correspondence, while ignoring the problems caused by the vocalism and the internal *-s-*.

43. H. Grassmann (1809–77), a schoolteacher who never succeeded in obtaining a University position, reached remarkable fame both as a mathematician and as comparativist. In mathematics he can count as the founder of linear algebra, though his achievements were mainly recognized after his death. He started publishing in Indo-European only in the 1860s but the discovery of the law of dissimilation of aspirates, or Grassmann's Law (Collinge 1985, 47ff.), was immediately seen as a remarkable achievement. We also owe him a dictionary of the RigVeda (1872–5), which is still indispensable, and a translation of, and commentary to, the RigVeda (1876–7). In addition, Grassmann anticipated remarkable discoveries in both physics and phonetics. It is notable that the article about him in the *Allgemeine deutsche Biographie* is jointly signed by Moritz Cantor, the famous mathematician, and by August Leskien, the Slavist who was regarded by the neogrammarians as their guru (Cantor and Leskien 1879).

44. Curtius's monographs are more useful at present and more widely consulted than Schleicher's *Compendium*; this is largely because they contain

a great deal of philological information which has not been superseded, even when the comparative interpretation is obsolete.

45. Pictet, who, *inter alia* was influential in inspiring the young Ferdinand de Saussure with interest in language (De Mauro 1970b, 288ff.), defined two aims of the *philologie comparée*: the first was to contribute to historical and ethnographic research, the second (perhaps less compelling for him) to identify the general laws of language (Pictet 1859–63, i, 11). About him see in general Vallini (1983), Bologna (1985).

46. Most of what precedes depends on Bologna (1988, *passim*). Max Müller ([1856] 1868–75, ii, 1ff.) discussed at length lexical reconstruction as used to determine the material culture of the Indo-Europeans in his 1856 paper about comparative mythology, where he also referred to previous work by Eichhoff (1836), Grimm (1848) and, obviously, Kuhn. How unsophisticated and purely linguistically based some of the inferences were is shown by the fact that Max Müller (*ibid.*, 47) attributes iron to Indo-European culture, while we would now assume that that was archaeologically impossible. Nor does he (or others) stop to consider two fundamental problems: (a) how do we know when we reconstruct an Indo-European form that its meaning is identical to that found in the later evidence, (b) is there a one-to-one connection between name and 'thing'? And, if not, are we entitled to use the 'name' to postulate the existence of the 'thing'? (Cf. Bologna 1988, 72.) These and other questions are seriously discussed in Schrader (1890) and in the preface of the *Reallexicon der indogermanischen Altertumskunde* (1901), also edited by Schrader. This is a book in which the most serious type of work about lexical reconstruction as a source for what we have called *realia* and *spiritualia* eventually converged and which was written in a mood of far greater methodological self-awareness than that which had prevailed earlier on. Cf. also Hehn (1870, 1976).

47. The evolution of the theory of *Ablaut* is full of sudden developments. For Grimm, as we have seen, the basic form of the root was that of the Germanic present, i.e. a root characterized by an *e*-vowel; the equivalent Sanskrit root would have had an *a*-vowel. Curtius (1869, 51) reported that the *neuere Sprachwissenschaft* would take as basic the form of the root without *a* in Sanskrit or without *e/o* in other languages; hence in the Greek verb for 'to leave' (λείπω) *lip*- rather than *leip*-, in that for 'to join' (ζεύγνυμι) *zug*- rather than *zeug*-; *Ablaut* was rather a *Zulaut*, an addition of vowel. For Geiger the reverse is true and this on the basis of a 'glottogonic' argument. Roots, in his view, represent the first words ever pronounced; if so, they must have been pronounceable and, among other things, have an accent. Yet forms such as *s*- (in *s-más* 'we are') are not pronounceable roots; hence it is necessary to start from *ás* 'to be' as the basic form. In its turn this view opens the possibility that a form such as *s-más* is due to the loss of the root vowel in a non-accented position. This provided a beautifully simple but 'mechanical' explanation of *Ablaut*; yet, as we shall see, such an explanation could not be acceptable to those who upheld Schleicher's and Curtius's views about the history and prehistory of language.

48. There were naturally some alternatives. Delbrück (1880, 61ff.) observes that the similarity between the pronouns and the verbal endings is a basic

point which everyone accepted; he then distinguishes between (a) evolutionary theories, such as those of the classicist and comparativist Rudolf Westphal, according to whom the roots (as for Friedrich Schlegel) 'sprouted' suffixes and endings; (b) 'adaptation' theories, such as those of the Sanskritist Alfred Ludwig, according to whom endings and pronouns arose separately and 'adapted' to each other (cf. De Meo 1987).

49. For a survey of the various 'glottogonic' hypotheses, cf. Vallini (1987). R. Wells (1987, 57ff.) distinguishes between primitivism (the oldest stage is the best), progressivism (the most recent stage is the best) and acmenism (things first improve and then deteriorate). From this point of view, Schleicher and Curtius are certainly acmenists, but Wells maintains (probably correctly) that Bopp was too. The problem is further complicated by the need to distinguish between linear and cyclical progress.

The theoretical discussion of the mid century

8.1 Historiographical assumptions

Three widespread historiographical assumptions need to be discussed before we summarize the more general efforts of the century's central decades. It is often stated that the linguists of the time:

(a) accepted in full Schleicher's naïve organicism: language was an independent organism subject to natural laws; it had no history, but a life similar to that of natural organisms.
(b) were anti-uniformitarian, i.e. believed that the earliest phases of language were not subject to the same processes of change as the later ones.
(c) obsessed as they were by the triumphs of comparative and historical work, not only had no interest in more general problems, but did not even realize that such problems existed. If and when they did, Schleicher's organic views satisfied them.

Predictably the real picture is more complicated; we shall consider each point in turn.

First, Schleicher's ontological organicism[1] is not as prevalent as is often assumed. A select list of dissenters could include A. F. Pott and H. Steinthal in Germany, the Latinist J. N. Madvig in Denmark, the comparativist and dialectologist G. I. Ascoli in Italy, the French linguists M. Bréal and G. Paris, and the American W. D. Whitney. Max Müller followed Schleicher only part of the way and Georg Curtius was too much of a philologist not to be critical. The very existence of this rejection implies that general issues were not altogether ignored.

Secondly, the uniformitarian issue is not clear-cut. The term was initially applied by the philosopher William Whevell to the geological theories of Charles Lyell and to his constant attempt 'to explain the former changes of the earth's surface by reference to causes now in operation' (Lyell 1830–3), but was not extended to linguistics.[2] It is clear that any linguist who postulated for language a period of growth according to different principles from those which determine the later decay was not a uniformitarian (see above), but we find uniformitarian practice and what amounts to declarations of uniformitarian faith in most of the scholars mentioned above, with the addition of e.g. Wilhelm Scherer and with the exception of Max Müller and Curtius. That we are not always dealing with black and white distinctions is shown exactly by these two: Max Müller has been taken both as a supporter and as an attacker of uniformitarianism and so, for that matter, has Schleicher (Christy 1983, 34ff.); we have seen above that Curtius was not a wholly coherent anti-uniformitarian.

Finally, even among the technicians there are requests for a broader and more theoretical outlook: Pott is an example, but Benfey too, in his history of linguistics (1869), while having little to report about German work in *allgemeine Sprachwissenschaft*, deplores that this science is only at the beginning (*ibid.*, 787). Work of a more general nature does in fact exist and is often accompanied by an explicit justification. In 1850, one of the most productive generalists, Heymann Steinthal ([1850] 1970, 114ff.), while exalting the importance of Bopp's discipline, stressed that historical linguistics is not self-sufficient; it cannot answer questions about the nature of language and has no autonomy; consequently it cannot be called a science (*Wissenschaft*). It takes its categories (e.g. noun, verb, case) from philosophical grammar and does not stop to ask how they have been reached (*ibid.*, 129).

8.2 General works

The first task now is to identify the relevant work. Some of it falls into a category which seems to be a typical creation of our period, the introduction to, or outlines of, linguistics. The starting point is provided by Max Müller's *Lectures on the Science of Language* (1861 and 1864), based on his famous performance at the Royal Institution (see above, p. 155); they provide a highly readable, but somewhat incoherent and superficial account of what was being discussed about language in a framework which is partly inspired by Schleicher's organicistic views. Later on, Max Müller's adversary, W. D. Whitney, threw himself into the field with two books, *Language and the Study of Language* (1867) and *The Life and Growth of Language* (1875), where the level of discussion is higher and more original and the emphasis is on language as an institution, the historical product of man's action. At an earlier stage, Steinthal had edited the posthumous *System der Sprachwissenschaft* by K. W. L. Heyse (1856), a work which in spite of its post-Humboldtian character and its incipient psychologism is closer in style, even if not in content, to the older accounts of language than to Max Müller's *Lectures*. Benfey (1869), though historiographical in nature, is also relevant. The very existence of the introductory work is important because, even when it is as superficial as Max Müller's *Lectures*, it calls for a level of generality and sustained reflection and for an effort of clarification which otherwise might have been absent from the prevailing technical contributions.[3] It certainly opens the way to a multiplicity of later introductions, some of which are theoretically very significant: in the last third of the century, Steinthal (1871), Sayce (1874, 1880), Hovelacque ([1876] 1922), Friedrich Müller (1876–88, Vol. I), Paul ([1880] 1920), Delbrück (1880), Gabelentz (1891), etc., and, in our century, e.g. Oertel (1901), Saussure's posthumous *Cours de linguistique générale* (1916) and Jespersen's, Sapir's and Bloomfield's books of the 1920s and 1930s, to quote but a few.

We also have specific, even if heterogeneous, work dedicated to the type of questions which would now be discussed under the heading of general or theoretical linguistics. Schleicher did of course defend his views in the extensive introductions to his numerous historical and comparative works, but he also wrote shorter and more general statements in descriptive and typological vein about the morphology of language (1859) or noun and verb (1865a). In two short pamphlets (1863, 1865b) he reiterated his biological views and highlighted his agreement with Darwin. In a very different book, his *Zur Geschichte der deutschen Sprache* (1868), the Germanist Wilhelm Scherer (1841–86) also introduced a number of methodological points.[4] Max Müller's linguistic essays oscillate in their adherence to Schleicherian line, but do not add much to the material summarized in the *Lectures on the Science of Language*. In France we find a group of believers in a biological view of language which concentrated round the Belgian Chavée (see above, pp. 156, 180 note 6, 320f.) and then his student Abel Hovelaque (1843–96) (cf. p. 320ff.; and see Auroux and Delesalle 1990; Nerlich 1992, 127ff.; Desmet 1994). If we look at those theoretical works which either were not influenced by Schleicher or reacted against him, again we find a series of divergent contributions. Classicists, who were probably more aware than other comparativists of the importance of description and of syntactical and semantic analysis, play a considerable role. Some of the essays written between the 1830s and 1870s by J. N. Madvig (above, p. 154) show a concept of language which is very different from that of both the early Romantics and Schleicher. The general anti-logical, anti-philosophical reactions are there but there is also a reaction against German Romanticism and organicism. They tackle general questions such as the need for a uniformitarian approach to language (the term is not used), the arbitrariness of the sign, the nature of language (which

Madvig sees as a social product arising from the need for communication between people who live together), the definition of grammatical categories, the importance of a functional approach, the concept of meaning as based on use, the incapacity of etymology to go back to the original meanings, the impossibility of establishing laws of semantic change, the mistake made in identifying the study of language with that of sound laws, the priority of syntax and of the study of meaning, etc.[5] Two other classicists, C. K. Reisig (1792–1829) and F. Haase (1808–67), whose work on Latin linguistics appeared posthumously (in 1839, 2nd edn 1881–90 and 1874–80), are now seen as the founders of German *Semasiologie*, the study of meaning and of its evolution, done in the first case in a Kantian framework joined to a Romantic form of historicism, in the second in a more evolutionary and historical context (Schmitter in Nerlich 1988, 101–19; Nerlich 1992, 33ff.; see below, p. 312f.). In France yet another classicist, Michel Bréal, starts in some essays of the late 1860s those discussions which will eventually lead to his *Essai de sémantique* (1897) and to yet another form of opposition to Schleicher's organicism. The monograph *De l'ordre des mots dans les langues anciennes comparées aux langues modernes* (1844) by the Hellenist Henri Weil, with its concern for syntax, offered an interesting combination of 'modern-sounding' empirical statements with views taken from the eighteenth-century work in the tradition of Condillac and from German syntactical work; in 1869 Bréal was responsible for its republication.[6] H. Steinthal's life work, which we shall discuss below, creates a tradition of its own and marks the beginning of that psychological and ethnopsychological view of language which characterizes the final part of the century.

Humboldt's views were not altogether forgotten. In Germany two scholars at least carried his torch: A. F. Pott, who re-edited the Kawi *Einleitung* with a lengthy commentary and discussion ([1876] 1880), and H. Steinthal, who, in spite of some sharp criticism, saw himself as a Theophrastus next to Humboldt as his Aristotle (Bumann 1965, 14). In addition to numerous short monographs and papers about Humboldt's *Sprachphilosophie*, Steinthal also produced an edition of his *sprachphilosophische* works (1883–4), while disputing with Pott about the nature of the task in hand (cf. also Haßler 1991b). Familiarity with Humboldt was not universal, as shown by Whitney's ([1872] 1971, 134) famous reference to him as 'a man whom it is nowadays the fashion to praise highly, without understanding or even reading him'. Max Müller's strictures point in the same direction: 'When I read a work of Steinthal's, and even many parts of Humboldt, I feel as if walking through shifting clouds' (1861 letter to Renan: G. Max Müller 1902, i, 257) or 'If you want to read obscure books about langage, read Humboldt, or should you wish to read obscure, superficial books read Steinthal' (1863 letter to Bernays; *ibid.*, 274). Yet some of the basic Humboldt concepts were influential even on those who attacked him (such as Madvig, Max Müller and Whitney) and a 'practicing' comparativist such as Ascoli repeatedly expressed his admiration for him (Timpanaro 1972b, 150, note 1). Humboldt's fortune would deserve a separate study, but, contrary to what is normally stated, we recognize in most of nineteenth-century linguistics echoes of his views.

In a Humboldt context we must remember the great quantity of general work about language classification and language typology done in the central decades of the century. The discussion follows on from that of the two Schlegels, of Humboldt, etc.: now Pott, Steinthal, Max Müller, Schleicher and then Friedrich Müller set the scene. Both genealogical and typological classifications are discussed but the later historiography has more or less deliberately forgotten the typological discussions. Yet it is in this context that we recognize the beginnings of that descriptive and general linguistics which will dominate the twentieth century.

Finally, the numerous monographs about the origin of language written between the 1840s and the 1870s (e.g. Renan [1848] 1883, Grimm 1851, Steinthal [1851] 1858, Farrar 1860, Wedgwood 1866, Geiger 1868–72, 1869, Marty 1875, Noiré 1877, etc.) reflect at various levels (from the highest to the most fantastic or the crankiest) strongly polarized views of a general nature; the questions which they dealt with – sometimes distinguishing them, often confusing them – concerned both languages as we know them and language as a general faculty. In discussing the origin of languages one could conclude that they were all descended from one single language (monogenesis) or that the differences were too great to support this view (polygenesis). In principle it would have been possible to use the comparative method to demonstrate the common origin of the various language families; in practice, in the course of the century the difficulties of such an enterprise became clear so that the problem remained open, in spite of occasional attempts; on this point evolutionary theory could not help. In so far as the institutionalized discipline ever reached a collective view, this tended towards polygenesis, though the racial problem interfered (cf. p. 182 note 18). Linguists could also assume that each language family (or language type) was linked to a race and if so the problem could be left to physiologists or anthropologists. More commonly, however, the roles were reversed and the anthropologist turned for help to the linguist.

In the discussion of the more general question, the origin of the language faculty, contrasting solutions were proposed which often resembled those of the previous centuries: language is a God-given gift, is innate and is what distinguishes human beings from animals so that evolution is not possible, is the product of human convention, is a natural evolutionary product (not necessarily in the Darwinian sense). In this context, however, serious discussion of general problems was possible: what is essential to the language faculty, what is its function, what role is played by communication needs, do we see the phonetic signs as playing (initially at least) an additional role or the primary role in communication? There was in addition the problem of how arbitrary signifiers had come to be used for the various meanings. Here linguists tended to take refuge in agnosticism (cf. Bopp's refusal to discuss the origin of the roots) or in the belief that the first expressions had been onomatopoeic, i.e. imitations of sounds (e.g. Whitney), or interjections, which were then conventionalized.[7] More sophisticated views, such as those of Noiré, were also propounded. It was possible, though not generally done, to admit that the more general problems belonged within physiology or psychology or philosophy, as Victor Henry (1896, 25–45) argued at the end of the century, but at two levels – that of monogenesis vs. polygenesis, and that of the origin of the roots – the practising comparativists felt frustrated; their method ought to have been relevant but did not go far enough nor was there any hope that it ever would. Some, like Max Müller and e.g. Geiger and Noiré, were at least confident that roots had existed at some stage as independent linguistic elements and that, in the case of Indo-European at least, it was possible to reconstruct for them general (non-concrete) meanings. But later on the neogrammarians challenged the very existence of independent roots. All this may perhaps explain why in the last third of the century the problem was marginalized and the various works forgotten.[8] As early as 1859, while writing a preface to the French translation of Grimm (1851), Renan, who had himself written a famous book on the subject, was relatively scathing about all work which removed attention from 'le problème essentiel de la philologie, qui est tout historique'. He nevertheless noted that all successful scientific work required the joining of those faculties which lead to the discovery of new facts and of the 'esprit philosophique', which sees the phenomena in their totality and defines their causes. He took comfort in the observation that many people no doubt found it more convenient to get involved in general questions instead of following 'les voies de l'analyse et de l'investigation', and that in all likelihood such people would not have had much talent for the elaboration of details.[9] Curtius and Schleicher, who had not written monographs of this type, but had theories about the origin of language, might have resented the implication. Nevertheless, Renan's statement may be relevant to the decision incorporated in the statutes of the new Société de Linguistique de Paris in 1866 not to entertain any communication about the origin of language and about universal languages (Vendryes 1955; cf. Auroux 1989).

In what follows we shall concentrate on the main linguistic (rather than philosophical) approaches to the nature of language and language change, fully aware that much more ought to be said than is possible here.[10] We shall then conclude this chapter with a brief look at linguistic typology and classification.

8.3 Schleicher's organicism

In German terms the main contrast is between the conceptions of language of Schleicher and his followers on the one hand, and of Steinthal and his smaller group of devotees on the other, i.e. between organicism and psychologism. Elsewhere, e.g. with Whitney and Madvig, the social and institutional nature of language comes to the fore. We start with Schleicher and Steinthal and shall discuss the French school in Chapter 10.

'Grammar is part of *Sprachwissenschaft* or *Glottik*. In its turn this is part of the natural history of man. Its method is in essence that of the natural sciences'. This sentence opens Schleicher's *Compendium* ([1861] 1871, 1) and summarizes what Schleicher had argued as early as 1850: 'The discipline which has language as its object but uses it as a way of access to the spiritual nature and life of one or more *Volksstämme* is *Philologie*, which belongs in essence to History. In contrast with it there is *Linguistik*, which has language as such as its object and has nothing to do with the historical life of the people who speak the languages; it is part of the natural history of men' (1850, 1). This is explained elsewhere: the object of linguistics is 'not a free mental activity (i.e. history), but language established by nature, subject to inalterable laws of formation, which is impossible to determine through individual will, just as it is impossible for the nightingale to change its song; in other words, the object of *Glottik* is a natural organism' (1860, 120). And further on: 'the use which is made of language has to do with the philologist, it is only the organism which has to do with the *Glottiker*' (*ibid.*, 121).

In Schleicher's early work, Hegelian terminology and concepts seem to dominate and historical linguistics is not yet seen as a natural science.[11] Later on, statements of the type quoted above are constantly reiterated, all the more so when the publication of the *Origin of the Species* (1859) raises the question whether linguists should conceive of the development of language in evolutionary terms comparable to those defined by Darwin. The two pamphlets written towards the end of Schleicher's life (1863, 1865b) answer the question in the affirmative and at the same time give the most explicit statement of Schleicher's views. As has often been noted (Koerner 1989, 324ff.; Maher 1983), Schleicher's evolutionism or, better, transformism, to use Greenberg's (1971) term, precedes Darwinism and is independent of it. There is, first of all, a view which Schleicher shared with most of his predecessors: 'such languages as we would call, in the terminology of the botanist or zoologist, the species of a genus, are for us the daughters of one common stock-language [*Grundsprache*], whence they proceeded by gradual variation' ([1863] 1983, 33). Here a language is identified with a species and a language family with a genus. Since languages change and yield new languages, it follows that the old dogma of the immutability of the species can be abandoned – as far as language is concerned. Yet no reference is made, at this stage, to typical Darwinian concepts such as the survival of the fittest, natural selection, etc., nor is there a discussion of why a language rather than a language family is to be treated as a species. There is, however, a firm statement that the various genera, i.e. language families, were not likely to be derived from one single language: Schleicher speaks firmly for polygenesis.[12] In the second of the two 'Darwinian' pamphlets, he takes further his view of language as an independent entity, a material thing. Language we are told is the result of neural activity in the brain and of the activity of speech organs. To treat language as if it had independent reality instead of as something which depends on the brain or the other organs is justifiable: scientists too study the properties of light on their own, even though light is dependent on the sun. But there is more: different languages are likely to correspond to different neural features or different organs; hence language is the most apt way to classify human races. Also, if the linguistic faculty is directly linked to certain biological characteristics, it may be treated as the result of a long process of evolution of the physical organism. When language first appears it is still in a very simple state. For Schleicher a prehistoric period of language development is followed by a historical period of language decay. During this time new forms are no longer created but the existing forms, as Chavée put it (1862, 21), are subject to chronic diseases according to fixed laws which can be scientifically formulated.

There are here a number of motifs which do not always form a coherent whole. If language is an organism, as Schleicher constantly stated, how can it also be a product of neural activity and of the speech organs? On the other hand, if language is not an organism, why should it have a period of obligatory growth followed by decay? How does this fit with Darwin's progressism? What is true of the individual organism need not be true of the species.[13] In fact, how cogent is the comparison of a language with a species and of a language family with a genus for other purposes than purely classificatory, static ones? The most important point, however, is that the theory, if seen in its stark nudity, is so counterintuitive that it can become the object of ridicule (as indeed has happened). Can it be made to make sense?

Max Müller, who in a number of points followed Schleicher, tried to provide an interpretation, largely repeating what Schleicher had already stated. The basic point, he argued, is that individuals have no power on language development; they cannot influence it through an act of will, and often are not aware of any change in progress ([1861] 1862, 28ff.). To say that language has no history does not imply that there is no change but that this change is not determined by human will. Language undergoes a form of growth which, for Max Müller (but not for Schleicher), is not comparable with that of a tree but rather with that of the crust of the earth; it is the result of natural agencies and is determined by 'continually new combination of given elements' (ibid., 68). Historical information in the conventional sense of the word may be useful for the linguist, but not essential: 'though every record were burned, and every skull mouldered, the English language, as spoken by any ploughboy, would reveal its own history, if analysed according to the rules of comparative grammar' (ibid., 72). This is further explained: it may be useful to recognize Celtic, Norman, Greek and Latin in the English vocabulary, 'but not a single drop of foreign blood has entered into the organic system of the English language. The grammar, the blood and soul of the language, is as pure and ummixed in English as spoken in the British Isles, as it was when spoken on the shores of the German ocean by the Angles, Saxons, and Juts of the continent' (ibid.). With unaccustomed thoroughness, Max Müller (ibid., 74) concludes defining two 'axioms' on which his other statements depend: (a) grammar is the most essential element of language; (b) there is no mixed language.

It now becomes clear (to the historical linguist at least) that the 'theory' must be taken in conjunction with the actual results of the concrete historical and comparative work which it serves to justify. Grammar refers to phonology and morphology (Schleicher had also said so) and is seen as the core element of language. It is not coincidental that grammar (in this sense) had taken the fundamental role in the definition of genetic kinship, and that genealogical comparison had successfully analysed phonological and morphological facts, but had mostly avoided a discussion of syntax and semantics. In its turn the insistence on the 'natural', unconscious development of language fulfils a number of needs. It first explains why, given sufficient data, historical phonology and morphology can be successfully studied and set out in the form of regularly recurring sets of events, even when we know nothing about the historical conditions in which the texts that we exploit have been produced. Without this possibility, reconstruction of the type practised by Schleicher would be unthinkable. Secondly, it justifies the move away from the study of literary languages, a move which linguistics needed in order to affirm its autonomy. Last but not least, it may even, and paradoxically, pander to the Romantic belief in the importance of spontaneous, unsophisticated development. The denial of the existence of mixed languages (or, more correctly, mixed grammars)[14] guarantees the validity of the tree model of language descent, which in its Schleicherian form did not allow for contamination; in its turn this speaks for the validity of reconstruction which is based on that model. Even Schleicher's glottogonic assumptions about a period of prehistoric linguistic growth followed by a period of decay are supported by the standard experience of the Indo-Europeanist that in the historical period languages 'lose forms' rather than acquiring them (Schleicher 1850, 10ff.; cf. Einhauser 1989, 202ff.).

In other words, there is more to Schleicher's views than is often admitted. But why was language treated as an independent organism, a view which even Max Müller found impossible to accept? Here the motivation is double. The whole of the previous generation, as we have seen, had spoken of the organic nature of language, but mostly had not clarified what that meant. It is typical of Schleicher to want to push a point as far as it can go and to wish to make his claims as definite as possible (his reconstruction technique offers further evidence for this attitude). In this instance, to do so meant to state, not only that language is organic, but also that it is an organism.[15] Secondly, Schleicher, like all his contemporaries, was exposed to the problem of language change: why do languages change and why do they change in the way they do? Change here referred both to internal language change (e.g. the loss of [k] in the English cluster [kn]) and to what Rulon Wells (1987, 44) has called change of kinds (Latin is replaced by French). Both types of change were typical of organic beings, and, if so, language could reasonably be compared with an organism. Yet change or development are part of the nature of the organism; the biologist does not need to explain why organisms develop. Similarly, if language is an organism, change will be part of its nature. Ontological organicism solves the problem of the why of change and at the same time justifies the search for regular patterns of development in the context of an autonomous and 'scientific' approach.

In general, the theory is neither as unmotivated nor as incoherent as is often assumed, but it is not acceptable either. Schleicher was ready to admit that there are links between language and the speakers, language and history, but relegated their study to *Philologie*, which was then also made responsible for lexical and syntactical studies. Yet the question concerns the nature of language, whatever the heading under which it is studied, and Schleicher's organic model simply did not allow for the interface between language and mankind.[16] The merit of his attempt, however, is that it revealed once and for all the ambiguity and inconsistence of the organicism of his Romantic predecessors; if language is indeed an independent organism, it cannot also be the true expression of the nation. But Schleicher had also made clear that the view of language as an autonomous organism only made sense (if it did) when language was identified with its most structured parts, phonology and morphology. In restricting *Glottik* to the study of grammar he had, deliberately or otherwise, started that programme of scholarly retrenchment which marked the work of the next generation.[17] He put forward, on the one hand, a grand general view that aimed at integrating the study of language into that of the sciences, on the other, a much more limited programme of work, based in fact on the experience of such work and its possibilities.[18] The conjunction of both caught the popular imagination (partly through the skilful attempts at 'haute vulgarization' made by his followers) and left its imprint on the way in which the layman thinks (or thought) of language as endowed with a life of its own. We now see Schleicher as very much at the meeting point of two tendencies: the excited fervour of the first part of the century, which looked at linguistics as the answer to, and a replacement for, philosophy, and the scholarly caution of the comparativists of the final decades of the century, who saw their task as that of defining the method of their work – and its limits.

8.3.1 Morphological description

Within this context we may now look at Schleicher's contribution to descriptive linguistics and his attempts at formalizing morphology. The aim is to provide a reliable basis for the purposes of language classification and typological description (Bynon 1986). A language, we are told in his 1859 essay *Zur Morphologie der Sprache*, consists of words; we must then establish what forms the words have and find a way to indicate these forms in a universally acceptable manner. The word 'morphology', which Schleicher popularized among linguists after having taken it from the natural sciences, where it had been used by Goethe,[19] is deliberately chosen in contrast with *Formenlere* (*sic*, Schleicher 1859, 35); the subject is concerned with forms and excludes all aspects of meaning except for the bare minimum necessary, e.g. to distinguish roots from relational forms (*ibid.*, 1). All languages must in some way express both meanings (such as 'say', 'red', etc.) and 'relations' of meanings (which include anything which is not lexical meaning, such as object, plural, etc.); a study of word structure will have to distinguish between these two types of forms. In a maximum model of the word we can indicate each different element with a letter and use the symbolism for classifying other words; thus R may indicate a basic 'root' which carries a meaning such as 'give'; Rs a 'root' + an inflectional affix ('gives'), R^x a 'root' with internal inflection (*Ablaut*), as in 'drove', etc.[20] It is not clear that the symbolism is much more than a form of shorthand, but the important point is that Schleicher is dedicating some thought to the basic problems of (synchronic) description. That becomes even clearer in his 1865 essay, which tries to demonstrate that a full and formal distinction of noun and verb is typologically rare and in fact is only found in Indo-European (Percival 1969). The paper starts with a basic question about the way in which grammatical categories are identified. Should we attribute a verb even to those languages which do not distinguish phonologically between verbs and nouns? In general, can there be grammatical categories which have no phonological expression? Schleicher answers negatively and points out that a positive answer would lead to the conclusion that all languages, however different, operate in terms of the same categories. The way in which the question is put and answered is impressive in its clarity; once again what matters is that, while comparativists and typologists tended to take for granted the categories of traditional grammar and apply them arbitrarily to all types of languages, Schleicher is aware that there is a problem. This does indeed fit with his statement (1859, 30) that grammar may have as its object the language abstracted from all change. However, before we turn Schleicher into a precocious Saussure or Bloomfield, we ought to underline how constricting his decision to limit grammar to phonology and morphology is: in this specific case no attempt is made to think in terms of those formal distinctions which are expressed syntactically or through word order.[21] And yet both Humboldt (e.g. GS, iv, 295) and Madvig (e.g. [1856] 1971, 121) had done so (cf. Johansen in Madvig 1971, 16, 22). Once again we find in Schleicher a mixture of the theoretically alert and the fettered mind.

8.4 Steinthal and psychologism

At the start of his booklet on *Sprachgeschichte und Sprachpsychologie* (1901), Wilhelm Wundt, the famous psychologist of the end of the century, gives credit to Heymann Steinthal for having introduced the psychological outlook in the discussion of language and points out that the very title of one of his books (*Grammatik, Logik und Psychologie*) breaks new ground in replacing the expected word 'philosophy' with 'psychology'.[22] The claim for priority may be disputed, but it is generally accepted that Steinthal made linguists aware of the psychological basis of their discipline. One first observation is that, while in Schleicher we recognize a practising comparativist who makes an effort at asking and answering some general questions about language, in Steinthal we have a general linguist or perhaps a philosopher of language who knows a great deal about language and languages (including language history), but whose concrete work ('objective' as he might have called it) concerns the description of 'exotic' languages, language classification, language typology, etc., rather than the detailed analyses of historical phonology and morphology favoured by the comparativists: his programme is that of Humboldt, rather than that of Bopp or Grimm. For him, as for

Humboldt, philosophical and historical (empirical) grammars are inter-dependent: the former needs theoretical input to define even the simplest categories (see above), the latter needs empirical data ([1850] 1970, 129). Graffi (1991, 21ff.) has referred to Steinthal's theoretical views as an 'original synthesis' whose sources are motifs originally found in Humboldt, in Hegel (through the mediation of Heyse, whose *Systeme der Sprachwissenschaft* Steinthal had edited), and, improbably, in the mechanistic psychology of an opponent of idealism such as Herbart. The contemporary practising linguist, i.e. the historical linguist, would have probably noticed in the first instance a number of observations, statements, beliefs which originally belonged to Humboldt: the concept of language as *energeia*, i.e. as constant creation, and that of language as the creative organ of thought.[23] On the view of language as continu-ous production, Steinthal builds his irreducible opposition to that form of organicism which treated language as an autonomous organism to be dissected and analysed, as *ergon* rather than *energeia*: 'the word organic can have for us only a metaphoric sense, since language belongs to the spirit [*Geist*], it is a spiritual production. Clearly it cannot have a purely natural meaning. . . . The word has outlived its fortune' (1855, 379).[24] Like Humboldt, Steinthal rejects the priority of logic over lan-guage and argues that logic and grammar are disparate entities. At an elementary level, if someone says: 'this round table is square', then 'the grammarian remains silent and content, the logician shouts "nonsense"' (1855, 220). The old philosophical grammar assumed that the differences between languages were trivial since they shared a common underlying logical structure. But if, as Humboldt argued, language is independent from logic, and indeed is prior to it, the importance of language differ-ences increases. Each language must be described in its own terms. It is common experience, even at the vocabulary level, that real trans-lation from one language to another is not possible, all the more so when the meanings are abstract and reference to something outside the language is not possible. If so, the abstract grammatical relations must be even more difficult to compare across languages and certainly do not warrant comparison with the abstract categories of logic. It makes no sense to try to identify a system of categories common to all languages; it would be far too superficial and indeed Humboldt is guilty of hold-ing onto a substantive notion of what is common to all languages (Trabant 1983). On the contrary, the real replacement for an *allgemeine Grammatik* is the classification of languages which sets out each lan-guage as an individual realization of the concept of language and, to use Steinthal's Hegelian terminology, is an expression of the idea of language in history (Steinthal 1855, 386ff.). Here too in Steinthal's eyes Humboldt is guilty of not having arrived at a real classification of languages (Ringmacher 1996, 129ff.).

Steinthal highlights here his dissociation, and that of the second part of the nineteenth century, from the old tradition of Port Royal which had been – and still was – important in grammatical description; this is part of his attack against Becker, who dominated the 'grammar market' in Germany with his mixture of organicism and logicism (see above, pp. 88 and 95 note 6). The consequences are noticeable at two different levels at least; first, as Humboldt had realized, language differences become much more intractable if they cannot be dismissed as due to superficial distinctions. Steinthal's own work constantly agonized about the problems of language classification and language typology (1850, [1852] 1970, 139ff.; 1860b, etc.). Secondly, if basic grammatical categories such as those of word, sentence, etc., cannot be linked to notions such as concept, judgement, etc., the whole of grammatical analysis must be rethought in the context of whatever conception of language is adopted. For Steinthal (and indeed for a number of his successors until Wundt) the conception of language as a form of mental activity is the basis for the assumption that psychology is the discipline which can properly study it (1858, 119). Psychology, in other words, must now assume the role previously held by logic.[25] The units of language (words or sentences) must be taken in conjunction with mental representations (*Vorstellungen*) which have their origin in sensation: 'Intuitions combine sensations into certain complexes, presentations [i.e. *Vorstellungen*] are intuitions of intuitions . . . always verbal in nature' (Nerlich 1992, 55). Steinthal accepts Herbart's view of the mind as dominated not by different mental faculties, but rather by the representations which through their interaction determine the mind's functioning (cf. Lazarus and Steinthal 1860, 70 = Steinthal 1970, 376). To perceive a horse involves the seeing of the horse and the recognition of the being in question as a horse; but this last act is a process, a coming together of the image of the horse before our eyes and of the images or representations of all horses that we have seen; we 'apperceive' the horse with, or through, these groups of previous representations, and from the coming together of the two sets of representations arises the product of the apperception, i.e. the recognition of the object perceived as, e.g. a horse. The existing representations play an active, apperceiving role and in their turn are enriched by the new perception. A word, then, is the phonetic expression of a *Vorstellung* or a group of *Vorstellungen*, but the sentence corresponds to a much more involved mental process, the apperception of a mental content. If we have a first impression of a blossoming tree, we may decompose it into two acts of apperception, that of a tree and that of blossoming (the analytic process), but then we apperceive the tree as blossoming and the blossoming as that of the tree; unity is restored and a sequence of subject and predicate, a sentence, 'the tree blossoms' is produced (Steinthal [1871] 1881, 419).[26]

This short summary may give an impression of the type of argument. However fragile and convoluted the theory (and however obscure the way in which it is expressed), on the one hand it shifts the emphasis from phonology and morphology to meaning, on the other it opens the way to an integrated account of both language production and language change. Schleicher concentrated on the latter and saw change as an irreversible process which somehow did not involve speech production as much as the produced speech. For Steinthal, by contrast, change can only be understood in terms of mental operations (cf. Steinthal 1860a). Speech is for him the result of impulses given by the mind and of the movements of the physical organs which react to these impulses. Change may occur because of purely physical causes: ease of articulation accounts for the dialect form *annere* instead of standard German *andere* (with progressive assimilation) or for the Latin *sumpsi* for the expected **sumsi*. Yet change may also result from a lack of coordination between impulses and reactions; the physiological mechanism is slower than the mental impulses and two of these may coalesce in their realization, as happens with regressive assimilation (*ad-pellare > appellare*). More important, changes are caused by the way in which the mental representations enter in various associations with each other due to 'objective' reasons (e.g. all members of a class such as that of colour words) or to the mediation of various factors ('white' is associated with 'snow' which is associated with 'cold') or through purely subjective individual connections (a famous event such as the battle of Leipzig is linked to the year 1813). Steinthal here adopts Herbart's views about the association of representations and also about the narrowness of our consciousness, which allows only a limited number of representations to be present in it at the same time, while the others descend to different levels of unconsciousness. The association partner of a representation when called into consciousness will also attract there the associated representation(s), which are then likely to influence each other. In Steinthal's view this explains large part of grammatical and syntactical change as well as part of sound change.

Various points seem to emerge from this form of association theory. First, there is once again a definite rejection of the view that language can be looked at separately from the mental processes which determine its functioning: words do not change; what may change are the mental representations which underlie them. Also, since the representations are in the last resort based on sensation and perception, language, or rather the speaking individual, is seen as capable, however mediately, of reacting to extralinguistic data, while at the same time providing a language-based way of organizing the new information, reacting to external events. Secondly, the theory makes it difficult, if not impossible, to explain change in terms of decay. For language to exist at all there must be associations, and associations lead to change in linguistic units; this must happen at all times and there is no reason to postulate a period in which the so-called laws of the language are broken (Steinthal 1860a, 100ff.).[27] Finally, it is notable that, just as Schleicher's organism could be interpreted in an anti-atomistic and structuralistic sense, so can Steinthal's associations.[28]

8.4.1 *Völkerpsychologie*

We cannot abandon this account without turning briefly to Lazarus's and Steinthal's view of *Völkerpsychologie*, the discipline which they created and to which they dedicated the *Zeitschrift für Völkerpsychologie und Sprachwissenschaft*, which they founded and edited from 1860 onwards. Ethnopsychology [29] tries to answer a problem which is shared by all social sciences: how do we explain the fact that language, customs, religion, morals, etc. seem to be inextricably tied to individual consciousness but at the same time depend on the existence of a community or at any rate a group of individuals? For Lazarus and Steinthal (1860 = Steinthal 1970, 307ff.) the social nature of man calls for a psychology of the *Volksgeist* (or rather 'Volksgeister') of the various peoples or nations or communities. This term, which had been extensively used by earlier authors, is now redefined and contrasted with *Seele* in an attempt to show that we are not dealing with an improbable metaphysical creation: the soul (*Seele*), which only belongs to the individual, is envisaged as having a substantial reality which must be studied by metaphysics or natural philosophy; *Geist* (mind), on the other hand, refers to the activity of the soul and the laws which determine it; its study is the domain of psychology. Thus *Volksgeist* simply indicates the coherent sum of laws or processes which govern or express the non-physical life of a people (*Volk*) (*ibid.*, 28). The *Völkerpsychologie* is concerned, on the one hand, with the interaction of the various forms of expression of the people; on the other hand, with the relationship of the individual minds among themselves and with the *Volksgeist*. Its laws and formulations are similar to those of the individual psychology. *Volk*, in its turn, is not defined in terms of origin or race but in purely subjective terms: 'the concept *Volk* is based on the subjective view which the members of the community have of themselves, of their identity and of their common links' (*ibid.*, 35). The development of the *Volksgeist* is partly free, partly determined by laws which require investigation. Language is the first product and condition of the *Volksgeist*, since it allows the individual minds to communicate with each other and influence each other. Yet language is also one of the constitutive influences on *Volksgeist*. The 'Geister' of the various peoples necessarily differ because of the different series of experiences and historical developments which they have undergone; it then follows that languages are different in a non-trivial manner and we are once again brought back to the problem of language classification and language typology.

In spite of the firm protestations to the contrary, it is clear that the concept of *Volksgeist* tends to acquire a metaphysical substance – which is of course what others (e.g. the neogrammarians) reproached Steinthal with. On the other hand, it would be a mistake to identify it with the earlier concept of *génie* or *esprit de la langue*. That of Lazarus and Steinthal was a new departure aimed at joining linguistics to a number of social and cognitive sciences. The difficulties and obscurities are considerable, but at least some of the problems are identified and discussed.

Whitney ([1872] 1971, 161), in reviewing the *Abriss der Sprachwissenschaft* or rather that part of it which discussed the origin of language, accused Steinthal of outdated metaphysical thinking and of ignoring all that had been accomplished in the historical study of language.[30] Later on (1875, 704) he pointed out that it was fortunate that 'theories so disconnected from the main scientific standpoint of the times as are those of Humboldt and Steinthal, have never had currency in America and in all likelihood never will.' The harshness is comprehensible but not justified – all the more so since Whitney was well aware of the need in Germany for more general discussions about language and Steinthal's work answered that specific need. Whitney must have also known that Steinthal's deliberate Humboldt-like request for a theory based on the differences of languages rather than on their fundamental identity was anything but outdated, though he may have felt that too little was specifically said about language change. Whatever Whitney's reasons, it may have given some pleasure to Steinthal's ghost to realize that, even if his specific views were repeatedly attacked, the psychologism which he had started had considerable influence. On the one hand, his contribution was explicitly recognized by W. Scherer and then by the neogrammarians, who adopted from Steinthal Herbart's associationism, while rejecting the concept of *Volksgeist* and ethnopsychology; on the other hand, Wundt, while rejecting Steinthal's individual psychology, stressed the need for a *Völkerpsychologie*. One of the people who had listened to Steinthal's lectures, Philipp Wegener (1848–1916), influenced the first English studies of pragmatics, i.e. Malinowski and Gardiner (Nerlich 1990, 157ff., at 162), while Wundt's psychology eventually reached America in a number of different ways – including the young Leonard Bloomfield (1914) in his pre-behaviourist days. Even before that, however, in a book paradoxically dedicated to the memory of Whitney and published by Yale University Press, Hanns Oertel (1868–1952) highlighted Steinthal's importance because 'he placed linguistics upon a definite psychological basis, and ... recognized that these linguistic phenomena were different in character from the psychological phenomena of the single individual' (Oertel 1901, 6off.). Oertel himself

believed that 'Linguistics is the psychological study of the facts of language . . . So conceived, linguistics is not a separate science, to be contrasted on the one hand with psychology, on the other with descriptive
historical grammar, but it forms part of the general field of psychology'
(*ibid.*, 83).[31]

8.5 Whitney and language as an institution

To an abrupt question 'What is language?' the mature Schleicher could
have replied 'an organism which has a life and development of its own',
while Steinthal would have produced a number of different formulae
mostly found in Humboldt: 'a forming organ of thought', 'continuous
production, energeia', and would then have proceeded to redefine them
in terms of individual and collective psychology, highlighting the difficulties and introducing new problems of increasing complexity (cf.
Steinthal 1875, 232ff.). In 1842 Madvig replied to the same question
from yet a different angle; he referred to language as due to the need
to make statements and to communicate and then asserted that language
is 'a system of signs for ideas [*Vorstellungen*] and their combinatory
relations expressed by articulate sound, interconnected and mutually
determined in regard to its parts. The signs have value through the
acknowledgement and sanction of those who participate in the language
and have their meaning only because of this acknowledgement and
by virtue of it'.[32] Much later, William Dwight Whitney, the Sanskritist
to whom we owe two 'introductory' books which formally continued
in the tradition of Max Müller, while disagreeing with him on most
subjects, argued along very similar lines:[33] '[The English language] is
the immense aggregate of the articulate signs for thought accepted by,
and current among, a certain vast community' ([1867] 1870, 22); 'The
desire of communication . . . is the only force that was equal to initi-
ating the process of language-making, as it is also the one that has kept
up the process to the present time' ([1872] 1971, 152f.). In the process
of language acquisition, 'every vocable' counts as 'an arbitrary and
conventional sign' ([1867] 1870, 14); 'A language . . . is a complex of
related and mutually helpful parts' (*ibid.*, 46). 'Language is, in fact, an
institution' (*ibid.*, 48). Concepts (often old concepts) which the German
scholars had either ignored (such as that of a linguistic sign which is
arbitrary and conventional) or given little importance to (that of communication), even when they did not reject them, here come to the fore,
as they had earlier done in Madvig, together with the view of language
as a means of communication and an institution. Similar points are
made very much at the same time by Bréal in his first essays but they
will not be collected in book form until much later. Among these authors
and their followers, Whitney was perhaps the most influential – in our

period at least. He is also easy to place among his contemporaries because of the force with which he reiterated his views and the polemical skill with which he fought those of his opponents: his reactions to Steinthal have been mentioned already; his attacks against Max Müller led to a stream of reviews, articles and eventually a short book (1892). Schleicher too was squarely confronted, since, Whitney argued, language is a human product and not a natural organism; consequently the study of language is not a natural science. In 1867 (1870, 48) Whitney treats the study of language as an 'historical or moral science', as 'a branch of the history of the human race and of human institutions'. In the article on 'Philology', which he wrote in 1885 for the *Encyclopaedia Britannica*, we are told that linguistics is 'a division of the general science of anthropology'. But what about Schleicher's and Max Müller's point about the incapacity of the speakers to exercise an influence on language and their lack of awareness of language change? Whitney's reply in his 1867 book offers one of his rare examples of grand style. The starting point is that 'everything in human speech is a product of the conscious action of human beings', but we are then told that:

> each separate item in the production or modification of language is a satisfaction of the need of the moment . . . is brought forth for the practical end of convenient communication . . . ; it is accepted by the community only because it supplies a perceived want . . . The language-makers are quite heedless of its position and value as part of a system. . . . A language is, in very truth, a grand system of a highly complicated and symmetrical structure; it is fitly comparable with an organized body; but this is not because any human mind has planned such a structure and skilfully worked it out. Each single part is conscious and intentional; the whole is instinctive and natural. The unity and symmetry of the system is the unconscious product of the efforts of the human mind, grappling with the facts of the world without and the world within itself, and recording each separate result in speech. ([1867] 1870, 50)

Anyone endowed with the wit which Whitney displayed in his attacks against Steinthal or Max Müller could have gone to town on this series of oxymora and argued that even the commonsensical Whitney had read too much metaphysics. Yet in the later book Whitney ([1875] 1882, 146) explains in simpler language. The reason why people tend to deny the importance of human will in language is that they see that it does not work consciously toward an end. 'No one says to himself or to others: "our language is defective in this and that particular; go to now, and let us change it."' When the need or the opportunity arises, one may add to or subtract from the language, but is not aware of it. Moreover it is true that all individuals are aware of their inability to effect changes in language on their own authority. The reason is that 'in a sense, it is not the individual, but the community, that makes and changes language'. Language is 'not an individual possession, but a social'. It exists 'not only partly, but primarily for the purpose of communication' and consequently any innovation must find acceptance in the community or part of it. To answer the perennial question about the nature of language which seems to exist only in the individual but also appears to have an objective nature and a life of its own, Whitney does not need to appeal to Steinthal's *Volksgeist*. The needs of communication are only served if the whole community accepts whatever linguistic features prevail. The process of language development will then start in the individual but before becoming effective will have to spread through the community. The individual's will is involved, in that he deliberately aims at communication, but if he innovates, he may not be aware of it; in any case he is not capable of knowing how the innovation will fare in the community.

What does linguistics study? For Schleicher the study of language was essentially study of change, i.e. in his terms, of the decay of the linguistic organism, though he was far more aware than others of the need to define in some way the categories used in language description; even his classification of languages, both genealogical and typological, was based on transformationist views. Steinthal, by contrast, was aware of change as much as his contemporaries, but his problems were more theoretical; he cared for the production of language, envisaged as a constant process, more than for historical change. As for Whitney, his view of language as a means of communication could have led him more easily towards synchrony and a theory of description than towards diachrony and a theory of change. Indeed, some of his important concerns (the English language, modern-language teaching, dialectology) called for synchronic material. Yet Saussure wrote in his notes that Whitney, whom he revered, never said a word that was not right, but, as everyone else, never thought that language needed 'une systématique' (Jakobson in Whitney 1971, xxxvii). Whitney did in fact share with his contemporaries (Steinthal and some of the other 'psychologists' were partial exceptions and so was the older Madvig) the form of historicism which dominated the century. How he envisaged the problem is clearly explained in his first theoretical book:

> every part and particle of every existing language is a historical product, the final result of a series of changes, working themselves out in time ... This fact prescribes the mode in which language is to be fruitfully studied. If we would understand anything which has *become* what it is, a knowledge of its present constitution is not enough: we must follow it backward from stage to stage, tracing out the phases it has assumed, and the causes which have

determined the transition of one into the other. Merely to classify, arrange, and set forth in order the phenomena of a spoken tongue, its significant material, usage and modes of expression, is grammar and lexicography, not linguistic science. The former state and prescribe only; the latter seeks to explain. And when the explanation is historical, the search for it must be of the same character. To construct, then, by historical processes, with the aid of all historical evidences within his reach, the history of the development of language, back to its very beginning, is the main task of the linguistic student; it is the means by which he arrives at a true comprehension of language, in its own nature and in its relations to the human mind and to human history. (Whitney [1867] 1870, 54)

In other words, the task of linguistics is to explain the facts of language and the only possible explanation is historical. This statement must be taken in conjunction with Whitney's anti-psychologism: it would have been possible to account for the facts of language in cognitive terms, but, although Whitney occasionally (if rarely) refers to mental associations, processes of thought, and even the nature of the mind (as above), he is in general unwilling to do so. His concern is rather with identifying in general terms the modes of language change while stressing that each specific instance of change must be historically defined.

But why and how does language change? Schleicher was able to take change for granted since it is a specific characteristic of all organisms. For Steinthal, on the other hand, the basic reason for change was found in the endless rearranging of the mental *Vorstellungen*, to which new units were constantly added as the result of new experiences; in this way, and through the introduction of the *Volksgeist,* Steinthal allowed for the influence of cultural and historical facts on language and language change. Whitney sees change as a natural result of use and transmission, but the precondition for it is the arbitrary nature of the signs which make up language. Change is change in words, but a word 'is not the natural reflection of an idea, nor its description, nor its definition; it is only its designation, an arbitrary and conventional sign with which we learn to associate it. Hence it has no internal force conservative of its identity, but is exposed to all the changes which external circumstances, the needs of practical use, the convenience and caprice of those who employ it, may suggest' ([1867] 1870, 70f.). If so, however, there is no reason to adopt Schleicher's distinction between a period of growth and one of decay: 'the forces which are at work in it [*sc.* language] are the same now that they have always been, and the effects that they are producing are of the same essential character: both are inherent in the nature of language, and inseparable from its use' (*ibid.,* 24f.). In the later book (1875, 196) it is repeated that 'The essential unity of linguistic history ... must be made the cardinal principle of the study of language, if this is to bear a scientific character'. The comparison with geology that follows is a clear pointer to Whitney's acceptance of Lyell's uniformitarianism. It follows that in the normal process of language change we find both growth and loss: loss of old forms or words, alteration of phonetic forms and meaning, creation of new words through reuse of old material in new combinations and of new forms and categories through what we would now call grammaticalization.

Phonetic change is seen as dominated by the principle of economy (1875, 69ff.; [1878] 1971, 249ff.), the 'tendency to ease', though it is also admitted that the cause of some changes (Grimm's Law is an example) escape us altogether. Analogy (OE *fōr* replaced by *fared*, etc.) is seen as a type of 'mental economy' which remodels forms which have been altered too much by phonetic corruption (1875, 74f.; cf. [1867] 1870, 27f., 82), but is also called (though little space is dedicated to it in the discussion) 'one of the most potent [*sc.* forces] in all language-history' (*ibid.*, 75). But in addition to phonological and morphological change, Whitney is also and above all interested in change of meaning: 'it may be even claimed . . . that change and development of meaning constitute the real interior life of language' ([1867] 1870, 100). And yet, while change in meaning is what determines the internal form of a language and its study is indispensable for etymology, we are reminded that etymology is not relevant to language use: 'a word, both in its direct significance and its suggestiveness, is just what our usage makes it' (*ibid.*, 133). In general Whitney contrasts the amount of work dedicated to phonetic change with the absence of a classification of 'the processes of significant change' ([1875] 1882, 76). His own attempt, as he states, is bound to be incomplete given the innumerable complications.[34]

It is easy to find in this conception a number of pointers to later developments; Whitney's views were influential on the neogrammarians, on Saussure, on the young Bloomfield, though in each case it is necessary to see what motifs are taken and how they are integrated in the new system. On the other hand, Whitney made no claim of originality for his views and indeed part of them can be traced back to other authors: Terracini (1949, 91ff.) stressed how much they were rooted in Anglo-Saxon empiricism and also argued (*ibid.*, 90) that Whitney was perhaps the first to emphasize that, alongside comparative grammar, there was a place (and a need) for a general linguistics built on empirical bases. This is certainly what Whitney did, but others (Humboldt, Madvig, Steinthal and even Pott) had felt the same need and Madvig had reached very similar conclusions. Whitney, however, has priority in actually attempting to set down in full (i.e. more diffusely than Madvig) a set of principles and attempting it, as it were, from the inside, i.e. from the viewpoint, on the one hand, of a practising Sanskritist who had gained immense respect among comparativists and was indeed one of them, on the other hand, of someone who was involved in the teaching of living European languages and in actual questions of English usage.[35] It is also true, as stated once again by Terracini, that Whitney's novelty is in the set of examples that he uses, taken from living rather than dead languages, pointing, not only to new pedagogical needs, but also to a desire for a first-hand intuitive experience of the object of study.

8.6 Linguistic typology and classification

So far we have deliberately kept apart the discussion of the structural classification of language from that of historical and comparative work. Some of the problems were mentioned earlier in connection with the two Schlegels (pp. 71ff.) and with Humboldt (pp. 165ff., cf. also pp. 91ff.); it is now time to reconsider them.[36]

At the beginning of the century, as we have seen, the new linguistics had been associated both with the realization that language variety could not be dismissed as a superficial phenomenon and with the definition of the historical-comparative method. The problem remained of how to put order in the multitude of new linguistic facts which were becoming available. Languages could be grouped according to their genealogical origin or according to their structural characteristics, i.e. in the view of most scholars, according to their grammar. The two types of classification – genealogical and structural (or physiological) – were not always clearly distinguished nor did this seem to be always essential: Schlegel's organic class comprised one language family only, Indo-European. By the middle of the century, after Humboldt's and Pott's pronouncements (p. 93), the position was different. The explicit form of reconstruction advocated by Schleicher must have had a powerful clarifying effect: it was possible to reconstruct an *Ursprache* comparing a number of languages which were genetically related, but not comparing languages that had similar structures only. It also became clear that while genetic kinship called for correspondences of sounds, for 'etymological kinship' (Pott 1856, 206), structural similarity did not; hence it would have been theoretically possible to demonstrate that two languages were related even if they were structurally different. Even if, as instinctively most scholars assumed, the genealogically related languages were structurally similar (cf. e.g. Pott 1856, 263), it was still necessary not to confuse the two types of classification.[37] At the same time the successes of the comparative method, the increasing sophistication of the technical work but also the realization that the chances of a full genealogical classification for all languages were limited, could lead to a parting of the ways: on the one hand the comparativists and historians whose work concentrated on specific languages, on the other those who were interested in the phenomenon of language variety *per se*. The latter included, of course, the fieldworkers who 'collected' languages for various purposes, but also those who, like Humboldt, were interested in analysing comparable linguistic categories in a number of different and unrelated languages, and those who, again like Humboldt, wanted to find an empirically based explanation of the contrast between the diversity of languages and their fundamental unity. It is within this framework that Steinthal argued, as Heyse (1856, 231) had done before him, that a classification of languages was the highest task of linguistics and that the study of language classification was the modern replacement for the old philosophical or general grammar. If discussions about e.g. the nature of linguistic categories arise in the context of classificatory or typological work, this is not only for pragmatic reasons but also because the most theoretically inclined or most speculative scholars turned to this task.

In 1876, in the first volume of his *Grundriß der Sprachwissenschaft* (1876–88, i, 63ff.), the largest linguistic collection after Adelung's *Mithridates*, the Vienna ethnologist and linguist Friedrich Müller (1834–98) summarized the various types of linguistic classification of the previous decades. His first distinction was between Steinthal's psychological classification and those forms of classification which were based on a conception of languages 'an und für sich', i.e. of languages as independent organisms. In this second category he listed, first, Schleicher's 'morphological classification' and, secondly, the genealogical classification which he himself adopted.

8.6.1 The 'morphological' classification
Among the structural types of classification, 'morphological classification' is certainly the best known; it is also the only one which Whitney ([1867] 1870, 360ff.) found useful to discuss in full. In its canonical form, which was established by Schleicher as early as 1848, redefined by him on later occasions, and popularized by Max Müller ([1861] 1862, 287ff.), it distinguished between isolating languages such as Chinese, where all forms have lexical meaning and there are no inflections or connecting (i.e. grammatical) elements, *zusammenfügende* or agglutinative languages such as Turkish, where the connecting elements are added to meaningful roots, and inflectional languages where the lexical elements and the connecting elements (the latter may have originally had lexical value) are fused and the roots or roots + suffixes may undergo regular alteration in order to indicate grammatical relations.[38] Using Schleicher's morphological algebra (see above, p. 200), we may say that the isolating languages have R ('roots' only), the agglutinative languages Rs ('roots' + affixes), and the inflectional languages $R^x s^x$ (internally modified 'roots' + affixes). In a different version, a class of incorporating or polysynthetic languages was added, though it was also

possible to include these languages in the agglutinative class.[39] The membership of each class was disputed: for Schleicher the inflectional class comprised Semitic and Indo-European, both of which used internal modifications of the root in grammatical function; the two Schlegels, whose schema was not all that different, had given inflectional status to Indo-European only, while Bopp (1833–6, I, 112f.) treated Semitic as belonging to a class of its own (cf. p. 148, note 12).

We do not need to discuss at length the wisdom or otherwise of basing a whole classification on the distinction between lexical meaning and *Beziehungen* 'connections' (i.e. grammatical elements).[40] Schleicher (1850, 6f.) defended his decision on the ground that just as the basic components of thought were concepts (or representations) and connections between concepts, in language the basic elements were meanings (expressed in lexical roots) and grammatical elements expressed either in separated words or in affixes or through the internal modification of the root. The argument was strongly reminiscent of the similar statements by Humboldt (p. 112ff.). Steinthal ([1850] 1970, 132ff.), who disliked the whole system and thought that Schleicher's Hegelianism made it worse, objected that in the Finnish or in the North American languages the cohesion of roots and endings was at least as strong as in Sanskrit. As early as 1856, Madvig (1971, 171) observed that some of the so-called grammatical elements (such as the plural ending) did in fact alter the actual meaning of words rather than their grammatical function. Whitney ([1867] 1870, 361ff.) complained that the agglutinative class was too huge for comfort, that he saw no reason to lump together Indo-European and Semitic, and that in any case no single trait or class of traits can be used as a criterion for ranking languages. Later on, Friedrich Müller (1876–88, i, 69) pointed out that, if thought was the basic criterion, then the classification was not as objective and 'organic' as it was supposed to be; there was a clear psychological element which was inconsistent with Schleicher's declared views.

The important point that distinguished Schleicher and Müller from the two Schlegels is their strong form of transformationism: in their view (and here the link with the problem of the origin of language is clear), all languages were originally of the simplest possible type, i.e. isolating; in progress of time some of them began to combine originally separate roots until they reached an agglutinative stage and, in some instances, an inflected one. The view was based on general considerations; as even the down-to-earth Whitney argued, it was far easier to envisage the origin of language in that way. Yet it was also supported by Bopp's findings about the supposed agglutinative origin of inflection. Max Müller went even further and mantained (against Pott) that 'there is hardly any language which is not at the same time *isolating, combinatory* [i.e. agglutinative], and *inflectional* (1868–75, iv, 121)';

this conclusion he then used in favour of transformationism, together with the semi-uniformitarian point that the same 'combinatory' forces are still at work in the present phases of languages.[41]

8.6.2 The psychological approach

The interest of the 'psychological' approach to classification is not so much in the actual classification produced (in Steinthal this changes e.g. from 1850 to 1860, and Misteli in 1893 further modifies Steinthal's account) as much as in the effort at general linguistic analysis which this involves. For Steinthal, as we have seen, there are no God-given logical or grammatical categories present in all languages. Humboldt's attempt to find out how all languages express the forms of the grammar is for him a mistake, because it gives to those forms an absolute value that they do not have. The answer to the question: 'How is this or that category represented in language?' is all too frequently: 'It is not'. What the linguist must do is to allow the languages to determine their own categories. Each individual *Volksgeist* is responsible for the expression into language of its own self-consciousness. Just as the various natural kingdoms can be seen as an expression of the idea of nature, the various languages can be seen as an expression of the idea of language; just as we can imagine the various natural beings on a sort of scale of development, we can also see the languages on a similar scale, though in no way we should see this as a straight line. Once again we are brought back to the point that to understand language we must consider all languages and the way in which they relate to each other (Steinthal 1860b, 104ff.).[42] If so, however, a classification based on the necessarily arbitrary choice of one or the other character will not do; the specific system of grammatical categories of each language, its *innere Sprachform*, which in itself is the expression of consciousness of the individual *Volksgeist*, must provide the only way of approach. For Steinthal then languages are first of all classified according to their form and above all to the presence or absence of form, provided this word is understood correctly. In some way all languages must express form but they may or may not make clear the distinction between form and matter (lexical meaning). Thus if a language indicates plurality with a word for 'many' or tense with a word for 'past', or uses substantives such as 'face', 'back' to indicate local relations, (lexical) meaning is not distinguished from form; the language is without form (*formlos*). Similarly in noun formation: if all place names include the word 'place', all tool names include the word 'tool', no distinction is made between lexical meaning and form. Further, the formal nature of a language reveals itself best in the construction, which is in essence a pure activity, a synthesis, i.e. in the expression of predication, attribution, objectivization (1860b, 318). Here the isolating/agglutinative/inflected distinction comes back into play, understood psychologically as marking the cohesion or otherwise of a meaningful element with a formal element. The isolating languages need not be without form, since they can exploit the ordering of their elements and have particles which guarantee the distinction between formal and meaningful elements. Yet the most significant criterion concerns the expression of subject and predicate. In languages which have only meaningful elements we may find sequences such as 'mountain high' which mean either 'the mountain is high' or 'the high mountain', a linguistic lack which hinders clear thought (*ibid.*, 325). It is languages with the grammatical categories of verb and noun and a formal marker of the subject such as the nominative case that best express the predicative relation. On the strength of these observations, Steinthal eventually produces his classification, based, as he puts it, on 'physiological characteristics' (the presence or absence of form and the distinction of noun and verb) and on morphological characteristics, namely the juxtaposition of words (which do not change their form), as in the isolating languages, and the modification of word-forms, as in agglutination and inflection. Semitic, Indo-European, Egyptian **and** Chinese are all languages with form while the Amerindian, Polynesian, Ural-Altaic languages are not. Chinese has form but is juxtaposing (*nebensetzend*), while Indo-European is a modifying (*abwandelnd*) language; among the languages without form, Thai is juxtaposing, while the Uralo-Altaic languages are modifying.

For all its obscurities, contradictions, obvious attempts at the justification of one's own prejudices, etc., the schema is more impressive and better thought out than that adopted by Schleicher. Above all the decision to define each language according to a number of characteristics instead of a single one is part of Steinthal's tendency to move away from the attempt to produce a partition of all languages and to think rather in terms of a typology.[43] An important consequence of this decision and of its background is also the realization that each linguistic system must be looked at as a whole because it is only in that way that its constitutive categories can be defined. Once again the problems of description raise their head, but in the case of Steinthal description is not limited to phonology and morphology and includes syntax as well.

8.6.3 Convergences and disagreements

In spite of their differences, Schleicher's and Steinthal's views have more in common than it may seem: the main point of agreement is in the total commitment (in theory, even if it does not always work in practice) to an analysis based on what we might now call the surface structure. This is true both when the concern is with morphological facts only, which is to be expected, and when the concern is with psychological facts. Schleicher had argued that functional distinctions can be admitted only when they find a formal (*lautliches,* i.e. phonetic/ phonological) expression, but, as his classification reveals, his definition of 'formal' was indeed based on segmental phonetics. Steinthal too is not prepared to argue in other terms, even if he has a more sophisticated view of 'formal' and allows e.g. word order to qualify. Heuristically his psychological distinctions are, or at least are meant to be, a reflection of the linguistic distinctions. Here language diversity acquires yet greater importance as the factor which allows the linguist to reintroduce in his analysis categories which he had debarred himself from using. How self-conscious this process is emerges from Steinthal's justification of his concern with predication. He asks himself whether it is contradictory to reject the use of logical categories and at the same time to speak of subject and predicate. The reply is that these are grammatical and not logical categories and that they have not been devised out of thin air but are based on the use of the nominative case in the Indo-European languages (1860b, 324f.). And the conclusion? 'This is purely empirical knowledge from which we derive the judgement that languages with a nominative are superior to all those without, because they bring more completely to representation the form of the content, since their force of synthesis is stronger' (*ibid.*, 325). The position is different for a scholar of the earlier period such as Madvig, who must count as a functionalist, but he too firmly refused to accept the existence of any preordained logical categories and, e.g. in his account of Latin cases was eager to point out that in each language there are no more cases than there are forms to distinguish them (Hauger 1994, 128ff.).

A second point of convergence – typical of the period – is the assumption, often not discussed, that genealogically related languages must share the same typological characteristics. The tabulated classification which Steinthal offers at the end of his *Characteristik der hauptsächlichsten Typen des Sprachbaues* (1860b, 327) provides, as examples of the eight types defined, not eight different languages but eight different language families (see above, pp. 216 and 223 note 27). The question whether genealogically related languages could belong to different structural classes had in fact been asked. Schleicher's answer ([1860] 1869, 31) was that in principle this was possible, in practice however no such languages were known. This meant, according to Schleicher, that the period of language growth was concluded before the division of the parent language. We noted earlier that Pott too asked the question, but was more hesitant in his reply (e.g. 1852, 514) and seemed to conclude that it was at least unlikely (e.g. 1856, 263). Steinthal himself, as we have seen (p. 223 note 27), excluded the possibility that a language changed class in the historical period. Madvig here differed, not least because he could not accept the whole basis of the morphological classification (e.g. [1856–7] 1971, 167ff.), but in general we shall have to wait to the end of the century and later to find a firm statement that languages can change 'class' while remaining the 'same language'.

In spite of this the various forms of transformism did not exclude the possibility of a development from one class to the other in the prehistoric period; indeed, Schleicher and Max Müller definitely favoured it (p. 214). Steinthal too argued for it: 'at a given time, perhaps 4000 or 5000 BC, the Sanskritic stock must have spoken a pure root language, which structurally was relatively similar to Chinese' (1860b, 277).

Finally, there seemed to be agreement in the assumption that the various languages could somehow be arranged in an ascending scale, parallel perhaps to the great chain of beings or at any rate to the increasing complexity of natural organisms: for Steinthal, Thai and the like were like the zoophytes of nature, while the Sanskritic languages were the roses among languages (1860b, 330); for Schleicher 'the inflectional languages occupy the highest level in the scale of languages' (1850, 9). The criteria varied, but the legitimacy of the arrangement was not normally doubted: Pott (1856, 197) pointed out that in the context of a physiological (i.e. structural) comparison it was possible to enquire about a scalar ordering and an evaluation of the languages from the lowest to the highest as in the animal kingdom. Whitney, as one might expect, was more cautious (e.g. [1867] 1870, 369); he doubted the wisdom of ranking languages on the basis of the morphological classification and emphasized the difficulty of the enterprise (pointing out *inter alia* the importance of considering lexical facts as well); he too, however, did not doubt its legitimacy. By contrast, Madvig, once again, was firmer: cultural facts at whatever level can equally well be expressed in an inflected and in a non-inflected language (e.g. [1856–7] 1971, 126).

A final quotation from Whitney may perhaps point the way for things to come. After having expressed his doubts about the validity of the morphological classification, while not necessarily denying its importance, he turned to a partial conclusion: 'There can be no question that, of all the modes of classification with which linguistic scholars have had to do, the one of first and most fundamental importance is the genetical, or that which groups together, and holds apart from others, languages giving evidence of derivation from the same original' ([1867] 1870, 369). In the famous preface to the *Langues du monde*, Meillet will echo these sentiments and advocate a complete rejection of morphological classification (Meillet and Cohen 1924, i, 1). On the other hand, while discussing the possibility of an evaluation and classification of languages, Whitney produced a brief account of what one may look for in the analysis of language, which reads to a certain extent as a blueprint for a linguistics of the future. We have seen already how questions of description were far more likely to arise in the actual work for linguistic classification (especially if this was moving towards typology) than in that for genealogical linguistics. The same point emerges: in the middle of the century classification and typology serve as training ground for description and theory.

Notes

1. See for this formulation Cassirer (1945, 109).
2. See in general Wells (1973), Christy (1983), Nerlich (1990a, 58ff.). In geology and other sciences a number of different distinctions were subsumed under the uniformitarian label (Mayr 1982, 375ff.): most importantly perhaps, there is no necessary connection between uniformitarianism, i.e. the belief that the same causes operate at all times, and an evolutionary, directional view of change in the world. In linguistics too the term, which has been introduced much more recently, is not easy to define and should not be confused, as it sometimes is, with transformationism, evolutionism or anti-prescriptivism; Schleicher's explicit acceptance of Darwinism does not make him a uniformitarian. Practice and theory often vary. It is also possible, without incoherence, to operate in terms of the same principles of change for modern and ancient language phases, while believing in a prehistoric period of growth in which those principles were not valid. In general, for the links between linguistics and geology, cf. the essays collected in Naumann, Plank and Hofbauer (1992).
3. The increase in published introductions is connected with the requirements of high-level popularization both in an academic and in a more general set-up. Three of the four books in English quoted (those by Max Müller, Sayce, and Whitney) were written in connection with lecture courses.
4. In the second edition (1878, 16ff.) Scherer introduced a chapter of *Principien* taken from his review of the 1874 German re-elaboration by J. Jolly of Whitney (1867). It contains *inter alia* a strong uniformitarian statement (with dutiful reference to geology), which reinforces the views expressed in the preface of the first edition.
5. Madvig's theoretical work was less influential than it could have been, largely because it was written in Danish and remained unread; in 1875, spurred by the fact that Whitney with much greater success had (independently) expressed many of the same views, he translated part of his essays into German, but their impact remained limited. See in general the introduction and commentary by K. F., Johansen in Madvig (1971), as well as Jespersen (1922, 84), Devoto (1958), de Mauro (1970a, 88f.), Aarsleff (1982, 299ff.), Knobloch (1988, *passim*). Two recent monographs counteract some of the previous neglect: Jensen (1981) is concerned with Madvig's life and work in general but above all with the classical work; Hauger (1994) offers the most detailed analysis of Madvig's linguistic thought, highlighting the contrasts with the comparativists and what she calls the 'historical' rather than 'genealogical' aspects of his work.
6. Cf. Scaglione (1978), Delesalle and Chevalier (1986, 179ff.), Graffi (1991, 276ff.).

7. We follow here the classification of the various theories proposed by Regnaud (1888), as quoted by Auroux (1989). Max Müller's (1862, 361) shorthand reference to the *bow-wow* (onomatopoeia) and the *pooh-pooh* (interjections) theories became famous (cf. Salmon 1996).

8. A discussion of the innumerable theories would take us too far. Stam (1976, 297) lists some fifty works published between 1860 and 1890, but the list is incomplete: cf. e.g. Scherer ([1868] 1878, 23f.). See in general Fano (1962), Stam (1976), G. A. Wells (1987) and above all Auroux (1989), as well as the articles collected in Gessinger and von Rahden (1989). For an earlier bibliography, cf. Hewes (1975). Some of this work is, of course, important for what we would now call philosophy of language or for cognitive theory, even if at the time it had no impact and the individual studies remained as isolated as their authors. A good account is that by Knobloch (1988, 93–181), who discusses in turn Steinthal and Lazarus, Gustav Gerber (1820–1901), Lazarus Geiger (1829–70), Ludwig Noiré (1829–89), Wilhelm Wundt, Anton Marty (1847–1914) and the upholders of a communicative theory of language, Herbart, Madvig, Whitney and Wegener. Geiger *inter alia* was concerned with identifying laws of semantic change starting with the first roots, which he did not see as nominal and concrete but as verbal, abstract and polysemous (cf. also Esper 1968, 85ff.). Noiré, another school-teacher greatly admired by Max Müller, whom he venerated (Noiré 1879a, b), is seen by Knobloch (1988, 126ff.) as one of the most original thinkers of the period and the one who came closer, before Wegener, to a functional vision of language as determined by the needs of communication. Anton Marty, Professor of Philosophy at Prague, and the author of a monograph *Über den Ursprung der Sprache* (1875), also shared with Madvig, Whitney and Wegener a view of language as a form of interaction aimed at communication (Knobloch 1988, 158ff.).

9. Madvig, who had firm ideas about the origin of language, attacked the second edition of Renan's book on the subject with no hesitations: 'The whole book by Renan is a superficial piece of rhetorics [*Schönrednerei*] characterized by some right observations taken from Grimm's *Abhandlung* quoted below and by one or the other sign of natural *bon sens*' (Madvig [1856/57 but 1874] 1971, 124, note).

10. Four important books (so recent that they have not yet been fully assimilated) have filled a gap in our historiography of the second part of the century, which so far had been mainly concerned with historical comparative work: Knobloch (1988) about the psychological conceptions of language from 1850 to 1920; Nerlich (1990a) about the views of language change in Whitney, Bréal and Wegener; Graffi (1991), a unique account of syntactical theory between the nineteenth and twentieth centuries; and Nerlich (1992) on semantic theories in Europe from 1830 to 1930.

11. Schleicher's Hegelianism, which is particularly obvious in the first works, goes beyond the standard patina of the period (Wilbur 1984). Later on Schleicher (1850, 10ff.) retracted some of his 1848 views about the spiritual nature of language, but Jaritz (1992) is probably right in arguing that, in origin at least, a good part of Schleicher's theories on a prehistoric period of language formation (*Ausbildung*) followed by a period of decay

represents a transformation of Hegel's ideas in terms which succeed in integrating rationalistic and Romantic positions. For Schleicher's theories about the position of linguistics, see also Streitberg (1897) and Einhauser's discussion (1989, 123ff.).

12. Schleicher was far more cautious in his earlier work (cf. 1850, 30f.).

13. Some of these perplexities are cogently discussed by Lepschy (1962) in an article which, together with Cassirer (1945), is still essential reading for the history of the concept of organism. Cf. also R. Wells (1987).

14. This view was soon challenged. Whitney ([1881] 1971, 172) noted that R. Lepsius had attacked the *communis opinio* in the preface to his Nubian grammar of 1880 adducing counterexamples from the African languages. However, in 1867 (p. 199) Whitney had stated: 'Such a thing as a language with a mixed grammatical apparatus has never come under the cognizance of linguistic students: it would be to them a monstrosity; it seems an impossibility.'

15. Heyse (1856, 58ff.), in his attack against Becker's organicism, explains that the shift is from the concept of organism as a formal characteristic to a substantive definition of language and that Becker had consistently concluded that scientific linguistics (*Sprachlehre*) had to be a physiology of language.

16. Esper (1968, 99) has some good observations about Schleicher and the organic model as well as a useful reference to Ernst Nagel's point about the role of a model as either a potential intellectual trap or an invaluable intellectual tool.

17. Geiger (1869, xiv ff.) quotes Schleicher's view (stated in the preface to a work by Johannes Schmidt) that 'when we come to the function, to the basic meaning of the roots, and to change of meaning in general during the life of the language, there reigns complete uncertainty and lack of method . . . At the risk of being dismissed as a "*glottischer* know-nothing" I do not hesitate to express my conviction that at present we must not treat etymology as one of the tasks of *Glottik* . . .' (Schleicher 1865c, vii f.; cf. Esper 1968, 102ff.).

18. Delbrück (1880, 54) concludes his puzzled discussion of Schleicher's scientific claims with the observation that, however much he would not have liked it, in his heart of hearts Schleicher 'was – just like Bopp and Grimm, Pott and Curtius – a philologist'.

19. Goethe was not first to use it in print; cf. Salmon (1974, 333, note 1). Dietze (1966, 52) thinks that the term was used in a linguistic sense for the first time in Schleicher (1859), but in fact we find a reference, without comment, to the 'Morphological coincidences of the Turanian languages' already in Max Müller ([1854] 1855, 89; cf. also [1861] 1862, 262). Here, as in Schleicher, the term, in contrast with the German *Formenlehre* or the English *accidence,* refers to the morphology of languages in the context of the attempts to classify them. The *Oxford English Dictionary* (s.v.) quotes as first instance of 'morphological' in a linguistic sense a passage by Farrar (1860), which again refers to morphological classification; for the noun 'morphology' the OED (s.v.) cites a later (1869) statement by Farrar: 'By the morphology of a language we mean the general laws of its grammatical structure'.

20. For clarity's sake, the symbolism used here is that which Schleicher used in the successive editions of the *Compendium* rather than the more complex one of the 1859 essay; for a good account of the system, see already Whitney ([1867] 1870, 364), who was impressed by it; more recently, cf. Bynon (1986).

21. Above, *lautliches* has been rendered with the anachronistic 'phonological', since 'phonetic' did not seem appropriate; 'formal' would be better, but has too wide a range. In Schleicher (1848, 7) accent and word order are mentioned, but the passage is not very clear.

22. H. Steinthal (1823–99; the forms of his first name vary) studied at the University of Berlin with Bopp, Lepsius and Boeckh, the great classicist. He obtained his doctorate from Tübingen with a thesis on the relative pronoun very much in Humboldt's style, and his *venia legendi* at Berlin with a work on Humboldt's linguistics and Hegel's philosophy. After a few years in Paris (1852–6), when he worked on Chinese and African languages, he taught in Berlin first as a Privat Dozent and then as an Extraordinarius in *Allgemeine Sprachwissenschaft*; as a Jew he was unlikely to obtain a full professorship and never did. Because of his subject or personality he had very few pupils and remained relatively isolated, in spite of the close links which he had with C. L. Heyse, whose posthumous work he edited, and with Moritz Lazarus, who became his brother-in-law, and with whom he shared his work in ethnopsychology. His *opus* includes a number of essays about Humboldt and a monumental commented edition of his work; he also wrote monographs of a more general nature such as *Grammatik, Logik und Psychologie* (1855), *Der Ursprung der Sprache* ([1851] 1858, 4th edn 1888), or of a philosophical descriptive nature such as *Die Mande-Neger Sprachen, psychologisch und phonetisch betrachtet* (1867), as well as the first volume of the *Abriss der Sprachwissenschaft* ([1871] 1881) and a very impressive account of linguistic thought in classical antiquity ([1863] 1890). See in general Bumann (1965, and in Steinthal 1970), Belke (1971–86), Trabant (1983), Knobloch (1988, *passim*), Christy (1989), Barba (1990), Graffi (1991, 21ff.), Haßler (1991a, 131ff., 1991b), Nerlich (1992, 53ff.), and most recently and in greater detail, Ringmacher (1996), a book which unfortunately I have not been able to exploit in full.

23. Steinthal is at times very critical of Humboldt, against whom he holds that he is too vague in his definition (or absence of definition) of terms such as language, *Geist*, intellectuality, individuality, identity; that he falls back too often into the use of ontological categories to understand language (1858, 118f.); and that he is incapable of escaping the dualism between the conclusions dictated by his a priori theory and those suggested by empirical data (*ibid.*, 114). Even so, for him, 'Humboldt is a genius because he has succeeded in identifying linguistics with his own person, so that to study linguistics or to study him is one and the same thing' (*ibid.*, 84). For the complex development of Steinthal's thought about Humboldt, see now Ringmacher (1996, 28ff.).

24. The first attacks are against Becker's organicism (cf. also Heyse 1856, 58ff.). The clearest statements against Schleicher's views are found in the lecture on *Philologie, Geschichte und Psychologie in ihren gegenseitigen*

Beziehungen ([1864] 1970, 436ff., esp. 452ff.), but similar views are expressed in earlier writings.

25. Psychology in the mid nineteenth century is not an experimental discipline, but is seen as part of philosophy. When we speak of scholars interested in the psychology of language, we refer to people who had positions either in philosophy (such as Moritz Lazarus or Wundt) or in historical linguistics (such as Paul and the other neogrammarians) or – in one case – 'general linguistics' (the title of Steinthal's position, which is, however, exceptional for the period); often they remained outside the Universities, as did e.g. Lazarus Geiger, Gustav Gerber and later Ludwig Noiré and Philipp Wegener (Knobloch 1988, 10). Earlier on, J. F. Herbart (1776–1841) had written about psychology (as based on experience, metaphysics and mathematics), while holding Kant's chair of Philosophy at Königsberg. On the other hand, e.g. Lazarus and Steinthal envisaged psychology (in theory, if not in practice) as an empirical (rather than experimental) discipline: 'psychology is not necessarily a philosophical discipline, or at least no more than the natural sciences. It has its own empirical or historical territory and in so far as it deals only with establishing facts and carefully representing them, it can well ignore all theoretical dissension' (Lazarus and Steinthal 1860, 59 = Steinthal 1970, 365).

26. Steinthal has a role in the history of syntax; for his definition of sentence and the later views which either built on him or opposed him, cf. Graffi (1991, 183).

27. Nevertheless Steinthal is not a full uniformitarian. Like Schleicher he accepts the possibility (indeed the necessity) that inflection is based on agglutination and this on juxtaposition, but finds it difficult to assume that this may have happened in historical times: 'the language of the builders of the Pyramids is fundamentally not very different from that which the Egyptians spoke under the Arabs. A change of the morphological principle, which introduces also a change of the psychological principle, is only thinkable in the prehistoric period, in the period of the establishment of the ethne'. This change, however, is not 'the result of a development, but of a new linguistic creation determined by natural and spiritual revolutions' (1860b, 323). The last point is of course part of the difference from Schleicher: for Steinthal after the change we are in fact dealing with a new *Sprachform*. Yet this form of catastrophism remains baffling.

28. For the very interesting way in which Steinthal and Lazarus deal with semantic change, cf. Nerlich (1992, 53–65).

29. Graffi (1991, 45ff.) speaks of 'etnopsicologia', which as a translation of *Völkerpsychologie* is preferable to Oertel's (1901, 76) 'social psychology'. The term and concept originate with Lazarus (cf. Knobloch 1988, 183).

30. Brugmann, in writing for Whitney's memorial volume (Whitney 1897, 78), produced a more sober and more balanced judgement. After having complained about the lack of real understanding of linguistic processes which prevailed in the previous generation and the misguided importance given to empty abstractions and metaphors (organism?), he pays tribute to Steinthal, who had not been similarly taken in. Yet, Brugmann continues, he was too much of a philosopher, he was too much concerned with generalities to

have impact on the detailed research, nor was he sufficiently involved in the question of language development. We have here in a nutshell Steinthal's successes and failures – or at least his successes and failures in the eyes of the neogrammarians.

31. There was other work important for a history of the psychological view of language. The names of Lazarus Geiger (1829–70), Gustav Gerber (1820–1901) and Ludwig Noiré (1829–89) come to mind, but cannot be discussed here. Cf. in general Knobloch (1988) and, for Geiger, Esper (1968, 86ff.).

32. Madvig ([1842] 1875, 55 = 1971, 86). This translation from the 1875 German version follows that by Aarsleff (1982, 299) with very minor modifications. For the coincidences between Madvig and Whitney, cf. Aarsleff (1982, 301f.) and Hauger (1994, 166ff.).

33. William Dwight Whitney (1827–94) belonged to a distinguished New England family; a chance purchase by his elder brother, a notable geologist, of Bopp's Sanskrit grammar introduced him to this language at the age of twenty. He then spent a year studying oriental languages at Yale with E. E. Salisbury and three years in Germany (at Berlin and Tübingen) specializing in Sanskrit with Weber and Roth (1850–3). On his return he settled in New Haven as a Yale professor and started a remarkable teaching activity, not only in Sanskrit and then in comparative philology, but also in modern languages, English, etc. As has been pointed out (Andresen 1990, 135), almost single-handed he succeeded in institutionalizing American linguistics. His Sanskrit work, which includes an outstanding Sanskrit grammar based both on Vedic and on classical Sanskrit and important editions of Vedic texts and grammatical texts, gave him a very high status among comparative linguists, though, as was noticed, his grammar was not comparative but purely descriptive in the style of Madvig's Latin grammar (Delbrück in Whitney 1897, 84). His more general works, and above all *Language and the Study of Language* (1867) and *The Life and Growth of Language: an Outline of Linguistic Science* (1875), had considerable influence and were translated one into German (in a modified version) and Dutch, the other into German, French, Italian, Dutch and Swedish. A number of his articles were collected in *Oriental and Linguistic Studies* (1873, 1874). See for further data his memorial volume (Whitney 1897), Terracini (1949, 73–121), De Mauro (1970b, 299ff. and *passim*), the prefatory material by Silverstein and Jakobson to Whitney (1971) and by Vincenzi to Whitney (1990), Koerner (1973a, 74–100; 1979), Nerlich (1990a; 1992, 225ff.), Andresen (1990, *passim*). McCawley ([1967] 1979) offers an interesting account of the phonological theory underlying Whitney's Sanskrit grammar.

34. Cf. in general for Whitney's analysis of change, Nerlich (1990a); and for his view of semantic change, Nerlich (1992, 225–31).

35. Yet Whitney showed relatively conservative views in his school English grammar (1877); cf. Wächtler (1991).

36. For brief introductions to the history of language classification and typology, cf. Jespersen ([1920] 1962), Lounsbury (1968), Horne (1966), Robins (1973) and the bibliography collected and discussed in Morpurgo Davies (1975). More recently, see Swiggers (1990), Plank (1991a) and the numerous works by Ramat.

37. In practice, even if not in theory, confusion did of course occur. Max Müller's account of the 'Turanian' family of languages, which were all agglutinative and included 'all languages spoken in Asia and Europe, and not included under the Aryan and Semitic families, with the exception of Chinese and its cognate dialects' ([1861] 1862, 290; cf. 1854), is just such a case which Pott (1855) did not hesitate to condemn.

38. Max Müller (1854, [1861] 1862) tried to link his classification with different stages in the evolution of society: the isolating languages with the family stage, the agglutinative languages with the nomadic stage and the inflectional languages with the 'political' stage. This view was attacked among others by Whitney (e.g. [1867] 1870, 363ff.), and Max Müller eventually abandoned it.

39. The ultimate source of the morphological classification is clearly the two Schlegels (p. 73ff.). Schleicher (1848, 6) attributed it to Humboldt and was rebuked by Steinthal (1860b, 10), though part of the terminology is probably due to Humboldt (cf. p. 122 note 30, and see in general Coseriu 1972). The paternity (at least in the four-classes version) was then attributed to Pott (e.g. by Madvig [1856–7] 1971, 168, who followed Steinthal, and by Max Müller 1876–88, I, 67f.), but he indignantly denied ever having produced a classification schema and argued that he had simply tried to report his interpretation of Humboldt's view (cf. Morpurgo Davies 1975, 663 for the references). Max Müller spoke of morphological classification in the eighth of his lectures on the science of language ([1861] 1862). For polysynthetic and incorporating languages, cf. Leopold (1984), Rousseau (1984).

40. Both Schleicher and Steinthal constantly refer to *Stoff* ('matter, material, substance') and *Form* ('form'); for clarity's sake we have often translated *Stoff* with '(lexical) meaning', which, in the context, is not as inaccurate as it seems.

41. Cf. also Madvig ([1856–7] 1971, 170).

42. Steinthal's works on classification continued through the whole of his life. Particularly important are his *Die Classification der Sprachen dargestellt als die Entwickelung der Sprachidee* (1850) and the *Charakteristik der hauptsächlichsten Typen des Sprachbaues* (1860b), which we have followed in most of our text. Bumann's (1965) account tends to follow the earlier book.

43. Cf. Lohmann (1960). In the preface to his remarkable *Sprache der Jakuten* (1851), Böhtlingk stressed that a grammar should be formulated so as to provide a characterization of the language for typological purposes; he also thought that for a 'physiological' classification both 'internal' and 'external' characters should be used.

9

The neogrammarians and the new beginnings

9.1 Successes and consolidation

The final part of the nineteenth century (the last thirty years) opened propitiously for linguistics, or at least for its historical-comparative branch. The successes of the discipline were universally acknowledged. Most – and eventually all – German Universities taught the subject; a number of other European countries followed suit and the United States also began to play an important role (see above, p. 207ff.). Outside Germany the previous expansion was partly due to German scholars who had sought and found academic positions abroad but now there was a new generation of native scholars and the periphery began to influence the centre. We have already mentioned some of the relevant events. A traditional history of 'linguistic science in the nineteenth century' such as that of Pedersen ([1931] 1962) lists for the generations born from the 1830s to the 1850s a number of linguists who originated in countries other than Germany: Britain, Denmark, France, Italy, Russia, the Scandinavian countries, Switzerland, etc. Work on Romance, after Diez, is cultivated by French scholars such as Paul Meyer (1840–1927) or Gaston Paris (1839–1903), by Danes such as K. Nyrop (1858–1931), by Swiss authors such as J. Gilliéron (1854–1926), by Italians such as Ascoli and Mussafia. The German Universities offer weighty contributions, but the archetypal German work, the real replacement for Diez's grammar and etymological dictionary, is due to W. Meyer-Lübke (1861–1936), who was a Swiss by birth and became professor at Vienna before moving to Bonn. We have seen already how cosmopolitan the work on phonetics was: Britain and France had an important role to play with, on the one hand, e.g. Alexander Melville Bell, Alexander Ellis and Henry Sweet,[1] and, on the other, Paul Passy (1859–1940), the initiator of the IPA transcription, and the abbé Pierre Rousselot (1846–1924), one of the founders of experimental phonetics. But there were also J. A. Lundell

(1851–1940) in Norway, Otto Jespersen (1860–1946) in Denmark, etc.
An experimental phonetics laboratory ('gabinetto di glottologia speri-
mentale') was founded by F. L. Pullé in the University of Pisa in 1890,
one year earlier than the institution of an equivalent laboratory at the
Collège de France (Bolelli 1965a). Even in the privileged field of Indo-
European studies, non-German influence had begun to be felt: once again
one may refer to the Italian Ascoli, but we should also consider the
Russian F. F. Fortunatov (1848–1914) and the Belgian E. Tegnér (1843–
1928) or the three great Danish scholars V. Thomsen (1842–1927), Karl
Verner (1846–1896), Hermann Möller (1850–1923), or the somewhat
younger Swiss scholars Jacob Wackernagel (1853–1938) and Ferdinand
de Saussure (1857–1913). Finally we cannot ignore a Sanskritist of the
calibre of the American W. D. Whitney (see above, p. 207ff.).

9.1.1 Diversity of approaches
We mentioned earlier the more general discussions which went on
in the middle of the century. Now the technical work continues and
becomes more specialized but the contribution of a number of scholars
of different origins also leads linguistics away from the strictly technical historical and comparative horizons, which had accompanied the
process of its institutionalization, towards new concerns and new problems. We have referred to some scholars who were influential in this
way:W. D. Whitney, with his social view of language, M. Bréal, with
his *sémantique*. Linguistic geography is associated with the name of the
Swiss Jules Gilliéron (1854–1926), who was largely responsible for the
linguistic atlas of France, and dialectology in general owes an immense
amount to Ascoli, with his *Saggi Ladini* and the *Archivio Glottologico* but
also to Rousselot and later on to the Swiss Louis Gauchat (1866–1942).
The work of the so-called Kazan' school, i.e. of the Polish linguists
J. Baudouin de Courtenay (1845–1929) and N. Kruszewski (1851–87)
to a certain extent anticipates the phonological theory which emerged
in the twentieth century with the Prague school; similarly, the Swedish
Germanist Adolf Noreen (1854–1925) also anticipated a number of
statements by the Prague school. Finally, even though Ferdinand de
Saussure's work in general linguistics belongs to the twentieth century,
when it appeared in print and had its maximum impact, surely it cannot
be entirely separated from that for the *Mémoire sur le système primitif des
voyelles dans les langues indo-européennes* (1879) and from Saussure's
teaching in Paris and Geneva.

It is tempting to argue that these more general developments arose
independently in the various non-German countries, perhaps as a reaction to German scholarship and a return to older concerns, but the dichotomy should not be pushed too far. There is no question of rejecting the
German achievements. Bréal, for instance, is one of the rare linguists

who referred to his eighteenth-century predecessors and, as has been argued, fits in a specifically French tradition, but at the same time he is not in a direct line of descent from the French Enlightenment or the *idéologues*. He was trained in Germany, translated Bopp, and, though by no means uncritical, saw himself as a practitioner of the new discipline which had arisen in Germany. *Mutatis mutandis* a number of other scholars, Ascoli included, adopted a similar attitude.[2] In the 1920s, Bréal's pupil, Antoine Meillet ([1923] 1938, 152ff.), while stressing the new initiatives which came from non-German scholars after the 1870s, recognized that the basic edifice had been built by the Germans. As for the Germans themselves, they knew that others were beginning to add to their achievements. More than ten years before Meillet, Karl Brugmann (1909b, 222), one of the main protagonists of the linguistics of the end of the century, had listed the indispensable books for a first approach to the subject: Whitney (1867 [1874]), Delbrück (1880, etc.), Paul ([1880] 1920), Oertel (1901), Jespersen (1894) and Wundt (1900), i.e. three German works (two of which were translated into English), and three books originally written in English by an American, a German settled in America and a Dane.

9.1.2 New developments and new directions

In general the last part of the century is marked by at least three new developments. First, we find in European institutions of higher learning, and to a certain extent in the United States, an almost general acceptance of the German model of historical and comparative linguistics. Secondly, the countries newly 'colonized' by German influence now come into their own and both request, and contribute to, a different slant in research. In some instances at least this produces an increasing awareness that even in a technical discipline more general questions exist and must be tackled. In its brief life the *Techmers Zeitschrift*, i.e. the *Internationale Zeitschrift für allgemeine Sprachwissenschaft*, published in Leipzig between 1884 and 1890, quoted on its title page a series of academic advisers together with the name of the place where they worked: three in France, one in Italy, one in Finland, four in the USA, two in Britain, two in Austria, one in India, one in Russia, one in Norway and nine in Germany.[3] Thirdly, in Germany itself the Universities supported an increasing number of linguists and a higher level of specialization. By 1887 the University of Leipzig, which had become pre-eminent in linguistics,[4] offered teaching by ordinary and extraordinary professors in Slavic philology (Leskien), Sanskrit and Celtic (Windisch), Indo-European comparative linguistics (Brugmann), general linguistics (G. von der Gabelentz), Sanskrit (Lindner), phonetics (Techmer), Germanic philology (Kögel), Romance philology (Koerting), Armenian philology (Wenzel), etc.[5] There is little doubt that these scholars, together with some of the classicists, were all competent (at different levels) to discuss problems of historical and comparative linguistics. Yet together with success there goes also the characteristic division in schools which had haunted other more long-lived disciplines such as classics. In linguistics, as in other subjects, the division is linked to specific theoretical or methodological views, but also, of course, to a wide network of personal and institutional patronage, mutual support, gossip and intrigues. This last set of circumstances influences both the development of the discipline and, even more consistently, the way in which that development is perceived, i.e. the contemporary historiography.[6]

9.2 The neogrammarian school

Both the technical work in historical and comparative linguistics and the more general approaches to language are dominated by one of the most influential developments of our period, the so-called *Junggrammatische Richtung* or, in the contemporary mistranslation, the neogrammarian school. The name *Junggrammatiker* was applied in the first instance to a group of young German scholars, originally based in Leipzig or closely connected with the University of Leipzig. Most of them had been taught by, or been in close contact with, the classicist and comparativist Georg Curtius (see above, p. 186 note 40) and the much younger August Leskien (1840–1916), an Indo-Europeanist and Slavicist who had been a student of Schleicher at Jena but had become Extraordinarius in Slavic philology at Leipzig as early as 1870. Against Curtius they reacted, of Leskien they made a friend and a guru who served in a sense as the focus of the group. This included at various times the Indo-Europeanists Karl Brugmann (1849–1919),[7] Hermann Osthoff (1847–1909) and the somewhat older Berthold Delbrück (1842–1922), as well as the Germanists Hermann Paul (1846–1921), Eduard Sievers (1850–1932) and Wilhelm Braune (1850–1926). Other Indo-Europeanists more loosely attached to the group, but also linked to Leipzig, were the Dane Karl Verner (1846–96), who had spent some time in Leipzig before becoming Librarian at Halle, and the German Iranianist and Armenologist J. H. Hübschmann (1848–1908), who took his *venia legendi* at Leipzig in 1875.[8] Ferdinand de Saussure (1857–1913), who went to study in Leipzig in 1876 at the age of nineteen, was too young to be a real part of what he called the *cénacle des docteurs*. The name *Junggrammatiker* was first used, probably in half-mocking, half-affectionate jest, by Friedrich Zarncke (1825–91), Professor of Germanistics at Leipzig, on the model of phrases with a political and literary connotation such as *Junges Deutschland*; the reference must have been to the young age of the protagonists and to their supposed tempestuous and revolutionary character. Initially the people to which the name referred used it as a banner, but later they too expressed the hope that the name be dropped (cf. e.g. Brugmann 1882) since it recalled contrasts which by that time were better forgotten (even if in fact they were not).

A number of contemporaries sided with this basic group but its membership was never very clearly defined, all the more so because, even at the time of most violent divergences, very similar work was done both by the neogrammarians and by their opponents. Individual attacks started in the late 1870s with the reviews of the first contributions but mostly concentrated in the mid 1880s.[9] By the end of the century it is perhaps fair to say that the neogrammarians had prevailed – but just in time to undergo another onslaught. From young revolutionaries they had turned into members of the establishment and as such were accused of stuffiness, dogmatism and inflexibility. Earlier on they were covered with opprobrium but they were also revered with the sort of devotion which is more suitable for the followers of a religious sect than for the members of a scholarly movement. On the one hand, we have accusations of mechanicism, narrow-mindedness, plagiarism, etc., all of which are repeated in the following decades, even before the additional reproach of atomism, which emerges in this century; on the other hand, the neogrammarians came to be seen as the instigators of a sort of Kuhnian revolution in both technique and methodology. Almost ninety years after their beginnings, in his 1965 presidential address to the Linguistic Society of America, Charles Hockett attributed to them the second of the four breakthroughs which he recognized in the history of modern linguistics, but also wrote that 'to this day, mention of the neogrammarians, no matter how disguised, can elicit so much emotional noise that no one can hear what you are saying' (Hockett 1965, 188). He had previously described them as a 'group of Young Turks, armed with a vitally important idea and with enormous arrogance, winning converts and making enemies as much through charisma as by reasonable persuasion' (ibid., 186), and had added: 'The price of the breakthrough was a bitter, intellect-blinding schism from which we have not yet recovered' (ibid.). We should look at these statements both as part of our evidence about the fortune of the neogrammarians and as a contribution to their historiography. The essential point for the historian of linguistics is that by the end of the century there was no linguistic theory which could afford to ignore the neogrammarians – even if that meant to attack them.[10]

9.2.1 The explosion of the controversy

Anecdotally the explosion of the controversy belongs in the late 1870s, with 1876 and 1878 counting as the two most significant years. In 1876 some of the basic tenets were stated by Leskien in his book about the

Slavic declension (1876) but the pieces which created scandal were two articles about Indo-European by Karl Brugmann (Brugman 1876a, b). In one of these he reconstructed for Indo-European a new set of phonemes, the so-called nasal sonants or vocalic nasals (*n, *m); in the other there was a discussion of some morphological problems accompanied by a reconstruction of Indo-European vocalism which differed considerably from that accepted by Schleicher and Curtius.

Brugmann published his articles in the *Curtius Studien*, the periodical which he temporarily edited in the absence of Georg Curtius, the founder and general editor. At his return, Curtius (1876) stated in print that he was not responsible for Brugmann's far-reaching conjectures and later stopped publication of the periodical. Brugmann's crime was two-fold. First, his reconstructions of Indo-European vocalism contradicted those of Curtius and in the last resort led to a very different form of the Indo-European tree. Secondly, he supported his points with repeated protestations about the correct methodology of historical and comparative research; the implication was that the previous work was methodologically unreliable. To some this must have sounded as a form of arrogant reproach, to others as an unnecessarily long-winded explanation of what was well known and could be taken for granted. In 1878, when Osthoff was already professor at Heidelberg but Brugmann still had only a precarious appointment, the two joined forces to edit a sort of periodical or collection of essays, the *Morphologische Untersuchungen*, which, in spite of its intermittent life (1–4, 1878–81; 5, 1890; 6, 1910) and of the fact that it only consisted of contributions by the editors, played an important role in the controversy. The introduction to the first number, signed by Osthoff and Brugmann but drafted by Brugmann, counts as the real manifesto of the neogrammarian movement and is written in a somewhat overemphatic and revolutionary style bound to irritate the older generations. The authors acknowledged the influence of W. Scherer[11] and H. Steinthal, but stated that they had developed their basic principles while listening to Leskien's lectures in Leipzig: first, language is not an object which has a reality of its own independent of its speakers (an attack against Schleicher); secondly, those mental and physical activities of human beings which impinge on language must have been always the same (the uniformitarian principle). For a real understanding of the principles of language development, the linguist must abandon 'the workshop ridden with hypotheses where Indo-European roots are hammered out' in order to step out into the 'clear light of the present and of understandable truth' (Osthoff and Brugman 1878, ix). The *Junggrammatiker* – the introduction continues (p. xiii) – attribute most importance to two of their methodological principles (*methodischen Grundsätzen*): (a) sound change occurs according to mechanical laws which suffer no exceptions (the regularity principle),[12] and (b) form-association, i.e. the creation of new forms through analogy, was as important a factor of language change in the past as it is in present-day languages. In the first and second pages of the preface the authors had pleaded for an increased awareness (à la Steinthal) of the psychological factors which determine the development of language.

We shall return to these statements, but let us first observe that what Osthoff and Brugmann do not say is as significant as what they do say. Instead of the standard pleading for the validity and the importance of 'Bopp's discipline', and instead of the usual genuflections to the memory of the founding fathers, the manifesto contains an attack against the current emphasis on reconstruction and Indo-European (i.e. an attack against Schleicher but also against the general tendency of most linguists after Bopp) and a plea for a move to the pure air of the present. Linguistics is now seen as an established discipline; there is no longer any need to make a case for it but it is necessary to reconsider its foundations and its methodology. There is no talk, however, of descriptive technique or theory. At this stage the neogrammarians share the historical interests (and bias) of the nineteenth century. Also, and in spite of the respectful references to Steinthal, there is no mention of typology and language classification – a fact which can be differently interpreted. Once again where the neogrammarians differ from their predecessors is in their concern for an explicit definition of the procedures and methods to be followed in the actual work of history and comparison. Ritschl, the Latinist who had brought new life to classical studies in Leipzig and had been the teacher of both Schleicher and Brugmann, listed among his ten commandments for the classicist: 'Du sollst den Namen Methode nicht unnütz im Munde führen' ('Thou shalt not take the name "Method" in vain').[13] This attitude certainly prevailed among classicists and had been adopted by the most technically minded of the linguists, who had done but little to define their techniques and method. Most of them were not interested; Pott was too obscure; Schleicher and Curtius, who were innovative in their methodology, were far too prone to mix discussions of procedure with a priori views such as Schleicher's Hegelianism and organicism or Curtius's anti-uniformitarianism. As for the 'theoreticians' (Steinthal and his followers), their concern was not with procedure but with more general questions. By contrast the editors of the *Morphologische Untersuchungen* were interested both in providing an explicit statement of the method which they used in their technical work and in the general principles which, in their view, justified that method. Whether they succeeded is of course a different matter.

The manifesto certainly does not provide a coherent model for linguistic analysis or even for the type of historical work which the neogrammarians favoured. Yet the points mentioned above are linked with each other, even if not obviously so. If language depends on the speaker, then it cannot be an autonomous organism with a life of its own, and consequently there is no reason to distinguish a period of growth from a period of decay. Uniformitarianism prevails and inevitably leads to the conclusion that modern languages are the best source of information about linguistic development – with the proviso, however, that, since the bias is entirely historical, 'modern languages' often refers to languages whose history is documented rather than to contemporary languages. There is no serious question at this point of Labov-like studies of sound change in progress. But modern languages, however the term is understood, also offer rich evidence for the study of what used to be called *falsche Analogie*, i.e. analogy. In a uniformitarian set-up this can no longer be treated as a symptom of decay missing from the earliest linguistic phases – hence its importance both for the historical linguist and the comparativist. In this scenario the odd man out is the regularity principle: why should the observation of modern languages support the view, so vociferously upheld, that at a given period the same sound changed in the same manner in all words in which it was found in the same phonological environment? Intuitively one has the opposite impression. Yet that the regularity principle was central to the whole undertaking is confirmed by the later reactions. The main attacks of the 1870s and 1880s concentrated both on the refusal to admit exceptions to sound laws and on the importance attributed to analogy. Later on, uniformitarianism and the consequent respectability of modern linguistic studies were tacitly accepted, as was the role of analogy in linguistic change. By contrast, the neogrammarians' conception of sound change remained highly controversial and was subject to the attacks of both the dialectologists (Gilliéron, etc.) and the idealists (Vossler, etc.). Ironically, the same neogrammarians who had fought against Schleicher's organicism and had clamoured for a shift of emphasis from the language to the speaker, became, in the eyes of their adversaries, the dogmatic upholders of a principle which denied the freedom of the individual. This paradoxical outcome leads us once again to consider why and how the neogrammarians reached their tenets. Yet to do so means to turn away from the more abstract definitions to the historical and philological work to which the neogrammarians and their contemporaries dedicated most of their intellectual efforts.

9.2.2 Who were the neogrammarians?

We start with a brief account of the life, works and careers of the most prominent neogrammarians: institutionally and intellectually they are all representative of the period in general and the school in particular.[14] Their teacher, August Leskien, was a Slavist who had started as a classicist; he was well acquainted with the modern languages (so much so that he could be taken for a native speaker of Serbo-Croat) and did fieldwork in Lithuania and Jugoslavia, but initially at least his work was largely historical. Most of it concerned Old Church Slavonic and, more generally, the historical phonology and morphology of the Slavic and Baltic languages. The Serbo-Croatian grammar which he wrote towards the end of his life remained incomplete, since he died before publishing the syntax volume.

Karl Brugmann and Hermann Osthoff were also trained as classicists. Osthoff had studied at Bonn and had then taken his *venia legendi* at Leipzig before moving to Heidelberg as Professor of Comparative Linguistics and Sanskrit. Before becoming more engrossed in etymological work, he too was mainly concerned with the historical phonology and morphology of Indo-European, as witnessed e.g. by his two volumes of *Forschungen im gebiete der indogermanischen nominalen stammbildung* (1875–76), the first of which was dedicated to Georg Curtius, and by his monograph on the Indo-European perfect (1884), dedicated to 'my friends Karl Brugmann and Hermann Paul'. His booklet on *Das physiologische und psychologische Moment in der sprachlichen Formenbildung* (1879) continues the general discussion from the point at which the manifesto had left it, and, as is usual with the 'non-philosophical' Osthoff, goes too far in its basic dualism.

In the annals of nineteenth-century linguistics, Brugmann counts as the Indo-Europeanist *par excellence* (Morpurgo Davies 1986). As we have seen, he was trained in Leipzig in the circle of Georg Curtius even if he then came under the influence of Leskien. From a series of minor notes about points of classical philology or etymology, he moved to the articles mentioned above which were instrumental in redefining the phonology of Indo-European and to a series of other papers on problems of phonology and morphology. The development of his career brought him from Leipzig to his first chair in Freiburg and then back to Leipzig (1887) shortly after the publication of the first edition of his *Griechische Grammatik* (1885a) and of the first volume of his *Grundriß* (1886–93), the *magnum opus* which replaced in five volumes Schleicher's *Compendium* and offered a detailed phonological and morphological reconstruction of Indo-European (see above, p. 166). The second edition of the great work appeared between 1897 and 1916. Meanwhile, Brugmann edited at least two periodical publications: with Osthoff the *Morphologische Untersuchungen* (see pp. 11, 231), and with W. Streitberg the newly founded and still-existing *Indogermanische Forschungen* (1892ff.), which soon acquired remarkable pre-eminence. He also wrote a second and third edition of his Greek Grammar (1885a, 2nd edn 1889, 3rd edn 1900) and an abbreviated version of the *Grundriß* (1902–4), as well as innumerable other works, some of which concerned semantic and syntactic development in the context of a psychological theory partly influenced by Wundt, while others defended the tenets of his school against the attacks of its adversaries.

The oldest of the Indo-Europeanists, Berthold Delbrück (36 in 1878) was trained at Halle, where Pott taught, and at Berlin, where he heard Bopp and Steinthal, but he then obtained at Jena the chair which had been held first by Schleicher and then by Leskien, and remained there until the end of his life (Hermann 1923). There are articles by him on Germanic phonology and morphology, but the bulk of his work concerns Sanskrit and Indo-European syntax, to which he made a unique contribution, as shown by his various monographs and by the three volumes which he wrote as a conclusion to Brugmann's *Grundriß*. The other strand of his activity is represented by his thoughtful accounts of contemporary linguistic work: the *Einleitung in das Sprachstudium* (1880, 6th edn 1919) offers a brief history of nineteenth-century linguistics and a summary of the main points disputed at the time; the later *Grundfragen der Sprachforschung, mit Rücksicht auf W. Wundts Sprachpsychologie erörtert* (1901) considers the dispute between Paul and Wundt about the role and nature of the psychological theory adopted by linguists. Much earlier he had written a short book which discussed the reasons why, and the ways in which, linguistics could be taught in Universities (Delbrück 1875).

The remaining three members of the core group, Hermann Paul, Wilhelm Braune and Eduard Sievers, were linked by their stronger interest in Germanic languages rather than in Indo-European *per se* and by their 'philological' activities, i.e. their text editions, their discussions of manuscripts, etc. They had all studied at Leipzig and, *qua* Germanists, had come into close contact with F. Zarncke, but also with Curtius and Leskien.[15]

Paul, who before reaching Leipzig had heard Steinthal in Berlin, became a Professor of German Language and Literature in Freiburg, where for a brief period he had Brugmann as a colleague, and then moved to Munich. The amount of work he produced is staggering: a series of articles which cover all stages of the history of Germanic, from Indo-European to Germanic and from Old High German to modern German; a theoretical book, the *Prinzipien der Sprachgeschichte* (1880, 5th edn 1920), which at some stage counted as the Bible of the contemporary linguist; an historical grammar of Middle High German (1881), which started as an analysis of phonology and morphology but acquired a section on syntax in the second edition (1884); a *Deutsches Wörterbuch* (1897) which concentrated on the development of lexical meaning; and the five volumes of a historical grammar of German (1916–20). We must also mention his contributions to, and editorial work for, the gigantic *Grundriß der germanischen Philologie* (1891–3, 2nd edn 1901–9).

Braune, who was the most 'philological' and the least theoretical of the three, started teaching at Giessen and then, with the help of Osthoff, moved to Heidelberg; to complement Paul's grammar he wrote a Gothic (1880) and an Old High German grammar (1886), which in updated versions are still in use. In 1874 he joined Paul in founding the *Beiträge zur Geschichte der deutschen Sprache und Literatur* (*Paul-Braune Beiträge* or PBB), which in effect were meant to introduce into the circles of Germanists the Leipzig principles, i.e. the views learned from Leskien, and which are still in existence. Sievers took over as editor in 1892.

We mentioned before Eduard Sievers, the youngest of the neogrammarians, who by the age of 25 had edited a number of medieval texts in Old English, Old High German, etc. and had written numerous articles on problems of Germanic historical linguistics. As early as 1876 he published the first edition of his *Grundzüge der Lautphysiologie*, which revolutionized the contemporary attitude to the study of phonetics and phonological change (cf. p. 162). The book opened a new series (*Bibliothek indogermanischer Grammatiken*) published at Leipzig and edited by a number of young scholars headed by the more senior Whitney (53) and by Franz Bücheler (43), then Professor of Latin at Bonn and author of, *inter alia*, a *Grundriß der lateinischen Declination* (1866).[16] With a slightly altered title (*Grundzüge der Phonetik*), Sievers' book reached its fifth edition in 1901. Sievers himself, who at the age of 21 was nominated Extraordinarius at Jena, held chairs successively at Jena, Tübingen and Halle before returning to Leipzig in 1892 as Zarncke's successor. He completed an Anglo-Saxon grammar (1882, 3rd edn 1898) which was highly innovative in its data and method though it was limited to phonology and morphology, but then dedicated great part of his work to the study of metre and accentuation in the Germanic languages.

Some points emerge even from this very superficial summary. The neogrammarians' extraordinary productivity is important. Together with their followers (and sometimes their enemies), and in the course of less than thirty years, they wrote or rewrote historical and comparative accounts of the grammar of Indo-European and of most Indo-European languages, including the Romance languages. Meyer-Lübke, the author of the monumental *Grammatik der romanischen Sprachen* (1890–1902) and of other grammars of the Romance languages, may count as one of the followers of the neogrammarians, as do other Romance specialists (Iordan-Orr 1970, 20ff.; cf. Malkiel 1989). Also important is the emergence of historical grammar on a par with comparative grammar. Bopp's great work (1833–52) was entitled 'Comparative grammar of Sanskrit, Zend, Greek, etc. . . . ', Schleicher (1861–2) wrote a 'Compendium of the comparative grammar of the Indo-European languages', but Brugmann's '*Grundriß* of the comparative grammar of the Indo-European languages', which obviously imitated the previous titles, had a significant subtitle: 'A concise exposition of the history of Sanskrit, Old Iranian . . .'. The standard scholarly account is now a historical grammar of individual languages where, as a classicist put it (Hoffmann 1905, 61), the 'Statistik der Formen' (i.e. the 'static' or synchronic description) is accompanied by a historical and explanatory grammar. Some of these works are still in use nowadays and all of them provide the foundation on which most modern historical work still depends. The priority given to the historical and comparative approach has consequences: most historical grammars include only phonology and morphology (*Laut- und Formenlehre*), since these were the levels of analysis to which the comparative and historical method had been applied most successfully. Yet it is mistaken to believe that syntax was neglected: Delbrück dedicated most of his life's work to it and Brugmann too turned to the subject in the second part of his life; Paul discussed syntax at length in his *Prinzipien* ([1880] 1920) and a relatively unknown scholar, Hermann Ziemer (1882), wrote a book entitled 'Neogrammarians' incursions into the field of syntax'. Once again the fact that, in contrast with Bopp's and Scheicher's works, Brugmann's *Grundriß* included three volumes on syntax (written by Delbrück) is significant. Similarly, we should not assume that all descriptive work was avoided. The neogrammarians knew very well that linguistic history had to be based on linguistic description. In the case of languages such as the classical ones, they assumed that descriptions existed, though they could and should be refined;[17] in other instances they recognized that the first task was that of collecting data, editing texts, if there were any, and eventually defining linguistic usage. Brugmann (1885b, 18) assumed that both description and history of languages belonged to the same discipline. The new emphasis on philological work makes sense in this context.[18] Among the neogrammarians a few, even if not all, were also concerned with editing texts; all Germanists for instance were accomplished philologists and textual critics.

9.2.3 The role of modern languages

The question of how the neogrammarians reached their views now becomes more, not less, pressing. The upholders of the theory that modern languages were the best field of enquiry were in fact Indo-Europeanists or medievalists; when they were not engaged in reconstruction they dealt with periods for which the evidence was scanty and needed to be discovered through advanced philological techniques. Moreover, the scholars who pleaded for a 'systematic exploration of the general conditions of the life of language' or for a 'Principienwissenschaft' (Brugmann 1885b, 33) in fact spent most of their working life dealing with 'Specialforschung', i.e. with minute problems of historical morphology or phonology. The inconsistency is obvious – but perhaps more apparent than real. An explanation comes once again from the link between data-oriented work and theory. We may consider first some of the 'practical' reasons for the new emphasis on modern languages.

First, historical linguists were increasingly aware of the importance of accurate phonetic statements. We saw earlier (p. 164) how strongly Scherer felt about this; his followers knew very well that phonetic work had to be done on the basis of existing spoken languages. Eduard Sievers' *Grundzüge der Lautphysiologie* appeared in 1876, the same year which saw Brugmann's revolutionary articles about Indo-European vocalism (cf. p. 231). In the preface Sievers pleaded for a systematic study of phonetic structure as contrasted with the odd checking up of phonetic details and he also referred extensively to the work by his pupil and friend J. Winteler, who had described with rich phonetic details his own Swiss dialect (1876). The reference to Winteler appears again in the preface to the *Morphologische Untersuchungen* (Osthoff and Brugman 1878, ix).

Secondly, an increased sophistication in Indo-European studies led to the conclusion that for a number of branches of the family the written texts were both late and inadequate and there was a crying need for contemporary descriptions of the languages in question. As early as 1850 (in *Die Sprachen Europas*, 191) Schleicher had regretted the absence of any scholarly grammar of Lithuanian and had proposed to study the language *in loco*. In 1852 he did so and the work yielded the two volumes of the *Handbuch der litauischen Sprache* (1856–7), which contained a remarkable descriptive grammar (phonology, morphology, syntax) of Lithuanian; the author commented that the efforts involved in fieldwork were compensated by 'the great joy to hear the magnificent forms of the language in living use' (1856–7, v). The journey to Lithuania in order to collect oral texts or linguistic data was repeated by other linguists: in, or around, 1880, Leskien, Brugmann and the young Saussure.

Finally, the scholarly interest in dialectology was increasing, spurred partly by political reasons or reasons of local or cultural prestige, partly by linguistic concerns: Ascoli's *Saggi Ladini*, which have been considered the starting point of Romance dialectology, date from 1873, and in France and Germany at this stage we begin to find similar work. Winteler's 1876 work has been mentioned above.

The conclusion is that at its new level of sophistication the actual work of comparison and reconstruction was instrumental in favouring an interest in modern or recently attested languages. In more general terms this had been advocated before by e.g. Whitney (see p. 207ff.) and Ascoli; in England in the early 1870s a group of phonetically inclined scholars such as the Anglicists A. J. Ellis and Henry Sweet had also spoken in similar terms. The neogrammarians were certainly influenced by the statements of these scholars (by Whitney and Ascoli, for instance), but the importance of the other factors which we have mentioned should not be underrated.[19] In its turn, this concern for modern languages could, as we have seen, lead to a reconsideration of the processes of linguistic change and in particular to a new assessment of the importance of analogical processes. If so, the primary requirement even for the Indo-Europeanist was an explicit methodology for the study of language change: comparative grammar had to yield to historical grammar (a statement which will have to be qualified). Within this context we must return to our original question (p. 237): What prompted the neogrammarians to affirm that sound laws suffered no exceptions, given that this view was not warranted by the study of contemporary languages?

9.2.4 Indo-European: reconstruction and phonetic development

Here too the initial motivation was that of data-oriented work, but this time the actual work of comparison, reconstruction, historical study was more directly relevant. As we have seen, by the 1870s in Indo-European studies the attention had shifted from the 'morphological' method of Bopp to the phonological reconstruction of Schleicher and Curtius. The task had then become that of linking the reconstructed forms to the attested ones and formulating the phonological processes involved. Some of the problems that arose were solved in quick succession between the 1860s and the 1880s. We must mention at least a few, even if it is difficult to re-create the highly charged atmosphere of the period, where a few scholars lived in the midst of a succession of 'discoveries' which was likely to change the starting point of their work from one day to the next.[20]

9.2.4.1 Consonantal reconstruction: Verner's Law, the velars

We have already discussed (p. 173) the ways in which Grimm's Law was gradually redefined. The original formulation was faulty from the point of view of phonetics (no distinction between fricatives and aspirated stops) and because it allowed too many exceptions. In the course of the century these were defined (Lottner, etc.) and in some instances explained (Grassmann, etc.). Yet there remained the basic problem referred to earlier. Why was an IE *t continued in Germanic sometimes as the fricative [θ] (<þ>) predicted by Grimm's Law and sometimes by a voiced dental stop [d] (<d>)? Gothic tunþu-, English tooth, correspond to Sanskrit dant-, Latin dent-, thus indicating a [θ] continuation of the reconstructed [t] which is preserved in Sanskrit and Latin, but Gothic þridja- 'third' with <d> corresponds to Latin tertius, Sanskrit tr̥tíya-, thus indicating a different treatment of internal [t]. Moreover, clearly related words showed a double treatment: 'to go' is in Gothic leiþan with <þ>, but the causative 'to lead' is laidja with <d>. Alternations occurred also in similar formations: Goth. broþar 'brother' with

<þ>, but *fadar* 'father' with <d> vs. Latin *fräter* and *pater* both with internal <t>. As we would now put it, there was a comparative problem caused by the unpredictability of the correspondences between cognate languages (Latin *t* vs. Gothic *þ*, but Latin *t* vs. Gothic *d*), a diachronic problem caused by the unpredictability of the treatment of Indo-European stops (IE **t* > Gothic *þ*, as predicted by Grimm's Law, but unpredictably we also have IE **t* > Gothic *d*), and a morphophonemic (synchronic) problem, caused by the difficulty in determining the rationale for the alternation between voiced and voiceless consonants in intervocalic position (*leiþan* and *laidjan*.) It was one of the scholars closest to the group of the Leipzig neogrammarians, the Dane Karl Verner, who objected that these could not be chance occurrences; the irregular changes were as frequent as the regular ones predicted by Grimm's Law. As he stated, there had to be a rule for the irregularity. Comparison provided him with the answer. In Germanic the Indo-European stops were voiced internally in words where they preceded the accent, but not when they followed the accent. The accent in question, however, was not the Germanic accent, which was word-initial, but the free accent of Indo-European still preserved in Sanskrit: notice the difference in accent in Sanskrit *bhrátar-* 'brother' and Sanskrit *pitár-* 'father' and compare the Gothic treatment with <þ> in the first word and <d> in the second. In the verbs mentioned above, the accent was on the suffix in the causatives but on the root in the basic verb. The article where Verner (1875) demonstrated the law which now carries his name is a model of clarity and could not fail to persuade. At one stroke he had eliminated the main remaining exception to Grimm's Law, had given an historical account of an important morphophonemic alteration and had demonstrated through a third *comparandum* (Germanic in addition to Sanskrit and Greek) that it was possible to reconstruct for the parent language not only the distribution of phonological segments but also that of suprasegmental features. He had also drawn attention to the importance of accentual studies.[21]

A similar success story was the reconstruction of two or three different velar series for Indo-European. Schleicher ([1861–2] 1871, 202ff.) thought in terms of one original series and derived from IE **k* e.g. Sanskrit *k, c, ś, p* (i.e. [k, ʧ, ʃ, p]) or Greek *κ, γ, π, τ* (i.e. [k, g, p, t]), apparently at random, i.e. without specifying why one or the other treatment occurred. Ascoli (1870) was the first to exploit the Iranian evidence to clarify the Sanskrit data, to draw attention to the similarity of developments in Indo-Iranian and Balto-Slavic, and to wonder whether setting up three different sound series in Indo-European would remove the apparently arbitrary developments. Somewhat later, August Fick (1873, 1ff.) firmly distinguished two sounds for Indo-European (*k* and *ḳ* in his notation); in his view the first of these was preserved as such in

Indo-Iranian but developed a labial element in the European languages (hence > Lat. *qu*), while the second yielded a fricative in Indo-Iranian (Sanskrit *ś*) and Balto-Slavic and a velar elsewhere. Generally accepted and more detailed conclusions were not reached until the 1890s and nowadays instead of Fick's *k* we reconstruct *k^w, a so-called labiovelar (or labial-velar). However, Ascoli's (and Fick's) work was sufficient to show that Schleicher's formulation was inadequate and that further work would lead to a much tighter and predictable account of the actual developments. The new views clarified e.g. the etymological links between words such as Greek τέτταρες, Latin *quattuor* and Sanskrit *catvāra-*, 'four', and in effect established clear rules for the derivation of the attested sounds from their Indo-European antecedents.

9.2.4.2 The reconstruction of the Indo-European vowels

If Ascoli's assumption that Indo-European had more than one type of velars eventually found general acceptance, and the validity of Verner's Law was immediately recognized, a solution to the problems of Indo-European vocalism was slow to come and proceeded in fits and starts. The problem was double because it concerned on the one hand the reconstruction of the Indo-European vocalic phonemes, on the other hand the understanding of the morphophonemic process known as *Ablaut*, that we have already had occasion to discuss (pp. 134ff., 144ff.). As we saw (p. 144), in 1822 Grimm had expressed the hope that further work would demonstrate that even the development of vowels showed some regularity. At a later stage this was tacitly accepted, but reconstructions and postulated developments were far from clear. All through the 1850s, the 1860s and most of the 1870s, the assumption was that Indo-European had three different vocalic qualities ([a, ā, i, ī, u, ū]) and that the *e* and *o* vowels of Greek and Latin were due to later developments: Greek *e, o, a* and Latin *e, i, o, u, a* all matched (or could match) Sanskrit *a* and were taken as derived from Indo-European *a*, but no attempt was made to explain why in any given word one or the other vowel appeared. It looked as if an original *a* had undergone a number of splits in a completely arbitrary fashion. This view came to be slowly eroded. First, Curtius ([1864] 1886, 2, 13ff.) demonstrated that the European languages (Greek and Latin, but also Germanic) showed a remarkable degree of agreement in vocalic quality: where Latin had *e* Greek also tended to have *e* (Sanskrit *sapta* 'seven' but Greek *hepta*, Latin *septem*).[22] He concluded that the European branch of Indo-European had altered some instances of the inherited *a*-vowel to *ä*, which yielded *e* in the various languages. At a later stage some of the remaining *a*-vowels were altered into *o*. The vocalism thus seemed to provide evidence for a first split of Indo-European into an Eastern branch (which preserved the original vocalism) and a Western branch marked by a series of common innovations; in the same way the split of a reconstructed European *a into a in e.g. Germanic and o in Greek and Latin (Sanskrit aṣṭau 'eight' but Greek oktō, Latin octō and Gothic ahtau) spoke in favour of a Graeco-Latin branch of the European languages, characterized by the a > o change. The obvious objection, and one which was soon raised, is that no rationale was given for the reconstruction. As the Germanist A. Amelung (1840–74) pointed out in 1871, if one reconstructed *a and *e for the European branch and *a for the Eastern branch there was no reason to assume a priori that the latter vocalism was that of the parent language. In one of those articles which angered Curtius, Brugmann (1876b) did in fact propose that the Indo-European system distinguished more than one type of a: it could be shown, he argued, that an e of Greek (and Latin) always corresponded to a Sanskrit a (acc. sg. Sanskrit pitaram 'father' vs. Greek patera), while an o in certain environments corresponded to Sanskrit ā (acc. sg. Sanskrit dātāram 'giver' vs. Greek dōtora); if so, the two sets of correspondences pointed at least to two different vowels for Indo-European, one which yielded Sanskrit a and Greek or Latin e and one which yielded Sanskrit ā and Greek or Latin o.[23] The real conclusion, even if not stated in those terms until later, was that Indo-European had e-vowels, o-vowels and a-vowels. That being so, however, the whole system of vocalic alternations (Ablaut) in Indo-European had to be reconsidered: one did not deal any longer with a simple alternation of zero (no vowel), a, ā, as in Sanskrit, but with a more complex alternation of zero, e, o, ē, ō. There was, however, a new series of problems which concerned the even more complicated alternations between ā and a or ā and i (in Sanskrit), etc. On the other hand some questions were clarified. In a first article, which we mentioned earlier (p. 231), Brugmann had tackled another series of irregularities which involved both the internal morphophonemic problems of e.g. Greek and Sanskrit and comparative problems: why did the Greek dialectal perfect λελόγχ-ατι 'they have obtained by lot' show an ending -ατι which differed from the ντι-ending of e.g. τέθνα-ντι 'they have died'; why did Latin decem 'ten' correspond to Greek deka, Sanskrit daśa, i.e. why did an -em of Latin correspond to an -a of Greek and Sanskrit? In the end Brugmann and Osthoff (the latter had worked on similar problems for the liquids) reconstructed for Indo-European a series of vocalic resonants (approximants) *r̥, *l̥, *n̥, *m̥, while showing that these had developed different supporting vowels in the daughter languages. At one blow a number of apparently arbitrary correspondences were removed while the origin of another set of morphophonemic alternations was explained (the original *-nti yielded -ati in post-consonantal position where -n- vocalized). Once again comparison and synchronic morphophonemics led to a new form of reconstruction. The novelty this time is that the reconstructed sounds *ṇ and *ṃ were not in fact attested as such in any of the early Indo-European languages, though, as Brugmann pointed out, Sievers had shown how phonetically plausible they were.[24]

The definitive proof that an e-vowel (different from a) had to be attributed to Indo-European came with the so-called law of the palatals (*Palatalgesetz*), discovered, perhaps independently, by a number of scholars of very different allegiance between 1874 and 1878 and first published by Hermann Collitz in 1878 and 1879.[25] In Sanskrit k and c [tʃ] alternated before a without an obvious explanation. It became possible to show that c appeared before those a-vowels that corresponded to an e of the European languages, while k occurred before those a-vowels which corresponded to a or o in those languages. The obvious explanation was that Sanskrit, or rather Indo-Iranian, the immediate ancestor of Sanskrit, had known an e which had triggered the palatalization of [k] to [k'] to [tʃ], just as i also caused the change of a preceding [k] to [tʃ] (contrast Sanskrit cid 'what' with ka- 'who'). In other words, in Indo-Iranian an earlier *ke (< *kʷe) was altered into [k'e] or [tʃe], while ka or ko were preserved as such. A later change then merged e, a and o into a, with the result that Indo-European *kʷe 'and' and *kʷo- 'who' appear in Sanskrit as ca and ka- respectively. If so, however, the three vowels had to be attributed to Indo-Iranian and, *a fortiori*, to Indo-European, the parent language.[26]

The work which pulled all new reconstructions of the Indo-European vocalism together and, through an impressive use of what we now call internal reconstruction, went much beyond a statement about the vocalic phonemes of Indo-European, moving towards a full interpretation of the original *Ablaut* alternations, was the *Mémoire sur le système primitif des voyelles dans les langues indo-européennes*, written by Ferdinand de Saussure when he was 21, and officially published in Leipzig in 1879, though it appeared in 1878. The general conclusion was that Indo-European had e and o vowels as well as six phonemes ([i, u, r, l, m, n]) which could appear in both vocalic and consonantal function, depending on the phonological environment: a normal root ablauted on the model of e.g. *bher-/*bhor-/*bhr- where each grade of the root corresponded to a different functional role. In addition, Saussure postulated two *coefficients sonantiques* A and O, not preserved as such in any attested language, which, in different phonological environments, either vocalised (mainly between consonants) or dropped (before a vowel) or dropped while lengthening a preceding vowel and in some instances changing its quality. These elements, whose exact phonetic nature remained obscure, form the basis on which the so-called laryngeal theory of the twentieth century will develop; as Saussure showed, they allowed a clear explanation of a number of morphophonemic alternations in the attested languages. Verbal forms as different as Sanskrit *yunak-ti* 'he joins' vs. the participle *yuk-ta-*; *śṛṇo-ti* 'he hears' vs. the participle *śru-ta-*; *punā-ti* 'he purifies' vs. the participle *pū-ta-* could all be brought back to ancient presents with a *-ne-* nasal infix which is absent in the participle: **yu-ne-k-* vs. **yuk-*; **kḷ-ne-u-* vs. **klu-*; **pu-ne-A-* (> **punā-*) vs. **puA-* (> **pū-*). At the same time all different types of *Ablaut* could be brought back to one single alternation between zero (no vowel) and *e/o*, since the odd *i*s of Sanskrit were due to the vocalization of A and O, and some of the long vowels were due to the contraction of a short vowel with A and O. Saussure's conclusions were not generally accepted – by the neogrammarians or their opponents – largely because they were too revolutionary and in a sense too speculative for the time, but partly because the whole edifice included some weak parts which were later put right.[27] However, apart from the qualitative as well as quantitative differences that characterize a work of genius, it is difficult to argue that Saussure's masterpiece belongs to a different paradigm from that of the neogrammarians. Admittedly it is often, and correctly, repeated that in the *Mémoire* the strong emphasis on the reconstruction of a system as contrasted with that of individual sounds foreshadows the later views of the founder of structuralism, but an interest in systemic observations is something which the neogrammarians shared too. The accusation of atomism is simply misguided – for this period at least and for the best neogrammarians (Lehmann 1994, 1002).

9.2.5 Empirical work and the regularity principle

The results which we have been describing may have been independent of each other but the problems and the methodology had a great deal in common. The starting point in all cases was a series of unexplained morphophonemic alternations and of irregular correspondences or derivations. Sound laws had been tentatively set up but either they could not be clearly defined or they had too many exceptions. However, it was possible to show that the exceptions were only apparent and that the formulation of the rules, the sound laws, could be sharpened. This was normally achieved through a restatement of the law's phonological conditions or of its chronology. Alternatively, the law itself could be redefined showing that the starting point, i.e. the reconstructed forms in the case of Indo-European or the earlier forms in the case of an attested language, had been wrongly identified. Confronted with this type of results, which were both obtained and recognized by scholars of very different persuasions, all contemporary linguists were bound to feel that the very concept of sound law had acquired a new validity. Most tiresome problems had been solved and eventually most, if not all, exceptions to the established sound laws were likely to disappear. But the development of Indo-European was not the only reason to think so. In the manifesto the editors of the *Morphologische Untersuchungen* (Osthoff and Brugman 1878, ix) also stressed, coherently with their principles, that the actual study of living dialects, if conducted on the basis of adequate phonetic knowledge, would yield a much clearer view of the regularity of phonetic alternation and derivation than any study conducted on written data. The example they produced was that of Winteler's 1876 study of his Swiss dialect – interestingly so in view of the later claims that dialect studies were responsible for the heaviest blow to the neogrammarians' doctrine (Iordan-Orr [1937] 1970, 36). Given the circumstances it is not surprising that initially the neogrammarians behaved as if the regularity principle was empirically based; in their mind it was closely linked with the work that they were doing about comparison, reconstruction and historical development and with the first analyses of individual dialects.[28]

9.3 The neogrammarians and their theoretical work

The preface to the *Morphologische Untersuchungen* (Osthoff and Brugman 1878) reflects the youthful enthusiasm of its authors but does not do justice to the later thinking of the neogrammarians. It is possible to offer a somewhat more coherent account of their views and of those of their contemporaries.

1875 and 1876, *anni mirabiles*, had seen the appearance of a series of concrete results: Verner's article, Hübschmann's impressive demonstration that Armenian was not an Iranian dialect, Leskien's *Declination*, Brugmann's syllabic nasals and his demonstration that Indo-European had *o*, Sievers' *Lautphysiologie* and Winteler's *Kerenzer Mundart*. 1878 is the year of the manifesto, which, we should not forget, is simply the preface to a number of technical articles. It is only to be expected that the serious theoretical work should come later. Two books appeared in the same year 1880: Delbrück's *Einleitung in das Sprachstudium. Ein Beitrag zur Geschichte und Methodik der vergleichenden Sprachforschung*, published as the fourth volume of the *Bibliothek indogermanischer Grammatiken*,[29] and Paul's *Prinzipien*. The former gave an account of the development of Indo-European studies from Bopp to Schleicher and then discussed individual problems characteristic of recent thought: the theory of the root and of agglutination, sound laws, language trees and language separation. The framework was deliberately that of Indo-European studies. Henry Sweet (1882–4, 107f.) remarked that the historical part was the best and that the book was too short to serve as a real guide for students; he also commented on the dogmatic and 'often dogmatically sceptical' attitude of the author. In general, though Delbrück's book had considerable importance, it did not contribute a great deal, nor was it meant to, to the theory of historical or descriptive linguistics. The author had taken as his task that of providing a background for the grammars in the series and wrote for those who 'do not make a special study of comparative linguistics' (1880, vi). Moreover, he was all too aware, as he put it, that 'the influence of research in the philosophy of language on the science founded by Bopp had been very limited and was still so at the time' (1880, v). By contrast, the theoretical book which is fundamental for the neogrammarians' thought is Paul's *Prinzipien*, which was frequently rewritten and updated until the author's death.[30] Sweet (1882-4, 105) hailed the first edition as 'the most important work on general philology appeared of late years', praised 'its extreme soundness' and remarked on Paul's ability to sum up the views of the neogrammarians 'more rigorously and consistently' and to add 'many original ideas of his own'. At the same time, however, he confessed to exasperation for the 'exaggeratedly German abstractness and cumbrousness' of the style (*ibid.*, 107). Both criticism and praise are correct but we should also notice the novelty of the enterprise. The earlier books by Max Müller, Sayce, Hovelacque, and to a certain extent Friedrich Müller (1876-88, vol. I) were introductory books; Whitney's general works too were meant to instruct and to enthuse (though the German translations are somewhat more ponderous). By contrast, Paul's work reads as if it was meant for colleagues.[31]

9.3.1 Paul's *Prinzipienlehre*

The recurring motif in Paul's book is the request for a more explicit account of methods and assumptions: not a philosophy of language but a statement of the basic principles which determine language functioning and language development; this *Prinzipienlehre* need not be any more or any less philosophical than e.g. physics or physiology.[32] The first sentence of the introduction can serve as a general summary of assumptions and aims: language, we are told, is subject to historical treatment like all products of human culture, but linguistic history, like all forms of history, must be accompanied by a discipline which is concerned with the general conditions of historical development and which investigates the nature and operation of all factors which remain constant through change. Paul's general programme calls for a distinction between natural sciences on the one hand and 'cultural sciences' on the other. The latter are characterized, in contrast with the former, by the importance of psychological factors, though these constantly interact with physical factors.[33]

Paul's influence was immense but we should not assume that the neogrammarians were happy to leave all thinking to him; it is enough to follow e.g. the successive versions of Brugmann's *Grundriß* or of his other Indo-European books to realize that, contrary to what is all too often assumed, at the end of the last century the neogrammarians' theoretical views were neither uniform nor static. Some points however are shared and of these perhaps the most important is the prevailing psychologism.[34] In 1887 Brugmann (cf. Gazdaru 1967, 58) wrote to Ascoli that the main controversy surrounding the neogrammarians concerned the relationship of the *Einzelforschung* with psychology. Two years earlier, in his inaugural lecture in Freiburg, he had explained (Brugmann 1885b, 37f.) that in the 1870s there had been a convergence of two directions in linguistics: on the one hand *Specialforschung*, i.e. concrete work of historical analysis, on the other *Sprachphilosophie*, i.e. general theoretical discussion.[35] This immediately follows the observation that Humboldt and above all Steinthal had long since established a *Prinzipienwissenschaft* of linguistics and that Steinthal had defined the fundamental role played in it by psychology. Linguistic theory is seen as linked to psychology. Psychology, however, is still to be defined.[36]

The beginning of the neogrammarians' psychologism must be seen in its context. It is a reaction against Schleicher – to be understood as a partial return to Humboldt mediated by Steinthal. If language is not an object with a life of its own, an organism, the attention necessarily shifts onto the speaker or speakers who is or are responsible for language production. Language is then treated as a mental phenomenon and the study of language as a part of psychology. When in 1901 Delbrück (1901, 43) observed that to adopt one or the other brand of psychology, i.e. Steinthal's or Wundt's views, did not make much difference to the praxis of the linguist,[37] he was in effect returning to this minimum model: the linguist had to assume that there was a link between mental processes and linguistic behaviour but in practice extrapolated the mental processes from linguistic behaviour. For Paul, however, the adoption of a psychological model prompted some extensive rethinking. The first task was that of determining whose psychology one should consider: did one think in terms of individual psychology or of collective psychology, *Völkerpsychologie*? At all stages Paul was adamant that the only psychology worth considering was that of the individual, the rest was unwarranted abstraction. Anachronistically we could say that the object of study was the idiolect and not the language. In the early editions of the *Prinzipien* this leads to an explicit rejection of Steinthal's *Völkerpsychologie*; in the fourth edition (1909) Paul attacks the views expounded by the famous psychologist W. Wundt in the first part of his monumental *Völkerpsychologie*, the first two volumes of which were dedicated to *Die Sprache* (1900). Paul's account is worth quoting. Not only does he disagree with Wundt in his assessment of Herbart's psychology and in his understanding of analogy (cf. below, p. 263), but he also finds that he is divided from Wundt by a much deeper and wider gap with respect to his attitude to *Völkerpsychologie*: for Wundt 'changes in language follow from changes in the *Volksseele*, not in the individual mind [*Einzelseele*]'. Consequently, the problem which for Paul is at the centre of the enquiry, the way in which reciprocal interactions and influences between individuals occur, is for Wundt no problem. 'He deals with language always from the point of view of the speakers, never from that of the hearers' (Paul [1909] 1920, v f.).

With respect to the individual, Paul followed entirely Herbart's associative psychology in the form adopted by Steinthal (p. 203). All linguistic activity leaves traces in the subconscious and these are differently grouped through associations of all possible types based on form, on meaning, on chance similarities, etc., so that the system of associations differs from individual to individual. In its turn the content of the subsconscious can be recalled to consciousness in different ways and at different times. However, for Paul, given the absence of a collective mind or psychology, and given the fact that minds cannot directly influence each other, the task of communication is entrusted to the physical element of language, which has as its main function that of allowing contact between the different psychological organisms and consequently of guaranteeing continuity in time and space. It follows that any study of language will have to investigate both psychological and physical factors. All sorts of conclusions depend on this: first, in Paul's view, the only possible analysis of psychological factors is through introspection; secondly, on the physical side, the most obvious factor is acoustic. It follows that in either case analysis must concentrate on contemporary speakers; the importance of living languages is re-emphasized once again. Even more important, since the content of *Vorstellungen* (ideas, representations) cannot be communicated as such, transmission of information requires by the receiver an act of re-creation, the results of which will depend on the mental and physical organization of each individual (Paul 1920, 15). There is a return here to Humboldt's creativity, but as much from the point of view of the hearer as from that of the speaker.

To focus on the individual has other consequences as well. If each individual has his or her own language and the language of each individual has its own history, the existence of language variety should not be surprising; what is more difficult to understand is the existence at any given moment of a linguistic norm (to use a more modern term), the fact that we speak of languages and not only of a multitude of idiolects. Paul's answer to the problem takes us back to his earlier statement that all 'cultural sciences' are in fact social sciences. Individuals do not live in isolation but in the same speech community influence each other through linguistic intercourse; in its turn this intercourse guarantees a degree of linguistic cohesion, helped by the fact that the essential psychological processes are the same for everyone; in addition to the speech of the individual we identify a *Sprachusus*, a linguistic norm. At the same time, however, language change can be explained by observing that each individual has a certain degree of freedom in his or her use of the language and that he or she may also be subject to different influences from other individuals. Major changes occur through the process of language acquisition and at the change of generation. When a number of idiolects move in the same direction the linguistic norm changes too. The novelty here with respect to most of Paul's German predecessors (but not e.g. Whitney) is the awareness of the need to explain not only why languages change in the way in which they do, but also why they change at all. As we have seen, not only an extreme organicism such as that of Schleicher, but even Bopp's more moderate version (p. 87) had previously been able to bypass that problem. On the other hand, Paul, as more modern authors, does not really solve the problem of the relationship of language and idiolect. What defines a speech community? What allows the linguist to select some idiolects and not others in order to identify a specific *Sprachusus*? How can different idiolects change in similar manner so that we can speak of a change in language or *Sprachusus*? Indeed what is *Sprachusus*? A construction of the linguist who indentifies an average between the various idiolects or a norm which influences the performance of the individual? (Cf. Knobloch 1988, 214.) One cannot but agree with one of Paul's conclusions: 'the whole *Prinzipienlehre* of linguistic history focusses on the question: What is the relation between *Sprachusus* and the linguistic activity of the individual? How is the one defined by the other and how does it influence it in its turn?' (Paul 1920, 33).

In spite of all the questions that are left open, Paul's model has the advantage that it combines (or aims at combining) both social and psychological factors under the umbrella of a single theory. But how is this set of views, which is in effect a theory of how language functions, compatible with the often repeated observation that Paul was only interested in language history? A famous passage of the *Prinzipien der Sprachgeschichte* (1920, 20) justifies the book's title, arguing that all **scientific** study of language is historical (*geschichtlich*). What does this mean? Marga Reis (1978, 175ff.) is certainly right in deploring the modern confusion of *geschichtlich* and diachronic. Paul was not arguing for the priority of diachrony over synchrony in linguistics, but simply for an integrated view of the study of language in which both description and the study of historical development played their part. In the passage quoted, he was reiterating his belief that linguistics is a 'cultural science', i.e. a social science, and consequently is not subject to the exact laws of the natural sciences: historical here is contrasted with nomothetic (Graffi 1991, 6off.), but is also equal to cultural and social. The point implicitly made is once again that the science of language is not merely part of psychology, since this is for Paul (1920, 6) an exact science, in fact the only *Geisteswissenschaft* dominated by natural laws. However, it is also true that Paul did not think that a purely syncronic description of a language provided an adequate account of that language. In general he felt that linguistic data call for an explanation and that no explanation was adequate unless it took into account the earlier history of the phenomenon.[38] To a colleague who objected that the book provided a blazing protest against his own thesis that 'Sprachwissenschaft is gleich Sprachgeschichte' ('linguistics equals language history'), Paul replied in a footnote to the fifth edition of the *Prinzipien* (1920, 21, note 1) that his *Prinzipienlehre* was concerned all through with the development of language. Yet the colleague was not altogether wrong; there is ample evidence of Paul's concern for linguistic description and of his awareness that a purely diachronic approach was not possible.[39]

To put it in other terms: What is the role of change in Paul's system? The answer is that Paul, or at least Paul as the author of the *Prinzipien*, was concerned with the functioning of language, and in his view no attempt to understand how language functioned was complete if one did not allow for change as one of the constituent factors of the linguistic phenomenon. Paul was also concerned with a causal explanation of the functioning of language and in his view this could only be provided in historical terms. Rosiello (1986, 24ff.) is certainly right in highlighting how the neogrammarians aimed at causal explanation just as the present-day generativists do, while the later structuralists aimed at a functional explanation. At the same time Paul's general theory prevented a study of change *per se*; this might have been possible as long as one saw the language as an independent object (or organism) but the perennial refrain by Paul and his colleagues is that 'what has been spoken has no development. It is erroneous to say that a word has arisen from a word of an earlier period' (Paul 1920, 28). Continuity, we are told, is only in the mental organism, which is indeed subject to change but whose functioning is infinitely difficult to describe; the linguist is obliged to think in terms of separate states situated in different points of time. Paul – as indeed his contemporaries – has no difficulty in distinguishing between a diachronic and a synchronic approach, even if these terms are not yet available; the contrast normally drawn is that between 'historical' (*geschichtliche* or *entwicklungsgeschichtliche*) and 'static' (*statistische*) or descriptive research.[40] The practical results of the distinction are also recognized. We saw earlier (p. 237) how necessary a purely descriptive approach was felt to be for phonetics or for those languages (such as Lithuanian) which were imperfectly known.[41] In addition, it did not escape the neogrammarians that a descriptive approach allowed systematic analyses, and that in their turn these could lead to a new interpretation of the historical data. Brugmann (1885b, 22) made clear that there were no Indo-European forms in Greek or Latin to be contrasted with new formations, since the old forms now belonged to a new psychological organism where they occupied a different position in the system and consequently were new in their role and value. Similarly, Paul (1920, 31) remarked that one of the standard mistakes of past work consisted in analysing a more recent state of the language in terms of grammatical categories which belonged to an earlier phase or to use etymology in order to understand the meaning of a word. Perhaps more interestingly Paul was also ready to accept the distinction originally drawn by Kruszewski (1881, 1884–90) between sound change and sound alternation: 'Lautwandel' in his terminology referred to change through time, while 'Lautwechsel' referred to allophonic or morphophonemic alternations which could be formulated in synchronic rules (Paul 1901, 201; 1920, 68).[42]

The bulk of the *Prinzipien* is dedicated to sound change, semantic change, analogy and syntax, with the latter (unexpectedly in view of the popular misapprehension about the neogrammarians' rejection of syntactical studies) taking a considerable share. Obviously, given the views expressed above, the main distinction is that between sound change and the rest of linguistic change, with analogy having a major role. We may now turn to a discussion of these topics, while also exploiting in addition to the *Prinzipien* the contributions of other neogrammarians – and of their opponents.

9.3.2 The 'sound laws' debate

All accounts of sound change in this period are necessarily dominated by the slogans found in the early writings of the neogrammarians: sound laws suffer no exceptions, they operate mechanically, they operate with blind necessity, etc. The attacks and the discussion that followed highlighted the difficulties but also clarified a number of problems in synchronic and diachronic phonology.[43] There was first of all disagreement in the assessment of the slogan and the concept. For some of Schleicher's devoted pupils, the statement that sound laws had no exception was simply a repetition of what Schleicher had always taught: Johannes Schmidt (1887), the great Indo-Europeanist professor at Berlin, conceded that Schleicher had not always followed his principles but argued in his defence that Rome had not been built in one day; practical mistakes had to be made before total consistency could set in. At the same time, Schuchardt (1885, 1) thundered from Graz that the only original statement of the neogrammarians concerned the sound laws – and that that was wrong!

An obvious difficulty concerned the obscurity of the wording and the loaded terminology. Sound laws were said to work mechanically but what did mechanically mean in this context? Why did one speak of 'blind necessity'? Mechanical in the first part of the century was contrasted with organic. Presumably in the 1870s the adjective was meant to be read as an anti-Schleicher declaration. And yet it could also be read as a concession to Schleicher's views. To treat language change as determined by irresistible forces external to the speaker was part of Schleicher's organicism, just as the increased importance attributed to sound laws was part of Schleicher's *modus operandi* (cf. pp. 172ff.). The slogans also reflected a dualistic model of language change. Physiological forces determined sound change, while analogy, which operated on grammar, obeyed psychological rules. If so, it was possible to compare the sound laws with the laws of the natural sciences. When Osthoff (1879, 16ff.), who admittedly was no great theoretician (Brugmann 1909a, 218), argued that sound change depended on changes in the organs of speech which were ultimately related to changes in climatic conditions, he was trying to provide a rationale for this view – even if, as was later observed, such statements were not supported by any evidence and were rejected by e.g. Paul. Moreover, it was soon pointed out that a decisive difficulty for the identification of sound laws and natural laws was that the latter had constant validity while sound laws operated only for a determinate period. After the first flush of enthusiasm, both the comparison with natural laws and the use of the adjective 'mechanical' were explicitly dropped, though they continued to influence – negatively – the most rabid of the anti-neogrammarians' reactions.

A different view (roughly that of Paul and Delbrück in the 1880s, which was shared by Brugmann at most stages) also aimed at formulating the phonetic history of a language in terms of sound laws and mantained that 'within a given speech community and in a given period a sound (or a combination of sounds) changes into another sound in all words in which it occurs, independently of their meaning, or alternatively is differently treated, provided that these differences are once more independent of meaning and are consistently conditioned by purely phonetic factors' (Paul 1901, 211).[44] However, it was also stated that the term sound law simply referred to empirically observable regularities and made no claim about their causes. Meaning was given no role in the formulation of sound laws, but the earlier dualism of physiological sound change and psychological analogy was abandoned in favour of a more humdrum attempt better to define the different levels of linguistic analysis; after all even the manifesto (Osthoff and Brugman 1878, iv) had referred to the importance of psychological factors in sound change. For Paul, sound change was determined by a combination of physiological, psychological and historical factors, all of which operated subconsciously. The phonetic performance of speakers is determined by the movements of their speech organs and by their mental

representation of sounds. The latter are more complex than at first supposed: on the one hand speakers form sound images (*Lautbilder*) based
on their auditory experience which act as the model or target or prototype of what sounds ought to be; on the other hand phonetic production
is controlled by the speakers' 'motor sensations' (*Bewegungsgefühle*),
which arise as the result of earlier experience of speech production.
Each one of these elements may undergo some form of displacement
and each one allows for a degree of latitude, which explains why gradual shifts in production or representation remain undetected by the
speakers. The natural tendency, however, is to realign *Lautbilder* and
Bewegungsgefühle when they get out of step, thus allowing for the
implementation of change. It is clear that in Paul's view the normal
mechanism for change within an idiolect would lead to 'regular' change,
i.e. to change which is not influenced by meaning. As he put it: 'a
motor sensation does not arise for each different word, but, wherever
the same elements recur in speech, their production is generated by the
same motor sensation. Thus if the motor sensation is changed because
of the pronunciation of an element in any given word, this change is
also influential for the same element in another word' (Paul 1920, 69).
The conclusion is that as long as we look at idiolects, the regularity
principle is generally observed, the unspoken assumptions being (in
more modern terms) that the pronunciation of all tokens of a given
allophone or phoneme change at the same time and that it changes
gradually since it is unconscious. Paul (1920, 73) nevertheless admitted
the possibility of sudden well-defined changes which were not regular
(metathesis, etc.), thus allowing his opponents to point out that after all
he did not differ from Curtius, who distinguished between sporadic and
regular sound change. Otherwise, according to Paul, possible reasons
for irregularity even within an idiolect may be found in dialect mixture:
a speaker may be influenced for the pronunciation of a certain word
by speakers of one dialect and for that of another word by speakers
of another dialect. In the community at large, again linguistic mixture
may be a cause of irregularity. Later on Brugmann (in Brugmann and
Delbrück 1897–1916, I, i, 70f.) and Delbrück (1902, 120) distinguished
between the primary onset of change (which is unconscious and regular) and the diffusion of change through imitation by other speakers –
which allowed far greater leeway for inconsistency. Sievers (1876, 127)
had previously assumed that the locus of change was the individual
speaker and that all innovations spread through the community at different speed.

A final agreement about the nature and validity of sound laws was
never reached. It was generally accepted (by the neogrammarians and
everyone else) that testing any sound law against the data was bound
to reveal a number of exceptions; in other words, there could not be an

immediate empirical demonstration of the regularity principle; Wundt (1886) argued that it had to be treated as a logical postulate. The neogrammarians did of course maintain that all the exceptions could be explained away by redefining the law, or by identifying a different starting point, or by recognizing the interference with an analogical process, but they were immediately accused of circularity. The objection runs as follows: consider the case of Indo-European *s in ancient Greek. We are told that it is lost in intervocalic position before our first documents. But if so, how do we account for forms such as the aorist ἔλυσα [ely:sa] 'I loosened', where the -s- is inherited from Indo-European and apparently is still there? An answer may be that ἔλυσα is a new analogical formation rebuilt on the model of other aorists where the -sa suffix occurred after a consonant and was not lost. But is this a legitimate procedure? We can say that the sound laws have no exceptions only because when we find an exception we eliminate it saying that there has been analogical interference. On the other hand, we also say that the only way in which we can prove that a form such as ἔλυσα is analogical is by pointing out that otherwise it would be an exception to the sound laws. There seemed to be no obvious counter objection and the problem remained open (see p. 262). Meanwhile, however, the practising historical or comparative linguist continued to, or began to, operate in terms of sound laws not too remote from those pleaded for by the neogrammarians. Sound change was described in formulae of the type $t > d$; further specification concerned the phonological environment of the change (including suprasegmentals) and the period in which the change was operative. In the discussion of the development of a specific language, sometimes it was intuitively felt suitable to derive a word X from a word Y. Yet if the phonological changes involved contradicted the sound laws previously established on the basis of other evidence, other possibilities had to be considered. There may have been two or more relevant sound laws for which a correct chronology had to be set up. If this was not the case, it might have been possible to redefine the relevant sound laws. If the remaining evidence spoke against taking this step, then one had to consider whether X was due to analogical reformation. For this to be plausible, the possible analogical models had to be identified. If these were missing, then X could not be treated as a direct descendant of Y; either there was no etymological connection between X and Y or, even if such connection existed, X had to be a borrowing or the like. The advantage of this model was that it provided clear guidelines for the actual work of the historian and for that of the reviewer of the work actually done. The willing student could be given explicit directions and told how to follow them. Part of the success of the neogrammarians depends on the fact that their students could be easily trained to apply the model, i.e. to identify the sound laws, recognize the exceptions and try to account for the exceptions. Part of the odium, however, arose from the fact that a good many followers applied the model mechanically without too much heart searching.[45]

9.3.3 The analogy debate

From the start all sorts of criticism surrounded the neogrammarians' *Analogisterei*, their desire to *veranalogisieren* everything, i.e. to explain everything through analogy. The difficulties normally mentioned were two: the lack of definition of the analogical process and the circularity of the way in which analogy was apparently invoked in order to preserve the exceptionless nature of sound laws. In addition, the uniformitarian statements made in the name of analogy were not popular in all quarters. Moreover, here too it was possible to challenge the neogrammarians' claim to originality: Curtius (1885, 33ff.) was quick to take the history of the concept back to the Greeks and to assert that no modern author (himself included) had neglected it, while at the same time deploring the use and abuse that the neogrammarians were making of it.[46]

It is indeed the case that analogical change had been identified and exploited by linguists well before the neogrammarians: the names of Pott, Benfey, Schleicher, Curtius, Whitney, Sayce, Ascoli have all been mentioned, but they are only a small subset of the names that could be quoted. Evidence is provided by the many words for analogy lovingly listed by Curtius in his polemical mood (*Analogiebildung*, 'mistaken analogy', *Formübertragung, Parallelbildung* or *Pendantbildung, Association, Angleichung* or *Ausgleichung, Verschleppung, Contamination, stumpfsinnige Übertragung*, etc.). However, for the neogrammarians analogy plays a far more important role than for most of the earlier authors. Osthoff and Brugman (1878) refer back to Steinthal and Scherer, but their immediate debt is to Leskien, who in 1876 (p. 2) stated that all inflectional forms of a language at a given period are the result of either sound change or analogy. In the same year, Brugmann (1876a, 317ff.) argued for the psychological nature of analogy and for its fundamental importance in language development. Analogical formations, according to him, have three characters in common: they are not the result of regular sound change, they are not 'new conceptual formations', and they come into existence because during a speech act speakers have in mind other forms which influence those which they are about to utter.

At this stage, we may note, analogy refers to the process through which new inflectional forms replace existing forms. The original plural of *cliff* is *clives* (which shows the same alternation which we find in *knife, knives*) but either *cliff* is replaced by *clive* or, more normally, *clives* is replaced by *cliffs* (the example is borrowed from Hoenigswald 1978). Cases such as this were unobjectionable, but the neogrammarians failed to make clear that there is no real parallelism (or antagonism) between analogy and sound laws and that Brugmann's first principle (analogical formations are not the result of sound change, i.e. they can be identified because they provide apparent exceptions to the sound laws) was merely heuristic, i.e. a discovery device. In analysing language change, linguists simply compare 'equivalent' (i.e. functionally similar) stretches of speech at different periods. They may first extract all possible regularities which can be expressed in the standard formula of the sound law (x > y) and then look closely at the remaining forms to try to classify them into various categories. No one confronted with the Italian *bello* 'beautiful', which, one may argue, replaced Latin *pulcher* 'beautiful', i.e. with a process which cannot be stated in terms of sound laws, would wish to speak of analogy rather than of lexical replacement. In other words, not all forms which could not be explained through sound laws were analogical and not all exceptions to sound laws could be eliminated advocating analogy. Moreover, Brugmann and his colleagues knew very well that there are instances of clear analogical formations, such as the substitution of Latin *filiabus* 'daughters' (dat. pl.) for Latin *filiis*, which no one had ever tried to treat as an instance of sound change.[47] Some of the difficulties raised by the opponents were bogus but others were not. Why is analogical change so unpredictable; why is *clives* replaced by *cliffs* but *knives* is not replaced by *kniffs*? Are there any constraints on the possible analogical processes? Can any form influence any other form? The neogrammarians agreed in explaining analogical change on the basis of Herbart's association theory. The representations of ideas in the mind join together in patterns of infinite intricacy; representations of sounds, of words, of syntactical patterns, of inflectional patterns, of meanings are grouped in various ways and the elements of each group are likely to influence each other (Paul 1920, 26f.). But this did not solve the question: Why did analogical change occur in some groups but not in others? Nor did it help to sort out the examples of analogical change from lexical change or other types of replacement.

In fact the problems of analogy were more complicated than the early Brugmann (1876a) had made them out to be. In a lengthy article, written one year later, Paul (1877) moved away from the purely historical approach. Analogy, we are now told, is an essential and indispensable factor of speech production. Speakers do not simply repeat parrot-wise forms that they have learned; they do not memorize separately all the inflectional forms of a noun or a verb. They constantly create or re-create forms and they do so on the basis of analogy with other forms. The so-called *falsche Analogie* may lead to the replacement of an existing form (*clives*) with a new form (*cliffs*), but analogy in general is far more pervasive; it is what allows us to create 'correct' or 'regular' forms that we have not heard before or we may have heard but not memorized. Here, and again in the *Prinzipien*, Paul is moving towards a synchronic theory of how language works, which he applies in the first instance to morphology but which could equally well be applied to syntax. Steinthal (1860a, 142f.) had assumed that speakers memorized words but he too had argued that sentences were continuously created or re-created as 'free creation, determined by laws'. Paul similarly assumes that speakers have memorized the basic lexical forms and then uses analogy to explain how the inflected forms are continuously created or re-created.

Analogy in speech production and analogy in language change should not be confused. The latter is relevant when replacement occurs in time (*cliffs* replaces *clives*); the former is, in Paul's view, present in every speech act. The latter, however, depends on the former; the creation of *cliffs* is no different from the creation of the plural of a word which the speaker has not used before. For both it is necessary to ask (and the neogrammarians did ask) how the analogical process works, what linguistic units are involved in it and under what constraints it operates. The historical question opens up further problems: not only, why are forms like *cliffs* created, but also why do such forms eventually replace the earlier *clives*? The first set of questions is, in our terminology, synchronic, the second diachronic. But there is a third set of questions: If analogy is responsible for (re)creating the 'standard' forms, how can it also lead to the creation of new forms. At a time when *clives* was still in use, could one and the same process account for the creation or re-creation of both *clives* and *cliffs*?

To these questions Paul tried to provide an answer in terms of associations and proportional analogy. To start from the end: two different forms may both arise analogically because each word enters into different sets of associations which may prompt different formations. Once the two forms have come into existence, one may be rejected and the other chosen for a variety of different motives, mostly, as we would now say, of a sociolinguistic nature. The new formation may occur in the language of an individual alone and if so it is not likely to spread; however, in suitable circumstances, if the same creation occurs in a number of individuals it may oust the form which was previously current and become acceptable. In other words, once the possibility of analogical creations, i.e. of synchronic analogy – in the sense described above – is accepted, the historical problem, that of analogical change, becomes easier to tackle, though of course there remains that margin of uncertainty which characterizes all historical events.

The real question concerns the operation of analogy as the primary factor in language production. Should we assume that analogy is simply another name for a set of rules which the speaker internalizes? Paul seems to reject this possibility mainly because any set of rules would operate in terms of abstractions to which he is not ready to attribute any validity. To say that *cliffs* is formed by adding a plural marker {s} to {cliff} would mean for Paul to give to {s} the same reality as to {cliff}, but for him one ({cliff}) is 'real', the other ({s}) is an abstraction since it never occurs as a free form. On the other hand, if we think in terms of analogical creations, the problem may be bypassed. Words, as free forms, influence each other; a proportion of the type *animus* : *animī* = *senātus* : *x* provides a model for the way in which new creation comes about. The first two forms are the nominative and genitive singular of the word for soul in Latin, and the third is the nominative singular of the word for 'senate'. To solve the proportion, i.e. to give a value to *x*, means to produce a new form (in this case *senātī*) for the genitive singular of 'senate'.[48] As Paul argued (1920, 110): 'a number of word forms and syntactical combinations which were never impressed onto the mind from outside not only can be generated with the help of proportional groups, but also can afterwards be confidently generated again and again, without the speaker having any inkling of the fact that he is abandoning the safe ground of what he had learned. For the nature of this process it is indifferent whether what emerges was previously current in the language or had never been there before. Nor does it matter if what is produced is in contradiction with what was previously current.'

The problem was naturally that of imposing constraints onto the proportional formula, i.e. of defining what the relationship was between its members; in the second edition of the *Prinzipien,* Paul argued that there must be 'material' and 'formal' agreement between the members of the proportion. This refers to his understanding of the associative groups as being either 'material', i.e. sharing a common lexical value (as in the various inflected forms of *animus*) or 'formal', i.e. sharing common grammatical and phonological properties (as *animus* and *senatus,* which are both nominative singular forms ending in -*us*). Later on Oertel (1901, 156) clarified the point, arguing that in order to account for the range of recognizable analogical formations it was necessary to speak of associations by sound, by sense and by function.

We should not underrate Paul's proportion, as it was often called, nor the general theory as summarized above: in order to recognize instances of analogical change, historical linguists still operate in terms of proportions. We may wish to ask why proportions still retain their (real or apparent) explanatory or definitory power against the background of very different linguistic theories from those advocated by Paul. It is worth noticing, however, that the proportion is a neutral form of notation, i.e. it may be interpreted in cognitive or structural terms and may or may not be reformulated in terms of morphological or morphophonemic rules. At the same time, it also offered an algorithm for a structurally based form of morphological segmentation, without making any claims about the status of the segments in question.[49] More important perhaps is that Paul's concept of analogy and of analogical proportion is a definite attempt at providing a generalized account at a certain level of detail of how language production occurs and of how the speaker and hearer can produce and analyse an infinite number of forms and sentences which they have not heard before.[50]

9.3.4 Language change

A full account of the neogrammarians' tenets should not be confined to a discussion of sound laws and analogy, even though these were the topics most discussed. Yet such an account would inevitably turn into a discussion of all the aspects of historical linguistics, an impossible task in the space available. What the neogrammarians were after was no more and no less than a programme for the study of language change together with an analysis of the history of those languages in which they were interested. The real object of study was language as such but the emphasis was on language change because in their view only a historical account had explanatory power, and their concept of science required that a scientific study offered an explanation of its object. Paul was ready to concede that some linguistic facts could be accounted for in universal psychological terms, but the laws of psychology were not sufficient to account for all the phenomena of language: linguistics, in the view of Paul and his colleagues, remained a historical discipline. The neogrammarians did of course know that all study of change was based on descriptive and 'static' analyses and, when necessary, they turned to the task of language description. Yet for the most part (there were exceptions) they saw description as a somewhat humdrum form of fact-finding, with the facts waiting there to be discovered and arranged in pre-existing slots, rather than as a difficult theoretical enterprise in its own right, which called for a justification of both the categories and the method of analysis to be used. Their historical phonology operated in quasi-phonemic terms, but that was largely because it depended heavily on written sources which tended to be quasi-phonemic. On the other hand, we detect even in the neogrammarians a move towards a 'phonology' different from phonetics. Sievers (1876, 1) was aware of the fact that: 'for the linguist . . . it is not the individual sound that matters but the sound systems of each linguistic unity, their relationship with each other and their gradual alteration'. Paul (1920, 51) commented on the difficulties encountered in dividing the phonetic continuum into segments and on the infinite variability of sounds. His dislike for abstractions leads him to what Lepschy ([1962] 1989, 35) called 'una posizione "antifonematica" *ante litteram*' (cf. Graffi 1988, 229), but his concept of a mental *Lautbild* which acts as a form of constraint on too high a level of variability was not too distant from the psychological definitions of the phoneme popular in the first part of the twentieth century. The position of morphology is not very different. The study of analogy called attention to morphophonemic questions but, as we have seen, there was considerable reluctance to discuss any criteria for segmentation and the basic unit remained the word, with all problems that that entailed. By contrast, the categories of morphosyntax were explicitly discussed not only by Paul and Delbrück, but also by e.g. Brugmann (1902–4). Yet here, as Graffi (1991, 124) has pointed out, uncertainty prevails following the general (but not total) scepticism about the usefulness of the old logical categories and the introduction of somewhat nebulous psychological categories which seem to exist both with logical and with grammatical categories. On the other hand, those grammars which added to *Laut- und Formenlehre* a syntactical part, used the traditional categories without too much agonizing.[51]

9.4 Reconstruction and history

Is the neogrammarians' emphasis on language change and historical linguistics as contrasted with reconstruction and comparative linguistics in any way a novelty? Kiparsky (1974) has argued that at some stage, before the neogrammarians, there was a paradigm shift in historical and comparative linguistics. Bopp had aimed at reconstructing proto-forms which could be explained in terms of logical forms; the linguists of the late 1860s or 1870s aimed at reconstructing proto-forms which provided an explanation for the attested forms. The distinction is not as sharp as Kiparsky suggests: in the case of Bopp, the aims of his youth were not those of his maturity. Moreover, some of his contemporaries – one thinks of Grimm and Humboldt – had different interests. It is true, however, that round 1870 the reconstruction of Indo-European could (though need not) be seen in a different light: no longer as the major aim but rather as a means to an end, i.e. a means for lengthening the history of a language and consequently providing better evidence to account for the existing forms. Delbrück (1880, 56, 100) quoted with approval Johannes Schmidt's statement that 'the task of Indo-European linguistics is to establish what the forms of the parent language were and in what way the forms of the individual languages have arisen from them'. It would be easy, of course, to explain the importance of reconstruction in Bopp by appealing to his rationalism, were it not for the fact that an interest in the earliest phases of language and a desire to go back to the origins is also typical of Romanticism. The later concentration on change, which naturally involves a comparison of language states, i.e. of 'static' descriptions, was better in tune with the prevailing psychologism. At the same time, the down-to-earth attitude engendered by the omnipresent positivism was more sympathetic to the study of attested facts than to that of speculative reconstructions.[52] However, the shift in attitude is also internally driven. On the one hand, among Indo-Europeanists the introduction of phonologically explicit reconstructions (which happened round the middle of the century) necessarily called for an account of the intermediate stages between the starred forms and the attested data. On the other hand, when a division of labour arose between Indo-Europeanists and Romance philologists, the latter naturally turned out to be more interested in development than in reconstruction; when they reconstructed they did it in order to explain the later developments.

Yet another factor helped to account for the shift in interests: the new developments in geology, anthropology, archaeology and biology. In the first part of the century it could still be assumed that man had been around, as the Bible indicated, for some 6000 years, but by the mid 1860s even Charles Lyell (1863) had had to admit on the basis of archaeological evidence that traces of human beings were present at a much earlier stage. Darwinism made the point even more forcefully. At this stage it could no longer be believed that the reconstruction of Indo-European, or, for that matter, of any language family, provided evidence for the language of the first men; the interest of the anthropologists in comparative philology evaporated,[53] and so did, to a certain extent, the concern of comparative philologists for reconstruction as an end in itself. The neogrammarians were certainly interested in the reconstructed language but were not eager to build too much on it.[54] In addition they were far more uncertain about the validity of their reconstructions than their predecessors. In some instances the evidence led to two alternative reconstructions and in others to no reconstruction: though it was clear that a specific word or morpheme had existed in the parent language, it was not possible to define its form with certainty. The question then arose whether what was reconstructed was a linguistic system or simply a construct by the linguist on the basis of a series of forms which perhaps had never coexisted.[55] Clearly the nature of the exercise had changed from the time of Bopp.

9.5 The programme and its outcome

Did the neogrammarians achieve their aim? Did they produce a viable programme for the study of language change? In 1932 Leonard Bloomfield reviewed – more in sorrow than in anger – Eduard Hermann's belated attack against the neogrammarians' concepts of sound law and analogical proportion (1931) and stated that 'the methods developed by the linguists of the nineteenth century are still the working methods of every competent linguist, including Hermann. They have been refined and supplemented, but not replaced, by later acquisitions, notably the phonemic principle and the mapping of dialect differences. Under these methods the phenomena of linguistic change, which baffled the scholars of the seventeenth and eighteenth centuries, can be compactly recorded and classified, and even subjected, within methodically defined limits, to inference and prediction. Like all scientific methods, they are justified by their performance and only by this' (Bloomfield 1932, 220). At the end he added: 'Regrettable as it is that a swing of fashion can lead a scholar of Hermann's metal to waste his time on such theories as these, one feels that in practice he will continue to use and refine the methods of our science' (*ibid.*, 232). The last sentence is significant: it is indeed difficult to think of any fundamental difference in the practice of historical work between the neogrammarians and their immediate followers, on the one hand, and the scholars of Hermann's or Bloomfield's generation on the other. It is also significant that at this stage Bloomfield was ready to jettison in full the psychological baggage which he had learned in Leipzig at the feet of Brugmann and Wundt, but was quietly confident that the techniques and methods of historical enquiry that he had applied both to Germanic and to American Indian languages were still valid.

Of the method Bloomfield (1932, 221) gave a masterly summary:

> the method of linguistic history classifies linguistic change into three great empirical types. One type is the change of phonemes or combination of phonemes, such as [þ] > [d] in older German, or, more recently, [st-] > [št-] in part of the German area. The second type is the extension of significant elements into new combinations, which we call analogic change (E *cow-s* beside older *kine*) or semantic change (E *bread and meat* beside older *bread and flesh* or *bread and flesh-meat*). The third type is the adoption of features and forms from foreign speech, as in E *rouge* from French, or Central-Western American E ['raðr] *rather* from New England, beside native ['reðr]. This classification, and all the technique that goes with it, is the common equipment and, up to the present day, the only methodical equipment, of all linguists, from Eduard Hermann down to the greenest student.

No doubt the 'nineteenth century masters' to whom Bloomfield later refers are those of the neogrammarians' persuasion. We may now enlarge on his summary, while trying to see where, if anywhere, the dividing line between the neogrammarians and their predecessors lies. The attacks, which either accused them of repeating older views or rejected their assumptions as wild and incoherent, are of little help in this task. Bloomfield was able to cut through the fuss and the verbiage (or, at least, we may assume that he did) and to realize that the regularity principle served the purposes of definition and its formulation was in fact tautological.[56] In a sense all linguistic change is sound change. Yet we call sound changes those changes which are regular and in this way we distinguish phonological change from the other types of change recognized by Bloomfield. As Hoenigswald (1978, 27) observed, by any pragmatic test this decision was singularly fruitful. If the role of sound laws is that of defining phonological change, it then becomes clear why Brugmann stated that analogical innovations are not the result of sound change (see above, p. 256); this followed from the basic distinction between phonological and non-phonological change. When Wundt later on treated under the heading of *Lautwandel* (sound change) phonological assimilation and dissimilation on the one hand, and analogical change on the other as examples of similar developments (*Associative Contactwirkungen der Laute* and *Associative Fernwirkungen der Laute* respectively), Paul (1920, 116, note 1) objected that this was impossible: if in modern German the old form *sturben* 'they died' is replaced by the new form *starben*, this is because *starben* is created on the model of *starb*, 'he died' as a wholly new form. Wundt, by contrast, assumed that the *u* of *sturben* was replaced by the *a* of *starb* through some form of assimilation at distance. If challenged, Bloomfield would probably have said that, in doing so, Wundt was jettisoning all chances of distinguishing between the various types of linguistic change.[57]

9.5.1 Language history and the causes of change

In his letter to Pietro Merlo about the neogrammarians, Ascoli (1886) implied that perhaps too much fuss was made about the regularity principle (with which he fundamentally agreed) and too little about the causes of sound change; he referred, of course, to his own theory of ethnic substratum, i.e. to his view that fundamental changes in language could be traced to the influence of submerged populations which somehow transmitted (through a far more complex process than that of borrowing) some of their phonological characteristics to the people superimposed (see p. 181 note 12 and cf. e.g. Silvestri 1982, 1986). Bloomfield (1932, 224), in the review of Hermann (1931) which we discussed above, states with his normal bluntness: 'Our assumptions (that is, to repeat, our working methods) leave a great many facts unexplained. . . . We do not know why a given change occurs when and where it does. . . . In this linguistics is no better off than the other branches of human study: we are forced to embody every descriptive or historical fact in a separate little assumption. Finally, we can co-ordinate our basic assumptions about linguistic change with our knowledge of non-linguistic processes only in the matter of linguistic borrowing, which is obviously a phase of cultural borrowing in general'. Ascoli was of course right in noticing the lack of interest shown by the neogrammarians for the causality of change as contrasted with its mechanism.[58] Bloomfield, who in diachrony was fundamentally a neogrammarian, knew that the

causes of change had not been established, i.e. no adequate generalization had been produced, even if 'separate little assumptions' might be
useful on occasion. This withdrawal from the major problems about the
causes of change and Bloomfield's acknowledgement that except in a
very limited area it is difficult, if not impossible, to coordinate the study
of language change and that of non-linguistic phenomena may well be
linked. They may also explain why, in spite of their immense productivity, the neo-grammarians never turned to the so-called 'history of the
language'; they wrote a number of historical grammars, but we shall
have to wait until the beginning of the new century to find Ferdinand
Brunot's *Histoire de la langue française* (Vol. 1, 1905) and the short
Growth and Structure of the English Language by Otto Jespersen (1905)
as well as the twenty pages about the history of ancient Greek published by Jacob Wackernagel (1905) in a collective volume. None of
these three authors can be properly labelled a neogrammarian.[59] To do
history of the language might have meant to return to the Romantic
beliefs about the inextricable connection of language and nation, language and *Geist*, or to develop a theory about the relationship of social
and linguistic facts or at the very least to accept an ethnically based
view of language change, but the neogrammarians, in spite of their all-
pervading energy, were not ready to move in this direction. It was not
cowardice or ignorance but rather a desire not to make hypotheses that
could not be verified.

9.5.2 The neogrammarians and the earlier problems

Abstract terms or analyses were avoided. But, if so, how did the neogrammarians answer the more specific questions which the linguists
had been asking from the beginning of the century? It is significant that
in 1880 Delbrück felt that some discussion of these problems was
necessary.

As we have seen (p. 131), Bopp himself had assumed that there was
no advantage in discussing the origin of roots; by the 1860s, 1870s such
problems tended to be regarded by established linguists as insoluble
and were ignored. Predictably the neogrammarians shared this view.
Indeed they went further and denied the historical existence of the roots
as such; they were simply abstractions from existing lexical forms (see
below). The position was different for questions such as the origin of
Ablaut and that of inflections. We may remember the importance attributed by Friedrich Schlegel (p. 68) to *Ablaut* as a mark of the superior
type of languages which generated inflections from their innermost
core or the quasi-mystical view of the Germanic *Ablaut* held by Grimm
(p. 144). The controversy which had started with Bopp's 'mechanical'
view (p. 135) now reaches an end, since it can be shown that in Indo-
European the simplest type of roots contained an *e-* or *o*-vowel which

was normally accented; if the accent was removed from the root (and fell e.g. on the ending), then the vowel was lost (*éi-mi 'I go' but i-més 'we go'). In this way Ablaut was seen as due to the grammaticalization of an Indo-European morphophonemic process originally determined by a phonetic change which had taken place in Indo-European itself – a view which had only recently become possible because, with the acceptance of uniformitarianism, it was no longer necessary to assume that all 'decay' was post-Indo-European. Thus what Schlegel had taken as the inflection par excellence was in the end seen to be not 'organic', but 'mechanical', even if prompted by a different 'mechanism' than that suggested by Bopp.

Was Bopp fundamentally right also about the origin of the normal inflectional forms? Did they originate through the agglutination of independent elements (pronouns or the copula) to the word root or stem? Or was it necessary to return to Schlegel's view of endings sprouting from roots all ready to fulfil their functional potential? It was difficult to accept Schlegel's view, which was too ill-defined for comfort and which had as a corollary that, in order to account for the similarity between endings and pronouns, somehow the pronouns had to be extracted from the inflectional forms. Yet we saw already (p. 176f.) the complications that arose from a simple agglutinative view according to which the pronouns were added to roots to yield inflectional forms. The phonology did not work: Schleicher (1871, 653–5) explained the second person singular endings of the Greek present -eis and -si, past -s, imperative -thi and perfect -tha as all derived from his reconstructed second person singular pronoun *tva 'thou', postulating phonetic changes which were not attested anywhere else. Similarly, the second person singular perfect leloipas 'you have left', according to Schleicher (ibid.) derived from *leloipta, with a somewhat implausible derivation, though not as implausible as that which derived the Greek second person plural ending -te from -tva-tva, i.e. 'thou thou' = 'you'. The young Brugmann (1878), who in this is representative of the neogrammarians, rejected most of these suggestions: (a) the phonology did not work, (b) the semantic development (especially in the plural) was implausible, (c) all existing languages show a variety of procedure which allow them to renew their inflectional morphology and there is no reason to suppose that Indo-European would not have done the same. If so, why should we assume that all personal endings derive from personal pronouns? It would be more plausible to assume that some did, but others had different origins. The example is representative of the cautious attitude taken by the neogrammarians; it goes together with a declared anti-glottogonic stance which almost becomes a declaration of faith. In his detailed reconsideration of the whole issue, the more mature Delbrück (1880, 100) concluded that in some instances it was possible – at best – to claim that the hypothesis had a certain likelihood; in most instances, however, the conclusion was a bare *non liquet*.

A final example of the contrast between the neogrammarians and their predecessors leads us back to the theory of the root. Agglutination theory had implicitly or explicitly assumed that the Indo-European roots (and presumably the roots of any other inflected or agglutinative language) had originally existed as independent items, as words in their own right. Pott (e.g. 1833–6, i, 148) had denied it but with little success. Max Müller ([1868] 1868–75, iv, 126) reiterated that 'Language ... begins with roots, which are not only the ultimate facts for the Science of Language, but real facts in the history of human speech'. We have also seen how Geiger (1868–72) had exploited the concept of free-standing independent root in order to tackle a problem of *Ablaut* and accentuation (p. 176). The new anti-glottogonic reaction was bound to object to the assumption, since there was no direct evidence for it. Delbrück (1880, 73ff.) discussed the question in the usual self-denying style, but was inclined to assume that in a very early period of Indo-European, before the creation of inflection, roots may have been free forms, though, if so, we would not be able to say anything about them. Brugmann returned to it again and again in the successive editions of his works, eventually reaching the conclusion that we had no right to assume that the roots were independent words in the parent language. Indo-European, in his view, could well have started as an uninflected language, but this did not imply that any individual root that we attribute to it had had a separate existence; we segment roots as etymological or morphological units without making any assumption about their earlier status (Brugmann and Delbrück 1897–1916, I, 1, 32ff.). At a later stage, Brugmann (1902–4, 282; in Brugmann and Delbrück 1897–1916, ii [1906], 5) was firmer: roots, at least in the sense in which we use the word, are grammatical constructs which point to the etymological relationship of a group of words. It is conceivable that at an earlier stage some of them had a separate existence as free forms, but it is impossible to reach such a conclusion for any specific case. In the earlier treatment, he had also noted, however, that roots, suffixes, etc. not only were morphological-etymological constructs, as he put it, but also had some psychological value; the naïve speaker could operate in terms of similar categories and, e.g. segment the German *Tages* 'of the day' into *Tag-es*, etc. (Brugmann and Delbrück 1897–1916, I, 1, 37f.). Yet it should be clear that these categories had nothing to do with any original form which could be deemed to have actually existed as such. We are approaching here a discussion about the synchronic value of morphemic analysis and its psychological implications (cf. also Paul 1920, 350). Years before, in the discussions about proportional analogy (see p. 257f.), it had also become clear that the proportional formula served not only to symbolize the process which led to analogical change but also to define the synchronic process which allowed morphological segmentation and was in the last resort responsible for the fact that the speakers were constantly (re)creating new combinations of morphemes. The starting point there was the reluctance of Paul (and before him Havet) to formulate their description of either historical or 'static' events in terms of abstract units (roots, suffixes, etc.; we would call them morphemes) which were not free forms (cf. note 48). Conceivably Bopp would have been equally reluctant to operate in terms of abstract segments, but behind his *Zergliederung* there lay the conviction that in the Indo-European period his roots and suffixes were separate words. Moreover, the tacit assumption prevailed that 'wordhood' in the 'organic' period was an adequate guarantee of independent status even in the later period. Once this set of beliefs had been called into doubt, as was done by the neogrammarians, the whole question of the units used in history and in description again raised its head – with beneficial effects. Paradoxically, the neogrammarians were brought back to problems of description by their own historical concerns and by the collapse (which to a certain extent they had engineered, but which was fundamentally data-driven) of the historical certainties with which they had been brought up.

9.6 The neogrammarians' legacy

The great Johannes Schmidt (1843–1901),[60] a pupil and supporter of Schleicher who would not have liked to be called a neogrammarian, had stated in a passage which Delbrück (1880, 57) selected for approval and to which we have already referred: 'Auf diesem Gebiete schreitet, wie es einer gesunden Wissenschaft geziemt, die Erkenntniss des Nichtwissens von Jahr zu Jahr fort' ('In this field the realization of our ignorance makes greater and greater strides every year, as is suitable for a healthy discipline'). The neogrammarians could have adopted this phrase as their motto. If we compare them with the scholars of the beginning of the century, with Grimm or Humboldt, or even Bopp, their ambitions were modest. They worked on language change, concentrating on what we would now call core linguistics: phonetics and phonology, morphology, syntax when possible, and sometimes lexical semantics. They pleaded for a study of modern and living languages and, if not them, at least some of their pupils turned to the living languages: Joseph Wright to English dialects, Leonard Bloomfield to Menomini, Meyer-Lübke to Romance, Thumb to Modern Greek. What they knew they systematized with that relentless hard work which characterized them. What they did not know in specific fields they found out (we still live on the results of their labours), but they maintained – and sometimes demonstrated – that there was a great deal which was not known and perhaps would never become known. Their programme was one of deliberate retrenchment. They did not work on comparative religion like Max Müller, they did not produce any extensive work on the *Urheimat*, or the *Ur*-culture, they did not consider the contribution of language to *Geistesgeschichte* or to philosophy. It is not due to chance that so far in this chapter we have had no occasion to discuss the typological classification of languages. The neogrammarians did not discuss it either. In general they worked on the languages which they knew and knew well. In the jargon of the market place they would have described the history of Bopp's discipline as similar to that of a large firm, which had started with a good new product, the comparative method, had expanded and had been successful but had overreached itself in the attempt to provide too wide a range of merchandise. The need, they would have said, was now for a new management who would know how to retract and concentrate on quality output, while exploiting the new technology to repackage the old products and improve the way in which they were manufactured. Like Bopp, the neogrammarians had no lightness of touch, but, like Bopp, they had the Kantian qualities: *Gründlichkeit, Beharrlichkeit und anhaltender Fleiss.*[61]

But what about the attacks, the praise and the denigration? How justified were they? Is it true that all the neogrammarians' tenets were taken from elsewhere? Is it true that the only original thought they had had, as Schuchardt (1885) had argued, concerned the principle of regularity and that that was wrong? In the case of Schuchardt, the sharpest of the serious opponents, the difficulty was that he would have raised similar objections against any form of generalization and that the principle of regularity lent itself to different interpretations, some of which he missed (see above, p. 262f.). On the other hand, there is a part of truth in the first of these indictments, as Brugmann (1885b) happily acknowledged. Curtius (1885) was right in saying that he had not been given enough credit for the use he had made of sound laws and analogy – but then Curtius was no uniformitarian. Ascoli (1886–8) was right in arguing that his method and that of the neogrammarians were fundamentally the same and that there was no great novelty in all the talk about analogical change, since the Romanists had always thought in those terms, but his concept of analogy was not the same as that of the neogrammarians (Vallini 1972, 37) and the uniformitarian fight was less important for those dealing with Romance than for the Indo-Europeanists. Above all, Kruszewski (1884–90: 1884, 299) was right in claiming precedence in this field for Baudouin de Courtenay, but his work on Polish was not sufficiently known. Johannes Schmidt (1877) spoke of Schleicher's strong belief in sound laws, but he had to admit that Schleicher did not practise what he preached. As for the attack against Schleicher's organicism and the defence of uniformitarianism, they had been preceded by Madvig, by Bréal, by Whitney, etc. (Aarsleff 1982, 293ff.) as well as by e.g. Steinthal and Baudouin de Courtenay. In general it is possible to find antecedents for most of the neogrammarians' statements in earlier work, and those who, like Ascoli, complained that there was no absolute novelty in their theoretical pronouncements cannot be faulted. The novelty, as was argued earlier, consisted on the one hand in defining a working method for the study of change with such clarity that it could be, and was, imitated – and produced results; on the other hand in realizing that the concrete work had to be accompanied by a statement of what was done: a *Prinzipienlehre*, not necessarily a philosophy. But perhaps the greatest achievement is that of having been able to concentrate on language *an und für sich*, as Bopp had wished, and to have done it with such thoroughness and such singlemindedness that both the merits and the weaknesses of the approach were revealed. Some of those in close contact with the neogrammarians went on to do what the neogrammarians had recommended, others went on to do what the neogrammarians had not done. It may not be chance that both Bloomfield and Saussure, who played such a role in the creation of linguistic structuralism, had passed through Leipzig.

Notes

1. Sweet (1888, xi) states that he and Ellis, the author of a number of volumes on early English pronunciation, 'were the first in England (with the brilliant exception of John Kemble) to apply German methods to English philology', although from the beginning they had 'set their faces against the "woodenness" which then characterized German philology: its contempt for phonetics and living speech and reverence for the dead letter, its one-sidedly historical spirit, and disregard of analogy.' In the next sentence he also affirms that he had been one of the first in England 'to welcome the "neo-philological" reformers who have rescued German philology from its earlier stagnation of methods' (the reference is to the neogrammarians, who are seen here as a positive force).
2. Savoia (1986) describes the tension among Italian dialectologists between the needs of synchronic description and the historical-comparative model of German inspiration.
3. The periodical was founded and edited by Friedrich Techmer (1834–91), who taught phonetics and general linguistics at Leipzig; the first number was dedicated to Humboldt's memory. It had a much wider range than the more specialized periodicals founded by the neogrammarians, since it dealt with general problems, with phonetics, with non-Indo-European languages, etc. It also made a point of reprinting important works of the past, such as John Wilkins' *Essay* of 1668, Bopp (1820), etc.. For its role in the history of linguistics, cf. Koerner (1973b) and Barozzi (1984).

4. The arrival of Curtius (in 1861) marked the beginning of Leipzig's importance in the field. Later on most foreign scholars in linguistics came to Leipzig
to study, attracted in succession by Curtius, Leskien, Brugmann and Wundt:
after Ferdinand de Saussure at a later stage one must at least mention Joseph
Wright, who then succeeded Max Müller at Oxford and worked extensively
on English dialectology as well as translating the first volume of Brugmann's
Grundriß. From America at different periods came Maurice Bloomfield,
the American comparativist and Sanskritist of German origin, who was a
pupil of Whitney and then became professor at Johns Hopkins', and his
nephew Leonard Bloomfield, one of the founders of American structuralism.

5. For our period, the *Literarisches Centralblatt* published lists of all lectures
given in German Universities.

6. The description of the contemporary German scene by the American classicist Basil Gildersleeve (1884, 354) applied to classics but no doubt to linguistics as well: 'I do not yield to anyone in admiration of German learning,
conscientiousness, inventiveness, grasp, but the more I have seen of the
arrogance, the jealousy, the hateful manoeuvering, the shameful backbit-
ing, the hatred, awry, malice and all uncharitableness, which a closer knowledge of the professor's life in Germany reveals, the more glad am I to live
where, if such abominations exist, they do not, like the frogs of Egypt, go
up and come into our houses and into our bedchambers and upon our beds
and upon our ovens and into our kneading troughs'.

7. Karl Brugmann published his first works under the name of Brugman,
but after 1882 the family adopted the alternative spelling with final -*nn*
(Streitberg 1919, 143). Here the later form has been used all through
except for the list of references.

8. The composition of the core group of the neogrammarians is disputed.
The list given here is that of Einhauser (1989); that there was a close link
between its members is shown by the letters which she publishes in the
appendix to her book (cf. also Einhauser 1992). A slightly different list is
offered by e.g. Jankowsky (1972, 128), who treats Leskien as one of the
neogrammarians and adds the Germanist Friedrich Kluge (1856–1926)
to the list.

9. Even an abbreviated list would include: Misteli (1880), Müller (1884),
Curtius (1885), Schuchardt (1885), Ascoli (1886–8), Collitz (1886), Jespersen
(1887), Schmidt (1887), etc. In the crucial period (1885) which followed
Curtius's last work (*Zur Kritik der neuesten Sprachforschung*), the neogrammarians replied in kind: cf. Brugmann (1885b), Delbrück (1885), Osthoff
(1886), etc.

10. The secondary literature on the neogrammarians is extensive, partly because
of the interest and importance of the subject, partly because the movement
keeps being quoted as evidence for or against the applicability of Kuhn's
model to the history of linguistics. Here we shall neglect the standard
histories of linguistics and give only selected indications for the remaining bibliography. There are some monographs and some collections of articles: on the one hand, Jankowsky (1972) (cf. also Jankowsky 1976, 1979),
Vennemann and Wilbur (1972), Schneider (1973), Einhauser (1989); on the
other, the articles by Robins, Hoenigswald, Morpurgo Davies, Collinge,

Allen, Bynon collected in the volume of *Transactions of the Philological Society* (1978) dedicated to the neogrammarians, and those by Rosiello, Ramat, Savoia, Silvestri, Campanile and Bolelli published in Quattordio Moreschini (1986). Hoenigswald, Rosiello and Bolelli provide general assessments which are more than summaries of previous work. Wilbur (1977) republishes with a long introduction some of the basic texts by the neogrammarians and their opponents about the sound-law controversy. Vallini (1972) concentrates on the history of analogy, giving pride of place to the neogrammarians; for the same subject, cf. also Esper (1973); Anttila and Brewer (1977) offer a useful checklist of references. Other articles will be quoted later on; here we may at least mention Putschke (1969, 1984), Graffi (1988) and various articles by Koerner (reprinted in Koerner 1978 and Koerner 1989); cf. also Koerner (1975, 776ff.). Amsterdamska (1987) is particularly interesting for her discussion of the neogrammarians' intellectual assumptions and institutional background; the correspondence between Brugmann and Osthoff published by Einhauser (1992) is very informative. Cf. also Graffi (1991) for the neogrammarians' theories about syntax, and Knobloch (1988) for their psychologism; Nerlich (1992, 87ff.) discusses Paul's views about semantics.

11. For Wilhelm Scherer, a Germanist who became professor at Berlin, cf. also pp. 192, 219 note 4. In the first edition of his *Zur Geschichte der deutschen Sprache* (1868) he pleaded for phonetics and for the importance of *Formübertragung* (analogy); in the second edition (1878) he reproduced a number of pages of his earlier (1875) review of Whitney-Jolly (1874; cf. Whitney 1867), where he had made a strong plea for uniformitarianism and had also stated that the sound changes which one can observe in attested data proceed according to firm laws which suffer no disturbance that is not itself determined by laws (Scherer 1878, 17). Though Scherer is quoted with respect in the manifesto, the relationship between him and Paul, or him and the Leipzig people in general, soon deteriorated, largely as the result of a bad review by Paul of the second edition of Scherer's book and of the fact that the Leipzig Germanists had taken an anti-Berlin side in the so-called *Nibelungenstreit*, which concerned the manuscripts of the *Nibelungenlied* (cf. Einhauser 1989, 61–83).

12. This is the first full formulation of the so-called regularity principle: 'Aller lautwandel, so weit er mechanisch vor sich geht, vollzieht sich nach **ausnahmslosen gesetzen**, d.h. die richtung der lautbewegung ist bei allen angehörigen einer sprachgenossenschaft, ausser dem fall, dass dialektspaltung eintritt, stets dieselbe, und alle wörter, in denen der der lautbewegung unterworfene laut unter gleichen verhältnissen erscheint, werden ohne ausnahme von der änderung ergriffen' (Osthoff and Brugman 1878, xiii).

13. Cf. Ribbeck (1879–81, ii, 450), but, as Henry Hoenigswald points out to me, Friedländer (1883, 158) rejects the joint attribution of the ten commandments to Ritschl and Lehrs and states that they were compiled by Karl Lehrs (1802–78), the Königsberg classicist, alone.

14. Here we ignore all secondary literature except for a few recent articles. For more detailed information and references, cf. Einhauser (1989, 9–60). For the correspondence between Osthoff and Brugmann, see Einhauser (1992).

15. In 1978 the *Paul-Braune Beiträge* (see below) celebrated the appearance of their one hundredth volume with a series of articles about the founders: cf. Reis (1978) and Huber (1978) on Paul, Ganz (1978) on Sievers, and Fromm (1978) on Braune. The volume also contains the publication of an exchange of letters between Paul, Braune and Sievers (Baur 1978) and of some letters by Zarncke (Pretzel 1978).

16. In 1876 the other editors, in addition to Leskien and Sievers, were H. Hübschmann (1848–1908), who was then Extraordinarius at Leipzig and produced outstanding work on Armenian (he demonstrated that it was not an Iranian dialect) and Iranian; Gustav Meyer (1850–1900), the Albanologist who also wrote for the series its third volume, the *Griechische Grammatik* (1880); E. Windisch (1844–1918), a pupil and biographer of Georg Curtius, Ordinarius for Sanskrit and Comparative Linguistics at Leipzig from 1877, a Sanskritist and Celticist who at a later stage at least was despised by Leskien and Brugmann (Einhauser 1989, 54, 372ff.). Later on, Delbrück, the author of the *Einleitung in das Sprachstudium*, which appeared as the fourth volume of the series (1880), is listed among the editors. The second volume was Whitney's Sanskrit grammar (1879), which, as G. Meyer ([1880] 1886, v) noted, was not comparative but descriptive (though it used both Vedic and Sanskrit evidence).

17. In an early review, Brugmann (1875) wrote 'the *statistische* method that recently has produced such convincing conclusions in the field of Greek syntax [the reference is to Tycho Mommsen's work on the prepositions σύν and μετά] here too has yielded something new and discovered widely accepted mistakes'.

18. Brugmann's inaugural lecture in Freiburg was entitled *Sprachwissenschaft und Philologie*, in constrast with, or imitation of, Curtius's inaugural lecture entitled *Philologie und Sprachwissenschaft* (cf. p. 186 note 40); Brugmann (1885b, 18ff.) pleaded for the non-separation of the two disciplines. As he said, it had been argued that descriptive or *statistische* grammar was the province of philology, and evolutionary historical (*entwicklungsgeschichtliche*) grammar that of comparative linguistics, but at least in Celtic and Lithuanian the linguists had done the philological work and indeed started it. Also there was no reason to believe that philology concerned itself with the higher and more developed forms of linguistic use, literature, and linguistics with the lower, more primitive forms, since current thinking assumed that the same factors operated in language at all stages. Finally, Brugmann argued, there is no distinction between early and late phases of a language; in principle at least the history of a language is a continuum from prehistory to modern days and any division is purely a matter of convenience (cf. also Brugmann in Brugmann and Delbrück 1897–1916, I 1, 28f.).

19. Amsterdamska (1987, 121ff., especially 134ff.) argues that, since the neogrammarians were operating within an institutional background in which academic positions in modern languages were fast increasing, their professed interest in modern languages and modern philologies was also a bid for institutional expansion. This is in some sense true but in my view the cognitive factors, to use Amsterdamska's terminology, are more important.

Moreover, the so-called modern philologies more often than not were medieval philologies and the Germanists such as Paul, Braune and Sievers were medievalists both *de facto* and *de jure*; no Indo-Europeanist who used Germanic evidence could fail to be a medievalist. Finally, this move towards modern languages was even more prominent in England – where the academic power game was entirely different. The same conclusions can be reached looking at the Italian scene.

20. It is impossible here to go into the details of this type of work. Pedersen ([1931] 1962) and Tagliavini (1963, 1968) offer the best accounts; for more detailed discussion, see Bechtel (1892) and the volumes in the series edited by Streitberg under the general title *Die Erforschung der indoger-manischen Sprachen* (1916–29). For the vocalism of Indo-European as such, see, in addition to Benware (1974), who does not cover our period, Hübschmann (1885) and again Bechtel (1892); cf. also Mayrhofer (1983).

21. For recent literature, cf. Collinge (1985, 203–16). Karl Verner (1846–96) himself was a remarkably unworldly scholar who in the whole of his life published practically nothing else (though his intellectual life continued vigorously and, e.g. he worked extensively in phonetics). He was for a while Librarian in Halle and then taught Slavic languages in Copenhagen. On the strength of his article he was awarded the Bopp medal of the Berlin Academy and an honorary degree by the University of Heidelberg (see Jespersen [1897] 1970, 12–23 = Sebeok 1966, i, 538–48).

22. Gothic *i* (cf. *sibun* 'seven'), which corresponded to *e* in other Germanic languages, was recognized as an innovation which reflected an earlier Germanic *e*.

23. For the so-called Brugmann's Law (whose validity and exact formulation is still disputed), cf. Collinge (1985, 13ff.) with references.

24. Saussure had reached the same conclusion while still at school, but in 1876 he heard in Leipzig from H. Hübschmann of Brugmann's discovery and of the fact that his idea was going to be published by another before he could do so (cf. De Mauro 1970b, 290ff. with references, Kohrt 1985, 113ff.).

25. Collitz (1855–1935) studied at Göttingen with August Fick and at Berlin with Johannes Schmidt; at some stage he replaced Verner as Librarian at Halle, but after that accepted an appointment at Bryn Mawr in the United States and from there moved to Johns Hopkins University in 1907. He was the first president of the Linguistic Society of America (1925).

26. In the history of linguistics the law of the palatals is a striking case. We still dispute which one of ten or six or five or, at best, three scholars discovered it first (Mayrhofer 1983, 137ff., Collinge 1985, 133ff.; Collinge 1987); Hermann Collitz, Ferdinand de Saussure, Johannes Schmidt, Esaias Tegnér, Vilhelm Thomsen, Karl Verner all compete for the honour. The interesting point is that these were scholars of very different persuasions. Karl Verner was to all effects and purposes a quasi-neogrammarian, while Collitz and Schmidt were very much on the other side of the fence.

27. For Saussure's *Mémoire*, see Vallini (1969), Vincenzi (1979) (with a long discussion of the history of *Ablaut*), Gmür (1980, 1986), Mayrhofer (1981, 1988), Koerner (1987). The book's centenary was commemorated in the

Cahiers Ferdinand de Saussure with a special number which includes articles by Kuryłowicz (1978), Redard (1978a, b), Vallini (1978) and Watkins (1978). The best reviews or accounts are by Havet in the *Journal de Genève* of 25 February 1879 (cf. Redard 1976, 1978b) and by Kruszewski (1880). Marchese (cf. Saussure 1995, xixff.) in editing a Harvard manuscript of Saussure's notes (*ca.* 1883/4) provides some important evidence about the links between the *Mémoire* and the *Cours*.

28. Weinreich, Labov and Herzog (1968, 115) wrote that Osthoff and Brugmann were mesmerized by Winteler's observation that e.g. all instances of [n] shifted to [ŋ] before [k, g] without any exception. In using this material to support the regularity principle they did not realize 'that they were extrapolating from a synchronic process to a diachronic one'. In fact Osthoff and Brugmann (1878) do not refer to this example so that it is not easy to know if what they have in mind is the diachronic or the synchronic part of Winteler's statements, both of which could have been used.

29. The book was translated into Italian by Pietro Merlo in 1881 and into English by Eva Channing in 1882. Graffi (1988, 223) highlights the difference between Delbrück (1880) and Paul (1880) and points out how it is only in the fourth edition of the book (1904) that Delbrück dedicates a chapter to analogy, and even so he adopts a restrictive definition of the phenomenon in comparison with Paul.

30. The book appeared in a number of editions; the most significant changes are those introduced in the second (1886) and in the fourth (1909) editions. The spelling of the title changed from *Principien* to *Prinzipien* in 1909. In what follows we mostly quote, as is customary, from the fifth edition of 1920 (reprinted in 1968), unless the passages quoted differ considerably from those of the earlier editions. An English translation of the second edition by H. A. Strong appeared in 1888. For Paul in general, see the bibliography quoted in notes 10 and 15 above. For a defence of his modernity, cf. Koerner ([1972] 1978, 73ff.) and Cherubim (1973), but see above all the discussion by Graffi (1988).

31. Perhaps the closest terms of comparison (for the genre of the book rather than its content) are Heyse's *System der Sprachwissenschaft* (1856) and Steinthal's *Einleitung in die Psychologie und Sprachwissenschaft* ([1871] 1881), though these are far more abstract and, in a sense, 'philosophical'.

32. In a period (the 1880s) when positivism prevailed and the atmosphere was strictly aphilosophical (Paul [1920, 1] spoke of 'unphilosophisches Zeitalter') it is not surprising to see Paul firmly distinguishing his *Prinzipienlehre* from *Sprachphilosophie* or stressing (*ibid.*) that this general part of linguistics is no less empirical than the historical part. When Brugmann and Delbrück (cf. pp. 247, 275 note 35) spoke of a *rapprochement* of technical work and philosophy, they were not disagreeing with Paul, but were using the word 'philosophy' as coterminous with theoretical linguistics or methodology.

33. Note, however, that for Paul psychology is an exact science.

34. Henry Sweet (1882–4, 105) refers to the fact that Paul mainly followed the 'psychological views of Steinthal'; much later, Kretschmer (1920, 256) spoke of the Brugmann period as of an era which had seen the foundation and development of the psychological methods of linguistics.

35. In 1901 Delbrück (1901, 176) concluded his book about *Grundfragen der Sprachforschung mit Rücksicht auf W. Wundts Sprachpsychologie erörtert* with a reference to the 'old truth, that philosophy and *Einzelforschung* belong together'.

36. See above, pp. 201ff., for the earlier psychologism of Steinthal and for some references to the relevant literature. For the psychologism of our period, cf. Esper (1968, 1973), Knobloch (1988, *passim*), Graffi (1991, 63ff.), Nerlich (1992, *passim*).

37. In his 1914 book *Introduction to the Study of Language*, Leonard Bloomfield declared himself an enthusiastic follower of Wundt, but in 1933, when he renounced all mentalism in favour of his own brand of 'mechanism', he referred back to Delbrück: 'we have learned . . . what one of our masters suspected thirty years ago, namely, that we can pursue the study of language without reference to any one psychological doctrine' (Bloomfield 1933, vii).

38. The emphasis on historical explanation is, of course, not new in the 1880s. By the 1860s in some quarters, and above all among Romance scholars, historical explanation (in our sense of the word) had taken over from the comparative explanation favoured by the early Indo-Europeanists (see p. 260); cf. Gaston Paris' statement quoted above, p. 165, and notice also his later (1868) observation, 'Là où la grammaire empirique constate, la grammaire historique explique', quoted by Savoia (1986, 93).

39. Graffi (1988, 277ff.) follows Reis (1978) in arguing that in Paul there is no real distinction between synchrony and diachrony, between 'creativity governed by rules' and 'creativity which changes rules'; in Paul, usage and change would be the same thing. This is not easy to follow since there is a social, interindividual side to the spreading of change.

40. The adjective *statistisch* is in current use at the time, but modern translations from German often render it wrongly with 'statistical'. An alternative adjective is *statisch*, which is used for instance in the German translation of Kruszewski (1884–90). Paul (1901, 201) speaks of *deskriptive Lautlehre*.

41. Winteler (1876, 85f.) distinguishes for speech sounds a physical (acoustic) analysis, a physiological (articulatory) analysis and a genetic analysis which arranges sounds in the sequence of their historical development. He concludes that the genetic approach is only possible after the others have taken place and due consideration has also been given to the subjective qualities of speech sounds.

42. Paul began to refer to Kruszewski's work in the third edition of the *Prinzipien* (1898), i.e. after the publication of Kruszewski's work in German in *Techmers Zeitschrift* (1884–90). Explicit references appear at least at the beginning of Chapter 3 (sound change) of the *Prinzipien* (of which we are told in the preface that it has been substantially modified) and of Chapter 10 (isolation and reactions against it).

43. For the basic literature, see above, note 10. The main texts are collected in Wilbur (1977); for general discussion, see Ramat (1986) and Graffi (1988) as well as the articles quoted below.

44. Gisela Schneider (1973, 19ff.) recognizes three basic models in the attempts made by the neogrammarians to define the regularity principle: (1) sound laws = natural laws; (2) sound laws = description of empirically observable

regularities; (3) sound laws = laws of grammar (as suggested by Brugmann and Delbrück in the later stages of their work). This is not a partition by authors or by periods: Osthoff may belong under (1) but also made different statements; Brugmann probably never really abandoned the second model. However, Schneider's models represent the poles between which most of the neogrammarians oscillated (cf. also Einhauser 1989, 219ff.). Naturally not only the neogrammarians but others too hesitated in their understanding of sound laws; cf. Desmet's (1992) account of Victor Henry's views on the subject.

45. It is striking in how many of the reviews written by Brugmann in the late 1870s and the 1880s the observance or otherwise of sound laws is treated as a touchstone by which to judge the work. Thus in his (partially favourable) review of Saussure's *Mémoire*, Brugmann (1879) points out (correctly) that at some point Saussure derives an ancient Greek *ū* from *ou*, though this is against the standard sound laws of Greek and though Saussure is normally consistent in this area. He then continues: 'apparently the author has not realized that in this way he calls in question the general foundations on which he builds his vocalic system'.

46. For analogy in general from Schleicher to Saussure, cf. Vallini (1972); for the use of analogy in the first neogrammarians, see Morpurgo Davies (1978).

47. Amsterdamska (1987, 184ff.) has some very interesting things to say about analogy but her statement (p. 293, note 18) that 'basically, analogical change as a mode of explanation was invoked in order to account for those linguistic forms which constituted apparent exceptions to exceptionless sound laws' reflects more the self-defence of the neogrammarians than the practice of their work. Analogical processes were frequently postulated (as in the case of *filiabus*) even when no one expressed any concern for a possible exception to the sound laws.

48. In all likelihood, analogical proportions of this type were introduced into contemporary linguistics by Louis Havet (1849–1925), a Paris professor of Latin and a friend of Saussure. The basic text is the preface that he wrote for his translation of F. Bücheler's book about the Latin declensions (Havet 1875), where he argued, before Paul, that all form of segmentation was artificial. The new Latin neuter plural *compluria* 'many', which replaced the expected *complura*, is, in Havet's terms, the proportional fourth in a formula of the type: *fortis : fortia = compluris : compluria* (*ibid.*, xiv); cf. also Havet's letter to Saussure published by Redard (1976, 322). Havet's point was similar to that made after him (and perhaps independently) by Paul, who also believed that we should not introduce abstract entities which do not correspond to any 'real' linguistic unit and that all forms of segmentation are artificial. Cf. also the following note.

49. The proportions set up before Havet and Paul but in circles relatively close to them had very different purposes. Cf. e.g. Curtius (1867, 193): ὁδός : ἑδ- = ποδός : πεδ-; here the aim is to show that a Greek nominative singular such as ὁδός 'road' built on the root ἑδ-, is formed in exactly the same manner as a genitive singular such as ποδός 'of the foot', built on the root πεδ-, and that this is only possible if the two inflections arose in different periods. Notice Curtius's use of roots in the proportion, something which

Paul would have found self-defeating. For Osthoff's attempt to introduce roots into proportions of the standard type, cf. Morpurgo Davies (1978, 52f.).

50. Further work on analogy by the neogrammarians and their contemporaries concentrated more on analogical change (the diachronic phenomenon) than on analogy as a synchronic process; the analogical proportion lived and prospered, but, as Paul had done, a distinction was normally made between (i) proportional analogy, (ii) folk etymology (*bridegroom* replacing the original *-guma* under the influence of *groom*), and (iii) contamination (*feets* from *foot* and *feet*). The American classicist B. I. Wheeler (1887) tried to produce a classification of analogical processes, and before him the French-man Victor Henry (1883) had also written in general terms about analogy, starting from German work. For the various attempts to introduce the techniques of psychology in the study of analogy and of linguistic change in general, see below, p. 294.

51. In their work practice the neogrammarians and their friends were much closer to structuralism than they normally are given credit for, but this emerged more in points of detail than in their programmatic declarations. We may refer, for instance, to Verner's statement (1875) that in setting up a specific sound law he did not mind whether he had to reconstruct a stage with an affricate or a spirant: what really mattered was the chronology of the changes and the type of the contrast. Verner does not explicitly say it but we are meant to understand that the phonetic substance is unimportant *vis-à-vis* the distribution and the distinctive features. Similar statements appear in Sievers, the phonetician *par excellence*.

52. Meillet ([1923] 1938, 156) also recognized that after the 1870s there was a shift in interests: no longer a wish to analyse the grammatical forms in their primitive elements or to understand how they had been created but rather a great concern for the way in which those forms developed in time: 'on a abandonné les vieilles préoccupations romantiques et l'on se limite strictement à l'étude positive des faits'.

53. Cf. e.g. Stocking (1987, 167 and *passim*). Whitney ([1875] 1882, 192) commented that there was no hope of dating the Indo-European commun-ity since the question 'whether the first man was born only 6,000 years ago, or 12,000, or 100,000 or 1,000,000, as the new schools of anthro-pology are beginning to claim' was not settled.

54. It is worth contrasting the space (steadily diminishing) dedicated to com-parison and reconstruction in Max Müller's *Lectures on the Science of Language* ([1861] 1862), Whitney's *Life and Growth of Language* ([1875] 1882) and Paul's *Prinzipien* ([1880] 1920): in the last book little or noth-ing is said about the subject.

55. 'We must stress that the reconstructed forms of Indo-European or at any rate of the period before the division, if taken together do not yield a language which was spoken by one single speech community at any given moment of time. These forms are more likely to have belonged to different regions and different periods' (Brugmann in Brugmann and Delbrück 1897–1916, I, i, 24).

56. This is a point that Hoenigswald has stated and clarified on various occa-sions, including the article quoted below (but see also Hoenigswald 1977,

179ff.). Whether Bloomfield really understood the regularity principle in this sense is of course doubtful, but not entirely implausible: cf. Hoenigswald (1977, 191f., note 17) and above all Hoenigswald (1987).

57. See in general Vallini (1972, 54ff.). Wundt considered the phenomenon in his *Die Sprache* ([1900] 1911–12, i, 444ff.). In his discussion of Wundt's psychology, Delbrück (1901, 107ff. at 110) referred to it, observing that for some forms he had come round to Wundt's view, which he had previously found unacceptable, though there were clear cases where this analysis could not apply. In his reply to Delbrück, Wundt (1901, 64) rejoiced at the newly found agreement, while reiterating his beliefs about the generality of his analysis. It is difficult to know what prompted Delbrück's change of mind, unless he decided to treat the case in question as an example of contamination (such as Italian *rendere* 'to give back' arisen from a contamination of Latin *reddere* 'to give back' and *prehendere* 'to take').

58. The problem is discussed in Delbrück (1880, 112ff.); cf. in general for a summary of the various proposals, Tagliavini (1963, i, 200f.).

59. We owe to Alberto Vàrvaro ([1972–73] 1984, 9ff.) a remarkable account of the beginnings of this genre (history of the language); he is absolutely right in commenting on the 'absence' of the neogrammarians, but I am not certain that Paul's individualistic psychologism is responsible for it. The neogrammarians considered more than once the questions of how individuals interreacted or how innovations spread, but probably did not feel prepared to tackle the sort of problem which would have obliged them to abandon their concentration on the most systematic parts of language.

60. The epitheton is traditional. The Latinist Eduard Fraenkel, who had studied in Berlin with Wilhelm Schulze, Schmidt's successor, used to refer to Johannes Schmidt as the great Schmidt or the great Johannes.

61. These are the Kantian words ('thoroughness, persistence and unceasing application') which Rulon Wells (1979, 32) used to describe Bopp. It is worth quoting, at this stage, the words written by A. Pagliaro (1930, 72ff.), an Italian scholar who had studied in Germany with the Iranist Bartholomae, but had a basically Crocian, i.e. idealistic and anti-positivistic, philosophy: 'It is necessary to stress that the principle of "sound laws" has been rich in results and we owe to the rigour with which it was applied by the neogrammarians the fact that it is now possible to do history of a language or of a linguistic fact without falling into approximation or arbitrariness'.

10

The end of the century:
general perspectives

10.1 Development and fragmentation of the discipline

In 1905 Antoine Meillet (1905, iii) prefaced the French translation of
Brugmann's *Kurze vergleichende Grammatik der indogermanischen
Sprachen* an account of the current state of affairs in comparative grammar (a term which clearly included historical and comparative linguistics). In spite of its length, it is worth quoting because better than any
more modern account it gives a view of the type of work done and of
the spread that the subject had reached.

We should not assume that Brugmann's doctrines are those of a small school:
Brugmann is not a theoretician with original and personal views of his own.
Also, strictly speaking, at present there are not two schools of comparative
grammar. No doubt the different groups of linguists differ in the way of presenting the facts, not everyone is interested in the same matters, and the ways
in which things are explained differ from one to the other. The students of
Johannes Schmidt (especially W. Schulze, Kretschmer) are particularly concerned with keeping as close as possible to the facts that are philologically
documented, to the material detail of things; the Göttingen group – Fick,
Bezzenberger, Hoffmann, Prellwitz, Bechtel, Collitz, etc. – is more interested in etymology and consequently is more prone to relax its phonetic
rigour; the Leipzig group: Brugmann, Osthoff, Leskien, Paul, G. Meyer,
Hübschmann, Thurneysen, Kluge, Bartholomae, Stolz – to quote only the
first generation – was characterized by the importance attributed to analogy
and by its wish to set up general laws. Consequently from this group have
emerged most of the manuals which have multiplied in recent years, beginning with the Greek grammar by G. Meyer, and continuing with the works
of Sommer, Berneker, Streitberg, Hirt, etc.; some of Brugmann's most
remarkable pupils, Streitberg and Hirt, have started sophisticated enquiries
on the accent and vocalism and have built up a whole system of complex
hypotheses. In Russia Fortunatov's teaching has created a small group which
has its special form of notation and its own way of working; in France Bréal's

influence has partly oriented the research towards questions of meaning, and, on the other hand, Ferdinand de Saussure's systematic and rigorous doctrines have left a deep impression on a whole group. The Swedish scholars, like Johansson, Persson, Lidén, have dedicated themselves above all to finding new etymologies as the Göttingen group, but independently from them. There are other scholars, like the famous Thomsen and more recently Pedersen in Denmark, Wackernagel, Solmsen, Zupitza in Germany, V. Henry in France, Zubatý in Bohemia, Bugge and Torp in Norway, Danielsson in Sweden, who could not be easily classified in any group. But all these various scholars are only separated by nuances; all agree on the fundamental principles, all argue in the same way and in the essential points they all reach the same conclusions.

Meillet continued with the observation that even if the principles of comparative grammar were solidly established and the method rigorous, it did not follow that everything had been done. Among the new developments, one could list the work in syntax started by Delbrück; the more accurate phonetic knowledge based on living languages as reflected in Jespersen's work and accompanied by the beginning of experimental phonetics as well as by the attempt to define the 'general and universal rules' of sound change as indicated by Maurice Grammont; the attempts to study the psychological conditions of linguistic phenomena made by Wundt and in part put into practice by Brugmann. 'As for the lexicon' – Meillet went on – 'Schuchardt, Meringer and Hoops have taught us to take facts into account [*à tenir compte des choses*], and the studies of dialects give us a glimpse of the complex conditionings on which lexical change depends. Finally, the study of societies, which becomes every day more precise and methodically more advanced, now begins to reveal the general laws of development to which language, a social fact *par excellence*, is subjected.'

Meillet's work does not belong in the nineteenth century; yet his words must be taken seriously. He was the most distinguished comparativist of twentieth-century France and in his time one of the three or four best comparativists in absolute. He was also someone who had general views of his own; an acute observer of the contemporary scene and an innovator because of his concern for the social nature of language. It is important that in mentioning the new developments he emphasized the work on syntax, phonetics, the psychological approach, the studies in historical semantics linked to the *Wörter und Sachen* movement, and above all the new sociological approach which he favoured in connection with the movement started by Durkheim in anthropology. In fact, as is perhaps implicit in Meillet's statement, the linguistics of the end of the century, after the neogrammarians' controversies had calmed down, is characterized on the one hand by a remarkable unity of intent and purposes, on the other hand by a parting of ways. This was prompted not so much by doctrinal disagreements as much as, on the one hand, by the increased specialization of the historical linguists and, on the other hand, by their programme of retrenchment, which was not limited to the neogrammarians and all too often led to a general reluctance to embark on great theoretical discussions. Delbrück's decision to change the title of the fourth edition (1904) of his 1880 introductory book from 'Introduction to the study of language' (*Einleitung in das Sprachstudium*) to 'Introduction to the study of the Indo-European languages' (*Einführung in das Studium der indogermanischen Sprachen*) is in a sense symbolic of the contemporary change in attitude and of the realization by historical and comparative linguists that there was more to the study of language than the detailed analysis of the history of Indo-European languages. Yet, even if the historical and comparative linguists realized that their subject was only a part, and not the whole, of linguistics, they still dominated the intellectual and institutional scene. The remaining efforts – in typology, phonology, morphology, semantics and syntax – are dispersed; they foreshadow the work of the next century often in very interesting ways, but do not signal as yet the serious creation of a new discipline with the same degree of coherence reached by historical linguistics.[1] When Saussure wrote to Meillet in 1894 (Benveniste 1964, 95–6; De Mauro 1970b, 322) about the difficulties that one experienced in writing even ten lines about language which made sense and about the need to reform the existing terminology and to show what sort of object language was, he was in effect subscribing to this view. A much less known Italian author, Francesco Scerbo (1891, 95), pointed out at the end of the century that: 'the nature of 'glottology' seems to be double: purely historical and positive, on the one hand; transcendental and metaphysic, on the other'. And he continued, noting that in the first field, that 'of the comparative history of individual languages', admirable and certain results had been achieved, but in the second field, 'for what concerns the speculation about the main principles and the inner laws of the life of language, both for the causes of change and for its origin and nature, there is complete and deep disagreement among linguists – so much so that one can in truth state that everything which concerns such difficult and all-important questions not only is full of uncertainty and vague hypotheses, but also seems to be deprived of a sound basis on which to rest anything positive and solid.'

It is impossible to give at this point an account of the various discussions, contributions, etc. which take place in the last decades of the nineteenth century and open the way to the different branches of twentieth-century linguistics. All that we can do, before concluding this account of nineteenth-century linguistics, is to mention a few strands, in full awareness of the inadequacy of this treatment. We start with language classification and discuss in this context the two competing models

(*Wellentheorie, Stammbaumtheorie*) of genealogical classification. We continue with a very brief account of the work of Hugo Schuchardt, one of the protagonists of the controversy, who advocated abandoning the organic or systemic view of language, which most of his predecessors had upheld, in favour of a much more individualistic position. We finally consider examples of the ways in which anthropology, ethnology, psychology and language teaching contribute to linguistics, before listing some of the more general works and giving a few references to the new developments in phonology, syntax and semantics.

10.2 The demise of typological classification

In the initial lecture for his 1891 Geneva course, Saussure observed that 'it is not linguists like Friedrich Müller, of the University of Vienna, who embrace almost all languages of the world, who have advanced even one step in our understanding of language; the names that one ought to quote in this context are those of Romanists like Gaston Paris, Paul Meyer and Schuchardt, of Germanists like Hermann Paul, or of the members of the Russian school who are mainly concerned with Russian and Slavic like Baudouin de Courtenay and Kruszewski' (Godel 1954, 66; De Mauro 1970b, 306). Coming from this quarter, the negative reference to Friedrich Müller may be surprising. We ended the discussion of the mid-century typological work with the observation that, in spite of the unsatisfactory and desultory nature of its results, it served as training ground for descriptive and theoretical linguistics (p. 219). How do we then explain Saussure's observation? The point is that by the 1890s the earlier faith in the possibility of a language classification which was both 'natural', i.e. meaningful, and not based on genetic considerations, had evaporated. Charles Darwin had written in the *Descent of Man* (1871, i, 188) that 'Classifications may, of course, be based on any character whatever, as on size, colour, or the element inhabited; but naturalists have long felt a profound conviction that there is a natural system. This system, it is now generally admitted, must be, as far as possible, genealogical in arrangement – that is, the co-descendants of the same form must be kept together in one group, separate from the co-descendants of any other form; but if the parent forms are related, so will be their descendants, and the two groups together will form a larger group.' Languages were then quoted as a parallel. Friedrich Müller, as we have seen (p. 213), described the various forms of morphological and psychological classification but opted for genealogical classification.[2] Yet this is just the type of classification which requires philological accuracy, but appears to be descriptively and theoretically uninteresting, since it is largely based on the application of a relatively well defined technique (the comparative method) to the formal (and most obvious) aspects of language.

Typological classification also suffered from the increased realization that two languages can be related even if they belong to different types. In 1870 Baudouin de Courtenay still declared that 'morphologically different languages cannot be genetically related' (1972, 65), but later on he expressed grave doubts about the possibility of morphological classification and e.g. in 1889 he underlined that the state of a language is not fixed but continuously changing (1972, 137f.). Still later (1910, 53), he stressed that English, an Indo-European language, was as isolating as Chinese.[3] For practical purposes, reference was constantly made to the one or the other form of morphological classification,[4] but other possibilities were also discussed – again without much faith in their validity. At the same time, however, there was some interest in providing a characterization, rather than a classification, of languages: the conclusion of Baudouin's 1910 paper pleaded for just such a characterization. Earlier, Raoul de la Grasserie, a French author who *inter alia* contributed to *Techmers Zeitschrift* a two-part article about language classification (La Grasserie 1889–90),[5] had reiterated that the most complete classification was genealogical, though it was possible to find other 'natural' criteria for grouping languages. In particular it was possible to recognize in language a principle similar to that of the 'subordination des caractères': languages with vowel harmony are also agglutinative (which was required by the need to have a link between empty words to define their function); monosyllabic languages are also tone languages (La Grasserie speaks of variation of accent) because otherwise the lexical resources would not be adequate, etc.[6] Thus we obtain groupings which may be said to be naturally justified. Georg von Gabelentz (1894), the Leipzig orientalist and general linguist (cf. p. 331, note 24), argued in a posthumous article that, though the possibility of doing for language what Cuvier had done for comparative anatomy (the reference is to the principle of *correlation des formes*) was remote, it was still worthwhile to establish on empirical basis which features clustered with which, in order to establish at least what the various grammatical possibilities were. La Grasserie had still the old aim, a classification of languages, but the others oscillated between linguistic classification, linguistic typology (a term created by Gabelentz) and more modest attempts at linguistic characterization. In general the loss of faith in non-genealogical classification, together with the fact that the theoretical problems of description were very much a minority interest with little or no institutional recognition, contributed to relegate typological classification and the whole of typology to a secondary role.

10.3 Genealogical classification and the wave theory

Genealogical classification had much greater prestige than the old 'mor-phological classification' and the work in the second part of the century had extended the methods applied to Indo-European to other family groups. Yet here too there were problems, even if of a different nature. Meillet (1905, v) stated that the Indo-European languages offered a model for comparative research which had to be pursued in the area of Semitic, Finno-Ugric, Bantu, Turkish, etc.[7] Yet for most languages the basic evidence was not comparable with that available for Indo-European. An immense amount of work was needed to establish the necessary links between the various languages of Africa, Asia and the Americas, not to mention the indigenous languages of Australia. Admittedly, a great deal had been done and in the course of the nineteenth century we witness a steady increase in the knowledge of 'exotic' languages, but reliable descriptions were not always available and, in the absence of any depth of historical evidence, all too often it was impossible to establish with any degree of reliability which languages were related.[8] F. Müller, whom we have already mentioned, assumed that there were some 78 original families or possibly more (he guessed 100), but in his attempt to link the linguistic classification to an anthropological classification (based on racial distinctions), he found himself at times deciding on linguistic affinities on racial bases – with the obvious dangers that this involved (Tagliavini 1963, i, 415ff.). By contrast, in 1905 the Italian A. Trombetti, who was interested in propounding his monogenetic theories, worked in terms of 11 basic linguistic groups only. Though the main non-Indo-European languages (Semitic, Hamitic, Dravidian, Caucasian, Chinese, etc.) were studied in the nineteenth century, it is striking that most of the fundamental work in these fields belongs to this century, i.e. is definitely later than the work on Indo-European.

At the end of last century, those who extolled the importance of genealogical classification were bound to think of Indo-European as the main model, even if they could refer, to a lesser extent, to Finno-Ugric, Semitic and perhaps Bantu, as Meillet was to do later. Yet, the Indo-Europeanists too had their difficulties – on two different scores at least. Once the existence of an Indo-European family had been established beyond any reasonable doubt and the main features of the parent lan-guage had been reconstructed, the wish to push further in reconstruc-tion was bound to arise. We mentioned earlier von Raumer's and Ascoli's belief that Indo-European and Semitic were originally related,[9] but they were not alone in holding these views. Towards the end of the century the suggestion was taken up with a series of new arguments by a remarkable scholar, the Dane Hermann Møller (Möller), who not only suggested that Saussure's *coefficients sonantiques* (see p. 243f.) should be identified with the Semitic laryngeals, but also argued that Saussure's new analysis made it possible to compare the Indo-European roots (including their laryngeals) with the Semitic ones. Another Dane, Holger Pedersen, a pupil and then colleague of Møller, went further and maintained that it was possible to postulate an original unit, which he called 'Nostratic', of Indo-European, Hamito-Semitic, Finno-Ugric, Altaic and perhaps Caucasian and Basque.[10] The problem is still debated and cannot be pursued here, but it created a major division between the majority of established Indo-Europeanists who saw these suggestions as much too speculative for comfort and those who, like Møller, were reacting on the one hand to their own isolation and on the other to the feeling that Indo-European studies were entering a period of stagnation: for them in the mid 1890s 'the carriage of Indo-European linguistics had begun to sink deeper and deeper into the bog' (Möller 1906, ix) and further comparison was the only way to salvation.[11]

If, on the one hand, the Indo-Europeanists felt threatened by those who wanted to carry comparison beyond the reconstruction of the Indo-European parent language, on the other hand they were bound to feel the ground cut under their feet by those who challenged the model of language relationship which in less than a generation had become traditional, Schleicher's family tree. In its simplest and most primitive form this was based on some fundamental assumptions: (a) languages or dialects were self-contained units easily identifiable, (b) after a language had split into two, no further contact between the two separate linguistic communities was normally assumed, (c) related languages would progressively diverge but never converge, (d) in order to establish whether two languages belonged to the same branch, shared innovations mattered more than the preservation of inherited features. Yet it had long since been observed that language and dialect boundaries were far from clear and that languages kept influencing each other, both if they were related and if they were not (cf. e.g. Pott 1856, 203, 213–20). Moreover, if one used shared innovations as a criterion for identifying the various forms of branching (two languages which shared the same innovation belonged to the same branch), the difficulty was that most languages shared innovations (different innovations) with a number of other languages and above all with those to which they were geographically adjacent. The question then arose whether the tree model offered the best way to illustrate the real connection of a group of related languages. Johannes Schmidt, in discussing the possible subgrouping of Indo-European languages, concluded in 1872 that it did not adequately express the facts: Latin, which according to the traditional view belonged to a Graeco-Italic branch, also had a number of common features with Celtic, while Greek shared features with the Asiatic languages and Celtic with Germanic. If so, the various reconstructions of *Grundsprachen* such as European, Slavo-Germanic, Italo-Celtic or Graeco-Italic, which were so essential for Schleicher's *Stammbaum*, had to be given up. A more realistic image of the relationship of the Indo-European languages would represent them as situated on concentric circles with the parent language at the centre and the individual languages more or less distant from it but still linked to each other; the model was that of waves in water which spread from a central point in concentric rings which progressively became weaker and weaker (Schmidt 1872, 27).[12] The so-called wave theory (*Wellentheorie*) had considerable repercussions, not least because it called attention to the partly arbitrary nature of the assumptions required by the *Stammbaumtheorie*. Similar conclusions had been earlier reached by Schuchardt for the Romance languages in a lecture which ended with the statement: 'I have wanted to speak about the classification of the Romance languages and have had to speak against it' (Schuchardt [1900] 1922, 166; the lecture was first read in 1870).[13] But Schmidt is not radically opposed to the standard genealogical classification or the reconstruction of the parent language as unitary, even if in his view the semi-automatic type of reconstruction allowed by the family-tree model is no longer viable. For him 'it is highly plausible that at some stage there was a unitary Indo-European language' (1872, 29f.); the question is whether we are able to reconstruct it and the conclusion is that with the present means the *Ursprache* is a scholarly fiction, a helpful one, but one which is not endowed with historical individuality (*ibid.*, 31). Schuchardt's position is far more radical and indeed comes close to the rejection of the concept of language or at least of language as a self-contained system; languages seems to be defined by the concentration of isoglosses but real boundaries are impossible to trace.

The problem – as set out by Schmidt – could be looked at in terms of the classification of the Indo-European languages or in more general terms; reviewers, attackers and supporters followed both ways. The Indo-Europeanists in general and the neogrammarians in particular were not inclined to give up the standard family tree, but acknowledged that the wave model was also plausible. Leskien (1876) argued that the two models were not incompatible and Brugmann (1884), in reconsidering the whole question, drew attention to the fact that similarity between related languages could depend on secondary contacts or influences but also on parallel but independent innovations. In his view the whole idea of branching did not have to be given up, but to establish a *Stammbaum* was far more complicated than was normally assumed; above all, like all forms of reconstruction, it required an understanding of the modality and, we could say, typology of change. Both at the concrete and the theoretical level, the *Wellentheorie / Stammbaumtheorie* controversy opened up for discussion a number of areas (and problems) which the

Indo-Europeanists (though not necessarily the Romance scholars) had all too often avoided: the distinction between language and dialect, the existence of unitary languages, the chances that reconstructed Indo-European was such a language, the likelihood that similar structural conditions might lead to similar but independent changes, the typology of change in general, etc. The technical work went on but the general problems were there and could no longer be forgotten. Above all, this is the period in which the existence of mixed languages begins to be accepted, in contrast with previous assumptions (cf. p. 198). It is not by chance that it is also the period in which Romance philology eventually obtains both intellectual and institutional recognition (Christmann 1993).

10.4 Hugo Schuchardt, language and dialect

The work of Hugo Schuchardt (1842–1927), one of the protagonists of the *Stammbaum* controversy, illustrates some of the directions in which linguistic thought was moving.[14] He was German by birth and studied at Jena (where he heard Schleicher) and Bonn, where he was influenced by the great Latinist Ritschl and by the Romanist Diez, before obtaining his *Habilitation* at Leipzig in 1870. His first permanent appointment was in Graz, where he remained until his death, publishing innumerable articles and pamphlets (the main book was his doctoral thesis) and pursuing an extensive correspondence all over the world. He did not belong to a school nor did he form one; the word 'isolated' has been used again and again in connection with him. His work ranged from detailed studies of Vulgar Latin and of various linguistic, and sometimes literary, problems in almost all Romance languages, to important studies of Basque conducted on the basis of fieldwork, to analyses of pidgins and creoles which in a sense started a new field of studies and provided evidence for language mixture, to theoretical discussions such as his pamphlet about sound laws and against the neogrammarians. But in addition there are studies of Caucasian and African languages, of Celtic, of artificial languages, and endless etymological studies which consider both form and meaning of the words with special concern for cultural facts – in his formula, not *Wörter und Sachen*, but *Sachen und Wörter*.[15] Fought (1982, 422) rightly sees Schuchardt's wave theory as based on two fundamental ideas, individualism and language mixture. The emphasis is on difference rather than on unity: each person is unique and each form of speech is unique; hence each language is a mixture of languages. There is no such thing as the coherent dialect envisaged by the neogrammarians. What we call dialect includes old and new forms at the same time. Schuchardt rejects the model of change which assumes that all members of a speech community gradually alter their linguistic performance: change spreads from individual to individual, but the various features spread in different directions, at different times and in different manners, so that it is not easy or possible to fix dialect boundaries.[16] Thus on structural bases it is difficult, if not impossible, to distinguish languages from dialects or dialects from other dialects. But Schuchardt's iconoclasm goes further: it is also difficult to draw a line between adjacent but unrelated languages. Language in general is a continuum and all so-called languages are in fact dialects, not because they have a common genetic origin, but because they share a number of features ([1917] 1922, 254ff.). In addition to the genetic relationship which we attribute to languages on the basis of formal external similarity, there is a basic relationship, an *Elementarverwandtschaft*, based on the *innere Sprachform* ([1917] 1922, 175ff.) and on common developments (sound symbolism plays a role) which allow languages to have similar features, while not being historically connected.

Starting in 1870 from the general belief, shared with Leskien, that linguists (*Sprachwissenschaftler*) were scientists (*Naturwissenschaftler*) (Richter [1928] 1977, 488), Schuchardt at a very early stage shifted not only to the anti-Schleicher views which the neogrammarians made popular but also to a much greater concern for the individual and social aspects of language. For him the neogrammarians' statements about sound laws showed a tendency to treat language as an object, which he could only deplore. In general he reacted against all attempts at classification which he saw as obvious sources of error: this applied to the classification of languages ([1884] 1922, 347), but also, in his view, to Saussure's attempt to treat linguistics as subordinate to semiology and social and general psychology, leaving aside sociology or cultural history ([1917] 1922, 348). Schuchardt is now considered one of the founders of sociolinguistics, but he would have been reluctant to identify linguistics with sociolinguistics exactly for the same reason for which he did not like to treat it as part of psychology only. Probably his reluctance to write the large theoretical work which he would have been uniquely capable of doing – his views are mostly formulated in throw-away remarks rather than in large theoretical constructions – is the result of this fear of abstraction and generalization.[17] Against this background the impression that sometimes one has in reading Schuchardt that the whole concept of language (in the sense of both *langage* and *langue*) is disintegrating is not altogether surprising. At the very end of the century the French comparativist Victor Henry (1850–1907) highlighted the problem in one of his *Antinomies linguistiques* (1896, 3ff.), which in the form of thesis and antithesis summarized the dilemmas of the time. Thesis: 'the category of language, that of a language and a dialect, even that of a simple word, as soon as one looks at them closely, are mere abstractions without external reality'. Antithesis: 'there is a science of language which takes as its object the study of the phenomena of the life of language, that is to say of the life of the various languages and of the life of the words'. And he added, wistfully, that normally no discipline starts by saying that it has no object. At the same time, however, he underlined that there is no language, only people who speak; that there is indeed infinite variation (as, we may add, the recent studies in dialectology were revealing) and that the various categories (language, dialect, etc.) are all abstractions. Henry concluded, however, that these were useful and indeed necessary abstractions. Others might have reached different results.

With hindsight it is not difficult to see what was happening. Once the idea of language as organism had been abandoned, the questions 'What is a language?', 'What is language?' were bound to raise their head again. At the same time there was an outburst of work in dialectology. Ascoli's *Saggi Ladini* and his 'Proemio' to the *Archivio Glottologico* date from 1873, the year in which the English Dialect Society was founded (Beyer 1981, 339ff.); Winteler's study of his Swiss dialect dates from 1876. The German Georg Wenker collected through questionnaires the data which he used in the linguistic map published as an appendix to his *Das rheinische Platt* (1877) and then began work towards a linguistic atlas of the German dialects. In France the Swiss linguist Jules Gilliéron prepared a first phonetic atlas of the Romance Valais (1881), and in 1887, in connection with a project for a French dialect atlas, together with the abbé Rousselot, the experimental phonetician, founded the *Revue des patois gallo-romains*. In 1891 Rousselot published in that periodical a study of his own dialect, based on his own speech and that of his family, in which he made large use of the techniques of experimental phonetics and *inter alia* observed distinctions and developments of which speakers were entirely unaware (*Les modifications phonétiques du langage étudiées dans le patois d'une famille de Cellefrouin (Charente)*). In England, Joseph Wright's description of his Yorkshire dialect was published in 1892 and was followed by the work for his monumental English dialect dictionary (Wright 1896–1905). What emerged, of course, from all this work is that the data were far more difficult to analyse than it had been suspected, that variation between individuals or generations occurred even in the smallest of dialects and that, if one traced on the map lines which joined the areas with similar phonetic developments, these lines (isophones) took some very odd shapes. Paul Passy wrote in his doctoral thesis (1891, 10f.) that, in principle at least, 'each individual speaks a special dialect, which he is the only person to speak'. Moreover, he continued, it would be possible to go further and say that 'each individual speaks *many dialects*, according to the circumstances, or even, to be rigorous, an *infinity of dialects*, none of which is identical to the dialects of other individuals'. For Schuchardt and others, this evidence, on the one hand, spoke against the neogrammarians and the regularity principle, on the other hand, supported their views about the mixed nature of all languages and, to go further, the impossibility of defining the boundaries of a language or dialect. This attitude, however, as Victor Henry knew, removed from linguistics its own object of study; in the new century Gilliéron and Mongin deny the very existence of the patois and conclude that the only possible study is that of words (Benincà 1996, 118f.). And yet the theoretical pronouncements of someone such as Schuchardt were not as remote from those of the neogrammarians as they are made out to be – something which Schuchardt himself hinted at (e.g. 1885, 34). Paul too was aware that the only 'real' language was that of the individuals, that dialects and languages were abstractions and that homogenous speech communities did not exist, but this did not prevent him and the other neogrammarians from exploiting those abstractions.[18] In their actual working practice the neogrammarians (or the best among them) treated the individual languages as systems (as the structuralists did), while Schuchardt was more concerned with the individual features of one or the other language on the one hand and with the general characteristics of language as such on the other. It is worthy of note that both camps produced outstanding work and that both acknowledged the validity of each other's results.

10.5 Linguistic core and linguistic periphery

Whoever tries to offer a bird's-eye view of linguistics at the end of the century must ask what work was being published at the time. The bulk of it was concerned with the historical and comparative analysis of the Indo-European languages in all their periods of attestation (including the more modern periods) and, to a lesser extent, of non-Indo-European languages: etymological essays, historical grammars, comparative grammars. In general this was work aimed at specialists, but other work, already mentioned, oscillates between the scholarly and the practical. We are in the period of Encyclopedias and the new status of linguistics is shown by the fact that the main linguists are asked to contribute simplified accounts of their subject. In the ninth edition of the *Encyclopedia Britannica* (1885), Whitney wrote the first part of the article *Philology* dedicated to *Science of Language in general*; the second part about the comparative philology of the Indo-European languages was written by Sievers. Bilingual and monolingual dictionaries keep increasing in number and so do grammars, both those aimed at non-native speakers and those aimed at the teaching of the native language. The historical approach often leaves its mark even on the simplest work. However, there were also more general contributions, prompted partly by the needs of vulgarization, partly by the wish to establish a serious methodological and theoretical background for the historical work, partly by a reaction against the historical approach or its dominance of the scene. Further discussions arise from the cross-fertilization of linguistics and other disciplines – a subject which would require a book on its own. In what follows we can produce only sketchy examples of how linguistics interacted with anthropology, ethnography, experimental psychology and practical language-teaching. We do so before turning to a brief account of the more general books and contributions.

10.5.1 Linguistics, anthropology, ethnography, etc.

In 1872 Max Müller stated that the Science of Language had become omnipresent in all spheres of knowledge (1868–75, iv, 234). This is of course exaggerated, but it was indeed the case that in England, for instance, anthropologists such as E. B. Tylor found it useful to turn to Max Müller to obtain information about linguistic facts and methods and that some of them became well acquainted, as Tylor did, with German linguistic scholarship (Leopold 1980, 1989a). Likewise the philosopher Herbert Spencer discussed extensively Max Müller's views in his works (Stocking 1987, 307ff.) Anthropologists borrowed or adapted from linguistics the comparative method in order to reconstruct the earliest stages of related civilizations (Leopold 1980, 58); in their search for evidence of human progress some of them were also happy to accept (e.g. from Max Müller) that brand of transformism which assumed a typological development in language from isolating to agglutinative to inflectional. However, as is clear from the language section in Chapter VI of Darwin's *Descent of Man* (1871), anyone who wished to make a case in evolutionary terms for a continuity between animals and human beings had to tackle the question of the origin of language: was it plausible that language had arisen as the result of evolutionary development? Max Müller denied it but Darwin and most anthropologists argued for it. Tylor was willing to speculate on onomatopoeia, sound symbolism, interjections, gestures, etc. as sources for the origin of language, as was Darwin (Leopold 1989a), but Max Müller (e.g. 1868–75, iv, 477) found it impossible to follow them. He was quick to point out that in most cases onomatopoeia was a mirage: a word such as *plunge* offers a perfect imitation of a body falling into water, but its history (it derives from *plumbicare*) shows that this is coincidental. The problem was further complicated by the different assumptions about thought and about the relative priority of language and thought; the like of Tylor, Darwin or Spencer moved within the framework of British empiricism in contrast with Max Müller, who was a Kantian with the difference (in his own words) that Kant took the categories 'as the *sine qua non* of thought in abstract', while he took them 'as the *sine qua non* of thought, as embodied in language' (Max Müller 1887, 477; cf. S. J. Schmidt

1976, 671). In consequence, for him animals who had no language also had no thought and the gap between human beings and animals seemed insurmountable (particularly within a scenario of gradual evolution). Darwin (e.g. 1871, i, 35ff.) disagreed, maintained that there was 'no fundamental difference between man and the higher mammals in their mental faculties' and argued that, though animals did not have articulate language, some of them had some form of language (*ibid.*, 53). Yet Max Müller stuck to his view that the Science of Language had proved that 'all our words are derived from roots, and that every one of these roots is the expression of a general concept'. Animals knew no roots and consequently had no language.[19] As we have seen, by the end of the century professional linguists were leaving some of these questions aside. We may again refer to Victor Henry's *Antinomies* (1896, 25). The thesis is that language must have had a beginning and we must find its origin. The antithesis states that the question of the origin of language is an impossible question. Henry concludes in his *synthèse* that the question of the origin of language, however interesting, is not a linguistic problem; it is in fact analysable into a number of questions which belong respectively in comparative anatomy, pure physiology, psycho-physiology and psychology.

A second instance of links between linguistics and ethnography, or again anthropology, is very different, but still tied to the first by personalities and intellectual trends. The native languages of North America had been studied in the first half of the century, partly under the auspices of the American Philosophical Society, by the like of Pierre Étienne Du Ponceau and John Pickering, but they had never gained adequate institutional recognition. In the second half of the century the type of linguistic work which had attracted attention was very much in the German tradition and dealt mainly with Sanskrit (Whitney) and the classical languages, though the occasional article on American Indian languages was also published. In 1879 the Bureau of American Ethnology was created within the Smithsonian in Washington under the direction of John Wesley Powell (1834–1902), a teacher of geology, a soldier and the head of a geographic expedition. Government funds were provided for ethnographic work on the assumption that this would help with the relocation of the natives in the reservations. Powell accepted the views of cultural evolution proposed by Lewis Henry Morgan (1818–81), which were close to those of Tylor, and assumed that it was possible to identify in human evolution three basic divisions: savagery, barbarism and civilization, with the first two being analysable into three levels. Morgan not only had produced one of the first thorough descriptions of kinship terminology in an Amerindian language but had also become an expert in Iriquois culture and was interested in all its aspects, including language. On that model Powell promoted the study of the various native cultures, including their linguistic aspects, and exploited the resources of the Bureau (which at times reached some fifteen members) for that purpose. The result was, in addition to a series of descriptive works of varying standards, also Powell's own *Introduction to the Study of Indian Languages* (1877 and 1880) and his classification (1891) of the languages north of Mexico into some 55 families, on the basis of an analysis founded more on lexical than on grammatical comparison.[20] In the same period, Daniel Brinton (1837–99), a physician who had become Honorary Professor of Archaeology and Linguistics at the University of Pennsylvania, also produced a classification, based on grammar, of the languages of North and South America, which competed, perhaps unfavourably, with that of Powell. The point here is that once again in a new field, which is different from that of the standard Indo-European studies, the first impulse towards a full collection of data and its implementation did not come from professional linguists. Indeed even Franz Boas (1858–1942), the man who put the description of American Indian languages on a really professional footing, was not a professional linguist: his original training in Germany was as a physicist and geographer and his later work in America was that of a fully fledged anthropologist and ethnographer rather than that of a specialized linguist. Conceivably this background (in addition to the influence of Humboldt and Steinthal) allowed Boas to develop, starting with the last decades of the nineteenth century, his form of linguistic relativism, i.e. to stress that the traditional grammatical categories could not be applied to languages very different from those for which they had been developed (as on the whole had been done) and that the phonological/phonetic interpretation which the fieldworkers set on the sounds that they heard was likely to be determined by their own system of sounds.[21] The later history of these studies merges witth the history of American structuralism.

10.5.2 Linguistics and experimental psychology

Our third set of data concerns linguistics and experimental psychology; though this link starts in our century it acquires momentum in the first decades of the twentieth century. The psychologism of the second part of the nineteenth century is well known; after Steinthal, this type of approach had been vociferously supported by the neogrammarians even if they did not believe in *Völkerpsychologie*. But this is also the period in which the Leipzig philosopher and psychologist Wilhelm Wundt turns his attention to language and Paul and Delbrück soon find themselves involved in courteous but firm debates about the nature of psychology and the importance or otherwise of a specific psychological theory for the linguist (cf. Delbrück 1901, Wundt 1901). However, Wundt was also eager to introduce experimental techniques in the study of individual psychology and some linguists felt moved to a somewhat different type of work from that which they were trained for. In the first substantial work on speech errors, the method is not experimental but observational. A monograph by the Vienna (and then Graz) linguist and Indo-Europeanist Rudolf Meringer and the neurologist and neuropsychiatrist Carl Mayer (1862–1936) on *Versprechen und Verlesen. Eine psychologisch-linguistische Studie* (1895) provided a classified collection, still useful, of speech mistakes.[22] The primary motivation for such work was the desire to identify evidence useful for the study of language change (Meringer had a long-standing interest in dissimilation), but the conclusion was that the data did not suggest that sound change arose from repeated speech errors (as had been suggested), though the same psychological causes could play a role in both errors and change. There are regularities in speech errors and an explanation for these must be found in the 'internal language', i.e. in those psychic processes which precede, and call forth, speech production. In a sense then a work which arose from an interest in historical linguistics turned into a contribution to general and descriptive linguistics.

The other work which saw the cooperation of a linguist, the neogrammarian Albert Thumb (1865–1915), with a psychologist (officially a philosopher), Karl Marbe (1869–1953), must at least be quoted here, even if it goes beyond our chronological limits, because it is closely linked with the neogrammarians' theories which we discussed earlier. The starting point was analogy and association theory, as stated e.g. by Paul, and the aim was to get away from the vicious circle which leads linguists to postulate mental associations on the basis of analogical change and then to explain analogical change as the result of mental associations. Fundamentally Thumb and Marbe analysed the responses and the reaction times to specific stimulus words and concluded that new analogical forms are more likely to arise in connection with associations which are more frequent (i.e. independently produced by a number of speakers) and have shorter reaction-times. Methods, conclusions, etc. were all challenged, but for a while various tests of this type were attempted (Esper 1973, 64ff.; Knobloch 1988, 463ff.). Once again some of this work, though meant to test historical conclusions, was more likely to have an influence on descriptive analysis.

10.5.3 Linguistics and language teaching

Finally, we may move from linguistics and psychology to linguistics and language teaching. In the nineteenth century academic linguistics and language teaching tend to move apart. Admittedly the historical bias of the century has some influence even on textbooks but normally we are dealing with a one-way movement. Yet the so-called Reform Movement of the late nineteenth century brought together the two fields

– even if at present not enough work has been done to establish the exact ways and means through which this *rapprochement* influenced the future developments of linguistics.[23] The starting point is perhaps the appearance in 1882 of the pamphlet *Der Sprachunterricht muss umkehren! Ein Beitrag zur Überbürdungfrage* ('Language teaching must start afresh! A contribution to the question of stress and overwork in school'), published under the pseudonym *Quousque tandem* by the young German teacher Wilhelm Viëtor (1850–1918), who had taught English in Germany and German in England before moving to University teaching first in Liverpool and then in Marburg. The reactions among teachers were important and the end result was the creation of a new movement which brought together a number of teachers and, in addition to Viëtor, at least three other linguists, all of whom mainly worked in phonetics and, with one exception, had had experience of school teaching: Henry Sweet (1845–1912), Paul Passy (1859–1940) and, somewhat later, Otto Jespersen (1860–1943). The recurring complaints, both in Viëtor's pamphlets and in the remaining literature by these authors, concerned the current teaching methods with their constant confusion between speech sounds and letters, their acceptance of old linguistic features as part of the modern language (even if no one ever used them), their nonsensical grammatical definitions mostly introduced on the basis of Latin grammar even when this was irrelevant (English was treated as if it had real cases, a productive subjunctive, etc.), their rote learning of rules rather than texts, etc. The desiderata for the classroom were intensive phonetic teaching, the priority of spoken language and the use of real sentences from the beginning. In reporting about this movement in 1884, Henry Sweet reiterated most of these points, attacked the idea that dead languages should be taught before the living ones and deplored all forms of historical explanations in the teaching of languages. 'The constant application of historical and comparative illustrations is often positively injurious, from the disturbing influence it has on the purity and definiteness of the groups of associations gained by the practical study. . . . happily the practice of throwing crumbs of philology into practical grammars, &c., seems to be falling more and more into discredit, even when the language is to be studied solely for scientific purposes' ([1884] 1913, 36ff.). The distinction between spoken and written language, the emphasis on phonetics, the sharp contrast between historical and non-historical study (we would say diachronic and synchronic) certainly permeate all the work of the authors cited but are found elsewhere. Yet the coming together of school teachers and academic phoneticians from a number of different countries and their attempt at implementing their views in the classroom were probably more influential than a purely academic debate would have been. Sweet's book *The Practical Study of Language* (1899), Passy's *De la méthode directe dans l'enseignement*

des langues vivantes (1899), Jespersen's *Sprogundervisning* (1901) with
its English version *How to teach a foreign language* (1904), Viëtor's
Die Methodik des neusprachlichen Unterrichts (1902) – all of these
represent the summing up of a number of debates, articles, etc. which
had considerable importance (Sørensen 1989). They also offer a synthesis of the work which went on in the phonetic association which
Passy had created, the others had joined, and eventually was to become
the International Phonetic Association (Bergounioux 1994, 238ff.).

10.6 General and theoretical work

So far, except for the neogrammarians and Schuchardt, we have neglected the less technical and/or more theoretical work aimed at providing general statements about linguistics. And yet this is the period in
which a number of general books appear, meant to explain to the interested layman or to the professional what linguistics is and what it has
achieved. In France a very incomplete list of such works written after
1870, or at least widely available in revised versions between 1870 and
1900, would include Abel Hovelaque, *La linguistique. Histoire naturelle
du langage* (1876, 5th edn 1922), an account in heavily organicistic
terms; Arsène Darmesteter, *La vie des mots* (1887, 15th edn 1925),
which first appeared in English translation in 1886; Victor Henry,
Antinomies linguistiques (1896); and Michel Bréal, *Essai de sémantique
(science des significations)* (1897), which collects the results of work
started in the 1860s and has in fact a broader scope than the title would
indicate. We have already discussed some of the German and Austrian
works: Delbrück (1880), Paul (1880) with all their successive editions,
translations, and adaptations, but also the heavily psychological H.
Steinthal, *Abriss der Sprachwissenschaft. I. Einleitung in die Psychologie
und Sprachwissenschaft* (1871, 2nd edn 1881), with the accompany-
ing volume by F. Misteli, *Charakteristik der hauptsächlisten Typen des
Sprachbaues* (1891). A slim monograph such as the *Untersuchungen
über die Grundfragen des Sprachlebens* (1885) by Philipp Wegener (see
below, p. 318ff.) and a much larger tome such as *Die Sprachwissenschaft,
ihre Aufgaben, Methoden und bisherigen Ergebnisse* (1891) by Georg
von der Gabelentz[24] represent new departures which are followed, at the
beginning of the new century, by the first two volumes on *Die Sprache*
in W. Wundt's *Völkerpsychologie* (1900).[25] The monumental *Grundriß
der Sprachwissenschaft* (1876–88) by Friedrich Müller is seen as the
replacement for Adelung's *Mithridates*, while the elderly Pott published
in successive numbers of *Techmers Zeitschrift* his *Einleitung in die
allgemeine Sprachwissenschaft* ([1884–90] 1974), a survey of the work
done in all linguistic fields. In the United States and in Britain there
are the innumerable editions, adaptations and translations of Whitney's

Language and the Study of Language (1867, 3rd edn 1870) and *The Life and Growth of Language* (1875), and the equally innumerable editions of Max Müller's *Lectures on the Science of Language* (7th edn with the title *The Science of Language*, 1891). In 1874 and 1880 Archibald Sayce, an Oxford Assyriologist who had at times acted as deputy for Max Müller, published a volume on *The Principles of Comparative Philology* (1874) and two volumes of *Introduction to the Science of Language* (1880), which, in spite of their discursive style, contain original and interesting criticism of current beliefs and, in the 1880 book, an original history of linguistic thought from the Babylonian period to modern times. Perhaps more important is the book which in a sense concludes our period, the *Lectures on the Study of Language* (1901) by Hanns Oertel, a German who had moved to the United States and become professor at Yale. Starting with the 1870s, Henry Sweet, the British phonetician and Anglicist, expressed in a series of papers (mostly addresses to the Philological Society) his views about the nature and development of language, pleading for an approach which started with the study of living languages (cf. Sweet 1913); another Anglicist and phonetician, the Dane Otto Jespersen, summarized in his *Progress in Language with Special Reference to English* (1894) his views about language evolution as teleologically driven towards greater economy and simplicity (Nielsen 1989).

A place of their own must be assigned to the publications of the Polish scholar Jan Baudouin de Courtenay (1845–1929) and his pupil Mikołaj Kruszewski (1851–87).[26] Most of their work was difficult to find and difficult to use because of the language in which it was written (mostly Polish and Russian), but Kruszewski's *Prinzipien der Sprachentwickelung*, an adaptation from the Russian original, appeared in *Techmers Zeitschrift* between 1884 and 1890 and influenced, for instance, the later editions of Paul's *Prinzipien* (cf. p. 275 note 42). As for Baudouin, doubtlessly he anticipated most of the conclusions of the neogrammarians (Kruszewski 1884–90, i, 299), but also aimed at producing a general theory of language which has surprisingly modern features. He and Kruszewski can certainly take the credit for the beginning of phonemic and morphophonemic theory, but also for serious, though different, attempts at understanding the nature of language change.[27]

10.6.1 Linguistic treatises and theoretical discussions

This is not the place to do so, but it would be useful to take a leaf from Malkiel's (1976b) study of etymological dictionaries and consider the typology of the more general accounts of linguistics in our period. We could then aim at establishing not only how opinions diverged, but also which subjects were discussed and which omitted. Suitable parameters

to use would be the definition of language (an organism, a social institution, etc.), that of linguistics (a natural science, a social science, a
historical subject, a part of psychology, etc.), the failure or otherwise to
distinguish between history and description, the role assigned to history
(on a par with description, the only way to explain linguistic facts, the
ultimate aim, etc.), the importance assigned to language classification,
the concern or otherwise for the definition of grammatical units and/or
for what we would now call language universals.

In general, Schleicher's organic views are abandoned or at least
toned down, even if Hovelacque and Darmesteter must count as exceptions. References to psychological and/or social factors dominate, but,
as we have seen, the increasing awareness of the differences between
individual speakers and of the inconsistencies in the speech of even one
individual, prompted by both phonetics and dialectology, generate considerable tension. A further, but perhaps welcome, level of complexity
is introduced by Wegener's view of language as essentially dialogic,
i.e. as arising in the interaction of speaker and hearer in a given context.

In the last three decades of the century the reactions to a view of
linguistics as a natural science seem to be negative or at least muted, but
there are attempts at a compromise which are soon forgotten. Friedrich
Müller (1876–88, i, 10ff.) lists linguistics among the *Geisteswissen-
schaften* (moral sciences) but assumes that its method is closer to that
of the natural sciences; the Frenchman Lucien Adam (1881) argues that
the study of phonetics and that of morphology do not depend on human
will and consequently belong to the natural sciences, while syntax and
'functionologie', i.e. semantics, are 'sciences de l'esprit'.[28]

In spite of the standard textbook presentation of the synchrony/
diachrony contrast as purely Saussurean, most of the general works of
our period have no difficulty in distinguishing between an approach
which considers the linguistic data at a given point of time (or perhaps
without regard to time) and an approach which looks at them as developing through time (see above, p. 250, for Paul). Practice and terminology differ: some authors simply put the distinction into practice but do
not mention it (Peeters 1988), while there are explicit statements by
Baudouin and Kruszewski,[29] by Henry Sweet and by the English phoneticians in general, and also by Winteler (1876), Gabelentz (1891; cf.
Coseriu 1967) and Schuchardt ([1874ff.] 1922, 264ff.), etc. (cf. Koerner
[1980] 1989, 257ff.). Obviously it does not follow that in these authors
synchrony plays the same role as in Saussure or is understood in the
same manner.

Together with a greater awareness of the contrast between 'static'
and 'dynamic' approaches we find some redimensioning of history. We
have seen that for Paul this is all important because of its explanatory
power. Yet we read in Gabelentz (1891, 61) that, though the prehistory

of the individual languages is instructive and whenever possible must be reconstructed, linguists should not forget that their task is to explain language as it is and to understand it as it lives in the mind of the speakers 'who manage their language without looking backwards to its prehistory, or sideways to its dialects or its foreign relatives'.

A concern for language change is omnipresent at the time but is certainly less prominent in Friedrich Müller, Steinthal and, to a certain extent, Wegener. As for the interest in language classification, at one extreme there were Hovelacque, Friedrich Müller and Misteli, who concentrated on language characterization and classification, and at the other e.g. Wegener, Bréal, Darmesteter and, up to a point, Paul, who tended to give it less importance – not to mention Schuchardt, who thought that classification was impossible. Problems of grammatical description are tackled in Gabelentz (1991) but also in e.g. Wundt and before him Wegener and indeed Paul. There is an increasing awareness of the inadequacy of the old grammatical categories for the description of different languages; as Bréal put it as early as 1868 (30f.), 'nowadays we do not look any longer for the nine parts of speech in Chinese, nor is there any question of a six case declension in French'.

A comparison between the list of contents of the first set of *Lectures on the Science of Language* by Max Müller ([1861] 1862) and the much later *Sprachwissenschaft* by Georg von der Gabelentz (1891) may illustrate how things had developed in the course of thirty years or so, even if we make allowance for the different audiences at which the two books aimed. The headings of Max Müller's chapters are: 'I. The Science of Language one of the physical sciences; II. The growth of language in contradistinction to the history of language; III. The empirical stage in the science of language; IV. The classificatory stage in the science of language; V. The genealogical classification of languages; VI. Comparative grammar; VII. The constituent elements of language [i.e. roots, etc.]; VIII. The morphological classification of language; IX. The theoretical stage in the science of language. – Origin of language'. Gabelentz's first section, by contrast, started with generalities about language and a brief history of linguistics but then turned to a discussion of various approaches with which the linguist must be familiar: phonetics, psychology, logic. The other three sections of the book deal with *einzelsprachliche Forschung* (the analysis of individual languages), 'genealogical-historical' linguistics, and finally general linguistics (*allgemeine Sprachwissenschaft*). Here the subjects discussed are the human capacity for language, the language of animals, etc., the analysis of discourse, the organization of morphological material, word order, intonation, grammatical categories, etc. – all this with reference to a number of non-Indo-European languages. In the arrangement there is an inescapable air of modernity that Max Müller lacks. The main difference is perhaps in the role explicitly assigned to historical linguistics. Gabelentz (1891, 12) acknowledges that historical linguists and comparativists have had such brilliant results that they may well be entitled to some complacency, but also envisages a situation in which they might say: 'In linguistics progress occurs entirely and exclusively within this school; those who remain outside it may call themselves philologists, philosophers of language, even language experts or polyglots, or whatever they like, but they must not pretend that they are linguists [*Linguisten*] and that their subject is linguistics [*Sprachwissenschaft*]'. Gabelentz's rebuke is immediate: 'Whoever speaks like that confuses the small field that he is ploughing with the meadows of a large community, and, to use a Chinese comparison, thinks like someone who sits in a well and maintains that the sky is small'.

The odds are that a bibliographical typology of the type that we have envisaged would reveal a much wider range of interests and opinions than is normally suspected. This area would also be a fruitful searching ground for enquiries, such as that envisaged by Formigari (1990), into the philosophical assumptions and background of the work of our period, not least because in addition to the works mentioned there were other articles or monographs, which in present terms would be normally described as contributions to the philosophy of language rather than to linguistics, while others tackled (again in a philosophical or psychological mode) the forbidden question of the origin of language, and still others were closer to rhetorical or literary studies.[30] Schmidt (1976) has argued that Gerber, Max Müller and the philosopher Georg Runze (1852–1922) saw thought as inextricably tied to language so that, in an extreme version, i.e. Max Müller's version, a solution of all philosophical problems could come from a new philosophical language, and, even more radically, 'if we fully understood the whole growth of every word, philosophy would have and could have no longer any secrets. It would cease to exist' (Max Müller 1887, 515).[31] Schmidt compares these authors with the first exponents of analytical philosophy, but see the objections by Knobloch (1988, 426). One may at least wonder whether for Max Müller, with his fundamentally monogenetic views, his rejection of Darwinism, and his concern for the fundamental, i.e. the earliest, roots, the important point is not rather the hope that the historical techniques which allow us to reconstruct those roots may also lead to a clarification of concepts, something which ties in with the very different attitude later supported e.g. by Kainz and Heidegger.

10.7 Core linguistics

Modern scholarship often distinguishes between core linguistics and the so-called linguistic subfields, which may include, e.g. historical linguistics. The coverage of core linguistics is debatable but phonology, morphology, syntax and semantics would appear in most lists, while phonetics, discourse analysis and pragmatics may also qualify. The approach, needless to say, is mostly synchronic. Before we conclude our sketchy panorama of the new departures at the end of the century we may ask what work was being done in these areas – though even with this anodine formulation the risk of anachronism is great, since for most linguists of our period core linguistics was indeed historical linguistics. While the standard historical and comparative works (e.g. Brugmann 1902–4 or Meyer-Lübke 1890–1902) regularly had separate sections for phonetics/phonology (*Lautlehre*), morphology (*Formenlehre*), syntax and, sometimes, lexical development (though the latter two were often missing), the more general books which we mentioned above did not follow this arrangement. Our categorization is open to challenge, but as early as 1870 Baudouin de Courtenay (1972, 61), who was writing in general (non-historical) terms, stated that grammar may be subdivided into three basic parts: phonology (phonetics) or the study of sounds; word formation in the broadest sense of the word, and syntax.[32]

10.7.1 Phonetics and phonology

We have already mentioned some of the early work in phonetics (p. 160ff.) and have also referred to the role of phoneticians in the Reform Movement for the teaching of foreign languages (p. 295). By the end of the century the various systems of phonetic transcription which proliferated earlier tend to gel round two basic models which still survive: that devised by Lepsius (see p. 161), which used letters of the Latin alphabet with various diacritics, and that of the newly formed (1888) International Phonetic Association (IPA), which is now more widely diffused (in an updated version) and uses a mixture of alphabetic and other symbols. The issues were of a double nature: on the one hand the progress in articulatory and acoustic phonetics was bound to have an influence on the type and number of symbols needed; on the other hand the choice of symbols required a series of practical decisions since not all symbols could easily be printed or recognized. In 1880 Henry Sweet, whose *Handbook of Phonetics* (1877) had appeared a few years earlier, declared himself confident that in the analysis of sounds there was 'a sufficient number of firmly established results to form the basis of an organic alphabet' ([1880] 1913, 291) and proceeded to consider the practical difficulties and the rationale behind the earlier proposals. Yet the practice of phonetic transcription called for a series of decisions not only about the symbols but also about the level of differentiation to be indicated in the transcription: Sweet (1877, 103) pointed out that it was not always necessary to go into minute details and that it was possible to distinguish between a narrow and a broad transcription. In a number of cases what was needed was an alphabet 'which indicates only those broader distinctions of sound which actually correspond to distinctions of meaning in language'. Similarly, if in a language two features always occur together, it is useless to symbolize them in the transcription; all that needs to be indicated is 'those distinctions of sounds . . . which are *independently significant*' (*ibid.*, 104). Sweet represents the acme of that English school of orthoepists and phoneticians (Bell, Ellis, etc.) who in this period, mostly starting from practical needs, were moving the first steps towards a concept of phoneme as a distinctive phonological unit.[33] Somewhat later, Paul Passy, in drafting the first formal statement of the aims of the IPA in 1888, stated in the *Phonetic Teacher* that 'there should be a separate letter for each distinctive sound; that is, for each sound which, being used instead of another, can change the meaning of a word' (Jones 1957, 5). This is of course the period in which both the articulatory and the acoustic study of the sounds of language become much more sophisticated and instrumental phonetics begins: we mentioned already Rousselot's work (cf. pp. 226, 289). What now emerges is the need (partly determined by practical considerations) to identify functional units and to distinguish between physical and physiological facts on the one hand, linguistic facts on the other; in other words, we come closer to the contrast between phonetics and phonemics though we cannot as yet speak of a theoretical distinction between the two levels of analysis.[34] From a different point of view but as early as 1870 Baudouin de Courtenay ([1920] 1922, 61) had made a distinction between 'the analysis of sounds from a purely physiological point of view' and 'the role of sounds in the mechanism of language, their value for the feeling of a speech community', but both he and Kruszewski went further in their Kazan' period. They tried to understand what they called at different times *Lautwechsel*, alternations, etc., i.e. synchronic alternations which are phonologically or morphologically determined as in *intolerant/impossible* with [n]/[m] or *electric/electricity* with [k]/[s] or *life/lives* with [f]/[v]. In so doing they developed the beginnings of both a phonemic and a morphophonemic theory. In Kruszewski the main analysis is synchronic (or static); the same is true for Baudouin though he finds it impossible to dispense with the concept of etymologically related sounds. A basic distinction which both Kruszewski and Baudouin make (though not exactly in these terms) is that between automatic, phonetically determined, alternations which in a given language are generally applicable, and morphologically determined alternations which may apply to some lexical items but not others. On the one hand, we have e.g. the Russian nominative *vodá* [vʌ'da] 'water' vs. the accusative *vódu* ['vodu], where the stressed vowel differs from the unstressed one ([o] does not occur in unstressed position), and on the other, the German singular *Buch* 'book' with [u] vs.

the plural *Büch-er* 'books' with [y], where the umlaut process (the [u]/[y] alternation) occurs only in some nouns but not in others. We do not find at this stage a clear distinction between allophonic variants ([pʰ] in *pin* vs. [p] in *spin*) and neutralization of phonemic contrasts ([n]/[m] in *intolerable*/*impossible*), but there certainly are the presuppositions for such distinctions.[35] The novelty is in the attempt to produce an explicit theory for linguistic description and to investigate in detail the relationship between phonetics and morphology. Not the least sign of modernity in both Kruszewski and Baudouin is their striving for explicitness – with the consequent outpouring of new technical terminology. Baudouin himself (1895, 6) regretted his terminological excesses, but, while most of the new terms were soon forgotten, some are still with us. Phoneme, morpheme, grapheme are among them: the first two deserve some attention; for the third, which is later, see Kohrt (1985, 168ff.).

10.7.2 Phonemes and morphemes

We owe our use of the term phoneme to the Prague school, which in turn owes it to Kruszewski and Baudouin (the latter confirms that he is indebted to his pupil for the term). Kruszewski certainly took it from Saussure's *Mémoire* (1879 but 1878), where *phonème* was far more frequent than the generic *son,* with which it occasionally alternated, but from which it probably differed in stressing the contrastive character of the 'sound' or 'sound sequence'.[36] For Kruszewski, *phoneme* provided the needed technical term to indicate an indivisible 'phonetic' unit (we would say 'morphophonemic' or in some cases 'phonological') in contrast with 'sound', which was an 'anthropophonic' unit (we would say 'phonetic'). As apparently is also the case in Saussure, for Kruszewski the phoneme could correspond to a single segment, but also to two or more segments which acted as a single entity in the alternations; from this point of view for Kruszewski both the Greek [i] in *elipon* 'I left' and the Greek [ej] in *leipō* 'I am leaving' counted as individual phonemes. This is still remote from the more modern distinction between phonemes and morphophonemes, though a start has been made highlighting the difference between the functional and the physiological/auditory level of analysis. Later on Baudouin also distinguished between sound (*Laut*) as an 'anthropophonic' (i.e. phonetic) unit and phoneme as a phonetic (we would say phonological) unit (Mugdan 1984a, 66), while still holding to the idea of the phoneme as defined by the alternations in which it takes part either within a language or in correspondences across languages. By 1895 (and, in fact, much earlier) the emphasis has shifted to psychology and the phoneme has become the mental counterpart of a speech sound.[37] At the same stage, phonetics is treated as subsuming two types of work: the anthropophonic work concerns articulatory and auditory phenomena while the psychophonetic work concerns the representations of those facts (i.e. the phonemes). Yet Baudouin still attributes considerable importance to his theory of alternations – i.e. in our terminology, to morphophonemic facts. Still later (1917) we are told that phonemes have no meaning but acquire linguistic importance when they are part of morphemes, i.e. of significant elements (Mugdan 1984a, 74). In other words, with the two Polish linguists we come near to a phonological theory not starting from phonetics (as was the case with the English linguists) or from language teaching, but from morphology, either static or historical; the decisive steps, however, belong to the twentieth century.

If 'phoneme' is an old term which Kruszewski and Baudouin redefined, 'morpheme' is a creation by Baudouin and appears in his work from the 1880s. In 1895 it is defined side by side with phoneme as 'that part of the word which is endowed with psychological autonomy and is for the very same reason not further divisible' (Baudouin de Courtenay 1895, 10 = 1972, 153). Clearly we are dealing with a unit which belongs, as we are told elsewhere, to the semasiological level; for Baudouin the basic units of grammar are the sentence and then the words, the morphemes and the phonemes. Baudouin does not distinguish, explicitly at least, between morpheme and allomorph, though in fact his theory of alternations depends on the identification of morphological units with no functional distinction.

Kruszewki died too early to complete his work; Baudouin's thought was better known in East Europe than in the West and even now must be reconstructed from lecture notes or short articles rather than from a coherent textbook-like work. Even so there is little doubt that these two linguists started a type of enquiry which was to dominate the following century.

10.7.3 Syntax

It is normally said that in the last part of the nineteenth century there was little or no interest in syntax: Saussure is acclaimed for having written a doctoral dissertation about Sanskrit syntax at a time when the subject was ignored. However, as Graffi's (1991) admirable work has shown, a number of scholars, including some of the leading figures among the neogrammarians (Delbrück, Brugmann), took very seriously the problems of syntax. The difficulty is, once again, that, while there was an agreed methodology for the analysis of **historical** phonology and morphology (*Lautlehre und Formenlehre*), the same unanimity and the same cumulative effects in the results were not available for either **descriptive** or **historical** syntax. All that we can do here is to refer briefly, on the one hand, to the type of syntactical analyses which were being published, and, on the other, to the general theoretical problems which were under consideration.[38]

Books, monographs and articles which described the syntax of a specific language or group of languages did of course exist. There was, first of all, a tradition of syntactical studies for the classical languages (Greek and Latin) which went back a long way and became more prominent in the nineteenth century. Round the middle of the century, books such as the Latin grammar (1841a) and the Greek syntax (1846) by Madvig were translated into a number of European languages: they were school grammars but created a bridge between the practical work aimed at school teaching and the more detailed scholarly works (cf. also Madvig 1841b, 1848). Madvig himself reflected about syntax in a more theoretical vein,[39] but otherwise the main concerns were often philological or practical: to understand the classical authors, to learn how to write Greek or Latin prose. The treatment was mostly synchronic but in some instances a historical element was introduced. In most textbooks or grammars a great deal was taken for granted and the description was couched in traditional terms, making use of categories which partly went back to the ancient grammarians, partly to the tradition of Port Royal, partly to eighteenth-century analyses. General problems were sometimes mentioned: the link between logical categories and syntactical categories, the role of psychological explanations, the theory of cases, the way in which the grammatical categories were identified or were assigned a 'basic meaning', etc.

A second source of syntactical work is provided by the school grammars and the more extensive reference works dedicated to modern languages (European and, less frequently, non-European). A possible generalization is that, while in the nineteenth century for phonology and morphology the new developments came from the scholarly work that we have been describing, in the first six or seven decades of the century for syntactical analysis the lead was taken by the school grammars.[40] Thus the graphic representation of sentence structure in the shape of a tree (which in this century was first adopted by Tesnière and then, in different manner, by American structuralism) goes back in the last resort to schoolbooks used to teach Latin (Coseriu 1980, Lepschy 1991), which influenced first Franz Kern (1830–94), who wrote about German syntax, and then H. Tiktin, the author of a Romanian grammar (1891–3) which included a volume dedicated to syntax (cf. p. 311).

In 1870 Georg Curtius, whose school grammar of Greek had been immensely successful, observed that, though his work had been very innovative in its morphological part, the same could not be said for syntax, where it did not differ very much from the standard treatments (Curtius 1870, 154); on the one hand, the preliminary work of fact-finding had not been done, on the other, syntax was beset by old assumptions (presumably reflecting its practitioners). However, within the historical and comparative tradition which we have been examining, syntax was not altogether neglected: Grimm's *Deutsche Grammatik* included a fourth volume on syntax (1837). Similarly, Diez dedicated to syntax the third volume (1843) of his *Grammatik der romanischen Sprache* (1836–44) and was followed by W. Meyer-Lübke with the third volume (1899) of his own grammar of Romance languages. The Swiss scholar Adolf Tobler (1835–1910), who became professor at Berlin, was mostly concerned with the historical syntax of French. Before Meyer-Lübke, Franz Miklosich had adopted Grimm's and Diez's model and dedicated to syntax the fourth volume (1868–75, 2nd edn 1883) of his *Vergleichende Grammatik der slavischen Sprachen* (1852–75, 2nd edn 1876–83), while also writing extensively about the so-called impersonal verbs such as 'it rains', etc. (1883). The same pattern must have also been the inspiration for Berthold Delbrück's three volumes of Indo-European syntax (1893–1900), written as a follow-up to Brugmann's *Grundriß* and based on Delbrück's earlier work, which included *inter alia* an *Altindische Syntax* (1888) and four other volumes of *Syntaktische Forschungen* (1871–88). Curtius had encouraged his classical pupils to write detailed, factual analyses of syntactical phenomena, and there are even from other schools a number of contributions of this type which oscillate between the descriptive and the historical approach. The most notable perhaps is Jacob Wackernagel's mammoth article 'about a law of Indo-European word order' (1892), which started from the detailed observation of the ordering of clitics in Greek, Latin, Sanskrit, etc., and defined a law of word order (Wackernagel's law: clitics take second position in the clause, whatever their meaning), which is now sometimes treated as a linguistic universal as well as being the only statement about Indo-European word order which is generally accepted. When later on the psychologist Wundt discussed syntactical problems in his *Die Sprache* (1900), the questions were looked at from yet another angle and from the perspective of languages other than the Indo-European ones, but Wundt was aware of the work done by the Indo-Europeanists and the Romanists.

10.7.3.1 Points of convergence: formalism and psychologism
In general, the discussion about syntax, conducted as it was within various disciplines (classical languages, modern languages, even 'exotic' languages, psychology, etc.), with various aims (language learning, scholarly research) and from various angles (historical, descriptive, comparative, psychological, philosophical), predictably led to disparate results, but in our period a few common features (mostly negative) begin to emerge. It is no longer legitimate to describe all languages on the model of Latin: English does not have cases (Sweet 1875–6). At the same time there is a general unease towards the 'logical' definitions which school grammars had inherited from the older tradition.[41] Henry Sweet (*ibid.*, 471) took as his starting point a plea for synchrony ('before history

must come a knowledge of what now exists. We must learn to observe things as they are without regard to their origin') and then observed that 'the ultimate ideas of language are by no means identical with those of psychology, still less with those of metaphysics' (*ibid.*, 484). In his view there was indeed a relation between language and logic, but only because a logical proposition is simply 'a stereotyped form of the linguistic sentence' (*ibid.*, 489ff.). Curtius (1870, 156) advocated the rejection of all preconceived notions and constructions still found in schoolbooks and continued in a critical vein: 'All those linguistic categories, forms of thought, relations between sentences, or however one may call them now or called them in the past, to which so much importance has been given and partly is still given, basically depend on the assumption that thought exists before language, that language forms are the product of sharp reflection, the discovery of individuals, of the founders of language, of the *inventores, constitutores sermonis*'. There followed a positive reference to Humboldt and expressions of praise for Steinthal's and Heyse's approach.

What all this meant in practice is best shown through an example which Curtius would have understood. The classical teacher Raphael Kühner (1802–78) began the section on the simple sentence in his monumental Greek grammar ([1834–5] 2nd edn 1869–70, ii, 28) with a series of firm statements: 'Syntax is the study of the sentence. A sentence is the expression of a thought in words . . . Thought is the mental act, through which man joins two concepts – a verbal concept and a substantival concept – into one unit . . . Thus the essence of each thought consists of three elements: two material ones, the substantival and verbal concepts, and a mental one, the combination of both into a unit. . . . The verbal concept which indicates what is stated (predicated) of the substantival concept, is called predicate; the substantival concept which indicates the object of which something is stated, is called subject'. The remote intellectual ancestry of these definitions is clear. The *Grammaire de Port Royal* (1660, 29), which we quoted apropos of Bopp (p. 134), stated: 'The judgement which we make of things, as when I say "the earth is round", is called proposition, and each proposition necessarily contains two terms, one called subject, which is that of which one affirms, like "earth", the other called attribute, which is what one affirms, like "round", and in addition the link between the two, "is" '.[42]

In 1897 F. B. Gerth (1844–1911), another *Gymnasium* teacher, who after Kühner's death had been entrusted with the revision of his Greek syntax, explained in his preface that Kühner had not been able to avoid the tendency, which still prevailed in his time, to derive all linguistic facts from philosophical categories. Thus, as Gerth (Kühner-Gerth 1898–1904, I, v f.) pointed out, Kühner operated in terms of three and not four Greek moods (indicative, subjunctive, imperative), treating the optative as a form of subjunctive of the past, because he wished to accommodate the moods within the standard tripartition of perception (*Wahrnehmung*), conception or representation (*Vorstellung*), desire (*Begehrungsvermögen*).[43] Gerth himself accepted the four-mood distinctions, while assuming that the subjunctive is the mood of expectation (*Erwartung*) and the optative that of conception (*Vorstellung*). There followed a cautious statement: 'naturally these are not definitions of so-called basic meanings (*Grundbedeutung*); they are simply general formulae which can comfortably cover the various usages of those moods' (Kühner-Gerth 1898–1904, I, vi; cf. *ibid.*, 200ff.).

Obviously, as soon as linguists moved away from phonology and morphology the difficulties multiplied, not least because the complexity of the earlier background could not be altogether ignored. On the one hand there were the different traditions of the *Grammaire de Port Royal* (1660) and of eighteenth-century philosophical grammar, which in our period were no longer known at first hand and were often seen – mistakenly – as identical; on the other hand there was the German Romanticism with its strong anti-rationalistic bias. With Steinthal and his attack against universal grammar, a psychological model had been introduced, but it was not altogether clear how this was to be implemented in the concrete work of syntactical description. Yet at this stage, partly because of the new psychological school, partly because of the general emphasis on language diversity, everything spoke against a view of language as reflecting 'les opérations de nôtre esprit'. The constant complaint was that logic imposed a strait-jacket onto language and led to a distortion of the data. Again Henry Sweet (1875–6, 487) pleaded for a clear distinction between formal definitions and definitions in terms of meaning or logical categories: 'We see now that the only satisfactory definition of a part of speech must be a purely formal one: "snow", for instance, is not a noun because it stands for a thing, but because it can stand as the subject of a proposition, because it can form its plural by adding *s*, because it has a definite prefix, &c., and "whiteness" is a noun for precisely the same reasons.' Similarly, Delbrück (1893–1900, i, 175–88) while trying to define the meaning of cases carefully explains Pāṇini's analysis, which started from the possible relations between nouns and verbs, even if he then prefers to return to the form and to give for each formal unit, i.e. for the traditional case forms, a *Grundbegriff*, i.e. a basic meaning (Lehmann 1980).

We may now return to the Port Royal assumption that propositions expressed judgements and that these required three elements, subject, predicate and the link between the two. Bopp had tried to provide historical evidence for this view, arguing that all verbs incorporated forms of the verb 'to be' (i.e. of the copula) and of the personal pronouns which could then serve as subjects. But Bopp's project had misfired

(Delbrück 1893–1900, i, 29) and the later discussions moved in the opposite direction, stressing the early existence of nominal sentences, i.e. of those sentences which included a subject and predicate but not the copula (Latin *omnia praeclara rara* 'all outstanding things [are] rare'), and of the early 'impersonal' constructions (Latin *pluit* '[it] rains') with no subject. There was no reason to believe that sentences formed of one single element (a vocative, an interjection, an 'impersonal' verb) were secondary creations. This opened the whole question of what a sentence was and at the same time of what the status was of categories such as subject and predicate. Sentences could be defined grammatic- ally as requiring a finite verb, which of course left nominal sentences, exclamations, etc. in a marginal position (Misteli, Kern), or could be seen as expressions which were understood by both speakers and hearers as coherent and complete units for the purposes of communication (Delbrück, Meyer-Lübke). In a more psychological vein, Paul defined the sentence as giving linguistic expression to the linking of a number of representations in the mind of the speaker and acting as the means to produce the same combination in the mind of the hearer. Wundt's own definition reacted, as usual, against the assumption of unconscious mental representations and started from the idea of a whole which was decomposed rather than of a number of units which were combined. The sentence was then taken as a linguistic expression which inten- tionally articulated into its component parts a whole, which was pres- ent in consciousness – a formulation which was attacked by Paul *inter alia* because it ignored the role of the hearer, as contrasted with the speaker. This multitude of views may be a sign of theoretical confusion, but also gives an indication of an active discussion, which sometimes combined – and sometimes contrasted – a functional, a grammatical, a psychological and, with Wegener (1885), a pragmatic approach. A complete account ought to go into a more detailed analysis and con- sider the work of the philosophers/psychologists such as Franz Brentano, Anton Marty (one of his pupils), and, obviously, Wilhelm Wundt (their opponent).[44]

The discussions about the nature and status of subject and predic- ate, the two elements which are present in the majority of sentences, if not in all, took place against this background. As early as 1844, Weil (cf. p. 193) had maintained that in ancient languages word order had a subjective purpose and highlighted a part of the utterance in prefer- ence to others; in modern languages it could do the same but it also served a syntactical purpose. Later on Gabelentz (1869) began to speak of a psychological subject and predicate: the speaker aims at draw- ing the attention of the hearer to a certain point (subject) and to make the hearer think a determinate thing about it; the psychological and grammatical categories do not need to overlap, though sometimes this happens. Word order – the psychological subject always occurs at the beginning of the sentence – offers a formal criterion for the identification of subject and predicate. With different terminology (and occasionally different analyses of the same examples), similar views were introduced by Wegener (1885), while Paul, who also spoke of psychological subject and predicate and contrasted them with the grammatical categories, still felt that it was not possible to ignore altogether the connections between grammatical and logical relations. The possibility then arises, even if it is not always exploited, of a three-layer distinction between grammatical, psychological and logical categories.[45] On the other hand a different path is followed by the Swedish Romanist Carl Svedelius (1861–1951), who in his doctoral thesis (1897) started unfashionably from content rather than form and developed a theory of communication which rejected entirely the notions of subject and predicate and came closer to the valence theory of the twentieth century (Knobloch 1988, 319ff.; Graffi 1991, 146ff.).

10.7.3.2 Syntax and morphosyntax: John Ries

There was yet another matter for debate. In 1894 John Ries, a Germanist, published a short monograph with the title *Was ist Syntax? Ein kritischer Versuch*, which took its starting point from the criticism of recent work in German syntax.[46] Ries noted that syntax had been left behind if compared with the other developments in linguistics and called for serious rethinking. A typology of previous works would distinguish between those which started from meaning as something given and enquired about the forms that expressed it and those which started from the forms and enquired about their meaning. According to Ries, the first approach (which would normally be associated with Becker) was definitely superseded; the second approach was on the right tracks but did not always lead to acceptable results. The difficulty arose in connection with scholars such as Miklosich, for whom syntax was the study of word classes or word forms and their meaning. For Ries this identification of syntax and morphosyntax must be at all costs resisted; in his view syntax is certainly closer to the study of sentences (*Satzlehre*) than to morphosyntax but is not identical to it either. The very concept of *Satz* 'sentence' is still based on the old logical definition according to which the sentence is the linguistic expression of a judgement. It is much better to assume that syntax, strictly speaking, is the study of word sequences, thus restoring the parallelism between the various units which are the object of linguistic study: the sounds, the words (which are sequences of sounds) and the word sequences (including the sentences). The words can be studied from the point of view of their form but also from that of their meaning; similarly, the word sequences can be studied formally or semantically. Here Ries (1894, 78ff.) assigns a new role to his *Bedeutungslehre,* which becomes not an optional part of grammar but an integral component of all linguistic analysis (Knobloch 1988, 318).

It is indeed true that not only Miklosich, but also most of the contemporary Indo-Europeanists, concentrated on questions of morphosyntax, i.e. preferred to discuss the meaning and distribution of the main categories (the cases, the moods, etc.), rather than the structure of the sentence or the utterance. One reason, as Graffi (1991, 128) has pointed out, is that, given the difficulties of Indo-European reconstruction, comparativists could hardly do anything else; another, also mentioned by Graffi, is the contemporary uncertainty about the validity of the logical or the psychological models of syntactical analysis. This last point may be pursued further. If, as Ries argued, contemporary linguistics, in contrast with universal grammar, preferred to start from the formal aspects of language in order to move to meaning, then the obvious step was to start with an enquiry into the meaning and function of e.g. cases, moods, etc. To start from the form of the sentence or the utterance was not easy because it was not clear how this should be analysed or classified. Ries (1894, 138f.) was aware of the difficulty and suggested that linguists could establish through formulae or diagrams a way to define the schemata of the various word-combinations in the language. The models that he quotes are the formulaic analyses of sentences offered by Paul and Gabelentz or the *Satzbilder* (images of the sentence) produced by Kern; in effect what he has in mind are the ancestors of the trees of immediate-constituent analysis or of Tesnière's stemmata (see p. 305). In general, Ries's contention is that this work, which is definitely understood as descriptive and not prescriptive, and, as far as one can judge, synchronic and not diachronic, is preliminary to any analysis of the meaning of sentences or utterances. The final aim is an integrated theory of form and meaning in which syntax implicitly acquires a primary role since the meaning and function of words can only be established starting from the utterance, and sounds can only be analysed starting from the words.[47]

10.7.4 The study of meaning

The term 'syntax' is a borrowing from Greek, where it was used in a sense not very different from the modern one. By contrast, 'semantics', or more exactly *sémantique,* is a deliberate creation (based on the Greek verb σημαίνω 'signify') by Michel Bréal in the last quarter of the century. It first appears in print in the context of an invitation made by Bréal (1883, 133) to his readers not to follow the majority of linguists and concentrate on the 'body and form' of words but rather to consider 'the laws that preside to the transformation of senses, the choice of new expressions, the birth and death of locutions'. Next to 'phonétique et morphologie' Bréal pleads for a *sémantique*, a 'science des signi-fications'.[48] This does not mean of course that Bréal was the first lin-guist to be concerned with meaning in the nineteenth century. We had occasion before to consider questions which could be broadly called semantic, from Bopp, who worried about how words or morphemes can acquire the meaning they have, to Humboldt's views about the way in which meaning is differently expressed in different languages, to Grimm's concern with the referent of words, i.e. with *Wörter und Sachen*, to Steinthal's psychological approach and his attempts to define the meaning of a word and the meaning of a sentence, to – at a more practical level – the various discussions about how to organize dic-tionaries, etc. It is true, however, that the historical work had largely concentrated on phonology and morphology. This was the immediate result of a series of concurrent factors: (a) the emphasis on language diversity was bound to highlight those aspects of language where divers-ity was most immediately identifiable, (b) the successes of the com-parative method privileged the comparison of forms, (c) the insistence on an empirical inductive approach coupled with a general (and gen-eric) anti-philosophical bias led to the rejection of any predetermined categorization of meanings. Of twentieth-century linguistics it has been said that its general tendency, exemplified in writers as diverse as Bloomfield, Jespersen and Hjemslev, is 'to insist that the semantic units of a language are those that have formal expression in it' (Matthews 1993, 14). In the nineteenth century the same point had been explicitly made by Schleicher; implicitly or explicitly it was accepted by most main-stream linguists (Bréal was an exception and so, to a certain extent, was Madvig), who assumed that in this view lay their major difference from their predecessors. None of these considerations prevented a study of meaning, but their combination helps to explain why this came to have lower priority. That no systematic attempt was usually made to provide an explicit description of meaning or a theory of meaning is not surprising in a period in which description and theory were not the primary aims.

     Yet semantics was not the only term devised for such a study. In German the standard expression was *Bedeutungslehre*, but we men-tioned before the two classicists of the beginning and middle of the century, Karl Reisig (1792–1829) and Friedrich Haase (1808–67), who, thanks to their posthumous books, count as the founders of the German *Semasiologie* in what Baldinger (1957, 5) has called its subterranean phase. There is indeed a continuous line of thought from Reisig to the end of the century, but its protagonists tend to be classicists rather than linguists and often school teachers rather than university teachers. For Reisig, grammar (*Sprachlehre*) consisted of its two traditional parts, etymology (i.e. according to the tradition in which he operated, the study of phonology, morphology, word formation and orthography) and syntax, to which it was necessary to add the study of the principles which explain the development of meaning and use of certain words, that is to say what he called *Bedeutungslehre* or *Semasiologie* (which included a study of synonymy). Words, for Reisig, correspond to extralinguistic concepts which change in time; a good classicist will meticulously establish the succession of meanings, but it is then possible to establish a logical classification in terms of the standard rhetorical figures (metonymy, etc.). Here the classicist's historicism is superimposed onto the basic 'philosophical' approach to grammar. In Haase, Reisig's pupil, the logico-philosophical apparatus disappears and the task of *Bedeutungslehre* is defined as that of establishing the rules for the alternation and transitions of word meaning ('die Regeln über den Wechsel und die Uebergänge der Wortbedeutung', Haase 1874–80, i, 74), but the subject is deemed to be in its infancy. To list in the correct historical order the various meanings for each word is not enough; we must identify the general laws and rules according to which change and extension of concepts and meanings have historically occurred (*ibid.*, 128). The new discipline acquires a much wider range than in Reisig: 'in my view the largest part of present-day syntax comes under *Bedeutungslehre*' (*ibid.*, 75), a statement which is immediately rejected by the third classicist who is listed as a major exponent of semasiology. Ferdinand Heerdegen (1845–1930), the re-editor of Reisig's lectures, pleads, in theory at least, for a *Semasiologie* which is exclusively concerned with the function of individual words.[49]

On the British side of the Channel the meaning of words had been studied, as we have seen, by Horne Tooke ([1786] 1798–1805), who argued that only etymology could bring us back to the true meaning of words either as signs of things or ideas or as signs of other words. Apart from the increasing realization of the weakness of Tooke's etymologies, in England as elsewhere other views begin to prevail which tie the notion of word meaning to that of use, and stress that the meaning of words is determined by the context in which they appear. We find similar statements in philosophers such as Dugald Stewart at the beginning of the century but also in Benjamin Smart, a grammarian, eloquence teacher and polymath, who created the word 'sematology' in the 1830s to refer to the study of signs and who was fundamentally concerned with meanings as expressed in sentences rather than in words. Later on, sematology was used to indicate the study of meaning by A. H. Sayce (1880, I, 339ff.) and by J. Murray in the introduction to the *New English Dictionary* (1884; cf. 1884–1928, I). Though less successful, the term came to be interchangeable with 'semasiology'. Round the turn of the century a number of other terms (glossology, comparative ideology, rhematology, etc.) make their appearance though with indifferent success (Read 1948); the only one which survived for a while was 'significs', which replaced the earlier 'sensifics' in the work of Lady Welby (1837–1912), a god-daughter of Queen Victoria who pleaded for a study of the meaning of meaning from a more general point of view than the philological and historical one and aimed at distinguishing sense, meaning and significance: the sense of a word is the sense in which the word is used, 'the circumstances, state of mind, reference, "universe of discourse" belonging to it', while its meaning is the 'intention of the user' and its significance is fundamentally the interest it has for us (Welby 1903, 5).[50]

This multitude of names for the study of meaning points to the need for a further definition of the nature of such study, but also to the multitude of approaches, to which the recent historiographical work has drawn attention (Nerlich 1992, Knobloch 1988, etc.). Towards the end of the century the range of interests increases: from lexical semantics to various forms of psychological analysis, to an attempt to produce a semantics of communication and usage (Wegener), to the diachronic generalizations of the French school. Any complete account should not ignore the contributions of philosophy. For the end of the last century the names of Gottlob Frege (1848–1925), the German philosopher of language whose work was influential in formal semantics, and that of Charles Sanders Peirce (1839–1914), who is associated with the philosophy of pragmatism and the beginnings of semiotics, must be mentioned. Yet with the exception of Lady Welby, who was in contact with Peirce and with a number of philosophers, the remaining work about meaning produced by professional linguists, or people who counted as such, remained separate from logic and philosophy.

10.7.4.1 The lexicon and lexicography
In the second part of the nineteenth century the most widespread concern was with the history of words and with what we now call historical lexical semantics (or semasiology) – not a surprising state of affairs given that this facet of the study of meaning was exactly the one which most impinged on the concrete historical work done at the time. A certain level of generality was reached in these discussions but the starting point was often within specific disciplines.

A first point of contact was with lexicography – with the explosion of lexica and, above all, of monolingual lexica, which is typical of the nineteenth century. By the last third of the century the best dictionaries were characterized by a number of features, some new, some old. First, the various senses of the words were normally illustrated by quotations; in this way the very structure of the dictionary drew attention to lexical polysemy and to the ways in which word meaning was contextually determined. Secondly, the idea of a non-prescriptive lexicon, though often controversial (then as now), was certainly well understood and largely accepted in scholarly circles. It was the hallmark of the *Deutsches Wörterbuch* by Jacob and Wilhelm Grimm (which began to appear in 1852); it was implicit in the various statements of Émile Littré's preface to his *Dictionnaire de la langue française* ([1863–72] 1889) and was highlighted by Bishop Trench (1857) in the essay *'On Some Deficiencies in our English Dictionaries'*, which anticipated the compilation of the *New English Dictionary* (the *Oxford English Dictionary*) (Murray 1884–1928) and which pleaded for a dictionary as a complete inventory of the language. In Trench's view it was not part of the lexicographer's task to select 'good' words. Both the emphasis on polysemy and the reaction against prescriptivism fed into (and were fed by) the prevailing historicism. Littré ([1863] 1889, vi) attacked the dictionary of the French Academy because each lemma started with the definition and exemplification of the most frequently attested sense rather than of the first-attested one. In that way, he argued, it was by no means clear how the various senses could be linked, while a historical ordering provided an obvious thread.[51] The *New English Dictionary* adopted the principle first expressed by Passow (p. 85) that 'every word should be made to tell its own story' (Aarsleff 1983, 255).

These various principles, which did not only belong to lexicography, were bound to have an influence both on historical and on synchronic semantics. Hermann Paul added a chapter about semantic change, or more exactly about change in the meaning of words, to the second edition of his *Prinzipien* ([1886] 1920), where he distinguished between 'usual' and 'occasional' meaning, i.e. between the general meaning of a word (we would say a lexeme) and the specific meanings of that word in the context(s), and argued that change in meaning must be correlated with the existence of 'occasional' meanings.[52] It is difficult to separate this view, which, though criticised, was influential (Nerlich 1992, 89ff.), from the experience of dictionary-writing, though Paul could go further than the lexicographer and argue that the specific meaning of a word was also defined by the non-linguistic context. In a later article (1894) about lexicography, which opened the way to the compilation of his *Deutsches Wörterbuch* (1897), Paul advanced in a synchronic/descriptive/structural direction and argued that the meaning of individual words (lexemes) can only be considered together with that of other words in the language. A systematic lexicon, in his view, would abandon the alphabetic order in order to reflect the real connections of meaning between words. What Paul did not state, however, is that this aim could only be achieved at the cost of not giving priority to the historical approach. Well after the appearance of the first edition of Paul's *Prinzipien*, Arsène Darmesteter (1846–88), a Semitist, medievalist and Romance philologist, extracted from the experience of his work for the

Dictionnaire général de la langue française (1890), which he edited together with Adolphe Hatzfeld, enough material for his immensely popular booklet on *La vie des mots étudiés dans leurs significations* (1886, 1887); he mixed with a Schleicher-type terminology (life of words, natural selection, etc.) the general assumption that change in meaning was psychologically determined and a dualism which was in tune with that of the early neogrammarians. As others after him, he envisaged the possibility of metaphors becoming fixed to the point where etymology did not have an influence on our understanding of the word and then proceeded to consider various types of meaning shifts which had diachronic repercussions, in other words to produce a typology of semantic change.[53]

10.7.4.2 The lexicon and etymology

All through the century two other types of technical work also had an impact on lexical semantics (we should not forget that most linguists were trained as Indo-Europeanists). With the new comparative approach of the nineteenth century the previously discredited art of etymologizing had acquired a new lease of life; there was almost general agreement (and not only among the neogrammarians) that it was the formal side of etymology, its ability to manipulate phonetic data, which gave it its validity. Yet, among the most thoughtful linguists it was also recognized that to link two words of two related languages or two different phases of the same language phonetically was not enough. The establishment of an etymological link also presupposed some view of semantic development; what was then required was the identification of semantic laws of development comparable to the phonetic laws. Here too Pott, the founder of Indo-European etymology, had from a very early stage highlighted the importance of a *Bedeutungslehre* (e.g. 1833–6, ii, 370); the attempt at a classification of the various types of semantic change which he inserted in the introduction to the second edition of his *Etymologische Forschungen* (1859–76, i) was widely quoted. Georg Curtius (1858–62, 75f.), in his *Grundzüge der griechischen Etymologie*, argued that it might be possible to find 'universal human laws and analogies for meaning shift, which naturally would be of the utmost importance for philosophical linguistics, and indeed for philosophy in general'. And he continued: 'Of what interest it would be, for instance, if the statement which is by and large accepted that the *abstractum* derives from the *concretum* could be supported by a rich quantity of examples from the individual languages!'.[54] Similar views are expressed by most of those who were concerned with etymology, though in some scholars, such as Schleicher (see p. 200), we find expression of scepticism about the very possibility of a study of meaning. Others, such as Lazarus Geiger (cf. p. 332 note 30), saw in correct etymology the way to a solution of the problem of the origin and nature of language and aimed at establishing 'exceptionless laws which determine the diachronic shift from one meaning to the other' (Knobloch 1988, 129; cf. Esper 1968, 85ff.). In this context, attempts are made (not always very successfully) to classify the various types of meaning change. Whitney (1875, 76), who deplored the fact that the processes of phonetic change had been classified, while those of meaning change had not, hinted that an exact classification was not possible, but recognized two major tendencies: specialization of meaning mainly occurs when generic terms are applied to individual objects ('the shiner' -> the moon), extension of meaning is partly due to figurative usage ('green' of a colour, but then 'unripe, immature'). However, the aims of etymology keep shifting and, while initially the purpose was to produce a reconstruction of how the first concepts were formed, later on the emphasis is on the development within attested languages.[55] While the meaning of a word was at some stage defined in terms of its etymology – and indeed some theorized that it is only etymology which can lead us back to a basic unitary meaning – later on it becomes almost commonplace to state that the meaning of a word is independent from its etymology. This is certainly what we find in Paul, but similar conclusions are reached by Whitney in America (cf. above, p. 211) and by Darmesteter and Bréal in France (Nerlich, 1992, 91, 158, 226, f.). Against this background the question of the word as sign and of its arbitrary nature re-emerges (e.g. in Whitney 1875, 102 and in Bréal 1897, 277) and the way is open for Saussure's conception of signs.

An alternative, and far more recondite, route to semantic thinking is also tied to etymology. We referred earlier to the attempts to reconstruct Indo-European culture; these inevitably led to an organization of the vocabulary into what we might call semantic fields (see Eichhoff 1836, Pictet 1859–63): words for animals, metals, kinship terms, etc. The result was a more structured study in reconstruction than that produced for e.g. the etymological dictionaries. However, in the last part of the century the criticism of the somewhat hasty etymologies and ill-founded conclusions reached by e.g. Pictet, also led to a reconsideration of the basic principles of semantic reconstruction and linguistic paleontology. The equation Sanskrit *aśvaḥ*, Greek ἵππος, Latin *equus* 'horse' undoubtedly called for the reconstruction of a similar word for Indo-European, but was it necessary to assume that the word referred to the domesticated horse as in the attested languages? How can we exclude the possibility that originally the word simply meant 'the swift one' and was applied to a horse-like animal, perhaps wild? The experience of this type of work was salutary not only for paleontologists but also for those who were too prone to establish a necessary link between the word and the object referred to; *inter alia* it called for serious reflection about the difference between sense and reference (or denotation), to use more modern terminology. It also highlighted, in practice if not in theory, the distinction between an approach to meaning which started from the words and one which started from the referents, i.e. the contrast between semasiology and onomasiology. In this field the end of the century is characterized by a level of caution and self-questioning which the great scholars of the mid century had not known; caution, in its turn, is prompted by a form of reflection, which even if not theoretically inclined, may lead to a rethinking of the assumptions on which lexical work was based. To read the arguments adduced against the old form of paleontology by someone such as Schrader ([1883] 1890) is as instructive for the history of historical semantics as it is for that of Indo-European reconstruction.[56]

10.7.4.3 Semantic development and Wegener's view of speech acts

The general aim of most of the work described, including that which goes under the German name of *Semasiologie*, is to establish laws of semantic development which have a certain level of generality. Knobloch (1988, 240) is right in stressing that the best outcome could only be a typology of semantic change, not a theory of meaning, but, as Nerlich (1992, 8) has emphasized, and as we have seen with Paul, the very fact of thinking about meaning – historically or otherwise – leads to a reconsideration of the principles according to which this is done. There is a clear link between the search for laws of semantic development and the beginning of a synchronic approach to semantics. On the other hand, more theoretical discussions come from outside institutionalized linguistics and most of them belong within the psychological framework which prevails in the last part of the century. We have seen Steinthal's approach to questions of meaning. He shares with many of his contemporaries the view of a word as a sign for a *Vorstellung*, a mental representation which is not to be identified with the object or the concrete referent, but in general there is a great deal of confusion between concepts and representations and about the nature of the representations, whether they exist without words or not. The multiplicity of word meanings also causes problems. The most radical solution is that by Gerber (see above, p. 302 note 8) who in *Die Sprache als Kunst* (1871–4) argues that all words are sound images (*Lautbilder*) and all are tropes; all use is figurative, there is no 'straight', 'prosastic' use (cf. Knobloch 1988, 119ff.). Further hesitation concerns the object of investigation: is it the meaning of words or that of expressions or sentences?

Against this background we must look at one of the rare theoretical books, the short monograph entitled *Untersuchungen über die Grundfragen des Sprachlebens* and published in 1885 by Philipp

Wegener (1848–1916), a classics school-teacher, who had studied at Marburg and Berlin, where he heard Steinthal. The book, which was not sufficiently philological for the contemporary taste, would have probably remained entirely unknown if some of its views had not been incorporated in the second edition (1886) of Paul's *Prinzipien*.[57] The starting point is an analysis of how communication is actually effected. In general the emphasis is on language as dialogue and on the aims of communication. To say that speech aims at the communication of thought is both too broad (why do we do it?) and too narrow (what about prayers, orders etc.?). For Wegener (1885, 67) the aim of speech is to influence the will or the cognitive processes of a person in a way which the speaker finds useful; the hearers in their turn are not passive but must be actively involved in communication. The first concern then is not for the word as such but for meaningful expressions which may consist of a word ('the child uses the word as a sentence', *ibid.*, 15) or a sentence. The basic distinction for Wegener is between what he calls the 'logical predicate' (though there is no hint of logic), which expresses what the speaker wants to convey, and the 'logical subject' or 'exposition', which provides the information necessary to understand the predicate (*ibid.*, 20). What matters here is that the preconditions for understanding may be expressed in speech (the 'exposition') but may also be clear through the 'situation', i.e. the circumstances (practical, spatial, temporal, psychological, etc.) in which the speech act takes place. At this point it is possible to move from a general theory of how meaning is conveyed to a theory of word meaning. Words have no unitary meaning: the meaning of a word may differ even for the same individual, depending on the representations with which a word is associated or can be associated and on the strength of emotion which accompanies it in the speech act (*ibid.*, 47ff.). Hence to understand a word in the sentence requires once again a work of interpretation on the basis of the data of the 'situation'. From this point of view, to understand metaphors is part of the same process. When confronted with a sentence such as 'Carthage was snuffed out by the younger Scipio', some will say that it is nonsensical, though perhaps those who know that the relationship of Scipio with Carthage is that he destroyed it will interpret the logical subject as being equivalent to 'the light of Carthage'. And yet all Romans understood *Carthago extincta est* (literally 'Carthage was snuffed out') without difficulties because for them the 'situation' was different, not because they had a different psychological organization (*ibid.*, 50f.). In other words metaphors are understood thanks to inferences from the linguistic data (logical subject and logical predicate) and from the 'situation' (the extralinguistic data), but the process is not different in nature from that of normal understanding. On the other hand, it is just this fluid situation which leads to change of meaning; metaphors 'fade away' and forms which were suitable to be logical predicates can now be used as 'expositions'. As Knobloch (1991, xxvf.) explains, according to the standard psychology of the time, language signs stood for representations which derived from sense perceptions; the speaker transmitted to the hearer knowledge of an event or action decomposed into signs and the hearer recomposed it; for Wegener, on the contrary, a verbal representation is 'an organized system of cues, fit only for the hearer who is willing and able to activate his practical knowledge of the world in order to fill in what linguistic representation has left open'. In general Wegener must count as a precursor of a pragmatic approach to the theory of speech acts and the author of an attempt to situate semantics within a more general framework than that adopted by the various exponents of *Semasiologie*. Yet his real followers belong to the twentieth century.[58]

10.7.4.4 Semantics and the French school: Michel Bréal

We have deliberately left aside until now a discussion of French linguistics. As we have seen (p. 156), in the second part of the century there were two contrasting French 'schools' of linguistics. The first group of scholars, who declared themselves positivists[59] and adopted Schleicher's positions, was headed by the Belgian Honoré Chavée (1815–1877) and then by the younger Abel Hovelacque (1843–96), the first holder of the chair of Linguistic Anthropology at the newly founded (1876) École d'Anthropologie (Desmet 1994). If contrasted with what survived of the grammatical tradition of the eighteenth century, they were innovative (in spite of their adoption of the word *idéologie*) since they adopted or perhaps anticipated the Schleicher model; if compared, on the other hand, with the group of Bréal and Gaston Paris they, or at least their head, Honoré Chavée, were antiquated simply because their historical work was not sufficiently sophisticated. Chavée dedicated large part of his work to the *lexiologie* or to the *idéologie lexiologique* or *positive*. The former was the study of words from a phonological or a semantic point of view; the latter was the study of the laws which determine the evolution of ideas when incorporated in words. In his *Lexiologie indoeuropénne* (1849), which is now entirely forgotten by Indo-Europeanists, Chavée aimed at reconstructing the basic vocabulary items of Indo-European[60] and developed a theory according to which meaning changed through individualization or assimilation of ideas. He started with some classes of meaning (we might speak of semantic fields) and analysed their development, but the absurdity of the reconstructions and etymologies makes it difficult to take the work seriously. The younger members of the school (Paul Regnaud and Julien Vinson among others) had different opinions, but shared the naturalistic views of Chavée and Hovelacque and consequently resented all the forms of mentalism, psychologism and intentionalism which they found in Bréal. At an even later stage, Raoul de la Grasserie, who was loosely associated with the group, kept the reference to ideas and ideology but also distinguished between static (i.e. synchronic) and dynamic semantics while maintaining that the former had logical priority, though it had curiously been ignored (La Grasserie 1908, 2; cf. Nerlich 1992, 194).

If the group of Chavée and Hovelacque had little impact outside France and on the later French generations, Michel Bréal and the scholars who were more or less loosely associated with him and associated with the foundation of the École Pratique des Hautes Études (from 1868) and of the Société de Linguistique de Paris (from 1866) had a more important role to play.[61] In effect what they were aiming at, largely under the impulse of Bréal and of Gaston Paris (1839–1903), seven years younger than Bréal, was the creation of a French school of linguistics which could absorb the results of German linguistics but also go beyond it with a character of its own. As we have seen (p. 156), Bréal's translation in 1866–74 of the *Vergleichende Grammatik* by Franz Bopp, with whom he had studied in Berlin, is matched by Gaston Paris' translation (1863, Diez 1874–76) of the *Grammatik der romanischen Sprachen* by Diez, his teacher. While the older Littré (p. 315) and Arsène Darmesteter (cf. note 53), who also gravitated towards the school of Gaston Paris, came to the study of meaning from the experience of lexicography and of modern French studies, Bréal, a classicist and comparativist by training, started his career with some studies of comparative mythology, strongly influenced by Kuhn and Max Müller, but soon turned either to more philological enterprises (his edition of the Igubine Tables, numerous specific articles about points of Greek or Latin linguistics) or to more general discussions, which opened the way to his own main work, the *Essai de sémantique (Science des significations)* of 1897. Bréal's achievements are certainly in his more general work as well as in his success in establishing linguistics in France. As Antoine Meillet ([1930] 1938, 218), his successor at the Collège de France, pointed out, he had deliberately cut himself out of the progress in comparative work which was going on in Germany, first by reacting against Schleicher's organicism and then by seeing in the insistence of the neogrammarians on sound laws without exceptions another side of that dry scientificism which he had deplored in Schleicher. But while others (e.g. the neogrammarians in the case of Schleicher, or Henry Sweet, in the case of both Schleicher and the neogrammarians) were ready to dissociate themselves from some of the general views of their theoretical opponents, while accepting their results in reconstruction and evolutionary studies, Bréal preferred to turn to more general discussions.[62] His – justified – complaint, from as early as the 1860s, was that contemporary historical linguistics concentrated on linguistic forms at the expense of function and meaningful content. In his view the aim of historical grammar is to seek in the mind the cause of language change; the method must join the study of forms with that of meaning ([1866] 1877, 247). He reproached not only Schleicher but Bopp too for giving the impression that language evolves according to natural laws as if it was a fourth kingdom of nature (*ibid.*, 248). Bréal himself firmly wanted to bring back language into the human domain and to make of linguistics an historical discipline. At this early stage he pleads for a strong uniformitarian position and for the realization that the history of language must not be envisaged merely as decay; there may be phonetic decay but the meaningful organization of language may actually improve. Meaning and sound do not move in unison: in Greek the participle ὤν, ὄντος 'being' (from *s-ont-*) etymologically is only an ending since the root (*s-*) was lost through phonetic change but this does not prevent it from carrying the expected meaning (*ibid.*, 254). Even phonetic change does not prevent the creation of new linguistic possibilities. On the contrary, sometimes it favours it: the French indefinite pronoun *on*, which forms impersonal constructions, derives from Latin *homo* 'man' (*ibid.*, 264). The study of syntax and of the meaning of words is necessarily tied not to natural laws but to a continuous and individual work of re-creation by the peoples, since all grammatical change has its starting point in our thought. There is no language outside people and (here Bréal appeals to Humboldt) words only exist when we think of them and understand them (*ibid.*, 265). In his essay about *Les idées latentes du langage* ([1868] 1877, 295ff.), Bréal returns to the same point and reiterates an earlier statement: we must combine the principles and observations of philosophical or general grammar (of which we have the first examples in Port Royal) with the new results of comparative grammar. 'Since the *grammaire générale* aims at showing the relationship between the operations of our mind and the forms of language, how could it be in contrast with a science whose aim is that of analysing those forms?'. It is clear, however, that Bréal does not propose a simple return to philosophical grammar, but rather a coexistence and interpenetration of the two types of approach. The *idées latentes* are for Bréal an example of how thought intervenes in the normal processes of speech; if we recognize that *prisonnier* 'prisoner' refers to someone who is kept in the prison while *geôlier* 'gaoler', which is formed in exactly the same manner, refers to someone who keeps a prison, it must be because we are able to introduce distinctions which have no formal expression in the language (*ibid.*, 302). According to Bréal (*ibid.*, 322), we do not want to go back to the assumption that all peoples in spite of their different languages classify and organize the ideas in the same manner, but we should not fall into the opposite excess and assume that in languages other than ours there are only those notions which are formally marked. 'To understand the structure of a language it is not enough to analyse its grammar and find the etymological value of words. We must enter into the people's thoughts and feelings.'

In the *Essai de sémantique* (1897), which includes much earlier material, Bréal aims at studying the intellectual causes which determine the evolution (he speaks of transformation) of languages. He discusses in turn a number of laws (the term is carefully defined in a non-naturalistic sense) such as specialization, repartition, analogy, etc.; a second part is concerned with the development of the sense of words; and a third with the formation of syntax. The *Essai* is not a work on the meaning of words, but a much wider discussion about most facets (except for phonology) of language and linguistic development. The emphasis is once again on the speaker, on the act of communication, and on speech acts. Indeed the parallelism with Wegener is sometimes striking: Bréal too argues that the first use of language is not to make statements but to express desires, give orders, indicate possession, etc. (1897, 264f.). We are told (Bréal 1897, 277) that words are signs, as was maintained by the *idéologues*, and through use keep acquiring new meanings while not necessarily shedding the old ones; for Bréal too, as for Wegener, the situation defines the specific sense or value of words ('Les mots sont placés chaque fois dans un milieu qui en détermine d'avance la valeur', *ibid.*, 156); both speaker and hearer select words or interpret words in the light of the situation in which they are. The etymological meaning is irrelevant. As has often been pointed out, much of this foreshadows the Saussure of the *Cours* (1916).

All through the *Essai* the emphasis is not only on the speakers, but on their subjectivity and individuality. Where Bréal differs from his contemporaries is in the belief that the speaker's intention has a role to play in the facts of language: 'though not premeditated, the facts of language are nevertheless inspired and directed by an intelligent will' ([1887] 1897, 337) – how this happens remains obscure.[63]

10.7.4.5 Convergences in the study of meaning

At this stage it is not easy to summarize the type of work which was being done. There is a degree of convergence: Madvig, Bréal, Whitney, Wegener (and Paul) all speak independently for the importance of a study of meaning. All of them (with the possible exception of Madvig and Wegener) are concerned with language development and consequently with change in meaning but their discussion is more synchronic and theoretical than one might have expected. Words are treated as signs, though their exact nature is not always clear. An aim shared by all exponents of *Semasiologie* and by e.g. Bréal is to establish laws of semantic development, though the last word may refer to how language changes or to how language functions. The discussion of polysemy is clearly important (because of the new vistas it opens on language production and understanding) and seems to go in parallel with the view that etymology after all is not the most useful tool to determine the meaning of a word – another move towards synchrony.[64] Most of these questions are discussed within a psychological framework,[65] but there is little agreement about the specific approach. Finally, meaning is no longer seen as a property of words or words only. The meaning of sentences or expressions is also brought into question and the roles of both speakers and hearers are considered: Wegener and Bréal move the first steps towards a theory of speech acts. Ries's view (p. 310f.) that a study of meaning must accompany all discussion of morphology and syntax, though not necessarily new, finds new support.

10.8 Conclusions: the evolution of historical linguistics

What precedes is necessarily inadequate, not only because of lack of space and of the writer's ignorance,[66] but also because there is no natural division between the general discussions of the late nineteeth century and the developments of the twentieth century: this is true for Baudouin de Courtenay and e.g. Schuchardt; it is even more true for the work in syntax and semantics. If nevertheless we have reached the end of this account we may well turn back and ask how the end fits the beginning. Should we assume, as e.g. Aarsleff has argued, that by the 1890s a sort of revolution starts in linguistics, the narrow comparativism and historicism are defeated and linguists, led by Bréal and the French school which influences Saussure, turn back to their true roots in the eighteenth century? Should we see the historical-comparative work as a brief (or perhaps not so brief) aberration in the history of linguistic thought, after which linguistics then moves back to its real concerns – unscathed by the interlude? No doubt, as we have stated, dissatisfaction with the current state of affairs surfaces at this point in time and no doubt also there is a yearning for a serious discussion of more general problems: from this point of view Saussure's discontent is representative. There is also an increasing realization that some problems cannot be discussed within a purely historical (i.e. diachronic) framework. In other words, the end of the century shows all the signs of the future change of direction (Brincat 1986, 215f.). But, in our view at least, there is not an intellectual break between the linguistics of the twentieth century and that of the nineteenth century which is in any way comparable to that between the latter and its eighteenth-century predecessor. By and large the like of Saussure, Bloomfield, Sapir, Trubeckoj were respectful of the earlier achievements and did not dispute their importance. Historical work, as we mentioned before, continued – and was accepted – in the twentieth century. The first president of the

Linguistic Society of America, founded in 1924, was Hermann Collitz, a German comparativist (even if not a neogrammarian); *Language*, its periodical, in its first ten volumes contained 172 papers of which 12 dealt with general topics and fewer than 10 are entirely descriptive; more than half concerned ancient Indo-European languages, i.e. were historical and philological (Matthews 1993, 10f.). As we have just been reminded 'one of the marvellous things about Bloomfield's *Language* is the way in which it reconciled so much that was already the established wisdom in the discipline, and therefore the main interest of most of the early membership of the Linguistic Society, with so much that was strikingly new' (*ibid.*, 11). In France, clear linguistic leadership is provided by Antoine Meillet, who was a pupil of Bréal and Saussure, but also the man whose main achievements are self-consciously in the historical and comparative field and who, in spite of his original bid for the foundation of a French *linguistique générale* (Auroux 1988c, 39), would never have disowned his intellectual ancestry. But if there is a form of continuity between the end of the century and the beginning of the next, should we nevertheless see the new beginnings which we have mentioned as due to a deliberate return to the eighteenth century? Here it is difficult to give a positive answer. Bréal did indeed appeal more than once to his predecessors, not least because he wanted the support of tradition for a French school of linguistics, but when he highlighted the importance of observation or of the philological analysis of the texts or of comparison he was deliberately taking his distance. The sentence in which, in his fight against Schleicher's organicism, he appeals to the *idéologues*' theory of signs is constantly quoted but no mention is made of the critical remark that immediately follows it.[67] Perhaps the final word can rest with Georg von der Gabelentz, who was not a neogrammarian nor predominantly a historical linguist. In *Die Sprachwissenschaft* (1891, 11) he referred to the period when people had believed that it was possible to establish deductively from their knowledge of the nature of language all that was necessary for human language and all that was possible in it. 'Thus arose the general or philosophical grammars, mostly children of our philosophical period, beautiful children but not sufficiently lively. Now we must count them among the dead and do not need to fight them any more. Their ways and means were mistaken, but their aims were right and deserve to be revindicated in our time.' What we are in effect being told is not 'let us return to Port Royal or to Condillac or the *idéologues*', but rather 'let us have a general linguistics (as philosophical grammar had auspicated) and let this include – but not be limited to – historical and comparative linguistics'. On this point most practising linguists of the end of the century (including the neogrammarians and certainly Paul) would have agreed, even if they then continued to work within their familiar historical and philological framework. Yet in the midst of the numerous fits and starts which characterize our period, no agreement was available about the way in which general linguistics was to be approached. The recent historiography is still rediscovering, almost daily, precursors of modern theories or supporters of interesting views who did not deserve the oblivion into which they fell. This dispersiveness of the more general discussion contrasted with the institutionally and intellectually more unified nature of the historical pursuits. No wonder then that these remained as the hallmark of the nineteenth century. A somewhat iconoclastic outsider such as Sayce (a popularizer and a non-neogrammarian) had put it well as early as 1880, with a rhetoric which is of course of German origin but by this stage had been generalized to most of Western linguistics: 'the many controversies excited by the science of language show how broadly and deeply the foundations of the science are being laid. On the phonological side the progress has been greatest and most certain; morphology and the investigation of roots still lag behind; comparative syntax is but beginning to be handled; and sematology, the science of meanings, has hardly been touched. But the method inaugurated by Bopp remains unshaken, the main conclusions he arrived at hold their grounds and the existence of the Aryan family of speech, with all its consequences, is one of the facts permanently acquired for science' (Sayce 1880, i, 87). We have here the familiar mixture of hyperbole and truth (with its fair share of non-sequiturs), but the last statement has not been really challenged. The nineteenth century introduced history and historical comparison into linguistics and did it with such enthusiasm and such success that all too often other approaches were ignored. Yet the historical work, if done in depth, was bound to lead back to the questions which had been left aside in the enthusiasm of the discovery. In the last decades of the century we noticed a move towards a 'static' (or synchronic) approach to language. This was not determined by a return to the philosophical grammar of the eighteenth century or the *Grammaire de Port Royal* or the Greek or the Indian grammarians, even if all of these had ignored diachrony and worked in a purely synchronic framework; rather it was prompted by the realization that some of the actual questions to which historical linguists were seeking an answer (including the questions of meaning) had to be tackled synchronically – in the first instance at least. Saussure said it more sharply than anyone else and was listened to, but the last decades of the nineteenth century had prepared the ground.

Notes

1. An exception should be made for phonetics and probably for dialectology, two fields which now begin to build up cumulative results similar to those which had characterized historical linguistics.

2. By contrast, the Swiss Franz Misteli, professor at Basel, in writing the second part of his and Steinthal's *Abriss der Sprachwissenschaft* (1893), which replaced Steinthal (1860b), continued the type of analysis proposed by Steinthal (1860b), though with modifications (cf. p. 215). He distinguished six major categories, all represented in his description by one or two definite **types** (the Mexican type, the Chinese type, the Dravidian type, the Indo-European type, etc.): incorporating (Mexican, Greenlandic), root-isolating (Chinese, Siamese), stem-isolating (Malayik-Dayak), ranking (*anreihende*: Egyptian and Coptic, Bantu), agglutinative (Ural-Altaic, Dravidian), inflectional (Semitic, Indo-European). The overriding consideration was that three of these categories (root-isolating, ranking and inflectional) had 'form' (see p. 215), while the others did not.

3. Observations of this type (which contrast with earlier beliefs) occur frequently at the beginning of the new century and in the preceding decade. Gabelentz (1894, 5) pointed out that there were isolating and agglutinative languages which belonged to the same genealogical family. Saussure (1967–74, i, 510) attacked the view that a language should keep its morphological character in the process of time. Even La Grasserie (see p. 321 and note 5), who fundamentally believed that typologically similar languages were related, acknowledged that this could not be proved.

4. This is often accompanied by the one or the other form of transformationism (Greenberg 1971, 106), i.e. by the assumption that monosyllabic or isolating languages evolved into agglutinative and then into inflected languages: cf. e.g. Hovelaque ([1876] 1922, 40ff.). For Georg von der Gabelentz (1891, 250ff.), languages followed this development in a sort of perennial spiral in which the inflected or agglutinative languages lost their affixes thus turning into isolating and the process started all over again. Cf. in general Morpurgo Davies (1975, 673ff.) and more recently Plank (1991a). Plank (1992) shows how in this image of the spiral Gabelentz was preceded by Rask.

5. Raoul Guérin de la Grasserie (1839–1914) was a learned judge, who wrote extensively about linguistic subjects (syntax, semantics, etc.), but remained outside the professional circles: see Delesalle (1990), Plank (1991a).

6. This type of statement anticipates, of course, more recent work by Jakobson, Greenberg, etc. about implicational universals. The important point, however, is that La Grasserie makes an attempt to explain why character A and character B co-occur and in doing so moves away from the standard historical explanations of the time (cf. Plank 1991a). For Humboldt's and Gabelentz's views, see Plank (1994).

7. Carl Meinhof (1857–1944) published in 1899 a *Grundriss einer Lautlehre der Bantu Sprachen*, which on the basis of exact phonetic correspondences between a number of Bantu languages proceeded to reconstruct an *Ur-Bantu*; his second book, *Grundzüge einer vergleichenden Grammatik der Bantusprachen*, appeared in 1906 and reconstructed the morphology of the parent language.

8. Perhaps the best way to find out what was known at the end of the century about the various languages of the world and what work had been done about them is to consult Pott's *Einleitung in die allgemeine Sprachwissenschaft* published in eight instalments (two of which appeared posthumously with

the help of Techmer and G. von der Gabelentz) in *Techmers Zeitschrift* from 1884 to 1890 (Pott 1974, 201–486). After a series of general considerations, Pott gives a *bibliographie raisonnée* of the work done on the various languages; the overriding classification is geographical (languages of Asia, Africa, America, Australia) but within each continent the languages are classified partly geographically (e.g. China, Japan, Korea, languages of the Himalaya), partly in families (in Asia: Uralo-Altaic, Finno-Ugric, Indo-European, Semitic). An account of the literature on the languages of Europe appears in Pott's *Zur Litteratur der Sprachenkunde Europas* (1887), also reprinted in Pott (1974). Tagliavini (1963, i, 230ff.) gives a brief account of the genealogical work done in the nineteenth and early twentieth centuries on non-Indo-European languages.

9. Ascoli summarized his views about the relationship of Indo-European and Semitic and replied to Max Müller's criticism in a very long note added to the reprint of one of his articles in the second volume of his *Studi Critici* (Ascoli 1877, 51–62). The methodological points made are impressive, but much of the positive argumentation is tied to a theory of the Indo-European root that became unacceptable after the later discoveries about Indo-European vocalism and *Ablaut*.

10. Møller (1850–1923) was from the start a supporter of the *Ablaut* theory proposed by the young Saussure in his *Mémoire*, though this was repeatedly attacked by Osthoff (cf. e.g. De Mauro 1970, 295ff.). Szemerényi ([1973] 1987–1991, i, 191ff.) has shown how he is in fact the real founder of what now goes under the name of laryngeal theory, which was then accepted and to a certain extent developed by Holger Pedersen (1867–1953) before the crucial contributions of later authors such as Albert Cuny and Jerzy Kuryłowicz. For the linguistic classification of Indo-European with Semitic and other languages, cf. Pedersen ([1931] 1962, 335–9) and for more recent developments, which, however, have found limited acceptance, cf. e.g. Bomhard (1984), and Shevoroshkin and Markey (1986), who provide an introduction to the Nostratic work by V. V. Illič-Svityč. About Pedersen in general, see Koerner (1989, 416–33).

11. Obviously the old question of monogenesis vs. polygenesis hovered in the background of these debates. Møller (Möller 1906, vi ff.) reported in full the objections which Osthoff had directed against him and which were typical of the cautious attitude of the neogrammarians: 'Möller must tell himself that the ultimate aim of Indo-European linguistics is not to demonstrate the original unity of our language family with the Semitic one ... If after an objective analysis of our vocalism there emerges no prospect of postulating a relationship between the two families ... this result would not be any more distressing than the opposite one' (Osthoff 1881, 343). For his part Møller (*ibid.*, vii) reacted: 'surely the ultimate aim of linguistics in general is to show the unity of the languages of mankind, even if this aim cannot be reached'. And he continued with the observation that he would have found it very difficult to accept arguments against the possible unity of Indo-European and Semitic, but, had he been obliged to do so, he would have indeed found this result much more distressing than the opposite one, because he would have then been obliged to give up his firm

conviction that the two languages were related and, consequently, his beliefs about the original unity of all languages.

12. Porzig (1954, 17–52) offers the most detailed account of the discussions about the internal classification of the Indo-European languages.

13. The priority for the *Wellentheorie* belongs to Schuchardt, who as early as 1866–8 drew, just a few pages apart, both a *Stammbaum* of the Romance languages and a series of concentric circles which represented the Romance area (Schuchardt 1866–8, i, 82, 94; cf. Malkiel 1955). Elsewhere in the same book (iii, 34) he compared language with a pool of water, which moved so that wave nuclei appear in different places and intersect with each other (Tagliavini 1963, i, 412). Schuchardt's discussion about classification belongs to a lecture given in Leipzig in 1870 for his *venia legendi*, but not published until 1900 (Schuchardt 1922, 144ff.).

14. With the exception of the three-volume *Der Vokalismus des Vulgärlateins* (1866–8), Schuchardt's work is dispersed in endless periodicals, pamphlets, etc. In the *Hugo-Schuchardt-Brevier* (1922, 2nd edn 1928) Leo Spitzer collected the most important passages of general interest. The 1885 essay against the neogrammarians has been most recently reprinted with a translation and additional essays in Vennemann and Wilbur (1972). Two modern works print in translation a selection of Schuchardt's essays on pidgin and creoles edited by Gilbert (Schuchardt 1980) and Markey (Schuchardt 1979). For his biography, cf. the two 1928 essays by Elise Richter (1977, 473ff., 505ff.). In general see Terracini (1949, 205–29), Iordan and Orr ([1937] 1970, 49ff.), Fought (1982), the essays collected in Lichem and Simon (1980), and above all Baggioni (1989b).

15. The reference is to a 1912 article by Schuchardt with the title *Sachen und Wörter* and to the periodical *Wörter und Sachen* started by Rudolf Meringer and others in 1909 and preceded by a 1905 article with the same title. Both Schuchardt and Meringer claimed priority for this approach (cf. Lochner von Hüttenbach 1980 and Timpanaro 1992, 158ff.).

16. The question whether there were dialect boundaries and consequently whether there were well-defined dialects was hotly debated, especially among Romanists. In an attack against Ascoli and his classification of the Franco-Provençal group, Paul Meyer (1875) maintained that dialects do not have a real existence. Ascoli replied, but Gaston Paris in 1888 supported Meyer and the controversy continued well into the new century until it got absorbed by the new fashion for linguistic geography; for a general account, cf. Horning (1893), and see also the famous article by Gauchat: 'Gibt es Mundartgrenzen?' (1903), which maintained that the dialects have a psychological reality of their own.

17. Schuchardt's fortune has been remarkable: he was idolized as a model and precursor by the idealists (Spitzer and Vossler) but also by the *Wörter und Sachen* movement. During the golden period of American structuralism he was almost forgotten (except of course for his Romance work and for his work on Basque) but more recently he has been rediscovered – with different results. Bickerton (in Schuchardt 1979, x) refers to his 'dilettantism and his atheoretical stance', though he approves of his work on pidgins and recognizes in it flashes of genius. Vennemann (in Vennemann and Wilbur

1972, 117f.) praises the deliberately theoretical approach of Schuchardt's essay against the neogrammarians, his 'demolition' of the neogrammarians' tenets and the demonstration of their 'utter uselessness', mentions his great contribution to linguistic science, but also compares his view of sound change which starts in a few words, spreads from there through conceptual analogy ('begriffliche Analogie') and is eventually generalized, with Kiparsky's rule generalization. Fought (1982), on the other hand, highlights the reasons why Schuchardt should count as one of the founders of modern sociolinguistics, and Baggioni (1989b) stresses that Schuchardt had a set of coherent theoretical views.

18. In the second edition of the *Grundriß*, Brugmann (in Brugmann and Delbrück 1897–1916, I 1, 70ff.) acknowledged that homogeneous speech communities did not exist, but in the context of the polemics about the regularity principle observed that all linguists were ready to recognize a certain level of regularity and that surely this had to be adopted as a working principle. Benincà (1994, 593; 1996, 118f.) refers to a remarkably subtle article by Jean Psichari (1888), who, in the second volume of the *Revue des patois gallo-romans*, defends the neogrammarians' hypotheses on the basis of dialect evidence and argues that one can only speak of mixed dialects if there is a 'pure' dialect. Benincà acutely comments that Psichari's argument runs into trouble because of the specific brand of positivism of the times which called for the empirical evidence of a pure dialect, and continues: ' "Pure" languages, like homogeneous linguistic communities and the ideal native speaker of Chomsky's paradigm, are empirically valid postulates not because they have an immediate counterpart in reality (on the contrary they are abstractions), but because the theory which postulates them reaches empirically valid results, which can in fact be checked on actual data'. It is legitimate to suppose that some at least of the neogrammarians (Psichari included) would have shared this view.

19. The discussions covered other areas as well, including the origin of myths: Spencer objected to Max Müller's assumption that the 'savages' had abstract words and concepts which were reinterpreted in the form of myths (see p. 175), since for him the only possible development was from concrete to abstract and not vice versa (Stocking 1987, 307ff.).

20. Haas (1969) analyses the lexical or grammatical bases on which the Amerindian languages were classified.

21. For the early work of the Bureau, see Andresen (1990, 190) with the earlier bibliography. For Boas, cf. Hymes and Fought (1975, 969ff., 981ff. and *passim*). Wells (1974) and Stocking (1974) convey the feeling of some of the work done at the end of the nineteenth century. For Humboldt, Steinthal and Boas, see Koerner (1990).

22. Meringer (1859–1931) is best known among linguists as the founding editor of the journal *Wörter und Sachen* (1909ff.), where he argued that the study of the meaning of words cannot be separated from that of their referent (see above, p. 287ff., for Schuchardt). From a very different angle the emphasis on words as basic units is also apparent in the 1895 book, where the relative independence of sound units is treated as a secondary development in the speakers, largely based on writing and schooling. Cf. in general

Cutler and Fay in the introduction to Meringer and Mayer (1978) and Knobloch (1988, 482ff.). Meringer returned to speech errors in *Aus dem Leben der Sprache* (1908) but the subject after that was neglected until the recent revival. The polemics between Meringer and Freud (Cutler and Fay 1978, xxviiiff.) are of more limited linguistic interest, but see Timpanaro (1992, 142ff.).

23. The literature on the movement is best found in the work on the history of teaching. Cf. in general Howatt (1984), who has a good bibliography and also prints an English translation of Viëtor (1882 [1886]).

24. Hans Georg Conon von der Gabelentz (1840–93), the son of the famous orientalist and expert in Melanesian languages Hans Conon von der Gabelentz (1807–74; cf. Plank 1996), taught at Leipzig and then Berlin and did important work on Chinese. His *Sprachwissenschaft* has a number of points which fit within a Humboldtian tradition, but is a substantially independent work, which, while recognizing the achievements of the neo-grammarians, does not side with them. It has been suggested (Rensch 1966, Coseriu 1967) that he anticipates Saussure in a number of important respects (*langue/parole*; synchrony/diachrony, etc.) but this has also been disputed (cf. Koerner 1975, 791f.); for his views on typology, cf. Plank (1991a, 1994) and for his critique of organicism, Haßler (1991a, 136ff.).

25. Wilhelm Wundt (1832–1920), who had studied physiology and medicine but had soon turned to philosophy and psychology, was immensely influential with philosophers, psychologists and linguists. To discuss him here would take too much space, but for a brief introduction see Eschbach (in Nerlich 1988, 183ff.) and Knobloch (1988, *passim*) with the earlier literature.

26. It is normal to speak of the Kazan' school in order to refer to Baudouin and his Kazan' colleagues and pupils, but it has been objected that Baudouin's and Kruszewski's views were not widely shared (Mugdan 1984a, 154ff.).

27. Baudouin de Courtenay studied at Warsaw, Jena (with Schleicher), Berlin, Prague, Leipzig and St Petersburg – though he thought of himself as self-taught. He had a complicated career and taught in Kazan' (1875–83) before moving to Dorpat and then Cracow, from where he went to St Petersburg. Eventually he returned to his native Poland to occupy the chair of Indo-European Linguistics in Warsaw. From his Kazan' period date his contacts with the orientalist V. Radloff and with M. Kruszewski, perhaps the most brilliant of his pupils, who came to study with him in 1878, but had only a very short and troubled life. Baudouin's contributions to general linguistics are scattered in individual articles and pamphlets and did not have in his lifetime the influence that they deserved. The general acknowledgement of his and Kruszewski's deep originality is recent and has led to a number of analyses, discussions, etc. See for the so-called Kazan' school Jakobson ([1960] 1971, 394–428); Albrow (1981); for Kruszewski, Jakobson (1965, 1971, 429–50), Koerner ([1986] 1989, 376–99, in Kruszewski 1995, xi–xxxix), Williams (1993), Adamska-Sałaciak (1996) and the works collected in Kruszewski (1967) (in Polish), with some English translations in Kruszewski (1995). For Baudouin's collected works, cf. Baudouin de Courtenay (1963, 1974–90). There are three useful anthologies in English, German and Italian respectively: Baudouin de Courtenay (1972) edited

by Stankiewicz; (1984) edited by Mugdan; Di Salvo (1975). Modern monographs and essays include Häusler (1968), Stankiewicz ([1972] 1976), Šaradzenidze (1980), Mugdan (1984a), Baudouin de Courtenay (1989), Adamska-Sałaciak (1996). For the development of morphophonemics, cf. Kilbury (1976); for Kruszewski's and Baudouin's views about language change, cf. above all Adamska-Sałaciak (1996).

28. See Nicolas (1988, 68), but notice that Schleicher too (e.g. 1850, 4) saw syntax as closer to philology, i.e. to a *Geschichtswissenschaft* (an historical science), since it depended more than morphology on thought and the will of individuals.

29. Mugdan (1984a, 86ff.) gives a detailed account of the various interpretations of the static/dynamic contrast in Baudouin de Courtenay and Kruszewski, from which it emerges clearly that the use of the two terms only partially overlaps with that of synchronic and diachronic.

30. Lazarus Geiger, the isolated scholar who wrote *Ursprung und Entwickelung der menschlichen Sprache und Vernunft* (1868–72) and *Der Ursprung der Sprache* (1869) was quoted earlier (pp. 176, 313). Knobloch (1988, 239ff.) discusses him together with Ludwig Noiré, who moved between linguistics and philosophy, in his chapter on psychological semantics, where he also analyses *Die Sprache als Kunst* (1871–4) by Gustav Gerber, who shared some of Max Müller's views (see Schmidt 1976).

31. Max Müller found a strong supporter in Ludwig Noiré (1879a, b), whom in his turn he had strongly praised for his book on the origin of language (Noiré 1877), and with whom he shared the belief in the importance of roots as real constituents of the earliest language and as endowed with a multiplicity of meaning (cf. Knobloch 1988, *passim*).

32. At the beginning of the new century (1900) Baudouin will divide grammar into phonology, semasiology, morphology (divided in its turn into morphology *stricto sensu* and syntax), lexicology and etymology (Mugdan 1984a, 50).

33. Naturally there are predecessors, even if mostly we deal with isolated statements: Grimm has been mentioned and Sievers and Winteler are frequently quoted in this context (cf. Jakobson [1966] 1971, 456ff.). On the other hand, as was pointed out, Jakobson's data are not always correct and there are some considerable differences between the views of these scholars and those of the English school (cf. Kohrt 1984, 1985, 213ff.). In particular Winteler is important because of his use of descriptive phonetics, not because he anticipated the results of the Prague school. For Winteler as Einstein's teacher and, according to Jakobson, supporter of a theory about the 'Relativität der Verhältnisse', which would have influenced the theory of relativity, see Kohrt (1984, 66ff.) who shows that once again the data are inadequate.

34. As in all disciplines, the question of names arises: in English, as in French and Italian, phonetics and phonology (French *phonétique, phonologie*; Ital. *fonetica, fonologia*) have had a chequered career and their meaning oscillates with apparent reversals of usage. For Saussure (1916, 55), *phonétique* indicates the evolution of sounds and he prefers to use *phonologie* for the physiology of sounds (De Mauro 1970b, 398); Sweet either uses the two terms as equivalent or reserves phonetics for the analysis and classification

of the actual sounds, while phonology includes the history and theory of sound change (cf. Henderson 1971, 26ff.). The current use of 'phonology' to indicate the study of the sound system of a language in its linguistic and functional aspects is largely based on the terminology of the Prague school, but Abercrombie (1967, 169ff.) refers to the posthumously published lecture by H. D. Darbishire (1863–93), a Cambridge lawyer and classicist, for whom phonetics is the 'science of vocal sounds' linked to acoustics and physiology, while phonology is the study of the spoken sounds of any language. To judge from the *Oxford English Dictionary*, the use of the two terms in English is likely to go back to the eighteenth century: phonology is attested from 1799 and the adjective *phoneticus*, admittedly in Latin, was used by an Egyptologist in 1797. For Italian, Tagliavini (1963, ii, 13) notes that at some stage *fonologia* was used to indicate historical phonetics, while others (Bertoni) used it for descriptive phonetics. In 1870 Ascoli (1870, 1) defined *fonologia* as 'the science of the sounds of which words are built'. Baudouin de Courtenay and Kruszewski make extensive use of *Anthropophonik* or the like, using the term adopted by Merkel in his 1857 book (cf. p. 164) to indicate what we would call phonetics, while Baudouin uses *Phonetik* and *Phonologie* more or less concurrently, sometimes to indicate the wider discipline (our phonetics and phonology), sometimes to indicate what he more specifically calls *Psychophonetik* (our phonology) (Mugdan 1984a, 61).

35. The Russian and German examples are taken from Kruszewski (1881), who also observes that, when the conditioning is phonetic, we must speak of sound alternation; when it is morphological, of form alternation. The distinction may go some way towards explaining the differences between sound change and analogical change.

36. Some notes by Saussure in a Harvard manuscript, probably of the period 1881–4, are a first attempt (not very clear) at a contrastive definition of the phoneme (Saussure 1995, 81; cf. Marchese in Saussure 1995, xxii ff.). The first use of the term *phonème* is normally attributed to the French linguist Dufriche-Desgenettes, who deliberately introduced it (as early as 1873 at least) to avoid, as far as one can see, the word *son* 'sound', which could be used both for linguistic and for physical phenomena, and which sometimes was applied to vowels only, in contrast with those consonants which were pure 'noise' (*bruit*); *phonème* could be used for vowels, consonants and for the 'intermediate' sounds such as semivowels (Kohrt 1985, 59–77). The term is then used from 1874 for all articulated sounds (both vowels and consonants) by Louis Havet, the French Latinist to whom we owe the formula of proportional analogy (cf. p. 276 note 48). Saussure may have taken it from the writings of either of these two linguists or from another French linguist of the period. Cf. in general Koerner (1978, 127ff., 177ff.); for the details and the earlier bibliography, see Mugdan (1987) and Kohrt (1985, 59–119), who, in spite of some differences, independently reach a number of common conclusions and correct the numerous earlier errors.

37. 'The phoneme – a unitary concept belonging to the sphere of phonetics which exists in the mind thanks to a psychological fusion of the impressions

resulting from the pronunciation of one and the same sound: it is the psychological equivalent of a speech sound. The unitary concept of the phoneme is connected (associated) with a certain sum of individual anthropophonic representations which are, on the one hand, articulatory, that is, performed or capable of being performed by physiological actions, and on the other hand, acoustic, that is the effects of these physiological actions, which are heard or capable of being heard' (Baudouin de Courtenay 1895, 9 = 1972, 152). The interpretation of Kruszewski's and above all Baudouin's theories is disputed; see here too Mugdan (1987) and Kohrt (1985, 19 162), quoted in the previous note. Williams (1993) discusses in detail Kruszewski's work and fortune but does not refer back to these two authors.

38. For an older account of the history of syntax from the Greeks to the last part of the nineteenth century, see Delbrück (1893–1900, i, 1–86); for more recent discussions, see Graffi (1991), with numerous references. Some useful information is also available in Drăganu ([1944] 1970).

39. For a detailed account, cf. Johansen's introduction to Madvig (1971), and Hauger (1994).

40. The school practice did not always differ from country to country. Becker's grammatical theory (see p. 95 note 6) was highly influential in German school-teaching and spread to England, where it introduced or confirmed the analysis of sentences into main and subordinate clauses (Michael 1987, 370). For some stronger statements about the importance of school grammar in general and Becker in particular, see Knobloch (1988, 318); for an analysis of the tradition of school grammars before and after Becker, see Knobloch (1989a, b).

41. 'Logic' is used here in the old sense of correct thought, *art de penser* – a sense in which the term was used by most linguists of the nineteenth century. Logic as calculus did not really impinge on linguistics nor did e.g. the work by Boole or Frege (Graffi 1991, 38f.).

42. The earlier history of this tradition (before Port Royal) is not relevant here. Notice, however, that in Port Royal *attribut* is used in the meaning of predicate and that in general, starting with the eighteenth century, to the French pair *sujet/attribut* in the grammatical sense correspond in Germany, under the influence of Christian Wolf, *subjectum* and *praedicatum* or *Subjekt* and *Prädikat* (Graffi 1991, 120f.; Lepschy 1991, 200ff.).

43. It is ironical that Kühner, the object of this criticism, in his time had rejected the 'logical' distinction between moods of reality (indicative), possibility (subjunctive) and necessity (imperative), which was that adopted by Gottfried Hermann and by Becker, because this form of explanation went against the nature of language, 'which starts in its development from sensory intuitions and not from philosophical and abstract concepts' (Kühner 1869–70, ii, 166f.).

44. What precedes is largely based on Graffi (1991, 183ff.).

45. The terminology is confusing and, as Graffi (1991, 142ff.) points out, Wegener uses 'logical' in a sense similar to that of 'psychological' in Gabelentz. Even someone as careful about terminology as Henry Sweet (1892–8, I, 6ff.) uses 'logical' as equivalent to 'semantic': 'There are ... two sides to language – two ways of looking at it: there is the **formal** side,

which is concerned with the outer form of words and sentences, and the **logical** side, which is concerned with their inner meaning. . . . The study of the formal side of language is based on **phonetics** – the science of speech-sounds; the study of the logical side of language is based on **psychology** – the science of mind.' The passage comes from *A New English Grammar Logical and Historical*; in the preface Sweet (*ibid.*, v) states that 'this grammar is not one-sidedly historical: it is at the same time a logical grammar. . . . I have taken considerable trouble to define accurately not only the parts of speech, but also the primary grammatical categories "word", "inflection", "sentence", etc., which have hitherto been often neglected, and sometimes ignored, by grammarians.'

46. Some thirty years later this was re-edited (1927) and was then followed by two further monographs about word groups (1928) and the sentence (1931) respectively. For John Ries (1857–1933) in general, cf. Drăganu ([1944] 1970, 76ff.), Knobloch (1988, 317ff.), Graffi (1991 *passim*).

47. It is obviously artificial to stop at this stage and not to consider the developments in the first part of the twentieth century, but even within the nineteenth century Ries had some influence; cf. for instance the statements by Meyer-Lübke in the introduction to the syntax volume of his *Grammatik der romanischen Sprachen* (1890–1902, iii [1899]). More recently Ries's view has certainly prevailed: a linguist such as McCawley (1988, i, 2) defines syntax as 'the system of rules . . . that determine what combinations of words into larger units, expecially into sentences, the language allows'.

48. Bréal's use of *sémantique* goes back at least to 1879, when he used the term in a letter to Angelo de Gubernatis (cf. Aarsleff 1982, 321, note 6). Kronasser (1952), Gordon (1982), Knobloch (1988), Haßler (1991, 139ff.) and, above all, Nerlich (1992 and 1993) provide indispensable help for the history of semantics in our period. In a number of instances their rich list of references makes it unnecessary for us to offer detailed bibliographical guidance.

49. For a more detailed account of German *Semasiologie* and of the role played in it by German classicists in general and classical school-teachers in particular, see Nerlich (1992, 29ff.). For the various conceptions of signs, cf. also Schmitter (1987b). Both Reisig and Haase were distinguished and prolific classicists. Karl Reisig, who was a pupil of Gottfried Hermann and taught classics at the University of Halle, wanted to introduce in the study of language philosophical (mostly Kantian) and historical (i.e. empirical) principles. His views about the study of meaning appeared posthumously in his *Vorlesungen über lateinische Sprachwissenschaft* edited by his pupil Haase (cf. Schmitter 1987b; and Schmitter in Nerlich 1988, 101ff.). Friedrich Haase started as a school teacher but ended his career as Extraordinarius (of classics) at the University of Breslau; his own book (with the same title as that by Reisig) appeared once again posthumously and contained only generalities and the semantic part (cf. Schmitter in Nerlich 1988, 111ff.). Heerdegen too was a classicist.

50. Lady Welby is better studied in the context of early-twentieth-century semantic and semiotic discussions in Anglo-Saxon countries and in the

Netherlands, where she influenced the so-called Dutch significs movement (cf. Schmitz 1985 and 1990; Nerlich 1992, 241ff.).

51. There was a certain amount of naïveté in these assumptions. All too often the historical picture was less complex than the synchronic one because the evidence was lacking and consequently the historical data conjured for each word the image of a simple family tree with a unitary trunk, i.e. a unitary meaning at the top and an increasing number of branches in the later period.

52. Paul was neither the first nor the last to make this type of distinction. An early predecessor, whom he was likely to have read, was A. F. Pott (1833–6, ii, 155), who in 1836 argued that polysemy (*Polysemantie*) of words could be taken as due to multiple use; the various meanings were *significationes* of one *vis, potestas, notio*, i.e. of a single underlying sense ('eines einzigen, jedem Worte unterliegenden Sinnes'). For Pott this polysemy is a potential characteristic of every word but only use (*Gebrauch*) makes it real. Later than Paul, Adolf Noreen (1854–1925), the author of *Vårt Språk* (1903–24), an impressive description of Swedish, repeated this distinction in the part of his book which dealt with 'semology', i.e. with the science of meaning in general (Noreen 1923, 199ff. and 211f.). Yet the distinction was not altogether clear – especially when it came to the usual meaning: see the detailed criticism by Stern (1932, 87ff.).

53. Darmesteter (1846–88), who during his short and difficult life was in close contact with Bréal and Gaston Paris, worked on Medieval Hebrew and on the history of French, but also wrote a *thèse de doctorat* on *De la création actuelle de mots nouveaux dans la langue française et des lois qui les régissent* (1877), which was the result of individual collections of new words. His booklet about *La vie des mots*, which first appeared in English (1886), had immense success: the 19th edition was published in 1937. For his biography, cf. Bergounioux (1986), for his thought, Delesalle (1987) and Nerlich (1992, 138ff.).

54. In the middle of the century Indo-Europeanists disputed whether the primitive roots, i.e. the roots reconstructed for Indo-European, had an abstract meaning (cf. Knobloch 1988, 249). Max Müller ([1861] 1862, 373ff.) referred to the old philosophical controversy about the *primum cognitum*, i.e. 'whether language originated in general appellations or in proper names' and concluded that no doubt words were first used for individual objects but such names were all derived from general ideas; in Sanskrit the snake is called *sarpa* (a concrete word) because it creeps (*sarp-*). The conclusion is not very different from Knobloch's point that the whole controversy is based on the failure to distinguish sense and reference. For nineteenth-century etymology in general, see the first chapter of Malkiel (1993).

55. Here too Madvig anticipates this trend. In 1871 he pointed out that etymology could not fulfil its task without the guidance of a special *Bedeutungslehre* and argued that the task of etymology was to pursue the history of a word in its own language and to establish the changes undergone by the forms while taking into account the meaning changes (Madvig [1871] 1875, 341f.).

56. For Chavée's earlier attempt at reconstructing the basic roots of Indo-European vocabulary, see above, pp. 156, 180 note 6, 185 note 30, and

below, note 60. Max Müller ([1861] 1862, 269) too had argued that all roots could be reduced to a small number of roots and consequently of concepts ('without roots, no language; without concepts, no roots', Müller 1868–75, iv, 477).

57. The remaining work by Wegener consists of a few articles and a chapter about modern dialectology (Wegener [1891] 1901) contributed to Paul's *Grundriß der germanischen Philologie*. In recent years he has been the object of much attention; cf. in general, Abse (1971), Knobloch (1988 and 1991), Nerlich (1990a, b, 1992) with the earlier bibliography. Knobloch (1991) offers a detailed analysis of Wegener's book and an attempt at situating it in the context of nineteenth-century psychology, while Nerlich (1990a) discusses Wegener's importance from the point of view of historical linguistics.

58. For Wegener's fortune, see the literature quoted in the preceding note (especially Knobloch 1991, xxxvii ff.). His functionalism and pragmatism were influential on British anthropologists and linguists: Malinowski, Gardiner, Firth. Alan Gardiner dedicated to his memory his *Theory of Speech and Language* (1932). In Germany, Karl Bühler often referred to him not only in the context of his work about the psychology of understanding, but also in the more general context of his *Sprachtheorie* (1934). As for the possible influences on Wegener, Knobloch (1991, xxxii) refers to Moritz Lazarus, Steinthal's friend and brother-in-law, and Whitney. Paul was obviously important (as Wegener was important for Paul) and we remain in doubt whether Wegener read Madvig's *Kleine philologische Schriften*, which appeared in 1875 and represent a similar approach. As for Bréal, who had very similar views, Wegener denied ever having read him (Nerlich 1992, 82).

59. In the context of an attempt at defining the role of positivism in nineteenth-century linguistics, Koerner ([1982] 1989, 194) points out that these linguists, who were the only ones to declare themselves positivists, i.e. followers of Auguste Comte, were snubbed by their contemporaries. A far more general definition of positivism is found in a note by Victor Henry to his *Langage Martien* (1901, 144); it is worth quoting it in full because it probably reflects the general feeling of Henry's contemporaries: 'J'entends "positiviste" au sens d'adepte d'une méthode scientifique qui rejette tout jugement préconçu et, à ce titre, s'impose à tout enquêteur sincère, quelles que puissent être ses convictions philosophiques ou religieuses; car, du positivisme érigé lui-même en doctrine philosophique, j'ai grand' peur, pour ma part, qu'il ne ressemble à la grenouille émule du boeuf'.

60. The final aim was to identify the original characteristics of each race. In his pamphlet on *Les langues et les races*, Chavée (1862, 60) concluded that through his linguistic analysis of Indo-European and Semitic he had definitively demonstrated 'the original diversity of the mental constitution and consequently of the cerebral organization of the two races' and had proved the original diversity of the human race. Hovelacque ([1876] 1922, 259) attributes to Chavée and Schleicher 'la première mise en réalisation de cette conception féconde d'une forme commune primitive des langues indo-européennes', i.e., one assumes, the discovery of reconstruction, but this forgets Pott and, for the vocabulary, Eichhoff.

61. Michel Bréal (1832–1915) after the École Normale studied in Berlin with Bopp and Weber and on his return worked at the Bibliothèque Impériale until he became *Chargé de cours* for *Grammaire comparée* at the Collège de France in 1864 and was eventually made the first professor of the subject at the Collège in 1866; he retired in 1905 at his own request. He was a member of the Société de Linguistique de Paris more or less from the beginning (was the secretary from 1868 until his death), was among the founder members of the École Pratique des Hautes Études in 1868 and later was its director, was heavily involved in questions concerning education and was public instruction inspector for higher education for almost ten years from 1879 to 1888 when the post was abolished. In this capacity he wrote a great number of articles, reports, etc. and an important book (cf. Delesalle and Chevalier 1986). The secondary literature about him has now become extensive after an initial period of neglect. Cf. Aarsleff ([1979] 1982, 293ff.; *ibid.* 382ff.), Delesalle and Chevalier (1986), Delesalle (1987, 1988). Nerlich (1990a, b, 1992) also provides earlier references. Wolf (in Bréal 1991) offers English translations of a wide choice of Bréal's linguistic essays, i.e. of those collected in Bréal (1877) and others. Two Italian translations of the *Essai de sémantique* (Bréal 1990 and 1992) include notes and further bibliography.

62. There is occasionally a slight coolness and a whiff of criticism in the way in which Meillet and others refer to Bréal; the reason is his rejection of the 'new' comparative grammar of Indo-European and the somewhat cavalier nature of his etymologies, both in the earlier work on religion and in the later articles (all the more ironical in view of Bréal's 1896 strictures about Nietzsche's etymologies – cf. Di Cesare 1986). This explains why Meillet ([1930] 1938, 212ff.) is at pains to emphasize the difference between Bréal and e.g. Havet or Saussure but also to stress his liberal attitude to his students and protégés (he mentions among them Louis Havet and James Darmesteter, the Iranist). Bréal was also responsible for creating a phonetic laboratory at the Collège de France and calling Rousselot to work in it, and for keeping in Paris the young Saussure in whose favour he relinquished in 1882 his teaching at the *Hautes Études*. That Bréal was aware of the ways of the academic market-place is shown by the public offices that he held and by his observation (1897, 279) that to link linguistics and the sciences could be a clever political move at a period when the sciences were in favour.

63. See Nerlich (1992, 149ff.) and above all Victor Henry's discussion of this matter in his *Antinomies* (1896, 64ff.), where a more conventional position is adopted.

64. Another subject which attracts attention is that of synonyms. The attempt to produce a formal analysis of their meaning (in terms close to those of set theory) by Carl Abel (1882, 137ff.) is particularly interesting. Cf. the next note.

65. It would be useful to study the traditional material used to define laws of semantic development and the way in which this was (or could be) reinterpreted in psychological key: the old rhetorical figures (metonymy, metaphor, etc.) would loom large in this context. At a simpler level, an interesting

example is that of enantiosemy, which Lepschy ([1982] 1989, 349ff.; cf. also *ibid.*, 277ff.) has studied with reference to the work of Carl Abel (1827–1906), a half dilettante, half professional German linguist, who lived part of his life in England, and who influenced Freud with his semantic theories. For Abel the *Urworte*, the words of the primitive language, are likely to have double and opposite meanings as if the word for 'good' meant both 'good' and 'evil' (Abel 1882, 235). Abel finds this feature in the vocabulary of ancient Egyptian and believes that he can prove that Egyptian, Semitic and Indo-European were related. Lepschy shows how the interest in words with opposite meanings has a long tradition and goes back to the Renaissance and much earlier, before playing a role in Romantic thought and eventually, through Abel, in Freud. Abel was attacked both for his general views and for his interpretation of Egyptian. Here we may simply notice that, when Victor Henry found in the *langage martien* which he was studying, i.e. in the language of a medium who spoke in tongues, obvious cases of enantiosemy (the use of a distortion of French *abondant* to mean *peu*), he explained it in terms of association theory: words are ordered in the memory through semantic contrasts, so that an idea recalls the opposite idea and consequently the speaker expresses e.g. the concept of pleasure with a word which indicates pain (Henry 1901, 49).

66. The omission of a serious discussion of Hanns Oertel (1901) and Wilhelm Wundt (1900) is particularly regrettable, as is that of Anton Marty's work.

67. Bréal (1897, 277): 'Nos pères de l'école de Condillac, ces idéologues qui ont servi de cible, pendant cinquante ans, à une certaine critique, étaient plus près de la vérité quand ils disaient, selon leur manière simple et honnête, que les mots sont des signes. Où ils avaient tort, c'est quand ils rapportaient tout à la raison raisonnante, et quand ils prenaient le latin pour type de tout langage'.

References

The following list does not aim at bibliographical completeness; it simply provides references for the citations in the text and in the notes, which are deliberately extensive. The hope is that the reader who wishes to pursue the subjects not discussed or inadequately discussed in the text or needs an introduction to the ever-increasing secondary literature will find this list helpful. For some nineteenth-century works I have mentioned earlier or later editions, translations, etc., both to make the basic texts more accessible and to give some indication of their availability and success in the period considered. For others this has not been done, because to obtain the relevant data would have been too difficult or because the fame of the work was such that it did not need further illustration.

AARSLEFF, H. (1975) The Eighteenth Century, Including Leibniz, in SEBEOK (ed.) (1975), 1, 383–479.

AARSLEFF, H. (1982) *From Locke to Saussure. Essays on the Study of Language and Intellectual History*, Athlone Press, London.

AARSLEFF, H. (1983) *The Study of Language in England, 1780–1860*, 2nd edn, University of Minnesota Press/Athlone Press, Minneapolis/London. 1st edn 1967.

AARSLEFF, H. (1988) Introduction, in HUMBOLDT (1988), vii–lxv.

AARSLEFF, H., KELLY, L. G., NIEDEREHE, H.-J. (eds.) (1987) *Papers in the History of Linguistics. Proceedings of the Third International Conference on the History of the Language Sciences (ICHoLS III), Princeton, 19–23 August 1984* (Studies in the History of the Language Sciences, 38), Benjamins, Amsterdam/Philadelphia.

ABEL, C. (1882) *Linguistic Essays* (Trübner's Oriental Series), Trübner, London.

ABEL, C. (1884) *Über den Gegensinn der Urworte*, Friedrich, Leipzig.

ABEL, C. (1885) *Sprachwissenschaftliche Abhandlungen*, Friedrich, Leipzig.

ABEL-RÉMUSAT, J. P. (1820) *Recherches sur les langues tartares ou mémoires sur différents points de la grammaire et de la littérature des mandchous, des mongols, des ouigours et des tibétains*, Imprimerie Royale, Paris.

ABERCROMBIE, D. (1949) What is a 'letter'?, *Lingua*, 2, 54–63. Reprinted in ID., *Studies in Phonetics and Linguistics*, Oxford University Press, London, 1965, 76–85.

ABERCROMBIE, D. (1967) *Elements of General Phonetics*, Edinburgh University Press, Edinburgh.

ABERCROMBIE, D. (1981) Extending the Roman Alphabet: Some Orthographic Experiments of the Past Four Centuries, in ASHER and HENDERSON (eds.) (1981), 206–24.

ABSE, D. W. (1971) *Speech and Reason: Language Disorder in Mental Disease. A Translation of 'The Life of Speech' by Philipp Wegener*, University of Virginia Press, Charlottesville.

ADAM, L. (1881) La linguistique est elle une science naturelle ou une science historique?, *Revue de linguistique et de philologie comparée*, 14, 373–95.

ADAMSKA-SAŁACIAK, A. (1996) *Language Change in the Works of Kruszewski, Baudouin de Courtenay and Rozdwadowski*, Motivex, Poznań.

ADELUNG, F. (1815) *Catherinens der Grossen Verdienste um die vergleichende Sprachenkunde*, Drechsler, St Petersburg.

ADELUNG, F. (1820) *Übersicht aller bekannten Sprachen und ihrer Dialekte*, Gretsch, St Petersburg.

ADELUNG, J. C. (1806–17) *Mithridates oder allgemeine Sprachenkunde mit dem Vater Unser als Sprachprobe in der nahe fünfhundert Sprachen und Mundarten (fortgesetz und bearbeitet von Dr Johann Severin Vater)*, 4 vols., Vossische Buchhandlung, Berlin.

AHLQVIST, A. (ed.) (1992) *Diversions of Galway. Papers on the History of Linguistics* (Amsterdam Studies in the History of the Language Sciences, 46), Benjamins, Amsterdam/Philadelphia.

AHRENS, H. L. (1839–43) *De graecae linguae dialectis*, 2 vols., Vandenhoeck & Ruprecht, Göttingen.

ALBROW, K. H. (1981) The Kazan' School and the London School, in ASHER and HENDERSON (eds.) (1981), 9–18.

AMELUNG, A. (1871) *Die Bildung der Tempustämme durch Vocalsteigerung im Deutschen: eine sprachgeschichtliche Untersuchung*, Weidmann, Berlin.

AMSTERDAMSKA, O. (1987) *Schools of Thought. The Development of Linguistics from Bopp to Saussure*, Reidel, Dordrecht.

ANDRESEN, J. T. (1990) *Linguistics in America 1769–1924* (Routledge History of Linguistic Thought), Routledge, London and New York.

ANONYMOUS (1805) *Philosophische Principien einer allgemeinen Sprachlehre nach Kant und Sacy*, Nicolovius, Königsberg.

ANQUETIL-DUPERRON, A.-H. (1771) *Zend-Avesta, ouvrage de Zoroastre, contenant les idées théologiques, physiques et morales de ce législateur, les cérémonies du culte religieux qu'il a établi, et plusieurs traits importants relatifs à l'ancienne histoire des Perses. Traduit en françois sur l'original Zend ... avec des remarques; & accompagné de plusieurs traités propres à éclaircir les matières qui en sont l'objet*, 3 vols., N. M. Tilliard, Paris. Reprinted Garland, New York, 1984.

ANTONSEN, E. H. (1962) Rasmus Rask and Jacob Grimm: Their Relationship in the Investigation of Germanic Vocalism, *Scandinavian Studies*, 34, 183–94.

ANTONSEN, E. H. (with MARCHAND, J. W., ZGUSTA, L.) (eds.) (1990) *The Grimm Brothers and the Germanic Past* (Amsterdam Studies in the History of the Language Sciences, 54), Benjamins, Amsterdam/Philadelphia.

ANTTILA, R., BREWER, W. A. (1977) *Analogy. A Basic Bibliography* (Library and Information Sources in Linguistics), Benjamins, Amsterdam.

ARENS, H. (1969) *Sprachwissenschaft. Der Gang ihrer Entwicklung von der Antike bis zur Gegenwart*, 2nd edn, Alber, Freiburg/München. Reprinted Athenäum Taschenbuch Verlag, Frankfurt a.M., 1974.

ASCOLI, G. I. (1861) *Studj critici*, I (Studi Orientali e linguistici, III), Il Politecnico/Brockhaus/Muenster, Milano/Lipsia/Trieste.

ASCOLI, G. I. (1870) *Lezioni di fonologia comparata del sanscrito, del greco e del latino date nella Regia Accademia Scientifico-Letteraria di Milano* (Corsi di Glottologia, 1), Loescher, Torino/Firenze. German translation by J. Bazziger and H. Schweizer-Sidler, Buchhandlung des Waisenhauses, Halle, 1872.

ASCOLI, G. I. (1873a) Proemio, *Archivio Glottologico Italiano*, 1, v–xli.

ASCOLI, G. I. (1873b) Saggi Ladini, *Archivio Glottologico Italiano*, 1, 1–556.

ASCOLI, G. I. (1876) P. Meyer e il franco-provenzale, *Archivio Glottologico Italiano*, 2, 385–95.

ASCOLI, G. I. (1877) *Studi critici*, II, Loescher, Roma/Torino/Firenze.

ASCOLI, G. I. (1886–8) Dei Neogrammatici. Lettera al prof. Pietro Merlo – Poscritta, *Archivio Glottologico Italiano*, 10, 18–73, 73–105. Partially reprinted in BOLELLI (1965b, 205–28).

ASCOLI, G. I. (1986) *G. I. Ascoli: Attualità del suo pensiero a 150 anni dalla nascita. Atti del XIII Incontro Culturale Mitteleuropeo, Gorizia, 24–25 novembre 1979*, Licosa, Firenze.

ASHER, R. E., HENDERSON, E. J. A. (eds.) (1981) *Towards a History of Phonetics. Papers Contributed in Honour of David Abercrombie*, Edinburgh University Press, Edinburgh.

AUROUX, S. (1973) *L'encyclopédie: 'grammaire' et 'langue' au XVIIIe siècle* (Repères linguistiques, 3), Maison Mame, Paris.

AUROUX, S. (1982) *Linguistique et anthropologie en France (1600–1900)* (Travaux d'histoire des théories linguistiques, 1), Département des recherches linguistiques, Paris.

AUROUX, S. (1983) La première société de linguistique – 1837?, *Historiographia Linguistica*, 10, 241–65.

AUROUX, S. (1984) Linguistique et anthropologie en France (1600–1900), in RUPP-EISENREICH, B. (ed.), *Histoires de l'anthropologie: XVI–XIX siècles*, Klincksieck, Paris, 291–318.

AUROUX, S. (1987) The First Uses of the French Word 'linguistique' (1812–1880), in AARSLEFF, KELLY and NIEDEREHE (eds.) (1987), 447–59.

AUROUX, S. (1988a) 'Histoire' et comparaison des langues. Connaissance des langues étrangères. Essai de bibliographie des publications françaises (1531–1804), in JOLY (ed.) (1988), 69–97.

AUROUX, S. (1988b) Modèles de l'âge classique pour la mobilité linguistique, in JOLY (ed.) (1988), 20–42.

AUROUX, S. (1988c) La notion de linguistique générale, *Histoire Épistémologie Langage*, 10:II, 37–56.

AUROUX, S. (1989) La question de l'origine des langues: ordres et raisons du rejet institutionnel, in GESSINGER and VON RAHDEN (eds.) (1989), 122–50.

AUROUX, S. (1990) Representation and the Place of Linguistic Change Before Comparative Grammar, in DE MAURO and FORMIGARI (eds.) (1990), 213–38.

AUROUX, S., DELESALLE, S. (1990) French Semantics of the Late Nineteenth Century and Lady Welby's Significs, in SCHMITZ (ed.) (1990), 105–31.

AUROUX, S., DÉSIRAT, C., HORDÉ, T. (1992) La question de l'histoire des langues et du comparatisme, in SCHLIEBEN-LANGE et al. (eds.) (1989–94), 3, 123–33.

AUROUX, S. et al., (eds.) (1984) *Matériaux pour une histoire des théories linguistiques / Essays Toward a History of Linguistic Theories / Materialien zu einer Geschichte der sprachwissenschaflichen Theorien*, Université de Lille III, Lille.

BAGGIONI, D. (1989a) La 'linguistique' française entre les Lumières et le positivisme (1816–68), in DUTZ (ed.) (1989), 139–59.

BAGGIONI, D. (1989b) Hugo Schuchardts Beitrag zur allgemeinen Sprachwissenschaft, *Historiographia Linguistica*, 16:3, 327–50.

BAHNER, W. (ed.) (1984) *Sprache und Kulturentwicklung im Blickfeld der deutschen Spätaufklärung. Der Beitrag Johann Christoph Adelungs* (Abhandlungen der sächsischen Akademie der Wissenschaften zu Leipzig. Philologisch-historische Klasse, Band 70, Heft 4), Akademie Verlag, Berlin.

BALBI, A. (1826a) *Introduction à l'atlas ethnographique du globe, contenant un discours sur l'utilité et l'importance de l'étude des langues appliquées à plusieurs branches des connaissances humaines; un aperçu sur les moyens graphiques employés par les différens peuples de la terre; des observations sur la classification des idiomes décrits dans l'atlas; un coup-d'-oeil sur l'histoire de la langue slave, et sur la marche progressive de la civilisation et de la littérature en Russie. Tome premier*, Rey et Gravier, Paris.

BALBI, A. (1826b) *Atlas ethnographique du globe ou classification des peuples anciens et modernes d'après leur langues, précédé d'un discours sur l'utilité . . . Russie* (cf. Balbi 1826a), *Et suivi du tableau physique, moral et politique des cinq parties du monde*, Rey et Gravier, Paris.

BALDINGER, K. (1957) *Die Semasiologie. Versuch eines Überblicks* (Deutsche Akademie der Wissenschaften zu Berlin. Vorträge und Schriften, 61), Akademie Verlag, Berlin.

BARBA, M. (1990) Lautform, innere Sprachform, Form der Sprachen. Il problema della comparazione e classificazione delle lingue in Heymann Steinthal, in DE MAURO and FORMIGARI (eds.) (1990), 263–80.

BAROZZI, M. (1984) La *Internationale Zeitschrift für allgemeine Sprachwissenschaft* di Friedrich Techmer nel dibattito linguistico di fine '800, *Studi e Saggi Linguistici*, 24, 11–78.

BARTHÉLEMY-ST HILAIRE, J. (1891) *Eugène Burnouf. Ses travaux et sa correspondance*, Imprimérie Durand (Chartres), Paris.

BAUDOUIN DE COURTENAY, J. (1895) *Versuch einer Theorie phonetischer Alternationen. Ein Capitel aus der Psychophonetik*, Trübner, Strassburg. Polish edition, Kraków 1894. Reprinted in Baudouin de Courtenay (1984).

BAUDOUIN DE COURTENAY, J. (1910) Klassification der Sprachen (in Bericht über die Grazer 50. Versammlung deutscher Philologen und Schulmänner), *Indogermanische Forschungen. Anzeiger*, 26, 51–8. Reprinted in Baudouin de Courtenay (1984), 190–7.

BAUDOUIN DE COURTENAY, J. (1963) *I.A. Boduèn de Kurtenè. Izbrannye trudy po obščemu jazykoznaniju*, ed. by V. P. Grigor'ev and A. A. Leont'ev, 2 vols., Izd. Akademii Nauk, Moskva.

BAUDOUIN DE COURTENAY, J. (1972) *A Baudouin de Courtenay Anthology. The Beginnings of Structural Linguistics*, translated and ed. with an introduction by Edward Stankiewicz (Indiana University Series in the History and Theory of Linguistics), Indiana University Press, Bloomington/London.

BAUDOUIN DE COURTENAY, J. (1974–90) *Dzieła wybrane [Selected Works]*, ed. by P. Zwoliński, 6 vols., Państwowe Wydawnictwo Naukowe, Warszawa. Reprint of select works.

BAUDOUIN DE COURTENAY, J. (1975) Cf. DI SALVO (1975).

BAUDOUIN DE COURTENAY, J. (1984) *Ausgewählte Werke in deutscher Sprache*. Mit einem Vorwort von Ewelina Malachowska, ed. by J. Mugdan, Fink, München.

BAUDOUIN DE COURTENAY, J. (1989) *Jan Niecisław Baudouin de Courtenay a lingwistyka światowa*, ed. by J. Rieger, M. Szymczak, S. Urbańczyk, Zakład Narodowy im. Ossolińskich, Wyd. Polskiej Akad. Nauk, Wrocław-Warszawa. Essays by different authors. *Non vidi*, cf. WILLIAMS (1991).

BAUMANN, H.-H. (1971) Die generative Grammatik und Wilhelm von Humboldt, *Poetica*, 4, 1–12.

BAUR, G. W. (1978) Aus der Frühzeit der 'Beiträge'. Briefe der Herausgeber 1870–1885, *Beiträge zur Geschichte der deutschen Sprache und Literatur (Paul-Braune-Beiträge)*, 100, 337–68.

BECHTEL, F. (1892) *Die Hauptprobleme der indogermanischen Lautlehre seit Schleicher*, Vandenhoeck & Ruprecht, Göttingen.

BECKER, K. F. (1827) *Organism der Sprache. Als Einleitung zur deutschen Grammatik – Deutsche Sprachlehre. I*, Reinherz, Frankfurt a. M. 2nd edn, with the title *Organism der Sprache*, 1841; reprinted Olms, Hildesheim, 1970.

BECKER, K. F. (1830) *A Grammar of the German Language*, John Murray, London. 2nd edn 1845, 3rd edn 1855.

BELARDI, W. (1990) *Linguistica generale, filologia e critica dell'espressione*, Bonacci, Roma.

BELKE, I. (1971–86) *Moritz Lazarus und Heymann Steinthal. Die Begründer der Völkerpsychologie in ihren Briefen* (Schriftenreihe wissenschaftlicher Abhandlungen des Leo Baeck Instituts, 21, 40, 44), 3 vols., Mohr, Tübingen.

BELL, A. M. (1867) *Visible Speech: the Science of Universal Alphabetics; or Self-interpreting Physiological Letters for the Writing of All Languages in One Alphabet*, Simpkin, Marshall & Co. / Trübner & Co., London / London & New York.

BENEŠ, B. (1958) *Wilhelm von Humboldt, Jacob Grimm, August Schleicher. Ein Vergleich ihrer Sprachauffassungen* (Diss. Basel), Keller, Winterthur.

BENFEY, T. (1839–42) *Griechische Grammatik. I Abth. Griechisches Wurzellexicon*, 2 vols., Reimer, Berlin.

BENFEY, T. (1869) *Geschichte der Sprachwissenschaft und orientalischen Philologie in Deutschland seit dem Anfange des 19. Jahrhunderts mit einem Rückblick auf die früheren Zeiten* (Geschichte der Wissenschaften in Deutschland, Neuere Zeit, 8), Cotta, München.

BENFEY, T. (1890–2) *Kleinere Schriften*. Ausgewählt und herausgegeben von Adalbert Bezzenberger, 2 vols. in 4 parts, Reuther, Berlin.

BENINCÀ, P. (1994) Linguistica e dialettologia italiana, in LEPSCHY, G. (ed.) (1990–4), 3, 525–644.

BENINCÀ, P. (1996) *Piccola storia ragionata della dialettologia italiana*, 2nd edn, Unipress, Padova. 1st edn 1988.

BENLOEW, L. (1858) *Aperçu général de la science comparative des langues pour servir d'introduction à un traité comparé des langues indo-européennes*, Durand, Paris.

BENSE, G. (1976) Bemerkungen zu theoretischen Positionen im Werk von A. F. Pott, *Zeitschrift für Phonetik, Sprachwissenschaft und Kommunikationsforschung*, 29, 519–22.

BENVENISTE, É. (1964) Lettres de Ferdinand de Saussure à Antoine Meillet, *Cahiers Ferdinand de Saussure*, 21, 89–130.

BENWARE, W. A. (1974) *The Study of Indo-European Vocalism in the 19th Century, from the Beginnings to Whitney and Scherer* (Studies in the History of Language Sciences, 3), Benjamins, Amsterdam.

BERGOUNIOUX, G. (1984) La science du langage en France de 1870 à 1885 du marché civil au marché étatique, *Langue française*, 63, 7–41.

BERGOUNIOUX, G. (1986) Arsène Darmesteter (1846–1888), *Histoire Épistémologie Langage*, 8:I, 107–23.

BERGOUNIOUX, G. (1990) *L'enseignement de la linguistique et de la philologie en France au XIXe siècle d'après les affiches de cours des facultés de lettres (1845–1897)* (Archives et documents de la société d'histoire et d'épistémologie des sciences du langage (SHESL). Seconde série, 2), SHESL, Paris.

BERGOUNIOUX, G. (1994) *Aux origines de la linguistique française*, Pocket, Paris.

BERNHARDI, A. F. (1801–3) *Sprachlehre*, 2 vols., Frölich, Berlin.

BERNHARDI, A. F. (1805) *Anfangsgründe der Sprachwissenschaft*, Fröhlich, Berlin. Reprinted 1981 (Olms, Hildesheim) and 1990 (with an introduction by R. Wild-Schedlbauer, Frommann-Holzboog, Stuttgart-Bad Cannstatt).

BEYER, A. (1981) *Deutsche Einflüsse auf die englische Sprachwissenschaft im 19. Jahrhundert* (Göppinger Arbeiten zur Germanistik, 324), Kümmerle Verlag, Göppingen.

BINGEN, J., COUPEZ, A., MAWET, F. (eds.) (1980) *Recherches de linguistique. Hommage à Maurice Leroy*, Université de Bruxelles, Bruxelles.

BJERRUM, M. (1959) *Rasmus Rask afhandlinger om det danske sprog. Bidrag til forståelse af Rasks taenkning*, Dansk Videnskabs Forlag, København.

BLEEK, W. H. I. (1862–9) *A Comparative Grammar of South African Languages*, 2 vols., Trübner & Co., London.

BLEEK, W. H. I. (1868) *Über den Ursprung der Sprache*. Herausgegeben mit einem Vorwort von Ernst Haeckel, Böhlau, Weimar. English translation by Thomas Davidson, L. W. Schmidt, New York, 1869; reprinted in Koerner (ed.) (1983). Italian translation by C. Emery, Testa, Napoli, 1872.

BLOOMFIELD, L. (1914) *An Introduction to the Study of Language*, Holt, New York. Reprinted Benjamins, Amsterdam/Philadelphia, 1983.

BLOOMFIELD, L. (1925) Why a Linguistic Society?, *Language*, 1, 1–5.

BLOOMFIELD, L. (1932) Review of Hermann (1931), *Language*, 8, 220–33.

BLOOMFIELD, L. (1933) *Language*, Holt, New York.

BÖHTLINGK, O. (ed.) (1840) *Pâṇini's acht Bücher grammatischer Regeln*, 2 vols., H. B. König, Bonn. New edn (*Pâṇini's Grammatik*) Haessel, Leipzig, 1887; reprinted Olms, Hildesheim, 1971.

BÖHTLINGK, O. (1851) *Über die Sprache der Jakuten*, 2 vols., Buchdruckerei der Kaiserlichen Akademie der Wissenschaften, St Petersburg.

BÖHTLINGK, O., ROTH, R. (1855–75) *Sanskrit Wörterbuch herausgegeben von der Kaiserlichen Akademie der Wissenschaften*, 7 vols., Buchdruckerei der Kaiserlichen Akademie der Wissenschaften, St Petersburg.

BOLELLI, T. (1962) Ascoli, G. I., in *Dizionario Biografico degli Italiani*, 4, Istituto della Enciclopedia Italiana, Roma, 380–4.

BOLELLI, T. (1965a) I settantacinque anni dell'Istituto di Glottologia dell'Università di Pisa, *Studi e Saggi Linguistici*, 5, 1–6.

BOLELLI, T. (1965b) *Per una storia della ricerca linguistica. Testi e note introduttive* (Collana di storia diretta da Arsenio Frugoni, 4), Morano, Napoli.

BOLELLI, T. (1986) I neogrammatici, in QUATTORDIO MORESCHINI (ed.) (1986), 159–73.

BOLOGNA, M. P. (1985) La 'paleontologia linguistica' di Adolphe Pictet fra realtà e irrealtà scientifica, in CAMPANILE, E., LAZZERONI, R., and PERONI, R. (eds.), *Scritti in onore di Riccardo Ambrosini*, Giardini, Pisa, 43–53.

BOLOGNA, M. P. (1986) Whitney in Italia, *Historiographia Linguistica*, 13, 43–70.

BOLOGNA, M. P. (1988) *Ricerca etimologica e ricostruzione culturale. Alle origini della mitologia comparata* (Testi Linguistici, 11), Giardini, Pisa.

BOLOGNA, M. P. (1990) Storia della linguistica e teoria linguistica: A. F. Pott e la ricostruzione, *Studi Classici e Orientali*, 40, 1–22.

BOLOGNA, M. P. (1992) Il 'dualismo' di Franz Bopp, *Incontri Linguistici*, 15, 29–48.

BOLOGNA, M. P. (1995) Langage et expressivité chez August Friedrich Pott, *Historiographia Linguistica*, 22: 1/2, 75–90.

BOLOGNESI, G. (1994) Sul termine 'Indo-Germanisch', in CIPRIANO, DI GIOVINE and MANCINI (eds.) (1994), 327–38.

BOMHARD, A. (1984) *Towards Proto-Nostratic: A New Approach* (Current Issues in Linguistic Theory, 27), Benjamins, Amsterdam/Philadelphia.

BONFANTE, G. (1953) Ideas on the Kinship of the European Languages from 1200 to 1800, *Cahiers d'histoire mondiale*, 1, 679–99.

BOPP, F. (1816) *Über das Conjugationssystem der Sanskritsprache in Vergleichung mit jenem der griechischen, lateinischen, persischen und germanischen Sprache*. Herausgegeben von K. J. Windischmann, Andreae, Frankfurt a. M. Reprinted Olms, Hildesheim, 1975.

BOPP, F. (1819) *Nalus carmen sanscritum e Mahâbhârato; edidit, latine vertit et adnotationibus illustravit F. Bopp*, Treuttel & Würtz, London. 2nd edn, Nicolai, Berlin, 1832; 3rd edn 1868.

BOPP, F. (1820) Analytical Comparison of the Sanskrit, Greek, Latin, and Teutonic Languages, Shewing the Original Identity of Their Grammatical Structure, *Annals of Oriental Literature (London)*, 1, 1–64. (Reprint ed. by E. F. K. Koerner, Benjamins, Amsterdam, 1974.)

BOPP, F. (1828–30) *Glossarium sanscritum a Francisco Bopp* (sic), Dümmler, Berolini. Cf. BOPP (1847).

BOPP, F. (1833–52) *Vergleichende Grammatik des Sanskrit, Zend, Griechischen, Lateinischen, Litthauischen, Gothischen und Deutschen*. 6 Abtheilungen, Dümmler, Berlin. For the 2nd edn, cf. BOPP (1857–61); for the English translation, cf. EASTWICK (1845–53).

BOPP, F. (1836) *Vocalismus oder Sprachvergleichende Kritiken über J. Grimm's deutsche Grammatik und Graff's althochdeutschen Sprachschatz mit Begründung einer neuer Theorie des Ablauts*, Nicolaische Buchhandlung, Berlin.

BOPP, F. (1847) *Glossarium sanscritum in quo omnes radices et vocabula usitatissima explicantur et cum vocabulis graecis, latinis, germanicis, lithuanicis, slavicis, celticis comparantur*, Dümmler, Berolini. Cf. BOPP (1828–30).

BOPP, F. (1857–61) *Vergleichende Grammatik des Sanskrit, Şend, Armenischen, Griechischen, Lateinischen, Litauischen, Altslavischen, Gothischen und Deutschen*. Zweite gänzlich umgearbeitete Auflage, 3 vols. (+ Register by Carl Arendt, 1863), Dümmler, Berlin. For the French translation, cf. BRÉAL (1866–72).

BORSCHE, T. (1981) *Sprachansichten. Der Begriff der menschlichen Rede in der Sprachphilosophie Wilhelm von Humboldts*, Cotta, Stuttgart.

BORSCHE, T. (1987) Die innere Form der Sprache, in HOBERG (ed.) (1987a), 193–216.

BORSCHE, T. (1990) *Wilhelm von Humboldt*, Beck, München.

BORSCHE, T. et al., (eds.) (1993) *Wilhelm von Humboldt e il dissolvimento della filosofia nei 'saperi positivi'* (Collana di Filosofia, nuova serie, 20), Morano, Napoli.

BORST, A. (1957–1963) *Der Turmbau von Babel: Geschichte der Meinungen über Ursprung und Vielfalt der Sprachen und Völker*, 6 vols., Hierschmann, Stuttgart.

BRAUNE, W. (1874) Zur Kenntnis der frankischen und hochdeutschen Lautverschiebung, *Beiträge zur Geschichte der deutschen Sprache und Literatur (Paul-Braune-Beiträge)*, 1, 1–56.

BRAUNE, W. (1880) *Gothische Grammatik*, Niemeyer, Halle. 19th edn (revised by A. Ebbinghaus), 1981.

BRAUNE, W. (1886) *Althochdeutsche Grammatik*, Niemeyer, Halle. 13th edn (revised by H. Eggers), 1975.

BRÉAL, M. (1864) *De la méthode comparative appliquée à l'étude des langues. Leçon d'ouverture du cours de grammaire comparée au Collège de France*, Librairie Germer Baillière, Paris. Reprinted in BRÉAL (1877, 217–41).

BRÉAL, M. (1866–72) *Grammaire comparée des langues indo-européennes par François Bopp. Traduite sur la deuxième édition et précédée d'une introduction par M. Michel Bréal*, 4 vols. (Vol. 5 *Registre detaillé par F. Meunier*, 1874), Imprimerie Impériale/Nationale, Paris.

BRÉAL, M. (1868) *Les idées latentes du langage. Leçon faite au Collège de France pour la réouverture du cours de grammaire comparée*, Hachette, Paris. Reprinted in BRÉAL (1877, 295–322).

BRÉAL, M. (1872) *Quelques mots sur l'instruction publique en France*, Hachette, Paris.

BRÉAL, M. (1877) *Mélanges de mythologie et de linguistique*, Hachette, Paris.

BRÉAL, M. (1897) *Essai de sémantique (Science des significations)*, Hachette, Paris. 3rd edn 1904; 7th or 8th edn 1924; reprinted Genève 1976, Saint-Pierre-de-Solerne 1983. English translation by H. Cust, Holt, London 1900 (reprinted 1964, Dover, New York). Italian translations in BRÉAL 1990 and 1992. Portuguese translation, Pontes, São Paulo, 1992.

BRÉAL, M. (1990) *Saggio di semantica. Introduzione, traduzione e commento di Arturo Martone*, Liguori, Napoli.

BRÉAL, M. (1991) *The Beginnings of Semantics. Essays, Lectures and Reviews.* Edited and translated by George Wolf, Duckworth, London.

BRÉAL, M. (1992) *Saggio di semantica (scienza dei significati).* Introduzione e cura di Renata Mecchia. Edizione critica e bibliografia brealiana di Domenico Russo, Métis, Chieti.

BREDSDORFF, J. H. (1817) *De regulis in classificatione rerum naturalium observandis commentatio. Diss. inauguralis,* Typis Andreae Seidelini, Hauniae.

BREDSDORFF, J. H. (1821) *Om Aarsagerne til Sprogenes Forandringer* (Indbydelsesskrift til den offentlige Examen i Roeskilde Kathedralskole i September 1821), Roskilde. Reprinted 1866, ed. by V. Thomsen, Gyldendal, Kjøbenhavn; reprinted also 1933, in *J. H. Bredsdorffs Udvalgte Afhandlinger inden for Sprogvidenskab og Runologi,* ed. by J. Glahder, Levin & Munksgaard, København, 3–27. German translation in BREDSDORFF (1970).

BREDSDORFF, J. H. (1970) *Über die Ursachen der Sprachveränderungen,* Übersetzen und herausgegeben von Uwe Petersen (Tübinger Beiträge zur Linguistik, 13), TBL, Tübingen. 2nd edn Narr, Tübingen, 1975; translation of BREDSDORFF (1821).

BRETTSCHNEIDER, G., LEHMANN, C. (eds.) (1980) *Wege zur Universalien Forschung. Sprachwissenschaftliche Beiträge zum 60. Geburtstag von Hansjacob Seiler,* Narr, Tübingen.

BRINCAT, G. (1986) *La linguistica prestrutturale,* Zanichelli, Bologna.

BRINTON, D. (1891) *The American Race: A Linguistic Classification and Ethnographic Description of the Native Tribes of North and South America,* Hodges, New York.

BROCKINGTON, J. L. (1989) Warren Hastings and Orientalism, in CARNALL, G., and NICHOLSON, C. (eds.), *The Impeachment of Warren Hastings. Papers from a Bicentenary Commemoration,* Edinburgh University Press, Edinburgh, 91–108.

BROGYANYI, B. (ed.) (1979) *Festschrift for Oswald Szemerényi on the Occasion of his 65th Birthday* (Current Issues in Linguistic Theory, 11), 2 vols., Benjamins, Amsterdam.

BROSSES, C. DE (1765) *Traité de la formation méchanique des langues et des principes physiques de l'étymologie,* 2 vols., Saillant-Vincent-Desaint, Paris.

BROWN, R. L. (1967) *Wilhelm von Humboldt's Conception of Linguistic Relativity* (Janua Linguarum. Series minor, 65), Mouton, The Hague / Paris.

BRÜCKE, E. W. (1856) *Grundzüge der Physiologie und Systematik der Sprachlaute für Linguisten und Taubstummenlehrer,* C. Gerold's Sohn, Wien.

BRUGMAN, K. (or BRUGMANN) (1875) Review of G. Koffmane, *Lexicon lateinischer Wortformen,* Göttingen, 1874, *Literarisches Centralblatt,* 1875, 651–2.

BRUGMAN, K. (1876a) Nasalis sonans in der indogermanischen Grundsprache, *Studien zur griechischen und lateinischen Grammatik (Curtius Studien),* 9, 285–338.

BRUGMAN, K. (1876b) Zur Geschichte der stammabstufenden Declinationen. Erste Abhandlung: Die Nomina auf *-ar-* und *-tar-, Studien zur griechischen und lateinischen Grammatik (Curtius Studien),* 9, 361–406.

BRUGMAN, K. (1877) Reviews of Marty (1876), Steinthal (1877) [3rd edn of Steinthal (1858)], Noiré (1877), *Jenaer Literaturzeitung,* 692–3.

BRUGMAN, K. (1878) Zur Geschichte der Personalendungen, *Morphologische Untersuchungen*, 1, 133–86.

BRUGMAN, K. (1879) Review of Saussure (1879), *Literarisches Centralblatt*, 773–4.

BRUGMANN, K. (or BRUGMAN) (1882) Review of Ziemer (1882), *Literarisches Centralblatt*, 401–2.

BRUGMANN, K. (or BRUGMAN) (1884) Zur Frage nach den Verwandtschaftverhältnissen der indogermanischen Sprachen, *Internationale Zeitschrift für allgemeine Sprachwissenschaft*, 1, 226–56.

BRUGMANN, K. (or BRUGMAN) (1885a) Griechische Grammatik, in MÜLLER, I. (ed.), *Handbuch der klassischen Altertumswissenschaft*, 2, Beck, München, 1–126. 2nd edn (much expanded) 1889; 3rd edn (an independent volume) 1900. 4th edn (with A. Thumb) 1913.

BRUGMANN, K. (or BRUGMAN) (1885b) *Zum heutigen Stand der Sprachwissenschaft*, Trübner, Strassburg. Reprinted in WILBUR (1977).

BRUGMANN, K. (or BRUGMAN) (1886–93) *Grundriß der vergleichenden Grammatik der indogermanischen Sprachen. Kurzgefaßte Darstellung der Geschichte des Altindischen, Altiranischen (Avestischen und Altpersischen), Altarmenischen, Altgriechischen, Lateinischen, Umbrisch-Samnitischen, Altirischen, Gotischen, Althochdeutschen, Litauischen und Altkirchenslavischen*, 5 vols., Trübner, Strassburg & London. English translation, Trübner, Strassburg & London, 1888–95. For the 2nd edn, cf. BRUGMANN and DELBRÜCK (1897–1916).

BRUGMANN, K. (or BRUGMAN) (1902–4) *Kurze vergleichende Grammatik der indogermanischen Sprachen. Auf Grund des fünfbändigen 'Grundrisses der vergleichenden Grammatik der indogermanischen Sprachen von K. Brugmann und B. Delbrück' verfaßt*. 3 Lieferungen, Trübner, Strassburg. For the French translation, cf. BRUGMANN (1905).

BRUGMANN, K. (or BRUGMAN) (1905) *Abrégé de grammaire comparée des langues indo-européennes*. Traduit par J. Bloch, A. Cuny et A. Ernout sous la direction de A. Meillet et R. Gauthiot, Klincksieck, Paris. Translation of BRUGMANN (1902–4).

BRUGMANN, K. (or BRUGMAN) (1909a) Hermann Osthoff, *Indogermanische Forschungen. Anzeiger*, 24, 218–23. Reprinted in SEBEOK (ed.) (1966), i, 555–62.

BRUGMANN, K. (or BRUGMAN) (1909b) Ein Wörterbuch der sprachwissenschaftlichen Terminologie, *Germanisch-romanische Monatsschrift*, 1, 209–22.

BRUGMANN, K., DELBRÜCK, B. (1897–1916) *Grundriß der vergleichenden Grammatik der indogermanischen Sprachen. Kurzgefaßte Darstellung der Geschichte des Altindischen, Altiranischen (Avestischen und Altpersischen), Altarmenischen, Altgriechischen, Albanesischen, Lateinischen, Oskisch-Umbrischen, Altirischen, Gotischen, Althochdeutschen, Litauischen und Altkirchenslavischen*, 2nd edn, 9 parts, Trübner, Strassburg. 2 vols. in 6 parts by Brugmann discuss phonology and morphology, while 3 vols. (1893–1900) by Delbrück discuss the syntax. Reprinted De Gruyter, Berlin, 1930 and 1967.

BRUNEAU, C. (1948) *Histoire de la langue française des origines à nos jours. XII. L'époque romantique*, Colin, Paris. 2nd edn 1968.

BRUNOT, F. (1905) *Histoire de la langue française*, 1, Colin, Paris.

BUCHHOLZ, U. (1986) *Das Kawi-Werk Wilhelm von Humboldts. Untersuchungen zur empirischen Sprachbeschreibung und vergleichenden Grammatikographie* (Studium Sprachwissenschaft Beihefte, 4), Institut für Allgemeine Sprachwissenschaft der Westfälischen Wilhelms-Universität, Münster.

BÜCHELER, F. (1866) *Grundriß der lateinischen Declination*, Teubner, Leipzig.

BÜHLER, K. (1934) *Sprachtheorie. Die Darstellungsfunktion der Sprache*, Fischer, Jena. Reprinted Fischer, Stuttgart, 1982. English translation by D. Fraser Goodwing, Benjamins, Amsterdam/Philadelphia, 1990; Italian translation, Armando, Roma, 1983.

BUMANN, W. (1965) *Die Sprachtheorie Heymann Steinthals: Dargestellt im Zusammenhang mit seiner Theorie der Geisteswissenschaft.* (Monographien zur philosophischen Forschung, 39), Anton Hain, Meisenheim am Glan.

BURKE, C. B. (1983) The Expansion of American Higher Education, in JARAUSCH (ed.) (1983), 108–30.

[BURNETT, JAMES, LORD MONBODDO] (1773–92) *Of the Origin and Progress of Language*, 2nd edn, 6 vols.; Vols. 1–3 Balfour/Cadell, Vols. 4–6 Bell/Cadell, Edinburgh/London.

BUSSE, W., TRABANT, J. (eds.) (1986) *Les idéologues. Sémiotique, théories et politique linguistiques pendant la révolution française*, Benjamins, Amsterdam/Philadelphia.

BUSTAMANTE, J. (1986) Apéndice con algunas notas complementarias, in TOVAR (1986), 73–87.

BYNON, T. (1986) August Schleicher: Indo-Europeanist and General Linguist, in BYNON and PALMER (eds.) (1986), 129–49.

BYNON, T., PALMER, F. R. (eds.) (1986) *Studies in the History of Western Linguistics in Honour of R. H. Robins*, Cambridge University Press, Cambridge.

CALDWELL, R. (1856) *A Comparative Grammar of the Dravidian or South-Indian Family of Languages*, Harrison, London. 3rd edn ed. by J. L. Wyatt and T. R. Pillai, London 1913.

CALVO PÉREZ, J. (1991) *Tres biografías lingüísticas en torno a Cuenca. III. Lorenzo Hervás y Panduro: Un científico a caballo entre dos mundos* (Lingüística, Filología, 4), Deputación Provincial de Cuenca, Cuenca.

CAMPANILE, E. (1986) Le pecore dei neogrammatici e le pecore nostre, in QUATTORDIO MORESCHINI (ed.) (1986), 147–57.

CANNON, G. (ed.) (1970) *The Letters of Sir William Jones*, 2 vols., Clarendon Press, Oxford.

CANNON, G. (ed.) (1979) *Sir William Jones: A Bibliography of Primary and Secondary Sources* (Library and Information Sources in Linguistics, 7), Benjamins, Amsterdam.

CANNON, G. (1990) *The Life and Mind of Oriental Jones: Sir William Jones, the Father of Modern Linguistics*, Cambridge University Press, Cambridge.

CANTOR, M., LESKIEN, A. (1879) Grassmann, Hermann, in *Allgemeine Deutsche Biographie*, IX, Duncker & Humblot, Leipzig, 595–8.

CARDINALE, U., PORZIO GERNIA, M. L., SANTAMARIA, D. (eds.) (1994) *Per Giovanni Flechia nel centenario della morte (1892–1992).* Atti del Convegno (Ivrea-Torino, 5–7 dicembre 1992), Edizioni dell'Orso, Alessandria.

CARDONA, G. R. (1981) *Antropologia della scrittura*, Loescher, Torino.

CARDONA, G., ZIDE, N. H. (eds.) (1987) *Festschrift for Henry Hoenigswald*, Narr, Tübingen.

CAREY, W. (1806) *A Grammar of the Sungskrit Language, Composed from the Works of the Most Esteemed Grammarians, to which are added, Examples for the Exercise of the Student, and a Complete List of the Dhatoos, or Roots*, 2nd edn, 2 vols., Mission Press, Serampore. 1st edn 1804.

CASSIRER, E. (1923) *Philosophie der symbolischen Formen; Die Sprache*, I, Bruno Cassirer, Berlin. English translation in CASSIRER (1953).

CASSIRER, E. (1945) Structuralism in Modern Linguistics, *Word*, I, 99–120.

CASSIRER, E. (1953) *The Philosophy of Symbolic Forms. Vol. 1; Language.* Translated by Ralph Manheim, Yale University Press, New Haven. Translation of CASSIRER (1923).

CASTRÉN, M. A. (1850) *De affixis personalibus linguarum altaicarum*, Litteris Frenckellianis, Helsingforsiae.

CHAMBERS, R. W. (1939) *Man's Unconquerable Mind*, Cape, London.

CHARLE, C. (1994) *La république des universitaires* (L'univers historique), Editions du Seuil, Paris.

CHARLE, C., VERGER, J. (1994) *Histoire des universités* (Que sais-je?), Presses Universitaires de France, Paris.

CHAUDURI, N. C. (1974) *Scholar Extraordinary. The Life of Professor the Rt. Hon. Friedrich Max Müller, PC*, Chatto & Windus, London.

CHAVÉE, H.-J. (1849) *Lexiologie indo-européenne ou essai sur la science des mots Sanskrits, Grecs, Latins, Français, Lithuaniens, Russes, Allemands, Anglais, etc.*, A. Franck, Paris, Leipzig.

CHAVÉE, H.-J. (1862) *Les langues et les races*, Chamerot, Paris.

CHERUBIM, D. (1973) Hermann Paul und die moderne Linguistik. Zur Studienausgabe von H. Pauls 'Prinzipien der Sprachgeschichte', *Zeitschrift für Dialektologie und Linguistik*, 40, 310–22.

CHERUBIM, D. (1992) Tradition und Modernität in der Sprachwissenschaft des 18. Jahrhunderts: Die Herausforderung der Natur- und Geowissenschaften. Am Beispiel der neugegründeten Universität Göttingen, in NAUMANN, PLANK and HOFBAUER (eds.) (1992), 193–219.

CHOMSKY, N. (1964) *Current Issues in Linguistic Theory* (Janua Linguarum. Series minor, 38), Mouton, The Hague.

CHOMSKY, N. (1965) *Aspects of the Theory of Syntax*, The MIT Press, Cambridge, Massachusetts.

CHOMSKY, N. (1966) *Cartesian Linguistics: a Chapter in the History of Rationalistic Thought*, Harper & Row, New York / London.

CHORLEY, J. A. (1984) *J. C. A. Heyse (1764–1829) and K. W. L. Heyse (1797–1855) and German School Grammar in the First Half of the Nineteenth Century*, Unpublished M. Litt. Thesis, University of Oxford, Oxford.

CHRISTIE, W. M. J. (1985) Rask's Lecture on the Philosophy of Language, in MAKKAI, A., and MELBY, A. K. (eds.), *Linguistics and Philosophy. Essays in Honor of Rulon S. Wells*, Benjamins, Amsterdam/Philadelphia, 77–83.

CHRISTMANN, H. H. (1967) *Beiträge zur Geschichte der These vom Weltbild der Sprache* (Abhandlungen der Geistes- und sozialwissenschaftlichen Klasse, 1966, 7 (pp. 441–69)), Akademie der Wissenschaften und der Literatur, Mainz.

CHRISTMANN, H. H. (ed.) (1977) *Sprachwissenschaft des 19. Jahrhunderts*, Wissenschaftliche Buchgesellschaft, Darmstadt.

CHRISTMANN, H. H. (1981) Neue Beiträge zur Geschichte der These vom Weltbild der Sprache; 'Praktische' Anwendungen in Frankreich und Deutschland am Ende des 18. Jahrhunderts, in TRABANT (ed.) (1981), 87–99.

CHRISTMANN, H. H. (1985) *Romanistik und Anglistik an der deutschen Universität im 19. Jahrhundert. Ihre Herausbildung als Fächer und Verhältnis zu Germanistik und Klassischer Philologie* (Akademie der Wissenschaften und der Literatur. Abhandlungen der Geistes- und sozialwissenschaftlichen Klasse, 1985, 1), Steiner, Mainz.

CHRISTMANN, H. H. (1993) L'entrée de la philologie romane dans les Académies des Sciences en Allemagne et en Autriche, in DROIXHE and GRELL (eds.) (1993), 319–27.

CHRISTY, T. C. (1983) *Uniformitarianism in Linguistics* (Amsterdam Studies in the History of Linguistics, 31), Benjamins, Amsterdam/Philadelphia.

CHRISTY, T. C. (1989) Reflex Sounds and the Experiential Manifold: Steinthal on the Origin of Language, in GESSINGER and RAHDEN (eds.) (1989), 523–47.

CIPRIANO, P., DI GIOVINE, P., MANCINI, P. (eds.) (1994) *Miscellanea di studi linguistici in onore di Walter Belardi*, 2 vols., Il Calamo, Roma.

COLEBROOKE, H. T. (1801) On the Sanscrĭt and Prácrĭt Languages, *Asiatic Researches*, 7, 199–231. Reprinted in *Miscellaneous Essays* by H. T. Colebrooke, 2 vols., Allen & Co., London, 1837, ii, 1–34.

COLEBROOKE, H. T. (1805) *A Grammar of the Sanscrĭt Language. Vol. 1*, Honorable Company's Press, Calcutta.

COLEMAN, W. (1977) *Biology in the Nineteenth Century. Problems of Form, Function, and Transformation* (The Cambridge History of Science Series), Cambridge University Press, Cambridge.

COLLINGE, N. E. (1985) *The Laws of Indo-European* (Current Issues in Linguistic Theory, 35), Benjamins, Amsterdam/Philadelphia.

COLLINGE, N. E. (1987) Who Did Discover the Law of the Palatals?, in CARDONA and ZIDE (eds.) (1987), 73–80.

COLLINGE, N. E. (1995) Further Laws of Indo-European, in WINTER, W., and GRELL, C. (eds.), *Languages and Language*, De Gruyter, Berlin and New York, 275–95.

COLLITZ, H. (1886) Die neueste sprachforschung und die erklärung des indogermanischen ablautes, *Beiträge zur Kunde der indogermanischen Sprachen*, 11, 203–42. Reprinted in WILBUR (ed.) (1977).

COLLITZ, H. (1926) A Century of Grimm's Law, *Language*, 2, 174–83.

CONDILLAC, E. B. abbé de (1947–51) *Œuvres philosophiques de Condillac. Texte établi et presenté par Georges Le Roy* (Corpus général des philosophes français. Auteurs modernes, 33), 3 vols., Presses Universitaires de France, Paris.

CONRAD, J. (1884) *Das Universitätsstudium in Deutschland während der letzen 50 Jahren. Statistische Untersuchungen unter besonderer Berücksichtung Preussens*, Fischer, Jena.

CONRAD, J. (1885) *The German Universities for the Last Fifty Years*. Authorised translation with Map, Notes and Appendix by John Hutchinson, MA

... and a Preface by James Bryce, MP, Regius Professor of Civil Law in the University of Oxford, David Bryce & Son, Glasgow.

CONRAD, J. (1893) Allgemeine Statistik der deutschen Universitäten, in LEXIS (ed.) (1893), 115–68.

CONSANI, C. (1991) *ΔΙΑΛΕΚΤΟΣ. Contributo alla storia del concetto di 'dialetto'* (Testi Linguistici, 18), Giardini, Pisa.

CONTE, M.-E. (1976) Wilhelm von Humboldt nella linguistica contemporanea. Bibliografia ragionata 1960–1976, in HEILMANN (ed.) (1976), 281–325.

CORSI, P. (1983) *Oltre il mito. Lamarck e le scienze naturali del suo tempo*, Il Mulino, Bologna.

COSERIU, E. (1967) Georg von der Gabelentz et la linguistique synchronique, *Word*, 23, 74–100. Reprinted in the 1969 reprint of GABELENTZ (1891).

COSERIU, E. (1968) Adam Smith und die Anfänge der Sprachtypologie, in BRECKLE, H. E. and LIPKA, L. (eds.), *Wortbildung, Syntax und Morphologie. Festschrift zum 60. Geburtstag von Hans Marchand*, Mouton, The Hague/Paris, 46–54.

COSERIU, E. (1970) Semantik, innere Sprachform und Tiefenstruktur, *Folia Linguistica*, 4, 53–63. Also in E. COSERIU, *Sprache – Strukturen und Funktionen*, Narr, Tübingen, 177–86.

COSERIU, E. (1972) Über die Sprachtypologie Wilhelm von Humboldts, in HÖSLE, J., and HEITEL, W. (eds.), *Beiträge zur vergleichende Literaturgeschichte. Festschrift für Kurt Wais zum 65. Geburtstag*, Niemeyer, Tübingen, 107–35. For the Italian version, see COSERIU (1976).

COSERIU, E. (1976) Sulla tipologia linguistica di Wilhelm von Humboldt. Contributo alla critica della tradizione linguistica, in HEILMANN (ed.) (1976), 133–64. Italian version of COSERIU (1972), originally published in *Lingua e Stile* 8 (1973), 235–66.

COSERIU, E. (1978) Hervás und das Substrat, *Studi şi cercetari linguistice*, 29, 523–30.

COSERIU, E. (1980) Un précurseur méconnu de la syntaxe structurale: H. Tiktin, in BINGEN, COUPEZ and MAWET (eds.) (1980), 48–62.

COURT DE GEBELIN, A. (1777–82) *Monde primitif analysé et comparé avec le monde moderne consideré dans son génie allégorique et dans les allégories auxquelles conduisit ce génie*, 2nd edn, 9 vols., Boudet, Paris.

CURTIUS, G. (1852) *Griechische Schulgrammatik*, Tempsky, Prag. 18th edn 1888. Translated into Czech, Polish, Serbian, Hungarian, Russian, Norwegian, Swedish, Spanish, Italian, English and French.

CURTIUS, G. (1858–62) *Grundzüge der griechischen Etymologie*, 2 vols., Teubner, Leipzig. 3rd edn 1869; 5th edn 1879. Translated into English by A. S. Wilkins and E. B. England, Murray, London 1875–6; 5th edn 1886.

CURTIUS, G. (1867) Zur Chronologie der indogermanischen Sprachforschung, *Abhandlungen der philologisch-historischen Classe der Königlichen Sächsischen Gesellschaft der Wissenschaften*, 5, 187–261. 2nd edn 1879. French translation by A. Bergaigne, Franck, Paris, 1869.

CURTIUS, G. (1870) *Erläuterungen zu meiner Griechischen Schulgrammatik*, 2nd edn, Tempsky, Prag. 1st edn 1863. Translated into Italian, Spanish and English.

CURTIUS, G. (1873–6) *Das Verbum der griechischen Sprache seinem Baue nach dargestellt*, 2 vols., Hirzel, Leipzig. 2nd edn 1877–80. English translation by A. S. Wilkins and E. B. England, Murray, London, 1880.

CURTIUS, G. (1876) Nachwort, *Studien zur griechischen und lateinischen Grammatik (Curtius Studien)*, 9, 436.

CURTIUS, G. (1885) *Zur Kritik der neuesten Sprachforschung*, Hirzel, Leipzig. Reprinted in WILBUR (1977).

CURTIUS, G. (1886) *Kleine Schriften*. Ed. by E. Windisch, 2 vols., Hirzel, Leipzig.

CUTLER, A., FAY, D. (1978) Cf. MERINGER and MAYER (1978).

DARDANO, M. (1974) *G. I. Ascoli e la questione della lingua* (Bibliotheca Biographica, 12), Istituto della Enciclopedia Italiana, Roma.

DARMESTETER, A. (1877) *De la création actuelle de mots nouveaux dans la langue française et les lois qui la régissent*, Vieweg, Paris. Reprinted Slatkine, Genève, 1972.

DARMESTETER, A. (1886) *The Life of Words as Symbols of Ideas*, Kegan Paul, Trench, London. French edn 1887.

DARMESTETER, A. (1887) *La vie des mots étudiée dans leurs significations*, Delagrave, Paris. 3rd edn 1889, 15th edn 1925.

DARMESTETER, A., HATZFELD, A. (eds.) (1890) *Dictionnaire général de la langue française du commencement du XVIIe siècle jusqu'à nos jours, précédé d'un traité de la formation de la langue ... (avec le concours de A. Thomas)*, 2 vols., Delagrave, Paris.

DARWIN, C. (1859) *On the Origin of Species by Means of Natural Selection or the Preservation of Favoured Races in the Struggle for Life*, Murray, London.

DARWIN, C. (1871) *The Descent of Man and Selection in Relation to Sex*, 2 vols., Murray, London.

DE CLERQ, J., DESMET, P., SWIGGERS, P. (1992) Idéologie et lexicographie à la fin du XVIII siècle, in SCHLIEBEN-LANGE *et al.* (eds.) (1989–94, 3, 135–56).

DE FELICE, E. (1954) *La terminologia linguistica di G. I. Ascoli e della sua scuola* (Comité international permanent des linguistes. Publication de la commission de terminologie), Spectrum, Utrecht-Anvers.

DEGÉRANDO, J.-M. (1800) *Considérations sur les diverses méthodes à suivre dans l'observation des peuples sauvages*, Paris (no publisher). Reprinted in *Revue d'anthropologie*, II série, 6, 1883, 152–82.

DEGÉRANDO, J.-M. (1969) *The Observation of Savage People. Translated by F. C. T. Moore with a Preface by E. E. Evans-Pritchard*, Routledge & Kegan, London. Translation of DEGÉRANDO (1800).

DELBRÜCK, B. (1871–88) *Syntaktische Forschungen*, 5 vols., Waisenhaus, Halle.

DELBRÜCK, B. (1875) *Das Sprachstudium auf den deutschen Universitäten. Praktische Rathschläge für studirende der Philologie*, Dufft, Jena.

DELBRÜCK, B. (1880) *Einleitung in das Sprachstudium. Ein Beitrag zur Geschichte und Methodik der vergleichenden Sprachforschung* (Bibliothek indogermanischer Grammatiken, 4), Breitkopf und Härtel, Leipzig. 6th edn 1919. The 4th and later edns have the title *Einführung in das Studium der indogermanischen Sprachen*. Translated into Italian (1881), English (1882), Russian (1904).

DELBRÜCK, B. (1885) *Die neueste Sprachforschung. Betrachtungen über Georg Curtius Schrift zur Kritik der neuesten Sprachforschung*, Breitkopf & Härtel, Leipzig. Reprinted in WILBUR (ed.) (1977).

DELBRÜCK, B. (1888) *Altindische Syntax* (Syntaktische Forschungen, 5), Waisenhaus, Halle. Reprinted Wissenschaftliche Buchgesellschaft, Darmstadt, 1968.

DELBRÜCK, B. (1893–1900) *Vergleichende Syntax der indogermanischen Sprachen*, in BRUGMANN and DELBRÜCK (1897–1916), V, Vols. 1–3.

DELBRÜCK, B. (1901) *Grundfragen der Sprachforschung mit Rücksicht auf W. Wundts Sprachpsychologie erörtert*, Trübner, Strassburg.

DELBRÜCK, B. (1902) Das Wesen der Lautgesetze, *Annalen der Naturphilosophie*, 1, 277–308.

DELESALLE, S. (1987) Vie des mots et science des significations: Arsène Darmesteter et Michel Bréal, *DRLAV. Revue de linguistique*, 36–7, 265–314.

DELESALLE, S. (1988) L'Essai de sémantique de Bréal. Du 'transformisme' à la diachronie, in JOLY (ed.) (1988), 43–55.

DELESALLE, S. (1990) Raul Guérin de la Grasserie, in NIEDEREHE and KOERNER (eds.) (1990), 677–87.

DELESALLE, S., CHEVALIER, J.-C. (1986) *La linguistique, la grammaire et l'école 1750–1914*, Armand Colin, Paris.

DE MAURO, T. (1970a) *Introduzione alla Semantica*, 2nd edn (Biblioteca di cultura moderna, 614), Laterza, Bari. 1st edn 1965.

DE MAURO, T. (1970b) *Ferdinand de Saussure, Corso di linguistica generale. Introduzione, traduzione e commento*, 3rd edn (Universale Laterza, 151), Laterza, Bari. 1st edn 1967. French version, Payot, Paris, 1972.

DE MAURO, T. (1980) *Idee e ricerche linguistiche nella cultura italiana*, Il Mulino, Bologna.

DE MAURO, T., FORMIGARI, L. (eds.) (1990) *Leibniz, Humboldt and the Origins of Comparativism* (Studies in the History of the Language Sciences, 49), Benjamins, Amsterdam/Philadelphia.

DE MAURO, T., FORMIGARI, L. (eds.) (1994) *Italian Studies in Linguistic Historiography. Proceedings of the Conference In Ricordo di Antonino Pagliaro – Gli studi italiani di storiografia linguistica, Rome 23–24 January 1992* (Materialen zur Geschichte der Sprachwissenschaft und der Semiotik, 6), Nodus, Münster.

DE MEO, A. (1987) Genesi della flessione e evoluzione dell'indoeuropeo nell'opera di Alfred Ludwig, *Annali dell'Istituto Orientale di Napoli, Sez. linguistica*, 9, 123–31.

DE MEO, A. (1990) Origine e evoluzione della lingua e della scrittura nella linguistica del XIX secolo, *Annali dell'Istituto Orientale di Napoli, Sez. linguistica*, 12, 281–300.

DENECKE, L. (1971) *Jacob Grimm und sein Brüder Wilhelm*, Metzler, Stuttgart.

DENECKE, L., TEITGE, I. (1989) *Die Bibliothek der Brüder Grimm: annotiertes Verzeichnis des festgestellten Bestandes* (erarbeitet von Ludwig Denecke und Irmgard Teitge; herausgegeben von Friedhilde Krause), Böhlau, Weimar.

DENINA, C. (1804) *La clef des langues ou observations sur l'origine et la formation des principales langues qu'on parle et qu'on écrit en Europe*, 3 vols., Mettra-Umlang-Quien, Berlin.

DENINA, C. (1985) *Storia delle lingue e polemiche linguistiche. Dai saggi berlinesi 1783–1804*, a cura di C. Marazzini, Edizioni dell'Orso, Alessandria.

DESMET, P. (1992) Victor Henry et les lois phon(ét)iques, in AHLQVIST (ed.) (1992, 237–50).

DESMET, P. (1994) *La Revue de linguistique et de philologie comparée* (1867–1916) – organe de linguistique naturaliste en France, *Beiträge zur Geschichte der Sprachwissenschaft*, 4.1, 49–80.

DESMET, P., SWIGGERS, P. (1996) Gaston Paris: aspects linguistiques d'une œuvre philologique, in LORENZO, R. (ed.), *Actas do XIX Congreso Internacional de Lingüística e Filoloxia Románicas, Universidade de Santiago de Compostela, 1989*, Fundación 'Pedro Barrie de la Maza, Conde de Fenosa', Coruña, 207–32.

DE STAËL, MME (Anne Louise Germaine Necker, baronne de Holstein) (1813) *De l'Allemagne*, John Murray, London. The 1st edn (Paris, 1810) was destroyed by Napoleon and the London edn is in effect a 1st edn.

DE STAËL, MME (1958–1960) *De l'Allemagne*. Nouvelle édition publiée d'après les manuscrits et les éditions originales avec des variantes, une introduction, des notices et des notes par la Comtesse Jean de Pange avec le concours de Mlle Simone Balayé, 5 vols., Hachette, Paris.

DESTUTT DE TRACY, A.-L.-C. (Antoine-Louis-Claude Destutt, comte de Tracy) (1826) *Elémens d'idéologie. Second Partie. Grammaire*, 4th edn, Auguste Wahlen, Bruxelles. 1st edn 1803; reprinted Vrin, Paris, 1870.

DEVOTO, G. (1958) Madvig grammairien et linguiste, in *Acta Congressus Madvigiani (Proceedings of the Second International Congress of Classical Studies)*, 1, Munksgaard, København, 57–63. Reprinted in *Scritti minori*, Le Monnier, Firenze, 1958, I, 379–85.

DI CESARE, D. (1986) Langage, oubli, vérité dans la philosophie de Nietzsche, *Histoire Épistémologie Langage*, 8:1, 91–106.

DI CESARE, D. (1988) Die aristotelische Herkunft der Begriffe ἔργον und ἐνέργεια in Wilhelm von Humboldts Sprachphilosophie, in ALBRECHT, J., LÜDTKE, J. and THUN, H. (eds.), *Energeia und Ergon. Studia in honorem Eugenio Coseriu*, 2, Narr, Tübingen, 29–46.

DI CESARE, D. (1990a) Origine del linguaggio e primitività delle lingue in Humboldt, *Annali dell'Istituto Orientale di Napoli, Sez. linguistica*, 12, 115–40.

DI CESARE, D. (1990b) The Philosophical and Anthropological Place of Wilhelm von Humboldt's Linguistic Typology. Linguistic Comparison as a Means to Compare the Different Processes of Human Thought, in DE MAURO and FORMIGARI (eds.) (1990), 157–80.

DI CESARE, D. (1991) Introduzione. Bibliografia, in HUMBOLDT (1991, xi–xcvi; 305–46).

DI CESARE, D., GENSINI, S. (eds.) (1987) *Le vie di Babele. Percorsi di storiografia linguistica (1600–1800)*, Marietti, Casale Monferrato.

DI CESARE, D., GENSINI, S. (eds.) (1990) *Iter Babelicum. Studien zur Historiographie der Linguistik 1600–1800*, Nodus, Münster. German translation of DI CESARE and GENSINI (1987).

DIDERICHSEN, P. (1960) *Rasmus Rask og den grammatiske tradition. Studier over vendepunktet i sprogvidenskabens historie* (Historisk-filosofiske

Meddelelser udgivet af Det Kongelige Danske Videnskabernes Selskab, Bind 38, nr. 2), Munksgaard, København. German translation Fink, München, 1976.

DIDERICHSEN, P. (1974) The Foundation of Comparative Linguistics: Revolution or Continuation?, in HYMES (ed.) (1974), 277–306.

DIDERICHSEN, P. (1976) *Ganzheit und Struktur. Ausgewählte sprachwissenschaftliche Abhandlungen*, Fink, München.

DIETZE, J. (1966) *August Schleicher als Slawist. Sein Leben und sein Werk in der Sicht der Indogermanistik* (Deutsche Akademie der Wissenschaften zu Berlin. Veröffentlichungen des Instituts für Slawistik, 43), Akademie Verlag, Berlin.

DIEZ, F. C. (1836–44) *Grammatik der romanischen Sprachen*, 3 vols., E. Weber, Bonn. 3rd edn 1870–2; 5th (posthumous) edn 1882. English translation by C. B. Cayley, William & Norgate, London and Edinburgh, 1863. French translation in DIEZ (1863 and 1874–6).

DIEZ, F. C. (1853) *Etymologisches Wörterbuch der romanischen Sprachen*, Weber, Bonn. 3rd edn 1869–70; 5th (posthumous) edn 1887.

DIEZ, F. C. (1863) *Introduction à la grammaire des langues romanes*, traduite de l'allemand par Gaston Paris, Franck, Paris/Leipzig. French translation of the first part of DIEZ (1836–44).

DIEZ, F. C. (1874–6) *Grammaire des langues romanes*. French translation from the 3rd German edn (1870–2) by Gaston Paris, Auguste Brachet, Alfred Morel-Fatio, 3 vols., Franck, Paris.

DI SALVO, M. (1975) *Il pensiero linguistico di Jan Baudouin de Courtenay. Lingua nazionale e individuale, con un' antologia di testi e un saggio inedito*, Marsilio Editori, Venezia/Padova.

DOVETTO, F. (1994a) Contributo alla storia del pensiero linguistico italiano della seconda metà dell'Ottocento. Giacomo Lignana (1827–1891) e la classificazione delle lingue, *Beiträge zur Geschichte der Sprachwissenschaft*, 4, 1, 31–48.

DOVETTO, F. (1994b) Il ruolo del Sanscrito nell'insegnamento della grammatica comparata da Flechia a Ceci, in CARDINALE, PORZIO GERNIA and SANTAMARIA (eds.) (1994), 131–55.

D'OVIDIO, F. (1876) and (1990) Cf. Whitney (1990).

DOWLING, L. (1982) Victorian Oxford and the Science of Language, *Proceedings of the Modern Language Association*, 97, 160–78.

DOWLING, L. (1986) *Language and Decadence in the Victorian Fin de Siècle*, Princeton University Press, Princeton.

DRĂGANU, N. (1970) *Storia della sintassi generale. Opera postuma. Traduzione dal rumeno della Dott. Paola Bardelli Plomteux, con note, premesse e illustrazioni di Carlo Tagliavini* (Linguistica, 1), Pàtron, Bologna. (1st edn in Romanian *Istoria sintaxei: lucrare postumă*, Institut de Linguistică Română, Bucureşti, 1945).

DROIXHE, D. (1978) *La linguistique et l'appel de l'histoire (1600–1800)*, Droz, Genève.

DROIXHE, D. (1984) Genèse du comparatisme indo-européen; Avant-propos, *Histoire Épistémologie Langage*, 6:II, 5–16.

DROIXHE, D. (1989) Boxhorn's Bad Reputation: A Chapter in Academic Linguistics, in DUTZ (ed.) (1989), 139–59.

DROIXHE, D. (1993) Wilkins et les langues européennes, in DROIXHE and GRELL (eds.) (1993), 41–54.

DROIXHE, D., GRELL, C. (eds.) (1993) *La linguistique entre mythe et histoire. Actes des journées d'étude organisées les 4 et 5 juin à la Sorbonne en l'honneur de Hans Aarsleff*, Nodus, Münster.

DÜCKERT, J. (ed.) (1987) *Das Grimmsche Wörterbuch. Untersuchungen zur lexicographischen Methodologie*, Hirzel, Stuttgart.

DUTZ, K. D. (ed.) (1989) *Speculum historiographiae linguisticae. Kurz Beiträge der IV. Internationalen Konferenz zur Geschichte der Sprachwissenschaft (ICHoLS IV), Trier 24–27 August 1987*, Nodus, Münster.

EASTWICK, E. B. (1845–53) *A Comparative Grammar of the Sanscrit, Zend, Greek, Latin, Lithuanian, Gothic, German, and Sclavonic Languages by Professor F. Bopp. Translated from the German Principally by Lieutenant Eastwick M.R.A.S., Conducted through the Press by H. H. Wilson*, 3 vols., Madden & Malcolm, London. 3rd edn, Williams and Norgate, London, 1862 (without reference to Wilson).

EICHHOFF, F. G. (1836) *Parallèle des langues de l'Europe et de l'Inde, ou Étude des principales langues romanes, germaniques, slavonnes et celtiques, comparées entre elles et à la langue sanscrite, avec un essai de transcription générale*, Imprimerie Royale, Paris. German translation by J. H. Kaltschmidt, J. J. Weber, Leipzig, 1840.

EINHAUSER, E. (1989) *Die Junggrammatiker: ein Problem für die Sprachwissenschaftgeschichtsschreibung*, Wissenschaftlicher Verlag Trier, Trier.

EINHAUSER, E. (with T. LINDKEN) (eds.) (1992) *Lieber Freund . . . . die Briefe Hermann Osthoffs an Karl Brugmann, 1885–1904*, Wissenschaftlicher Verlag Trier, Trier.

ELLIS, A. J. (1848) *The Essentials of Phonetics: Containing the Theory of a Universal Alphabet, together with its Practical Application as an Ethnical Alphabet to the Reduction of All Languages, Written or Unwritten, to one Uniform System of Writing; with Numerous Examples; Adapted to the Use of Phoneticians, Philologists, Etymologists, Ethnographists, Travellers, and Missionaries. In Lieu of a Second Edition of the 'Alphabet of Nature'*, Pitman, Phonetic Depot, London. Title transliterated from the phonetic alphabet used by Ellis.

ELLIS, A. J. (1869–99) *Early English Pronunciation*, 5 vols., The Philological Society, London.

ELLIS, A. J. (1873–74) First Annual Address of the President to the Philological Society, Delivered at the Anniversary Meeting, Friday 17th May, 1872, *Transactions of the Philological Society*, 1873–4, 1–34.

ENGEL, A. J. (1983) *From Clergyman to Don. The Rise of the Academic Profession in Nineteenth Century Oxford*, Clarendon Press, Oxford.

ERLINGER, H. D., KNOBLOCH, C., MEYER, H. (eds.) (1989) *Satzlehre – Denkschulung – Nationalsprache. Deutsche Schulgrammatik zwischen 1800 und 1850*, Nodus, Münster.

ESCHBACH, A., TRABANT, J. (eds.) (1983) *History of Semiotics* (Foundations of Semiotics, 7), Benjamins, Amsterdam/Philadelphia.

ESPER, E. A. (1968) *Mentalism and Objectivism in Linguistics. The Sources of Leonard Bloomfield's Psychology of Language* (Foundations of Linguistics, 1), American Elsevier, New York.

ESPER, E. A. (1973) *Analogy and Association in Linguistics and Psychology*, University of Georgia Press, Athens, Georgia.

FANO, G. (1962) *Saggio sulle origini del linguaggio, con una storia critica delle dottrine glottogoniche* (Saggi, 312), Einaudi, Torino. Reprinted 1973. English translation, Indiana University Press, Bloomington, 1992.

FARKAS, J. VON (1952) August Ludwig Schlözer und die finnisch-ugrische Geschichts-, Sprach- und Volkskunde, *Ural-Altaische Jahrbücher*, 24, 1–22.

FARRAR, F. W. (1860) *An Essay on the Origin of Language, Based on Modern Researches*, Murray, London.

FAUST, M. (1983) Jean Paul's Essay on Word Formation, in FAUST, M. *et al.* (eds.), *Allgemeine Sprachwissenschaft, Sprachtypologie, und Textlinguistik. Festschrift für Peter Hartmann*, Narr, Tübingen, 237–48.

FERBER, C. VON (1956) *Die Entwicklung des Lehrkörpers der deutschen Universitäten und Hochschulen 1864–1914* (Untersuchungen zur Lage der deutschen Hochschullehrer, hsg. von Dr Helmuth Plessner, Vol. 3), Vandenhoeck & Ruprecht, Göttingen.

FERRARIS, M. (1989) *Storia dell'ermeneutica*, Bompiani, Milano.

FICHTE, J. G. (1808) *Reden an die deutsche Nation*, Realschulbuchhandlung, Berlin.

FICK, A. (1868) *Wörterbuch der indogermanischen Grundsprache*, Vandenhoeck & Ruprecht, Göttingen. 2nd edn 1870.

FICK, A. (1873) *Die ehemalige Spracheinheit der Indogermanen Europas. Eine sprachgeschichtliche Untersuchung*, Vandenhoeck & Ruprecht, Göttingen.

FIESEL, E. (1927) *Die Sprachphilosophie der deutschen Romantik*, Mohr, Tübingen.

FIRTH, J. R. (1957) *Papers in Linguistics 1934–1951*, Oxford University Press, London.

[FISHLAKE, J. R.] (1834) Greek-and-English Lexicography, *Quarterly Review*, 51 (March–June), 144–77.

FODOR, I. (1975) *Pallas und andere afrikanische Vokabularien vor dem 19. Jahrhundert. Ein Beitrag zur Forschungsgeschichte* (Kommentare zu Peter Simon Pallas, *Linguarum totius orbis vocabularia comparativa*, 1), Buske, Hamburg.

FORMIGARI, L. (ed.) (1977a) *La linguistica romantica* (Filosofia, 9), Loescher, Torino.

FORMIGARI, L. (1977b) *La logica del pensiero vivente. Il linguaggio nella filosofia della Romantik* (Biblioteca di Cultura Moderna, 800), Laterza, Bari.

FORMIGARI, L. (1988) De l'idéalisme dans les théories du langage. Histoire d'une transition, *Histoire Épistémologie Langage*, 10:I, 59–80.

FORMIGARI, L. (1990) Philosophies of Language in the Heyday of Comparativism, in HÜLLEN, W. (ed.), *Understanding the Historiography of Linguistics. Problems and Projects. Symposium at Essen, 23–25 November 1989*, Nodus, Münster, 277–85.

FORMIGARI, L. (1993) *Signs, Science and Politics. Philosophies of Language in Europe 1700–1830* (Studies in the History of Language Sciences, 70), Benjamins, Amsterdam/Philadelphia.

FORMIGARI, L. (1994) XIXth- and XXth-Century Philosophical Linguistics, in DE MAURO and FORMIGARI (eds.) (1994), 225–44.

FORMIGARI, L., LO PIPARO, F. (eds.) (1988) *Prospettive di storia della linguistica. Lingua linguaggio comunicazione sociale.* Prefazione di Tullio de Mauro (Nuova biblioteca di cultura, 291), Editori Riuniti, Roma.

FORSGREN, K.-Å. (1973) *Zur Theorie und Terminologie der Satzlehre. Ein Beitrag zur Geschichte der deutschen Grammatik von J. C. Adelung bis K. F. Becker, 1780–1830* (Göteborger Germanistische Dissertationsreihe, 4), Göteborgs Universität, Institut für deutsche Sprache, Göteborg.

FORSGREN, K.-Å. (1990) *Satz, Satzarten, Satzglieder; zur Gestaltung der deutschen traditionellen Syntax von Karl Ferdinand Becker bis Konrad Duden, 1830–1880*, Nodus, Münster.

FORSTER, H. P. (1810) *An Essay on the Principles of Sanskrit Grammar*, I, Ferris & Co., Calcutta.

FOUCAULT, M. (1966) *Les mots et les choses. Une archéologie des sciences*, Gallimard, Paris. English translation, London, 1970.

FOUGHT, J. (1982) The Reinvention of Hugo Schuchardt (Review Article), *Language in Society*, 11, 419–36.

FOURQUET, J. (1948) *Les mutations consonantiques du germanique: Essai de position des problèmes*, Les Belles Lettres, Paris.

FREESE, R. (1986) *Wilhelm von Humboldt. Sein Leben und Wirkung dargestellt in Briefen, Tagebücher und Dokumenten seiner Zeit*, Wissenschaftliche Buchgesellschaft, Darmstadt.

FRIEDLÄNDER, L. (1883) Lehrs, Karl, in *Allgemeine Deutsche Biographie*, 18, Duncker & Humblot, Leipzig, 152–66.

FROMM, H. (1978) Wilhelm Braune, *Beiträge zur Geschichte der deutschen Sprache und Literatur (Paul-Braune-Beiträge)*, 100, 4–39.

GABELENTZ, [H.] G. [C.] VON DER (1869) Ideen zu einer vergleichenden Syntax, *Zeitschrift für vergleichende Sprachforschung*, 6, 376–84.

GABELENTZ, [H.] G. [C.] VON DER (1891) *Die Sprachwissenschaft, ihre Aufgaben, Methoden und bisherigen Ergebnisse*, Weigel Nachfolger, Leipzig. 2nd edn, Tauchnitz, Leipzig, 1901. Reprinted Narr, Tübingen, 1969, 1972, 1984.

GABELENTZ, [H.] G. [C.] VON DER (1894) Hypologie [*sic*] der Sprache, eine neue Aufgabe der Linguistik, *Indogermanische Forschungen*, 4, 1–7.

GABELENTZ, H. C. VON DER (1861) 'Über das Passivum. Eine sprachvergleichende Abhandlung', *Abhandlungen der Königlich Sächsischen Akademie der Wissenschaften zu Leipzig, Phil.-hist. Classe*, 3, 449–546.

GABELENTZ, H. C. VON DER (1861–73) 'Die melanesischen Sprachen nach ihrem grammatischen Bau und ihrer Verwandtschaft unter sich und mit den malaiisch-polynesischen Sprachen untersucht', *Abhandlungen der Königlich Sächsischen Akademie der Wissenschaften zu Leipzig, Phil.-hist. Classe*, 3, 1–266; 7, 1–186.

GAMKRELIDZE, T. V., IVANOV, V. V. (1973) Sprachtypologie und die Rekonstruktion der gemeinindogermanischen Verschlüsse, *Phonetica*, 27, 150–6.

GAMKRELIDZE, T. V., IVANOV, V. V. (1984) *Indoevropejskij jazyk i indoevropejcy (Rekonstrukcija i istoriko-tipologičeskij analiz prajazyka i protokul'tury)*, 2 vols., Izdatel'stvo tbilisskogo universiteta, Tbilisi. English translation Mouton / de Gruyter, Berlin / New York, 1994–5.

GANZ, P. (1973) *Jacob Grimm's Conception of German Studies. An Inaugural Lecture Delivered before the University of Oxford on 18 May 1973*, Clarendon Press, Oxford.

GANZ, P. (1978) Eduard Sievers, *Beiträge zur Geschichte der deutschen Sprache und Literatur (Paul-Braune-Beiträge)*, 100, 40–85.

GÁRATE, J. (1933) *Guillermo de Humboldt. Estudio de sus trabajos sobre Vasconia*, Imp. Provincial, Bilbao.

GARDINER, A. H. (1932) *The Theory of Speech and Language*, Clarendon Press, Oxford. 2nd edn 1951.

GARNETT, R. (1859) *The Philological Essays of the Late Rev. Richard Garnett of the British Museum. Edited by his Son*, Williams and Norgate, London.

GAUCHAT, L. (1903) Gibt es Mundartgrenzen?, *Archiv für das Studium der neueren Sprachen und Literaturen*, 111, 365–403.

GAZDARU, D. (1967) *Controversias y documentos lingüísticos*, Instituto de Filología. Universidad Nacional de la Plata, Buenos Aires.

GEIGER, L. (1868–72) *Ursprung und Entwickelung der menschlichen Sprache und Vernunft*, 2 vols., Cotta, Stuttgart.

GEIGER, L. (1869) *Der Ursprung der Sprache*, Cotta, Stuttgart.

GENSINI, S. (1984) *Linguistica leopardiana. Fondamenti teorici e prospettive politico-culturali* (Studi linguistici e semiologici, 22), Il Mulino, Bologna.

GENSINI, S. (1993) *Volgar favella. Percorsi del pensiero linguistico italiano da Robortello a Manzoni*, La Nuova Italia, Firenze.

GENSINI, S. (1994) The History of Linguistic Ideas in the Age of Enlightenment and the Early 19th Century in Italy, in DE MAURO and FORMIGARI (eds.) (1994), 167–90.

GÉRANDO, J.-M. DE (1800). Cf. DEGÉRANDO (1800).

GÉRARD, R. (1963) *L'orient et la pensée romantique allemande* (Germanica, 4), Didier, Paris/Bruxelles.

GERBER, G. (1871–4) *Die Sprache als Kunst*, 2 vols. (in 3 parts), Mittler, Bromberg. 2nd edn, Berlin, 1885.

GESSINGER, J. (1990) August Ferdinand Bernhardi, in NIEDEREHE and KOERNER (eds.) (1990), 561–75.

GESSINGER, J. (1994) *Auge & Ohr. Studien zur Erforschung der Sprache am Menschen 1709–1850*, De Gruyter, Berlin / New York.

GESSINGER, J., RAHDEN, W. VON (eds.) (1989) *Theorien vom Ursprung der Sprache*, 2 vols., De Gruyter, Berlin / New York.

GILBERT, G. (1980) Cf. SCHUCHARDT (1980).

GILDERSLEEVE, B. (1884) Friedrich Ritschl, *American Journal of Philology*, 5, 339–55.

GILLIÉRON, J. (1881) *Petit atlas phonétique du Valais roman (sud du Rhône)*, Champion, Paris.

GINSCHEL, G. (1967) *Der junge Jacob Grimm, 1805–1819* (Veröffentlichungen der Sprachwissenschaftlichen Kommission, 7), Akademie Verlag, Berlin.

GIPPER, H. (1965) Wilhelm von Humboldt als Begründer moderner Sprachforschung, *Wirkendes Wort*, 15, 1–19.

GIPPER, H. (1972) *Gibt es ein sprachliches Relativitätsprinzip? Untersuchungen zur Sapir-Whorf-Hypothese*, Fischer, Frankfurt a.M.

GIPPER, H. (1981) Schwierigkeiten beim Schreiben der Wahrheit in der Geschichte der Sprachwissenschaft. Zum Streit um das Verhältnis Wilhelm von Humboldts zu Herder, in TRABANT (ed.) (1981), 101–15.

GIPPER, H. (1986) Understanding as a Process of Linguistic Approximation: The Discussion between August Wilhelm von Schlegel, S. A. Langlois, Wilhelm von Humboldt and G. W. F. Hegel on the Translation of the *Bhagavadgita* and the concept of 'Yoga', in BYNON and PALMER (eds.) (1986), 109–28.

GIPPER, H. (1987) Sprache und Denken in der Sicht Wilhelm von Humboldts, in HOBERG (ed.) (1987a), 53–85.

GIPPER, H., SCHMITTER, P. (1979) *Sprachwissenschaft und Sprachphilosophie im Zeitalter der Romantik. Ein Beitrag zur Historiographie der Linguistik* (Tübinger Beiträge zur Linguistik, 121), Narr, Tübingen. A first version appears in SEBEOK (ed.) (1975), I, 480–606.

GIPPERT, J. (1994) Zur indogermanistischen Ausbildung in der zweiten Hälfte des 19. Jahrhunderts, *Münchener Studien zur Sprachwissenschaft*, 54 (1993 [1994]), 65–121.

GIRARD, G. abbé (1747) *Les vrais principes de la langue françoise ou La parole reduite en méthode, conformément aux Lois de l'Usage, en seize discours*, Le Breton, Paris. New edn with an introduction by P. Swiggers, Droz, Genève & Paris, 1982.

GIRAULT-DUVIVIER, C. P. (1812) *Grammaire des grammaires ou Analyse raisonnée des meilleurs traités sur la langue françoise*, 2 vols., Janet et Cotelle, Paris. 9th edn 1840, 21st edn 1879.

GLINZ, H. (1947) *Geschichte und Kritik der Lehre von den Satzgliedern in den deutschen Grammatik*, Francke, Bern.

GMÜR, R. (1980) *Das Mémoire von F. de Saussure* (Arbeitspapier, 18), Universität Bern, Institut für Sprachwissenschaft, Bern.

GMÜR, R. (1986) *Das Schicksal von F. de Saussures 'Mémoire'. Eine Rezeptionsgeschichte* (Arbeitspapier, 21), Universität Bern, Institut für Sprachwissenschaft, Bern.

GOBINEAU, A. (Joseph-Arthur, comte de Gobineau) (1853–55) *Essai sur l'inégalité des races humaines*, 4 vols. in 2 parts, Didot, Paris. 2nd edn 1884, 5th edn 1930 (reprinted 1940). Reprinted Belford, Paris 1967. German translation, Frommann, Stuttgart, 1898, 3rd edn 1902, 5th edn 1939. English translation of Vol. 1, Lippincott, Philadelphia, 1856 (reprinted Garland, New York, 1984). Other English translation, Heinemann, London, 1915; reprinted Britons, London and Noontide Press, Torrance CA, 1966, 2nd edn 1993.

GODEL, R. (1954) Notes inédites de Ferdinand de Saussure, *Cahiers Ferdinand de Saussure*, 12, 49–71.

GOMBRICH, R. (1978) *On Being Sanskritic. A Plea for Civilized Study and the Study of Civilization. An Inaugural Lecture Delivered before the University of Oxford on 14 October 1977*, Clarendon Press, Oxford.

GORDON, W. T. (1982) *A History of Semantics* (Studies in the History of Linguistics, 30), Benjamins, Amsterdam/Philadelphia.

GOTTSCHED, J. C. (1748) *Grundlegung einer Deutschen Sprachkunst, nach den Mustern der besten Schriftsteller des vorigen und jetzigen Jahrhunderts abgefasset*, Breitkopf & Sohn, Leipzig. 6th edn 1776; reprinted Olms, Hildesheim / New York, 1970.

GRAFFI, G. (1988) Luoghi comuni su Hermann Paul e la scuola neogrammatica, *Lingua e Stile*, 23, 211–34.

GRAFFI, G. (1991) *La sintassi tra Ottocento e Novecento*, Il Mulino, Bologna.

GRASSI, C. (1975) *Graziadio Isaia Ascoli. Scritti sulla questione della lingua* (Piccola Biblioteca Einaudi. Testi, 7), Einaudi, Torino.

GRASSMANN, H. (1863) Über die Aspiraten und ihr gleichzeitiges Vorhandensein im An- und Auslaute der Wurzeln, *Zeitschrift für vergleichende Sprachforschung*, 12, 81–138. English translation in LEHMANN (ed.) (1967), 111–31.

GREENBERG, J. H. (1971) *Language, Culture and Communication. Essays by Joseph H. Greenberg. Selected and Introduced by Anwar S. Dil*, Stanford University Press, Stanford.

GRIMM, J. (1819) *Deutsche Grammatik, I.*, Dieterich'sche Buchhandlung, Göttingen. Cf. GRIMM (1822, 1822–37, 1840).

GRIMM, J. (1822) *Deutsche Grammatik. Erster Teil*, 2nd edn, Dieterich'sche Buchhandlung, Göttingen. Cf. GRIMM (1819, 1822–37, 1840).

GRIMM, J. (1822–37) *Deutsche Grammatik*, 4 vols., Dieterich'sche Buchhandlung, Göttingen. It includes the 2nd edn of Vol. I. New edn (ed. by W. Scherer, G. Roethe and E. Schröder) 1870–98 (Dümmler, Berlin; Bertelsmann, Berlin & Gütersloh). Reprinted 1967, Olms, Hildesheim.

GRIMM, J. (1824) *Wuk's Stephanowitsch Kleine Serbische Grammatik verdeutscht und mit einer Vorrede*, Reimer, Leipzig und Berlin.

GRIMM, J. (1840) *Deutsche Grammatik. Erster Teil*, 3rd edn, Dieterich'sche Buchhandlung, Göttingen. Cf. GRIMM (1819, 1822, 1822–37).

GRIMM, J. (1848) *Geschichte der deutschen Sprache*, 2 vols., Weidmann, Leipzig. 2nd edn 1853, 4th edn 1880. Reprinted 1970, Olms, Hildesheim.

GRIMM, J. (1851) *Über den Ursprung der Sprache, gelesen in der Preussischen Akademie der Wissenschaften am 9. Januar 1851* (Abhandlungen der königlichen Akademie der Wissenschaften zu Berlin, Philosophisch-historische Classe, 32, 2), Dümmler, Berlin. 4th edn 1858. Reprinted 1958 (Insel-Verlag, Wiesbaden); also in GRIMM (1864–90), i, 255–98, GRIMM (1984), 64–100. French translation by F. de Wegmann, Franck, Paris, 1859; English translation by R. A. Wiley, Brill, Leiden, 1984; Italian translation by L. Lun, 1962, and by T. Weddinger in MORETTI (ed.) (1991).

GRIMM, J. (1864–90) *Kleinere Schriften*, 8 vols., Dümmler, Bertelsmann, Berlin, Gütersloh.

GRIMM, J. (1984) *Reden in der Akademie, Ausgewählt und herausgegeben von Werner Neumann und Hartmut Schmidt*, Akademie Verlag, Berlin.

GRIMM, J., GRIMM, W. (eds.) (1854–1960) *Deutsches Wörterbuch*, 16 tomes, Hirzel, etc., Leipzig. The first fascicle appeared in 1852. Vol. i (1854), ii (1860), iii (1864). The remaining volumes (16 tomes in 32 vols.) were not ed. by the two Grimm.

GRIMSLEY, R. (ed.) (1971) *Maupertuis, Turgot, Maine de Biran, Sur l'origine du langage. Etude de Ronald Grimsley suivie de trois textes*, Droz, Genève. Contains texts by Maupertuis 1748 and 1750, Turgot 1750 (published 1805), Maine de Biran 1815.

GULYA, J. (1974) Some Eighteenth Century Antecedents of Nineteenth Century Linguistics: The Discovery of Finno-Ugrian, in HYMES (ed.) (1974), 258–76.

GUTIERREZ-CUADRADO, J. (1987) L'introduction de la philologie comparée dans les universités espagnoles (1857–1900), *Histoire Épistémologie Langage*, 9:II, 149–68.

GYARMATHI, S. (1799) *Affinitas linguae hungaricae cum linguis fennicae originis grammatice demonstrata nec non vocabularia dialectorum tataricarum et slavicarum cum hungarica comparata*, Dieterich, Göttingen. Reprinted Indiana University, Bloomington, 1968; English translation with an introduction and notes by Victor E. Henzeli (Amsterdam Classics in Linguistics, 15), Benjamins, Amsterdam/Philadelphia, 1983.

HAARMANN, H. (ed.) (1979) *Wissenschaftsgeschichtliche Beiträge zur Erforschung indogermanischer, finnisch-ugrischer und kaukasischer Sprachen bei Pallas* (Kommentare zu Peter Simon Pallas, *Linguarum totius orbis vocabularia comparativa*, 2), Buske, Hamburg.

HAAS, M. R. (1969) Grammar or Lexicon? The American Indian Side of the Question from Duponceau to Powell, *International Journal of American Linguistics*, 35, 239–55.

HAASE, H. G. F. C. (1874–80) *Vorlesungen über lateinische Sprachwissenschaft, gehalten ab 1840*, 2 vols., Simmel, Leipzig. 1st part (*Einleitung und Bedeutungslehre*) ed. by F. A. Eckstein, 2nd part (*Bedeutungslehre*) ed. by Hermann Peter.

HALHED, N. B. (1776) *A Code of Gentoo Laws, or, Ordinations of the Pundits, from a Persian Translation, Made from the Original, Written in the Shanscrit Language*, publisher not stated, London.

HALHED, N. B. (1778) *A Grammar of the Bengal Language*, no publisher, Hoogly, Bengal. Reprinted Scholar Press, Menston, 1969; Ananda, Calcutta, 1980.

HARRIS, R., TAYLOR, T. J. (1989) *Landmarks in Linguistic Thought. The Western Tradition from Socrates to Saussure*, Routledge, London and New York.

HASELBACH, G. (1966) *Grammatik und Sprachstruktur. Karl Ferdinand Beckers Beitrag zur allgemeinen Sprachwissenschaft in historischer und systematischer Sicht*, De Gruyter, Berlin.

HAßLER, G. (1986a) Die These der Sprachrelativität des Denkens in der Aufklärung und bei Wilhelm von Humboldt, in WELKE (ed.) (1986), 154–77.

HAßLER, G. (1986b) Zur Stellung von Humboldts 'sprachlicher Weltansicht' und seiner Konzeption der Sprache als organisches Ganzes in der Geschichte der Sprachtheorien, in SPREU, A., and BONDZIO, W. (eds.), *Sprache, Mensch und Gesellschaft – Werk und Wirkungen von Wilhelm von Humboldt und Jacob und Wilhelm Grimm in Vergangenheit und Gegenwart* (Humboldt-Grimm Konferenz, Berlin 22–25 Oktober 1985), I, Humboldt-Universität, Sektion Germanistik, Berlin, 263–74.

HAßLER, G. (1991a) *Der semantische Wertbegriff in Sprachtheorien von 18. bis 20. Jahrhundert*, Akademie Verlag, Berlin.

HAßLER, G. (1991b) Die Kontroverse Pott – Steinthal: Ausdrückliche und stillschweigende Voraussetzungen in der Rezeption von Humboldts Sprachtheorie, *Zeitschrift für Phonetik, Sprachwissenschaft und Kommunikationsforschung*, 44, 34–42.

HAUGER, B. (1994) *Johan Nicolai Madvig. The Language Theory of a Classical Philologist* (Studium Sprachwissenschaft, Beiheft, 22), Nodus, Münster.

HÄUSLER, F. (1968) *Das Problem Phonetik und Phonologie bei Baudouin de Courtenay und in seiner Nachfolge*, Niemeyer, Halle (Saale).

HAVET, L. (1875) Préface du traducteur, in *Précis de la déclinaison latine par M. François Bücheler, traduit de l'allemand par M. L. Havet* (Bibliothèque de l'École des Hautes Études. Sciences philologiques et historiques, 24), Vieweg, Paris, i–xxii.

HAVET, L. (1879) Review of SAUSSURE (1879), *Journal de Genève*, 50, no. 47 (25 February 1879), Suppl. 1–2. Reprinted in *Cahiers Ferdinand de Saussure* 32, 1978, 103–22.

HAYM, R. (1856) *Wilhelm von Humboldt. Lebensbild und Charakteristik*, Gaertner, Berlin.

HAYM, R. (1920) *Die romantische Schule: Ein Beitrag zur Geschichte des deutschen Geistes*, 4th edn, Gaertner, Berlin. 1st edn 1870.

HEERDEGEN, F. (1875–1881) *Über Umfang und Gliederung der Sprachwissenschaft im Allgemeinen und der lateinischen Grammatik insbesondere. Versuch einer systematischen Einleitung zur lateinischen Semasiologie*, 3 vols., Deichert, Erlangen.

HEHN, V. (1870) *Kulturpflanzen und Haustiere in ihrem Übergang aus Asien nach Griechenland und Italien sowie das übrige Europa*, Gebr. Borntraeger, Berlin. 2nd edn 1874, 4th edn 1883, 6th edn ed. by O. Schraeder 1894. English translation, Sonnenschein, London, 1885; for the reprint cf. HEHN (1976).

HEHN, V. (1976) *Cultivated Plants and Domesticated Animals in their Migration from Asia to Europe. Historico-Linguistic Studies*, new edn ed. by James P. MALLORY (Amsterdam Classics in Linguistics, 7), Benjamins, Amsterdam/Philadelphia. Cf. HEHN (1870).

HEILMANN, L. (ed.) (1976) *Wilhelm von Humboldt nella cultura contemporanea* (Quaderni della rivista 'Lingua e Stile', 1), Il Mulino, Bologna.

HELMHOLTZ, H. L. F. VON (1863) *Die Lehre von den Tonempfindungen als physiologische Grundlage für die Theorie der Musik*, F. Vieweg und Sohn, Braunschweig. 3rd edn 1870, 4th edn 1877, 6th edn 1913. English translation by A. J. Ellis, Longmans, Green & Co., London, 1875; 2nd edn 1885; reprinted Dover, New York, 1954.

HENDERSON, E. J. A. (ed.) (1971) *The Indispensable Foundation. A Selection from the Writings of Henry Sweet*, Oxford University Press, London.

HENNE, H. (1985) 'Mein Bruder ist in einigen dingen . . . abgewichen'. Wilhelm Grimms Wörterbucharbeit, *Zeitschrift für Phonetik, Sprachwissenschaft und Kommunikationsforschung*, 38, 533–43.

HENNE, H. (1990) Jacob Grimm and Wilhelm Grimm at Work on their Dictionary, in ANTONSEN (with MARCHAND and ZGUSTA) (eds.) (1990), 89–96.

HENRY, V. (1883) *Étude sur l'analogie en général et sur les formations analogiques de la langue grecque; thèse pour le doctorat présentée à la Faculté des Lettres de Paris*, Danel, Lille.

HENRY, V. (1896) *Antinomies linguistiques* (Bibliothèque de la Faculté des Lettres de Paris, 2), Félix Alcan, Paris. Reprinted Didier, Paris s.d. (1989?).

HENRY, V. (1901) *Le langage martien. Étude analytique de la genèse d'une langue dans un cas de glossolalie somnambulique*, Maisonneuve, Paris. Reprinted Didier, Paris, s.d. (1989?).

HERDER, J. G. VON (1877–1913) *Sämtliche Werke, herausgegeben von Bernhard Suphan*, 33 vols., Weidmann, Berlin.

HERMANN, E. (1923) *Berthold Delbrück. Ein Gelehrtenleben aus Deutschlands großer Zeit*, Frommann, Jena.

HERMANN, E. (1931) *Lautgesetz und Analogie* (Abhandlungen der Gesellschaft der Wissenschaften zu Göttingen. Philologisch-historische Klasse, Neue Folge, 23, 3), Weidmann, Berlin.

HERVÁS Y PANDURO, L. (1778–87) *Idea dell'Universo, che contiene la Storia della vita dell'uomo, elementi cosmografici, viaggio estatico al mondo planetario, e Storia della Terra*, 21 vols., Gregorio Biasini all'Insegna di Pallade, Cesena.

HERVÁS Y PANDURO, L. (1784) *Catalogo delle lingue conosciute e notizia della loro affinità, e diversità*, Gregorio Biasini all'Insegna di Pallade, Cesena. Vol. XVII of HERVÁS Y PANDURO (1778–87); reprinted in TOVAR (1986).

HERVÁS Y PANDURO, L. (1800–5) *Catálogo de las lenguas de las naciones conocidas y numeración, división y clases de éstas segun la diversidad de sus idiomas y dialectos*, 5 vols. in 6 parts, Impr. Administración del Real Arbitrio de Benificencia, Madrid. Reprinted Atlas, Madrid, 1979.

HEWES, G. W. (1975) *Language Origins; A Bibliography*, 2nd edn, 2 vols., Mouton, The Hague.

HEYSE, K. W. L. (1856) *System der Sprachwissenschaft*, nach dessen Tode herausgegeben von Dr H. Steinthal, Dümmler, Berlin. Italian translation by E. Leone, Botta, Torino, 1864.

HIRT, H. (1939) *Die Hauptprobleme der indogermanischen Sprachwissenschaft*. Herausgegeben und bearbeitet von Helmut Arntzt (Sammlung kurzer Grammatiken germanischer Dialekte. Ergänzungsreihe, 4), Niemeyer, Halle/Saale.

HJELMSLEV, L. (1950–1) Commentaires sur la vie et l'œuvre de Rasmus Rask, *Conférences de l'Institut de linguistique de l'Université de Paris*, 10, 143–57. Reprinted in SEBEOK (ed.) (1966), i, 179–99.

HOBERG, R. (ed.) (1987a) *Sprache und Bildung. Beiträge zum 150. Todestag Wilhelm von Humboldts*, Technische Hochschule Darmstadt, Darmstadt.

HOBERG, R. (1987b) Die sprachlichen Weltansichten gleichen sich an. Ein Begriff Wilhelm von Humboldts und die gegenwärtige Sprachenentwicklung, in HOBERG (ed.) (1987a), 217–35.

HOCKETT, C. F. (1965) Sound Change, *Language*, 41, 185–204.

HOENIGSWALD, H. M. (1963) On the History of the Comparative Method, *Anthropological Linguistics*, 5, 1–11.

HOENIGSWALD, H. M. (1974) Fallacies in the History of Linguistics: Notes on the Appraisal of the Nineteenth Century, in HYMES (ed.) (1974), 346–58.

HOENIGSWALD, H. M. (1975) Schleicher's Tree and its Trunk, in ABRAHAM, W. (ed.), *Ut Videam: Contributions to an Understanding of Linguistics. For Pieter Verburg on the Occasion of his 70th Birthday*, Peter de Ridder, Lisse, 157–60.

HOENIGSWALD, H. M. (1977) Intentions, Assumptions, and Contradictions in Historical Linguistics, in COLE, R. W. (ed.), *Current Issues in Linguistic Theory*, Indiana University Press, Bloomington, 168–93.

HOENIGSWALD, H. M. (1978) The *annus mirabilis* 1876 and Posterity, *Transactions of the Philological Society*, 1978, 17–35.

HOENIGSWALD, H. M. (ed.) (1979) *The European Background of American Linguistics. Papers of the Third Golden Anniversary Symposium of the Linguistic Society of America*, Foris, Dordrecht.

HOENIGSWALD, H. M. (1984) Etymology against Grammar in the Early 19th Century, *Histoire Épistémologie Langage*, 6:II, 94–100.

HOENIGSWALD, H. M. (1986) Nineteenth-Century Linguistics on Itself, in BYNON and PALMER (eds.) (1986), 172–88.

HOENIGSWALD, H. M. (1987) Bloomfield and Historical Linguistics, *Historiographia Linguistica*, 14, 73–88.

HOENIGSWALD, H. M., WIENER, L. F. (eds.) (1987) *Biological Metaphor and Cladistic Classification. An Interdisciplinary Perspective*, University of Pennsylvania Press, Philadelphia.

HOFFMANN, O. (1905) Griechische Grammatik, in KROLL, W. (ed.), *Die Altertumswissenschaft im letzen Vierteljahrhundert. Eine Übersicht über ihre Entwicklung in der Zeit von 1875–1900 im Verein mit mehreren Fachgenossen* (Jahresbericht über die Forschritte der klassischen Altertumswissenschaft, begründet von Conrad Bursian, herausgegeben von Wilhelm Kroll. Supplementband, 124), Reisland, Leipzig, 50–83.

HOLTZMANN, A. (1841) Review of Grimm, Deutsche Grammatik I, 3 (1840), *Heidelberger Jahrbücher der Literatur*, 34, 770–7.

HORNE, K. M. (1966) *Language Typology: 19th and 20th Century Views*, Georgetown University Press, Washington DC.

HORNING, A. (1893) Über Dialektgrenzen im Romanischen, *Zeitschrift für romanische Philologie*, 17, 160–87. Reprinted in SPITZER (ed.) (1929–30), ii, 264–98.

HOVELACQUE, A. (1922) *La linguistique. Histoire naturelle du langage*, 5th edn (Bibliothèque des sciences contemporaines), Alfred Costes, Paris. 1st edn 1876. English translation, Chapman & Hall, London, 1877.

HOWATT, A. P. R. (1984) *A History of English Language Teaching*, Oxford University Press, Oxford.

HUBER, W. (1978) Hermann Paul und die Kasusgrammatik, *Beiträge zur Geschichte der deutschen Sprache und Literatur (Paul-Braune-Beiträge)*, 100, 86–109.

HÜBSCHMANN, H. (1875) Über die stellung des armenischen im kreise der indogermanischen sprachen, *Zeitschrift für vergleichende Sprachforschung*, 23, 5–49. Reprinted in HÜBSCHMANN (1976, 1–45). English translation in LEHMANN (ed.) (1967), 166–89.

HÜBSCHMANN, H. (1885) *Das indogermanische Vocalsystem*, Trübner, Strassburg. Reprinted Oriental Press, Amsterdam, 1975.

HÜBSCHMANN, H. (1976) *Kleine Schriften zum Armenischen*. Herausgegeben von Rüdiger Schmitt (Collectanea, XXXVI), Olms, Hildesheim / New York.

HÜLTENSCHMIDT, E. (1987) Paris oder Berlin? Institutionalisierung, Professionalisierung und Entwicklung der vergleichenden Sprachwissenschaft im 19. Jahrhundert, in SCHMITTER (ed.) (1987a), 178–97.

HUMBOLDT, W. VON *Einl.* Cf. HUMBOLDT (1836–9), I, i–ccccxxx.

HUMBOLDT, W. VON GS = HUMBOLDT (1903–36).

HUMBOLDT, W. VON (1817), *Berichtigungen und Zusätze zum ersten Abschnitte des zweyten Bandes des Mithridates über die Cantabrische oder Baskische Sprache*, in ADELUNG (1806–17), iv, 273–360.

HUMBOLDT, W. VON (1836–9) *Über die Kawi-Sprache auf der Insel Java nebst einer Einleitung über die Verschiedenheit des menschlichen Sprachbaues und ihren Einfluss auf die geistige Entwickelung des Menschengeschlechts* (Abhandlungen der Königlichen Akademie der Wissenschaften zu Berlin. Aus dem Jahre 1832), 3 vols., Königliche Akademie der Wissenschaften / F. Dümmler, Berlin.

HUMBOLDT, W. VON (1903–36) *Gesammelte Schriften, im Auftrag der Königlichen Preußischen Akademie der Wissenschaften*, ed. by A. Lietzmann *et al.*, 17 vols., Akademie der Wissenschaften, Berlin. Reprinted De Gruyter, Berlin, 1968.

HUMBOLDT, W. VON (1960–81) *Werke in fünf Bänden*. Herausgegeben von Andreas Flitner und Klaus Giel, 3rd edn, Wissen-schaftliche Buchgesellschaft, Darmstadt. Vol. 3 contains the major linguistic works, but other works on the subject are reproduced in Vol. 5 and, sporadically, in other vols.

HUMBOLDT, W. VON *Einl.* (1971) *Linguistic Variability & Intellectual Development*. Translated by George C. Buck and Frithjof A. Raven (Miami Linguistics Series, 9), University of Miami Press, Coral Gables, Florida. Translation of Humboldt GS, vii, 1–344, or rather of the Dümmler separate edition of the *Einleitung* (*Einl.*) to HUMBOLDT (1836–9).

HUMBOLDT, W. VON (1985) *Über die Sprache. Ausgewählte Schriften*. Ed. by J. Trabant, DTV, München.

HUMBOLDT, W. VON (1988) *On Language. The Diversity of Human Language-Structure and its Influence on the Mental Development of Mankind*. Translated by Peter Heath with an Introduction by Hans Aarsleff (Texts in German Philosophy), Cambridge University Press, Cambridge.

HUMBOLDT, W. VON (1989) *Scritti sul linguaggio (1795–1827)*, ed. by A. Carrano (Micromegas, 22), Guida, Napoli.

HUMBOLDT, W. VON (1991) *La diversità delle lingue*. Introduzione e traduzione a cura di Donatella di Cesare. Premessa di Tullio de Mauro (Biblioteca Universale Laterza, 344), Laterza, Roma-Bari.

HUMBOLDT, W. VON *Einl.* Cf. HUMBOLDT (1994) *Mexicanische Grammatik* (Schriften zur Sprachwissenschaft, Abt 3, Bd 2), Schöningh, Paderborn. *Non vidi.*

HUXLEY, T. H. (1971) *T. H. Huxley on Education. A Selection from his Writings with an Introductory Essay and Notes by Cyril Bibby*, Cambridge University Press, Cambridge.

HYMES, D. (ed.) (1974) *Studies in the History of Linguistics. Traditions and Paradigms*, Indiana University Press, Bloomington.

HYMES, D., FOUGHT, J. (1975) American Structuralism, in SEBEOK (ed.) (1975), 2, 903–1176. Reprinted as *American Structuralism*, The Hague, 1981.

IHRE, J. (1769) *Glossarium suiogothicum in quo tam hodierno usu frequentata vocabula, quam in legum patriarum tabulis aliisque aevi medii scriptis obvia explicantur*, 2 vols., Typis Edmannianis, Uppsala.

IORDAN, I., ORR, J. (1970) *An Introduction to Romance Linguistics, its Schools and Scholars*. Revised with a supplement 'Thirty Years on' by R. POSNER (Language and Style Series, 8), Blackwell, Oxford.

ISING, E. (1956) Die Begriffe 'Umlaut' und 'Ablaut' in der Terminologie der frühen deutschsprächigen Grammatik, *Sitzungsberichte der deutschen*

Akademie der Wissenschaften zu Berlin, Klasse für Sprache, Literatur und Kunst, Jahrgang 1955, Nr 3, 21–45.

ITKONEN, E. (1991) *Universal History of Linguistics. India, China, Arabia, Europe* (Studies in the History of the Language Sciences, 65), Benjamins, Amsterdam/Philadelphia.

JACOBI, T. (1843) *Beiträge zur deutschen Grammatik*, Trautwein, Berlin.

JÄGER, L. (1987) Philologie und Linguistik. Historische Notizen zu einem gestörten Verhältnis, in SCHMITTER (ed.) (1987a), 198–223.

JAKOBSON, R. (1965) L'importanza di Kruszewski per lo sviluppo della linguistica generale, *Ricerche Slavistiche*, 13, 3–23. Russian version printed in JAKOBSON (1971), 429–50.

JAKOBSON, R. (1971) *Selected Writings. II. Word and Language*, Mouton, The Hague / Paris.

JAMIESON, J. (1808) *An Etymological Dictionary of the Scottish Language, Illustrating the Words in their Different Significations by Examples from Ancient and Modern Writers; Shewing their Affinity to those of Other Languages, and Especially the Northern; Explaining Many Terms, which, though Now Obsolete in England, Were Formerly Common to both Countries; and Elucidating National Rites, Customs and Institutions in their Analogy to those of Other Nations; to which is Prefixed a Dissertation on the Origin of the Scottish Language*, Printed at the University Press for W. Creech, Edinburgh. 2nd edn 1840–1; 3rd edn 1879–82.

JAMIESON, J. (1814) *Hermes Scythicus: or, The Radical Affinities of the Greek and Latin Languages to The Gothic: Illustrated from the Moeso-Gothic, Anglo-Saxon, Francic, Alemannic, Suio-Gothic, Islandic, &c. To which is Prefixed, A Dissertation of the Historical Proofs of the Scythian Origins of the Greeks*, Edinburgh University Press (for Longman, Hurst, Rees, Orme & Brown, London, and Bell & Bradfute; Doig & Stirling, etc.), Edinburgh.

JANKOWSKY, K. R. (1972) *The Neogrammarians* (Janua Linguarum, Series minor, 116), Mouton, The Hague / Paris.

JANKOWSKY, K. R. (1976) The Psychological Component in the Work of the Early Neogrammarians and its Foundations, in CHRISTIE, W. M. (ed.), *Current Progress in Historical Linguistics. Proceedings of the Second International Conference on Historical Linguistics, Tucson, Arizona, 12–16 January 1976*, North Holland, Amsterdam, 267–82.

JANKOWSKY, K. R. (1979) Typological Studies in the Nineteenth Century and the Neogrammarian Sound Law Principle, *Forum Linguisticum*, 4, 159–73.

JARAUSCH, K. H. (1982) *Students, Society and Politics in Imperial Germany. The Rise of Academic Illiberalism*, Princeton University Press, Princeton.

JARAUSCH, K. H. (ed.) (1983) *The Transformation of Higher Learning 1860–1930*, University of Chicago Press, Chicago.

JARITZ, P. (1992) August Schleicher und Hegel, der vielgeschmähte Meister, *Beiträge zur Geschichte der Sprachwissenschaft*, 2, 57–76.

JENSEN, P. J. (1981) *J. N. Madvig. Avec une esquisse de l'histoire de la philologie classique au Danemark*, Odense University Presse, Odense. Traduit du Danois par André Nicolet.

JESPERSEN, O. (1887) Zur Lautgesetzfrage, *Internationale Zeitschrift für allgemeine Sprachwissenschaft*, 3, 188–217. Reprinted in JESPERSEN (1970, 160–92) and in WILBUR (ed.) (1977).

JESPERSEN, O. (1894) *Progress in Language, with Special Reference to English*, Swan Sonnenschein, London. Reprinted (with an introduction by James McCawley) Benjamins, Amsterdam/Philadelphia, 1994.

JESPERSEN, O. (1901) *Sprogundervisning*, Gyldendal, København. 2nd edn 1933. English translation: *How to Teach a Foreign Language*, Allen & Unwin, London, 1904. 12th reprint 1961.

JESPERSEN, O. (1905) *Growth and Structure of the English Language*, Teubner, Leipzig. 2nd edn 1912; 9th edn 1938 and numerous reprints.

JESPERSEN, O. (1922) *Language. Its Nature, Development and Origin*, Allen and Unwin / Holt & Co., London / New York.

JESPERSEN, O. (1962) The Classification of Languages. A Contribution to the History of Linguistic Science, in *Selected Writings of Otto Jespersen*, Allen & Unwin / Senjo Publishing Co., Ltd, London/Tokyo, 693–704.

JESPERSEN, O. (1970) *Linguistica. Selected Papers in English, French and German*, 2nd edn, McGrath, College Park, Maryland. 1st edn 1933.

JOLY, A. (ed.) (1988) *La linguistique génétique. Histoire et théories*, Presses Universitaires de Lille, Lille.

JONES, D. (1957) *The History and Meaning of the Term 'Phoneme'*, International Phonetic Association, London.

JONES, SIR WILLIAM (1790) On the Spikenard of the Antients, *Asiatick Researches*, 2, 405–17.

JONES, SIR WILLIAM (1807) *The Works of Sir William Jones with the Life of the Author by Lord Teignmouth*, ed. by John Shore, Baron Teignmouth, 13 vols., Stockdale, Walker, London.

JOST, L. (1960) *Sprache als Werk und wirkende Kraft. Ein Beitrag zur Geschichte und Kritik der energetischen Sprachauffassung seit Wilhelm von Humboldt*, Haupt, Bern.

JUNKER, K. (1986) Zur Kritik an der Humboldt-Adaptation der Neuhumboldtianer, in WELKE (ed.) (1986), 68–93.

JUUL, A., NIELSEN, H. F. (eds.) (1989) *Otto Jespersen: Facets of his Life and Work* (Studies in the History of the Language Sciences, 52), Benjamins, Amsterdam/Philadelphia.

KALTZ, B. (1985) Christian Jacob Kraus' Review of 'Linguarum totius orbis vocabularia comparativa' ed. by Peter Simon Pallas (St Petersburg, 1787). Introduction, Translation and Notes, *Historiographia Linguistica*, 12, 229–60. Cf. KRAUS (1787).

KANT, I. (1798) *Der Streit der Facultäten in drey Abschnitten*, Nicolovius, Königsberg. Reprinted in Kant's *Gesammelte Schiften*, herausgegeben von der Königlich Preußischen Akademie der Wissenschaften, 7, 1–116, Reimer, Berlin 1907.

KEJARIWAL, O. P. (1988) *The Asiatic Society of Bengal and the Discovery of India's Past 1784–1838*, Oxford University Press, Delhi.

KEMP, J. A. (1981) Introduction to Lepsius's 'Standard Alphabet', in LEPSIUS (1981), 1*–88*.

KEMPELEN, W. VON (1791) *Mechanismus der menschlichen Sprache, nebst Beschreibung einer sprechenden Maschine*, Degen, Wien. Reprinted with an introduction by H. E. Breckle and Wolfgang Wildgreis, Frommann-Holzboog, Stuttgart-Bad Cannstatt, 1970. French translation Bauer, Vienna, 1791.

KILBURY, J. (1976) *The Development of Morphophonemic Theory* (Studies in the History of Linguistics, 10), Benjamins, Amsterdam.

KIPARSKY, P. (1974) From Paleogrammarians to Neogrammarians, in HYMES (ed.) (1974), 331–45.

KIRCHER, A. (1667) *China monumentis quà sacris quà profanis, nec non variis naturae et artis spectaculis aliarumque rerum memorabilium argumentis illustrata*, apud J. Janssonium a Waesberge & E. Weyerstraet, Amstelodami. Reprinted Minerva, Frankfurt a.M., 1966.

KIRKNESS, A. (1980) *Geschichte des deutschen Wörterbuches 1838–1863. Documente zu den Lexicographen Grimm. Mit einem Beitrag von Ludwig Denecke*, Hirzel, Stuttgart.

KISPERT, R. J. K. (1978) Sir William Jones: A New Perspective on the Origin and Background of his Common Source, *Georgetown University Papers on Language and Linguistics*, 14, 1–68.

KLAPROTH, J. VON (1823) *Asia polyglotta*, J. M. Eberhart, Paris.

KNOBLOCH, C. (1988) *Geschichte der psychologischen Sprachauffassung in Deutschland von 1850 bis 1920* (Germanistische Linguistik, 86), Niemeyer, Tübingen.

KNOBLOCH, C. (1989a) Die deutsche Schulgrammatik vor dem Erscheinen von Karl Ferdinand Beckers 'Organism der Sprache' (1827), in ERLINGER, KNOBLOCH and MEYER (eds.) (1989), 63–86.

KNOBLOCH, C. (1989b) Einige Entwicklungstendenzen der deutschen Schulgrammatik nach Karl Ferdinand Becker, in ERLINGER, KNOBLOCH and MEYER (eds.) (1989), 87–113.

KNOBLOCH, C. (1991) Introduction, in WEGENER (1991), xi*–li*.

KOEPKE, W. (ed.) (1990) *Johann Gottfried Herder. Language, History and the Enlightenment*, Camden House, Columbia / South Carolina.

KOERNER, [E. F.] K. (1973a) *Ferdinand de Saussure: Origin and Development of his Linguistic Thought in Western Studies of Language. A Contribution to the History and Theory of Linguistics* (Schriften zur Linguistik, 7), Friedrich Vieweg & Sohn, Braunschweig. Reprinted 1974.

KOERNER, [E. F.] K. (1973b) *The Importance of F. Techmer's Internationale Zeitschrift für Allgemeine Sprachwissenschaft in the Development of General Linguistics* (Studies in the History of Linguistics, 1), Benjamins, Amsterdam.

KOERNER, [E. F.] K. (1975) European Structuralism: Early Beginnings, in SEBEOK (ed.) (1975), 2, 717–827.

KOERNER, [E. F.] K. (1978) *Toward a Historiography of Linguistics: Selected Essays*, Foreword by R. H. Robins, Benjamins, Amsterdam.

KOERNER, [E. F.] K. (1979) L'importance de William Dwight Whitney pour les jeunes linguistes de Leipzig et pour F. de Saussure, in BROGYANYI (ed.) (1979), 1, 437–54.

KOERNER, [E. F.] K. (ed.) (1983) *Linguistics and Evolutionary Theory. Three Essays by August Schleicher, Ernst Haeckel, and Wilhelm Bleek, with an*

Introduction by J. *Peter Maher* (Amsterdam Classics in Linguistics, 1800–1925, 6), Benjamins, Amsterdam/Philadelphia.

KOERNER, [E. F.] K. (1987) The Importance of Saussure's 'Mémoire' in the Development of Historical Linguistics, in CARDONA and ZIDE (eds.) (1987), 201–17.

KOERNER, [E. F.] K. (1989) *Practising Linguistic Historiography. Selected Essays* (Studies in the History of the Language Sciences, 50), Benjamins, Amsterdam/Philadelphia.

KOERNER, [E. F.] K. (1990) Wilhelm von Humboldt and American Ethnolinguistics, Boas (1894) to Hymes (1961), in DINNEEN, F. P., S. J., and KOERNER, E. F. K. (eds.), *North American Contributions to the History of Linguistics* (Amsterdam Studies in the History of the Language Sciences, 58), Benjamins, Amsterdam/Philadelphia, 111–28.

KOERNER, [E. F.] K. (ed.) (1994) *Giulio Panconcelli-Calzia, Geschichtszahlen der Phonetik. Quellen Atlas der Phonetik. New Edition with an English Introduction* (Amsterdam Studies in the History of Language Sciences, 16), Benjamins, Amsterdam/Philadelphia.

KOERNER, [E. F.] K. (1995) *Professing Linguistic Historiography* (Studies in the History of the Language Sciences, 79), Benjamins, Amsterdam/Philadelphia.

KOHLER, K. (1981) Three Trends in Phonetics: the Development of the Discipline in Germany since the Nineteenth Century, in ASHER and HENDERSON (eds.) (1981), 161–78.

KOHRT, M. (1984) *Phonetik, Phonologie und die 'Relativität der Verhältnisse'. Zur Stellung Jost Winterlers in der Geschichte der Wissenschaft*, Steiner, Stuttgart.

KOHRT, M. (1985) *Problemgeschichte des Graphembegriffs und des frühen Phonembegriffs* (Reihe Germanistische Linguistik, 61), Niemeyer, Tübingen.

KOHRT, M. (1990) 'Sound Inventory' and 'Sound System' in 19th Century Linguistics, in NIEDEREHE and KOERNER (eds.) (1990), 589–603.

KRAPF, V. (1993) *Sprache als Organismus: Metaphern – Ein Schlüssel zu Jacob Grimms Sprachauffassung* (Schriften der Brüder Grimm-Gesellschaft, NF, 26), Brüder Grimm-Gesellschaft, Kassel.

KRAUS, C. J. (1787) Review of ST PETERSBURG: Srawniteljnjije Slowari wsjech Jasikow i Narjetschii sobrannije Desnizeju wsewisotschaisei Osobji, etc., das ist: Vergleichendes Glossarium aller Sprachen und Mundarten, gesammelt auf Veranstaltung der allerhöchsten Person. Erster Band, *Allgemeine Literaturzeitung*, 4 (numm. 235, 236, 237a, 237b), cols.1–29. Review of PALLAS (1787–89), I. Partly reprinted in ARENS (1969, 136–145). English translation in KALTZ (1985).

KRETSCHMER, P. (1896) *Einleitung in die Geschichte der griechischen Sprache*, Vandenhoeck & Ruprecht, Göttingen. Reprinted 1970.

KRETSCHMER, P. (1920) Nekrolog von Prof. Karl Brugmann, *Almanach der Akademie der Wissenschaften in Wien*, 70, 256–61.

KRONASSER, H. (1952) *Handbuch der Semasiologie. Kurze Einführung in die Geschichte, Problematik und Terminologie der Bedeutungslehre*, Winter, Heidelberg. 2nd edn 1968.

KRUSZEWSKI, M. (1880) Lingvističeskie zametki. I. Novejšie otkrytija v oblasti ario-evropejskogo vokalizma [Newest Discoveries in the Field of Ario-

European Vocalism], *Russkij filologičeskij vestnik*, 4, 33–45. Review of BRUGMANN (1876a) and SAUSSURE (1879).

KRUSZEWSKI, M. (1881) *Über die Lautabwechslung*, Universitätsbuchdruckerei, Kazan. English translation in KRUSZEWSKI (1995).

KRUSZEWSKI, M. (1884–90) Prinzipien der Sprachentwickelung, *Internationale Zeitschrift für allgemeine Sprachwissenschaft*, 1, 295–307; 2, 258–68; 3, 145–87; 5, 133–44, 339–60. Translated from Polish original of 1883. English translation in KRUSZEWSKI (1995).

KRUSZEWSKI, M. (1967) *Wybór pism [Selected Writings]*, Zakład Narodowy im. Ossolińskich, Wrocław/Warszawa/Kraków.

KRUSZEWSKI, M. (1995) *Writings in General Linguistics*. Edited with an introduction by Konrad Koerner (Amsterdam Classics in Linguistics, 11), Benjamins, Amsterdam/Philadelphia.

KÜHNER, R. (1869–70) *Ausführliche Grammatik der griechischen Sprache*, 2nd edn, 2 vols., Hahnsche Buchhandlung, Hannover. 1st edn 1834–5.

KÜHNER, R., GERTH, B. (1898–1904) *Ausführliche Grammatik der griechischen Sprache. Zweiter Teil: Satzlehre*, 2 vols., Hahnsche Buchhandlung, Hannover. Reprinted Wissenschaftliche Buchgesellschaft, Darmstadt, 1966.

KURYŁOWICZ, J. (1978) Lecture du 'Mémoire' en 1978: un commentaire, *Cahiers Ferdinand de Saussure*, 32, 7–26.

LA GRASSERIE, R. G. DE (1889–90) De la classification des langues. I. Partie: Classification des langues apparentées. II. Partie: Classification des langues non apparentées, *Internationale Zeitschrift für allgemeine Sprachwissenschaft*, 4, 374–87; 5, 296–338.

LA GRASSERIE, R. G. DE (1908) *Essai d'une sémantique intégrale*, Leroux, Paris.

LAKÓ, G. (1970) Janos Sajnovics und die finnisch-ugrische Sprachvergleichung, *Sovetskoe Finno-ugrovedenie*, 6, 239–47.

LAKS, A., NESCHKE, A. (eds.) (1990), *La naissance du paradigme herméneutique: Schleiermacher, Humboldt, Boeckh, Droysen* (Cahiers de philologie, Série Apparat critique, 10), Presses universitaires de Lille, Lille.

LANJUINAIS, J. D., comte. (1832) *Œuvres*, 4 vols., Dondey-Dupré, Paris.

LANMAN, C. R. (ed.) (1897) Cf. WHITNEY (1897).

LAW, V. (1993) Processes of Assimilation. European Grammars of Sanskrit in the Early Decades of the Nineteenth Century, in DROIXHE and GRELL (eds.) (1993), 237–61.

LAZARUS, M., STEINTHAL, H. (1860) Einleitende Gedanken über Völkerpsychologie, als Einladung zu einer Zeitschrift für Völkerpsychologie und Sprachwissenschaft, *Zeitschrift für Völkerpsychologie und Sprachwissenschaft*, 1, 1–73. Reprinted in STEINTHAL (1970), 307–79.

LEFMANN, S. (1870) *August Schleicher. Eine Skizze*, Teubner, Leipzig.

LEFMANN, S. (1891–7) *Franz Bopp, sein Leben und seine Wissenschaft.* 2 vols. + *Nachtrag*, Reimer, Berlin.

LEHMANN, W. P. (ed.) (1967) *A Reader in Nineteenth Century Historical Indo-European Linguistics*, Indiana University Press, Bloomington and London.

LEHMANN, W. P. (ed.) (1980) Case Syntax at the Turn of the Century in Relation to Universals, in BRETTSCHNEIDER and LEHMANN (eds.) (1980), 145–50.

LEHMANN, W. P. (ed.) (1994) The Continuity of Theory in Linguistics, in CIPRIANO, DI GIOVINE and MANCINI (eds.) (1994), ii, 985–1009.

LEHMANN, W. P., ZGUSTA, L. (1979) Schleicher's Tale after a Century, in BROGYANYI (ed.) (1979), i, 455–66.

LEITNER, G. (ed.) (1991a) *English Traditional Grammars. An International Perspective* (Studies in the History of the Language Sciences, 62), Benjamins, Amsterdam/Philadelphia.

LEITNER, G. (ed.) (1991b) Eduard Adolf Maetzner (1805–1902), in LEITNER (ed.) (1991a), 232–55.

LEITZMANN, A. (ed.) (1908) *Briefwechsel zwischen Wilhelm von Humboldt und August Wilhelm Schlegel. Mit einer Einleitung von B. Delbrück*, Niemeyer, Halle.

LEOPOLD, J. (1974) British Applications of the Aryan Theory of Race to India, 1850–1870, *English Historical Review*, 89, 578–603.

LEOPOLD, J. (1980) *Culture in Comparative and Evolutionary Perspective: E. B. Tylor and the Making of Primitive Culture*, Dietrich Reimer, Berlin.

LEOPOLD, J. (1983) *The Letter Liveth: The Life, Work and Library of August Friedrich Pott (1802–87)* (Library and Information Sources in Linguistics, 9), Benjamins, Amsterdam/Philadelphia.

LEOPOLD, J. (1984) French–German Connections in Linguistics: August Friedrich Pott (1802–87) and his French Friends, in AUROUX *et al.* (eds.) (1984), 415–25.

LEOPOLD, J. (1989a) Anthropological Perspectives on the Origin of Language Debate in the Nineteenth Century: Edward B. Tylor and Charles Darwin, in GESSINGER and RAHDEN (eds.) (1989), 2, 151–75.

LEOPOLD, J. (1989b) The Last Battle over the Tower of Babel: The Controversy between August Friedrich Pott and Franz Kaulen, in GESSINGER and RAHDEN (eds.) (1989), 2, 548–60.

LEPSCHY, G. C. (1962) Osservazioni sul termine struttura. A proposito di Sens et usage du terme structure dans les sciences humaines et sociales, édité par R. Bastide, *Annali della Scuola Normale di Pisa*, 31, 137–97. Reprinted in LEPSCHY (1989), 283–323.

LEPSCHY, G. C. (1982) Freud, Abel e gli opposti, in FORNARI, F. (ed.), *La comunicazione spiritosa. Il motto di spirito da Freud a oggi*, Sansoni, Firenze, 39–68. Reprinted in LEPSCHY (1989), 349–78.

LEPSCHY, G. C. (1989) *Sulla linguistica moderna*, Il Mulino, Bologna.

LEPSCHY, G. C. (ed.) (1990–4) *Storia della linguistica*, 3 vols., Il Mulino, Bologna.

LEPSCHY, G. C. (1991) Appunti sul soggetto e sull'oggetto nella storia della linguistica, *BioLogica*, 5, 193–211.

LEPSCHY, G. C. (ed.) (1994–) *History of Linguistics*, 5 vols., Longman, London.

LEPSIUS, R. (1855) *Das allgemeine linguistische Alphabet. Grundsätze der Übertragung fremder Schriftsysteme und bisher noch ungeschriebener Sprachen in europäische Buchstaben*, Hertz, Berlin. English translation, Seeleys, London, 1855. Cf. LEPSIUS (1981).

LEPSIUS, R. (1861) Über die Umschrift und Lautverhältnisse einiger hinterasiatischer Sprachen, namentlich der Chinesischen und der Tibetischen, *Abhandlungen der Königlichen Akademie der Wissenschaften zu Berlin*, 1860, 449–96.

LEPSIUS, R. (1981) *Standard Alphabet for Reducing Unwritten Languages and Foreign Graphic Systems to a Uniform Orthography in European Letters*.

2nd revised edn (London, 1863) ed. with an introduction by J. Alan Kemp (Amsterdam Classics in Linguistics, 5), Benjamins, Amsterdam. Reprinted from the 2nd English edn, Williams & Norgate, London, 1863; W. Hertz, Berlin; 1st (German) edn, Berlin, 1855.

LEROUX, R. (1958) *L'anthropologie comparée de Guillaume de Humboldt* (Publications de la Faculté des Lettres de l'Université de Strasbourg, 135), Les Belles Lettres, Paris.

LEROY, M. (1971) *Les grands courants de la linguistique moderne*, 2nd edn, Université de Bruxelles, Bruxelles. 1st edn 1963. Translations into Italian 1965 (2nd edn 1969), English 1967, Spanish 1969, Portuguese 1970.

LEROY, M. (1985) Honoré Chavée et l'édification de la grammaire comparée, in AMBROSINI, R. (ed.), *Tra Linguistica Storica e Linguistica Generale. Scritti in onore di Tristano Bolelli* (Quaderni della cattedra di linguistica dell'Università di Pisa. Serie Monografica, 6), Pacini, Pisa, 209–25.

LESKIEN, A. (1876) *Die Declination im Slavisch-Litauischen und Germanischen*, Hirzel, Leipzig.

LEVENTHAL, R. S. (1987) Language Theory, the Institution of Philology and the State: The Emergence of Philological Discourse 1770–1810, in AARSLEFF, KELLY and NIEDEREHE (eds.) (1987), 349–63.

LEVI DELLA VIDA, G. (1938) *Les Sémites et leur rôle dans l'histoire religieuse. Trois leçons au Collège de France*, Librairie Orientaliste Paul Geuthner, Paris.

LEXIS, W. (1893) *Die deutschen Universitäten*, 2 vols., Asher, Berlin.

LICHEM, K., SIMON, H. J. (eds.) (1980) *Hugo Schuchardt: Schuchardt Symposium 1977 in Graz* (Veröffentlichungen der Kommission für Linguistik und Kommunikationsforschung. Heft 10. Österreichische Akademie der Wissenschaften, Sitzungsberichte, Philosophisch-Historische Klasse, 373), Österreichische Akademie der Wissenschaften, Wien.

LIDDELL, H. G., SCOTT, R. (1843) *A Greek – English Lexicon. Based on the German Work of Francis Passow*, The Clarendon Press, Oxford. 4th edn 1855, without mention of Passow in the title page; 9th edn ed. by H. S. Jones and R. McKenzie, 1940.

LIEBRUCKS, B. (1965) *Sprache und Bewußtsein. II. Sprache. Wilhelm von Humboldt*, Lang, Frankfurt a.M.

LIGHT, D. W. (1983) The Development of Professional Schools in America, in JARAUSCH (ed.) (1983), 345–65.

LITTRÉ, É. (1889) *Dictionnaire de la langue française*, 3rd edn, 4 vols., Hachette, Paris. 1st edn 1863–72.

LOCHNER VON HÜTTENBACH, F. (1980) Sachen und Wörter – Wörter und Sachen, in LICHEM and SIMON (eds.) (1980), 159–72.

LOEWE, M. L. (1829) *Historiae criticae grammatices universalis seu philosophicae lineamenta*, Typis Birkianis, Dresdae.

LOHMANN, J. (1960) Die Entwicklung der allgemeinen Sprachwissenschaft an der Friedrich-Wilhelms-Universität zu Berlin bis 1933, in LEUNINK, H., NEUMANN, E., KOTOWSKI, G. (eds.), *Gedenksschrift der Westdeutschen Rektorenkonferenz und der Freien Universität Berlin: zur 150. Wiederkehr des Gründungsjahres der Friedrich-Wilhelm-Universität zu Berlin. 2. Studium Berolinense. Aufsätze und Beiträge zu Problemen der Wissenschaft und zur*

Geschichte der Friedrich-Wilhelms Universität zu Berlin, De Gruyter, Berlin, 449–58.

LÖTHER, B. (1984) Zum Organismus-Begriff bei Jacob Grimm, *Zeitschrift für Phonetik, Sprachwissenschaft und Kommunikationsforschung*, 34, 11–8.

LOTTNER, C. (1862) Ausnahmen der ersten Lautverschiebung, *Zeitschrift für vergleichende Sprachforschung*, 11, 161–205. English translation in LEHMANN (ed.) (1967), 97–108.

LOUNSBURY, F. G. (1968) One Hundred Years of Anthropological Linguistics, in BREW, J. O. (ed.), *One Hundred Years of Anthropology*, Harvard University Press, Cambridge MA, 150–225, 256–64.

LOWE, R. (1983) The Expansion of Higher Education in England, in JARAUSCH (ed.) (1983), 37–56.

LUDOLF, H. (1702) *Grammatica Aethiopica. Ab ipso Auctore solicite revisa, & plurimis in locis correcta & aucta*, 2nd edn, Zunner & Helvig, Frankfurt a.M. Reprinted Halle, Martin-Luther-Universität-Halle-Wittenberg, 1986.

LÜDTKE, J. (1978) *Die romanischen Sprachen im Mithridates von Adelung und Vater. Studie und Text* (Lingua et Traditio, Beiträge zur Geschichte der Sprachwissenschaft, 4), Narr, Tübingen.

LÜHR, R. (1989) Bemerkungen zur Grammatiktheorie Jacob Grimms und Karl Ferdinand Beckers, *Sprachwissenschaft*, 14, 126–60.

LYELL, SIR CHARLES (1830–3) *Principles of Geology; Being an Attempt to Explain the Former Changes of the Earth's Surface by Reference to Causes Now in Operation*, 3 vols., John Murray, London. 11th edn 1872.

LYELL, SIR CHARLES (1863) *The Geological Evidences of the Antiquity of Man with Remarks on Theories of the Origin of Species by Variation*, John Murray, London. 4th edn 1873.

MADVIG, J. N. (1841a) *Latinsk Sproglære til Skolebrug*, Gyldendal, Kjöbenhavn. Translations into German 1843, English 1849, Dutch 1849, French 1870, Italian 1870, Portuguese 1872, etc.

MADVIG, J. N. (1841b) *Bemærkninger i Anledning af Professor Madvigs latinske Sproglære, af dens Forfatter*, Gyldendal, Kjöbenhavn. German translation 1843.

MADVIG, J. N. (1846) *Græsk Ordføiningslære, især for den attiske Sprogform*, Reitzel, Kjøbenhavn. German translation 1847, 2nd edn 1857; English 1853, French 1884.

MADVIG, J. N. (1848) *Bemerkungen über einige Puncte der griechischen Worfügungslehre* (Suppl. Philologus), Dieterich, Göttingen.

MADVIG, J. N. (1875) *Kleine Philologische Schriften*, vom Verfasser Deutsch bearbeitet, Teubner, Leipzig.

MADVIG, J. N. (1971) *Sprachtheoretische Abhandlungen* im Auftrage der Gesellschaft für Dänische Sprache und Literatur herausgegeben von Karsten Friis Johansen, Munksgaard, no place (but København).

MAGGI, D. (1986) Il sanscrito e gli inizi della linguistica comparata indo-europea, a proposito di M. Mayrhofer, *Sanskrit und die Sprache Alteuropas*, *Archivio Glottologico Italiano*, 71, 135–45.

MAHER, J. P. (1983) Introduction, in KOERNER (ed.) (1983), xvii–xxxii.

MAJEED, J. (1992) *Ungoverned Imaginings: James Mill's The History of British India and Orientalism*, Clarendon Press, Oxford.

MALKIEL, Y. (1955) An Early Formulation of the Linguistic Wave Theory, *Romance Philology*, 9, 31.

MALKIEL, Y. (1974) Friedrich Diez's Debt to Pre-1800 Linguistics, in HYMES (ed.) (1974), 315–30.

MALKIEL, Y. (1976a) Friedrich Diez and the Birth Pangs of Romance Philology, in TUTTLE, E. F. (ed.), *Friedrich Diez Centennial Lectures (delivered May 24, 1976)* (Supplement to *Romance Philology* XXX, no 2. Center for Medieval and Renaissance Studies Contributions, 9), University of California Press, Berkeley, London and Los Angeles, 1–15.

MALKIEL, Y. (1976b) *Etymological Dictionaries. A Tentative Typology*, Chicago University Press, Chicago.

MALKIEL, Y. (1979) Review of LÜDTKE (1978), *Kratylos*, 24, 117–26.

MALKIEL, Y. (1988) *Prospettive della ricerca etimologica*, Liguori, Napoli.

MALKIEL, Y. (1989) *Die sechs Synthesen im Werke Wilhelm Meyer-Lübkes* (Veröffentlichungen der Kommission für Linguistik und Kommunikationsforschung, 23), Oesterreichische Akademie der Wissenschaften, Wien.

MALKIEL, Y. (1993) *Etymology*, Cambridge University Press, Cambridge.

MALMBERG, B. (1991) *Histoire de la linguistique de Sumer à Saussure*, Presses Universitaires de France, Paris.

MANCHESTER, M. L. (1985) *The Philosophical Foundations of Humboldt's Linguistic Doctrines* (Amsterdam Studies in the History of the Language Sciences, 32), Benjamins, Amsterdam/Philadelphia.

MARAZZINI, C. (1984) Langue primitive et comparatisme dans le système de Carlo Denina, *Histoire Épistémologie Langage*, 6:II, 117–29.

MARAZZINI, C. (1988) Conoscenze e riflessioni di linguistica storica in Italia nei primi vent'anni dell'Ottocento, in FORMIGARI and LO PIPARO (eds.) (1988), 405–21.

MARAZZINI, C. (1989) *Storia e coscienza della lingua in Italia dall'umanesimo al romanticismo*, Rosenberg & Sellier, Torino.

MARAZZINI, C. (1991) Linguistique Vaticane: les missionaires et le sanskrit à Rome et en Italie à la fin du XVIIIe siècle, in DI CESARE and GENSINI (eds.) (1991), 85–97.

MARAZZINI, C. (1992) Carlo Denina e il paleocomparativismo europeo del Sei e Settecento, in NEGRI and ORIOLES (eds.) (1992), 29–48.

MARAZZINI, C. (1993) Le teorie, in SERIANNI, L. and TRIFONE, P. (eds.), *Storia della lingua italiana, I: I luoghi della codificazione*, Einaudi, Torino, 231–329.

MARINI, G. (1972) *Jacob Grimm* (Gli Storici, 1), Guida Editori, Napoli.

MARINO, L. (1976) Wilhelm von Humboldt e l'antropologia comparata, in HEILMANN (ed.) (1976), 11–41.

MARKEY, T. (1979) Cf. SCHUCHARDT (1979).

MARSDEN, W. (1796) *A Catalogue of Dictionaries, Vocabularies, Grammars, and Alphabets*, 2 vols., privately printed, London.

MARSDEN, W. (1827) *Bibliotheca Marsdeniana philologica et orientalis, a Catalogue of Works and Manuscripts Collected with a View to the General Comparison of Languages, and to the Study of Oriental Literature*, J. L. Cox, London.

MARTY, A. (1875) *Über den Ursprung der Sprache*, Stuber, Würzburg. Reprinted Minerva, Frankfurt a.M., 1976.

MATTHEWS, P. H. (1993) *Grammatical Theory in the United States from Bloomfield to Chomsky* (Cambridge Studies in Linguistics, 67), Cambridge University Press, Cambridge.

MAX MÜLLER, F. Cf. MÜLLER, F. MAX.

MAYR, E. (1982) *The Growth of Biological Thought. Diversity, Evolution, and Inheritance*, The Bellknapp Press of Harvard University, Cambridge, MA.

MAYRHOFER, M. (1981) *Nach hundert Jahren. Ferdinand de Saussures Frühwerk und seine Rezeption durch die heutige Indogermanistik. Mit einem Beitrag von Ronald Zwanziger* (Sitzungsberichte der Heidelberger Akademie der Wissenschaften. Philosophisch-historische Klasse. Jahrgang 1981. Bericht 8), Winter, Heidelberg.

MAYRHOFER, M. (1983) *Sanskrit und die Sprachen Alteuropas. Zwei Jahrhunderte des Widerspiels von Entdeckungen und Irrtümern* (Nachrichten der Akademie der Wissenschaften in Göttingen. I. Philologisch-historische Klasse. Jahrgang 1983. Nr 5), Vandenhoeck & Ruprecht, Göttingen.

MAYRHOFER, M. (1988) Zum Weiterwirken von Saussures 'Mémoire', *Kratylos*, 33, 1–15. Reprinted in *Ausgewählte kleine Schriften*, Reichert, Wiesbaden, 1996, 271–85.

MCCAWLEY, J. D. (1979) The Phonological Theory behind Whitney's *Sanskrit Grammar*, in *Adverbs, Vowels, and Other Objects of Wonder*, University of Chicago Press, Chicago/London, 10–19. First publication, 1967.

MCCAWLEY, J. D. (1988) *The Syntactic Phenomena of English*, 2 vols., The University of Chicago Press, Chicago and London.

MEILLET, A. (1905) Avertissement, in BRUGMANN (1905), i–v.

MEILLET, A. (1938) *Linguistique historique et linguistique générale*, 2, Klincksieck, Paris.

MEILLET, A., COHEN, M. (eds.) (1924) *Les langues du monde par un groupe de linguistes sous la direction de A. Meillet et M. Cohen*, 2 vols., Société de Linguistique de Paris, Paris. 2nd edn 1952.

MEINHOF, C. (1899) *Grundriß einer Lautlehre der Bantu Sprachen, nebst Anleitung zur Aufnahme von Bantusprachen*, Brockhaus, Leipzig. 2nd edn 1910. English translation, Reimer/Vohsen, Berlin, 1932.

MEINHOF, C. (1906) *Grundzüge einer vergleichenden Grammatik der Bantusprachen*, Reimer, Berlin. 3rd edn 1967.

MERINGER, R. (1908) *Aus dem Leben der Sprache*, Behr, Berlin.

MERINGER, R., MAYER, C. (1895) *Versprechen und Verlesen. Eine psychologisch-linguistische Studie*, Göschen'sche Verlagshandlung, Stuttgart. Cf. MERINGER and MAYER (1978).

MERINGER, R., MAYER, C. (1978) *Versprechen und Verlesen. Eine psychologisch-linguistische Studie*. New edition with an introductory article by Anne Cutler and David Fay (Amsterdam Classics in Psycholinguistics, 2), Benjamins, Amsterdam. For the 1st edn, cf. MERINGER and MAYER (1895).

MERKEL, C. L. (1857) *Anatomie und Physiologie des menschlichen Stimm- und Sprach-Organs (Anthropophonik) nach eigenen Beobachtungen und Versuchen wissenschaftlich begründet und für Studirende und ausübende Ärtze, Physiologen, Akustiker, Sänger, Gesanglehrer, Tonsetzer, öffentliche Redner, Pädagogen und Sprachforscher dargestellt*, A. Abel, Leipzig.

MERKEL, C. L. (1866) *Physiologie der menschlichen Sprachen (physiologische Laletik)*, Wigand, Leipzig.

METCALF, G. J. (1974) The Indo-European Hypothesis in the 16th and 17th Centuries, in HYMES (ed.) (1974), 233–57.

METCALF, G. J. (1984) Adelung Discovers the Languages of Asia, *Histoire Épistémologie Langage*, 6:II, 101–15.

MEYER, G. (1886) *Griechische Grammatik*, 2nd edn, Breitkopf & Härtel, Leipzig. 1st edn 1880.

MEYER, P. (1875) Review of *Archivio Glottologico Italiano*, 3 n. 1, *Romania*, 4, 293–6.

MEYER-LÜBKE, W. (1890–1902) *Grammatik der romanischen Sprachen*, 4 vols., Reisland, Leipzig. French translation by E. Rabiet, A. and G. Doutrepont, Paris, 1890–1906.

MICHAEL, I. (1987) *The Teaching of English. From the Sixteenth Century to 1870*, Cambridge University Press, Cambridge.

MICHAEL, I. (1991) More than Enough English Grammars, in LEITNER (ed.) (1991), 11–26.

MICHELENA, L. (1976) Guillaume de Humboldt et la langue basque, in HEILMANN (ed.) (1976), 113–31.

MIKLOSICH, F. (1852–75) *Vergleichende Grammatik der slavischen Sprachen*, 4 vols., Braumüller, Wien. 2nd edn 1876–83. Reprinted Biblio-Verlag, Osnabrück, 1973.

MIKLOSICH, F. (1883) *Subjektlose Sätze*, Braumüller, Wien.

MIKLOSICH, F. (1886) *Etymologisches Wörterbuch der slavischen Sprachen*, Braumüller, Wien.

MILL, J. (1820) *The History of British India*, 2nd edn, 6 vols., Baldwin, Cradock and Joy, London. 1st edn 1817–18, 5th edn 1858. Reprint ed. by W. Thomas, University of Chicago Press, Chicago, 1975.

MILLER, R. L. (1968) *The Linguistic Relativity Principle and Humboldtian Ethnolinguistics* (Janua Linguarum, Series minor, 67), Mouton, The Hague / Paris.

MISTELI, F. (1880) Lautgesetz und Analogie. Methodologisch-psychologische Abhandlung von Prof. Franz Misteli bei Gelegenheit der Schrift: Morphologische Untersuchungen auf dem Gebiete der indogermanischen Sprachen von Dr Hermann Osthoff und Dr Karl Brugman. Erster Teil. Leipzig 1878, *Zeitschrift für Völkerpsychologie und Sprachwissenschaft*, 11 and 12, 365–475, 1–27.

MISTELI, F. (1893) *Abriss der Sprachwissenschaft. Zweiter Teil. Charakteristik der hauptsächlichsten Typen des Sprachbaues*. Neubearbeitung des Werkes von Prof. H. Steinthal (1861) [but 1860?], Dümmler, Berlin.

MÖLLER, H. (MØLLER) (1906) *Semitisch und Indogermanisch. Erster Teil. Konsonanten*, H. Hagerup, Kopenhagen. Reprinted Olms, Hildesheim / New York, 1978.

MONBODDO Cf. BURNETT, JAMES, LORD MONBODDO.

MOON, P. (1989) *The British Conquest and Dominion of India*, Duckworth, London.

MORETTI, G. (ed.) (1991) *Jacob Grimm, Friedrich Wilhelm Schelling, Sull' origine del linguaggio* (Biblioteca filosofica, Testi, 4), Gallio, Ferrara. Italian translation by T. Weddingen of GRIMM (1851) and of an essay by Schelling.

MORPURGO DAVIES, A. (1975) Language Classification in the Nineteenth Century, in SEBEOK (ed.) (1975), i, 607–716.

MORPURGO DAVIES, A. (1978) Analogy, Segmentation and the Early Neogrammarians, *Transactions of the Philological Society*, 1978, 36–60.

MORPURGO DAVIES, A. (1986) Karl Brugmann and Late Nineteenth-Century Linguistics, in BYNON and PALMER (eds.) (1986), 150–71.

MORPURGO DAVIES, A. (1987) 'Organic' and 'Organism' in Franz Bopp, in HOENIGSWALD and WIENER (eds.) (1987), 81–107.

MORPURGO DAVIES, A. (1994) Early and Late Indo-European from Bopp to Brugmann, in DUNKEL *et al.* (eds.) (1994), 245–65.

MOURELLE-LEMA, M. (1968) *La teoría lingüística en la España del siglo XIX*, Prensa Española, Madrid.

MUELLER-VOLLMER, K. (1976) Wilhelm von Humboldt und der Anfang der amerikanischen Sprachwissenschaft: Die Briefe an John Pickering, in HAMMACHER, K. (ed.), *Universalismus und Wissenschaft im Werk und Wirken der Brüder Humboldt*, Klostermann, Frankfurt a.M., 259–334.

MUELLER-VOLLMER, K. (1990a) From Sign to Signification: The Herder-Humboldt Controversy, in KOEPKE (ed.) (1990), 9–24.

MUELLER-VOLLMER, K. (1990b) Eine Einleitung zuviel. Zur Hermeneutik und Kritik der Editionen von Humboldts Einleitung in die Kawi Sprache, in *Kodikas/Code/Ars Semiotica*, 13, 1–2, 3–19.

MUELLER-VOLLMER, K. (1991) Die Vaskische Haupt- und Muttersprache. Zwei unveröffentlichte Stücke aus Humboldts baskischen Arbeitsbüchern 1800–1801, in SCHMITTER (ed.) (1991a), 111–30.

MUELLER-VOLLMER, K. (1993) *Wilhelm von Humboldts Sprachwissenschaft: Ein kommentiertes Verzeichnis des sprachwissenschaftlichen Nachlasses*, Schöningh, Paderborn.

MUGDAN, J. (1984a) *Jan Baudouin de Courtenay (1845–1929). Leben und Werk*, Fink, München.

MUGDAN, J. (ed.) (1984b) Cf. BAUDOUIN DE COURTENAY (1984).

MUGDAN, J. (1987) The Origin of the Phoneme: Farewell to a Myth, *Lingua Posnaniensis*, 28, 137–50.

MUKHERJEE, S. N. (1968) *Sir William Jones: A Study in Eighteenth Century British Attitudes to India*, Cambridge University Press, Cambridge.

MÜLLER, F. (1876–88) *Grundriß der Sprachwissenschaft*, 6 vols., Hölder, Wien.

MÜLLER, F. (1884) Sind die Lautgesetze Naturgesetze?, *Internationale Zeitschrift für allgemeine Sprachwissenschaft*, 1, 211–14.

MÜLLER, F. MAX (1854) Letter of Professor Max Müller to Chevalier Bunsen; Oxford, August 1953; On the Classification of the Turanian Languages, in C. C. J. BUNSEN (ed.), *Christianity and Mankind, Their Beginnings and Prospects. Third part. Outlines of the Philosophy of Universal History, Applied to Language and Religion*, 1, Longman, Brown, Green and Longmans, London, 263–521.

MÜLLER, F. MAX (1855) *The Languages of the Seat of War in the East. With a Survey of the Three Families of Language, Semitic, Arian, and Turanian*, 2nd edn, Williams and Norgate, London. 1st edn 1854.

MÜLLER, F. MAX (1862) *Lectures on the Science of Language Delivered at the Royal Institution of Great Britain in April, May, & June 1861*, 2nd edn,

Longman, Green, Longman and Roberts, London. 1st edn 1861, 9th edn 1891 with the title *The Science of Language*. Cf. MÜLLER (1864) and for the various editions SALMON (1996).

MÜLLER, F. MAX (1864) *Lectures on the Science of Language Delivered at the Royal Institution of Great Britain in February, March, April, & May 1863*. *Second Series*, Longman, Green, Longman, Roberts, & Green, London. This volume and/or MÜLLER (1862) were translated into German 1863–6, Italian 1864, French 1864–7, Russian 1865, etc.

MÜLLER, F. MAX (1868–75) *Chips from a German Workshop*, 4 vols., Longmans, Green & Co., London. 1st edn of Vols. 1–2, 1867; new edn 1894–5.

MÜLLER, F. MAX (1887) *The Science of Thought*, Longmans, Green & Co., London. German translation, Engelmann, Leipzig, 1888.

MÜLLER, G. MAX (1902) *The Life and Letters of the Right Honourable Friedrich Max Müller, Edited by his Wife*, 2 vols., Longmans, Green & Co., London.

MULLER, J.-C. (1984a) Quelques repères pour l'histoire de la notion de vocabulaire de base dans le précomparatisme, *Histoire Épistémologie Langage*, 6:II, 37–43.

MULLER, J.-C. (1984b) Saumaise, Monboddo, Adelung: vers la grammaire comparée, in AUROUX *et al.* (eds.) (1984), 389–96.

MULLER, J.-C. (1986) Early Stages of Language Comparison from Sassetti to Sir William Jones (1786), *Kratylos*, 31, 1–31.

MULLER, J.-C. (1993) Die Sanskritgrammatiken europäischer Missionare. Aufbau und Wirkung, in DUTZ, K. D. (ed.), *Sprachwissenschaft im 18. Jahrhundert. Fallstudien und Überblicke*, Nodus, Münster, 143–68.

MÜLLER-SIEVERS, H. (1993) *Epigenesis. Naturphilosophie im Sprachdenken Wilhelm von Humboldts* (Humboldt-Studien, 2), Schöningh, Paderborn. *Non vidi*.

MURR, S. (1987) *L'Inde philosophique entre Bossuet et Voltaire* (Publications de l'Ecole Française d'Extrême-Orient, 146), 2 vols., Ecole Française d'Extrême-Orient, Paris.

MURRAY, J. A. H. (1970) *The Evolution of English Lexicography*, McGrath, College Park, Maryland. First printed Clarendon Press, Oxford, 1900.

MURRAY, J. A. H. *et al.* (eds.) (1884–1928) *A New English Dictionary on Historical Principles, Founded Mainly on the Materials Collected by the Philological Society*, 10 vols., Clarendon Press, Oxford. Reprinted in 12 vols. with a Supplement and the title *The Oxford English Dictionary*, 1933; 2nd edn ed. by J. Simpson and E. Weiner, 20 vols., 1989.

MUSSAFIA, A. (1983) *Scritti di filologia e linguistica*, a cura di Antonio Daniele e Lorenzo Renzi (Medioevo e Umanesimo, 50), Antenore, Padova.

NAUMANN, B. (1986) *Grammatik der deutschen Sprache zwischen 1781 und 1856* (Philologische Studien und Quellen, 114), Erich Schmidt, Berlin.

NAUMANN, B., PLANK, F., HOFBAUER, G. (eds.) (1992) *Language and Earth. Elective Affinities between the Emerging Sciences of Linguistics and Geology* (Amsterdam Studies in the History of Language Sciences, 66), Benjamins, Amsterdam/Philadelphia.

NEGRI, M., ORIOLES, V. (eds.) (1992) *Storia, problemi e metodo del comparativismo linguistico. Atti del convegno della Società Italiana di Glottologia, Bologna, 29 novembre – 1 dicembre 1990*, Giardini, Pisa.

NERLICH, B. (ed.) (1988) *Anthologie de la linguistique allemande au XIXe siècle*, Nodus, Münster.

NERLICH, B. (1990a) *Change in Language. Whitney, Bréal and Wegener* (Routledge History of Linguistic Thought Series), Routledge, London and New York.

NERLICH, B. (1990b) From Form to Function. The Contribution of Bréal, Wegener and Gardiner to a Semantics of Communication and Comprehension, in SCHMITTER, P. (ed.), *Essays towards a History of Semantics*, Nodus, Münster, 105–28.

NERLICH, B. (1992) *Semantic Theories in Europe, 1830–1930* (Amsterdam Studies in the History of the Language Sciences, 59), Benjamins, Amsterdam/ Philadelphia.

NERLICH, B. (1993) Avant propos; la sémantique historique au XIXe siècle, en Allemagne, en Angleterre et en France, *Histoire Épistémologie Langage*, 15:I, 5–30.

NEUMANN, G. (1967) *Indogermanische Sprachwissenschaft 1816 und 1966* (Innsbrucker Beiträge zur Kulturwissenschaft, 24), Leopold-Franzens-Universität, Innsbruck.

NICOLAS, A. (1988) La notion d'histoire dans la linguistique française du XIXe siècle, in JOLY (ed.) (1988), 57–68.

NIEDEREHE, H.-J., KOERNER, [E. F.] K. (eds.) (1990) *History and Historiography of Linguistics. Papers from the Fourth International Conference on the History of the Language Sciences (ICHoLS IV), Trier, 24–28 August 1987* (Amsterdam Studies in the History of the Language Sciences, 51), 2 vols., Benjamins, Amsterdam/Philadelphia.

NIELSEN, H. F. (1989) On Otto Jespersen's View of Language Evolution, in JUUL and NIELSEN (eds.) (1989), 61–78.

NISBET, H. B. (1970) *Herder and the Philosophy and History of Science* (Modern Humanities Research Association, Dissertation Series, 3), Modern Humanities Research Association, Cambridge.

NOIRÉ, L. (1877) *Der Ursprung der Sprache*, Zabern, Mainz.

NOIRÉ, L. (1879a) *Max Müller und die Sprach-Philosophie*, Zabern, Mainz. Reprinted Minerva, Frankfurt a.M., 1983. English translation in NOIRÉ (1879b).

NOIRÉ, L. (1879b) *Max Müller and the Philosophy of Language*, Longmans, Green, London. Translation of NOIRÉ (1879a).

NOORDEGRAAF, J. (1977) A few remarks on Adam Smith's Dissertation (1761), *Historiographia Linguistica*, 4, 59–67.

NOORDEGRAAF, J. (1992) Dutch Linguists and the Origin of Language: Some Nineteenth-Century Views, in AHLQVIST (ed.) (1992), 279–89.

NOORDEGRAAF, J. (1993) From Myth to History. On the Reception of German Historical Grammar in Nineteenth-Century Dutch Linguistics, in DROIXHE and GRELL (eds.) (1993), 297–317.

NOORDEGRAAF, J. (1994) Dutch Linguistics around 1800. Between France and Germany, in SCHLIEBEN-LANGE et al. (eds.) (1989–94), 4, 223–44.

NOORDEGRAAF, J., VERSTEEGH, K., KOERNER, E. F. K. (eds.) (1992) *The History of Linguistics in the Low Countries* (Amsterdam Studies in the History of Language Sciences, 64), Benjamins, Amsterdam/Philadelphia.

NORDENSKIØLD, E. (1929) *The History of Biology: a Survey*, Kegan, Trench, Trübner, London.

NOREEN, A. G. (1903–24) *Vårt Språk. Nysvensk grammatik i utförlig framställning*, 10 vols., Gleerup, Lund.

NOREEN, A. G. (1923) *Einführung in die wissenschaftliche Betrachtung der Sprache. Beiträge zur Methode und Terminologie der Grammatik*. Von Verfasser genehmigte und durchgesehene Übersetzung ausgewählter Teile seines schwedischen Werkes 'Vårt Språk' von Hans W. Pollak, Niemeyer, Halle (Saale).

NOWAK, E. (1994) From the Unity of Grammar to the Diversity of Language. Language Typology around 1800, *Beiträge zur Geschichte der Sprachwissenschaft*, 4, 1, 1–18.

NÜSSE, H. (1962) *Die Sprachtheorie Friedrich Schlegels*, Winter, Heidelberg.

OERTEL, H. (1901) *Lectures on the Study of Language*, Charles Scribner's Sons, New York.

OESTERREICHER, W. (1981) Wem gehört Humboldt? Zum Einfluss der französischen Aufklärung auf die Sprachphilosophie der Romantik, in TRABANT (ed.) (1981), 117–35.

OESTERREICHER, W. (1986) Ère française et Deutsche Bewegung. Les idéologues, l'historicité du langage et la naissance de la linguistique, in BUSSE and TRABANT (eds.) (1986), 97–143.

OLENDER, M. (1989) *Les langues du paradis: Aryens et Sémites: un couple providentiel*. Preface de Jean-Pierre Vernant, Gallimard / Editions du Seuil, Paris. English translation by A. Goldhammer, Harvard University Press, Cambridge MA / London, 1992.

OPPENBERG, U. (1965) *Quellenstudien zu Friedrich Schlegels Übersetzungen aus dem Sanskrit* (Marburger Beiträge zur Germanistik, 7), Elwert, Marburg.

OPPENBERG, U. (1975) Cf. STRUC-OPPENBERG (ed.) (1975).

OSTHOFF, H. (1875–76) *Forschungen im gebiete der indogermanischen nominalen stammbildung*, 2 vols., Hermann Costenoble, Jena.

OSTHOFF, H. (1879) *Das physiologische und psychologische Moment in der sprachlichen Formenbildung* (Sammlung gemeinverständlicher wissenschaftlicher Vorträge. XIV Serie, Heft 327), Carl Habel, Berlin.

OSTHOFF, H. (1881) Die tiefstufe im indogermanischen vocalismus, *Morphologische Untersuchungen*, 4, 1–406.

OSTHOFF, H. (1884) *Zur geschichte des perfects im indogermanischen mit besonderer rücksicht auf griechisch und lateinisch*, Trübner, Strassburg/London.

OSTHOFF, H. (1886) *Die neueste Sprachforschung und die Erklärung des indogermanischen Ablautes. Antwort auf die gleichnamige Schrift von Dr Hermann Collitz*, Otto Petters, Heidelberg. Reprinted in WILBUR (ed.) (1977).

OSTHOFF, H. (1992) Cf. EINHAUSER (1992).

OSTHOFF, H., BRUGMAN, K. (1878) Vorwort, *Morphologische Untersuchungen*, 1, iii–xx.

OTT, R. (1975) *Satz und Urteil: sprachphilosophische Untersuchungen über das Verhältnis von Grammatik und Logik in den deutschen Grammatik von Karl Ferdinand Becker (1775–1849)*, Lang, Bern.

PACHORI, S. S. (ed.) (1993) *Sir William Jones. A Reader*, Oxford University Press, Delhi / Oxford / New York.

PÄTSCH, G. (1960) Franz Bopp und die historisch-vergleichende Sprachwissenschaft, in GRÖBER, W., HERNECK, F. (eds.), *Forschen und Wirken. Festschrift zur 150. Jahr-Feyer der Humboldt-Universität zu Berlin 1810–1960*, 1, VEB Deutscher Verlag der Wissenschaften, Berlin, 211–28.

PAGLIARO, A. (1930) *Sommario di linguistica arioeuropea. Fasc. I. Cenni storici e questioni teoriche*, 'L'Universale' Tipografia poliglotta, Roma. Reprinted Novecento, Palermo, 1993.

PALLAS, P. S. (1787–89) *Sravitel'nye slovari vsex jazykov i narečij, sobrannye desniceju vsevysočajšej osoby. Otdelenie pervoe, soderžasčee v sebe evropejskie i aziatskie jazyki. Linguarum totius orbis vocabularia comparativa. Augustissimae cura collecta. Sectionis primae, Linguas Europae et Asiae complexae*, 2 vols., Schnoor, Petropoli. 2nd edn ed. by F. I. Jankovic de Mirievo with the title *Sravitel'nyi slovar' vsex jazykov i narečij, po azbučnomu porjadku raspoložennyi*, 4 vols., St Petersburg, 1790–1. Reprinted Buske, Hamburg, 1977–8. Cf. WENDLAND (1992), 2, 954f.

PANCONCELLI-CALZIA, G. (1940) *Quellenatlas zur Geschichte der Phonetik*, Hassischer Gildenverlag, Hamburg. Reprinted in KOERNER (ed.) (1994).

PANCONCELLI-CALZIA, G. (1941) *Geschichtszahlen der Phonetik. 3000 Jahre Phonetik*, Hassischer Gildenverlag, Hamburg. Reprinted in KOERNER (ed.) 1994.

PARIS, G. (1863) Préface, in *F. Diez, Introduction à l'étude des langues romanes*, traduite de l'allemand par Gaston Paris, Franck, Paris/Leipzig, i–xix.

PARIS, G. (1888) Les parlers de France, *Revue des patois gallo-romans*, 2, 161–75. Text of an 1888 lecture first printed as a separate pamphlet, then in two other periodicals before this reprint.

PASQUALI, G. (1968) *Pagine Stravaganti*, 2 vols., Sansoni, Firenze. 1st edn in 4 separate collections: *Pagine Stravaganti di un filologo*, 1933 (2nd edn *Pagine Stravaganti vecchie e nuove*, 1952), *Pagine meno stravaganti*, 1935; *Terze Pagine Stravaganti*, 1942; *Stravaganze quarte e supreme*, 1951. New edn ed. by C. F. Russo, *Pagine stravaganti di un filologo*, Le Lettere, Firenze, 1994.

PASSOW, F. (1812) *Über Zweck, Anlage und Ergänzung griechischer Wörterbücher*, Maurer, Berlin.

PASSOW, F. (1819–23) Johann Gottlob Schneider, *Handwörterbuch der griechischen Sprache*. Nach der dritten Ausgabe der grössern Griechisch–deutschen Wörterbuchs ... ausgearbeitet von Franz Passow, 2 vols., Vogel, Leipzig. 4th edn 1831, without Schneider's name; 5th edn ed. by V. C. F. Rost, F. Palm *et al.*, 4 vols., 1841–57; reprinted Wissenschaftliche Buchgesellschaft, Darmstadt, 1970.

PASSY, P. (1891) *Étude sur les changements phonétiques et leurs caractères généraux. Thèse pour le doctorat présentée à la Faculté des Lettres de Paris*, Firmin-Didot, Paris.

PASSY, P. (1899) *De la méthode directe dans l'enseignement des langues vivantes*, Colin, Paris.

PÄTSCH, G. (1967) Humboldt und die Sprachwissenschaft, in HARTKE, W., MASKOLAT, H. (eds.), *Wilhelm von Humboldt 1767–1967. Erbe – Gegenwart – Zukunft*, Niemeyer, Halle/Saale, 1967, 101–25.

PAUL, H. (1874) Zur Lautverschiebung, *Beiträge zur Geschichte der deutschen Sprache und Literatur (Paul-Braune-Beiträge)*, 1, 147–201.

PAUL, H. (1877) Die vocale der flexions- und ableitungs-silben in den ältesten germanischen dialecten, *Beiträge zur Geschichte der deutschen Sprache und Literatur (Paul-Braune-Beiträge)*, 4, 315–475.

PAUL, H. (1880) Cf. PAUL (1920).

PAUL, H. (1881) *Mittelhochdeutsche Grammatik*, Niemeyer, Halle. 2nd edn 1884; 22nd edn ed. by Hugo Moser, Ingeborg Schröbler and Siegfried Grosse, Niemeyer, Tübingen, 1982.

PAUL, H. (ed.) (1891–3) *Grundriß der germanischen Philologie*, 2 vols., Trübner, Strassburg. 2nd edn (4 vols.) 1901–9.

PAUL, H. (1894) Über die Aufgaben der wissenschaftlichen Lexicographie mit besonderer Rücksicht auf das deutsche Wörterbuch, *Sitzungsberichte der philosophisch-philologischen und der historischen Classe der Königlich-Bayrischen Akademie der Wissenschaften zu München*, 1, 53–91.

PAUL, H. (1897) *Deutsches Wörterbuch*, Niemeyer, Halle. 5th edn 1966.

PAUL, H. (1901) Methodenlehre, in PAUL, H. (ed.), *Grundriß der germanischen Philologie*, 2nd edn, Trübner, Strassburg, I, 159–247. 1st edn 1891.

PAUL, H. (1916–20) *Deutsche Grammatik*, 5 vols., Niemeyer, Halle. Reprinted Niemeyer, Tübingen, 1968.

PAUL, H. (1920) *Prinzipien der Sprachgeschichte*, 5th edn, Niemeyer, Halle/Saale; 1st edn as *Principien der Sprachgeschichte*, 1880; numerous reprints, e.g. Niemeyer, Tübingen, 1970. English translation of the 2nd edn by H. A. Strong, Swan Sonnenschein, Lowrey & Co., London, 1888. Adaptation in STRONG, LOGEMAN and WHEELER (1891).

PAULINUS A SANCTO BARTHOLOMAEO (J. P. WESSDIN) (1790) *Sidharubam seu Grammatica Samscrdamica cui accedit dissertatio historico-critica in linguam samscrdamicam vulgo samscret dictam. In qua huius linguae existentia, origo, praestantia, antiquitas, extensio, maternitas ostenditur, libri aliqui ea exarati critice recensentur, & simul aliquae antiquissimae gentilium orationes liturgicae paucis attinguntur et explicantur*, Ex typographia Sacrae Congregationis de propaganda fide, Romae. The *Dissertatio* is reprinted and translated in PAULINUS A SANCTO BARTHOLOMAEO (1977).

PAULINUS A SANCTO BARTHOLOMAEO (J. P. WESSDIN) (1798) *De antiquitate et affinitate linguae zendicae, samscrdamicae et germanicae dissertatio*, Typis seminarii, Patavii. Published in 1798 according to the title page, but in 1799 according to the colophon (cf. p. lvi).

PAULINUS A SANCTO BARTHOLOMAEO (J. P. WESSDIN) (1804) *Vyàcaranam seu locupletissima sanscrdamicae linguae institutio in usum fidei praeconum in India orientali, et virorum litteratorum in Europa adornata a p. Paulino a S. Bartholomaeo*, Typis S. Congregationis de propaganda fide, Romae.

PAULINUS A SANCTO BARTHOLOMAEO (J. P. WESSDIN) (1977) *Dissertation on the Sanskrit Language*. A Reprint of the Original Latin Text of 1790, together with an Introductory Article, a Complete English Translation, and an Index of Sources by Ludo Rocher (cf. PAULINUS A SANCTO BARTHOLOMAEO 1790) (Amsterdam Studies in the History of Linguistics, 12), Benjamins, Amsterdam/Philadelphia.

PECA CONTI, R. (1978) *Carteggio G. I. Ascoli – E. Teza* (Orientamenti Linguistici, 6), Giardini, Pisa.

PEDERSEN, H. (1916) *Et blik på sprogvidenskabens historie med særligt hensyn til det historiske studium av sprogets lyd*, Universiteitsbogtrykkeriet (J. H. Schultz A/S), København. Cf. PEDERSEN (1983).

PEDERSEN, H. (1924) *Sprogvidenskabe i det Nittende Aarhundrede. Metoder og Resultater*, Gyldendalske Boghandel, København. Cf. PEDERSEN (1962).

PEDERSEN, H. (1962) *The Discovery of Language. Linguistic Science in the Nineteenth Century.* Translated by John Webster Spargo, Indiana University Press, Bloomington. English translation of PEDERSEN 1924, first appeared with the title *Linguistic Science in the Nineteenth Century*, Harvard University Press, Cambridge MA, 1931.

PEDERSEN, H. (1983) *A Glance at the History of Linguistics with Particular Regard to the Historical Study of Phonology.* Translated from the Danish by C. C. Henriksen, Benjamins, Amsterdam/Philadelphia. English translation of PEDERSEN (1916).

PEETERS, C. (1988) 'Grammaire historique' et 'linguistique génétique'; un malentendu persistant, in JOLY (ed.) (1988), 69–72.

PENN, J. M. (1972) *Linguistic Relativity versus Innate Ideas. The Origin of the Sapir–Whorf Hypothesis in German Thought* (Janua Linguarum, Series minor, 120), Mouton, The Hague / Paris.

PERCIVAL, W. K. (1969) Nineteenth Century Origins of Twentieth Century Structuralism, *Papers from the Fifth Regional Meeting of the Chicago Linguistic Society*, 5, 416–20.

PERCIVAL, W. K. (1974a) Rask's View of Linguistic Development and Phonetic Correspondences, in HYMES (ed.) (1974), 307–14.

PERCIVAL, W. K. (1974b) Humboldt's Description of the Javanese Verb, in HYMES (ed.) (1974), 380–9.

PERCIVAL, W. K. (1987) Biological Analogy in the Study of Language Before the Advent of Comparative Grammar, in HOENIGSWALD and WIENER (eds.) (1987), 3–38.

PERKIN, H. (1983) The Pattern of Social Transformation in England, in JARAUSCH (ed.) (1983), 207–18.

PETERSEN, U. (ed.) (1992) R. K. Rask. *Von der Etymologie überhaupt. Eine Einleitung in die Sprachvergleichung* (Lingua et traditio, 11), Narr, Tübingen.

PEZZI, D. (1877) *Glottologia aria recentissima; cenni storico-critici*, Loescher, Torino. English translation, Trübner, London, 1879.

PEZZI, D. (1888) *La lingua greca antica. Breve trattazione comparativa e storica*, Loescher, Torino.

PEZZI, D. (1889) La vita scientifica di Giorgio Curtius (Approvata nell'adunanza del 27 giugno 1886), *Memorie della Reale Accademia di Torino (Scienze Morali, Storiche e Filologiche)*, Serie II, Vol. 39, 1–47.

PFEIFFER, R. (1968–76) *History of Classical Scholarship*, 2 vols., Clarendon Press, Oxford.

PHILIPS, C. H. (1940) *The East India Company 1784–1834*, Manchester University Press, Manchester.

PICARDI, E. (1973) Organismo linguistico e organismo vivente, *Lingua e Stile*, 8, 61–82.

PICARDI, E. (1977) Some Problems of Classification in Linguistics and Biology, 1800–1830, *Historiographia Linguistica*, 4, 31–57.

PICARDI, E. (1992) The Chemistry of Concepts, in NAUMANN, PLANK and HOFBAUER (eds.) (1992), 125–46.

PICTET, A. (1859–63) *Les origines indo-européennes ou les Aryas primitifs. Essai de paléontologie linguistique*, 2 vols., Joël Cherbuliez, Paris. 2nd edn, Sandoz & Fischbacker, Paris, 1877.

PLANK, F. (1987a) The Smith–Schlegel Connection in Linguistic Typology: Forgotten Fact or Fiction?, *Zeitschrift für Phonetik, Sprachwissenschaft und Kommunikationsforschung*, 40, 198–216.

PLANK, F. (1987b) What Friedrich Schlegel could have learned from Alexander ('Sanscrit') Hamilton besides Sanskrit?, *Lingua e Stile*, 22, 367–84.

PLANK, F. (1989) On Humboldt On the Dual, in CORRIGAN, R., ECKMAN, F., NOONAN, M., (eds.), *Linguistic Categorization* (Current Issues in Linguistic Theory, 61), Benjamins, Amsterdam/Philadelphia, 293–333.

PLANK, F. (1991a) Hypology, Typology: the Gabelentz Puzzle, *Folia Linguistica*, 25, 421–58.

PLANK, F. (1991b) Rasmus Rask's Dilemma, in PLANK, F. (ed.), *Paradigms. The Economy of Inflection* (Empirical Approaches to Language Typology, 9), Mouton / De Gruyter, Berlin / New York, 161–96.

PLANK, F. (1992) Language and Earth as Recycling Machines, in NAUMANN, PLANK and HOFBAUER (eds.), (1992) 125–46.

PLANK, F. (1993) Professor Pott und die Lehre der Allgemeinen Sprachwissenschaft, *Beiträge zur Geschichte der Sprachwissenschaft*, 3, 94–128.

PLANK, F. (1994) Aus der Geschichte der Abhängingkeiten: Wilhelm von Humboldt zu Mehrheitsbezeichnung und Einverleibungssystem, in ZIMMERMANN, TRABANT and MUELLER-VOLLMER (eds.) (1994), 229–55.

PLANK, F. (1996) 'Gabelentz, Hans Conon von der', in H. Stammerjohann (ed.), *Lexicon Grammaticorum*, Niemeyer, Tübingen, 319–20.

POPE, M. (1975) *The Story of Decipherment. From Egyptian Hieroglyphic to Linear B*, Thames and Hudson, London.

POPE, M. (1989) Ventris's Decipherment – First Causes, in *Problems in Decipherment* (Bibliothèque des Cahiers de l'Institut de Linguistique de Louvain, 49), Peeters, Louvain-la-Neuve, 25–37.

POPPE, E. (1992) Lag es in der Luft? – Johann Kaspar Zeuß und die Konstituierung der Keltologie, *Beiträge zur Geschichte der Sprachwissenschaft*, 2, 41–56.

PORT ROYAL (1660) *Grammaire generale et raisonnée contenant les fondemens de l'art de parler; expliquéz d'une maniere claire et naturelle; Les raisons de ce qui est commun à toutes les langues, & des principales differences qui s'y rencontrent; Et plusieurs remarques nouuelles sur la Langue Françoise*, Le Petit, Paris. Reprinted Scolar Press, Menston, 1968; Slatkine, Genève, 1980; Italian edn of the 3rd edn of 1846, ed. by R. Simone, Ubaldini, Roma, 1969, 2nd edn 1985.

PORZIG, W. (1954) *Die Gliederung des indogermanischen Sprachgebiets*, Winter, Heidelberg.

POSNER, R. (to appear) Language Studies in Oxford 1880–1914, in *History of the University of Oxford. Nineteenth Century*, 8, Clarendon Press, Oxford.

POTT, A. F. (1833–6) *Etymologische Forschungen auf dem Gebiete der Indo-Germanischen Sprachen mit besonderem Bezug auf die Lautumwandlung im Sanskrit, Griechischen, Lateinischen, Littauischen und Gothischen*, 2 vols., Meyer, Lemgo. For the 2nd edn, cf. POTT (1859–76).

POTT, A. F. (1852) Die neuere Sprachwissenschaft, *Blätter für literarische Unterhaltung*, 22, 505–17.

POTT, A. F. (1855) Max Müller und die Kennzeichen der Sprachverwandtschaft, *Zeitschrift der deutschen morgenlandischen Gesellschaft*, 9, 405–64.

POTT, A. F. (1856) *Die Ungleichheit menschlicher Rassen, hauptsächlich vom sprachwissenschaftlichen Standpunkte unter besonderer Berücksichtigung von der Grafen von Gobineau gleichnamigem Werke – mit einem Überblicke über die Sprachverhältnisse der Völker. Ein ethnologischer Versuch*, Meyer, Lemgo & Detmold.

POTT, A. F. (1859–76) *Etymologische Forschungen auf dem Gebiete der indogermanischen Sprachen, unter Berücksichtigung ihrer Hauptformen, Sanskrit; Zend-Persisch; Griechisch-Lateinisch; Littauisch-Slawisch; Germanisch und Keltisch*, 6 vols. in 10 parts (including II 2–V, 1867–73, *Wurzel-Wörterbuch der Indogermanischen Sprachen*; VI *Register*, ed. by H. E. Bindseil), 2nd edn, Meyer, Lemgo & Detmold. 2nd edn of POTT (1833–6).

POTT, A. F. (1863) Zur Geschichte und Kritik der sogenannten Allgemeinen Grammatik, *Zeitschrift für Philosophie und philosophische Kritik*, 43, 102–41, 185–245.

POTT, A. F. (1880) *Wilhelm von Humboldt und die Sprachwissenschaft. Über die Verschiedenheit des menschlichen Sprachbaues und ihren Einfluss auf die geistige Entwickelung des Menschengeschlechts, mit erläuternden Anmerkungen und Excursen, sowie als Einleitung: Wilhelm von Humboldt und die Sprachwissenschaft*, 2nd edn, 2 vols., Calvary, Berlin. Edition with long introduction and commentary of Humboldt (1836–9), I. 1st edn 1876.

POTT, A. F. (1884–90) Einleitung in die allgemeine Sprachwissenschaft, *Internationale Zeitschrift für allgemeine Sprachwissenschaft*, I, 1–68, 329–54; 2, 54–115, 209–51; 3, 110–26, 249–75; 4, 67–96; 5, 3–18. Reprinted in POTT (1974).

POTT, A. F. (1887) *Zur Litteratur der Sprachenkunde Europas* (Internationale Zeitschrift für Allgemeine Sprachwissenschaft, Suppl. 1), Barth, Leipzig. Reprinted in POTT (1974).

POTT, A. F. (1974) *Einleitung in die allgemeine Sprachwissenschaft, preceded by the same author's Zur Li<t>teratur der Sprachenkunde Europas*. Newly ed. together with a Bio-bibliographical Sketch of Pott by Paul Horn by E. F. K. Koerner, Benjamins, Amsterdam. Reprint of POTT (1884–90 and 1887).

POWELL, J. W. (1877) *Introduction to the Study of Indian Languages, with Words, Phrases, and Sentences to be Collected*, Government Printing Office, Washington. 2nd edn, with charts, 1880.

POWELL, J. W. (1891) Indian Linguistic Families of America, North of Mexico, *US Bureau of American Ethnology, 7th Annual Report* (1885–1886), 1–142.

PRETZEL, U. (1978) Der Lehrer. Aus Briefen Friedrich Zarnckes, *Beiträge zur Geschichte der deutschen Sprache und Literatur (Paul-Braune-Beiträge)*, 100, 369–86.

PRICHARD, J. C. (1831) *The Eastern Origin of the Celtic Nations Proved by a Comparison of Their Dialects with the Sanskrit, Greek, Latin and Teutonic Languages*, Sherwood, Gilbert and Piper, London.

PROSDOCIMI, A. L. (1969) Carteggio di G. I. Ascoli ad A. Mussafia, *Archivio Glottologico Italiano*, 54, 1–48.

PROST, A. (1968) *Histoire de l'enseignement en France 1800–1967*, 2nd edn, Colin, Paris.

PSICHARI, J. (1888) Quelques observations sur la phonétique des patois et leur influence sur les langues communes, *Revue des patois gallo-romans*, 2, 7–30.

PUTSCHKE, W. (1969) Zur forschungsgeschichtlichen Stellung der Junggrammatischen Schule, *Zeitschrift für Dialektologie und Linguistik*, 36, 19–48.

PUTSCHKE, W. (1984) Die Arbeiten der Junggrammatiker und ihr Beitrag zur Sprachgeschichtsforschung, in BESCH, W., REICHMANN, O., SONDEREGGER, S. (eds.), *Sprachgeschichte. Ein Handbuch zur Geschichte der deutschen Sprache und ihrer Erforschung*, 1, De Gruyter, Berlin, 331–47.

QUATTORDIO MORESCHINI, A. (ed.) (1986) *Un periodo di storia linguistica: i Neogrammatici. Atti del Convegno della Società Italiana di Glottologia (1985)*, Giardini, Pisa.

QUILIS, A., NIEDEREHE, H. J. (eds.) (1986) *The History of Linguistics in Spain* (Amsterdam Studies in the History of the Language Sciences, 34), Benjamins, Amsterdam/Philadelphia.

QUILLIEN, J. (1987) *Problématique, genèse et fondements anthropologiques de la théorie du langage de Guillaume de Humboldt. Jalons pour une nouvelle interprétation de la philosophie et de son histoire*, Thèse d'État, Lille. *Non vidi.*

QUILLIEN, J. (1990) Pour une autre scansion de l'histoire de l'herméneutique. Les principes de l'herméneutique de W. von Humboldt, in LAKS and NESCHKE (eds.) (1990), 69–117.

QUILLIEN, J. (1991) *L'anthropologie philosophique de Guillaume de Humboldt*, Presses Universitaires de Lille, Lille.

RAICICH, M. (1970–74) Momenti di politica culturale dopo l'Unità (De Sanctis e Ascoli), *Belfagor*, 25, 495–529; 29, 33–55, 250–81.

RAICICH, M. (1981) *Scuola, cultura e politica in Italia da de Sanctis a Gentile* (Saggi di varia umanità, 24), Nistri-Lischi, Pisa.

RAMAT, P. (1976) Del problema della tipologia linguistica in Wilhelm von Humboldt e d'altro ancora, in HEILMANN (ed.) (1976), 43–65.

RAMAT, P. (1985) Wilhelm von Humboldts Sprachtypologie, *Zeitschrift für Phonetik, Sprachwissenschaft und Kommunikationsforschung*, 38, 590–610.

RAMAT, P. (1986) La querelle sulle 'leggi fonetiche', in QUATTORDIO MORESCHINI (ed.) (1986), 51–61.

RAMAT, P. (1992) La comparazione tipologica, ieri, oggi (e domani?), in NEGRI and ORIOLES (eds.) (1992), 55–70.

RAMAT, P., NIEDEREHE, H. J., KOERNER, [E. F.] K. (eds.) (1986) *The History of Linguistics in Italy* (Amsterdam Studies in the History of Language Sciences, 33), Benjamins, Amsterdam/Philadelphia.

RAPP, K. M. (1836–41) *Versuch einer Physiologie der Sprache nebst historischer Entwickelung der abendländischen Idiome nach physiologischen Grundsätzen*, 4 vols., Cotta, Stuttgart und Tübingen.

RAPP, K. M. (1852–9) *Vergleichende Grammatik (Grundriß der Grammatik der indisch-europäischen Sprachstammes)*, 6 vols., Cotta, Stuttgart und Tübingen/Augsburg.

RASK, R. K. (1818) *Undersögelse om det gamle Nordiske eller Islandske Sprogs Oprindelse. Et af det Kongelige Danske Videnskabers-Selskab kronet Prisskrift*, Gyldendalske Boghandlings Forlag, Kjöbenhavn. German translation in VATER (ed.) (1822; only in part) and in PETERSEN (ed.) (1992); English translation *Investigation of the Origin of the Old Norse or Icelandic Language*, Linguistic Circle of Copenhagen, Copenhagen, 1993.

RASK, R. K. (1830) *A Grammar of the Anglo-Saxon Tongue with a Praxis. A New Edition Enlarged and Improved by the Author*, Translated from the Danish by B. Thorpe, Møller, Copenhagen.

RASK, R. K. (1932–7) *Ausgewählte Abhandlungen (Udvalgte Afhandlinger)*, herausgegeben auf Kosten des Rask-Orsted Fonds, auf Anregung von Vilhelm Thomsen, für Det danske Sprog- og Litteraturselskab, von Louis Hjelmslev, mit einer Einleitung von Holger Pedersen, 3 vols., Munksgaard, Kopenhagen.

RASK, R. K. (1941–68) *Breve fra og til Rasmus Rask*. 3 vols., Vols. I–II ed. by L. Hjelmslev, Vol. III ed. by M. Bjerrum, Munksgaard, Kopenhagen.

RAUMER, R. VON (1863) *Gesammelte sprachwissenschaftliche Schriften*, Heyder & Zimmer, Frankfurt a.M. & Erlangen.

RAUMER, R. VON (1870) *Geschichte der germanischen Philologie* (Geschichte der Wissenschaften in Deutschland. Neuere Zeit, 9), Oldenbourg, München.

READ, A. W. (1948) An account of the word 'Semantics', *Word*, 4, 78–97.

REDARD, G. (1976) Ferdinand de Saussure et Louis Havet, *Bulletin de la Société de Linguistique*, 71, 313–49.

REDARD, G. (1978a) Deux Saussure?, *Cahiers Ferdinand de Saussure*, 32, 27–41.

REDARD, G. (1978b) Louis Havet et le Mémoire, *Cahiers Ferdinand de Saussure*, 32, 103–22.

REGNAUD, P. (1888) *Origine et philosophie du langage, ou principes de linguistique indo-européenne*, Fischbacher, Paris.

REICHMANN, O. (1990) Einige Thesen zur Bedeutungerläuterung in dem von Jacob Grimm bearbeiteten Teil des *Deutschen Wörterbuches* und im *Wörterbuch der deutschen Sprache* von Daniel Sanders, in ANTONSEN (with MARCHAND and ZGUSTA) (eds.) (1990), 97–113.

REIS, M. (1978) Hermann Paul, *Beiträge zur Geschichte der deutschen Sprache und Literatur (Paul-Braune-Beiträge)*, 100, 159–204.

REISIG, C. K. (1839) *Vorlesungen über lateinische Sprachwissenschaft (abgehalten ab 1825)*, herausgegeben mit Anmerkungen von Friedrich Haase, Lehnhold, Leipzig.

REISIG, C. K. (1881–90) *Vorlesungen über lateinische Sprachwissenschaft*, 3 vols., Calvary, Berlin. First part (*Etymologie*) ed. by Hermann Hagen (1881), 2nd part (*Lateinische Semasiologie oder Bedeutungslehre*) ed. by Ferdinand Heerdegen (1890), 3rd part (*Lateinische Syntax*) ed. by J. H. Schmalz and G. Landgraf (1888).

RENAN, E. (1858) *Histoire générale et système comparé des langues sémitiques. Première partie. Histoire générale des langues sémitiques*, 2nd edn, Imprimerie Impériale, Paris.

RENAN, E. (1859) Introduction, in *De l'origine du langage par M. Jacob Grimm, traduit de l'allemand par Fernand de Wegmann*, Franck, Paris, 1–3.

RENAN, E. (1883) *De l'origine du langage*, 6th edn, Calmann Lévy, Paris. 1st edn 1848, 2nd edn 1858. Reprinted Didier Erudition, Paris, no date (but 1987).

RENSCH, K. H. (1966) Ferdinand de Saussure und Georg von der Gabelentz. Übereinstimmungen und Gemeinsamkeiten dargestellt an der langue–parole Dichotomie sowie der diachronischen und synchronischen Sprachbetrachtung, *Phonetica*, 15, 32–41.

RENSCH, K. H. (1967) Organismus – System – Struktur in der Sprachwissenschaft, *Phonetica*, 16, 71–84.

RIBBECK, O. (1879–81) *Friedrich Wilhelm Ritschl*, 2 vols., Teubner, Leipzig.

RICHERT, G. (1914) *Die Anfänge der romanischen Philologie und die deutsche Romantik*, Niemeyer, Halle/Saale.

RICHTER, E. (1977) *Kleinere Schriften zur allgemeinen und romanischen Sprachwissenschaft*. Ausgewählt, einleitet und kommentiert von Yakov Malkiel. Mit einer Bibliographie von B. M. Woodbridge, Jr. Gesamtredaktion: Wolfgang Meid (Innsbrucker Beiträge zur Sprachwissenschaft, 21), Institut für Sprachwissenschaft der Universität Innsbruck, Innsbruck.

RICKEN, U. (1978) *Grammaire et philosophie au siècle des lumières. Controverses sur l'ordre naturel et la clarté du français* (Publications de l'Université de Lille III), Université de Lille, Lille.

RICKEN, U. (1984) Linguistik und Anthropologie bei Adelung, in BAHNER (ed.) (1984), 124–34.

RICKEN, U. (ed.) (1990a) *Sprachtheorie und Weltanschauung in der europäischen Aufklärung. Zur Geschichte der Sprachtheorien des 18. Jahrhunderts und ihrer europäischen Rezeption nach der Französischen Revolution*. Ed. by Ulrich Ricken in Zusammenarbeit mit Patrice Bergheaud, Lia Formigari, Gerda Haßler, Boris A. Ol'chovikov und Jurij V. Roždestvenskij (Sprache und Gesellschaft, 21), Akademie Verlag, Berlin.

RICKEN, U. (1990b) Sprachtheoretische und weltanschauliche Rezeption der Aufklärung bei August Friedrich Pott (1802–1887), in NIEDEREHE and KOERNER (eds.) (1990), ii, 619–45.

RICKEN, U. (1990c) Wilhelm von Humboldt, Jacob Grimm und das Problem des Sprachursprungs. Zur sprachtheoretischen Rezeption der Aufklärung im 19. Jahrhundert, in DI CESARE and GENSINI (eds.) (1990), 141–57. Earlier Italian version in DI CESARE and GENSINI (eds.) (1987), 102–12.

RIES, J. (1894) *Was ist Syntax? Ein kritischer Versuch*, Elwert, Marburg. 2nd edn Taussig & Taussig, Prag, 1927.

RIES, J. (1928) *Zur Wortgruppenlehre*, Taussig & Taussig, Prag.

RIES, J. (1931) *Was ist ein Satz?*, Taussig & Taussig, Prag.

RIESE, B. (1994) Buschmann und die utoatzekischen Sprachen, in ZIMMERMANN, TRABANT and MUELLER-VOLLMER (eds.) (1994), 269–80.

RINGMACHER, M. (1996) *Organismus der Sprachidee. H. Steinthals Weg von Humboldt zu Humboldt* (Humboldt-Studien, 4), Schöningh, Paderborn.

ROBINS, R. H. (1973) The History of Language Classification, in SEBEOK, T. A. (ed.), *Current Trends in Linguistics*, 11, Mouton, The Hague / Paris, 3–41.

ROBINS, R. H. (1987a) Duponceau and Early Nineteenth Century Linguistics, in AARSLEFF, KELLY and NIEDEREHE (eds.) (1987), 435–46.

ROBINS, R. H. (1987b) The Life and Work of Sir William Jones, *Transactions of the Philological Society*, 1–23.

ROBINS, R. H. (1997) *A Short History of Linguistics*, 4th edn, Longman, London / New York. 1st edn 1967.

ROCHER, L. (1957–58) Les philologues classiques et les débuts de la grammaire comparée, *Revue de l'Université de Bruxelles*, 10, 251–86.

ROCHER, R. (1968) *Alexander Hamilton (1762–1824). A Chapter in the Early History of Sanskrit Philology* (American Oriental Series, 51), American Oriental Society, New Haven.

ROCHER, R. (1979) The Past up to the Introduction of Neogrammarian Thought: Whitney and Europe, in HOENIGSWALD (ed.) (1979), 5–22.

ROCHER, R. (1980a) Lord Monboddo, Sanskrit and Comparative Linguistics, *Journal of the American Oriental Society*, 100, 12–17.

ROCHER, R. (1980b) Nathaniel Brassey Halhed, Sir William Jones and Comparative Indo-European Linguistics, in BINGEN, COUPEZ and MAWET (eds.) (1980), 173–80.

ROCHER, R. (1983) *Orientalism, Poetry and the Millennium: The Checkered Life of Nathaniel Brassey Halhed 1751–1830*, Motilal Banarsidass, Delhi.

ROMASCHKO, S. A. (1991) Sprachwissenschaft, Ästhetik und Naturforschung der Goethe Zeit. Theorie und Empirie im Ursprung der vergleichenden Grammatik, *Historiographia Linguistica*, 18, 301–20.

RÖMER, R. (1985) *Sprachwissenschaft und Rassenideologie in Deutschland*, Fink, München.

ROSIELLO, L. (1967) *Linguistica Illuminista*, Il Mulino, Bologna.

ROSIELLO, L. (1986) Spiegazione e analogia: dai neogrammatici ai generativisti, in QUATTORDIO MORESCHINI (ed.) (1986), 23–50.

ROSIELLO, L. (1987) Tipologia sintattica delle lingue (Girard) e degli stili (du Marsais) nel pensiero linguistico dell'Illuminismo, *Lingua e Stile*, 22, 315–40.

ROSIELLO, L. (1992) Grammatica generale e comparativismo, in NEGRI and ORIOLES (eds.) (1992), 11–25.

RÖSSING-HAGER, M. (1986) Zur Stellenwert der Syntax in Jacob Grimm, in SPREU and BONDZIO (eds.) (1986), 86–104.

ROTH, H. (1988) *The Sanskrit Grammar and Manuscripts of Father Heinrich Roth, S. J. (1620–1668)*. Facsimile edition of Biblioteca Nazionale, Rome, Mss.gr. 171 and 172. With an Introduction by Arnulf Camps and Jean-Claude Muller, Brill, Leiden.

ROUSSEAU, J. (1980) Flexion et racine: trois étappes de leur constitution. J. C. Adelung, F. Schlegel, F. Bopp, in KOERNER, E. F. K. (ed.), *Progress in Linguistic Historiography. Papers from the International Conference on the History of the Language Sciences (Ottawa, 28–31 August 1978)* (Studies in the History of Linguistics, 20), Benjamins, Amsterdam/Philadelphia, 235–47.

ROUSSEAU, J. (1981) R. Rask (1787–1832) et la transcription des langues amerindiennes – une lettre inédite à J. Pickering, *Histoire Épistémologie Langage*, 3:II, 69–83.

ROUSSEAU, J. (1984) La naissance de la typologie chez P. E. Du Ponceau et A. W. Schlegel (1816–1819), in AUROUX *et al.* (eds.) (1984), 399–413.

ROUSSELOT, P.-J. abbé (1891) Les modifications phonétiques du langage etudiées dans le patois d'une famille de Cellefrouin (Charente), *Revue des patois gallo-romains*, 5, 65–208.

SAJNOVICS, J. [J.] (1770) *Demonstratio idioma Ungarorum et Lapponum idem esse*, Collegium Academicum Societatis Jesu, Tyrnavia. Reprinted, Indiana University, Bloomington, 1968.

SALMON, P. B. (1974) The Beginnings of Morphology: Linguistic Botanizing in the 18th Century, *Historiographia Linguistica*, 1, 313–39.

SALMON, P. B. (1996) Max Müller and the Origin of Language, in LAW, V., HÜLLEN, W. (eds.), *Linguists and their Diversions*, Nodus, Münster, 333–60.

SANDERSON, M. (1975) *The Universities in the Nineteenth Century*, Routledge and Kegan Paul, London and Boston.

SANTAMARIA, D. (1981) *Bernardino Biondelli e la linguistica preascoliana*, Cadmo, Roma.

SANTAMARIA, D. (1983) *Contributi di Linguistica*, Galeno, Perugia.

SANTAMARIA, D. (1986a) Orientamenti della linguistica italiana del primo Ottocento, in RAMAT, NIEDEREHE and KOERNER (eds.) (1986), 195–225.

SANTAMARIA, D. (1986b) G. I. Ascoli e la linguistica italiana del primo Ottocento, in ASCOLI (1986), 215–47.

SANTAMARIA, D. (1993) Interessi linguistici in storici ed eruditi del primo Ottocento italiano, in *Lo studio storico del mondo antico nella cultura italiana dell'Ottocento*, Edizioni Scientifiche Italiane, Napoli, 81–128.

SANTAMARIA, D. (1994) A Case Study in Italian Linguistic Historiography. Benvenuto Terracini on Graziadio Isaia Ascoli, in DE MAURO and FORMIGARI (eds.) (1994), 207–24.

SAPIR, E. (1921) *Language*, Harcourt, Brace, New York.

ŠARADZENIDZE, T. S. (1980) *Lingvističeskaja teorija I.A. Boduena de Kurtene i ee mesto v jazykoznanii XIX–XX vekov*, Nauka, Moskva. Russian translation from original Georgian version, Tbilisi 1978.

SARMIENTO, R. (ed.) (1987) *La tradition espagnole d'analyse linguistique* (Histoire Épistémologie Langage, 9:II), HEL, Paris.

SARMIENTO, R. (1990) Lorenzo Hervás y Panduro (1735–1809): Entre la tradición y la modernidad, in NIEDEREHE and KOERNER (eds.) (1990), ii, 461–82.

SAUMAISE, C. (1643) *Commentarius de lingua hellenistica*, Ex officina Elseviriorum, Lugduni Batavorum.

SAUSSURE, F. DE (1879) *Mémoire sur le système primitif des voyelles dans les langues indo-européennes*, Teubner, Leipsick. Published in 1878 with 1879 date.

SAUSSURE, F. DE (1916) *Cours de linguistique générale*, publié par Charles Bally et Albert Sechehaye avec la collaboration de Albert Riedlinger, Payot, Lausanne et Paris.

SAUSSURE, F. DE (1970) Cf. DE MAURO (1970b).

SAUSSURE, F. DE (1967–74) *Cours de linguistique générale. Edition critique par Rudolf Engler*, 4 vols., Harrassowitz, Wiesbaden.

SAUSSURE, F. DE (1979) *Saggio sul vocalismo indoeuropeo*. Edizione italiana (introduzione, traduzione e note) a cura di Giuseppe Carlo Vincenzi, Libreria Universitaria Editrice, Bologna. Italian translation of SAUSSURE (1879).

SAUSSURE, F. DE (1995) *Phonétique. Il manoscritto di Harvard Houghton Library bMS Fr266 (8)*, edizione a cura di Maria Pia Marchese (Quaderni del dipartimento di linguistica, Università di Firenze – studi 3), Unipress, Padova.

SAUTER, C. M. (1989) *Wilhelm von Humboldt und die deutsche Aufklärung* (Historische Forschungen, 39), Duncker & Humblot, Berlin.

SAVIGNY, F. K. VON (1814) *Vom Beruf unsrer Zeit für Gesetzgebung und Rechtswissenschaft*, Mohr und Zimmer, Heidelberg.

SAVIGNY, F. K. VON (1815) Ueber den Zweck diser Zeitschrift, *Zeitschrift für geschichtliche Rechtswissenschaft*, 1, 1–17.

SAVOIA, L. M. (1981) Appunti per la storia della linguistica fra '700 e '800, in *Studi di linguistica italiana per Giovanni Nencioni a cura degli allievi*, Le Monnier, Firenze, 351–420.

SAVOIA, L. M. (1986) La formazione di un modello descrittivo 'neogrammaticale' nella linguistica italiana dell'Ottocento, in QUATTORDIO MORESCHINI (ed.) (1986), 67–121.

SAYCE, A. H. (1874) *The Principles of Comparative Philology*, Trübner & Co., London. 2nd edn 1875.

SAYCE, A. H. (1880) *Introduction to the Science of Language*, 2 vols., Kegan Paul, London. French translation as *Principes de philologie comparée*, Delagrave, Paris, 1884.

SCAGLIONE, A. (1978) Introduction, in WEIL (1978), vii–xvii.

SCALIGER, I. I. (1610) Diatriba de Europaeorum linguis, in *Opuscula varia antehac non edita*, apud Hadrianum Beys, Parisiis, 119–22. A first version appears in P. Merula, *Cosmographiae generalis libri tres*, 2 vols., [Lugduni Batavorum], Ex Officina Plantiniana Raphelengii, Lugduni Batavorum / ap. Cornelium Nicolai, Amstelodami, 1605, I, 271–2 (Merula says that he reproduces a letter *Magni Scaligeri* of March 1599).

SCERBO, F. (1891) *Saggi glottologici*, Successori Le Monnier, Firenze.

SCHARF, H.-W. (1983) Das Verfahren der Sprache. Ein Nachtrag zu Chomskys Humboldt-Reklamation, in ESCHBACH and TRABANT (eds.) (1983), 204–49.

SCHARF, H.-W. (1994) *Das Verfahren der Sprache: Humboldt gegen Chomsky* (Humboldt-Studien, 1), Schöningh, Paderborn. *Non vidi*.

SCHENKER, A. M., STANKIEWICZ, E. (1980) *The Slavic Literary Languages; Formation and Development*, Yale Concilium on International and Area Studies, New Haven.

SCHERER, W. (1868) *Zur Geschichte der deutschen Sprache*, Duncker, Berlin. 2nd edn Weidmann, Berlin, 1878.

SCHERER, W. (1885) *Jacob Grimm*, Weidmann, Berlin. 1st edn as a reprint of separate articles, Reimer, Berlin, 1865; reprinted with additions, 1921. 3rd edn with introduction by L. E. Schmitt, Olms-Weidmann, Hildesheim, 1985.

SCHERER, W. (1886) *A History of German Literature*, translated from the third German edn by Mrs F. C. Conybeare, ed. by F. Max Müller, 2 vols., Clarendon Press, Oxford. Translation of SCHERER, W., *Geschichte der deutschen Litteratur*, Weidmann, Berlin, 1883.

SCHERER, W. (1893) *Kleine Schriften*, herausgegeben von Konrad Burdach und Erich Schmidt, 2 vols., Weidmann, Berlin.

SCHLANGER, J. (1971) *Les métaphores de l'organisme*, Vrin, Paris.

SCHLEGEL, A. W. (1817) *Über dramatische Kunst und Litteratur, Grundzüge einer Kultur- und Völkergeschichte Alteuropas*, 2nd edn, 3 vols., Mohr und Winter, Heidelberg. 1st edn 1809–11; critical edn by G. V. Amoretti, Bonn 1923; reprinted by E. Lohner in *Kritische Schriften und Briefe*, 6–7, Kohlhammer, 1966–7; translated into Dutch, 1810, French, 1814, English, 1815, Italian, 1817.

SCHLEGEL, A. W. (1832) *Réflexions sur l'étude des langues asiatiques adressées à Sir James Mackintosh, suivies d'une lettre à M. Horace Wayman Wilson*, Weber/Maze, Bonn/Paris. Reprinted in SCHLEGEL (1846), iii, 95–275.

SCHLEGEL, A. W. (1846) *Oeuvres écrites en français et publiées par Edouard Böcking*, 3 vols., Weidmann, Leipzig.

SCHLEGEL, A. W. (1846–7) *Sämmtliche Werke*, herausgegeben von Eduard Böcking, 12 vols., Weidmann, Leipzig.

SCHLEGEL, F. (1808) *Über die Sprache und Weisheit der Indier. Ein Beitrag zur Begründung der Alterthumskunde*, Mohr & Zimmer, Heidelberg. Re-edited

1975 in *Kritische Friedrich-Schlegel-Ausgabe,*ˑ8, 105–433; cf. STRUC-OPPENBERG (ed.) (1975). English translation in *The Aesthetic and Miscellaneous Works of Frederick von Schlegel*, ed. and translated by Ellen J. Millington, Bohn, London, 1849, 425–465; reprinted in SCHLEGEL (1977).

SCHLEGEL, F. (1977) *Über die Sprache und die* [sic] *Weisheit der Indier*. New edition with an introductory article by Sebastiano Timpanaro (translated from the Italian by J. Peter Maher), prepared by E. F. K. Koerner (Amsterdam Classics in Linguistics, 1800–1925, 1), Benjamins, Amsterdam/Philadelphia. Reprint of SCHLEGEL (1808) and of its English translation.

SCHLEICHER, A. (1848) *Sprachvergleichende Untersuchungen. I. Zur vergleichenden Sprachengeschichte*, König, Bonn.

SCHLEICHER, A. (1850) *Die Sprachen Europas in systematischer Uebersicht* (Linguistische Untersuchungen, II), König, Bonn. Reprinted with an introductory article by [E. F.] K. Koerner, Benjamins, Amsterdam/Philadelphia, 1983.

SCHLEICHER, A. (1856–7) *Handbuch der litauischen Sprache*, 2 vols., Calve'sche Verlagsbuchhandlung, Prag.

SCHLEICHER, A. (1859) Zur Morphologie der Sprache, *Mémoires de l'Académie des Sciences de St-Pétersbourg*, 1, 1–38.

SCHLEICHER, A. (1860) *Die Deutsche Sprache*, Cotta, Stuttgart. 2nd edn 1869, 5th edn 1888; reprinted Sändig, Niederwalluf, 1974.

SCHLEICHER, A. (1861–2) *Compendium der vergleichenden Grammatik der indogermanischen Sprachen. Kurzer Abriss einer Laut- und Formenlehre der indogermanischen Ursprache, des Altindischen, Alteranischen, Altgriechischen, Altitalischen, Altkeltischen, Altslawischen, Litauischen und Altdeutschen*, 2 vols., Böhlau, Weimar. 2nd edn 1866, 3rd edn 1871, 4th edn 1876, reprinted Olms, Hildesheim, 1975. Italian translation by D. Pezzi, Loescher, Torino, 1869; English translation by H. Rendall, Trübner, London, 1874–7.

SCHLEICHER, A. (1863) *Die Darwinsche Theorie und die Sprachwissenschaft. Offenes Sendschreiben an Herrn Dr Ernst Häckel*, H. Böhlau, Weimar. Reprinted in CHRISTMANN (ed.) (1977), 85–105. English translation by A. V. M. Bikkers, Camden Hotten, London, 1869; reprinted in KOERNER (1983). Also translated into French, Paris, 1868, and Italian, in BOLELLI (1965b), 113–36.

SCHLEICHER, A. (1865a) Die Unterscheidung von Nomen und Verbum in der lautlichen Form, *Abhandlungen der philologisch-historischen Classe der Königlichen Sächsischen Gesellschaft der Wissenschaften*, 4 (Nr iii), 495–587.

SCHLEICHER, A. (1865b) *Über die Bedeutung der Sprache für die Naturgeschichte des Menschen*, Böhlau, Weimar.

SCHLEICHER, A. (1865c) Vorwort, in SCHMIDT, J., *Die Wurzel ak im Indogermanischen*, Böhlau, Weimar, iii–x.

SCHLEICHER, A. (1868) Eine fabel in indogermanischer ursprache, *Beiträge zur vergleichenden Sprachforschung*, 5, 206–8.

SCHLEICHER, A. (ed.) (1869a) *Indogermanische Chrestomathie. Schriftproben und lesestücke mit erklärenden glossaren zu August Schleichers compendium der vergleichenden grammatik der indogermanischen sprachen*. Bearbeitet von H. Ebel, A. Leskien, Johannes Schmidt und August Schleicher, Nebst zusätzen und berichtigungen zur zweiten auflage des compendiums herauß gegeben von August Schleicher, Böhlau, Weimar.

SCHLEICHER, A. (1869b) *Die deutsche Sprache*, 2nd edn, Cotta, Stuttgart. 1st edn 1860.

SCHLEICHER, A. (1871) Third edn of SCHLEICHER (1861–2) ed. by A. Leskien and J. Schmidt, Böhlau, Weimar.

SCHLEICHER, A. (1983) Cf. KOERNER (1983) for the reprint of the English translation of SCHLEICHER (1863).

SCHLEIERMACHER, F. (1977) *Hermeneutics: the Handwritten Manuscripts by Friedrich Schleiermacher*. Ed. by Heinz Kimmerle. Translated by James Duke and Jack Forstman (American Academy of Religion Texts and Translation Series, 1), Scholars Press, Missoula, Montana.

SCHLERATH, B. (1986) Eine frühe Kontroverse um die Natur des Ablauts, in ETTER, A. (ed.), *o-o-pe-ro-si. Festschrift für Ernst Risch zum 75 Geburtstag*, De Gruyter, Berlin / New York, 3–19.

SCHLIEBEN-LANGE, B. *et al.* (eds.) (1989–94) *Europäische Sprachwissenschaft um 1800. Methodologische und historiographische Beiträge zum Umkreis der 'idéologie'*, 4 vols., Nodus, Münster.

SCHLIEBEN-LANGE, B., WEYDT, H. (1988) August Ferdinand Bernhardi (1770–1820), *Histoire Épistémologie Langage*, 10:I, 81–100.

SCHMIDT, H. (1986) *Die lebendige Sprache. Zur Entstehung des Organismuskonzepts* (Linguistische Studien des Zentralinstitut für Sprachwissenschaft, A 151), Akademie der Wissenschaften der DDR, Berlin.

SCHMIDT, H. (1989) Metapherngebrauch in deutschen sprachwissenschaftlichen Texten des 19. Jahrhunderts, in SCHLIEBEN-LANGE *et al.* (eds.) (1989–94), i, 203–27.

SCHMIDT, H. (1992) Sprachauffassung und Lebensmetaphorik im Umkreis von Friedrich Schlegel, Jacob Grimm und Alexander von Humboldt. Eine Kontaktzone von Naturphilosophie, Geowissenschaften und Linguistik, in NAUMANN, PLANK and HOFBAUER (eds.) (1992), 1–27.

SCHMIDT, J. (1869) Nachruf für August Schleicher, *Zeitschrift für vergleichende Sprachforschung*, 18, 315–20. Also in *Beiträge zur vergleichende Sprachforschung* 6 (1870), 251–6.

SCHMIDT, J. (1872) *Die Verwantschaftverhältnisse der indogermanischen Sprachen*, Böhlau, Weimar.

SCHMIDT, J. (1887) Schleichers auffassung der lautgesetze, *Zeitschrift für vergleichende Sprachforschung*, 28, 303–12.

SCHMIDT, J. (1890) Schleicher, August, in *Allgemeine deutsche Biographie*, 31, Duncker & Humblot, Berlin, 402–15. Reprinted in SEBEOK (ed.) (1966), i, 374–95.

SCHMIDT, S. J. (1976) German Philosophy of Language in the Late 19th Century, in PARRET, H. (ed.), *History of Linguistic Thought and Contemporary Linguistics*, De Gruyter, Berlin / New York, 658–84.

SCHMITTER, P. (1977) Zeichentheoretische Erörterungen bei Wilhelm von Humboldt. Vorstudien zum Problem der Intergrierbarkeit von divergierenden Bedeutungstheorien, *Sprachwissenschaft*, 2, 151–80. Reprinted in SCHMITTER (1987b), 43–78.

SCHMITTER, P. (1982) *Untersuchungen zur Historiographie der Linguistik. Struktur – Methodik – theoretische Fundierung* (Tübinger Beiträge zur Linguistik, 181), Narr, Tübingen.

SCHMITTER, P. (ed.) (1987a) *Geschichte der Sprachtheorie. I. Zur Theorie und Methode der Geschichtsschreibung der Linguistik*, Narr, Tübingen.

SCHMITTER, P. (1987b) *Das sprachliche Zeichen. Studien zur Zeichen- und Bedeutungstheorie in der griechischen Antike sowie im 19. und 20. Jahrhundert*, Institut für Allgemeine Sprachwissenschaft der Westfälischen Wilhelms-Universität, Münster.

SCHMITTER, P. (ed.) (1991a) *Multum non multa? Studien zur 'Einheit der Reflexion' im Werk Wilhelm von Humboldts. Mit der Edition zweier bisher unveröffentlicher Texte aus Humboldts baskischen Arbeitsbücher* (Studium Sprachwissenschaft, Beiheft 14), Nodus, Münster.

SCHMITTER, P. (1991b) Einheit und Differenz im Werk Wilhelm von Humboldts. Eine Vorbemerkung, in SCHMITTER (ed.) (1991a), 7–28.

SCHMITTER, P. (1992a) 'Machine' vs. 'Organismus'. Einige Überlegungen zur Geistes- und Sprachwissenschaftsgeschichte im 18. und 19. Jahrhundert, in AHLQVIST (ed.) (1992), 291–307.

SCHMITTER, P. (1992b) Zur Wissenschaftskonzeption Georg Forsters und dessen biographischen Bezügen zu den Brüdern Humboldt. Eine Vorstudie zum Verhältnis von allgemeiner Naturgeschichte, physischer Weltbeschreibung und allgemeiner Sprachkunde, in NAUMANN, PLANK, and HOFBAUER (eds.) (1992), 91–124.

SCHMITTHENNER, F. (1826) *Ursprachlehre. Entwurf zu einem System der Grammatik mit besonderer Rücksicht auf die Sprachen des indisch-teutschen Stammes: das sanscrit, das persische, die pelasgischen, slavischen, und teutschen Sprachen*, Hermann, Frankfurt a.M. Reprint ed. by H. E. Brekle (Grammatica Universalis, 2), Frommann-Holzboog, Stuttgart-Bad Cannstatt, 1976.

SCHMITZ, H. W. (ed.) (1985) *Significs and Language. The Articulate Form of our Expressive and Interpretative Resources, by V. Welby*. Ed. and introduced by H. Walter Schmitz (Foundations of Semiotics, 5), Benjamins, Amsterdam/Philadelphia.

SCHMITZ, H. W. (ed.) (1990) *Essays on Significs. Papers Presented on the Occasion of the 150th Anniversary of the Birth of Victoria Lady Welby (1837–1913)*, Benjamins, Amsterdam/Philadelphia.

SCHNEIDER, G. (1973) *Zum Begriff des Lautgesetzes in der Sprachwissenschaft seit den Junggrammatikern* (Tübinger Beiträge zur Linguistik, 46), Narr, Tübingen.

SCHOTT, W. (1849) *Über das Alta'ische oder Finnisch-Tatarische Sprachengeschlecht*, Reimer, Berlin.

SCHRADER, O. (1890) *Sprachvergleichung und Urgeschichte. Linguistisch-historische Beiträge zur Erforschung des indogermanischen Altertums*, 2nd edn, Costenoble, Jena. 1st edn 1883, 3rd edn 1906–07. English translation, London 1890.

SCHRADER, O. (1901) *Reallexicon der indogermanischen Altertumskunde. Grundzüge einer Kultur und Völkergeschichte Alteuropas*, Trübner, Strassburg. 2nd edn 1917–23.

SCHREMPP, G. (1983) The Re-education of Friedrich Max Müller: Intellectual Appropriation and Epistemological Antinomy in Mid-Victorian Evolutionary Thought, *Man*, 18, 90–110.

SCHUCHARDT, H. (1866–68) *Der Vokalismus des Vulgärlateins*, 3 vols., Teubner, Leipzig.

SCHUCHARDT, H. (1885) *Ueber die Lautgesetze – Gegen die Junggrammatiker*, Oppenheim, Berlin. Reprinted and translated into English in VENNEMANN and WILBUR (1972); reprinted in WILBUR (ed.) (1977).

SCHUCHARDT, H. (1905) Sachen und Wörter, *Zeitschrift für romanische Philologie*, 29, 620–2.

SCHUCHARDT, H. (1912) Sachen und Wörter, *Anthropos*, 7, 827–39.

SCHUCHARDT, H. (1922) *Hugo Schuchardt-Brevier. Ein Vademekum der allgemeinen Sprachwissenschaft*. Als Festgabe zum 80. Geburtstag des Meisters zusammengestellt und eingeleitet von Leo Spitzer, Niemeyer, Halle (Saale). 2nd edn 1928; reprinted 1976.

SCHUCHARDT, H. (1979) *The Ethnography of Variation. Selected Writings on Pidgins and Creoles*, ed. and translated by T. L. Markey, Introduction by D. Bickerton (Linguistica extranea. Studia, 3), Karoma, Ann Arbor.

SCHUCHARDT, H. (1980) *Pidgin and Creole Languages: Selected Essays*, ed. and translated by Glenn G. Gilbert, Cambridge University Press, Cambridge.

SCHWAB, R. (1950) *La renaissance orientale*, Payot, Paris. English translation, *The Oriental Renaissance. Europe's Rediscovery of India and the East 1680–1880*, Columbia University Press, New York, 1984.

SEBEOK, T. A. (ed.) (1966) *Portraits of Linguists. A Biographical Source Book for the History of Western Linguistics, 1746–1963*, 2 vols., Indiana University Press, Bloomington and London.

SEBEOK, T. A. (ed.) (1975) *Current Trends in Linguistics, 13. Historiography of Linguistics*, 2 vols., Mouton, The Hague / Paris.

SEIDEL, S. (ed.) (1962) *Der Briefwechsel zwischen Friedrich Schiller und Wilhelm von Humboldt*, 2 vols., Aufbau-Verlag, Berlin.

SGALL, P. (1971) On the notion 'Type of Language', *Travaux linguistiques de Prague*, 4, 75–87.

SHEVOROSHKIN, V. V., MARKEY, T. L. (eds.) (1986) *Typology, Relationship and Time*, Karoma, Ann Arbor.

SIEVERS, E. (1876) *Grundzüge der Lautphysiologie zur Einführung in das Studium der Lautlehre der indogermanischen Sprachen* (Bibliothek indogermanischer Grammatiken, 1), Breitkopf und Härtel, Leipzig. 2nd edn with the title *Grundzüge der Phonetik*, 1881; 5th edn 1901.

SIEVERS, E. (1882) *Angelsächsische Grammatik*, Niemeyer, Halle. 3rd edn 1898.

SILVERSTEIN, M. (1971) Whitney on Language, in WHITNEY (1971), x–xxiii.

SILVESTRE DE SACY, A. I. (1799) *Principes de grammaire générale mis à la portée des enfans et propres à servir d'introduction à l'étude de toutes les langues*, Imprimerie de A. A. Lottin et chez J. J. Fuchs, Paris. 2nd edn 1803, 7th edn 1840, 8th edn 1852; reprint ed. by H. E. Brekle and B. Asbach-Schnitker, Frommann-Holzboog, Stuttgart-Bad Cannstatt, 1975. English translation Andover, New York, 1834; German translation, cf. VATER (ed.) (1804).

S[ILVESTRE DE] S[ACY], A. I. (1808) Review of Recherches critiques et historiques sur la langue et la littérature de l'Aegypte par Et. Quatremère, *Magasin encyclopédique ou journal des sciences, des lettres et des arts*, 4, 241–82.

SILVESTRI, D. (1977–82) *La teoria del sostrato. Metodi e miraggi* (Biblioteca della Parola del Passato, 12), 3 vols., Macchiaroli, Napoli.

SILVESTRI, D. (1982) La teoria ascoliana del sostrato e la sua rilevanza metodologica, *Annali dell'Istituto Orientale di Napoli, Sez. linguistica*, 4, 15–33.

SILVESTRI, D. (1986) Epilegomena a Graziadio Isaia Ascoli Sostratista, in QUATTORDIO MORESCHINI (ed.) (1986), 131–45.

SIMMONS, J. S. G. (1980) Slavonic Studies at Oxford, 1844–1909, *Oxford Slavonic Papers*, 13, 1–27.

SIMONE, R. (1997) The Early Modern Period, in LEPSCHY (ed.) (1994–), iii, 149–236.

SKÁLA, E. (1961) Zur Entwicklung der deutschen grammatischen Terminologie, *Zeitschrift für Phonetik, Sprachwissenschaft und Kommunikationsforschung*, 14, 214–30.

SMITH, A. (1761) Considerations Concerning the First Formation of Languages, and the Different Genius of Original and Compounded Languages, in *The Philological Miscellany (London)*, I, 440–79. Reprinted as an appendix to the 3rd edn (1767) and later editions of the *Theory of Moral Sentiments*, e.g. in the 6th edn, Strahan or Cadell, London; Creech or Bell, Edinburgh, 1790, 2 vols., 2, 401–62. Reprint ed. by G. Narr, Narr, Tübingen. French translations 1784, 1796, 1809; 1798 reprinted in 1830, 1860 and in *Varia linguistica*, ed. by C. Porset, Ducros, Paris, 1970, 305–44. Cf. NOORDEGRAAF (1977).

SMITH, M. D. (1983) Peter Stephen Du Ponceau and his Study of Languages, a Historical Account, *Proceedings of the American Philosophical Society*, 127, 143–79.

SOMMARIO (1958) *Sommario di statistiche storiche italiane*, Istituto Centrale di Statistica, Roma.

SPITZER, L. (ed.) (1922) Cf. SCHUCHARDT (1922).

SPITZER, L. (ed.) (1929–30) *Meisterwerke der romanischen Sprachwissenschaft*, 2 vols., Max Hueber, München.

SPREU, A., BONDZIO, W. (eds.) (1986) *Sprache, Mensch und Gesellschaft – Werk und Wirkungen von Wilhelm von Humboldt und Jacob und Wilhelm Grimm in Vergangenheit und Gegenwart* (Humboldt-Grimm Konferenz, Berlin 22–25 Oktober 1985), Humboldt-Universität, Sektion Germanistik, Berlin.

STAAL, J. F. (ed.) (1972) *A Reader on the Sanskrit Grammarians*, Massachusetts Institute of Technology, Cambridge, MA.

STAËL (1810) Cf. DE STAËL.

STAM, J. H. (1976) *Inquiries into the Origin of Language. The Fate of a Question* (Studies in Language), Harper & Row, New York.

STANKIEWICZ, E. (ed.) (1972) Cf. BAUDOUIN DE COURTENAY (1972).

STANKIEWICZ, E. (1974) The Dithyramb to the Verb in 18th and 19th Century Linguistics, in HYMES (ed.) (1974), 157–90.

STANKIEWICZ, E. (1976) *Baudouin de Courtenay and the Foundations of Structural Linguistics*, De Ridder, Lisse. Revised version of the Introduction to BAUDOUIN DE CORTENAY (1972).

STEHR, A. (1957) *Die Anfänge der Finnisch-Ugrischen Sprachvergleichung*, 1669–1771, Unpublished Dissertation, Göttingen.

STEINTHAL, H. (1848) *Die Sprachwissenschaft Wilhelm von Humboldt's und die Hegel'sche Philosophie*, Dümmler, Berlin. Reprinted Olms, Hildesheim / New York, 1971.

STEINTHAL, H. (1850) *Die Classification der Sprachen dargestellt als die Entwickelung der Sprachidee*, Dümmler, Berlin. Cf. STEINTHAL (1860b).

STEINTHAL, H. (1855) *Grammatik, Logik und Psychologie. Ihre Principien und ihr Verhältniss zu einander*, Dümmler, Berlin.

STEINTHAL, H. (1858) *Der Ursprung der Sprache im Zusammenhange mit den letzen Fragen alles Wissens. Eine Darstellung, Kritik und Fortentwickelung der vorzüglichsten Ansichten*, 2nd edn, Dümmler, Berlin. 1st edn 1851 (. . . *Eine Darstellung der Ansichten Wilhelm von Humboldts, verglichen mit denen Herders und Hamanns*), 3rd edn 1877, 4th edn 1888.

STEINTHAL, H. (1860a) Assimilation und Attraction, psychologisch beleuchtet (Auf Anlaß von: Jacob Grimm, Ueber einige Fälle der Attraction. Aus den Abh. d. Akad. d. Wissensch. zu Berlin 1858), *Zeitschrift für Völkerpsychologie und Sprachwissenschaft*, 1, 93–179.

STEINTHAL, H. (1860b) *Charakteristik der hauptsächlichsten Typen des Sprachbaues*, Dümmler, Berlin. 2nd edn of STEINTHAL (1850).

STEINTHAL, H. (1867) *Die Mande-Neger-Sprachen psychologisch und phonetisch betrachtet*, Dümmler, Berlin.

STEINTHAL, H. (1881) *Einleitung in die Psychologie und Sprachwissenschaft (Abriß der Sprachwissenschaft. Erster Teil: Die Sprache im allgemeinen)*, 2nd edn, Dümmler, Berlin. 1st edn 1871.

STEINTHAL, H. (1890–91) *Geschichte der Sprachwissenschaft bei den Griechen und Römern mit besonderer Rücksicht auf die Logik*, 2nd edn, 2 vols., Dümmler, Berlin. 1st edn 1863. Reprinted Dümmler, Bonn, 1961.

STEINTHAL, H. (1970) *Kleine sprachtheoretische Schriften*. Neu zusammengestellt und mit einer Einleitung versehen von Waltraud Bumann, Olms, Hildesheim / New York.

STERN, G. (1932) *Meaning and Change of Meaning, with Special Reference to the English Language* (Göteborgs Högskolas Årsskrift, XXXVIII), Elanders Boktryckeri Aktiebolag, Göteborg. Reprinted Indiana University Press, Bloomington and London, 1968.

STERNEMANN, R. (1984a) *Franz Bopp und die vergleichende indoeuropäische Sprachwissenschaft* (Innsbrucker Beiträge zur Sprachwissenschaft. Vorträge und Kleinere Schriften, 33), Institut für Sprachwissenschaft, Innsbruck.

STERNEMANN, R. (1984b) Franz Bopps Beitrag zur Entwicklung der vergleichenden Sprachwissenschaft, *Zeitschrift für Germanistik*, 5, 144–58.

STETTER, CH. (1990) Wilhelm von Humboldt und das Problem der Schrift, in DE MAURO and FORMIGARI (eds.) (1990), 181–97.

STIPA, G. J. (1990) *Finnisch-ugrische Sprachforschung von der Renaissance bis zum Neupositivismus* (Mémoires de la société finno-ougrienne, 206), Suomalais-ugrilainen Seura, Helsinki.

STOCKING, G. W., JR (1974) The Boas Plan for the Study of American Indian Languages, in HYMES (ed.) (1974), 454–84.

STOCKING, G. W., JR (1987) *Victorian Anthropology*, The Free Press / Collier Macmillan, New York / London.

STREITBERG, W. (1896) *Urgermanische Grammatik*, Winter, Heidelberg.

STREITBERG, W. (1897) Schleichers Auffassung von der Stellung der Sprachwissenschaft, *Indogermanische Forschungen*, 7, 360–72.

STREITBERG, W. (ed.) (1916–29) *Geschichte der indogermanischen Sprachwissenschaft seit ihrer Begründung durch Franz Bopp. II. Die Erforschung der indogermanischen Sprachen*, 4 vols., Trübner / De Gruyter, Straßburg / Berlin and New York.

STREITBERG, W. (1919) Karl Brugmann, *Indogermanisches Jahrbuch*, 7, 143–8. Reprinted in SEBEOK (ed.) (1966), i, 565–80.

STROHBACH, M. (1984) *Johann Christoph Adelung. Ein Beitrag zu seinem germanistischen Schaffen mit einer Bibliographie seines Gesamtwerkes*, De Gruyter, Berlin / New York.

STRONG, H. A., LOGEMAN, W. S., WHEELER, B. I. (1891) *Introduction to the Study of the History of Language*, Longmans, Green & Co., London. Adaptation of PAUL ([1880] 1920). Reprint with a preface by W. K. Percival, AMS Press, New York, 1973.

STRUC-OPPENBERG, U. (1965) Cf. OPPENBERG (1965).

STRUC-OPPENBERG, U. (ed.) (1975) Über die Sprache und Weisheit der Indier, in BEHLER, E., STRUC-OPPENBERG, U. (eds.), *Kritische Friedrich-Schlegel-Ausgabe*, 8, Schoningh/Thomas, München, Paderborn, Wien/Zürich, cxxxvii–ccxiii.

SVEDELIUS, C. (1897) *L'analyse du langage appliquée à la langue française*, Almqvist & Wiksell, Uppsala.

SWEET, H. (1875–6) Words, Logic and Grammar, *Transactions of the Philological Society*, 1875–6, 470–503. Reprinted in SWEET (1913), 1–33.

SWEET, H. (1877) *A Handbook of Phonetics Including a Popular Exposition of the Principles of Spelling Reform* (Clarendon Press Series), Clarendon Press, Oxford.

SWEET, H. (1882–4) Report on General Philology, *Transactions of the Philological Society*, 1882–4, 105–15. Reprinted in SWEET (1913), 153–67.

SWEET, H. (1888) *A History of English Sounds from the Earliest Period with Full Word-lists*, Clarendon Press, Oxford.

SWEET, H. (1892–8) *A New English Grammar Logical and Historical*, 2 vols., Clarendon Press, Oxford.

SWEET, H. (1899) *The Practical Study of Language. A Guide for Teachers and Learners*, Dent & Sons, London. Reprinted Oxford University Press, London, 1964.

SWEET, H. (1910) Grimm, Jacob Ludwig Carl, in *Encyclopaedia Britannica*, 11th edn, The Encyclopaedia Britannica Company, New York, XI, 600–2.

SWEET, H. (1913) *Collected Papers*. Arranged by H. C. Wild, Clarendon Press, Oxford.

SWEET, H. (1971) Cf. HENDERSON (ed.) (1971).

SWEET, P. R. (1978–80) *Wilhelm von Humboldt: A Biography*, 2 vols., Ohio University Press, Columbus, Ohio.

SWEET, H. (1988) Wilhelm von Humboldt, Fichte, and the *idéologues* (1794–1805). A Re-examination, *Historiographia Linguistica*, 15, 349–75.

SWIGGERS, P. (1989) Linguistique générale et linguistique romane chez Hugo Schuchardt, in KREMER, D. (ed.), *Actes du XVIIIe Congrès International de Linguistique et de Philologie Romanes*, 7, Niemeyer, Tübingen, 80–91.

SWIGGERS, P. (1990) Comparatismo e grammatica comparata, tipologia linguistica e forma grammaticale, in DE MAURO and FORMIGARI (eds.) (1990), 281–99.

SWIGGERS, P. (1992) Peter Stephen Du Ponceau et la philologie définie comme science comparative des langues, *Cahiers de l'Institut de linguistique de Louvain*, 18 (3–4), 5–16.

SWIGGERS, P. (1993) L'étude comparative des langues vers 1830. Humboldt, Du Ponceau, Klaproth et le baron de Mérian, in DROIXHE and GRELL (eds.) (1993), 275–95.

SWIGGERS, P. (1994) Réfraction et dépassement de l'Idéologie aux Etats-Unis: le cas de Peter S. Du Ponceau, in SCHLIEBEN-LANGE *et al.* (eds.), 4, 245–65.

SWIGGERS, P. (1996) A Note on the History of the Term Linguistics With a Letter from Peter Stephen Du Ponceau to Joseph von Hammer-Purgstall, *Beiträge zur Geschichte der Sprachwissenschaft*, 6, 1–17.

SØRENSEN, K. (1989) The Teaching of English in Denmark and Otto Jespersen, in JUUL and NIELSEN (eds.) (1989), 29–41.

SZEMERÉNYI, O. (1980) About Unrewriting the History of Linguistics, in BRETTSCHNEIDER and LEHMANN (eds.) (1980), 151–62. Reprinted in SZEMERÉNYI (1987–91), i, 355–66.

SZEMERÉNYI, O. (1987–91) *Scripta Minora. Selected Essays in Indo-European, Greek and Latin.* ed. by P. Considine and J. T. Hooker (Innsbrucker Beiträge zur Sprachwissenschaft), 4 vols., Institut für Sprachwissenschaft der Universität Innsbruck, Innsbruck.

TAGLIAVINI, C. (1963) *Introduzione alla glottologia*, 5th edn, 2 vols., Pàtron, Bologna.

TAGLIAVINI, C. (1968) *Panorama di storia della linguistica*, Pàtron, Bologna.

TELEGDI, Z. (1966) Zur Geschichte der Sprachwissenschaft ('Historische Grammatik'), *Acta Linguistica Hungarica*, 16, 225–37.

TELEGDI, Z. (1970) Humboldt als Begründer des Sprachtypologie, in DESZÖ, L., HAJDU, P. (eds.), *Theoretical Problems of Typology and the Northern Eurasian Linguistics*, Grüner / Akadémiai Kiadó, Amsterdam/Budapest, 25–34.

TERRACINI, B. (1949) *Guida allo studio della linguistica storica. 1. Profilo storico-critico* (Studi e guide di filologia e linguistica, 1), Edizioni dell'Ateneo, Roma.

THIÉBAULT, D. (1802) *Grammaire philosophique, ou la métaphysique, la logique et la grammaire réunies en un seul corps de doctrine*, 2 vols., Courcier, Paris. Reprinted Frommann-Holzboog, Stuttgart–Bad Cannstatt, 1977.

THOMSEN, V. (1902) *Sprogvidenskabens historie: en kortfattet fremstilling af dens hovedpunkter*, Gad, København. Cf. THOMSEN (1927).

THOMSEN, V. (1927) *Geschichte der Sprachwissenschaft bis zum Ausgang des 19. Jahrhunderts. Kurzgefasste Darstellung der Hauptpunkte.* Translated by H. Pollack, Niemeyer, Halle (Saale). German translation of THOMSEN (1902).

THUMB, A., MARBE, K. (1901) *Experimentelle Untersuchungen über die psychologischen Grundlagen der sprachlichen Analogiebildungen*, Engelmann, Leipzig. Reprinted with an introduction by David J. Murray, Benjamins, Amsterdam, 1978.

TIKTIN, H. (1891–93) *Gramatica romînă pentru învătămîntul secundar. Teorie şi practică*, 2 vols., Librariei Şcoalelor Fraţii Şaraga, Iaşi. 2nd edn 1895, 3rd edn 1945.

TIMPANARO, S. (1959) Graziadio Isaia Ascoli. Note letterario-artistiche minori durante il viaggio nella Venezia, nella Lombardia, nel Piemonte, nella Liguria, nel Parmigiano, Modenese e Pontificio. Maggio-Giugno 1852, *Annali della Scuola Normale Superiore di Pisa*, 28, 151–91.

TIMPANARO, S. (1969) *Classicismo e illuminismo nell'Ottocento italiano*, 2nd edn, Nistri-Lischi, Pisa. 1st edn 1965.

TIMPANARO, S. (1972a) Friedrich Schlegel e gli inizi della linguistica indoeuropea in Germania, *Critica Storica*, 9, 72–105. Translated in TIMPANARO (1977).

TIMPANARO, S. (1972b) Graziadio Ascoli, *Belfagor*, 27, 149–76.

TIMPANARO, S. (1972c) Il primo cinquantennio della 'Rivista di Filologia e d'Istruzione classica', *Rivista di Filologia e di Istruzione Classica*, 100, 387–441.

TIMPANARO, S. (1973) Il contrasto tra i fratelli Schlegel e Franz Bopp sulla struttura e la genesi delle lingue indoeuropee, *Critica Storica*, 10, 553–90.

TIMPANARO, S. (1977) Friedrich Schlegel and the Beginnings of Indo-European Linguistics in Germany, in SCHLEGEL, F. (1977), xi–lvii. English translation of TIMPANARO (1972a).

TIMPANARO, S. (1978) *La filologia di Giacomo Leopardi*, 2nd edn, Laterza, Roma-Bari.

TIMPANARO, S. (1979) Giacomo Lignana e i rapporti tra filologia, filosofia, linguistica e darwinismo nell'Italia del Secondo Ottocento, *Critica Storica*, 16, 406–503.

TIMPANARO, S. (1980a) *Aspetti e figure della cultura ottocentesca*, Nitri-Lischi, Pisa.

TIMPANARO, S. (1980b) Il Carteggio Rajna-Salvioni e gli epigoni di Graziadio Ascoli, *Belfagor*, 35, 45–67.

TIMPANARO, S. (1981) *La genesi del metodo del Lachmann*, 2nd edn, Liviana Editrice, Padova. 1st edn Firenze 1963. German translation, Buske, Hamburg, 1971.

TIMPANARO, S. (1992) *La 'fobia romana' e altri scritti su Freud e Meringer*, ETS Editrice, Pisa.

TONFONI, G. (1988) Problemi di teoria linguistica nell'opera di Hervás y Panduro, *Lingua e Stile*, 23, 365–81.

TONNELAT, E. (1912) *Les frères Grimm – Leur oeuvre de jeunesse*, Colin, Paris.

TOOKE, J. H. (1798–1805) *ΕΠΕΑ ΠΤΕΡΟΕΝΤΑ*, or The Diversions of Purley, 2nd edn, 2 vols., printed for the author, London. 1st edn of Vol. 1, 1786; later edns ed. by R. Taylor until 1860.

TOVAR, A. (1986) *El lingüista español Lorenzo Hervás. Estudio y selección de obras básicas (Edición al cuidado de Jesús Bustamante)*, Sociedad General Española de Librería, Alcobendas (Madrid).

TPS (1978) The Neogrammarians. ('Transactions of the Philological Society'. Commemorative Volume), Blackwell, Oxford.

TRABANT, J. (ed.) (1981) *Logos Semantikos. Studia linguistica in honorem Eugenio Coseriu 1921–1981*, 1, De Gruyter / Gredos, Berlin / New York, Madrid.

TRABANT, J. (1983) Ideelle Bezeichnung. Steinthals Humboldt-Kritik, in ESCHBACH and TRABANT (eds.) (1983), 251–76.

TRABANT, J. (1985a) Humboldt zum Ursprung der Sprache. Ein Nachtrag zum Problem des Sprachursprungs in der Geschichte der Akademie, *Zeitschrift für Phonetik, Sprachwissenschaft und Kommunikationsforschung*, 38, 576–89.

TRABANT, J. (1985b) Cf. HUMBOLDT (1985).

TRABANT, J. (1986) *Apeliotes oder Der Sinn der Sprache. Wilhelm von Humboldts Sprach-Bild* (Supplemente, 8), Fink, München. French translation, *Humboldt ou le sens du langage*, Mardaga, Paris, 1992.

TRABANT, J. (1990a) Le concept intérieur de la linguistique, in DE MAURO and FORMIGARI (eds.) (1990), 135–56.

TRABANT, J. (1990b) *Traditionen Humboldts*, Suhrkamp, Frankfurt a.M.

TRABANT, J. (1994) Ein weites Feld: 'Les langues du nouveau continent', in ZIMMERMANN, TRABANT and MUELLER-VOLLMER (eds.) (1994), 11–25.

TRENCH, R. C. (1857) *On Some Deficiencies in Our English Dictionaries. Being the Substance of Two Papers Read before the Philological Society Nov. 5, and Nov. 19, 1857*, J.W. Parker & Son, London. 2nd edn 1860.

TROMBETTI, A. (1905) *L'unità d'origine del linguaggio*, Treves, Bologna.

TURGOT, A.-R.-J., baron de l'Aulne (1913–23) *Oeuvres de Turgot et documents le concernant, avec biographie et notes par Gustave Scheller*, F. Alcan, Paris.

TURNER, R. S. (1975) University Reformers and Professional Scholarship in Germany, 1760–1806, in STONE, L. (ed.), *The University in Society*, 2, Princeton University Press, Princeton, 495–531.

VAL-ALVARO, J. F. (1987) La notion de langue dans le *Catálogo de las lenguas*, *Histoire Épistémologie Langage*, 9:II, 99–115.

VALLINI, C. (1969) Problemi di metodo in Ferdinand de Saussure indoeuropeista, *Studi e Saggi Linguistici*, 9, 1–85.

VALLINI, C. (1972) *Linee generali del problema dell'analogia dal periodo schleicheriano a F. de Saussure* (Biblioteca dell'Italia Dialettale e di Studi e Saggi Linguistici, 5), Pacini, Pisa.

VALLINI, C. (1978) Le point de vue du grammairien ou la place de l'étymologie dans l'œuvre de F. de Saussure indo-européaniste, *Cahiers Ferdinand de Saussure*, 32, 43–57.

VALLINI, C. (1983) Etimologia come φαντασία: il paradiso indoeuropeo di Adolphe Pictet, *Fabrica*, 1, 221–44.

VALLINI, C. (1987) Speculazioni e modelli nell'etimologia della grammatica, *Annali dell'Istituto Orientale di Napoli, Sez. linguistica*, 9, 15–81.

VAN COETSEM, F. (1990) Grimm's Law: A Reappraisal of Grimm's Formulation from a Present-Day Perspective, in ANTONSEN (with MARCHAND and ZGUSTA) (eds.) (1990), 43–59.

VAN DRIEL, L. (1992) 19th-Century Linguistics: the Dutch Development and the German Theme, in NOORDEGRAAF, VERSTEEGH and KOERNER (eds.) (1992), 221–51.

VÀRVARO, A. (1984) *La parola nel tempo. Lingua, società e storia* (Studi linguistici e semiologici, 20), Il Mulino, Bologna.

VATER, J. S. (1801) *Versuch einer allgemeinen Sprachlehre. Mit einer Einleitung über den Begriff und Ursprung der Sprache und einem Anhange über die Anwendung der allgemeinen Sprachlehre auf die Grammatik einzelner Sprachen und auf Pasigraphie*, Renger, Halle/Saale. Reprinted with an introduction and commentary by H. E. Breckle, Frommann-Holzboog, Stuttgart–Bad Cannstatt, 1970.

VATER, J. S. (ed.) (1804) *A. I. Silvestre de Sacy, Gründsätze der allgemeinen Sprachlehre in einem allgemein fasslichen Vortrage, als Grundlage alles Sprachunterrichts und mit besonderer Rücksicht auf die französische Sprache bearbeitet*. Nach der 2. Ausgabe übersetzt, und mit Anmerkungen und Zusätzen besonders in Rücksicht auf die deutsche Sprache herausgegeben von Johann Severin Vater, Ruft, Halle & Leipzig.

VATER, J. S. (1805) *Lehrbuch der allgemeinen Grammatik besonders für höhere Schul-Classen, mit Vergleichung älterer und neuerer Sprachen entworfen*, Renger, Halle.

VATER, J. S. (1815) *Litteratur der Grammatiken, Lexica und Wörtersammlungen aller Sprachen der Erde nach alphabetischer Ordnung der Sprachen, mit einer gedrängten Uebersicht des Vaterlandes, der Schicksale und Verwandtschaft derselben*, Nicolai, Berlin. 2nd edn ed. by B. Jülg, 1847.

VATER, J. S. (1820–1) *Analekten der Sprachenkunde*, 2 vols., Dyck, Leipzig.

VATER, J. S. (ed.) (1822) *Vergleichungstafeln der europäischen Stamm-Sprachen und Süd- West-Asiatischer*; R. K. Rask *über die Thrakische Sprachclasse*, aus dem Dänischen; *Albanesische Grammatik* nach Fr. Mar. de Lecce; *Grusinische Grammatik*, nach Maggio, Ghai und Firalow, herausgegeben von Johann Severin Vater; und *Galische Sprachlehre* von Christian Wilhelm Ahlwardt, Renger, Halle.

VENDRYES, J. (1955) La société de linguistique de Paris (1865–1955), *Orbis*, 4, 7–21.

VENNEMANN, T., WILBUR, T. H. (1972) *Schuchardt, the Neogrammarians, and the Transformational Theory of Phonological Change. Four Essays by Hugo Schuchardt, Theo Vennemann, Terence H. Wilbur* (Linguistische Forschungen, 26), Athenäum, Frankfurt a.M.

VENTURI, F. (1972) *Italy and the Enlightenment. Studies in a Cosmopolitan Century*, ed. with an introduction by Stuart Woolf. Translated by Susan Corsi, Longman, London.

VERBURG, P. A. (1950) The Background to the Linguistic Conception of Franz Bopp, *Lingua*, 2, 438–68. Reprinted in SEBEOK (ed.) (1966), i, 221–50.

VERNER, K. (1875) Eine Ausnahme der ersten Lautverschiebung, *Zeitschrift für vergleichende Sprachforschung*, 23, 97–130. English translation in LEHMANN (ed.) (1967), 132–63.

[VIËTOR, W.] (1882) *Der Sprachunterricht muss umkehren! Ein Beitrag zur Überbürdung Frage*, Henninger, Heilbronn. Published under the pseudonym 'Quousque tandem'. 2nd edn 1886 with the name of the author added. English translation in HOWATT (1984), 344–63.

VIËTOR, W. (1902) *Die Methodik des neusprachlichen Unterrichts*, Teubner, Leipzig.

VINCENZI, G. C. (1979) Cf. SAUSSURE (1979).

VINCENZI, G. C. (1990) Cf. WHITNEY (1990).

VITALE, M. (1984) *La questione della lingua*, 2nd edn, Palumbo, Palermo.

VOLNEY, C. F., comte de (1820) *Discours sur l'étude philosophique des langues*, 2nd edn, Baudouin, Paris. 1st edn 1819.

WACHTER, J. G. (1737) *Glossarium Germanicum*, J. F. Gleditschii filius, Leipzig.

WACKERNAGEL, J. (1892) Über ein Gesetz der indogermanischen Wortstellung, *Indogermanische Forschungen*, I, 333–436. Reprinted in WACKERNAGEL (1955–79), i, 1–104.

WACKERNAGEL, J. (1904) Vergleichende Sprachwissenschaft, in LEXIS, W. (ed.), *Das Unterrichtswesen im deutschen Reich, I, Die Universitäten*, Asher, Berlin, 202–7. Reprinted in WACKERNAGEL (1955–79), iii, 1852–7.

WACKERNAGEL, J. (1905) Die griechische Sprache, in HINNEBERG, P. (ed.), *Die Kultur der Gegenwart*, I, Teubner, Berlin-Leipzig, 286–312. Reprinted in WACKERNAGEL (1955–79), iii, 1676–702.

WACKERNAGEL, J. (1955–79) *Kleine Schriften*, 3 vols., Vandenhoeck & Ruprecht, Göttingen. Vols. 1–2 (1955) ed. by the Akademie der Wissenschaften zu

Göttingen (preface by K. Latte); Vol. 3 (1979) ed. by Bernhard Forssman for the Akademie der Wissenschaften zu Göttingen.

WÄCHTLER, K. (1991) W. D. Whitney's Essentials of English Grammar, for the Use of Schools (1877), in LEITNER (ed.) (1991), 39–55.

WARD, W. H. (1897) Address, in WHITNEY (1897), 47–56.

WATKINS, C. (1978) Remarques sur la méthode de Ferdinand de Saussure comparatiste, Cahiers Ferdinand de Saussure, 32, 59–69.

WATKINS, C. (1983) New Directions in Indo-European: Historical Comparative Linguistics and Its Contribution to Typological Studies, in HATTORI, S., INONE, K. (eds.), Proceedings of the XIIIth International Congress of Linguists, Sanseido Book Store Ltd, Tokyo, 270–7.

WEDGWOOD, H. (1866) On the Origin of Language, Trübner, London.

WEGENER, P. (1885) Untersuchungen über die Grundfragen des Sprachlebens, Niemeyer, Halle. Reprinted in WEGENER (1991). Translated into English in ABSE (1971).

WEGENER, P. (1901) Die Bearbeitung der lebenden Mundarten. I. Allgemeines, in PAUL, H. (ed.), Grundriss der germanischen Philologie, 2nd edn, Trübner, Strassburg, i, 1465–82. 1st edn 1891.

WEGENER, P. (1991) Untersuchungen über die Grundfragen des Sprachlebens. Newly edited with an introduction by Clemens Knobloch by Konrad Koerner (Amsterdam Classics in Psycholinguistics, 5), Benjamins, Amsterdam/Philadelphia.

WEIGAND, G. (1966) Karl Ferdinand Becker – ein hessischer Pädagoge und Sprachphilosoph des 19. Jahrhunderts, Diesterweg, Frankfurt.

WEIL, H. (1844) De l'ordre des mots dans les langues anciennes comparées aux langues modernes (thèse française), Joubert, Paris. 2nd edn Franck-Vieweg, Paris, 1869; 3rd edn Vieweg, Paris, 1879. Reprinted with a preface by Simone Delesalle, Didier Erudition, Paris, 1991. English translation in WEIL (1978).

WEIL, H. (1978) The Order of Words in the Ancient Languages Compared with that of the Modern Languages. Translated with Notes and Additions by Charles W. Super. New Edition with an Introduction by Aldo D. Scaglione (Amsterdam Classics in Linguistics, 1800–1925, 14), Benjamins, Amsterdam. 1st edn, Ginn & Co., Boston, 1887.

WEINREICH, U., LABOV, W., HERZOG, M. I. (1968) Empirical Foundations for a Theory of Language Change, in LEHMANN, W. P., MALKIEL, Y. (eds.), Directions for Historical Linguistics. A Symposium, University of Texas Press, Austin/London, 95–195.

WEISZ, G. (1983) The Emergence of Modern Universities in France, 1863–1914, Princeton University Press, Princeton.

WELBY, LADY VICTORIA (1903) What is Meaning? Studies in the Development of Significance, Macmillan, London / New York. Reprinted with an introduction by Gennit Mannoury, Benjamins, Amsterdam 1983.

WELKE, K. (ed.) (1986) Sprache – Bewußtsein – Tätigkeit. Zur Sprachkonzeption Wilhelm von Humboldts, Akademie Verlag, Berlin.

WELLS, G. A. (1987) The Origin of Language. Aspects of the Discussion from Condillac to Wundt, Open Court, La Salle, Illinois.

WELLS, R. (1973) Uniformitarianism in Linguistics, in WIENER, P. R. (ed.), Dictionary of the History of Ideas, 4, Charles Scribner's Sons, New York, 423–31.

WELLS, R. (1974) Phonemics in the Nineteenth Century, 1876–1900, in HYMES (ed.) (1974), 434–53.

WELLS, R. (1979) Linguistics as a Science: The Case of the Comparative Method, in HOENIGSWALD (ed.) (1979), 23–61.

WELLS, R. (1987) The Life and Growth of Language: Metaphors in Biology and Linguistics, in HOENIGSWALD and WIENER (eds.) (1987), 39–80.

WENDLAND, F. (1992) *Peter Simon Pallas, 1741–1811: Materialien einer Biographie*, 2 vols., De Gruyter, Berlin / New York.

WENKER, G. (1877) *Das rheinische Platt*, Selbstverlag, Düsseldorf.

WESSDIN, [J.] P. Cf. PAULINUS A SANCTO BARTHOLOMAEO.

WHEELER, B. I. (1887) *Analogy and the Scope of its Application in Language* (Cornell University, Studies in Classical Philology, 2), John Wilson & Son, Ithaca NY.

WHITER, W. (1822–5) *Etymologicon universale; or, Universal Etymological Dictionary: on a New Plan. In which it is Shewn, that Consonants are Alone to be Regarded in Discovering the Affinities of Words, and that the Vowels are to be Totally Rejected; that Languages Contain the Same Fundamental Idea; and that they are Derived from the Earth, and the Operations, Accidents, and Properties, Belonging to it. With Illustrations Drawn from Various Languages, etc.*, 3 vols., Cambridge University Press, Cambridge.

WHITNEY, W. D. (1867) *Language and the Study of Language: Twelve Lectures on the Principles of Linguistic Science*, Charles Scribner & Co., New York. 3rd edn 1870. Partial re-edition, London 1876. German translation by J. Jolly, Ackermann, München, 1874; Dutch translation by J. Beckering Vinckers, Bohn, Haarlem, 1877–81.

WHITNEY, W. D. (1870) 3rd edn of WHITNEY (1867).

WHITNEY, W. D. (1873) *Oriental and Linguistic Studies: the Veda; the Avesta; the Science of Language*, Scribner, Armstrong & Co., New York.

WHITNEY, W. D. (1874) *Oriental and Linguistic Studies. Second Series: the East and West; Religion and Mythology; Orthography and Phonology; Hindu Astronomy*, Scribner, Armstrong & Co., New York.

WHITNEY, W. D. (1875) *The Life and Growth of Language: an Outline of Linguistic Science* (International Scientific Series, 16), Appleton & Co., New York. Reprinted Olms, Hildesheim, 1970; Dover, New York 1979. Translated into French 1875, German 1876, Italian 1876, Dutch 1879, Swedish 1880. Cf. WHITNEY (1882).

WHITNEY, W. D. (1879) *A Sanskrit Grammar, Including Both the Classical Language and the Older Dialects, of Veda and Brahmana*, Breitkopf & Härtel, Leipzig. German translation by H. Zimmer, Leipzig, 1879. 2nd edn 1889.

WHITNEY, W. D. (1882) *The Life and Growth of Language*, 3rd edn, Kegan Paul, Trench & Co., London. 1st edn 1875.

WHITNEY, W. D. (1885) Philology. Part I – Science of Language in General, in *Encyclopaedia Britannica*, 9th edn, Adam & Charles Black, Edinburgh, XVIII, 765–80.

WHITNEY, W. D. (1892) *Max Müller and the Science of Language: A Criticism*, D. Appleton & Co., New York.

WHITNEY, W. D. (1897) *The Whitney Memorial Meeting. A Report of That Session of the First American Congress of Philologists, which was Devoted to the Memory of the Late Professor William Dwight Whitney of Yale University;*

Held at Philadelphia, Dec. 28, 1894. Edited for the Joint Committees of Publication by Charles R. Lanman, Ginn & Company, Boston.

WHITNEY, W. D. (1971) *Whitney on Language. Selected Writings of William Dwight Whitney*, ed. by Michael Silverstein. Introductory Essay by Roman Jakobson, The MIT Press, Cambridge MA and London.

WHITNEY, W. D. (1990) *La vita e lo sviluppo del linguaggio*, nella traduzione di Francesco D'Ovidio. Presentazione di Luigi Rosiello, introduzione e note di commento di Giuseppe Carlo Vincenzi, Rizzoli, Milano. Italian translation and commentary of WHITNEY (1875); 1st edn of the translation 1876.

WIEGAND, H. E. (1990) Dictionary Styles: A Comparison between the Dictionary of Jacob Grimm and Wilhelm Grimm and the Revised Edition, in ANTONSEN (with MARCHAND and ZGUSTA) (eds.) (1990), 115–39.

WILBUR, T. H. (ed.) (1977) *The Lautgesetz-Controversy: A Documentation (1885–86)* (Amsterdam Classics in Linguistics, 1800–1925, 9), Benjamins, Amsterdam.

WILBUR, T. H. (1984) Hegelian Thought and the Development of Linguistic Theory in the Mid-19th Century, in AUROUX *et al.* (eds.) (1984), 427–36.

WILEY, R. A. (ed.) (1971) *John Mitchell Kemble and Jakob Grimm: A Correspondence, 1832–1852*, Brill, Leiden.

WILEY, R. A. (1984) Cf. GRIMM (1851).

WILEY, R. A. (1990) Grimm's *Grammar* gains ground in England, 1832–1852, in ANTONSEN (with MARCHAND and ZGUSTA) (eds.) (1990), 33–42.

WILKINS, SIR CHARLES (ed.) (1785) *The Bhăgvăt-gēētā, or, Dialogues of Krĕĕshnă and Arjŏŏn; in Eighteen Lectures, with Notes*, C. Nomse, London. Reprinted Scholars' Facsimilies and Reprints, Gainesville, Florida, 1959.

WILKINS, SIR CHARLES (1808) *A Grammar of the Sanskrĭta Language*, Printed for the Author by Bulmer & Co. and sold by Black, Parry and Kingsbury, London.

WILLIAMS, J. R. (1991) Baudouin de Courtenay and his Place in the History of Linguistics, *Historiographia Linguistica*, 18, 349–67.

WILLIAMS, J. R. (1993) *A Paradigm Lost. The Linguistic Theory of Mikołaj Kruszewski* (Amsterdam Studies in the History of the Language Sciences, 72), Benjamins, Amsterdam/Philadelphia.

WILLSON, A. L. (1964) *A Mythical Image; the Ideal of India in German Romanticism*, Duke University Press, Durham NC.

WILSON, H. H. (1819) *A Dictionary, Sanskrit and English, Translated and Edited from an Original Compilation Prepared by Learned Natives for the College of Fort Williams*, P. Pereira at the Hindostanee Press, Calcutta. 2nd edn 1832, Education Press, Calcutta; Allen, London.

WINDISCH, E. (1917–1920) *Geschichte der Sanskrit Philologie und indischen Altertumskunde* (Grundriß der Indo-Arischen Philologie und Altertumskunde, 1), 2 vols., Trübner / De Gruyter, Straßburg/Berlin/Leipzig.

WINDISCH, E. (1966) Georg Curtius, in SEBEOK (ed.) (1966), i, 311–73. Originally appeared in *Biographisches Jahrbuch für Altertumskunde* 9 (1886), 75–128.

WINTELER, J. (1876) *Die Kerenzer Mundart des Kantons Glarus in ihren Grundzügen dargestellt*, Winter, Leipzig/Heidelberg.

WRIGHT, J. (1892) *A Grammar of the Dialect of Windhill of the West Riding of Yorkshire* (English Dialect Society, Series C, Original Glossaries, 67), Kegan Paul, Trench, Trübner & Co, London.

WRIGHT, J. (1896–1905) *The English Dialect Dictionary, Being the Complete Vocabulary of All Dialect Words Still in Use or Known to Have Been in Use During the Last Two Hundred Years*, 6 vols. By private subscription, Oxford. 1st fascicle 1896, 1st vol., 1898; first printed by H. Frowde, London; then by Oxford University Press, Oxford.

WUNDT, W. (1886) Über den Begriff des Gesetzes, mit Rücksicht auf die Frage der Ausnahmlosigkeit der Lautgesetze, *Philosophische Studien*, 3, 195–215.

WUNDT, W. (1900) *Völkerpsychologie. Eine Untersuchung der Entwicklungsgesetze von Sprache, Mythus und Sitte. I. Die Sprache*, 2 vols., Engelmann, Leipzig. 2nd edn 1904, 3rd edn 1911–12, 4th edn 1921–2.

WUNDT, W. (1901) *Sprachgeschichte und Sprachpsychologie*, Wilhelm Engelmann, Leipzig.

WUNDT, W. (1911–12) 3rd edn of WUNDT (1900).

WYSS, U. (1979) *Die wilde Philologie. Jacob Grimm und der Historismus*, Beck, München.

[YOUNG, T.] (1813–14) Review of ADELUNG (1806–17), Vol. I, *Quarterly Review*, 10 (October 1813), 250–92.

ZELDIN, T. (1967) Higher Education in France 1848–1940, *Journal of Contemporary History*, 2, 53–80.

ZELDIN, T. (1993) *A History of French Passions*, 2 vols., Clarendon Press, Oxford. Reprint of original edn of 1973 entitled *France 1848–1945*.

ZEUSS, J. C. (1853) *Grammatica Celtica e monumentis vetustis tam hibernicae linguae quam britannicae dialecti cornicae armoricae nec non e gallicae priscae reliquiis construxit J. C. Zeuss*, 2 vols., Weidmann, Leipzig.

ZIEMER, H. (1882) *Junggrammatische Streifzüge im Gebiete der Syntax*, Post'sche Buchhandlung, Colbert. 2nd edn 1883.

ZIMMERMANN, K., TRABANT, J., MUELLER-VOLLMER, K. (eds.) (1994) *Wilhelm von Humboldt und die amerikanischen Sprachen* (Humboldt-Studien, 3), Schöningh, Paderborn.

ZSIRAI, M. (1951) Samuel Gyarmathi, Hungarian Pioneer of Comparative Linguistics, *Acta Linguistica Academiae Scientiarum Hungaricae*, 1, 5–16. Reprinted in SEBEOK (ed.) (1966), I, 58–70 and in the 1968 reprint of GYARMATHI (1799), v–xvii.

ZWIRNER, E., ZWIRNER, K. (1966) *Grundfragen der Phonometrie. Erster Teil*, 2nd edn (Bibliotheca Phonetica, 3), S. Karger, Basel.

Index

This index includes the authors of works quoted in the list of references, but not the names of editors, publishers, etc. and those quoted in the titles.